WITHDRAWN

If You're Thinking of Living In . . .

If You're Thinking of Living In...

*All About 115 Great
Neighborhoods in and
Around New York*

**EDITED BY MICHAEL J. LEAHY,
REAL ESTATE EDITOR**

The New York Times

RANDOM HOUSE

Copyright © 1999 by The New York Times Company.

All rights reserved under International and Pan-American Copyright Conventions. Published in the United States by Times Books, a division of Random House, Inc., New York, and simultaneously in Canada by Random House of Canada Limited, Toronto.

Library of Congress Cataloging-in-Publication Data
If you're thinking of living in— : compiled columns from the New York times.
    p.   cm.
  Includes index.
  ISBN 0-8129-2983-7 (alk. paper)
  1. New York Region—Guidebooks.   2. New York Region—History, Local.   3. Moving, Household—New York Region—Handbooks, manuals, etc.   I. New York times.
  F128.18.I34   1998
  974.7'043—dc21   98-46272

Random House website address: www.atrandom.com
Printed in the United States of America

98765432

First Edition

Maps: Natasha Perkel
Book Design: Cindy La Breacht

Times Books are available at special discounts for bulk purchases for sales promotions or premiums. Special editions, including personalized covers, excerpts of existing books, and corporate imprints, can be created in large quantities for special needs. For more information, write to Special Markets, Times Books, 201 East 50th Street, New York, N.Y. 10022, or call 800-800-3246.

CONTENTS

INTRODUCTION

One of the pleasures of walking along Manhattan's streets is the mix of people rushing, strolling, or idling by. Mink-coated and pin-striped, wearing ragged jeans (but just-so in their raggedness) and purple hair, buttoned-down and laid-back, all share the same space. It is a variety that also marks the housing choices available to those who live in New York City and its suburbs.

These neighborhoods, hamlets, villages, towns, and cities each have their own personalities, though, like members of sprawling families or clans, their similarities are frequently as striking as their differences. There are few guideposts to these individual personalities, and those that exist are sometimes hard to decipher. Classified ads are a help—house descriptions and figures preceded by dollar signs quickly direct most house hunters in making some basic decisions—but even these are frequently written in code. In the city, an apartment described as having a "townhouse feel" probably means that it is on a low floor. The phrase "lots of light" frequently translates to "no view." Whether in city or country, "riv vu" may assume a contortionist's ability to swivel the neck. References to "t.l.c." have nothing to do with the Taxi and Limousine Commission, except to suggest a blinking yellow caution light. And, of course, "needs work" invariably means "needs *lots* of work."

Names may or may not provide clues. Manhattan's West End Avenue, a block from the bustle of Broadway, seems to occupy a different universe from that of the tranquil (some West Siders would say dull) high-rise village of East End Avenue. Brooklyn Heights and Staten Island's Lighthouse Hill do, as their names suggest, offer splendid views, but the names of Manhattan's TriBeCa and New Jersey's Ho-Ho-Kus are more puzzling than descriptive. On Long Island, Port Washington, Port Jefferson, Northport,

Centerport, and Oyster Bay accurately suggest nautical surroundings, but Locust Valley may put those unfamiliar with its leafy privileged lanes in mind of less appealing biblical images. For those who live in them, however, the New Jersey communities of Alpine and Summit may well occupy the housing niches that these names suggest.

In many New York suburbs, looks and boundary lines can be misleading. Identical-seeming houses on the same street will sell for differences of tens of thousands of dollars because they are in different towns or school districts. Many towns are served by more than one school district, and the differences in reputations of the districts will translate into significant differences in housing prices. Access to such desirable facilities as golf clubs and beaches may be controlled by the municipal boundary lines that run through otherwise identical neighborhoods. Taxes can vary sharply from municipality to municipality, even when a visitor would be hard put to see many differences between them.

All of these factors are part of what makes each community different from its neighbors. Beyond these attributes, though, are others that are harder to measure, but that give each place its personality. The hamlet of South Salem, just an hour from Manhattan, takes part of its Norman Rockwell character from a town center consisting of a general store, an antiques shop, and the remnants of a one-pump gas station that no longer operates; across the street, standing on a slight rise, is the South Salem Presbyterian Church. Part of the character of the surrounding boomerang-shaped Town of Lewisboro comes from a network of horse trails allowing riders free access to 1,500 acres of private property. The Long Island village of Northport has chosen to preserve the tracks of the long-departed trolleys along a still-thriving Main Street that leads down to Long Island Sound.

Montclair, with its wide range of housing, its stress on education, and its devotion to making multiracial society more than a lip-service term, has long drawn so many former Manhattan residents that it is known as the Upper West Side of New Jersey. The space and modest rents of the Brooklyn neighborhood of Williamsburg have helped form an urban mix that includes Polish immigrants, Italian, Hispanic, and Hasidic families, and artists (some of whose works are exhibited in the Brooklyn Brewery's gallery), all one subway stop away from Manhattan. The Tudor half-timbers, extensive brickwork, and red-tiled roofs of the Queens neighborhood of Forest Hills Gardens owe much to the turn-of-the-century Garden Cities movement. Nearby, in the heart of another Queens neighborhood, the 600 two-story row houses of Sunnyside Gardens cluster around landscaped gardens in one of the first planned communities in the United States, a 77-acre enclave that is listed in the National Register of Historic Places.

Every week since March 28, 1982, writers for the Real Estate section of *The New York Times* have set out to describe the communities of the New York area, seeking to identify and describe such specifics as the costs of homes, school spending, and local history, as well as such harder-to-define qualities as the look and feel of the neighborhoods and the ways in which they are changing, or keeping the qualities that have drawn residents to live in them. This book collects 115 of these pieces, all of which have been updated.

A word about the statistics used in this book: All are current as of the end of 1997 or early 1998, with a few figures from mid-1998. And all will surely be out of date by the time you read this—though whether the current figures will be much different from these, or even if they will be higher or lower, is impossible to forecast. Despite their seeming precision, real estate statistics can only approximate a market. In the suburbs, multiple-listing services make a thorough and conscientious effort to track prices, but not every house is sold through agents whose real estate brokerages are members of those services. In New York City, unlike most other real estate markets in the United States, there is no comprehensive multiple-listing service. And sales of the co-op apartments that are a major part of the housing market in New York City, especially in Manhattan, are not a matter of public record; our figures for these sales are estimates from a variety of real estate brokerages. Gazetteer figures for taxes on median-priced houses are approximations; property taxes can vary markedly on houses selling for roughly the same price. In a few cases, where the data were insufficient or misleading, the estimates were omitted. Estimates of population and median household income were prepared by the Queens College Applied Social Research Program, and are as of 1997.

The variety of housing choices in the New York area is not exhausted in the 115 places described in this book, but it is suggested. Within these pages are communities that have long been the first stop for immigrants, and others where multimillion-dollar homes are so common as to be unremarkable. There are many communities in which outstanding schools are regarded as both a responsibility and a good community investment. There are others in which residence (which in these cases usually means ownership) also buys membership in, or at least eligibility for, the village country club, mooring rights at the municipal marina, and—perhaps sweetest of all—a guaranteed parking spot at the railroad station.

There are many people whose offstage work has gone into these articles, and into this book. Among those to whom thanks are due are each of the staff members of and contributors to the Real Estate section of *The New York Times*, especially Bill Hollander, the original editor on almost all of these pieces; Alan S. Oser, who sets the standard for perceptive and knowledgeable real estate coverage, and who is the most generous of colleagues; and Rosalie Radomsky, who would bring sunshine into a windowless room. Also at *The Times*, Steve Hadermayer and his expert colleagues in the Map Department, including Natasha Perkel, who prepared the maps in this volume; Don Donofrio, resident technology wizard; Charles Robinson, information services director; Linda Amster and her research staff, who may not know everything, but who know how to find it; Mitchel Levitas, whose determination saw this book into being; and Arthur Gelb, Timesman nonpareil. Outside *The Times*, the list should include Susan Weber of Queens College, and the many local officials, real estate professionals, and municipal staff members and academics who have helped reporters who come into an area and try to capture its life. The names of two New York City borough historians, Richard B. Dickenson of Staten Island and John H. Manbeck of Brooklyn, can represent those of many others who have been generous with their knowledge. Sybil Pincus, production editor at Times Books, has shepherded this book into print with a sure hand and a watchful eye.

The "If You're Thinking of Living In . . ." column was the idea of the late Michael Sterne, a reporter, foreign correspondent, and editor who made contributions that can still be seen in the pages of *The New York Times*. As a boss and colleague, he was more demanding of himself than he was of anyone else. The name of the column, as Mike noted in his introduction to an earlier compilation of columns in 1985, was the idea of A. M. Rosenthal, who was then the executive editor of *The Times*.

Finally, thanks to my family: my wife, Blitz, and our children, Christine, Thomas, and Christopher. I want to live wherever they live.

Michael J. Leahy
Real Estate Editor
The New York Times
July 1998

If You're Thinking of Living In . . .

New York City

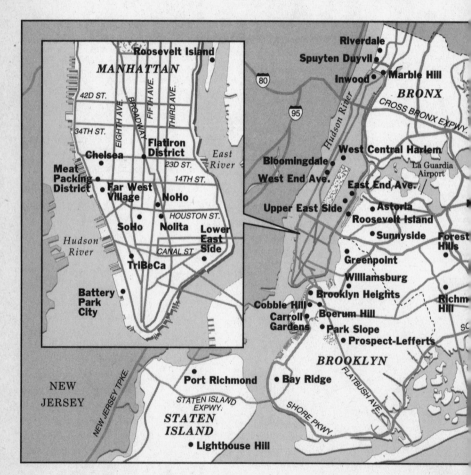

The Lower East Side

Marble Hill

The Meat Packing District

NoHo

Nolita

Roosevelt Island

SoHo

TriBeCA

The Upper East Side

West Central Harlem

West End Avenue

THE BRONX

City Island

Riverdale

Sputen Duyvil

BROOKLYN

Bay Ridge

Boerum Hill

Brooklyn Heights

Carroll Gardens

Cobble Hill

Greenpoint

Park Slope

Prospect Lefferts Gardens

Williamsburg

QUEENS

Astoria

Bayside

Briarwood

Douglaston

Forest Hills Gardens

Jamaica Estates

Richmond Hill

Sunnyside

STATEN ISLAND

Lighthouse Hill

Port Richmond

Long Island Sound

0   Miles   4

y Island

25A

Douglaston

LONG ISLAND EXPWY.

495

NORTHERN STATE PKWY.

Jamaica Estates

CROSS ISLAND PKWY.

NASSAU

ood

EENS

SOUTHERN STATE PKWY.

MEADOWBROOK STATE PKWY.

N PKWY.

27

nedy rnational oort

SUNRISE HWY.

Atlantic Ocean

BATTERY PARK CITY

An urban suburb, with yacht basin

BY PETER MALBIN

Where else in Manhattan can you sail away from a harbor only steps away from your apartment building, as well as plant and tend your own small plot of land with advice from a horticulturist? Not to mention walk five minutes to a corporate job in a financial center? With a yacht basin, a 1.2-mile-long esplanade, and a third of its 92-acre site devoted to open space, it is hard to imagine that you are in one of the world's most densely populated cities.

Battery Park City is an urban suburb designed to include some of the best features of New York's architecture. Tree-lined, wide streets lead to the esplanade hugging the Hudson River, which offers views of the Statue of Liberty, Ellis Island, and the New Jersey riverfront. Cool breezes off the Hudson lower the temperature by 10 degrees throughout the year. Its five public parks and its gardens and plazas are patrolled around the clock by officers in green ranger uniforms. Whimsical bronze sculptures of animals, musical instruments, and hands enliven the area.

"I love the open space," said Maria Smith, who has lived in a one-bedroom condominium on Rector Place for 10 years. "Within two minutes, I am on the river and I can watch the tankers and sailboats go by." *The Battery Park City Broadsheet* publishes a column called "Riverwatch," listing the sailing times of passing liners.

Retail stores on South End Avenue, the main shopping area of the complex, include two supermarkets, several cleaners, a pharmacy, a liquor store, a hair salon, and a deli. On Thursdays, a farmers' market sets up shop on Liberty Street at the south end of the neighboring World Trade Center.

By comparison with the usual cornucopia of older residential neighborhoods, however, shopping leaves something to be desired. "Services

POPULATION: 7,615.

AREA: 1.7 square miles.

MEDIAN HOUSEHOLD INCOME: $110,000.

MEDIAN PRICE OF A ONE-BEDROOM CONDO: $231,000.

MEDIAN PRICE OF A TWO-BEDROOM CONDO: $346,000.

MIDRANGE RENT FOR A ONE-BEDROOM APARTMENT: $2,330.

MIDRANGE RENT FOR A TWO-BEDROOM APARTMENT: $3,450.

DISTANCE FROM MIDTOWN MANHATTAN: 4.5 miles.

RUSH-HOUR TRAVEL TO MIDTOWN: PATH train, 15 minutes, $1 one way; 20 minutes on the 1, 2, 3, 9, A, E, C, N, or R subway train.

CODES: Area, 212; ZIP, 10280.

have improved vastly in the 10 years I've been here, but we could use a video rental store and a bakery," said Ms. Smith.

Casual neighborhood restaurants like Steamer's Landing and Wave offer a view of the sun setting on the Hudson. A stroll away in the World Financial Center are the more up-scale Hudson River Club as well as a plethora of other restaurants, and stores such as the Rizzoli bookstore, Barneys, Ann Taylor, and Gap Kids. Orchestras, jazz bands, circus troupes, and dancers provide free entertainment in the Winter Garden, where 16 giant palm trees reach toward the top of the 120-foot glass-enclosed atrium.

Battery Park City is built on land-fill, some from the excavation for the World Trade Center. Gov. Nelson A. Rockefeller envisioned it as a futuristic residential and commercial neighborhood along the Hudson River. In 1968, the state legislature formed the Battery Park City Authority to develop the community in several stages.

The first residential complex was Gateway Plaza—six rental buildings that opened in 1982–83. Young single professionals who wanted to be close to financial jobs downtown were attracted to the area. Many of those singles from the pioneer days are now raising young families in the area, often combining condominium apartments. Charles Wolstein, his wife, Miriam Chernick (who lived in Gateway Plaza in the '80s), and their baby daughter moved into a 1,550-square-foot three-bedroom apartment at 280 Rector Place from a one-bedroom in a next-door building at 200 Rector Place. Mr. Wolstein, a management consultant, works in midtown, and Ms. Chernick is in the marketing department of a financial-services company in the World Financial Center. "There are very few large apartments here," Mr. Wolstein said. "We were lucky to find it. We wanted to stay in the neighborhood. It's one of the most serene communities in the city."

"It's an unusual market," said Julie Stevens, a broker with Douglas Elliman, referring both to the types of buildings and to the fact that the area is exempt from the various laws that regulate many rental apartments elsewhere in the city. "There are no walk-up brownstones or tenements, no rent control or rent stabilization."

Instead there are 11 condominium and eight rental buildings. All have concierges and exercise rooms and three provide parking. Asking prices for typical 625- to 775-square-foot one-bedroom condominiums are $150,000 to $350,000, brokers say. Two-bedrooms are in short supply, they say, costing anywhere from $275,000 for a 900-square-foot apartment with no view to $800,000 for a penthouse with a river-view terrace.

Combined common charges and taxes generally range from $1 to $2 per square foot, typical for Manhattan, said Norman Horowitz, a broker with Halstead Property Company. But the monthly charges are considerably higher in smaller buildings because there are fewer tenants. Part of the proceeds from common charges and taxes goes to the Battery Park City Authority, which maintains the parks.

The rental market is tight, brokers say, a situation that may be alleviated somewhat by current construction of three rental buildings in the "north neighborhood," which is a short walk from TriBeCa's restaurants, bakeries, and nightlife. Two nine-story rental buildings in the south section are also in the advanced planning stage.

"The population is going to increase significantly," said John La Mura, president and chief executive of the Battery Park City Authority. "There are about 1,400 units coming into play in the next two years." One-third of these units will be two- and three-bedroom apartments.

Rents announced for the 43-story, 340-unit TriBeCa Pointe at 41 River Terrace, expected to be completed in October of 1998, ranged from $1,670 to $2,550 for studios, $1,860 to $2,795 for one-bedroom apartments, and $2,895 to $4,155 for two-bedroom units. Two 1,300-square-foot, three-bedroom penthouse apartments are to rent for about $5,000, according to the developer, Rockrose.

The second rental property under development in the north section, TriBeCa Park, at 34 River Terrace, is expected to be completed in June 1999. Market rents for studios in the 28-story, 396-unit building were estimated to start at $1,700, one-bedrooms from $1,950, and two-bedrooms from $3,195. The Related Companies building is being designed by Robert A. M. Stern Architects.

A third new building, TriBeCa Bridge Tower, developed by the Battery Park City Authority, will have subsidized apartments for middle-income tenants, with funds generated by the market-rate apartments. The income range for those who win the right to a subsidized apartment in a lottery is to go from $32,000 a year for an individual to $108,000 for a family of three to six persons. Rents for such tenants will range from $800 a month for a one-bedroom unit to $1,800 for three bedrooms.

The building has been modified at its base to house two new public schools, P.S. 89 for kindergarten through fifth grade, and I.S. 89 for sixth through eighth grade.

Many children in Battery Park City currently attend the overcrowded P.S. 234 in TriBeCa, a highly rated progressive school with an extensive arts program. "There is every indication that P.S. 89 will function as a sister school to P.S. 234," said Dorothy Baratta, president of the Battery Park City Parents Association. Another school popular with Battery Park City parents is the Early Childhood Center (E.C.C.), a kindergarten-through-grade 2 public school in TriBeCa.

At the private Battery Park City Nursery School, parents of children aged 1 to 5 pay $365 to $1,010 a month. Many students attend private schools uptown.

The prestigious Stuyvesant High School, which admits students through a rigorous entrance examination, is at the north border of Battery Park City, at 345 Chambers Street. The Battery Park community can use Stuyvesant's basketball courts and swimming pool at nonacademic times. There are also two free tennis courts nearby, as well as fields for Little League and Soccer League play.

"It's like a Club Med in the summertime," said Susan Beckert, who lives at Gateway Plaza with her husband, Pierric, and two children. Co-ed Downtown Little League, for children 5 to 14, runs from April to the end of June. The Battery Park City Parks Corporation sponsors a host of activities from May through October, including traditional American folk dancing; fishing in the Hudson River; a Swedish midsummer festival of music, dancing, food, and games; West African dance; and horticultural tours showcasing the gardens of Battery Park City. Co-ed Downtown Soccer League, for children ages 5 to 12, lasts from September to the end of November. And all year round, the World Financial Center offers a program of free exhibitions, fairs and festivals, music, modern dance, ballet, and square dancing.

BLOOMINGDALE

A family enclave that some call SoCo

BY JOYCE COHEN

When people ask Susanna Frazer where she lives, she feels she must explain. "It always seems a little unclear to people," said Ms. Frazer. "It's too far north for the Upper West Side, but not quite as far up as Morningside Heights."

Her neighborhood, Bloomingdale—sometimes called the Upper Upper West Side—lies between 96th and 110th Streets, west of Amsterdam Avenue. The name Bloomingdale—Broadway was once called Bloomingdale Road—is mentioned infrequently these days, though a handful of institutions still use it. Newcomers have even been known to call the neighborhood SoCo, for "South of Columbia," a name Ms. Frazer coined several years ago, when she sold real estate.

Some say it is one of Manhattan's best family neighborhoods, where people know nearly everyone in their building and really feel a sense of belonging. Dog owners congregate for evening walks. Parents' groups abound. "It's a very homey, unpretentious area," said Ms. Frazer, an actress. "It has its own certain charm and has a really good mix politically and socially. It is not quite as gentrified as the Upper West Side below," she added, referring to the neighborhood that is sometimes called the Lower Upper West Side.

Nor are the streets as congested as they are farther south. "There's not a lot of traffic from other parts of the city," said Hedy Campbell, a mother of two for whom a trip to the West 80s counts as an urban excursion. "People don't come flocking here to go to a store or a museum," she said. "It doesn't have a major attraction. It's very much our own neighborhood."

The housing stock includes plenty of spacious prewar apartments, along with brownstones on the side streets. Prices tend to be a bit lower than they are farther downtown, said Laurie Bloomfield, a sales agent at

POPULATION: 31,489.

AREA: 0.5 square mile.

MEDIAN HOUSEHOLD INCOME: $55,715.

PRICE OF A MIDRANGE TWO-BEDROOM CO-OP: $550,000.

MIDRANGE RENT FOR A ONE-BEDROOM APARTMENT: $2,000.

DISTANCE FROM MIDTOWN MANHATTAN: 3.5 miles.

RUSH-HOUR TRAVEL TO MIDTOWN: 10 minutes on the 1 or 9 subway train connecting to the 2 or 3 express train at 96th Street; 30 minutes on buses on Broadway and Riverside Drive.

CODES: Area, 212; ZIP, 10025.

Douglas Elliman who has lived in Bloomingdale for more than two decades. In the late 1990s, a "classic six," with two bedrooms and 2½ baths, might sell for $500,000 to $600,000, she said, compared with $700,000 or more for a similar home 30 blocks south. Rentals start at $1,000 for a studio, $1,500 for a one-bedroom apartment, and $2,000 for a two-bedroom.

"It's very mixed professionwise—musicians, artists, writers, yuppies, political activists," said Ms. Bloomfield. "A lot of people went to Columbia and fell in love with the neighborhood and never left."

Geographically and conceptually, the Upper West Side splits at 96th Street. That's where traffic gets on and off the Henry Hudson Parkway, and where the subway lines branch. The ride to Times Square takes only about 10 minutes from 96th Street, where both the express and local trains stop; only local trains stop at the 103d and 110th Street stations. Also at 96th Street, the land dips into a little valley near the Hudson River, at what used to be called Stryker's Bay.

The area's reputation dips, too. Just a few years ago, the streets were filled with vagrants, panhandlers, drug dealers, and peddlers. There is still an east-west barrier created by Broadway, with areas to the east decidedly more commercial and downscale than those to the west. On the west side of Amsterdam Avenue between 100th and 101st Streets, there is a 158-unit, 20-story public housing building.

Over a three-year period, crime has fallen by half, said Capt. Kevin Barry, commanding officer of the 24th Precinct, though pockets of drug dealing remain, primarily on Amsterdam Avenue between 101st and 110th Streets. One ongoing problem is car thefts and break-ins along Riverside Drive, which feels eerily deserted at night. Residents have taken their own steps to allay fears of crime. Several block associations hire guards, generally to patrol at night. And a force of 160 auxiliary police officers patrols on weekdays from 6 to 10 P.M., communicating with the regular police by radio.

The auxiliary force, all volunteers, is one of the most active in the city—a testament to the neighborhood's cohesiveness, said Lisa Lehr, a police auxiliary and co-chairwoman of the West 90s/West 100s Neighborhood Coalition. "This is a mixed neighborhood that works," she said. "This is a tolerant, sophisticated, intellectual neighborhood of many cultures. It's a real melting pot. People are so truly caring. This is not an anonymous neighborhood where nobody knows their neighbors."

About half a dozen blocks have strong block associations. Members prune and water the nearby trees, and plant flowers in the tree beds. Some paint over the graffiti on the mailboxes along the streets, a practice encouraged by the Postal Service, which provides the paint. Some associations run summer block picnics, where people convene on the sidewalk for snacks and socializing.

Those are not the only neighborhood groups. The Broadway Mall Association maintains the landscaped traffic islands in the middle of Broadway. The West Side Arts Coalition occasionally hosts weekend art shows at the Broadway Mall Community Center, in the center island at 96th Street. One group is devoted to reviving the 105th Street Tot Lot in Riverside Park.

Riverside Park serves as the neighborhood's great backyard. Many people feel it is less congested and more homey than Central Park. Bloomingdale residents say that their part of the park is even "more woodsy, a little more wild," than Riverside Park farther south, "with more services for kids," said Teresa Elwert of the West 104th Street Block Association. Indeed, there are basketball courts, dog runs, playgrounds, a soccer field, and places to jog and skateboard.

Some people, though, feel that Riverside Park can be a bit unwelcoming at times. Most building entrances are on the side streets, and a brutal winter wind whips up from the river. Those facing west along Riverside Drive can hear traffic roaring and buses lurching; when the weather is bad, there are foghorns on the Hudson.

In the spring of 1997, Straus Park, the small triangular park near 106th Street, was reopened, neatly outfitted with new benches, shrubs, pavement, and fencing. The sitting area, complete with fountain, is named for Isidor Straus—co-owner with his brother, Nathan, of Macy's and a partner in the Abraham & Straus department store—and his wife, Ida. Isidor and Ida, who lived on West 105th Street, went down on the *Titanic*, with Ida choosing to remain with her husband rather than join the women and children in the lifeboats. The park's ribbon-cutting was held on April 15, 1997, the 85th anniversary of the *Titanic*'s sinking.

Broadway is the neighborhood's main commercial strip. This far north, it is largely devoid of national retailers, though there is a popular Starbucks at 102d Street, as well as a nearby Blockbuster Video and Radio Shack. Some people complain about a lack of certain stores—bookstores, clothing stores, well-stocked supermarkets—though there is no shortage of restaurants, delis, and greengrocers. A branch of Gourmet Garage, the upscale food specialty market, is located just north of 96th on the west side of Broadway, and many people make weekly shopping trips to the cavernous uptown Fairway on West 132d Street.

There are two two-screen movie houses and even an Off-Off-Broadway theater near 100th Street—the 70-seat Homegrown Theater Company, which also gives acting classes.

Residents sometimes worry that the area is a dumping ground for social-service agencies, since there are several residences for people who were formerly homeless and mentally ill. But anticipated problems with crime and drugs have not developed, said Toni Rachiele, who founded Neighborhood Survival, a group devoted to making sure people housed in the neighborhood are given adequate support services.

The neighborhood is within Community School District 3. P.S. 163 and 145 (also known as the Bloomingdale School) feature programs for the gifted and talented, as do some of the district's other schools. The prekindergarten-through-grade 8 Ascension School, with about 200 pupils, is associated with the Roman Catholic Church of the Ascension on 107th Street east of Broadway. The Roman Catholic Holy Name School, with 600 pupils, features a Montessori preschool and grades kindergarten through 8. Its parent, the Holy Name of Jesus Church, dominates its corner at Amsterdam and 96th Street; its "little room" is rented out to such groups as Overeaters Anonymous and Alcoholics Anonymous.

The most prominent synagogue is Congregation Ansche Chesed ("Caring People") at 100th Street and West End Avenue. Participants in its many adult programs need not be Jewish. The synagogue hosts several different preschool and nursery programs, along with a small homeless shelter. A bit farther north, on Riverside Drive, is the New York Buddhist Church. Outside the nondescript two-story building is a 12-foot-tall bronze statue of Shinran Shonin, founder of a Buddhist sect in Japan, that was brought from Hiroshima in 1955. The church is adjacent to a turn-of-the-century town house in the Beaux Arts style, one of several in the West 105th–106th Street Historic District. St. Michael's Episcopal Church on Amsterdam Avenue and 99th Street is known for its Tiffany windows.

Bloomingdale takes its name from Bloemendael, or "Vale of Flowers," a district in Holland. Bloomingdale Road, later called the Boulevard, opened in 1703. It was renamed Broadway in 1899. The Bloomingdale name lives on in the Bloomingdale Library on 100th Street; the Bloomingdale House of Music, a private music school on 108th Street; and the Bloomingdale Coalition, founded nearly 20 years ago to improve the area's quality of life.

And, no, the name has nothing to do with the store. That was started by brothers Lyman and Joseph Bloomingdale in 1872.

CHELSEA

Brownstones, bistros, lofts, galleries, and a seminary

BY PETER MALBIN

Signs of renewal are everywhere in Chelsea. Few stores are vacant, which was hardly the case several years ago. Bistros like Le Gamin, Trois Canards, and the Chelsea Bistro & Bar have sprouted all over the neighborhood, along with espresso bar–bookstores, attracting Manhattanites from uptown and downtown. Barnes & Noble and Burlington Coat Factory are among stores revitalizing the historic retail district on the Avenue of the Americas. Art galleries are adding luster to an abandoned part of the neighborhood. And not surprisingly, commercial and residential real estate prices are rising. "Prices have been accelerating over the past three years," said Ed Ferris, a broker with the William B. May Company. "In the luxury category, Chelsea is only slightly less expensive now than the West Village."

Around Seventh Avenue in the teens, light-filled low-rise buildings are magnets for photographers, artists, and designers, some of whom work out of their converted lofts. Premium converted loft spaces are in the Hellmuth and other deceptively nondescript buildings from 15th to 18th Street, between the Avenue of the Americas and Eighth Avenue. In the final quarter of 1997, a 1,350-square-foot loft on West 15th Street with a private roof sold for $527,000. Above 23d Street, loft prices drop significantly, brokers say. Median prices of 2,200-square-foot lofts were $667,000 in 1997, up from $509,000 in 1994, said Scott Durkin of the Corcoran Group.

Eighth Avenue between 14th and 23d Streets has had a face-lift, amazing longtime residents. Somewhat seedy only a few years ago, it is now Chelsea's bustling Main Street by day and restaurant row by night. It is also the neighborhood's and the city's gay hub, where "Chelsea Boys" patronize a variety of businesses.

Four abandoned piers on the Hudson River from 17th to 23d Street

POPULATION: 44,932.

AREA: 1 square mile.

MEDIAN HOUSEHOLD INCOME: $46,293.

MEDIAN PRICE OF A 2,200-SQUARE-FOOT LOFT: $667,000.

RUSH-HOUR TRAVEL TO MIDTOWN: 5 minutes by subway.

TRANSPORTATION: 1, 2, 3, 9, A, C, E, and F subway lines; buses on Sixth, Seventh, Eighth, Ninth, and 10th Avenues and 14th and 23d Streets.

CODES: Area, 212; ZIP, 10001 and 10011.

have been transformed into the 30-acre Chelsea Piers sports and entertainment complex, providing a variety of activities. Two outdoor rollerblade and roller-skating rinks are available until mid-November, and disco skaters take to the rink on weekend nights. Two indoor ice-skating rinks, open all year, are home to figure skaters, hockey leagues for players of all ages, and visiting professional hockey teams practicing before hitting the ice at Madison Square Garden. Golfers practice their shots from several levels rising above a 200-yard driving range.

"It's nice to have more amenities in Chelsea, but I think the people who live here don't want it to become as slick as SoHo or as polished as the West Village," said Tony Sheldon, a financial adviser who lives on 24th Street.

"There's a bit of a small-town atmosphere," said Rowena Doyel, who has lived in Chelsea's oldest surviving house at 404 West 20th Street for 43 years. Children play in the newly renovated and fenced Clement Clarke Moore Park on 22d Street at 10th. The McBurney Y.M.C.A. on 23d offers day care, among other programs. Next to the Y, the small Muhlenberg Library has a well-stocked children's section.

Chelsea offers a selection of nursery schools and public schools, including P.S. 11, P.S. 33, I.S. 70, the Bayard Rustin High School for the Humanities, and the Fashion Industries High School. There are two Roman Catholic elementary schools in Chelsea, Guardian Angel and St. Columba. Chelsea's private Corlears School at 324 West 15th Street educates 142 children from a variety of backgrounds through fourth grade. Tuition is $9,300 to $13,610.

"It's a real community here," said Jeremy Berkovits, one of Chelsea's ubiquitous dog walkers, who lives on 15th Street. "The guys in the Korean grocery store and the dry cleaner know my name." Mr. Berkovits and other residents also said they felt safe in their neighborhood, a feeling seconded by Steve Galasso, crime-prevention officer at the 10th Precinct.

Chelsea has a substantial population of elderly people, particularly centered around the middle-income Penn Station South co-ops between Eighth and Ninth Avenues in the 20s. There is also a residence for blind people, Selis Manor, at 135 West 23d Street. On Ninth Avenue in the teens is one of Chelsea's two subsidized public housing developments, the Robert Fulton Houses. The other is the Elliott-Chelsea Houses, from 25th to 27th, between Ninth and 10th.

Several residences for people with AIDS have opened in recent years, including the Flemister House at 527 West 22d Street. Chelsea is particularly supportive of AIDS services. The Gay Men's Health Crisis organization has its headquarters on 24th Street.

Loft buildings are the primary residences between the Avenue of the Americas and Seventh Avenue, and there are many 19th-century brownstones between Seventh and 10th Avenues. The mix adds character to the area, said Edward Kirkland, a member of Community Board 4, "because we don't want it to be homogenized like the Upper East Side."

Chelsea was rural farmland in 1750 when Capt. Thomas Clarke bought a tract there for his retirement. He named his farm Chelsea after the Chelsea Royal Hospital, an old soldiers' home in London. In the 1830s, Captain Clarke's grandson, Clement Clarke Moore, a poet best known for "A Visit from St. Nicholas," reluctantly decided to develop Chelsea as a garden suburb. Moore, who is revered as Chelsea's founding father, established guidelines for residential building that are still in force between the avenues. That concern for Chelsea's architecture and housing stock is firmly echoed today by Community Board 4 and civic groups, whose Chelsea Plan seeks to preserve the neighborhood's scale, historic character, and diversity.

The architectural jewel especially worth preserving is the Historic District, which encompasses parts of West 20th, 21st, and 22d Streets between Eighth and 10th Avenues. The serene district includes the Gothic-style General Theological Seminary, a stunning refuge in the middle of Chelsea. Moore, who was a professor at the seminary, donated the Chelsea square block it occupies, between Ninth and 10th Avenues from 20th to 21st Street. Opposite, the Greek Revival Cushman Row town houses (1839–40) are set back from 20th Street with 10-foot front yards.

This is prime Chelsea real estate, and brownstone prices in the Historic District have been climbing. There has been at least an appreciation of 15 to 20 percent in town house values over the last three years, said Mr. Ferris, the real estate broker. In the Italianate-style Fitzroy Place co-ops, which extend from 22d to 23d Street in the midblock between Ninth and 10th Avenues, two-bedroom apartments fetched $450,000 in late 1997. The outsides of these town houses contain or reflect much of their original detail, with ornamental front gardens, imitation gas lamps, cast-iron railings, and big rear gardens.

Vacant town houses are difficult to find in Chelsea, and there are few quality prewar doorman buildings. Four of these are at the landmark

London Terrace Complex, opened in 1930. A two-bedroom co-op at London Terrace sold for $390,000 at the end of 1997, with maintenance of $1,235. The complex, home to many in the fashion industry, has an indoor swimming pool and a gym. The central buildings are rentals.

The rental market in Chelsea is tight, brokers say, with average studios renting for $1,100 in 1997 compared with about $850 in 1994. One-bedroom apartments rent for between $1,500 and $2,200, while two-bedroom apartments fetch between $2,300 and $3,200. The Chelsea Coalition on Housing and the Chelsea Housing Group advise and represent tenants.

There is something for most pocketbooks in Chelsea, but demand is especially fierce for some real estate. Waiting lists for the 2,820 units at the moderate-income Penn South co-op have been closed since 1987, said Brendan Keany, general manager, and sublets are not allowed.

Near Penn South on 23d Street is Chelsea's commercial center. The busy street was once the city's liveliest entertainment district. While clubs like Roxy and Tunnel are thriving in Chelsea, other clubs in western Chelsea have closed after residents' complaints. Less contentious forms of entertainment include the nine-screen Cineplex Odeon on 23d Street, the Off-Broadway W.P.A. Theater, and the Joyce Theater for dance productions.

Many people in the theater and the arts worlds call Chelsea home. At one time, the Chelsea Hotel on 23d Street was a residence for Arthur Miller and Dylan Thomas. Joni Mitchell was inspired to write "Chelsea Morning" in the hotel. Notoriety, as well as the literati, attracts tourists to the Chelsea Hotel, where the girlfriend of the aptly named Sid Vicious was murdered.

Iconoclastic 23d Street is also the headquarters of the Communist Party U.S.A. and its Unity bookstore (no espresso bar).

Despite significant gentrification, Chelsea still has plenty of quirky niches. But long gone are the days when Chelsea was home to sailors and longshoremen who occupied rooming houses in brownstones scattered about the neighborhood. Fading, too, is a prevailing immigrant presence, although there is still a Greek Orthodox church at 359 West 24th Street, and a Lutheran church on 22d Street conducts services in German. Remnants of Little Spain exist on 14th Street near Eighth Avenue, including the Spanish Benevolent Society and Our Lady of Guadalupe Church, which offers Mass in Spanish and English.

Around the corner on 15th Street, El Cid Tapas Bar & Restaurant serves fine Spanish dishes, and diners can still savor Chinese-Cuban cuisine at several Eighth Avenue spots.

"Chelsea," said Lori Bezahler, director of development at the Hudson Guild, a 100-year-old Chelsea settlement house, "is a fabulous microcosm of what I like to think New York City is."

EAST END AVENUE

Upscale Manhattan, with small-town touches

BY BRET SENFT

Twin lanes of cars pass along the Franklin D. Roosevelt Drive and disappear beneath the wedge of the elevated John H. Finley Walk that curves close to East End Avenue. John Marshall's seventh-floor window looks out toward Astoria's low-level terrain to the east, the Queensboro Bridge to the south. He is unhappy about the lights on Roosevelt Island that dim the skies for his terrace telescopes, but Mr. Marshall, a widower retired from his job as a supervisor with the Singer Company, is otherwise pleased with his accommodations: a two-bedroom apartment he and his wife, Anna, rented in 1954 and bought, for a fraction of its current value, in 1960. "If I were to move," he said, "although I would make a huge paper profit, I would gain nothing—because I wouldn't get anything as good as this."

Susan Coleman, a lifelong neighborhood resident whose family has owned a delicatessen at 50 East End for 45 years, works behind the deli's counter, where she holds customers' extra apartment keys and Federal Express or shopping packages. Her store, Ms. Coleman said, has been described as "a psyche-deli," because she ministers to emotional needs. "People come in and tell me all their troubles," she said. "We're very involved in people's lives."

Monro Wines & Spirits, the next block up, does likewise. Both proffer cab fare for East Enders arriving late with no small change. Such small-town customs, with little commercial traffic (there are two dry cleaners, a gift shop, a laundry, and a Sloan's supermarket), afford a virtual suburban lifestyle within Manhattan. Transportation includes the York Avenue M31 bus to 57th Street, and crosstown buses on 86th Street and 79th Street.

Three or four decades ago, Ms. Coleman said, the neighborhood consisted largely of "small buildings and families with eight kids." Many of those people have relocated, she said, but side streets still contain rent-

POPULATION: 19,162.

AREA: 0.14 square mile.

MEDIAN HOUSEHOLD INCOME: $78,865.

PRICE OF A MIDRANGE TWO-BEDROOM CO-OP: $557,500.

MEDIAN PRICE OF A TOWN HOUSE: $1.45 million.

RUSH-HOUR TRAVEL TO MIDTOWN: 30 minutes.

TRANSPORTATION: York Avenue M31 to 57th Street; crosstown M86 and M79 buses connect with subways and uptown and downtown buses.

CODES: Area, 212; ZIP, 10128, 10028, and 10021.

controlled and rent-stabilized railroad flats whose longtime tenants may pay less than $300 a month and live a wall away from recently arrived young professionals who pay multiples of that amount for the same type of unit.

East End Avenue runs from 79th to 90th Street; it is part of the neighborhood of Yorkville, which was established by German immigrants in the late 18th century. Archibald Gracie built a mansion in 1799 at what is now 88th Street; it is now the residence of New York City's mayor. According to the urban historian Val Ginter, estates near Gracie Mansion owned by the Astor, Gracie, Rhinelander, and Schermerhorn families were divided in the mid-19th century after the city created its street grid. Light industry (a lime yard, a cigar factory) was established in the late 19th century. Working-class tenements filled the side streets.

In 1881, John C. Henderson built 32 Queen Anne red-brick town houses for "persons of moderate means." The houses, most of them on East End between 86th and 87th Streets, run into a mews, Henderson Place, on 86th Street. In summer 1996, the renovated No. 146 sold for $1.325 million, according to Sieglinda G.-S. O'Donnell of the William B. May Company.

The west side of the mews was leveled in 1961 for the 22-story luxury high-rise Henderson House at 535 East 86th Street; the remaining 24 houses attained landmark status in 1969. Henderson House "has no mortgage, therefore very low maintenance," said Barbara Freehill of the Corcoran Group. In 1995, a second-floor, seven-room apartment sold for $635,000; the same amount bought only 4½ rooms on that floor in early 1998. The most recent penthouse sale was in 1995, when a seven-room penthouse with river views changed hands for $1.05 million.

By the standards of other parts of the city, the neighborhood is quiet, an attribute that its residents cherish. "Some people consider this dull, but I'm at a stage in my life where I cherish 'dull,'" said Laura Palmer, a freelance producer for NBC who spent her 20s in the West Village and now lives with her daughter and two poodles in a rental building nearby. "There are two schools, and in the morning the streets are filled with children,"

Ms. Palmer said. "There's a lot of life, without there being a trendiness to go with it—there is absolutely no scene here."

At the top of East End Avenue sits the largest parabolic cement building in the world, built in 1944 as an asphalt-mixing plant. Converted 40 years later into the George and Annette Murphy Center, it is part of a sports/community center under the rubric Asphalt Green. It houses a 90-seat theater, art studios, and two gyms. Outside are an Astroturf playing field stretching from East End to York Avenue, a perimeter running track, and basketball courts. Adjacent is the AquaCenter, which opened in July 1993 and has an Olympic-standard indoor pool, a 750-seat stadium, a health/fitness center, saunas, and steam rooms. The pool, said Ms. Palmer, is "like a little slice of Aruba."

The author Susan Cheever, who lives with her daughter and son in an apartment below Ms. Palmer's, walked by with her corgi, Lydia, and joined the discussion of her neighborhood. "There is something of a literary scene," Ms. Cheever said. It includes Jean Stein, the editor and publisher of *Grand Street* magazine; Jane Hitchcock, a novelist; the journalist Terry McDonnell and his novelist wife, J. M. Among other residents are Walter Cronkite, Willard Scott, and Patricia Neal.

The City and Suburban Homes, a complex of six-story tenements from York Avenue to the river along 79th Street, was constructed in sections from 1901 to 1913. But luxury-apartment-house developers hesitated to go so far east until the pioneering Chapin School built its own Georgian-style building in 1928 at 100 East End, at 84th Street. (Today, tuition is $14,025 for kindergarten, $15,375 for grades 1–12.)

The Brearley School moved to its building at 610 East 83rd Street, near East End, in 1929. A two-floor addition to the existing 10 stories was built in 1995 for grades 9–12, and includes a student desktop publication office, two computer labs, and art studios for ceramics and photography. A 12,000-square-foot field house was built in 1997 at 353 East 87th Street, with a regulation-size basketball court (convertible to two practice courts or two regulation-size volleyball courts); the roof is used as a practice area for field sports. School tuition is $15,400 for kindergarten through fourth grade, $15,700 for fifth through 12th grade.

One block down from City and Suburban, at 1458 York Avenue, P.S. 158 provides a literacy-based enrichment program in a heterogeneous learning environment for grades K–5. The Parent Association, its roughly $200,000 budget the result of year-round fund-raising, pays for classroom materials and cultural enrichment programs.

Upstairs, on the fifth floor, is the East Side Middle School, with admission based on test scores, interviews, and submitted written work. The school has affiliations with science and art museums and with concert-band and cultural programs. Each year, more than 80 percent of East Side Middle School's graduates proceed to either the city's total-educational-option high schools (such as the Beacon School at 227 West 61st Street) or the four specialized high schools, to which entrance is by highly competitive examination, according to District 2 spokesman Andrew Lachman.

Roman Catholic schools in the neighborhood include St. Joseph's School of Yorkville (pre-K is $3,200 a year; K–8, $2,650 a year), at 420 East 87th Street, and St. Stephen of Hungary School, at 408 East 82d Street (K–8, $2,000 a year for parishioners, $2,500 for nonparishioners).

In 1928, a Board of Estimate ruling restricted development on East End Avenue to residential use below 84th Street. The 14-story building at 25 East End, at 80th Street, was first up (a six-room apartment on the ninth floor recently closed for $1.05 million). It was followed by No. 120, at 85th Street, built by Vincent Astor (who had earlier built 520 and 530 East 86th Street); it has 17 stories, large rooms, and views of the park and the river. Its 23-room penthouse sold in summer 1994 for $5.85 million. A 13-room apartment on the 15th floor recently went to contract for $4.75 million.

Buildings along Gracie Square, on the park's southern border, also date from the late 1920s/early 1930s, the most coveted being No. 10, a 15-story co-op facing the river. The south penthouse was on the market in early 1998 for $4.995 million; an 11-room duplex (14 and 15F), with views to the east, had an asking price of $3.65 million.

The East River Park, originally from 84th to 86th Street, was designed by Samuel Parsons of Vaux & Parsons in 1876; it was expanded to 90th Street in 1891 and renamed Carl Schurz Park in 1911 for the German immigrant and statesman. The John H. Finley Walk, over the Franklin D. Roosevelt Drive since 1941, serves as a promenade from 81st to 90th Street, continuing as a joggers' path along the river.

Since the mid-1970s, the Carl Schurz Park Association has supplemented Parks Department maintenance by setting new drainage pipes and cherry trees in the mall; restoring entrances, stairways, and a children's playground; and creating a dog run. A dog subculture has grown up around the run, where residents congregate and set their dogs to frolic.

THE FAR WEST VILLAGE

Bohemian, with Hudson breezes

BY PETER MALBIN

Open-sky vistas that stretch to the river and beyond provide a serene contrast to the Greenwich Village bustle that lies to the east of Hudson Street. On the west side of Hudson, every day feels like a Sunday. Homey neighborhood take-out stores do a thriving business catering to artists, photographers, and designers working from studios in converted warehouses. On Hudson Street are quaint neighborhood stores like Myers of Keswick, a haven for British expatriates in search of Cornish pasties and Scotch eggs. Mrs. Hudson's Video Library has an extensive catalog of BBC television shows and foreign-language films. Residents without doormen stop on their way home at the Golden Rabbit stationery store at 561 Hudson to collect their packages and dry cleaning at a cost of $1 per item.

"It's magical down here," said Jo Hamilton, who moved in 1994 with her family and pets into an 1840s Greek Revival town house on Jane Street, which they restored under strict historical guidelines. "It's the ultimate in Village living. When I walk the dog, I see four people I know and I meet people I didn't know."

The neighborhood's history has been one of mixed uses. Dutch settlers developed a tobacco plantation in the area in the late 17th century. Sir Peter Warren, a British naval commander, bought the plantation in different parcels from 1731 through 1744 and renamed his estate Greenwich. Gradually, a village with farmers' markets sprang up near the shoreline. A maritime industry centering around the Hudson River piers attracted immigrant longshoremen and artisans, who occupied rooms in tenements between factories and warehouses. Remnants of the elevated freight line that ran through the third floor of some industrial buildings along Washington Street into the Meatpacking District just south of 14th Street are a reminder of a bygone era.

POPULATION: 12,896.

AREA: 0.9 square mile.

MEDIAN HOUSEHOLD INCOME: $77,161.

MEDIAN PRICE OF A ONE-BEDROOM CO-OP: $242,000.

MEDIAN PRICE OF A TOWN HOUSE: $2 million.

PRICE OF A 2,000-SQUARE-FOOT LOFT: $888,000.

MIDRANGE RENT FOR A ONE-BEDROOM APARTMENT: $2,000.

RUSH-HOUR TRAVEL TO MIDTOWN: Buses on Seventh and Eighth Avenues, 20 minutes; A, C, E, 1, 2, 3, and 9 subway trains, 5 minutes; PATH train at Christopher and Hudson Streets, 10 minutes.

CODES: Area, 212: ZIP, 10014.

"When I moved here, you felt like there were more trucks than people, and there were meat carcasses everywhere," said Marjorie Colt, who bought a town house in 1959 on Horatio Street for $37,000. "In the last 10 years, the neighborhood has become fashionable—we could probably get close to 1 million today."

Most of the former industrial and institutional buildings in the Far West Village converted to high-end residential real estate in the 1980s, when the low-rise neighborhood quietly became gentrified. Brokers say the real estate market is hot, with more buyers than available properties. "You will have to pay a premium to live in the neighborhood," said Joan Kadushin, a broker with Eychner Associates. A premium, that is, for housing that's anything but run-of-the-mill. "The wonderful ghosts of history are all around you in the Far West Village," said Ben Green, chairman of Community Board 2. "It's like living in a museum."

The eclectic real estate mix includes a former printing house on Hudson Street that is now a condominium loft building with a doorman, and the former Federal Archives Building—bounded by Christopher, Greenwich, Barrow, and Washington Streets—which has been converted into rental apartments. The printing presses have stopped at 155 Perry Street for the Italian newspaper *Il Progresso*, but the building was renovated into lofts with 12-foot ceilings. The Sapolia soap factory at 166 Bank Street is now a high-end co-op loft dwelling, as is a former stable on Horatio Street. The aroma of eclairs baking once wafted from what is now the co-op residence at 68 Jane Street, while the former Sixth Precinct station house at 135 Charles Street has been converted into Le Gendarme rentals.

Peter Rippon lives with his family in a 3,000-square-foot duplex loft on West 12th Street, near West Street, where he designs furniture. "We get the breezes off the Hudson, and you get more air and light here," he says of the neighborhood. There is a D'Agostino supermarket nearby, but subways are a 10-minute walk east. It is a 10-minute commute to midtown by train.

Real estate prices in the neighborhood have risen 10 to 20 percent in the last several years, brokers say. In the fourth quarter of 1997, a 1,200-square-foot historic brownstone co-op in "mint condition" at 69 Perry Street sold for $565,000. A 1,200-square-foot two-bedroom prewar co-op with a balcony and terrace at 256 West 10th Street sold for $600,000. An 1,850-square-foot loft at 380 West 12th Street sold for $780,000.

Co-op lofts command upward of $300 per square foot (and condominiums upward of $350), depending on size, light, windows, floor, location, and condition of the building, said Ed Ferris, a broker with the William B. May Company.

One of the earliest conversions of industrial space into residential apartments took place in the late '60s at Westbeth, the 13 buildings bounded by Washington, Bank, Bethune, and West Streets. Formerly a Bell Laboratories research center, this is where scientists pioneered long-distance telephone service and talking pictures. Creative juices still flow at Westbeth, now a subsidized artists' residence with an on-site gallery, sculpture studio, and graphic workshop. Residents pay from $380 for efficiencies to $660 for highly coveted three-bedroom apartments. Artists who are eligible for housing join an eight-year waiting list.

The wait is also long for the cherished rent-regulated apartments at the five-story West Village Houses, which opened 19 years ago for moderate-income families. The cluster of 42 buildings, with courtyards and gardens, stretches between Washington and West Streets from Morton to Bank Street. The maximum rent for a two-bedroom apartment is $897, and families must earn between $35,000 and $85,000 to qualify.

Market rentals in the Far West Village are rarely a bargain. Studios start at $1,150 (add $100 for a doorman or an alcove), one-bedrooms range between $1,500 and $2,200 (with doormen and dining areas), and two-bedrooms are priced from $2,300 to $3,200. Three-bedroom apartments for rent can fetch between $3,300 and $3,800, according to the Corcoran Group.

Many families moved into spacious loft buildings in the '80s, raising the number of neighborhood children under the age of 9 by 32 percent. The pre-K–6 P.S. 3, the alternative arts-oriented 540-pupil elementary school, occupies a landmark building at 490 Hudson Street, at Grove Street. Residents can also send their children to P.S. 41 at 116 West 11th Street, at Sixth Avenue.

The West Village Nursery School, a parent-owned co-op at 73 Horatio Street, was established in 1962. Tuition ranges from $1,700 to $5,430. Far West Village neighborhood parents raised money to establish the progressive, independent K–8 Village Community School in 1973. Housed in a five-story, 19th-century building at 272 West 10th Street, the school has 267 pupils. Tuition ranges from $12,400 to $13,350.

St. Luke's School, an independent Episcopal day school established in

1945, offers small classes for 4-year-olds through eighth grade. Tuition for 190 students ranges from $12,350 to $12,960. Nature classes at St. Luke's often take place in the verdant St. Luke's Garden on the school's two-block campus. The St. Luke's campus also includes the Episcopal Church of St. Luke-in-the-Fields, the city's third-oldest church, established 1822, when the site was literally a field. It was restored and expanded after it was destroyed by a fire in 1981.

On the first balcony of the Roman Catholic Church of St. Veronica at 149 Christopher Street are brass memorial plaques dedicated to people who have died of AIDS-related causes. The former rectory of the parish at 657 Washington Street has been converted into the Gift of Love hospice for 15 men with AIDS, staffed by the Missionaries of Charity founded by Mother Teresa. At the Bailey Holt House, at 180 Christopher Street, there are 44 formerly homeless men and women living with AIDS. Opened in December 1985, it was the first residential support program in the country.

In warmer months, passersby may watch residents doing the slow-motion tai chi chuan exercises at Corporal Seravalli Park in the morning. Children enjoy several playgrounds along Hudson Street.

Congregation Beth Simchat Torah, which claims the largest gay and lesbian membership of any synagogue in the country, leases space at 57 Bethune Street in the Westbeth complex. Westbeth also leases space to two Off-Off-Broadway theaters and the Merce Cunningham Dance Company.

"We are currently being overrun by models," said George Kroon, who teaches marketing at New York University and lives on Horatio Street. Industria, the fashion photography studio at 775 Washington Street, and other photo studios have added a glamorous new industry to the neighborhood.

On weekend nights, there is a vibrant bar and club scene on Christopher Street and in the Meatpacking District. The funky Florent Restaurant at 69 Gansevoort Street is buzzing at all hours. On Greenwich Street, Le Zoo attracts a trendy crowd. Other restaurants include the Au Troquet bistro on West 12th Street and El Faro, specializing in tapas. Neighborhood hangouts include Nadine's and Tortilla Flats. Among the artists and painters who live in the Far West Village these days are Lanford Wilson, the playwright; Paul Rudnick, the playwright and screenwriter; RuPaul, the drag artist; Gregory Hines, the actor and dancer; and Jennifer Bartlett, the painter.

"The neighborhood is still partly bohemian," Mr. Kroon said. "If you're the slightest bit nonhomogenized milk, it's a wonderful place to be."

INWOOD

A polyglot island on Manhattan's northern tip

BY MAGGIE GARB

On a clear day, the view from the terrace of Jane Kinney's co-op in the Inwood neighborhood on Manhattan's northern tip spans the Hudson River to the wooded hills of the Palisades. Tired of high rents and tiny box-like apartments downtown, Ms. Kinney, an editor at a downtown publishing house, moved to Inwood in 1995. "I came up here expecting to rent," she said. "But I realized I could afford to buy. One of the things I wanted was an unobstructed view of the sky and I got it here."

Nestled between the Harlem and Hudson Rivers just north of Fort Tryon Park and its Cloisters medieval museum, and edged to the east with the craggy bluffs of Inwood Hill Park, Inwood has long attracted those seeking lower-priced housing and a slice of nature in Manhattan. "The neighborhood feels almost isolated from the rest of Manhattan," said Federico Camilo, a graphic designer who with his wife, Malgorzata, and two children has lived in Inwood for a decade. "We decided we didn't want to do the suburban thing, but we wanted to be near a park and away from the high stress of downtown."

In the '30s, working-class people of Irish and German descent settled in the neighborhood's low-rise buildings, which were then abutted in some cases by farmland. By the '60s, the farms had disappeared and Cuban and Puerto Rican families moved into the prewar six- and seven-story buildings east of Broadway. More recently, Dominican immigrants have flocked into Inwood, and the seven-block area bordered by Broadway, Post Avenue, and Dyckman and 207th Streets now houses what is considered the nation's largest concentration of Dominicans.

Inwood is changing again. Just a 30-minute commute to midtown on the A train, 45 minutes on the 1 or 9 line, the neighborhood has become a

POPULATION: 58,289.

AREA: 1 square mile.

MEDIAN HOUSEHOLD INCOME: $30,928.

MEDIAN PRICE OF A TWO-BEDROOM CO-OP: $60,000–$70,000.

MIDRANGE RENT FOR A TWO-BEDROOM APARTMENT: $950–$1,000.

DISTANCE FROM MIDTOWN MANHATTAN: 8 miles.

RUSH-HOUR TRAVEL TO MIDTOWN: 30 minutes on the A train from Broadway and 207th or Dyckman Street; 45 minutes on the 1 or 9 train from St. Nicholas Avenue and 215th, 207th, or Dyckman Street; 30 minutes on the express Liberty Lines bus from 207th Street and Broadway, $3 one way.

CODES: Area, 212; ZIP, 10040 and 10034.

refuge for actors, musicians, and artists seeking to escape pricey downtown rents. Like the immigrants who arrived with dreams of a better life, the artists have brought a host of plans for revitalizing the neighborhood.

New homeowners have banded together to sponsor street fairs and neighborhood cleanups in parks and playgrounds. Musicians play regular gigs in neighborhood bars, and residents are increasingly volunteering their time in after-school arts programs.

Michael Petelka, a longtime resident, owns six buildings in Inwood. "The neighborhood is hungry for cafes and places for artists," he said, noting that over the last five years he has rented apartments to two filmmakers, a composer, a Broadway actor, several Off-Broadway actors, and three painters. "A lot of these people are moving from Chelsea and the West Village, where prices have gone out of control," he said.

With rents as low as $500 to $600 for a studio in 1997, struggling artists and medical students working at Columbia-Presbyterian Medical Center have moved in. Large one- and two-bedroom apartments rent for $750 to $1,200. East of Broadway, where recent immigrants from the Dominican Republic and Central America tend to settle, rents are slightly less, said Philip C. Moya, who owns an Inwood real estate agency. The neighborhood's rental market is thriving, said Mr. Moya and other brokers.

Sales of co-ops began increasing in early 1997, with prices going up slowly. One-bedroom co-ops range in price from $30,000 to $40,000. More common are sales of two- and three-bedroom co-ops west of Broadway in the Art Deco buildings overlooking Inwood Hill Park. Prices in those buildings began climbing in the mid-nineties. Depending on the condition of the co-op, two-bedrooms are priced from $45,000 to $90,000. Duplex and three-bedroom co-ops run from $105,000 to $150,000, with maintenance fees ranging from $875 to $1,200.

Charles and Lisa Stephenson moved from midtown into a duplex with a 300-square-foot terrace three years ago. "Our sophisticated friends with their chichi apartments in Lincoln Center walk in and take a look at the staircase and say, 'What's that?' " Mr. Stephenson said. "To have a duplex with a terrace in Manhattan is something we never thought would happen."

A handful of row houses line Payson Avenue and Park Terrace West. Built in the '20s, the narrow brick houses are prized by many seeking a house in Manhattan. A two-family house in need of extensive renovations sold for $150,000 in 1996. Another, a single-family in better condition, was sold for $240,000 in 1993, said Robert Kleinbardt, a broker with New Heights Realty. But, he added, very few single-family homes ever go on the market.

Once a fertile hunting ground for Weckquasgeek Indians, Inwood was settled by Dutch farmers in the late 18th century. Much of the fighting during the Battle of Harlem Heights, a major Revolutionary War battle, took place in Inwood.

A legacy of the neighborhood's rural history is Manhattan's last standing colonial farmhouse, the Dyckman House at the northwest corner of Broadway and 204th Street. It was built in 1784, and in the early 19th century the Dyckman family owned about 450 acres of cherry, pear, and apple orchards in the surrounding hills. But by midcentury, when the pastures around the house were used to graze herds of cattle on their way to market downtown, the Dyckman family moved to 225th Street and the house fell into disrepair. Restored by the family and donated to the city in 1915, the farmhouse today is a museum.

Inwood got its name from the verdant woods that once blanketed northern Manhattan. The only remnant of natural forest in Manhattan lies in Inwood Hill Park, a 197-acre rocky expanse covered with oak, tulip, maple, hickory, and dogwood trees. The park features six miles of hiking trails, the only accessible salt marsh in Manhattan, ball fields, and tennis and basketball courts. There are three newly refurbished playgrounds in adjoining Isham Park.

Inwood Hill Park's rangers offer regularly scheduled walking tours on Indian history, park geology, and native birds. An urban ecology center, located in a renovated boathouse near the park entrance at 218th Street and Indian Road, offers after-school programs, exhibits on park life, and a computerized guide to various sites in the park.

Jane Schachat, director for North Manhattan Parks, says Inwood Hill Park rivals Central Park for bird-watching. "In the fall, hawks come down the river, their migration path," she said. "There may be some days when you'll see several thousand hawks."

As in much of the city, crime in Inwood has diminished in recent years, but residents warn against walking alone in the neighborhood at night. "The muggings really are it," said Police Lieut. Ralph Robinson, noting that there was little violent crime. "Seniors seem to be the ones targeted." He added that car thefts and break-ins had risen "a little bit."

Inwood is in Community School District 6, which includes Washington Heights. All of Inwood's schools—P.S. 98, 5, and 152 and I.S. 52—are overcrowded. Residents have been fighting for new schools and for renovations of existing schools for several years. Three years ago, an alternative K–4 school, the Muscota New School, opened with 185 students on two floors of P.S. 5 at Broadway and 204th Street. Two other alternative schools for intermediate grades are also housed in the building. All offer "hands-on learning, bolstered by computers, with an emphasis on the arts," said the school's interim principal, Lydia Bassett. The schools are open to all students living in Inwood.

The closest secondary school is George Washington High School in neighboring Washington Heights. But because the school has long operated well over its 2,715 capacity, with a current student population nearing 4,000, many students go to school elsewhere in Manhattan.

Many recent immigrants attend Liberty 2 High School, also called Gregorio Luperon in honor of the late-19th-century leader of a Dominican nationalist movement, which offers intensive English-language training.

There is one Roman Catholic school in the neighborhood, the pre-K–8 Good Shepherd School in the heart of Inwood on Isham Street.

Two long-standing community organizations are among groups offering an array of programs designed to bring the neighborhood together. Good Shepherd Church, which has been in Inwood since 1912, sponsors Scout troops, an after-school program, and visits with the elderly, and provides a food pantry and small shelter for the homeless. Inwood Community Services, which opened in 1988, offers English-as-a-second-language classes, a youth tutoring program, and mental-health, drug, and alcohol clinics.

The neighborhood's commercial streets, Broadway, Dyckman, and 207th, show signs of the many changes Inwood has seen. Amidst the bodegas and Latin music stores are a handful of boutiques selling goods imported from Ireland. The Piper's Kilt, an Irish pub on Broadway, is popular for its burgers and beers. El Lina Restaurant on 207th Street offers upscale Dominican food and the Carrot Top bakery on 211th Street is known for its carrot cake. The Chanting House Cafe on 207th Street, one of the most recent and popular additions to the neighborhood, serves beer, wine, and Irish-style food.

"Physically, the neighborhood has changed only slightly in the last few years," said Mr. Camilo, the graphic designer who has lived here for 10 years. "But the social ramifications of all these people moving here, coming together, and talking will blossom."

THE LOWER EAST SIDE

Reinventing the first stop for immigrants

BY JANICE FIORAVANTE

The Lower East Side, long the first home of immigrants, is being redis-covered by new immigrants—artists who are joining earlier homesteaders from the late '80s and are moving from the East Village or reeling from SoHo prices. "The community keeps reinventing itself," said Susan Fleminger, director of visual arts and arts education at the Henry Street Settlement, one of six century-old settlement houses that continue to help new immigrants, providing day care and programs for the young and old, as well as cultural activities. "Just when you think it's over, it revives itself."

The changes in the area are reflected in tenements that were built in the 1860s to the early 1900s, but were boarded up in the mid-1930s when owners felt new requirements for renovations to bring in more light and air too costly to undertake during the Depression. "They couldn't rehabili-tate them; they didn't have the money," said Matthew Bauer, executive director of the Lower East Side Business Improvement District (BID). Ground-floor stores remained opened, however, and now the upper floors are being renovated, preserving such elements as window surrounds and cornices and bringing closer-to-market-rate prices to the neighborhood.

But what some people view as a renaissance others see as displace-ment of the poor. As the middle class moves in and prices rise, some locals fear gentrification is driving out poorer residents of the neighborhood, stretching from Houston Street to the Brooklyn Bridge and the Bowery to the East River and taking in a large part of Chinatown, including the 44-story Confucious Plaza, just south of the Manhattan Bridge ramp. "It's a very divisive issue," said Ann Bobco, a resident and a member of Commu-nity Board 3.

"People are screaming about gentrification," said Lyn Pentecost,

POPULATION: 98,000.

AREA: 0.85 square mile.

MEDIAN HOUSEHOLD INCOME: $26,300.

MEDIAN PRICE OF A ONE-BEDROOM CONDO: $110,000.

PRICE OF A MIDRANGE ONE-BEDROOM APARTMENT: $1,400 (exclusive of public housing).

DISTANCE FROM MIDTOWN MANHATTAN: 2.25 miles.

RUSH-HOUR TRAVEL TO MIDTOWN: 10 minutes on the F, D, B, or Q subway train; 25 minutes on the M9 or M15 buses.

CODES: Area, 212; ZIP, 10002 and 10038.

chairwoman of the Lower East Side Coalition for Housing Development. But Ms. Pentecost, a 35-year resident who teaches metropolitan studies at New York University, said that for every market-rate apartment, there's low-income housing coming online. "There's a strong nonprofit sector in the neighborhood keeping affordable housing here," she said.

On Ms. Bobco's Suffolk Street block, for example, the Asian Americans for Equality (A.A.F.E.), a community-development organization, is building 12 four-story houses with 48 for-sale units. Their two- and three-bedroom units will sell for $125,000 to $140,000. The units will be limited to households earning $40,000 to $70,000.

"Ownership gives residents a stake in the community," said Christopher Kui, executive director of A.A.F.E. "Why should people have to move out to Queens to own a home?" His agency acts as a tenant advocate as well as a developer and refurbishes existing buildings.

Originally, Irish and German immigrants came here, followed by eastern Europeans and southern Italians. "By the 1890s, the residents were mostly eastern European Jews," said Sharon Seitz of the Tenement Museum, at 97 Orchard Street, near Delancey Street, which occupies a building built in 1863. Today, Dominicans, Mexicans, Colombians, Bengalis, and Chinese are among the residents.

Schools are a problem. In Community School District 1, five of nine schools have been cited for corrective action for poor performance. Sonia Diaz Salcedo, who became superintendent in August 1997, has removed three principals from troubled schools, instituted professional-development programs for assistant principals and staff, and is focusing on improving the physical plants of schools.

But at the pre-K–6 P.S. 20, the principal, Dr. Leonard Golubchick, said that 90 percent of his 1,010 pupils scored at or above the 90th percentile in state reading and math tests. Moreover, he said, grades 4, 5, and 6 are connected to the Internet; all classrooms have at least one computer, the technology lab has 34 Macintosh terminals, the library has five computers, and a multimedia center with computers is imminent. In 1997, the school received a $75,000 Annenberg grant for each of five years for arts programs, provided through the Henry Street Settlement.

Among the school's graduates are the Gershwin brothers; Louis J. Lefkowitz, the longtime New York State attorney general; George Burns; and Edward G. Robinson.

I.S. 131, one of six schools in District 2 that serve the community, is known as the Dr. Sun Yat-sen School. It enrolls 1,400 students, of whom 85 percent are Chinese, said Alice Young, its principal. "English is a second language for most kids here, even the native born, because they speak Chinese at home," she explained. The school offers a Saturday program to inspire literacy. Called "Walk, Talk, Think, Write," it exposes students to their community and beyond. A recent program included a tour of the uptown and SoHo Guggenheim Museums for children and parents.

The 2,300-student, 70-year-old Seward Park High School has long been regarded as a troubled school. In 1993, Councilwoman Kathryn E. Freed attended the funeral of a student who had been knifed to death. But now, she said, there is an effort to turn the school around.

"Our printing and publishing program includes tours of printing presses and teaches word processing, computer graphics, and desktop publishing," said Kenneth Harvey, assistant principal for guidance. And, he said, a medical technology program offers internships for seniors in labs at New York Downtown Hospital and Bellevue.

Among the private schools are Tifereth Jerusalem, a K–12 yeshiva with 150 students, where tuition is $3,900 a year, and the pre-K–8, 210-student Roman Catholic St. James School, where tuition is $1,930 to $3,500, depending on the number of children in a family.

There are seven public housing projects in the neighborhood, with a total of 9,465 apartments. And running along Grand Street from Essex Street to the river are 28 12- to 20-story co-ops, with a total of 4,400 units, many with spectacular views. Celia Honig, assistant principal at I.S. 131, who grew up in the area, now lives in a one-bedroom co-op at East Broadway. "They were originally financed by garment industry unions," said Ms. Honig, referring to the International Ladies' Garment Workers' Union and the Amalgamated Clothing Workers.

The co-ops were built from the 1930s to the late 1960s as affordable housing for the middle class, added Joel Kaplan of the United Jewish Council. "Co-ops could be bought for $3,000 a room and had to be sold back to the co-op," he said. "But in November 1996, co-op members voted to reconstitute the cap to $15,000 a room and allow sales to outsiders."

But demand far outstrips supply, said Sion Misrahi, owner of a real estate firm by the same name. "One-bedroom co-ops cost from $45,000 to $57,000, but they're hard to come by," he said. Heshey Jacob, general manager for three of the co-ops, Seward Park, Hillman, and East River, with

4,200 apartments, said that 150 apartments had sold in nine months, "so you can see the turnover rate is not high." He cited sales of two-bedroom units for $60,000 and three-bedrooms for $85,000.

"Rentals of one-bedroom apartments in refurbished tenements are going for $1,100 to $1,500, while two-bedrooms run from $1,500 to $2,000," noted Mr. Misrahi.

Mr. Misrahi's own life mirrors the neighborhood's. "I was a merchant on Orchard Street and my father also had a store here," he said. Then in August 1994, he opened his firm as its only employee and now has 17 people working with him. "My office played a role in pushing for renovations as buildings became valuable." He was the founding president of the BID.

Buildings being bought for renovation for market-rate rentals or co-ops are selling for $80 and $120 a square foot, Mr. Misrahi added. The stores themselves, which five years ago ran anywhere from $20 to $80 a square foot, now go for as much as $120 a square foot. If the store is "on Orchard Street between Delancey and Rivington Streets, or Essex and Delancey, there's more shopping traffic and the price is higher," he explained.

The higher prices reflect the influx of designer clothing stores and trendy restaurants such as the Living Room Cafe, which features folk music. They join such institutions as Katz's Delicatessen, at 205 East Houston Street, at Ludlow Street, and Ratner's, the kosher dairy restaurant, at 138 Delancey Street, near Suffolk Street, that itself has become a part of the '90s Lower East Side by opening Lansky's Lounge, a hip nightspot suggesting a speakeasy.

MANHATTAN

MARBLE HILL

It's in the Bronx, but it's still Manhattan

BY JENNIFER KINGSON BLOOM

Yes, you have crossed the Harlem River and, yes, that is the northern tip of Manhattan Island that you can see to the south. But, as residents of Marble Hill are quick to point out, you are not in the Bronx: Because of a 19th-century public works project that reshaped Manhattan Island and severed its topmost land, Marble Hill is across the river and into what logically should be the Bronx.

It is a quirky and little-known neighborhood whose residents consider it a well-kept secret. "I've been watching Marble Hill for years and saying, 'Why doesn't it catch fire?' " said John Brown, an agent with the Robert E. Hill Agency. "We don't do a lot of business there and I don't know any broker who does."

Few properties come on the market, he said. And those that do, sell for well below market rates in Manhattan or neighboring Riverdale. A single-family house with a yard and a couple of bedrooms, in good condition, sells for about $250,000, Mr. Brown said. Realtors link the low prices to the fact that the homes are aging and may need repairs, as well as to the fact that part of the small neighborhood is a giant public housing project. But Mr. Brown offers another explanation. "Many people don't even know it exists," he said.

Lying on a rocky hillside overlooking the Harlem River, the neighborhood is bounded to the north by 230th Street, to the east by Exterior Street, and to the west by Johnson Avenue. It was the site of a marble quarry in the early 19th century and did not draw a large residential population until the turn of the century, when the West Side subway was extended along Broadway to 225th Street. Many of the neighborhood's one- and two-family frame houses were built before World War I.

Marble Hill **31**

POPULATION: 8,152.

AREA: 52 acres.

MEDIAN HOUSEHOLD INCOME: $28,860.

MEDIAN PRICE OF A SINGLE-FAMILY HOUSE: $145,000.

TAXES ON A MEDIAN-PRICED HOUSE: $1,350.

DISTANCE FROM MIDTOWN MANHATTAN: 8 miles.

RUSH-HOUR TRAVEL TO MIDTOWN: 40 minutes on the No. 1 IRT local or Liberty Lines express bus to the East and West Sides, $3 one way; 22 minutes on the Metro-North Hudson line, $4.75 one way, $108 monthly.

CODES: Area, 718; ZIP, 10463

Today, there are 4,000 households in Marble Hill, but just 157 private homes.

The neighborhood is divided, both physically and socially: Clustered near the commercial spine of Broadway are the Marble Hill Houses, an 11-building public housing development, while up on "the hill," the former site of marble quarries, are the attractive turn-of-the-century houses that lend the neighborhood its cachet.

Rental apartments are easy to come by, but houses do not come on the market with great regularity. Rents range from $600 for a one-bedroom to $1,000 for two-bedroom apartments. Some homeowners and landlords choose only to advertise their properties in the classified section of the local paper, *The Riverdale Press*, and many transactions are done even more informally. "People just don't move out, and when they do, they often sell their homes to their neighbors," said H. Michael Pichardo, executive director of the Marble Hill Neighborhood Improvement Corporation.

In what many residents view as a vote of confidence for Marble Hill, City Councilman Guillermo Linares bought a house on Van Corlear Place in 1993. "We just went driving around and looking, and we saw this house that had a sale sign," Mr. Linares said. "We talked to the owner, we looked at the area, we fell in love with it, and we have been very happy." But even Mr. Linares, who was elected to represent the neighborhood in 1991, had not been aware of its existence or its status as part of Manhattan before he began campaigning for office. "Even though I had lived in Washington Heights all this time, I thought that on the other side of the 225th Street Bridge was the beginning of the Bronx," he said.

The confusion is extremely common. While Marble Hill residents vote in Manhattan, do jury duty there, and are represented by Manhattan officials, their municipal services come from the Bronx. Their fight for recognition as a Manhattan neighborhood has persisted for years. As recently as this decade, neighbors turned out in force to oppose the move to change their telephone area code from 212 to 718 (they lost).

Marble Hill was lopped from Manhattan in 1895, when the northern channel of the Harlem River was redug to make way for a ship canal. Soon after, the Spuyten Duyvil Creek was filled in, cementing Marble Hill to the Bronx. The Greater New York Charter of 1897 designated Marble Hill as part of Manhattan but not of New York County, producing decades of headaches and squabbles.

In 1984, the matter was settled with some finality when Assemblyman J. Brian Murtaugh and State Senator Franz Leichter sponsored successful legislation declaring the neighborhood part of Manhattan. Mr. Murtaugh, an Inwood resident, is a longtime Marble Hill enthusiast. "It's just a very unusual niche," he said. "It is one of the most ethnically and economically mixed neighborhoods in New York City, and yet they operate like a small town." A community council meets monthly.

Formerly an Irish and Jewish bastion, Marble Hill's population is now about 35 percent black and 55 percent Hispanic. In the '50s, the construction of the Marble Hill Houses brought about the radical demographic change. The neighborhood's population of middle-class Hispanic people has continued to grow in recent years, and the first Asians have begun moving in. While whites make up only about 8 percent of the population now, their influence still permeates the neighborhood: Broadway is still dotted with Irish pubs that draw a loyal clientele, and just over the Kingsbridge border are a kosher bakery and an Orthodox synagogue.

Rev. Leonis Quinlan, the pastor of St. Stephen's United Methodist Church on the southeast corner of Marble Hill Avenue and 228th Street, moved to Marble Hill in 1991 and said that its heavily Dominican flavor came as a pleasant surprise. "It is Dominican in its essence," he said. "You can smell the foods in the air, you can hear the music. You see older men playing dominoes in front of the bodegas, and women in traditional dress."

During the day, the neighborhood is populated—some would say inundated—by students from John F. Kennedy High School, a school of 4,500 that was built in 1972 for a student body of 3,400. Residents complain that the students generate noise and litter and crowd the local markets at lunchtime. But aside from the annoyance factor, the school's multiracial student body has caused no racial tensions.

"You don't have racial problems here—there are no bias crimes," Mr. Pichardo of the neighborhood group said. "Show me another neighborhood in the city with this racial composition, this mix, where people get along." Relations are somewhat less harmonious between homeowners and residents of the housing projects.

Elementary school students attend P.S. 37 on 230th Street or P.S. 7 in neighboring Kingsbridge. Both school buildings are in need of significant repairs and both are overcrowded. Reading scores in both schools are fairly low. But, noted Milton Fein, the principal of P.S. 7, many children in both schools are recent immigrants with a limited command of English. "By fifth grade, our scores improve significantly," he said. P.S. 7 was listed among the top public elementary schools in the city in *The Parents' Guide to New York City's Best Public Elementary Schools* by Clara Hemphill, a senior research fellow at the Public Eduction Association.

There are also several private schools, including two Catholic and three Jewish schools, in the surrounding neighborhoods.

Uphill from the boxy housing projects is a cluster of attractive homes, many of them fixer-uppers. Houses in poor condition sell for $65,000 to $70,000, Mr. Brown said. When they come on the market, he added, run-down houses often are sold to young couples who intend to spend a few years slowly fixing them up and then starting a family.

Most of the shops that serve the neighborhood lie over the Bronx border, but within easy walking distance. Residents also point with pride to the Allen Pavilion, a community hospital operated by Columbia-Presbyterian Medical Center just across the river in Inwood. And they note the abundance of transportation options: Both Metro-North and the IRT have stations in Marble Hill. The trip to midtown runs about 25 minutes on Metro-North. Numerous express buses run from Broadway and 230th Street to midtown Manhattan, and highways are close by.

On the downside, the neighborhood has no movie theaters, and dining options are limited to pubs and the Riverdale Diner. Two longtime neighborhood favorites are the midpriced Land and Sea restaurant and Piper's Kilt, a homey Irish pub.

As with any urban area, the neighborhood has its share of drug problems and blighted properties. Until several years ago, the neighborhood was included in Manhattan's 34th Police Precinct, but Bronx police from the 50th Precinct now protect Marble Hill's streets. Officials there say the neighborhood's crime rate is low, with drug-related arrests falling dramatically in the past few years.

One neighborhood stalwart is Dr. Jeffrey L. Gurian, a dentist and comedy writer whose practice lies across the street from St. Stephen's. Through his career as a professional comedian, he has lured various celebrities to his office for dental work. "When they see the private homes and the trees, they all say it's much nicer than they ever expected," Dr. Gurian said.

On the flip side, Dr. Gurian said, the neighbors are equally astonished by some of his clients. When the actor Charlie Sheen and his bodyguard drove to the office in a stretch limousine, the police came over to check out the situation. "They don't expect to see a big stretch limo up here," Dr. Gurian said.

THE MEATPACKING DISTRICT

Once-gritty neighborhood comes alive

BY JOYCE COHEN

Gansevoort Street marks the great divide. To the north is New York's meat market, a largely nocturnal link in the city's food chain, where meat is cut, packaged, and distributed for delivery. To the south are narrow residential streets, filled with historic brownstones, converted factories, and high-rise apartment houses.

The Meatpacking District, a curious mix of commerce and community, is finally living down its reputation as a seamy, threatening segment of the Far West Village, a place where trade was in flesh when not in meat. Certainly, some indelicate elements remain. But a crackdown on crime and the expansion of housing and small businesses have combined to make the area more desirable. "When we moved here 25 years ago, it was like Christopher Columbus and the end of the world," said Kathleen Pustarfi, who lives on Horatio Street.

Not anymore.

The meat market itself, extending north from Gansevoort to West 15th Street, is zoned for light manufacturing. Because of this, few people live there. But the area is changing quickly, with a boom in restaurants, bars, art galleries, antiques stores, and dance clubs.

South of Gansevoort, the residential areas have two distinct personalities. Toward the east are historic residential blocks that have, for years, been soldered together with active block associations.

"We're a mixed bag—gay, straight, single, married, children, elderly," said Carol Yankay, an officer of the Horatio Street Association. "You know everyone. Even if you're not a friendly person, they'll make it their business to know who you are. We consider that an asset."

Near the Hudson River are the former quarters of meatpackers and other industries. Many of the buildings have been converted to housing,

POPULATION: 6,166.

AREA: 1 square mile.

MEDIAN HOUSEHOLD INCOME: $62,208.

MEDIAN PRICE OF A ONE-BEDROOM CO-OP: $275,000.

DISTANCE FROM MIDTOWN MANHATTAN: 2 miles.

RUSH-HOUR TRAVEL TO MIDTOWN: 5 minutes on the 1, 2, 3, 9, A, C, or E subway train.

CODES: Area, 212; ZIP, 10014, 10011, and 10012.

and some new residential buildings have gone up.

The continuing changes are a mixed blessing for residents. On the one hand, they enjoy the liveliness, the shopping, the cleaned-up streets. On the other, they fear developmental overkill, with high-rises boxing in their homes, or megastores attracting excessive crowds and traffic.

The area has a century-long history as a marketplace. The Gansevoort Market opened in 1882, with farmers from neighboring states peddling their produce. The author Herman Melville worked as a customs inspector on a nearby pier. The current era of change began in 1969, when work began on Westbeth. The blond brick complex, dating from the turn of the century, had been the site of Bell Telephone Laboratories, where, among other things, the vacuum tube was invented. Today, with 384 units of federally subsidized housing for artists—and a screening committee to verify artistic authenticity—Westbeth has an eight-year waiting list.

The conversion of Westbeth "proved people would live this far west," said Michael Levine, director of planning studies for the Department of City Planning. Previously, he said, "Westbeth was the boundary beyond which you didn't go. It introduced residences west of Washington Street and north of Bank Street where there had never been residences before."

"A lot of people uptown are finding downtown really appealing," said Elaine Young, a broker at Patton Young Properties. "The housing stock is not conventional. The area offers a lot of different types of housing—lofts, brownstones, postwar, prewar."

By early 1998, one-bedroom units in a doorman co-op building were selling for a minimum of $200,000, she said, with two-bedrooms starting at $350,000. But there wasn't much available. "Unfortunately there are not a lot of large buildings that lend themselves to being converted," she said.

Prices surged around 25 percent between early 1996 and early 1998, said Edward C. Ferris, a vice president at the William B. May real estate brokerage. "In spite of its extreme west location and reputation for being a marginal area, the people who do buy in the Meatpacking District are willing to pay the same kind of premium all real estate is commanding in the city," he said. The median price of a one-bedroom apartment in a doorman building would be about $275,000, Mr. Ferris said, with a two-bedroom going for $425,000.

Mr. Ferris said the area is like the new Central Park West, with the Hudson River waterfront analagous to Central Park. Others tout the Meatpacking District as the new SoHo. Far west 14th Street is something of a food mecca, with a big Western Beef supermarket, Patisserie J. Lanciani, a Belgian restaurant called Petite Abeille, and Dizzy Izzy's Bagels, a 24-hour deli. Just north of the Meatpacking District, between 15th and 16th Streets and Ninth and 10th Avenues, is the new Chelsea Market, a former Nabisco bakery whose brick interior walls now surround a parade of food markets, take-out stores, bakeries, and stores selling kitchen equipment, wine, or flowers.

In 1994, local businesses formed the Far West 14th Street Association to encourage occupants to keep the streets garbage-free and to watch for crime. But crime is nowhere as bad as people think, said Lynne Funk, whose architectural firm is on West 14th Street. It might just be that "people are unused to the character of the neighborhood, which is a little bit grimy," she said. "And it's on a different schedule from a lot of the city," with most meatpacking activity occurring between midnight and dawn.

Fears of crime were intensified in the summer of 1990 after an advertising executive was killed at a telephone booth on Jane Street. The incident, never solved, prompted several neighborhood groups to employ a private security patrol, which now covers portions of Gansevoort, Horatio, Jane, West 12th, and Bethune Streets after dark.

Crime in the area has dropped, said Michael Singer, community affairs officer for the Sixth Precinct, partly because of a crackdown on the transvestite prostitutes notorious for frequenting the area, and partly because the prostitutes are being driven out by the new round-the-clock activity. "We still have some prostitution," Officer Singer said. "They do their business in cars that people and their families can see." The real problem, he said, comes not from prostitutes but from the drug dealers and robbers they attract.

Zoning on some blocks permits adult-related businesses, and there are several sex clubs, both gay and straight. The Liberty Inn Motel on West Street between 13th and 14th Streets charges in three-hour increments.

The nightlife scene makes for some late-night noise. Rowdy crowds sometimes gather, and motorcycles roar through. That's in addition to the noise generated by convoys of meat trucks passing by certain blocks for hours on end. What's more, refrigerated tractor-trailers, laden with meat cargo, sometimes idle noisily all night long.

Another reason residents are glad to have the meat market remain is that it prevents high-rises from moving in. The Greenwich Village Historic

District does not extend north of Gansevoort Street or west of Washington Street, so those areas lack the barriers to development that accompany historic designation. Several organizations hope to create a Waterfront Historic District, which would curtail development along the river.

"We do not want to see new residential development," said Marie Dormuth, former chairwoman of Community Board 2's zoning committee. "The area can't handle any increase in demands on services and traffic."

The neighborhood's concerns about traffic congestion have been incorporated into the reconstruction of Route 9A, which is coterminous with West Street. Neither Jane nor Horatio Street connects directly to 9A. Through-traffic, however, is apparently shifting onto Washington and Greenwich Streets, said Charle Cafiero, chairman of Community Board 2's traffic and transportation committee. Residents are lobbying for so-called traffic-calming measures, including stoplights and safer crosswalks.

Hudson River Park, a contentious project for years, is going forward, though plans are still subject to change. The park, a joint project of the city and the state, includes a walkway and a bikeway from the Battery to 59th Street.

The area's largest open space is the one-acre Corporal John A. Seravalli Playground, near the east end of Gansevoort Street.

Local preschools include the well-known West Village Nursery School for children 2 to 4 years old, and the Chelsea Day School, for children 2 to 5. Public school pupils are in a double zone: They may attend P.S. 3, with its informal atmosphere, or P.S. 41, with its fine academic reputation. Both cover kindergarten through grade 5.

St. Bernard's Parish School, covering prekindergarten through grade 8, connects to the parish church on West 14th Street. The area's other house of worship is Congregation Beth Simchat Torah, a gay and lesbian synagogue in the Westbeth courtyard.

No one minds that the neighborhood is a bit out of the way. A subway ride to midtown takes just five minutes or so, but it requires a good 10- or 15-minute walk to the station (Christopher Street or 14th Street and Seventh Avenue for the 1, 2, 3, and 9 trains; 14th Street and Eighth Avenue for the A, C, E, and L trains).

"It's a haven, especially when you come back from being uptown," said Ms. Pustarfi, of Horatio Street. "The atmosphere just envelops you."

NOHO

Spacious lofts, cast iron, and ultrachic

BY PETER MALBIN

Antiques stores have replaced crack vials on Bond Street, stylish restaurants are opening all over NoHo, and loft prices continue to climb, making it a vibrant, viable neighborhood. So much so that when the sign went up on the Bond Street block in January 1996 for "The Cynthia Swann Griffin Crisis Center for Women," some neighbors were surprised to find that yet another social-service agency had taken root. Then they saw the cameras and crews, somebody spotted Diane Keaton, and the word was soon out that the sign was just a front for the movie *The First Wives Club*, shooting in NoHo.

The sense of relief was palpable. Residents remember only too well the period in the late 1980s when social problems seemed to overwhelm the small neighborhood, which is north of Houston Street to Astor Place, and from Mercer Street to the Bowery. Drug dealing was rife on certain blocks. In response, neighbors armed with walkie-talkies patrolled Bond and Great Jones Streets twice a night for months. "It was a bit of grass-roots democracy in action," recalled Herbert Wells, a real estate developer who lives on Great Jones Street.

"I wouldn't say NoHo is drug-free, but it's pretty quiet now," said Marilynn Geyer, who heads the NoHo Neighborhood Association.

Artistic NoHo has neither the history of the neighboring Village nor the glamour or glitz of SoHo, but Bond Street, one of the city's most fashionable streets in the 1830s, is again becoming chic. Il Buco, in the mid-1990s the first antiques store to open on the street, doubles as a wine-and-food bar after 6 P.M.

In the 19th century, when Lafayette Street was Lafayette Place, the Vanderbilts, Astors, and Delanos had town houses on the broad thoroughfare. Now spacious loft apartments in cast-iron and Romanesque Revival

POPULATION: 9,405.

AREA: 0.083 square mile.

MEDIAN HOUSEHOLD INCOME: $66,413.

MEDIAN PRICE OF A LOFT APARTMENT: $350 a square foot; $700,000 for a typical 2,000-square-foot loft.

RUSH-HOUR TRAVEL TO MIDTOWN: 15 minutes or less.

TRANSPORTATION: No. 6 subway train at Astor Place and Bleecker Street; R and N at Eighth Street and Broadway; Q at Broadway and Lafayette; F at Houston Street; M1, M2, M3, M13, and M101 buses.

CODES: Area, 212; ZIP, 10012 and 10014.

buildings line the street. Favorite haunts of NoHo residents include the colorfully columned NoHo Star restaurant and the Time Cafe, with its striking Southwestern mural. The 1888 brick-and-terra-cotta loft building that houses the Time Cafe was the work of Henry J. Hardenbergh, architect of the Plaza Hotel and the Dakota apartment building on Central Park West.

At night, Temple Bar is packed with upscale singles, the Fez has poetry readings and bands, and the Bowery Bar on Fourth Street is so hip that its sign is almost impossible to detect. Near the Joseph Papp Public Theater on Lafayette Street is a Brazilian rotisserie, Riodizio. Nudged between an auto-parts store and a loft building is the retro-chic Marion's on the Bowery. The landmark Bouwerie Lane Theater, home of the Jean Cocteau Repertory, stages classic plays, and across the street is the intimate Amato Opera Theater, New York's third-oldest opera house, which opened in 1948.

Tower Records sparked a retail resurgence in NoHo when it opened on Broadway and East Fourth Street in 1983. A Barnes & Noble superstore moved to Astor Place in October 1994.

The neighborhood lacks amenities such as supermarkets, but is within walking distance of great food shopping. "You can take a Saturday-morning stroll with your grocery cart to Raffetto's on Houston Street and to Joe's Dairy on Sullivan Street for fresh mozzarella," said Judith Gerard, an architect who has been living in a former-hat-factory-turned-loft apartment on Great Jones Street since 1978. "There's a wonderful kosher bakery on Second Avenue. We buy fish in the morning at the Union Square market on Saturdays and frequently run into people we know."

Which is not the case on Broadway. From Houston Street to Astor Place, Broadway is a passing parade of New York University students en route to the East Village and a conduit for tourists going down to SoHo. The revolving doors at Tower Records keep spinning until midnight. But Shakespeare & Co. Booksellers provides a quiet respite on the busy thoroughfare.

The redbrick building at the northeast corner of Broadway and Bond, now the Reebok Store, was the site of the Brooks Brothers store from 1874 to 1884. Residents say they would like to see a better caliber of retail stores on Broadway. "We don't want Broadway to become like Eighth Street," said George Schwarz, who owns and lives above the NoHo Star restaurant on the corner of Bleecker and Lafayette Streets.

Since the mid-nineties, real estate prices have risen steadily in NoHo. Co-ops are more plentiful than condominiums, particularly on Broadway and Lafayette Street. A typical co-op loft has 2,000 square feet of space and sells for $700,000. Some condominiums on East Fourth Street and Bond Street sell for $300 to $400 a square foot, said Norman Horowitz, a broker with Halstead Property Company. Toward the end of 1997, a 2,700-square-foot loft at 620 Broadway sold for $750,000, while a 1,167-square-foot, one-bedroom duplex loft in the Silk Building at 14 East Fourth Street sold for $310,000. Prices of lofts have risen by as much as 30 percent in the last three years, according to Scott Durkin of the Corcoran Group.

Loft prices depend on factors such as ceiling height, noise level, functional space, and charm, with such variables as skylights and archways inflating prices.

There is a quick turnover of rentals in conventional apartments, walk-ups, and loft buildings, which are priced according to square footage. In late 1997, studios rented from $1,100 to $1,500 (with alcoves); one-bedrooms were priced between $1,500 and $2,200, and two-bedrooms between $2,200 and $3,200.

Like SoHo, most of mixed-use NoHo is still zoned for light manufacturing, with joint living-and-work quarters for artists. Almost all the former warehouse buildings have become residential and require resident artists to be certified by the city's Department of Cultural Affairs. Amy Fusselman, a certified artist, and her fiancé, Frank Sneider, bought a bright 2,000-square-foot co-op loft on East Fourth Street. A writer, she creates a homemade periodical called *Bunnyrabbit*, which she describes as a "funky fiction and music" magazine. "Getting certification required a lot of documentation," she said. "Our building was quite strict about it."

A significant portion of NoHo from Broadway to the Bowery, excluding small pockets, is reserved for certified artists. Others who live there face the risk of eviction, said David Ratner, a lawyer specializing in loft law.

In the pioneer loft-living days of the '60s and '70s, SoHo and NoHo streets were deserted at night, recalled Ruth McMurray, a graphic designer who in the late '60s slowly moved into the 2,000-square-foot loft where she had been working for two years. "It was spooky to walk here," she said. "We moved in illegally with the tacit understanding of the landlord. We didn't have heating in the evenings or weekends. And the city didn't collect garbage."

The artist Robert Rauschenberg was an early NoHo resident and maintains a studio on Lafayette Street, and Robert Mapplethorpe, the photographer, worked on Bond Street. Another NoHo resident is Chuck Close, the painter.

In the mid-1970s, artists adopted the acronym "NoHo" and petitioned Community Board 2 to ask the city to rezone their neighborhood similarly to SoHo, which had been zoned for artists in 1971. After NoHo was granted residential zoning for artists in 1976, some residents opted for co-op conversions. Owners and landlords were required to bring buildings up to a residential code when the 1982 Loft Law was enacted—artists were now legal tenants and rents became regulated. People interested in moving to NoHo should check with the New York City Loft Board to see whether their building is in compliance with the Loft Law before finalizing their plans, advised Chuck DeLaney, the Loft Board's tenant representative.

Ms. Gerard, who lives in the former hat factory, and her husband, Robert Tan, who is also an architect, moved to NoHo in the late 1970s and were "grandfathered" in by the Loft Law. Despite not having a park, library, or school, Ms. Gerard said NoHo was a good place to raise a family. "We have good nursery schools and elementary schools nearby," she said. "And N.Y.U. and Cooper Union are a great source for baby-sitters. My child enjoyed going to art galleries, and there are good bookstores nearby."

Parents who live in Community School District 2 may opt to send their children to schools outside the zone. In the district's zoned elementary schools, P.S. 3, P.S. 40, and P.S. 41, two-thirds of children are at grade level or above for reading and math, according to Kathleen Berger, president of Community School Board District 2.

Grace Church School, affiliated with the landmark Grace Episcopal Church at Broadway and 10th Street, offers prekindergarten to eighth-grade education.

NoHo has a number of nonprofit organizations and social-service agencies, which community leaders say are well run.

Among Lafayette Street's rich variety of public and commercial buildings is the Joseph Papp Public Theater, an Italian Renaissance palazzo at No. 425. The theater was originally built as a library, the city's first, with funds bequeathed by John Jacob Astor. The library closed in 1895 and its books were eventually incorporated into the New York Public Library. From 1921 to 1965, the building became the headquarters of the Hebrew Immigrant Aid and Sheltering Society (H.I.A.S.), an agency responsible for sheltering and relocating thousands of Jewish refugees. The building was landmarked on October 26, 1965. When H.I.A.S. moved uptown, Joseph Papp and others persuaded the City Council to recommend municipal purchase of the building for the New York Shakespeare Festival. The Public Theater opened on October 17, 1967, with the rock musical *Hair*. The building contains six theaters.

NOLITA

A slice of Little Italy moving upscale

BY JOYCE COHEN

No one is quite certain what to call this part of town. Nolita—north of Little Italy, that is—certainly pinpoints it geographically. The not-quite-acronym was apparently coined several years ago by real estate brokers seeking to give the area at least a little cachet. It no longer needs their help. Nolita has begun to attract a young and trend-setting clientele of artists and professionals. As they set up shop and home, they are recasting the neighborhood with an up-to-the-minute mix of retailing and nightlife.

Historically, this northern edge of Little Italy was a sleepy family neighborhood, home to several waves of immigrants who settled in its five- and six-story tenement buildings. Some of them moved up and out, but others turned into the gray-haired grandmothers who still sit out on the sidewalk in pleasant weather.

Within recent years, however, boutiques, galleries, cafes, and nightclubs have sprouted in once-vacant storefronts, and several midsize apartment houses have gone up. Community Board 2, hoping to retain the area's character, is urging the city to limit the height of new construction and crack down on zoning violations.

"The neighborhood is at an old-guard, new-guard kind of moment," said Laurie McLendon, the owner of Shi, a pioneering home-furnishings store that opened in a vacant storefront on Elizabeth Street two and a half years ago. "It's changing in a way that remains to be seen."

Gentrification might liven the place up, but it brings with it noise, trash, traffic, rising rents, and big buildings. These threats have given Nolita's inhabitants a newfound civic consciousness. When the community board held its first "town hall meeting" for the area at St. Patrick's Old Cathedral on March 30, 1998, hundreds of people turned out. Some are

POPULATION: 4,850.

AREA: 0.1 square mile.

MEDIAN HOUSEHOLD INCOME: $32,500.

PRICE OF A MIDRANGE ONE-BEDROOM CO-OP: $175,000.

MIDRANGE RENT FOR A ONE-BEDROOM APARTMENT: $2,000.

DISTANCE FROM MIDTOWN MANHATTAN: 2.5 miles.

RUSH-HOUR TRAVEL TO MIDTOWN: 10 minutes on the 6, F, B, D, or Q train; 25 minutes or more on the M1 or M103 bus.

CODES: Area, 212; ZIP, 10012.

now planning to form a neighborhood association.

"It's a great neighborhood—you know your neighbors, you know the people who own the coffee shop, you know the kids," said Suzan Schaefer, who belongs to the Cleveland Place Neighborhood Association, a group formed in 1997 to oppose Jet 19, a new nightclub that brought all-night noise and crowds to the tiny street. "It has retained that neighborhood characteristic," Ms. Schaefer said. "We would like to keep it that way so it doesn't turn into a tourist strip."

The area, originally farmland, was generally considered downscale. Its eastern border, the Bowery, was named for Peter Stuyvesant's farm, or *bouwerij*. In 1805, a canal was dug to drain water into the Hudson River; it became a breeding ground for mosquitoes and a decade later was filled in to become Canal Street.

European immigrants populated the area, with the Irish followed by the Italians in the 1850s. The Bowery was a main commercial artery, but it deteriorated into a home for vagrants and drunks after being shrouded by the Third Avenue el in 1878. Ever since the late 1960s, when the United States opened its doors to Chinese immigrants, Chinatown has been creeping northward from its traditional Canal Street boundary. Though plenty of Italian restaurants and stores remain, much of Little Italy—the blocks between Canal and Kenmare Streets—has the feel of Chinatown. Locals continue to refer to the whole area, including Nolita, as Little Italy.

Nolita is centered around St. Patrick's Old Cathedral, founded by Irish immigrants in 1809. "It has really been the gateway for every immigrant class that's come through Manhattan," said Michael Pitts, the church's development officer. "For years, this was considered not-very-nice-property." The cathedral became a parish church in 1879 when it was eclipsed by the new St. Patrick's Cathedral on Fifth Avenue. The old church achieved a measure of cinematic fame as the childhood parish of Martin Scorsese and as a backdrop for several movies, including two in Francis Ford Coppola's *Godfather* series. The church has embarked on a major capital campaign to restore the building as well as its organ, dating from the mid–19th century.

"In the past few years, extremely upwardly mobile young men and women have moved into the neighborhood and put a brand on it that is not ethnic and not monolithically religious in nature," said Mr. Pitts. "Now the hallmark is that they're affluent. It causes some interesting dynamics.

"My concern is that they're changing the character from a family neighborhood to the Mulberry Street mall. I'll have breakfast with people who have been here their entire lives. Where else can you hear people complaining that their rent is going up to $180 a month?"

Those rents, of course, are not for newcomers. Cheap tenement apartments hardly ever become available.

"A lot of the tenants have occupied the apartment for 20, 30, or 40 years," said Andy Mak of Mak's Avenue Realty. Even if these aging residents die or move in with relatives, their families hang on to the apartments, he said. And if the apartments do become vacant, brokers say, the landlords renovate them and raise the rents. The community board says it has received several complaints of landlords trying to force rent-regulated tenants out.

"People think there's this fountain of cheap listings over there," said Maria Enns, a broker at Elias/Hyde Real Estate Ltd. But bargains don't exist "unless people know someone who has lived in a tenement for 15 years and the landlord will let them flip the lease," she said.

The apartments that most new residents live in are "every bit as expensive as rentals in Greenwich Village," said Douglas Wagner, vice president of Benjamin James Associates.

But even these rental units are limited in number. They tend to be in the several new buildings that have gone up in the last decade, including 284 Mott Street and 259 Elizabeth Street. A 375-square-foot studio rents for nearly $1,500 a month and a one-bedroom starts at $2,000, Mr. Wagner said.

The sale market is even smaller than the rental market. There are just a handful of co-op and condominium buildings in the area, said Glenn J. Norrgard, a real estate broker at William B. May, and units in these rarely become available. When they do come on the market, one-bedrooms go for $175,000 to $200,000.

Brokers say that most newcomers do not have children, and are not interested in the schools. The neighborhood school is P.S. 130 on Baxter Street, which has about 950 pupils in prekindergarten through grade 5. It offers bilingual classes in Chinese and English, as well as English as a second language. In the spring of 1997, statewide school rankings showed that 98 percent of the school's third graders were at or above the standard for math, while 43 percent read at or above grade level.

At the Roman Catholic St. Patrick's School, there are more than 600 pupils in prekindergarten through grade 8. Fewer than half of the students are Catholic; many come from low-income families. Tuition is $140 a month for one pupil, $165 for two in the same family, and $190 for three or more.

St. Patrick's also runs free youth programs that take advantage of the area's lone playground, the De Salvia Playground on Spring Street near Mulberry Street. It has basketball hoops, jungle gyms, and chess tables.

While the neighborhood offers little outdoor recreation, there are plenty of places to eat and shop. Dozens of Italian restaurants and cafes serve such specialties as coal-oven pizza and chocolate cannoli. If people find the stores in the immediate area too specialized, they can buy virtually anything they need along the commercial corridors of East Houston and Canal Streets. Lower Broadway, just a few blocks west, teems with stores.

The big annual event is the San Gennaro Festival, which starts the Thursday after Labor Day. For 10 days from 11:30 A.M. to 11:30 P.M., Mulberry Street from Canal to East Houston is open to pedestrians only. For many locals, the festival is an ongoing sore spot. The community board receives complaints of rowdy and drunken behavior, and merchants say they lose business to the street vendors.

The police have been criticized for their ineffective handling of noise complaints but credited for reducing crime and cleaning up the old drug-dealing area near East Houston Street. Even the Bowery has forsaken its skid-row past and become a cheery commercial artery.

"Since SoHo started, I see a lot of people on vacation coming down with maps and guides," said John Buffa, owner of Buffa's, a coffee shop at 54 Prince Street founded in 1928 by his grandfather Augustino Buffa. "Before that, it was just people who worked around here. We've seen everything change."

ROOSEVELT ISLAND

A cable-car ride off Manhattan,
an urban island

BY BRET SENFT

Roosevelt Island is a mix of Sinclair Lewis (its main street, appropriately, is Main Street) and utopia, a middle-class development where once stood a penitentiary, a lunatic asylum, and other institutions on a two-mile-long, 147-acre East River strip. Just 300 yards from both Manhattan and Queens, it was planned as a model community, but all is not paradise: Tenants have said they are increasingly unable to absorb rising rents, resulting in rent strikes. And there are strains on school and community among 9,000 residents of mixed backgrounds and incomes living together.

State subsidies for the island have been eliminated by the administration of Gov. George E. Pataki, who wants to see the island become self-sufficient. The Roosevelt Island Operating Company (RIOC), led by its president, Dr. Jerome Blue, has attempted to raise revenue, through commercial leases (a Gristede's supermarket opened on Main Street in December 1997), and increased rates at the 2,000-car Motorgate garage, where a reserved space is $210 a month and a nonreserved space is $162.

As the RIOC director of communications, Michael Greason, explained, RIOC has also increased soccer and baseball field fees from $5 to $25 per hour for off-island groups. But public outcry thwarted attempts to cut late-night hours on the island's tramway service (to and from Manhattan at 59th Street), and to rescind free tram passes for students attending off-island schools.

Residents enjoy an atmosphere of modern housing and open space, parks, recreation, and promenades with views of the city's eastern skyline. Cars are parked in the Motorgate garage, with transportation offered by little red buses for 25 cents a ride, 10 cents for seniors and the disabled. Public safety officers patrol the quiet streets.

POPULATION: 9,063.

AREA: 147 acres (2 miles long, less than 800 yards wide).

MEDIAN HOUSEHOLD INCOME: $53,091.

MIDRANGE RENT FOR A TWO-BEDROOM APARTMENT: $1,700.

CO-OP PRICES: All co-ops on the island, which were built with government assistance, have income restrictions, and long waiting lists. Future development is expected to include some market-rate apartments.

DISTANCE FROM MIDTOWN MANHATTAN: 300 yards.

RUSH-HOUR TRAVEL TO MIDTOWN: 5 minutes on the aerial tram ($1.50) and on the Q or B subway line.

CODES: Area, 212; ZIP, 10044.

Carole Kleinknecht, a 19-year resident, and her husband, Glenn, have raised two children here. "We can walk anywhere, anytime," she said. "Another thing—you don't have to drive your kids to tap, piano lessons, children's theater, Little League. It's all in walking distance."

Patrick Stewart is a 15-year resident and president of the Roosevelt Island Residents Association. He is no fan of the present RIOC administration, but said, "Overall, it's a pleasant, bucolic kind of neat place. There is a fresh, island mentality here—yet we're 300 yards from the most sophisticated city in the world."

In a distant, far quieter time, the Canarsie Indians named the island Minnahannock (loosely translated as "It's Nice to Be on the Island"). After a brief Dutch settlement, the Robert Blackwell family took possession in 1686. The 18th-century Blackwell farmhouse still stands in a park south of Town Center. Sold to the city in 1828, Blackwell Island became a repository for insane, infirm, and criminal populations and was named Welfare Island in 1921. The only hospitals remaining are the 925-bed Goldwater Memorial to the south and the 1,045-bed Coler Memorial to the north, both for long-term care. Patients are seen throughout the wheelchair-accessible community.

In 1969, the Urban Development Corporation announced "a new town in town" with a master plan from the architects Philip Johnson and John Burgee. The first group of residential buildings, Northtown I, with 2,100 apartments, opened in 1975. Island House and Westview are middle-income rental buildings; for studios, rent is $700 to $775, with income limits between $27,000 and $59,000; the waiting list is three to four years long. For a two-bedroom, tenants with incomes within $48,000 to $123,840 pay $1,150 to $1,300 a month; the waiting list for Island House and Westview is approximately 18 months.

The federally subsidized Eastwood Building includes units for the elderly and the disabled; studios rent for $476 or 30 percent of income, with an income ceiling of $34,302. A two-bedroom rents for $873; income ceilings are either $44,100 or $49,000, depending on household numbers; the waiting period is approximately three months.

In Rivercross, a Mitchell-Lama co-op, a large two-bedroom with Manhattan views costs $25,000; 1,500-square-foot three-bedrooms are priced at $30,000. Maintenance charges range from $650 to $1,400. The waiting list has remained closed for several years.

Disputes over rent increases in the subsidized buildings in recent years have led to rent strikes and an agreement between renters and the New York State Division of Housing and Community Renewal—which regulates the island independently of New York State rent-regulation guidelines—on a new system of rent increases for the buildings that will go into effect at the end of 1998.

The second group of apartments, the five-building Manhattan Park, known as Northtown II, opened north of Town Center in 1989 with 884 market-rate units and 223 with subsidized rent under the Federal Section 8 program. Unsubsidized rents in the buildings, which have concierges, range from $1,995 to $2,400 for a two-bedroom and $2,995 to $3,400 for a 1,300-square-foot three-bedroom.

A subway station opened in late 1989 with service to midtown in under five minutes. Or residents can take the tram—at $1.50, the most affordably spectacular transportation in town; its two cabins run every 15 minutes during most of the day, and every seven minutes during rush hour.

The Roosevelt Island Racquet Club opened south of the tram in 1992, with 12 indoor, air-conditioned, Har-Tru courts (residents get a 50 percent discount on annual $1,000 dues). The northern Octagon Park surrounding the landmarked 1839 lunatic asylum tower, now known as the Octagon Tower, features a 124-plot community garden, soccer and baseball fields, and tennis courts.

Behind the subway station is the future site of Southtown, its 2,000 mixed-income units to fulfill the housing portion of the master plan. In 1997, the Roosevelt Island Operating Corporation, the state agency responsible for operating and maintaining the island, secured developers for the site, but building plans had not yet been announced a year later.

There is almost full retail occupancy along Main Street, including the recently expanded Gristede's supermarket, a diner, a bakery, a general store, a jewelry store, a pharmacy, and a Chinese restaurant.

Toddlers attend the Roosevelt Island Day Nursery (with a parent board of directors) for fees ranging from $5,200 for half days (9 A.M. to noon) for 3-year-olds, to $6,900 for full days (8 A.M. to 3 P.M.) for 5-year-olds. Financial aid is available. "And all the upper-middle-class parents of 5-year-olds stand around discussing where they're sending their kids off-island next year," said one upper-income resident. "The local school . . . well, it's controversial."

The controversy at P.S./I.S. 127 surrounds lower reading scores and the perception among some parents that children from the subsidized housing disrupt classes. Such perceptions are not accurate, said Katherine Teets Grimm, a Rivercross resident with two children who attend off-island schools. Dr. Teets Grimm's children once attended the island school, which runs from kindergarten through grade 8. A faculty member at Mount Sinai Medical Center and a local pediatrician since 1987, Dr. Teets Grimm hears all the latest school news from parents.

"I do pediatric work with P.S. 171 in East Harlem," said Dr. Teets Grimm, "and they have a lot of ghetto kids, but the school operates very well. Here, it's always the Section 8 kids who get blamed, but I don't accept that. I think there's a leadership problem on behalf of the adults here—learning how to nurture kids and maintain order at the same time. But I hope the school does well. I think it has a lot of potential."

The K–8 school was originally in five minischools on Main Street. In September 1992, P.S./I.S. 217 moved into a $28 million building designed by the architect Michael Fieldman. The air-conditioned school has a gym and dining hall with tall windows facing Manhattan and a library with computers, plus two computer labs. Programs include interdisciplinary teaching and an accelerated math program in junior high, an after-school program for gifted and talented students, French (beginning in fifth grade), and band and chorus in the performing arts theater.

The school has suffered because of a lack of permanent leadership—it has had two interim principals in recent years, said Karen Smith, president of the PTA and two-year resident of Manhattan Park with one child in the local school. "But we have a very active PTA, which fund-raises for the after-school programs," such as cultural and gymnastics programs, a Career Day, and a part-time guidance counselor. The after-school program includes tutorials for eighth graders taking the examination for New York City's highly selective specialized high schools; a third of those taking the exams were accepted into those schools in 1997.

Some 36 nationalities—many of them children of United Nations staff and diplomats—are among the school's 560 pupils. But the loss of upper-middle-class pupils to off-island schools troubles Rev. Oliver T. Chapin, pastor of the island's 1889 Chapel of the Good Shepherd, an Episcopal church. "That," he said, "has to be examined carefully—whether you can come to Roosevelt Island and expect it to be the suburbs."

SOHO

Art, commerce, and their complications

BY BRET SENFT

Behind the graffiti-covered cast-iron facades of SoHo's cold 19th-century factory buildings, above the trendy boutiques and restaurants and their crowds, are artists and their allies in art-related fields who provide a support system for this center of the international art market.

The desolate Dickensian streets—part of the ambience of inverse snobbism adopted by residents attracted to the look of postindustrial decay—are a distant cry from the farmland and meadows that the area south of Houston Street (thus: SoHo) to Canal Street was in the 18th century. As the city moved north, the area became first a suburb, then, in the 1850s, an elegant shopping district along Broadway. When the stores moved still farther north, to Chelsea, they were replaced by Italianate or Palladian warehouses and factories built between 1860 and 1900. The neighborhood became, in the words of the Historic District's 1973 designation report, "the largest concentration of full and partial cast-iron facades anywhere in the world."

Light industry—furriers; doll, rag, and box makers—remained in the buildings through the 1950s. By then, the cluster of warehouses was known as Hell's Hundred Acres for its frequent fires. As manufacturers left the city, artists looking for low rents and large studio space moved in from Greenwich Village, stealthily, because commercial zoning made such residential use illegal.

The abstract painter Deborah Remington moved into her first loft in 1965 for $42.50 a month, but not without certain precautions. "My boyfriend found the parts on Canal Street and literally built a periscope in a black box that hung out the window," she recalled. Spied from above, building inspectors at the front door would find only a strangely quiet building.

POPULATION: 10,322.

AREA: 48 blocks.

MEDIAN HOUSEHOLD INCOME: $54,477.

PRICE OF A MIDRANGE TWO-BEDROOM (2,000-SQUARE-FOOT) LOFT: $900,000 ($450 per square foot).

MIDRANGE RENT FOR A TWO-BEDROOM LOFT: $5,000.

DISTANCE FROM MIDTOWN MANHATTAN: 2.25 miles.

RUSH-HOUR TRAVEL TO MIDTOWN: 12 minutes on the 6, E, N, or R subway line.

CODES: Area, 212; ZIP, 10012.

In 1968, Paula Cooper opened the first gallery in SoHo, and in 1971, Leo Castelli and several partners opened the first gallery building, on West Broadway. "And this was a real desert," said the 90-year-old Mr. Castelli, sitting in a small conference room off the gallery. "I remember, there was only one restaurant, Fanelli's, on Spring Street [a workingman's bar then, a popular hamburger joint now]. But the fears that no one would come down here—museum curators, collectors, the art public—proved completely unfounded."

Ms. Remington moved down her block, where tenants formed a co-op and bought their West Broadway building in 1969, even as the SoHo Artists Association (later folded into the SoHo Alliance, a community group) lobbied City Hall for tenants' rights. By 1972, zoning amendments established joint living/work quarters, permitting artists certified by the city's Department of Cultural Affairs legal residence in SoHo buildings under the rubric of "light manufacturers."

The 1982 Loft Law set a 10-year timetable for loft building compliance with the state's Multiple Dwelling Law, though the state legislature granted a four-year extension in 1992. A Loft Board was established to enforce the law and monitor the progress of Interim Multiple Dwellings in their trek toward certification. As to particulars—setting rents and allocating costs among owners and tenants in getting a building up to code—a long-time community activist, Terry Sullivan, said: "When it comes to the Loft Law, if you're not confused, you're not paying attention."

Shael Shapiro, a 25-year resident and partner in WYS Design Partnership Architects, which specializes in rehabilitating and legalizing loft buildings, advises potential tenants and buyers to do research on costs. "Here, it's very important to know what you're getting into," Mr. Shapiro said. "You have to ask: How much construction still needs to be done, what it's going to cost, and how much you'll be expected to pay."

The law permits only certified artists to live in SoHo. But severe budget cutbacks at the Department of Cultural Affairs, plus a Loft Board mired in owner-tenant disputes, have meant a gray area in enforcement of the requirement that artists be certified by the city. "In my experience," said Ingrid Wiegand, a loft resident from 1968 to 1985 and a broker with

Eychner Associates, "10 percent of the boards demand it, 40 percent request a letter of indemnity"—waiving co-op liability in case of a cited violation—"and one-half don't give a damn."

As a result, she said, there is a mix of early pioneers, arts-related residents from the 1980s, and the most recent influx, "the sons and daughters of the wealthiest Germans and Japanese, creating a sort of finishing school for the internationally rich.

"And now, in the late '90s, they are joined by a growing French population, and an influx of American and international Wall Street people," she said.

Susan Penzner, president of Susan Penzner Real Estate, notes that "all the new conversions are condominiums, eliminating a board of directors, so there is no enforcement of the artist-certification rules. But I would say there are more celebrities than stockbrokers who want to be in SoHo." Sales in August 1997 included 47 Mercer Street: "Clean, raw spaces—but very nice. New floors, wood-burning fireplaces." She sold four apartments of 4,000 square feet, with prices ranging from $1.2 million on the second floor to a penthouse with roof terrace for $1.65 million.

Said Susan Meisel of Meisel Real Estate, "I think a lot of people who are purchasing are less concerned with the issue of artist certification than the horrible stories they've heard about co-op boards in general. I think they prefer the flexibility of having a condo—of being able to rent, and not having to answer to a board." At 42 Wooster Street, where she is exclusive selling agent, 12 of 14 lofts were sold through the fall of 1997, their sizes ranging from 2,100 to 3,800 square feet, at prices of $350 to $400 per square foot.

In rentals, Ms. Weigand quotes $3,500 to $5,000 as the range for 1,500 to 2,000 square feet—and "for a big, beautiful loft, you can easily pay $7,000 to $9,000 per month."

Recently, a 2,200-square-foot loft sold for $800,000. "And not a high floor, nothing spectacular. Not a rough loft—it was in very nice condition. But we're not talking marble baths with gold-plated faucets here." Top-floor lofts with roof space and/or great views command $500-plus per square foot.

High-priced European boutiques line Prince and Spring Streets, with upscale restaurants like Zoe (American) at Prince and Mercer, Savoy (nouvelle American) at Prince and Crosby, and Balthazar (French) at Spring and Crosby Streets. At the intersection of Prince Street and Broadway are the 10,000-square-foot Dean & DeLuca fine foods store, the chic Armani A/X Exchange, and the 40,000-square-foot SoHo Guggenheim gallery. A Victoria's Secret on the fourth corner completes the quadrangle of art and commerce.

The SoHo Grand Hotel at 310 West Broadway between Canal and

Grand Streets opened early 1996. At 15 stories, it provides pet-friendly accommodations and an elegant bar and two-star restaurant on the second floor, and the upscale prices ($269 to $369 per night depending on season) have diminished neighborhood fears of tour buses lined up to unload middle-class tourists planning a cheap stay in SoHo.

On Broadway between Houston and Prince Streets is a miniature Museum Mile. At 583, the New Museum of Contemporary Art, founded in 1977, provides a constantly updated venue for emerging artists, with group shows or single-artist projects. Next door, at 593, the Center for African Art, formerly on East 68th Street, opened in early 1993 as the Museum of African Art. Across the street, at 594, the Alternative Museum is an artists-administered institution focusing on issue-oriented exhibitions.

There are no supermarkets in the neighborhood (Dean & DeLuca offers an array of prepared and luxury foods, and many residents patronize the Gourmet Garage at Broome and Mercer). There are several pharmacies on Broadway, but no dry cleaners—nor newsstands, parks, schools, police or fire stations.

There are no schools in SoHo itself, but there are three schools nearby: the progressive P.S. 3 at 490 Hudson Street; P.S. 41 at 116 West 11th Street; and P.S. 234 at 292 Greenwich Street—the latter two featuring active learning with hands-on material in science and mathematics, and cooperative study groups.

Among the many downtown private schools are the progressive, inter-disciplinary Little Red Schoolhouse on Bleeker Street and its upper division Elisabeth Irwin High School, on Charlton Street. Tuition, pre-K to 12th grade, is $12,800 to $14,800 a year.

Intense police ticketing has reduced truck traffic along Broome Street in recent years, and late-night motorcycle gang revelry has moved from such lower West Broadway clubs as La Jumelle and Lucky Strike to the newer Spy, Scratch, and Boom in central SoHo on Greene and Spring Streets. The blast of roaring motorcycle engines sends noise "reverberating against the cast-iron facades of the buildings," said Susan Fortgang, a Greene Street resident. "It becomes magnified, like a giant echo chamber," she said. "It makes you jump out of your skin.

"The reason all the galleries are here is because people want to visit artists' studios," Ms. Fortgang said, "and the artists want to be near the market." But for some residents, she said, the crowds and noise make it "increasingly harder to stay here."

TRIBECA

From quiet, desolate streets to high-priced
neighborhood

BY MAGGIE GARB

To hear the old-timers tell it, TriBeCa has gone from a quiet community to a glitzy, high-priced urban neighborhood in a scant 15 years. The old-timers are those who moved in before property values began a steady and precipitous climb, before lofts three times the size of an average New York City apartment became fashionable, and before amenities like groceries and dry cleaners could be found nearby.

That was in the '70s. Rents were low, space was abundant, and views of the Hudson River or the midtown skyline were affordable. Many poor artists unfazed by desolate streets were willing to invest some sweat equity to install kitchens and bathrooms in raw warehouse space. That was when the neighborhood, 40 blocks from Canal to Murray Street and from Broadway to West Street, acquired its name, an acronym for Triangle Below Canal Street. It's actually shaped more like a triangle with a flattish top and an indentation at one end, but the name remains.

By the mid-eighties, TriBeCa began appearing on maps, and property values began to rise as celebrities, developers, and professionals recognized the advantages of vast residences not far from Wall Street or midtown. Trash pickups became more regular, and in 1988 a Food Emporium supermarket opened at the three-building, 1,332-unit Independence Plaza rental complex on Greenwich Street between Harrison and Duane Streets.

TriBeCa has been in the vanguard of rising Manhattan real estate prices in the latter part of the '90s, with 3,000- and 4,000-square-foot condominium conversions selling for more than $1 million, two- and three-bedroom co-op resales into the high six figures and beyond, and rents up to $3,000 and more. "We're getting people bidding almost at the asking price where we couldn't give away the apartments three years ago," said

POPULATION: 10,106.

AREA: 40 blocks.

MEDIAN HOUSEHOLD INCOME: $78,477.

MEDIAN PRICE OF A LOFT CO-OP: $550,000.

MEDIAN PRICE OF A LOFT CONDO: $600,000.

DISTANCE FROM MIDTOWN MANHATTAN: 3 miles.

RUSH-HOUR TRAVEL TO MIDTOWN: 10 minutes on the 1, 9 or C subway line; 7 minutes on the 2, 3, or A line.

CODES: Area, 212; ZIP, 10007 and 10013.

Jeff Tabak of Tabak Real Estate. "There is no bargain property here anymore."

The changes generated strife, as residents fought rent increases and condominium developments. Battles were fought over efforts to rezone much of TriBeCa from manufacturing to residential and commercial. The changes were approved in 1995, covering TriBeCa south of North Moore Street and sparking a wave of condominium conversions. "It was an eight-year battle," said Judy Duffy, assistant district manager for Community Board 1. "A lot of the old-timers were afraid of big money coming in, pretty much like what's happened here."

The battles of the early '90s have given way to resigned acceptance. "I'm ambivalent about these changes," said Dan Lenchner, who has a catering business on Harrison Street and has lived in TriBeCa since 1984. "In some ways the neighborhood has improved. The services are better and it is very much a family neighborhood." Indeed, as tenants scramble for a diminishing supply of rental property, couples with young children are bidding up the prices on condominiums. "It seems like everybody who has kids and a half-million dollars moves here," said Michel Cohen, a pediatrician with offices and a duplex loft in a converted warehouse on Harrison Street.

Prices began climbing in the mid-eighties, as some of the stately 19th-century warehouse buildings along Hudson Street were converted to co-ops. Now, about 70 percent of the resales are co-ops, while newer conversions are almost always condominiums.

New condominiums tend to be large, like the 3,600-square-foot lofts developed by Savannah Partners at 50 Warren Street. In the spring of 1996, they sold quickly for over $900,000, Mr. Tabak said.

Buyers are not deterred. "In 1990, you'd be with people who had seen 60 or 70 places," said Edward Ferris of the William B. May Company. "There was so much available, they couldn't decide. Now we have 100 buyers and maybe 10 spaces. It's created a very vicious market with bidding wars."

Rental units are hard to find, with rents rising as fast as condominium prices. A 1,200-square-foot two-bedroom loft on Greenwich Street that had been rented for $2,100 in 1993 went for $2,900 in the summer of 1997, said Andrew Melnick of Tabak Real Estate. Apartments in doorman buildings can be found from $1,900 to $2,000, and 400-square-foot studios are $1,000 to $2,000, he said.

In what might seem a bitter irony to TriBeCa's current renters, the area's earliest Colonial property owner, Trinity Church, helped set the model for long-term low-cost leases that typified the Manhattan housing market for two centuries. In 1705, the church secured a patent from Queen Anne for 32 acres of land west of Broadway between Fulton and Duane Streets. Seeking a steady stream of revenue to cover expenses, the church vestry began a program to divide the farmland into lots and offer long-term leases. Tenants could construct homes and shops on the lots.

As Elizabeth Blackmar wrote in *Manhattan for Rent*, other large landowners like Henry Rutgers, James De Lancey, and a British admiral, Sir Peter Warren, took up the idea of leasing rather than selling land, and established Manhattan's real estate market on leases of 15 to 93 years. Well into the 19th century, the city's aldermen complained about congestion in the streets, as artisans moved their homes from one leased lot to another.

By the late 18th century, artisans and shopkeepers unable to pay higher rents along the East River began building wooden houses to shelter their families and business activities on land leased from Trinity Church. The opening of the Erie Canal in 1825 initiated a change in the artisan neighborhood. By 1851, when Cornelius Vanderbilt built a railroad terminal on Hudson and Chambers Streets, houses were being replaced by freight terminals.

After the Civil War, the area became the city's leading wholesale produce outlet, Washington Market. In the 1880s and 1890s, wealthy merchants built warehouses to hold midwestern agricultural goods, as well as spices, nuts, and coffee. Washington Market closed in the early '60s. "What killed the market was you couldn't bring trucks down here; the streets were too narrow," said Steven Wils, owner of a family wholesaling business, Harry Wils & Company, and the last of the large wholesalers in the neighborhood.

When Mr. Wils moved into one of his father's buildings on Duane Street in 1973, he had just a handful of neighbors. "There was nothing going on here," he said. "It's sad, because it was such a small neighborhood. Now you kind of look around and see all these people and think, 'Who are they?' "

Some of them are celebrities such as Robert De Niro, who set up his film production company in TriBeCa nearly a decade ago, and John F. Kennedy Jr., who owns a condominium.

"It used to be there was nobody on the street and now it's rocking," said Karen Waltuck, owner of Chanterelle, the restaurant that the

Waltucks moved from SoHo to the Mercantile Building at Hudson and Harrison Streets in 1989. Chanterelle, along with the four-star Bouley, now closed, Montrachet, and TriBeCa Grill, has made the area a mecca for fine dining. Less expensive restaurants include Bubby's at 120 Hudson and the Independent and the Odeon on West Broadway. Yaffa's Tea Room at 19 Harrison Street is a longtime neighborhood place known for its Casbah-style decor.

These days, park space, overcrowded schools, and the expansion of the neighborhood's Little League program are the subjects of debate in the cafes along West Broadway. Community efforts of the last 10 years brought a new public library, a new building for Public School 234 at Greenwich and Chambers Streets, and the establishment of four historic districts.

P.S. 234, with kindergarten through fifth grade, is at 120 percent capacity, with 650 students, said the principal, Anna Switzer. Some crowding is expected to be alleviated in the fall of 1999, when a combined elementary and middle school will open a block away. Begun as a three-room alternative school in 1977, P.S. 234 is now in a modern building with air-conditioning and a well-stocked library. It has retained its progressive mission, shunning textbooks and replacing formal grades with an individualized assessment system. The curriculum has generated some controversy, but most parents seem pleased with its approach. "My kids love the school and are thriving there," Dr. Cohen said.

The nonprofit Washington Market School, a Montessori-influenced early childhood center on Hudson Street, is at capacity, with 200 children from 1½ to 5 years old. Annual tuition is $6,500 for half a day, $9,000 for a full day. Parents raise about $25,000 each year for scholarships, and the school sponsors a street fair each May to raise money, said the director, Ronnie Moskowitz.

Some longtime residents worry that the neighborhood will become another SoHo, with a Gap and a Starbucks on every corner. "From the day we got here, people were saying this was the next SoHo," Mr. Lenchner said. "That's not really happening. It used to be a place for poor pioneers; now it's a place for wealthy pioneers. But it still has a lot of character."

THE UPPER EAST SIDE

Urban elegance and world-class cachet

BY JOYCE COHEN

The Upper East Side boasts perhaps the most coveted street addresses in the United States. Its southernmost ZIP code, 10021, contains the nation's highest density of humanity and its largest concentration of wealth. It is, for many, the place to move up to.

And it is where the city exists at its urban best. The upscale and the downtrodden march the same sidewalks, which empty and fill with the pace of the day. There is little that is not within a few minutes' walk: schools and stores, mansions and museums, public parks and private clubs.

With its abiding images of silk stockings, white gloves, and school uniforms, the Upper East Side is possibly the only place in the city that could be imagined to have a dress code. The housing stock is varied—the area is crammed with plush new condominiums, single-family town houses, small apartment buildings, and tenement-style walk-ups.

Third Avenue is lined with postwar high-rises, many erected in a flurry of construction in the early '60s hastened by the imminent change to a more restrictive citywide zoning. But the predominant residential structures are the prewar buildings, many of which are co-ops.

Typically, the co-op apartments have "large rooms, high ceilings, thick walls, gracious service, and very constraining house rules," said Clark Halstead, founder of the Halstead Property Company.

Prices for a classic six—with two bedrooms, kitchen, living room, dining room, maid's quarters, and two or three bathrooms—cluster in the $500,000 to $1.5 million range, with a monthly maintenance of $2,000 to $3,000, said Mr. Halstead. Prices tend to rise as buildings get nearer to Fifth Avenue. On the high end, a full-floor co-op with something like 18 rooms might sell for $14 million. But there are also studios, "400 or 500

POPULATION: 69,315

AREA: 0.75 square mile.

MEDIAN HOUSEHOLD INCOME: $117,793.

PRICE OF A MIDRANGE TWO-BEDROOM CO-OP: $750,000.

DISTANCE FROM MIDTOWN MANHATTAN: 1.5 miles.

RUSH-HOUR TRAVEL TO MIDTOWN: Up to 10 minutes on the 4, 5, or 6 subway line; up to 30 minutes by bus on Fifth, Madison, Lexington, and Third Avenues.

CODES: Area, 212; ZIP, 10021 and 10028.

square feet in size, that can be purchased for $70,000 or $80,000 in a walk-up building," Mr. Halstead said.

The Upper East Side has "an enormous price variation," said Elizabeth Stribling, president of Stribling & Associates Ltd., who added that there were multiple bids on nearly half the properties her company sells.

The rental market is even tighter, as tight as it has been in nearly two decades, said Nancy Packes, president of Feathered Nest, a rental company. In a postwar doorman building on Third Avenue, a plain one-bedroom would rent for around $2,300 a month, she said, and a two-bedroom for $3,200. Going west, prices typically rise a few hundred dollars each block, with a one-bedroom, prewar apartment facing Central Park renting for up to $5,000, said Ms. Packes, and a two-bedroom as high as $8,000.

By and large, the streetscape reflects the area's affluence. The carefully tended Park Avenue malls—blooming with tulips in the spring, begonias in the summer, and white lights at holiday time—have an annual budget of $300,000, financed by voluntary contributions.

Preserving the atmosphere is important to many residents, with community groups concerned that new construction fit in. Much of the Upper East Side is protected from new development by historic-district designation.

Residents have successfully lobbied against what they consider the malling of Third Avenue, one of the main commercial arteries. In late 1996, they prevented the opening of a big Toys "R" Us at 80th Street. Lexington Avenue is another shopping hub that people are monitoring.

"I've watched the deterioration of Lexington Avenue over the years," said Nikki Henkin, a resident for more than three decades. Madison Avenue, with its exclusive boutiques and specialty shops, "has a great deal of cachet," she said. "But if you walk on Madison and turn east at 79th Street, there is such a falloff, you think you are in another world. There are all these teeny, tiny stores, no plan about signage and no cohesive plan about awnings. It gets tacky." In 1996, she helped start Lexington Neighbors to improve the avenue from 74th to 79th Street. The group hopes to replace ordinary street lamps with bishop's-crook lampposts, and to add hanging foliage to building facades.

Ms. Henkin also helped found the 100–299 East 77th Street Block Association, devoted to cleaning up East 77th Street, a curious amalgam of residence and commerce. Though not a major crosstown street, it has a subway stop at Lexington Avenue, a jumble of stores, and Lenox Hill Hospital, with its concomitant traffic congestion. The block association is lobbying to prohibit street vendors on much of East 77th Street plus parts of Lexington and Third Avenues. "We need the sidewalk space for walking," said Ms. Henkin.

Unlike in some city neighborhoods, there is not much of a close-knit feel; people tend to value their privacy. There are pockets of places where "people do know one another," said Teri Slater, a resident for two dozen years and co-chairwoman of the East 78th Street Block Association for the Park/Lexington block, which is filled with brownstones and has no doormen. "But where you have nothing but tall apartment buildings, people are more anonymous."

Historically, the Upper East Side has been a place of privilege. Until the 1840s, it was primarily pastureland. That changed with the opening of Central Park in 1860. In the late 19th century, mansions and the Metropolitan Museum of Art rose on Fifth Avenue, and brownstones lined the side streets. In 1906, when the New York Central Railroad converted from steam to electricity, the Park Avenue tracks were moved underground. In 1955–56, the Third Avenue el was demolished; within a few years, many of the artery's tenements vanished, too.

Today, the area is filled with museums, embassies, and private schools; there are public institutions like Hunter College and membership-only ones like the New York Society Library ($135 a year for a household). The local elementary school, P.S. 6, is hot. Third-grade reading and math scores are among the highest in the city; the school ranked first in the city in 1996–97, and second in 1997–98. The school emphasizes the arts, music, dance, and computers; there are no separate programs for gifted students. There's a "strong focus on academics," said its principal, Carmen Farina, but pupils are "not separated according to ability."

Pupils living in the local zone can automatically attend P.S. 6, at Madison Avenue and 81st Street, as can siblings of enrolled children. About a quarter of the 900-student body, which includes grades kindergarten through 5, comes from elsewhere in Community School District 2. There's space because so many children within the zone attend private schools, said Ms. Farina.

An excellent public school is just one of the neighborhood's benefits, said Gail Feher, former president of the school's Parent-Teacher Association, whose family lived on the Far East Side before moving to Park Avenue a half-dozen years ago. Her new neighborhood is a bit more residential and less commercial, she said.

"Most of the shops are small shops," she said. "Everything you need is within blocks. You're near everything," including Central Park, movie theaters, and museums with children's programs. About the only things she feels are missing are everyday restaurants that are not too expensive. "There's such a concentrated area of wonderful things," she said. "I feel very fortunate living here."

For those who do not walk to work, the Lexington Avenue subway is convenient, though seriously overcrowded. A trip to midtown takes approximately 10 minutes on the 4, 5 or 6 train. Buses run along Fifth, Madison, Lexington, and Third Avenues.

Most crimes in the area involve property, said Officer Stephen Petrillo of the 19th Precinct. Robbers snatch bags dangling from restaurant chairs and break car windows to get at laptops and cell phones.

But the preponderance of doormen adds to safety of the streets. Operation Interwatch, run by the nonprofit Association for a Better New York, has a radio network that allows doormen direct access to police dispatchers, bypassing the 911 system. Police report one or two such calls a day. "The door personnel know the neighborhood," said Jo-Ann Polise, the program's director. "They know who belongs there, and have a strong sense of responsibility."

WEST CENTRAL HARLEM

Abandonment down, refurbishment up

BY MAGGIE GARB

After decades of housing decay and lagging residential real estate values, the low-rise neighborhood of West Central Harlem is reviving, according to real estate brokers and longtime residents. The neighborhood, which the poet Langston Hughes called "a dusky sash across Manhattan," is benefiting from city- and state-financed housing programs and an influx of middle-class black and Latino families, young artists, and professionals, many of whom have been displaced by rising residential prices in Lower Manhattan.

The area, a slice of 19th-century brownstones, prewar walk-ups, and small elevator buildings bounded by 110th and 125th Streets, Morningside Park, and Adam Clayton Powell Jr. Boulevard, appears on city maps as the western part of Central Harlem. Some residents call it Manhattanville, the name of the post office on 125th Street near the boulevard.

Most blocks are still marked by a couple of abandoned buildings, and sections of Frederick Douglass Boulevard remain rundown and marred by trash-strewn vacant lots. The 1990 census found that nearly 50 percent of the neighborhood's residents received some form of public assistance. Crime, while still higher than in many areas of the city, has declined in recent years. Since 1995, said Police Officer Leslie Cardona, a headquarters spokeswoman, reported homicides in the 28th Precinct, which includes West Central Harlem, dropped from 30 in 1995 to 9 last year, rapes from 50 to 41, and armed robberies from 602 to 512.

Housing prices in West Central Harlem have risen 20 percent in five years, said R. Kenyatta Punter, a broker with the Myers, Smith & Granady Realty Agency. Brownstones, hard to sell in 1993, ranged in price from $200,000 for a gutted, long-abandoned building to $450,000 for one in mint condition in mid-1998, said Mr. Punter. Some brownstones are being

POPULATION: 12,000.

AREA: 45 blocks.

MEDIAN HOUSEHOLD INCOME: $24,260.

MEDIAN PRICE OF A TWO- OR THREE-FAMILY BROWNSTONE: $350,000.

MIDRANGE RENT FOR A ONE-BEDROOM APARTMENT: $850.

DISTANCE FROM MIDTOWN MANHATTAN: 3.5 miles.

RUSH-HOUR TRAVEL TO MIDTOWN: 20 minutes on the A, C, or D subway train; 50 minutes by bus.

CODES: Area, 212; ZIP, 10026 and 10027.

renovated into a mix of rental and owner-occupied apartments, he said, while others are marketed as condominiums priced from $80,000 to $90,000 for a one-bedroom. Two-bedroom duplexes sell for about $165,000 and three-bedroom duplexes for $175,000 to $215,000, depending on the block, Mr. Punter said.

Many of the well-preserved brownstones have been purchased, leaving long-abandoned, nearly gutted buildings on the market. "Some of these buildings have been abandoned for as long as 20 years," said Willie Kathryn Suggs, owner of a realty agency that bears her name. "In the '70s, you couldn't give these buildings away. Now we have loads of callers."

Rents in the neighborhood's brownstones and walk-ups run from $600 for a one-bedroom to $800 to $1,000 for a two-bedroom. Three-bedrooms, which are harder to find, cost as much as $1,800, depending on the condition of the building, said Edward Poteat, co-owner of Horsford & Poteat Realty.

Brenda Burton, a nursing home administrator, rented a floor-through in a brownstone on 118th Street three years ago. "The apartment was so big and the rent was so good that it sold me on the neighborhood," she said. "I've never felt afraid on the street here. There are some abandoned buildings on my block, which are intimidating. But it's a great location, close to the park, close to Columbia, close to the subways."

A handful of nonprofit housing development corporations, working with city and state subsidies, have been active in the area for some years. The Harlem Community Development Corporation and the Abyssinian Development Corporation, among other nonprofits, are building and renovating properties for low- and moderate-income families with the help of public subsidies. In recent years, the city's Department of Housing Preservation and Development initiated several programs to encourage home ownership in the neighborhood. "Our aim is to increase home ownership opportunities for people in Harlem," said Ibo Balton, the H.P.D. director of Manhattan planning.

Tracy Butler, a neurology resident at Columbia Presbyterian Hospital, and her husband, Mark Silberg, a public school teacher, recently paid $345,000 for a brownstone on 123d Street through the city's Homeworks program, in which small, vacant city-owned buildings are turned over to developers who must show that they have financing for renovation. Buyers, in turn, must demonstrate to H.P.D. that they qualify for mortgages for a market-rate purchase. When Dr. Butler and Mr. Silberg bought their brownstone from Cross Construction, a Manhattan developer chosen by the program, nothing but the brick walls and an ornate mantel remained in its interior.

For Dr. Butler and Mr. Silberg, one attraction of the brownstone was the ability to live in a duplex on the top two floors and to rent a studio and a one-bedroom apartment on the lower floors. Another was the neighborhood. "We wanted a street with a lot of brownstones and we liked the proximity to Columbia and the fact that the neighborhood is racially mixed," she said.

There is a handful of restaurants in the neighborhood, including Perk's, an upscale jazz and supper club on 123d Street, and M&G, a 24-hour soul-food diner, on 125th Street. The neighborhood is within walking distance of Columbia University, City College, and the Studio Museum of Harlem.

At the heart of West Central Harlem is a thriving West African community, centered around 116th Street and Adam Clayton Powell Jr. Boulevard. Recent immigrants often gather at the tiny Cafe Soleil on Frederick Douglass Boulevard at 118th Street, which serves West African food. "I've seen a lot of changes here in the last few years," said Ibrahim Traore, who with Lacine Diaide opened Cafe Soleil in 1997. "Harlem has always been a family neighborhood, but now you see more and more people on the streets. People aren't afraid to go out anymore."

Residents and city officials hope that the influx of middle-class families will increase public pressure to improve the neighborhood's public schools. P.S. 180, the neighborhood elementary school, was ranked among the city's lowest in reading scores in 1997, with just over 10 percent of the students performing at or above grade level. There are no high schools in the neighborhood.

Some parents send their children to one of two nearby K–8 Roman Catholic schools, St. Joseph's and Corpus Christi, where tuition ranges from $1,600 to $2,200 a year.

Settled in the 17th century by Dutch farmers who named it Nieuw Haarlem, the area was a farming community well into the 19th century. The extension of the elevated railroads along Eighth and Ninth Avenues in the 1880s set off a construction boom. Rows of brownstones and a handful of spacious apartment buildings were constructed in the area north of Central Park for German immigrants and, by the turn of the century, for eastern European Jews escaping the squalor of the Lower East Side.

Blacks from the South and from the Caribbean began moving into some sections of Harlem in the early 20th century. By the 1920s, writers like Langston Hughes, Countee Cullen, and Zora Neale Hurston helped launch the literary movement known as the Harlem Renaissance. Over the next quarter century, jazz musicians like Duke Ellington and Fletcher Henderson performed in Harlem's nightclubs, and many, like Louis Armstrong and Bessie Smith, lived in Harlem.

But it wasn't until the late '20s and early '30s that black families began moving into the brownstones edging Morningside Avenue south of 125th Street.

Margaret Wyke, whose father bought a brownstone on 122d Street in 1936, said that hers was the first black family on the block. By the end of World War II, all of her neighbors were black, she said. Although her family has occupied their home continuously, many middle-class black families sold their homes in the '50s, or subdivided them and rented out apartments. "Harlem was abandoned in the '50s and '60s," Mrs. Wyke said. "Middle-class people just left for Westchester and Long Island. Then the drug problems started. It was like an abandoned area, it really was."

In 1981, when Eric Sawyer bought his first brownstone on Manhattan Avenue, his was one of three occupied buildings on the block. Mr. Sawyer, a former investment consultant and founding member of the AIDS activist group Act Up, paid just $26,000 for the four-story building. He spent the next couple of years renovating it. The building had no heat and no hot water, and only one or two electric outlets worked, he said. "I moved in and lived in it that first winter. I spent most nights doing demolition work and Sheetrocking and spent the next seven years making the building habitable."

Later he bought a second building, renting out floor-through apartments in both to Columbia students, artists, and, more recently, young professionals. "I basically toughed out living here and watched the entire neighborhood come back to life," he said. "There was a period of time when there were a lot of crack sales in the neighborhood. There were a couple of murders because of drug wars. But those gangs were pushed out of the area and it is again quite safe."

On the block that had only three occupied buildings when Mr. Sawyer moved in 17 years ago, there is now only one unoccupied building. Its owner says that he plans to renovate it.

WEST END AVENUE

A calm oasis near the buzz of Broadway

BY PETER MALBIN

Leaving the buzz of Broadway behind, residents carrying food-laden shopping bags from Zabar's and Fairway walk one block west to a gentler, tree-lined world of distinguished doormen buildings, churches, and schools. In the morning, school buses are the only large vehicles permitted on the avenue, and baby strollers parade the sidewalks. With Riverside Park one block to the west for much of its length and Broadway close by, West End Avenue is residential yet close to transportation, shopping, and entertainment. "For the most part, once people move to the avenue, they nest," said Cathy Blau of the Corcoran Group, a real estate agency. "In many cases, both partners are serious professionals and don't want to be one hour away from Manhattan."

One nester, Julie Sakellariadis, moved to New York City after college and is raising four children in two combined apartments on West End Avenue at 91st Street. "Everything's right here," Ms. Sakellariadis said. "The grocery stores are one block away. Our church is across the street from us. My children go to school in the neighborhood."

A continuation of 11th Avenue, West End Avenue goes from 59th Street through 107th Street, where it connects with Broadway. The avenue is well known—and sought-after—for its classic six- and seven-room co-op apartments, which have two or three bedrooms and bathrooms, a living room, a formal dining room, and a maid's room.

Such apartments are in short supply, according to brokers. Classic six-room co-ops ranged from $580,000 to $850,000, while seven-room co-ops averaged $810,000 in mid-1997, according to the Corcoran Group. Co-op prices depend on condition, square footage, views, the building's financial condition, maintenance, and location. "Even though the avenue looks homogenous, there's quite a variation," said JoAnne Kennedy of Coldwell Banker Hunt Kennedy.

POPULATION: 73,979.

AREA: 2.37 miles.

MEDIAN HOUSEHOLD INCOME: $64,633.

PRICE OF A MIDRANGE SIX-ROOM CO-OP: $825,000.

DISTANCE FROM MIDTOWN MANHATTAN: 1.5 miles.

TRANSPORTATION: The M57 bus travels on 11th and West End Avenues between 57th and 72d Streets. Other buses are a block away, on Riverside Drive, Broadway, and Amsterdam Avenue. No. 1, 2, 3, and 9 subway lines with express stops at 72d and 96th on Broadway, local stops at 66th, 72d, 79th, 86th, 96th, and 103d.

CODES: Area, 212; ZIP, 10023, 10024, and 10025.

The avenue's solid prewar apartments were built with walls thick enough to absorb the sounds of musicians, of which the avenue has many. Most of West End's prewar buildings went co-op in the last 15 years, leaving only a few condominium buildings and rent-stabilized apartments. "The prime location on West End is from 73d to 90th Street," said Greta Walker of the Stribling & Associates real estate agency. "Part of it has to do with Broadway, which is at its nicest at that point." An address further uptown may not carry the same cachet, but the apartments are often as spacious and may be less expensive, depending on such factors as the elegance of the building.

Philip Bentley, a lawyer, and his wife, Joann, who teaches business at Columbia University, bought a 2,200-square-foot seven-room apartment at 103d and West End for $505,000 in the spring of 1995. "We were looking in the 70s and 80s, but you get a lot more space for the same amount of money in the 100s," Mr. Bentley said.

While West End between 70th and 107th is solidly prewar, new development is taking place down the avenue. Many apartments at the 1,000-unit West End Towers, two rental buildings from 61st to 64th, are occupied by young professionals, with 20 percent reserved for moderate-income tenants. Market-rate rents range from $1,700 to $1,900 a month for a one-bedroom and from $2,700 to $3,200 for a two-bedroom. The complex has a one-acre public park.

On the other side of the avenue from West End Towers, the public Amsterdam Houses development, with its many Hispanic residents, stretches from 61st to 64th Street, backing onto West End Avenue.

The 1961 movie *West Side Story* was partly filmed in abandoned tenement lots, some now home to Lincoln Towers, a complex of eight high-rise buildings on either side of West End between 66th and 70th Streets. The well-maintained buildings, which were built as rentals and became co-ops in the mid-eighties, have gardens, playgrounds, and their own security force. Several years ago, studios at Lincoln Towers were priced at $60,000; at the end of 1997, they were trading between $90,000 and $135,000. One-bedrooms that sold for $115,000 in 1995 were bringing between $160,000 and $300,000 in 1997. Two-bedrooms, meanwhile, which were priced at $250,000 in 1995, changed hands between $375,000 and $425,000 in late 1997, according to the Corcoran Group. Prices have risen dramatically in the last two years at Lincoln Towers, said Ms. Blau of the Corcoran Group, despite the emergence of the first towers of Donald J. Trump's Riverside South development to the west, which cut off the Hudson River views of many Lincoln Towers residents.

Developers were drawn to the Upper West Side in 1879 when the Ninth Avenue line of the New York Elevated Railroad extended north of 59th Street. "In the 1890s, West End Avenue was becoming the residential street par excellence for prosperous families," said Peter Salwen, author of *Upper West Side Story*. Opulent row houses were the first homes on the avenue and side streets. On the west side of the avenue between 76th and 77th Streets are some surviving speculative row houses, designed with gables, arches, and bay windows in the late 19th century. They are part of a historic district that includes the Flemish-style West End Collegiate Church (1891–92) and Collegiate School on the blockfront between 77th and 78th. The opening of New York's first subway in 1903 and a trend toward apartment living was an impetus for development of West End buildings with grand lobbies, high ceilings, and 10- and 12-room apartments.

Some of the earliest residents in the West End area were affluent Protestants who attended the Methodist or Episcopal churches on West End between 86th and 87th Streets. Large numbers of Jewish families also moved into the neighborhood and commissioned a site on West 88th between Broadway and West End for Congregation B'nai Jeshurun, the oldest Ashkenazic congregation in New York.

Several religious institutions have recorded large increases in attendance in recent years. Attendance, particularly among young families, has tripled in the last decade at the St. Paul and St. Andrew United Methodist Church at 86th and West End, said Rev. Edward Horne, the pastor, largely because young parents want their children to be part of a religious community. B'nai Jeshurun, a Conservative synagogue, has been meeting at the church because its building suffered structural problems; the synagogue's membership has increased more than tenfold in the last decade.

In recent years, a burgeoning Orthodox and Conservative Jewish community has emerged in the neighborhood. With more than a dozen synagogues and a variety of kosher businesses, the neighborhood is a focal point for Orthodox Jewish life, said Rabbi Ephraim Buchwald, director of the National Jewish Outreach Program.

In the realm of arts and entertainment, there is much to do. The not-for-profit Symphony Space theater at 95th and Broadway has readings and music and dance performances. Residents brush shoulders with artists at neighborhood stores and catch their performances at Lincoln Center. The latest foreign film releases are likely to be playing at the Lincoln Plaza Cinemas at 63d and Broadway. And there are the Sony multiplexes at 84th and Broadway and 68th and Broadway.

West End Avenue has been associated with many writers. Joseph Heller wrote most of *Catch-22* in the foyer of a West End Avenue apartment, and a section of West 84th Street off West End bears Edgar Allan Poe's name because Poe visited the area frequently.

"Seven in the evening is prime Chinese food delivery time on West End Avenue, and you take your life in your hands crossing the street," said one longtime, and quick-footed, bookstore manager. Residents not ordering takeout have their choice of many restaurants, among them Docks and Zen Palate.

Nearby Columbia University adds a scholarly flavor to the neighborhood. "One of the reasons to live here is the fabulous schools," said Ms. Sakellariadis. Private schools on West End include Collegiate at 78th, the country's oldest independent school (established 1628). Tuition at the male-only kindergarten-through-12th-grade school is from $15,600 to $16,850. A striking modern building that resembles a television screen houses the co-ed Calhoun School at West End and 81st. Tuition for the 503 students ranges from $11,200 to $17,700 annually.

Tuition at St. Agnes Boys High School, a parochial high school at 87th and West End, is $3,400 a year. Many of the 320 students are from immigrant families, and more than 85 percent of graduating seniors go on to higher education, said Christopher Farmer, a guidance counselor. Other private schools in the neighborhood include Trinity School, founded in 1709; three Montessori pre- and elementary schools; and a Jewish day school, the Abraham Joshua Heschel School.

Public School 75 (the Emily Dickinson School), on 96th Street and West End Avenue, was one of 91 schools in the country listed for overall excellence by *Redbook* magazine in both 1993 and 1995. There are also other public schools near the avenue, and youngsters can attend public and private schools all over Manhattan.

Part of the neighborhood's appeal is its proximity to Riverside and Central Parks. "In the last three years, neighborhood community policing and block groups in the West 90s and 100s have succeeded in alleviating many problems," including crime and homelessness, said Aaron Biller, co-chairman of the West 90s/West 100s Neighborhood Coalition.

West End does not have the celebrity status of Central Park West, but Penny Marshall, Debra Winger, Bernadette Peters, Garrison Keillor, and Harry Belafonte are among the celebrities who have had homes on the avenue. And on more than one occasion, Mick Jagger has been spotted in the neighborhood going into a brownstone he owns on West 81st Street, just west of the West End.

CITY ISLAND

*A water-bounded village
that's part of the Bronx*

BY MAGGIE GARB

On a gray day recently, the talk on City Island, the mile-and-a-half-long marine village off Pelham Bay Park in the north Bronx, was of an approaching storm. The last big storm, in 1992, damaged scores of small boats, knocked tree limbs through the roofs of several houses, and submerged the island's only link to the mainland, the bridge to the park. Yet to many of the island's 4,100 residents, a big storm is just part of life near the water. "It's the wind blowing," said Robert T. Carmody, director of the chamber of commerce and a broker with Atlantic Emeritus Realty on City Island. "You get wet, pump out the basement, and then go back to work."

Once the home of oystermen and boatbuilders, the island has become a haven for artists, police officers, doctors, and working-class families seeking a Cape Cod–like environment with low real estate taxes and a highly regarded public elementary school. Its only commercial street, City Island Avenue, is lined with seafood restaurants. Among the more popular are the Lobster Box, the Seashore, and the Crab Shanty.

On narrow side streets, gabled brick and frame mansions stand next to four- and five-room cottages. No house is more than a short walk from the water.

"It's one of the few places in New York where rich and poor live right next to each other," said Jane Protzman, a 15-year resident of the island. "You go to a party and can be next to a postdoc from Einstein Hospital and someone who works for the phone company."

Most islanders are homeowners, although there are a growing number of rental units, many leased to interns and residents working at Bronx hospitals. Most rental units are one-bedrooms, where rents start at $700 and go as high as $1,500 for a few, depending largely on location.

Housing prices remained relatively stable until the mid-nineties, when

POPULATION: 4,100.

AREA: 230 acres.

MEDIAN HOUSEHOLD INCOME: $50,750.

MEDIAN PRICE OF SINGLE-FAMILY HOUSE: $220,000.

TAXES ON A MEDIAN-PRICED HOUSE: $1,200–$2,000.

DISTANCE FROM MIDTOWN MANHATTAN: 13 miles.

RUSH-HOUR TRAVEL TO MIDTOWN: 50 minutes by New York Bus Service express, $4 one way; bus to Pelham Bay station and No. 6 subway train to Grand Central, 1 hour.

CODES: Area, 718; ZIP, 10464.

the rise in the Manhattan real estate market began pushing up prices elsewhere in the city. Prices of large Victorian houses on the waterfront run from about $450,000 to $650,000, said Jacqueline Kyle Kall, who runs Port of Kall Realty, a firm started by her grandfather in 1894.

Ms. Kall noted that waterfront houses tend to come on the market about every 30 years, when the owners decide to move to Florida after their children have grown up. "The waterfront properties don't have a lot of turnover because once you get in, you stay," she said.

Off the waterfront, three-bedroom brick houses in good condition are priced from $200,000 to $250,000, said Ms. Kall. Smaller one- and two-bedroom cottages run from $115,000 to $145,000.

Over the last dozen years, a handful of condominium developments have been built along the waterfront. At the 72-unit Boat Yard, units run from about $205,000 for a two-bedroom simplex to $220,000 for a duplex. At the Sailmaker Complex, which includes 34 studios and one-bedroom units, prices range from about $89,000 to $149,000.

The developments initially caused some concern among longtime residents who worried that the island's waterfront would become overdeveloped and its already crowded streets even more congested. "People worried that the island would lose its charm or its small-town style, but that's not what happened," Ms. Kall said. "Nobody ever wants anything to change too quickly."

Some changes are welcome, like the recent arrival of young artists and galleries. Residents point to CIAO, an acronym for City Island Arts Organization, the three-year-old artists' cooperative and gallery on City Island Avenue. The group, which has more than 50 members, sponsors workshops, exhibits, and a Mardi Gras party. Two other galleries, the Focal Point and the Starving Artist, sell paintings, crafts, and photographs. "It's definitely become a very artsy community and that's great," said Carla Perlowin Chadwick, a jewelry maker and owner of Down by the Sea, one of a handful of craft and gift shops to open on City Island Avenue in the last couple of years.

There is no movie theater on City Island, but there are monthly poetry readings at Laura's Cafe and local musicians have formed a blues band, which performs at some of the yacht clubs.

The island's only bed-and-breakfast, Le Refuge, was opened five years ago by Pierre St. Denis, chef and owner of both the inn and the restaurant of the same name on the Upper East Side. Its restaurant serves elegant French meals Wednesday through Saturday evenings.

Though some see the onslaught of artists as a sign of gentrification, the glitter of high-priced island resorts like Martha's Vineyard is still years away. Celebrities are such a rare sight that last summer when a Hollywood film company was shooting a movie on City Island, residents brought lawn chairs to the sidewalk to watch the filmmakers and actors at work. The island's most prominent celebrity is Dr. Oliver Sacks, a neurologist and author of *Awakenings* and *The Man Who Mistook His Wife for a Hat*.

Many of the island's families have lived on City Island for three and four generations, working in the eight boatyards and a dozen marinas and two sailmaker lofts along the island's shores.

The island, which was settled by German and Scandinavian fishermen and oystermen in the 18th century, became the hub for some of the East Coast's premier yacht builders in the late 19th century. "All the yards here were custom builders," said Tom Nye, a sailmaker whose great-grandfather moved to City Island in the 1860s to work in the shipyards. "They built yachts for Morgans, Vanderbilts, Astors, all the richest families."

During World War II, the boatyards produced warships for the Navy. But after the war, Mr. Nye said, boating changed as small, moderately priced boats became popular. Two sailmakers, about eight boat repair yards, a dozen small marinas, and several yacht clubs remain.

A lot of the younger people went to work for the city Mr. Nye said, many becoming firefighters or policemen. Many young people also left the island, only to return a few years later. They find they miss friends and family and they want good schools and they want to live near the water in a place they can afford, said Mr. Carmody of the chamber of commerce.

The island's only public school, P.S. 175, was built in 1972 on the site of the former Nevins Boat Yard, a firm that built several America's Cup contenders. The school covers kindergarten through eighth grade with open classrooms for second through eighth grades. In 1994, P.S. 175 was one of 31 New York–area schools to receive a grant from the Annenberg Foundation to pay for educational workshops, programs to encourage parental involvement, and school trips, said Rose Rodstrom, a former Parent-Teacher Association president.

St. Mary's Star of the Sea School, a Roman Catholic school, covers prekindergarten through eighth grade. There is no high school on the island, but two Bronx high schools, Herbert H. Lehman and Harry S Truman, are just a 10-minute bus ride away. At the 3,500-student Lehman High School, 93.9 percent of the graduating seniors went on to higher education in 1997. Judith Klemperer, director of college counseling, said the school had strong computer, math, and performing arts programs. At the 2,700-student Truman High School, just 47.9 percent of the freshman class of 1993 graduated four years later. Of the graduates, 74 percent went on to higher education, said Angela Fernandez, a spokeswoman for the Central Board of Education. She said the school had its own television and radio stations.

City Islanders have a few complaints. In the summer, the island is so packed with tourists that traffic crossing the bridge is sometimes backed up for miles. Parking can be hard to find, especially on holiday weekends.

Many also complain about noise on Rodman's Neck, a New York City Police firing range and bomb-squad detonation site in Pelham Bay Park. After several years of pressure from residents, city officials allocated $1.5 million to build a sound barrier around the site to be completed by the end of 1999.

Charlene Schulz-Campbell and her husband, Malcolm, bought a house on City Island two and a half years ago. Both worked in Manhattan but wanted to live where they could own a sailboat and be near the water.

"We heard City Island had more sailboats than people, so we started looking out here," she said. "There's definitely a salty atmosphere out here. It's so close to the city and it seems so far away."

RIVERDALE

Winding streets, high-rises, mansions, and open space

BY MAGGIE GARB

Residents of the rambling Riverdale neighborhood in the northwest corner of the Bronx have long fought to retain its special character. And with good reason. Situated on the rocky bluffs overlooking the Hudson River, many of its narrow, winding streets offer magnificent views of the river and the rugged Palisades beyond. It borders the 1,146-acre Van Cortlandt Park, and several of the neighborhood's stately 19th-century mansions have been designated as city landmarks.

"We're actively trying to keep Riverdale the way it is," said Laura Spalter, co-president of the Riverdale Community Association and a 30-year resident of the neighborhood. "We're trying to keep Riverdale from becoming overdeveloped."

Just a 25-minute ride on Metro-North from midtown Manhattan, Riverdale has long served as a haven for urbanites seeking some green space with easy access to Manhattan. "We're all people who like urban living and want easy access to the city, but we also have a great appreciation for the natural environment," said Anthony Thoman, a history teacher at John F. Kennedy High School who recently bought a co-op in Riverdale.

"Riverdale is really like a small town," said City Councilwoman June M. Eisland, whose district includes Riverdale, where she lives.

Although residents tend to head to Manhattan for an evening out, there is an abundance of Japanese and Chinese restaurants and kosher delis on Riverdale Avenue for those preferring to dine in the neighborhood. Other popular food establishments are the Corner Cafe and Josephina on Johnson Avenue and Bella Vista on 235th Street, the latter two Italian restaurants.

Interest in Riverdale has surged in the last few years as more and

POPULATION: 41,620.

AREA: 3 square miles.

MEDIAN HOUSEHOLD INCOME: $53,390.

MEDIAN PRICE OF A SINGLE-FAMILY HOUSE: $425,000.

MEDIAN PRICE OF A TWO-BEDROOM CO-OP: $84,000.

DISTANCE FROM MIDTOWN MANHATTAN: 10 miles.

RUSH-HOUR TRAVEL TO MIDTOWN: No. 1 or 9 subway train, 50 minutes; Liberty Lines express bus (routes to the East Side, West Side, and Wall Street), 45 minutes, one way $3 monthly pass $120; about 25 minutes on Metro-North Hudson line, one way $4.75, monthly pass $108.

CODES: Area, 718; ZIP, 10463 and 10471.

more people discover that it is a refuge for those seeking to escape Manhattan's soaring real estate prices, said Bradford Trebach, a lawyer and associate broker with his family's firm, Trebach Realty.

On Riverdale's southern tip, wide boulevards like Independence and Palisades Avenues are lined with high-rise apartment houses. Built as rentals in the '60s and '70s, many were converted to condominiums or co-ops in the '80s. While there is a large population of the elderly in the high-rises, an increasing number of young couples with children, priced out of Manhattan, are buying Riverdale apartments. Co-ops sell from about $40,000 for a one-bedroom to as much as $300,000 for a three-bedroom in a building with doormen and a pool. Rents run from about $850 for a one-bedroom to as much as $2,500 for a three-bedroom in a building with doormen and a pool.

North of the high-rises, the streets narrow and curve past large estates. Often set on rolling lawns, massive stone homes run from $500,000 to several million dollars. To the east, in the exclusive Fieldston section, where a cluster of houses designed by the noted architect Dwight James Baum were built in the '20s, Colonials and Tudor-style homes with five or more bedrooms range in price from $500,000 to more than $2 million.

Along the Yonkers border, houses are smaller, with lots averaging 25 by 100 feet. There, brick and stucco houses can be found for about $250,000. "These houses are like old battleships," said Vivian J. Oleen, an associate broker with Sopher Reality. "The houses are sturdy and the neighborhood is stable and quiet."

Most of Riverdale was farmland until the 1840s, when wealthy New Yorkers fleeing the turmoil of the city began building homes on the hills above the Hudson. Cholera epidemics in lower Manhattan in the 1830s and 1840s gave added impetus to those who could afford to move their families out of the densely packed borough. Among the earliest estates was Wave Hill, a two-story Greek Revival manor built in 1836 by the lawyer William Lewis Morris and his wife, Elizabeth Babcock. Purchased by

George Waldridge Perkins in 1903, the home and its lush grounds were rented to many distinguished tenants, including Samuel L. Clemens and Arturo Toscanini.

In 1960, the Perkins family donated the 28-acre property to the City of New York. Today, it features an environmental center, a small art gallery, beautiful gardens, and wooded paths overlooking the 97-acre Riverdale Park and the river.

A century and a half ago, affluent families were attracted to Riverdale by what Kenneth Jackson, a professor of American history at Columbia University, calls the suburban ideal, an environment that combined the best of both rural and urban life. As he noted in his history of the suburbs, *Crabgrass Frontier*, communities such as Riverdale were dependent on new transportation systems, which made possible a commute to a city's business centers.

Riverdale became an affluent suburb after a bridge was built across Spuyten Duyvil Creek in 1853 for the Hudson River Railroad. By 1870, the hills below what is now 254th Street were covered with spacious villas, including Greyston, a mansion designed by James Renwick, Jr., the architect of St. Patrick's Cathedral, for William Earl Dodge, an industrialist who was the founder of the Young Men's Christian Association; and Alderbrook, a Gothic Revival mansion built for Percy Pyne, president of the National City Bank of New York.

The neighborhood was annexed to the City of New York in 1874, a move that sparked a public battle over remapping the neighborhood's streets. Frederick Law Olmsted, co-designer of Central Park, argued for preserving Riverdale's winding roads, an effort that proved successful. But protests against further change were unavailing when New York City Parks Commissioner Robert Moses announced plans to construct the Henry Hudson Parkway and the Henry Hudson Bridge in the mid-thirties, which led to a wave of residential construction after World War II.

Recently the Riverdale Nature Preservancy began a campaign for rezoning the neighborhood to limit construction of such projects as nursing homes or homes for the elderly, several of which have recently expanded. "We did a study and asked if everyone built as much as allowable under law, what would it look like?" said Paul Elston, chairman of the Riverdale Nature Preservancy. "The answer was horrific."

A primary target for activists is a 20-story building that has housed Soviet and then Russian diplomats and their families since 1974. Recently the Russians announced plans to remove the top 11 floors and build four adjoining towers of nine to 13 stories. "Community groups have been meeting with them and we're hoping to reach a compromise," said Mr. Elston.

But Riverdale residents also have more esoteric interests. Sixty to 70 people show up for poetry readings at the An Beal Bocht Cafe each

Tuesday night. Exoterica, a nonprofit literary group founded in 1991, sponsors poetry workshops for all ages as well as poetry readings.

The neighborhood's public elementary schools, P.S. 24 and P.S. 81, were rated among the best elementary schools in the city in last year's *The Parents' Guide to New York City's Best Public Elementary Schools*, compiled by Clara Hemphill, a senior research fellow at the Public Education Association. Both schools are well equipped with computer labs and libraries, and P.S. 24 has a planetarium.

Of the 4,500 students at John F. Kennedy High School in neighboring Kingsbridge, the only public high school in the district, 150 are in the highly selective Kennedy Institute of Society and Science program, which emphasizes the sciences and offers year-long internships at research institutes. Gino Silvestri, the principal, said that many graduates of this program get full scholarships to four-year colleges. But the school was built for just 3,400 students and there is a serious overcrowding problem.

"We're exploring efforts to build another high school for the area, but we're still in the early stages of that discussion," said Councilwoman Eisland.

Riverdale is also home to the 3,600-student Manhattan College and the 1,100-student College of Mount St. Vincent, and there are several well-known private schools in the neighborhood. Fieldston, Horace Mann, and the Riverdale Country School include prekindergarten through 12th grade. Tuition at the schools ranges from $11,000 to $18,500.

There are two Roman Catholic parochial schools in Riverdale, St. Gabriel's, with 260 students, and St. Margaret of Cortona, with 350. Both include prekindergarten through eighth grade; tuition ranges from $1,800 for the lower grades to $2,800.

In the last 50 years, there has been a growing Jewish community in the neighborhood. Its three Jewish schools, the Kinneret Day School, the Yeshiva of the Telshe Alumni High School (across from Wave Hill in the former Campagna estate), and the S/A/R Academy are among the top Jewish schools in the country, according to Rabbi Jonathan Rosenblatt of the Riverdale Jewish Center. Tuition ranges from $7,000 at Kinneret to $10,500 at the S/A/R Academy. At the Telshe Yeshiva, a boarding school that also includes a rabbinical college, board and tuition costs $8,900. "This has become one of the choice neighborhoods for very educated, very committed, young Jewish families," said Rabbi Rosenblatt. "The parks on a Saturday afternoon are great; they're filled with kids."

SPUYTEN DUYVIL

Sunsets over the Palisades, and legends

BY ROSALIE R. RADOMSKY

Ferne LaDue can tell it's spring when she hears the coxswains rhythmically barking strokes to Columbia University shell teams practicing on the Hudson River below her duplex in Spuyten Duyvil. Her co-op in Villa Charlotte Brontë, where she and her family have lived since 1968, is perched 150 feet above the river. "I feel like I'm on a ship," said Mrs. LaDue, who can see magnificent sunsets over the Palisades across the river.

Views of the Palisades and the Henry Hudson and George Washington Bridges are noteworthy elements of the hilly northwest Bronx neighborhood. So is its Dutch name. Over the centuries, the name (pronounced SPY-ten- DIE-vul) has been grist for legends—usually linked to the fierce confluence of the Harlem and Hudson Rivers below.

Rev. William A. Tieck, an expert on the area's history who died in 1997, favored the explanation given in Washington Irving's *Knickerbocker's History of New York*. In 1664, according to Irving, Antony Van Corlear was dispatched by Peter Stuyvesant, governor of Nieuw Amsterdam, to warn Dutch settlers across the swirling Harlem River where it joins the Hudson River ("in spite of the devil," or *"spyt den duyvel,"* in Dutch) of an impending invasion by the British. When no ferry could be found, the messenger, trumpet in hand, tried to swim across. He never made it, drowning after one last blast of his trumpet.

Many refer to Spuyten Duyvil, divided by the Henry Hudson Parkway, as a section of Riverdale, as well as lower or south Riverdale. But the late Dr. Tieck wouldn't hear of it. "People think everything west of the Grand Concourse is Riverdale," said Dr. Tieck, who once served as the pastor of the Edgehill Church of Spuyten Duyvil and as the official Bronx historian, and whose books on the borough included *Riverdale, Kingsbridge and Spuyten Duyvil*.

POPULATION: 23,461.

AREA: 4 square miles.

MEDIAN HOUSEHOLD INCOME:
$56,101.

**MEDIAN PRICE OF A TWO-
BEDROOM CO-OP:** $130,000.

**MEDIAN PRICE OF A TWO-
BEDROOM CONDO:** $380,000.

**MIDRANGE RENT FOR A TWO-
BEDROOM APARTMENT:**
$1,450.

**DISTANCE FROM MIDTOWN
MANHATTAN:** 8 miles.

**RUSH-HOUR TRAVEL TO
MIDTOWN:** 6 minutes on the
B24 or B10 bus to West 231st
Street subway stop, then 32
minutes on the No. 1 or No. 9
line; 26 minutes on the
Metro-North train, $4.75 one
way, $108 monthly; 45
minutes by Liberty Lines
express bus service, $3.00; or
by Mosholu van, $6.

CODES: Area, 718; ZIP, 10463.

To him, Spuyten Duyvil was the heights from the Spuyten Duyvil Creek by the Henry Hudson Memorial Bridge to the Memorial Bell Tower at 239th Street, where Riverdale begins. To the east, the boundary is roughly Waldo and Johnson Avenues.

Spuyten Duyvil was essentially a wilderness until Isaac Johnson set up an iron foundry on a peninsula jutting into Spuyten Duyvil Creek about 1853. During the Civil War, the foundry turned out cannon, ammunition, and the first American torpedo boat. The Spuyten Duyvil Rolling Mill Company was built next to it. The rolling mill shut down in 1883, but the Johnsons ran the foundry for 40 years more.

Most of the peninsula was destroyed by 1937 to widen the Harlem River Ship Canal. The remaining wedge, between a railroad cut and water, became known as the Columbia Rock, and now bears a 60-foot-high faded blue and white "C," freshened up every few years by Columbia shell crews.

Surviving as a designated landmark with a small congregation and four Tiffany windows is the countrylike Edgehill Church of Spuyten Duyvil, established by the Johnson family in 1889. It has about 18 regular members. Below it are five 19th-century wood-frame houses along Edsall Avenue (formerly Spuyten Duyvil Road) in the shadow of the Henry Hudson Memorial Bridge, which connected Spuyten Duyvil to Manhattan in 1936.

"This area is a very affordable alternative for people with a Manhattan mentality, and offers a suburban lifestyle without the necessity of owning a car," said Susan E. Goldy, president of Susan E. Goldy, Inc., in Riverdale.

"There are probably no more than a dozen houses west of the parkway that afford a river view," she said, "and generally one to three come on the market each year. Prices for those houses would begin in the $800,000 range. East of the Parkway, we probably list five to nine houses a year. They begin at around $350,000."

During 1997, a three-bedroom Tudor house with a nanny suite and river views on a private cul-de-sac near West 231st sold for $699,000, and a three-bedroom brick Colonial along Arlington Avenue sold for $450,000.

There are about 55 co-ops and four condominiums in the neighborhood. In 1984, the Association of Riverdale Cooperatives was set up to assist local co-op owners. According to Ms. Goldy, two-bedroom co-ops ranged from $79,000 to $275,000 and one-bedrooms went from $45,000 to $127,000 in the spring of 1998. Two-bedroom condominiums were pricier, ranging from $133,000 to $450,000, and one-bedrooms went from $95,000 to $135,000.

"My dream was a southwest river view on Riverside Drive," said Linda Sproule, a physiotherapist, "but Manhattan real estate agents laughed when we wanted to spend $200,000." She and her husband, Jack, a controller for the Franciscan Friars of the Atonement-Graymoor, a Catholic order of men based in Garrison, New York, in Westchester County, left the Upper West Side in 1993 to buy a junior four-room co-op with a terrace and a Hudson River view for $105,000.

In the spring of 1998, a 1,600-square-foot two-bedroom co-op, which could be converted into a three-bedroom, along the Henry Hudson Parkway was on the market for $165,000. It also offered a terrace, panoramic views, and a 24-hour doorman. The median sales price of a two-bedroom co-op was $130,000 in the spring, and $125,000 in 1997. About two dozen two-bedroom co-ops were still available for under $115,000, according to Ms. Goldy, and two-bedroom apartments in luxury high-rises started at $130,000.

Along the Hudson River, a 3,000-square-foot, three-bedroom, triplex town house condominium with parking was on the market for $695,000 in the spring of 1998. The median price of a two-bedroom condominium was $380,000 in early 1998 and $295,000 in 1997.

The midrange price of a two-bedroom rental was $1,450 and a one-bedroom was $950 in early 1998.

Parents pitch in to run the library at P.S. 24 (the Spuyten Duyvil School). The K–5 school had the top reading scores in the Bronx in the last decade. With 88.5 percent of the children scoring at or above grade level last year, the school ranked 13 out of 676 schools in 1997. The school, with 922 students, also hones special interests of fourth and fifth graders in enrichment clusters, clublike groups including art, chess, French, and Spanish. It also offers 12 special education classes and gives everyone a chance to work with computers.

Murals by students cover three stairwells and hallways at Middle School 141 (the David A. Stein Riverdale Middle School), across the street. The school, whose enrollment totaled 1,430, is for grades 6 through 8 and offers eighth graders accelerated English, high school math, languages, and earth science.

Some students go on to John F. Kennedy High School in Kingsbridge, which emphasizes multiculturalism. About 70 nations are represented among its 4,500 students, and 70 percent of its seniors went on to four-year colleges and 12 percent to two-year colleges in 1997. It has 26 intramural teams, and offers nine advanced placement courses for college credit, as well as science honors programs.

Several private schools are in the area, including the pre-K–12 Riverdale Country School, the pre-K–6 Fieldston Lower School, the Fieldston School (7–12), and the Horace Mann School (K–6 and 7–12). Students may also attend the pre-K–8 Roman Catholic St. Gabriel School or the Orthodox Jewish pre-K–8 S/A/R Academy in upper Riverdale.

Spuyten Duyvil has its own Metro-North station and post office. Shopping is mainly along Johnson Avenue, from 235th to 236th Street, and paralleling those streets along Riverdale Avenue, between 235th and 238th Streets. Another shopping area can be found outside the 231st Street No. 1 train subway stop.

Among the parks is nine-acre Henry Hudson Memorial Park, easy to spot by the monument at its northern end. A sitting area surrounds the 106-foot-high granite Doric column topped by a sculpture of the explorer. At the other end, separated by Kappock Street, are four basketball courts, a softball field, and a playground.

Red maples, Japanese cherry trees, shrubs, and Boston ivy can be found amid the seven-acre Spuyten Duyvil Shorefront Park, where dog walkers, strollers, and joggers wend their way along its winding gravel path, which runs along Edsall Avenue, passes Thompson Pond, and ends at the railway station. Nannies or parents with children in tow usually congregate on two large cement benches situated above the Hudson on the park's overlook—also a popular vantage point for artists and camera-toting visitors.

Fishermen catch striped bass, eels, and white perch in the river near the old Penn Central tracks and Harlem River Ship Canal. And joggers who run along scenic Palisade Avenue are apt to pass an old unmapped private country road where a red fox lived in a yard in the 1950s, and an ancient tulip tree still stands.

Among the many preschools in the area is the Spuyten Duyvil Infantry, set up as a parent co-op in 1928 in Kingsbridge. The name is said to have been suggested by a parent who said at the time: "Well, they're a bunch of infants. And it's a school. Why not call it the Spuyten Duyvil School of Infantry?" It was later shortened to Spuyten Duyvil Infantry. The program, which accepts only 2- to 5-year-olds, is now often referred to as Spuyten Duyvil Preschool to avoid confusion.

BAY RIDGE

Where many ethnic currents
meet beside the Narrows

BY JANICE FIORAVANTE

Bay Ridge, on the Narrows in the shadow of the graceful Verrazano-Narrows Bridge, is as compelling to its contemporary year-round residents as it was to the summer émigrés who built mansions by its waters in the last century. Like Brooklyn itself, it is marked by social diversity. Yet the stamp of its ethnic history is still upon it, as reflected in its shops. On Third Avenue, Nordic Delicacies, a deli, sits next to the Middle Eastern Family Store. On Fifth Avenue, Leske's Bakery, with its German, Danish, Swedish, and Italian pastries, faces Mejander & Mulgannon's, a Norwegian and Irish food store across the street. Many residents point to this ability to absorb each new group—the Irish in the early 1800s, Germans and Scandinavians later in the century, Italians and Greeks in this century—as a striking and positive characteristic of Bay Ridge.

Since the '20s, its one- and two-family homes and mid-rise apartment buildings along Shore Road and Fourth Avenue have helped it retain what Mary Sempepos, former district manager of Community Board 10, calls its "small-town character." Mrs. Sempepos has lived in the neighborhood for 26 years; her husband, James, is a lifelong resident.

Before the '20s, Bay Ridge was a mix of farms and large mansions built after the Civil War, said Susan Pulaski, president of the Bay Ridge Historical Society. It originally was settled by the Dutch. A cemetery on McKay Place and Narrows Avenue dates to Revolutionary War days, with names of families who settled Bay Ridge, including the Cortelyous and Barkaloos. "This was a homestead cemetery and farms surrounded it," said Rita Unz, treasurer and corresponding secretary of the society. Other early family farms were owned by the Bennetts and the Van Brunts. Today, the Roman Catholic Xaverian High School for boys, built in the '50s, fronts the cemetery.

POPULATION: 70,980.

AREA: 4.5 square miles.

MEDIAN HOUSEHOLD INCOME: $45,489.

MEDIAN PRICE OF A SINGLE-FAMILY HOUSE: $275,000.

TAXES ON A MEDIAN-PRICED HOUSE: $2,000.

DISTANCE FROM MIDTOWN MANHATTAN: 15 miles.

RUSH-HOUR TRAVEL TO MIDTOWN: 55 minutes on the R subway line; 65 minutes on the M.T.A. x27 express bus, $3 one way.

CODES: Area, 718; ZIP, 11209, 11219, and 11220.

Bay Ridge was originally called Yellow Hook for the yellow clay found in its soil. "It probably was Yellow Hoch, from the Dutch, which means bay or cove, Americanized to *hook*," added Peter Scarpa, vice president of the society. But in 1848–49, a yellow fever epidemic gave Yellow Hook a bad connotation. "Businesspeople met to choose a better name," said Mr. Scarpa, "and a florist named James Weir devised Bay Ridge in 1853, from the little bays and big ridge of the landscape." Much of the history has been gathered in a book, *The Bay Ridge Chronicles*, written by Jerome Hoffman and available through the society.

The bays have been filled in for Shore Road Park's 58 green acres of swings and slides, ball fields, and basketball and tennis courts. A shore promenade along the Belt Parkway for walking and bicycling was added in the late '30s. But it was the coming of the subway in 1916 that changed the neighborhood's character. Before then, dirt roads and huge trees were the norm, said Ms. Pulaski. "Large estates were sold to developers, ponds were drained, and houses were built," she added, including attached homes and apartment houses.

"The neighborhood was really peopled in the '20s and '30s," Ms. Pulaski continued. "The population shot up from a few thousand before the '20s to tens of thousands afterward."

The area's Norwegian heritage is apparent in the annual Norwegian Day parade, culminating in Leif Ericsson Park with the crowning of Miss Norway alongside the monument of Ericsson donated by the Prince of Norway in 1939. Irish residents hold a St. Patrick's Day parade in March.

Residents say a sense of community pervades Bay Ridge. Merchant and civic groups monitor the conditions of the streets and even have designated cleanup days, scheduled in spring. Their effort is designed to maintain the vitality of the shopping thoroughfares, Third and Fifth Avenues and 86th Street.

For residents, the fact that most stores are within walking distance is one of the neighborhood's appeals. "So is its suburban landscape," said Ms. Pulaski, who moved away after college in the 1960s and lived in Virginia, but returned in the mid-seventies. In fact, 85 percent of new home buyers are from Bay Ridge, said Dorothy Maguire, co-owner with her husband, John, of John A. Maguire Real Estate. Their three sons, Tom, Bob, and Steven, have taken over much of the day-to-day running of the firm. "These are people who could live anywhere and are here by choice," she said. "Largely we deal in reshuffles—people who want a bigger house or are selling their home and want an apartment."

Timothy and Maria Cochrane are two such people. In 1994, they moved into 10 78th Street, a $355,000 one-family house, from an apartment on 71st Street. Mrs. Cochrane was born and reared in Bay Ridge, Mr. Cochrane in Sunset Park, the neighboring community. "Our house is a block from Shore Road Park with water views," she noted. And in 1997, they bought a new home three blocks away on Harbor Lane, with five bedrooms to accommodate their growing family—Stephanie, their third child, is a year old.

Although the bulk of homes are one- and two-families, there are three- to six-family houses available as well. Basil Capetanakis, former chairman of Community Board 10, explained that many families of Greek descent moved here in the '70s after the construction of Holy Cross Greek Orthodox Church. Mr. Capetanakis, owner/broker of 14 Apollo Real Estate, commented on the strong recent demand for houses and apartments. "It seems to be an influx from Manhattan," he said, explaining that prices have increased 5 percent to 7 percent in the mid-nineties.

While the median sale price for a one-family home was $245,000 in 1996, for the third quarter of 1997, it was $275,000. Annual taxes on a typical house valued at $275,000 would be $2,000 to $2,100, he said.

Apartment-house conversions helped supply the co-op market. "It's easier to convert apartment houses than to find land for new construction, so we have many more co-ops than condominiums," Mrs. Maguire noted, adding that "new" homes in Bay Ridge were 30 years old. She estimated that there were about 2,000 co-ops and 200 condominiums in the neighborhood.

Over the last nine years, public school enrollment has risen in the five elementary schools, three middle schools, and two public high schools, said the School District 20 superintendent, Vincent Grippo. "We opened a new middle school this September, I.S. 30, with grade 6 and 120 students only," he said. Eventually, it will be a grade 6–8 school with about 400 enrollment.

Among pre-K–5 schools is P.S. 102 (the Bayview School) which has computers in every classroom linked to the Internet.

The High School of Telecommunications Arts and Technology continues the high-tech emphasis for its 1,300 students. The former president of the school's Parent-Teacher Association, Audrey Tumbarello, who now works at the school in its College Now program, credits the small size of the school—and thus the greater attention paid to each student—for the fact that when her son Vito was 15, his reading scores soared from the 84th to the 97th percentile in just one year. Recently Vito was offered two teaching assistantships at the State University of New York's Binghamton campus, where he is an undergraduate: one in Russian literature, the other in feminist cinema.

Fort Hamilton High School, with 4,100 enrollees and typically 85 percent going on to college, has a computer science institute for grades 9 and 12, culminating in up to 12 advanced college credits for qualified students. While 2,000 to 3,000 children apply, only 34 out-of-zone spots are available, said the principal, Dr. Alice Farkouh.

Among the neighborhood's private schools are two college prep schools: the 27-acre, grades 5–12 Poly Prep Country Day School, with a tuition of $14,000, which recently purchased a lower school in Park Slope for pre-K to grade 4; the pre-K–12 Adelphi Academy in what had been the Norwegian Children's Home for Orphans, with a tuition of $10,000; and the pre-K–8 Lutheran Elementary School of Bay Ridge and the Leif Ericsson Day School for grades pre-K to 8, which have a tuition of $3,000 to $3,500.

There are also two Roman Catholic girls' schools—the Visitation Academy, covering pre-K through grade 8, which has a tuition of $4,000 a year, and Fontbonne Hall, a high school that was once the villa of the entertainer Lillian Russell. The high school, celebrating its 60th anniversary, currently has 512 students enrolled at a tuition of $4,800 a year; of its 1997 graduating class of 134, 99 percent went on to college.

Parks are plentiful, including McKinley Park, scheduled for refurbishing, Owls Head Park, recently renovated, Dyker Beach Park, also a candidate for renovation, and the city-owned Dyker Beach Golf Course.

The southerly anchor of Bay Ridge is the Fort Hamilton Army base, whose original stone fort was built in 1820, not long after the War of 1812, to guard the Narrows against foreign incursion. It is in the National Register of Historic Places.

Almost 10 years ago, the city's Landmarks Preservation Commission designated as a landmark a large stone cottage with an imitation thatch roof at 8220 Narrows Avenue. The privately owned residence, built in 1917 by Howard E. Jones, a shipping entrepreneur, is known locally and variously as the Mushroom House, the Witch's House, and the Hansel and Gretel House.

BOERUM HILL

Restoration in a mixed ethnic district

BY JANICE FIORAVANTE

For Michael Armstrong, a pioneering town house purchaser in the 1960s, Boerum Hill was, when he first arrived, "more than a conscious neighborhood, more like a state of mind."

"We bought our house at 453 State Street in 1966, a 16-foot-wide four-floor row house where we raised three kids," said Mr. Armstrong, public affairs director for Howard Golden, the Brooklyn borough president. "Before us, 30 people lived in this house." The downtown Brooklyn neighborhood had, in the '50s, consisted of many single-room-occupancy rooming houses. "The docks were still going," he noted. "The S.R.O.'s allowed workers to live cheaply."

When a moratorium on S.R.O.'s was declared in the '60s, he continued, buildings became available to town-house hunters from Manhattan on the lookout for homes. These people, primarily middle-class professionals, restored not only homes but the area's prestige. Part of the transformation was renaming the neighborhood Boerum Hill—after a family that had owned a large farm in the area in Colonial days.

Mr. Armstrong and his wife, Dnynia, who in 1972 founded *The Phoenix*, a Brooklyn downtown weekly, paid $12,000 25 years ago and put $120,000 to $130,000 in restoration and renovation.

Randall Thomas, who with his wife moved into 230 Wyckoff Street in August 1993, bought his fully restored four-floor home for $215,000. Mr. Thomas's house was built in the 1860s. The couple's two-bedroom duplex has a working fireplace and a backyard for barbecues. His two-bedroom rental upstairs, Mr. Thomas says, makes the couple's net monthly layout for taxes and mortgage about equal to the rent they had been paying for their one-bedroom apartment on the Upper West Side.

G. Dennis Holt, a local historian who is a senior editor at two area

GAZETTEER

POPULATION: 12,476.

AREA: 0.23 square mile (30 blocks).

MEDIAN HOUSEHOLD INCOME: $50,830.

MEDIAN PRICE OF A TOWN HOUSE: $390,000.

TAXES ON A MEDIAN-PRICED HOUSE: $1,850.

DISTANCE FROM MIDTOWN MANHATTAN: 5.6 miles.

RUSH-HOUR TRAVEL TO MIDTOWN: 25 minutes on the 2, 3, 4, 5, A, B, C, D, F, G, M, N, Q, or R subway train.

CODES: Area, 718; ZIP, 11201 and 11217.

newspapers, *The Brooklyn Heights Press* and *The Brooklyn Daily Eagle*, thinks that there's probably more wealth among the 17,550 people of Boerum Hill today than there ever was. "Houses date from the 1850s to the 1870s and they were peopled by middle-class merchants," Mr. Holt explained. "But the wealth was never as profound as the Heights or Cobble Hill."

Among the advantages of living in Boerum Hill, said JoAnne Simon, president of the Boerum Hill Association, is easy access to 10 subway lines and the Long Island Rail Road in the Atlantic Terminal; cheap cab fare home from Manhattan; and only 15 minutes to Wall Street by subway.

"It's quiet, convenient, friendly—and liberal," said Ms. Simon, a lawyer on Fulton Street who rents in the neighborhood. "We tend to stay for eight, 10, or 15 years and many home-owning neighbors have been here for 25 to 30 years. It's the first time since I was a kid that I know everyone on my block." She noted, too, that people who live here care about architectural detail. "The homes on my block, Dean Street, were built in 1852," said Ms. Simon. "A few of my neighbors have working gas-burning chandeliers."

William Harris, a real estate broker at Renaissance Properties who has lived in Boerum Hill since 1970, calls the dominant architectural styles "post-Federal to Italianate." In general, he said, prices in the neighborhood are half those for comparable housing in Brooklyn Heights and about three-quarters those of Cobble Hill or Park Slope.

In 1973, the New York City Landmarks Preservation Commission designated as a historic district a six-block irregularly shaped area bounded by Pacific, Nevins, Wyckoff, and Hoyt Streets. Buildings on State Street between Smith and Hoyt Streets have been individually designated by the commission.

Christopher Thomas, vice president of William B. May Company, noted that these "spectacular" four-story town houses ranged in price from $500,000 to $750,000. Rents for one-bedrooms run from $950 to $1,200 and the market is extremely tight, said Mr. Harris of Renaissance Properties. A two-bedroom ranges from $1,100 to $1,600.

As for co-ops and condominiums, Mr. Harris said sales are picking up from their lows in the early 1990s, an 8 percent increase each year in the mid-nineties. He added that two-bedroom condominiums ranged from $100,000 to $150,000, while two-bedroom co-ops were from $90,000 to $140,000.

Mr. Thomas said that recently "there was a big Federal-style 25-foot-wide National Register house bought for $625,000, the top price paid for a brownstone in the neighborhood" despite the fact that it was in terrible shape. Seven doors down the street, a very similar, beautifully restored Federal-era 25-foot National Register house sold for $495,000 in 1996, and came back on the market in 1998 for $750,000.

And Mr. Harris put the median sale price of a house in 1996 at $350,000, while it was $390,000 in the fourth quarter of 1997. "This reflects an 8 percent yearly increase for prices in the mid-nineties," he said. Annual taxes on a median-priced house would be about $1,850.

There are two public housing complexes in Boerum Hill: The Gowanus has 1,139 apartments in 16 buildings; the Wyckoff has 529 in three buildings.

There are two elementary schools in the 30-block neighborhood—P.S. 38 on Pacific Street between Nevins Street and Third Avenue, and P.S. 261, on Pacific Street between Smith and Hoyt Streets. "We have two full-day pre-K classes as well as full-time day and evening adult education classes," said Millicent Goodman, the P.S. 38 principal, adding that all students have access to computers. An Annenberg School grant of $75,000 for five years—"We're in our second year," said Mrs. Goodman—is being used to connect art to the curriculum. When third-grade students studied Asian traditions, ribbon dancers from China performed; children made their own ribbons and learned the dance.

P.S. 261 offers three small kindergarten-through–grade 5 schools: Children's Learning Cooperative, New Program, and Multicultural Learning Connection. "We have 884 students on our campus and this breakdown allows teachers more collaboration and connection with students, their parents, and the community," said the principal, Judi Aronson. "It's the small one-room concept of teaching more intimately."

Middle School 293, with 630 students, and the Brooklyn School for Global Studies, with 525, share the same building on Baltic Street, but the latter is both a middle and a high school, serving grades 6 through 12. Its June 1998 graduating class was its first. "We're expecting 90 percent of our 25 graduates to go on to college," said Larry Abrams, principal. Students are expected to produce exit portfolios to show their skills, using research papers, literary essays, and interviews on such themes as "Men and Women in Transition," "The Color Line," and "Clinging/Letting Go," about cities and suburbs. M.S. 293 has a fine and performing arts academy and a math academy that are open to students throughout Brooklyn.

Community and block associations get high marks from the police. The cooperation is so good, said Sgt. James McGrath, community relations officer at the 84th Precinct, "that we are devoting resources in a preventive mode rather than problem solving.

"There have been sporadic incidents with drugs, but we've been able to catch it early because of the block associations," he explained. "Boerum Hill residents keep us well informed about daily happenings."

A History of Boerum Hill, written by a former resident, L. J. Davis, for the Boerum Hill Association in 1987, notes that a major impetus to the growth of the area was the construction of the Gowanus Canal, which was begun in 1845. The canal, estimated to have cost $78,600, drained the swamps south of Warren Street and spurred the development of both Cobble Hill and Boerum Hill.

"It led to the brownstoning of Brooklyn," said William C. May's Mr. Thomas. "Brownstones were quarried on the banks of the wetlands of New Jersey, put on barges, and shipped through the canal."

The area historically was called downtown Brooklyn, South Brooklyn, or North Gowanus. "During the 1920s, there were lots of Irish here," said Mr. Holt, the historian, who noted that he and his wife, Susan, bought their house at 137 Bergen Street in 1968 from Anna Murphy. "That changed during the '40s and '50s, when poor people from Puerto Rico moved into rooming houses. The house next door was still a rooming house until eight or 10 years ago."

Third-generation Italians and Irish, as well as Puerto Ricans, Arabs, and blacks, live in this area, pointed out Mr. Harris. "About 15 percent of brownstones are owned or rented by blacks and Latinos," he said.

Atlantic Avenue is known for its antiques shops and restaurants, especially those with a Middle Eastern flavor. Groceries like Sahadi and El Asmar and restaurants like Moustache (Middle Eastern pizzas a specialty) are redolent of lamb, cumin, cardamom, hummus, and tabbouleh.

A few blocks to the east is the Fulton Street Mall, adequate for some serious shopping but lacking what Boerum Hill sorely needed—a supermarket. But when the 400,000-square-foot, $85-million Atlantic Center opened in fall 1996, it brought a 24-hour Pathmark, along with such stores as Caldor's. The center, next to the Long Island Rail Road terminal at Atlantic and Flatbush Avenues, is planning an expansion that would bring in a Sears store, among others.

"It's transformed the way we live," Mr. Armstrong said, "to have national chains on the edge of our neighborhood."

Next door to the Atlantic Center is Metrotech, a high-tech office/academic complex that opened its first building in September 1990. Both Metrotech and Atlantic Center are key elements of the revitalization of downtown Brooklyn.

BROOKLYN HEIGHTS

Serenity and stunning vistas

BY JOHN RATHER

Brooklyn Heights is in some ways like a historic theater with no cheap seats and a center aisle, busy Montague Street, leading to a blockbuster scene like no other. Rising from the opposite shore of the same bend in the East River that George Washington's retreating army stole across to safety after losing the Battle of Long Island in 1776 is Wall Street and the thickly gathered, soaring commercial towers of lower Manhattan.

From the Brooklyn Heights Esplanade, a strollers' perch above the Brooklyn-Queens Expressway, the nonpareil riverfront view also takes in the Battery, Governors Island, and the Statue of Liberty to the south, and the Brooklyn and Manhattan Bridges, the Chrysler and the Empire State Buildings, and midtown Manhattan to the north.

The protecting river and the vicissitudes of Brooklyn's southward-tending urban development played a trick here, keeping immensity at bay and sparing the ever-appreciating architectural virtues of mid-19th-century Brooklyn Heights. While skyscrapers rose across the water, the Heights stayed low, with some hotel exceptions, and maintained an air of peace and tranquillity from one epoch to the next.

In a small park by the esplanade, also called the promenade, sounds of children playing ring out. On interior streets of brownstone and brick attached housing, low-rise, leafy serenity reigns.

People complain of rush-hour overflow traffic, and late-night trucks rumble through certain unfortunate streets, but the community, built on a bluff by the river, is essentially a cul-de-sac. And when, in 1965, Brooklyn Heights won designation as the city's first historic district, protection was assured for brick and brownstone row houses on streets sometimes little altered since the Civil War.

With steam-propelled ferries easing passage to Manhattan, Brooklyn

POPULATION: 19,120.

AREA: 0.5 square mile.

MEDIAN HOUSEHOLD INCOME: $62,970.

MEDIAN PRICE OF SINGLE-FAMILY HOUSE: $1.25 million.

MEDIAN PRICE OF A TWO-BEDROOM CO-OP: $325,000.

DISTANCE FROM MIDTOWN MANHATTAN: 3 miles.

RUSH-HOUR TRAVEL TO MIDTOWN: 20 minutes on the A, C, F, M, N, R, 2, 3, 4, or 5 subway line.

CODES: Area, 718; ZIP, 11201.

Heights became a redoubt for the working rich even before the mid–19th century. Moderate decline set in when the Brooklyn Bridge, in 1883, the IRT subway, in 1908, and the Manhattan Bridge, in 1909, brought Manhattan too close and sent patricians packing.

Hotels and rooming houses began a transformation that was halted in the '50s and '60s, when young families moved in to restore architecturally diverse but fading brownstone and brick row houses. By the '80s, hotels and apartment buildings were swept by co-op conversions.

Among the hotels that converted was the St. George, which is now two co-ops—the 292-unit St. George Tower & Grill and the 71-unit 60 Pineapple Street. There are also 433 rooms for students and 30 rooms for others.

"The hotels were deteriorating and the co-op conversions had a fairly dramatic effect in stabilizing them," said Kevin J. Carberry, a real estate broker and lifelong resident of Brooklyn Heights. Today, buyers who cannot afford row houses often turn to co-ops instead. Even at $1 million, attached houses are hard to find. A five-story brick fixer-upper, in need of extensive renovation, is on the market for $1.2 million.

But co-ops, too, can be costly. Prices have been rising swiftly, and in 1997 there was a record $1.6 million sale, Mr. Carberry said. Two-bedroom rentals for $2,000 can be found and there are a small number of condominiums. River views, naturally, always cost more.

In a housing market that mirrors the long bull market on Wall Street, well-heeled buyers are increasingly cobbling together adjoining co-ops and reconverting two- and three-family brownstones to their original one-family use, shrinking what is, to begin with, a limited housing stock.

"There is a lot of money chasing too little product," said Christopher Thomas, vice president and director of sales for the Brooklyn offices of William B. May Company. The inevitable result, he said, was higher prices.

The Metrotech Complex and other projects in downtown Brooklyn have brought rapid change during the '90s to Brooklyn Heights's doorstep, but no farther.

"It can't change much here because of the historic-landmarking and zoning restrictions," said Judy Stanton, executive director of the Brooklyn

Heights Association. "New construction is highly unlikely. Restoration, of course, goes on all the time."

Montague Street, the commercial core, is lined with shops, chain stores, and restaurants and clogged with midday traffic exacerbated by double-parking.

The idle East River piers jutting out below the esplanade raise some trepidation. The Brooklyn Bridge Park Coalition, of which the Brooklyn Heights Association is a leading member, has formally proposed a riverfront park. The future of the piers will be determined by the governor and the mayor. Most of the land is owned by the Port Authority of New York and New Jersey.

Brooklyn Heights is split between Community School Districts 13 and 15.

P.S. 8, in Brooklyn Heights, is dedicated to fusing the arts into the curriculum, said Irene Gluck, the principal. Music, fine arts, dance, and song flute instruction is available. There are 400 students enrolled in kindergarten through grade 6. Students have scored above average in reading and in the top quarter in math on standardized tests in recent years, Mrs. Gluck said.

P.S. 29, in neighboring Cobble Hill, counts some Brooklyn Heights children among its 750 students in prekindergarten through grade 6. Students routinely score very high on standardized tests.

But many young families move to Brooklyn Heights for its private schools.

At St. Ann's School on Pierrepont Street, 1,045 students attend preschool through grade 12. Tuition ranges from $13,600 for kindergarten through grade 3 to $15,900 in grade 12, and admission is competitive. Virtually all graduates go on to higher education. Five members of the Class of '98 were named National Merit Scholarship Program finalists. In lower grades, a middle school math team recently finished third out of 60 teams in a state competition. The five-building campus includes a computer center.

St. Ann's preschool has full-day programs for 4-year-olds and half-day programs for 2- and 3-year-olds. Music, art, and dance movement are offered to 72 students currently enrolled. Tuition is $10,900 for 4-year-olds, $7,300 for 3-year-olds, attending five days a week.

The Packer Collegiate Institute on Joralemon Street, founded in 1845 and now the oldest independent school in Brooklyn, has 800 students in prekindergarten through grade 12. Advanced placement courses in many subjects are given in the Upper School, for grades 9 through 12. Community service is required for graduation. Tuition ranges from $6,500 for 3-year-olds attending mornings to $14,400 in grade 12. Admission is competitive.

The four-building campus includes two libraries, two computer labs with more than 200 computers, seven science labs, and one language lab. Forty-nine percent of 1997 graduates were accepted at colleges and universities rated most competitive.

The 210-student St. Charles Borromeo, a Roman Catholic school covering prekindergarten through grade 8, is soon to celebrate its 150th anniversary. Spanish and computer science are taught in all grades. Annual tuition is $2,550.

Arts at St. Ann's, a performing arts group, offers musical and puppet theater and operates a stained-glass studio at St. Ann's Church on Montague Street, a Gothic-style Episcopal church listed as a national landmark. The church has the country's first complete ensemble of stained-glass windows.

Another performing arts group, the Heights Players, stages plays and musicals. There are also a number of small arts groups and a music society. The Brooklyn Historical Society, currently under renovation, is on nearby Pierrepont Street.

Other famous churches include the Church of the Pilgrims at Remsen and Henry Streets, where Henry Ward Beecher fulminated against slavery; and the Gothic Revival Grace Church at Grace Court and Hicks Street.

The Canarsie Indians called Brooklyn Heights Ihpetonga, meaning high sandy bank, before the Dutch arrived in the mid–17th century. During the Battle of Long Island in August 1776, Washington gathered his routed troops for a fog-shrouded soundless retreat across the river to Manhattan. The British, advancing next morning, found an empty campsite.

Quiet, a key to the American escape, remains a leading attribute of Brooklyn Heights.

BROOKLYN

CARROLL GARDENS

A neighborly neighborhood

BY JANICE FIORAVANTE

Often a neighborhood includes a place central to its life; for Carroll Gardens, such a place is Carroll Park. Since its creation in the 19th century, the park has unified the Brooklyn community's residents. In November 1994, a rededication ceremony celebrated the park's renovation, which included renewing play areas, adding benches and trees, and restoring the Carroll Park Monument honoring neighborhood residents killed in World War I. The efforts that led to the renovation crystallized in 1990, when Glenn Kelly, who has lived in Carroll Gardens since 1977, helped form the Committee to Improve Carroll Park. "I wanted to get it back to the way I remember neighborhood parks," Mr. Kelly said, "so that when someone's home on a Friday night, they can say, 'Let's go see what's happening at the park.' "

The efforts to restore the park typify the activities of residents who care, are neighborly, and join groups to keep the neighborhood viable. Among the neighborhood's efforts on behalf of the park have been Halloween parties, wine tastings, and dinner parties to raise money for park upkeep.

In the late 1840s, Carroll Park was a private garden. The land for a park was secured through an act of the New York State Legislature in 1850, but the creation of a park was not approved until 1870. The park spurred development of the surrounding area, which became highly prized for its residences. Earlier, the opening of the Hamilton Avenue Ferry to and from Manhattan in 1846 and the draining of the swampland near the Gowanus Canal in the 1860s also stimulated land speculation.

Until the 1960s, the neighborhood was considered part of Brooklyn's Red Hook section. Then, partly in response to the flight of many people to the suburbs, neighborhood residents formed an organization to improve the area; they called it the Carroll Gardens Association. When, also in the

GAZETTEER

POPULATION: 13,609.

AREA: 0.33 square miles.

MEDIAN HOUSEHOLD INCOME: $51,548.

MEDIAN PRICE OF A TOWN HOUSE: $500,000.

TAXES ON MEDIAN-PRICED HOUSE: $2,900.

DISTANCE FROM MIDTOWN MANHATTAN: 5 miles.

RUSH-HOUR TRAVEL TO MIDTOWN: 20 minutes on the F or G subway line.

CODES: Area, 718; ZIP, 11231.

'60s, the neighborhood was cut off from Red Hook by the Brooklyn-Queens Expressway, it took its new name from the association.

"Charles Carroll was one of the original signers of the Declaration of Independence," said Salvatore J. Scotto, president of Scotto Funeral Home and founder of the association. Carroll, who never lived in the area, led a Maryland regiment that defended the Old Stone House at Gowanus, a local landmark, against the British in the Revolutionary War. Carroll's name was appropriated for both the park and Carroll Street, which crosses the neighborhood.

And Gardens? "Most houses here have front and rear gardens," said Mr. Scotto, a community leader who many residents consider the neighborhood's unofficial mayor. The association counts among its accomplishments a successful campaign for the building of a $458 million sewage-treatment plant that has cleaned up the Gowanus Canal, and the construction of housing for senior citizens on Carroll Street. It has also fostered a sense of local pride by giving the neighborhood an identity.

Carroll Gardens has long had a strong Italian-American flavor, and that flavor is still very much in evidence. Court Street, the area's commercial district, "has more Italian restaurants and pizza stores per square inch than almost any other New York neighborhood," said Salvatore Capozucca, a resident since birth who as a real estate broker goes by the name Sal Cappi. "Within two blocks, there's Helen's, Red Rose, Marco Polo, and Casa Rosa."

This influenced Craig and Mylene Pollock to buy their home at 47 Third Street in 1997. "We'd been renting an apartment in the neighborhood for four years," Mr. Pollock said. "We love the people here, who are nice, warm, and friendly, the Italian markets and Italian butchers." Among their favorite haunts are Caputo's on Court Street, for homemade sauces and pastas, and Leonardo's Pizza at Court Street and First Place.

Mr. Pollock said he was also pleased with the area's convenience to Manhattan. "We both work in advertising," he said. "I'm an associate creative director in the Flatiron District and Mylene works in midtown, both just a few subway stops on the F line."

The Pollocks have a 4-year-old son, Grant, and in March 1998 a new baby boy, Trey, was born. Their home is a three-story one-family house with three bedrooms, hardwood floors, a basement, and a backyard, for which they paid $275,000.

The Pollocks, like others in this community of 13,609 people, are savoring the additions to Smith Street, where Refinery, a handmade handbag and furniture shop; Montgomery Antiques; Patois, a French bistro; and Rosina's Bistro, serving pan-Mediterranean cuisine, are new attractions in a four-block stretch from President to Douglass Street.

Christopher Thomas, a broker at William B. May Company, a real estate brokerage, described the town houses in Carroll Gardens as more diminutive than those in the nearby brownstone neighborhoods of Cobble Hill and Brooklyn Heights. There are more 20-foot-, 18-foot-, and 15-foot-wide three- and four-story houses in Carroll Gardens, as opposed to the more prevalent 20-foot- to 25-foot-wide homes in Cobble Hill.

For this reason, houses often cost less than in those neighborhoods, Mr. Thomas said. But he added that because the neighborhood is considered very safe, rents of comparable apartments are higher than those in some of the surrounding areas. Mr. Thomas said a one-bedroom rental would start at $975 and run to $1,100, while a two-bedroom ranges between $1,300 and $1,500.

One-family homes can be purchased for $325,000 to $750,000, while two-family houses cost from $350,000 to $850,000, said Jean Austin of Brooklyn Bridge Realty. "A three-family house starts at around $300,000 and goes to about $700,000," she said.

Price increases averaged 4 percent to 5 percent in the early '90s, then rose sharply beginning in mid-1996. The median sale price in 1997 was $400,000; in the first quarter of 1998, it was $500,000. Annual taxes on the median house would be $2,900.

Mr. Thomas said that "a high price for a corner house on Union and Clinton Streets was $775,000 in 1995 and in 1998 it would be worth $850,000, while a house close to the Gowanus Canal at Hoyt and Bond Streets, which sold for $200,000 in 1995, would be $250,000 in 1998." The former is at the boundary of Carroll Gardens and Cobble Hill, while proximity to the Gowanus Canal, which functions as a catch basin for sewage when rainstorms overwhelm the capacity of treatment plants and counts "Perfume Creek" among its nicknames, is still not a selling point.

But a tunnel to circulate the water is scheduled to begin operation in 1998, for the first time since the 1960s. "The tunnel will bring fish traffic into and out of the canal again," said Mr. Scotto of the Carroll Gardens Association.

As the canal gets a new life, so do surrounding buildings. While co-ops and condominiums "didn't extend here like the numbers of these units in Brooklyn Heights," Mr. Thomas said, "there are several interesting examples." A former seamen's church, now the Old Westminster Church

Apartments at 450 Clinton Street, has been renovated and turned into a co-op. Co-op prices in the neighborhood range from a half-floor one-bedroom for $135,000 to a larger three-bedroom on President Street for $300,000 to $335,000.

Angela Vita, owner of Vita Realty, said a former jute factory on President Street between Hoyt and Bond Streets had become a condominium called the Mill, with 57 units. "It has two-bedroom units whose median price would be $250,000," she said.

Part of the neighborhood was designated the Carroll Gardens Historic District by the New York City Landmarks Preservation Commission in 1973. The district, which contains more than 160 buildings, includes houses on President and Carroll Streets between Smith and Hoyt Streets as well as adjacent parts of the four streets and a bit of First Street east of Hoyt. All the district's brownstone row houses were erected between 1869 and 1884. In making the designation, the commission cited "the impression of space," the result of "the surveyor Richard Butts's plan devised in 1846, which created building lots with unusually deep front yards."

P.S. 58, at 330 Smith Street, has an all-strings music program for grades 2 through 6, to which it has added a percussion program via an affiliation with the Brooklyn College Conservatory of Music. The school, with 727 students, placed 201st in reading scores among 1,084 New York City public schools in 1998. P.S. 29, at 425 Henry Street, offers its 756 pre-K–grade 6 students special classes for gifted pupils as well as a special education program.

Middle School 293, at 284 Baltic Street, enrolls 630 students and shares its building with the School for Global Studies, which serves grades 6 through 12. With 525 students enrolled, the School of Global Studies expects 90 percent of its 25 graduates to go on to college. "We keep classes under 25 students," said its principal, Larry Abrams. "Our theme is the study of understanding ourselves and the world and how to change our perspectives."

Also in the area is Sacred Heart/St. Stephen's Catholic School. Its principal, Allan Degnan, said that until 10 or 11 years ago, enrollment was 95 percent Italian-American, but that now "we're much more multicultural, with blacks and Latinos as well as Asians." The school serves prekindergarten through eighth grade, enrolling about 145 students.

Children can also attend one of two private prekindergarten-through-12th-grade schools nearby. Tuition at Packer Collegiate Institute, a prep school, is $6,500 to $14,400, depending on grade. At St. Ann's School, a private school for gifted students, tuition ranges from $13,600 for kindergarten to third grade to $15,900 for grade 12. Preschool tuition also ranges from $3,900 for two half days to $10,900 for five full days a week. Typically, 100 percent of graduates go on to college.

COBBLE HILL

New settlers alter an old ethnic mix

BY JANICE FIORAVANTE

When Joanne Nicholas and her husband, Peter, moved to the Cobble Hill section of Brooklyn in 1976, she thought of the neighborhood as a mixture of "new people" and "old people." The new people were artists, professors, and "people willing to homestead." The old people were the Italians and Middle Easterners who had been there for generations.

Ms. Nicholas worked in the community for 12 years, in communications for Long Island College Hospital, which opened in 1858 as one of the nation's first hospital-based medical schools. She also wrote a column, "Cobble Hill News and Views," which ran in *The Brooklyn Heights Press* for more than 11 years. Today she is in communications at Memorial Sloan-Kettering Cancer Center.

And what does she think of Cobble Hill today?

"It's quieter now," she said. "It was livelier and noisier when I came." It's very likely, Ms. Nicholas said, that homes that once housed four or five families with many children now are home to a husband and wife who work and have one or two children, as she does. Where once there were tables and chairs with domino players in the schoolyard, she said, today you're more likely to see tennis and lacrosse.

But the neighborhood, most of which is part of a New York City historic district designated in 1969 and slightly extended in 1988, hasn't changed in its basics, residents say. There is still a strong sense of community. Gary Aagaard, a 48-year-old illustrator originally from Seattle, moved from Park Slope, where he lived for seven years, to a rented four-room floor-through apartment at 159 Warren Street. He shares it with Nancy Stangeland, who works for the New York City comptroller. "Here people have lived for generations," he said. "If you were in trouble here, people would actually help." He described Cobble Hill Park, at Clinton and

POPULATION: 20,457.

AREA: 1 square mile.

MEDIAN HOUSEHOLD INCOME: $60,290.

MEDIAN PRICE OF A SINGLE-FAMILY HOUSE: $725,000.

TAXES ON A MEDIAN-PRICED HOUSE: $2,500.

MIDRANGE RENT FOR A TWO-BEDROOM APARTMENT: $2,000.

DISTANCE FROM MIDTOWN MANHATTAN: 5 miles.

RUSH-HOUR TRAVEL TO MIDTOWN: 30 minutes on the N, R, F, 4, or 5 subway line.

CODES: Area, 718; ZIP, 11201 and 11231.

Congress Streets, as a testament to the community's spirit. "People take care of it, plant flowers, clip trees," he said.

The park won a Municipal Art Society Award for a renovation effort early in this decade. It is paved in bluestone, and through the Friends of Cobble Hill Park, more than 300 trees have been planted in the area, said Jerry Armer, first vice president of the Cobble Hill Association.

Prices of houses vary sharply block by block, said Carl Peek, a broker at Brooklyn Landmark Realty. He said that some houses have been restored with historic authenticity and can sell for as much as $1.5 million. But the average price for a brownstone or an attached redbrick town house, most of them more than a century old, is about $750,000. The houses generally have one to four apartments, often with an owner's duplex or triplex and one or more rentals.

There are few apartment houses in the area. One 1950s high-rise is a co-op where units sell for $100,00 to $160,000, said Andy Friedman, another Cobble Hill broker at that same agency. There are only a handful of condominium units. A typical two-bedroom sells for about $215,000.

Rents in general run from $900 a month for a studio to $1,800–$2,200 for a two-bedroom. "A duplex can run as high as $3,000 a month," Mr. Friedman said.

The median sale price in 1996 was $685,000, Mr. Friedman noted; in the third quarter of 1997, it was $725,000. "And annual taxes on that house would be $2,500."

His colleague Mr. Peek is also a past president of the Court Street Merchants Associates, which has parking on its agenda. "We're always worried about parking," he said. A question mark is the reconstruction of the Gowanus Expressway and its effect on business. "The Department of Transportation has approved this 12-year project—that's all we know," he said. "We expect chaos."

If parking is high on the list of problems, crime is not. "Cobble Hill has one of the lowest crime rates," said Capt. Roger Peterson, commanding officer at the 76th Precinct. "It ranks third or fourth lowest in the city." Car thefts and house break-ins, while still the main crime concerns of residents, he said, have followed the recent pattern of the rest of the city in fewer incidences.

Settlement of the area began in the mid-1660s when the Dutch governor, Willem Kieft, granted permits for farms north of Red Hook. "Cobleshill" first comes up in a 1767 survey of Brooklyn and refers to a steep hill in the area where Atlantic Avenue and Pacific Avenue meet. On this hill, the site of Cobble Hill Fort, the Revolutionary Army met defeat in the Battle of Long Island.

Residential development mushroomed in the 1830s as groups of English, Irish, Italians, and Greeks set down roots. One reason was that ferry service to Manhattan began in 1836 from the foot of Atlantic Avenue. Small estates and farms began at the time to be divided into lots for row houses. As the century progressed, row house construction moved northward from Atlantic Avenue.

In the 1930s, Thomas Wolfe lived on Verandah Place. Jenny Jerome, the mother of Winston Churchill, was born on Amity Street in 1854. And Louis Comfort Tiffany in 1917 designed the windows, high altar, and other appointments of the Episcopal Christ Church and Holy Family at 326 Clinton Street, a Greek Revival structure built in 1842.

In addition to the landmark architecture, Cobble Hill's schools continue to be an attraction for new residents. Margaret Kelley, former president of the Parents Association of Public School 29, has a son, Daniel, 12, in eighth grade and son Timothy, 8, in third grade. Mrs. Kelley is now vice president of Community School Board 15. P.S. 29 offers classes from pre-K through grade 6. "The parents are very active in the school," she said. "Parents pay for whatever needs funds, whether it be art, music, or physical education programs. Many parents volunteer in classrooms and help with reading."

P.S. 29 has gifted and special education programs and offers its 700 students computer lab periods. "Students also take geography, physical education, advanced math, and art classes once a week," Mrs. Kelley said. Among extracurricular activities are field day and an art show. All children win ribbons on field day and have artwork in the show.

Mrs. Kelley's example of Cobble Hill's community feeling is the lollipops and other small gifts Timmy gets from shopkeepers at Halloween and when he graduates from each grade. "All the kids know the shopkeepers and the people in the homes on their route to school," she said.

Other schools in the area include St. Ann's School on Pierrepont Street, with 1,045 students and a tuition range for grades K–12 from $13,600 to $15,900 a year. The Packer Collegiate Institute on Joralemon Street enrolls 800 students, with a tuition range from $6,500 for a half-day preschool to $14,400 for grade 12. The Brooklyn Friends School on Pearl Street has an enrollment of 520 students, with tuition from $5,000 to $15,000.

Among merchants are a handful each of butchers, greengrocers, and bakeries. Mr. Peek mentioned Mazzola's Bakery on Court Street and the many coffee bars in Cobble Hill and neighboring areas. Arabic restaurants and specialty food shops dot Atlantic Avenue in a section known as Little Arabia, offering Middle Eastern delicacies, particularly from Egypt, Yemen, and Morocco. Atlantic Avenue is also well known for its antiques stores. Restaurants in the area also offer Italian, Continental, French, and American cuisine.

David Berger, who moved to Cobble Hill in 1994, described Cobble Hill as an oasis not too far from Manhattan. He and his wife, Tracey Altman— both are lawyers and native Manhattanites—lived in Brooklyn Heights for a year and a half. "I loved Brooklyn Heights, but I love Cobble Hill even more because it's really a neighborhood," he said. "You know your neighbors and they really do talk to you." He said he liked the local merchants, citing Jim & Andy's on Court Street, a greengrocer, and the "wonderful places to buy food on Atlantic Avenue."

Mr. Berger and Ms. Altman bought an 1842 Federal-style house. "We took the easy way out," he said, because the four-story house on Clinton Street between Baltic and Kane Streets had been renovated. Their apartment has five bedrooms, some of which Ms. Altman uses as an art/photography studio and one of which is for their daughter, Tashi, who is 2 years old.

Accessibility is another word that residents use in talking about Cobble Hill. "Four train lines are within walking distance," said Mr. Amer of the Cobble Hill Association. Rush-hour commuting to midtown averages 30 minutes.

The Cobble Hill Cinema on Court Street has five screens. Newsstands run by Middle Eastern immigrants also add to the neighborhood's character.

Craig Hammerman, manager of Community Board 6, said that the area has waged a successful battle to preserve the neighborhood's bluestone sidewalks. "They were being ripped out when tree roots upended them," he said. "People tended to replace them with concrete. The Department of Transportation has put a moratorium on replacement with other than bluestone. And today we are looking at replacing streetlights with historic replicas like those on Atlantic Avenue, working with the Cobble Hill Neighborhood Association."

GREENPOINT

Ethnic and artistic in North Brooklyn

BY JOHN RATHER

Rimmed by an industrial area that long ago wiped the green off this Brooklyn peninsula to make way for cauldrons of commerce, residential Greenpoint was built in another age to house the workers who stoked its fires. Now many of the factories along the waterfront are abandoned or gone, but the sturdy railroad flats of the workers and the more substantial brownstones of their bosses and the local gentry remain. Greenpoint, population about 46,000, churns on as a distinctly Polish enclave peppered with Hispanic, Italian, and Irish influences and enlivened by a growing artistic community gathered on its loosely defined southern border with Williamsburg.

The Polish community has been a distinctive part of Greenpoint for generations. For immigrant Poles of recent years, Greenpoint has been a magnet because of its low-to-moderate rents, good prospects for ownership, and a milieu where Polish culture sometimes presides and English is a second language. Figures of the New York City Planning Department show Greenpoint was the destination for 27 percent of the 7,267 Polish immigrants arriving in the city between 1983 and 1989. Signs in Polish on shops and restaurants everywhere look strange to English-only eyes but seem synergistic with the gibberish tags of graffiti artists, who have been hard at work here.

In sturdy Greenpoint, graffiti and the yawning, trash-strewn decrepitude along parts of the East River and Newtown Creek waterfronts are more ignored than worried over. Both are poor indexes of a quality of life on interior streets that is orderly, intimate, thrift-minded, safe, and Old World.

For the legitimate artists and craftspeople of Bedford Avenue, Berry Street, and elsewhere within a gray area some call Greenpoint and others

POPULATION: 45,689.

AREA: 2.7 square miles.

MEDIAN HOUSEHOLD INCOME: $39,605.

MEDIAN PRICE OF A SINGLE-FAMILY HOUSE: $150,000.

TAXES ON A MEDIAN-PRICED HOUSE: $900.

DISTANCE FROM MIDTOWN MANHATTAN: 2 miles.

RUSH-HOUR TRAVEL TO MIDTOWN: 15 minutes on the G train, 10 minutes on the L train, both with transfers to the E or F train.

CODES: Area, 718; ZIP, 11222.

call Williamsburg, the attraction is escape from the high rents and congestion across the East River. The L line subway, which lends its name to the L Cafe, one of the bistros that enrich the youthful ambience of the area, keeps Manhattan close, only a 10- or 15-minute ride away. When it can be glimpsed, the view across the river is spectacular.

"Everyone here is an artist or a writer or a cabinetmaker," said Michele Bertomen, an architect at the Brooklyn Architects Collective off Bedford Avenue. "We're the new SoHo. SoHo got too commercial." The collective was founded in 1994 by a group of young architects involved in real and theoretical projects, including alternative transportation plans for the metropolitan area. By 1998, the artistic migration from Manhattan was continuing apace, Ms. Bertomen said, and rents were beginning to climb. Apartments that rented for $700 in 1995 were up to $800 or $900 as 1998 began.

Owner-occupied, one-family houses are the exception in a housing market dominated by renters. In low-rise, residential Greenpoint, the owner of a multifamily building is often in residence and not infrequently a prior tenant. Garages are rare. Outdoor plots are small when they exist at all in this unapologetically urban place of attached housing. Many buildings are wood-frame structures built before or near the turn of the century, covered now in a crazy-quilt of siding. "The trend here is that people have an apartment first, they work very hard, and within a pretty short amount of time they save enough money to purchase a home," said Yolanda J. Zawisny, manager of Century 21 Polonia on Driggs Avenue.

The median price for a one-family house was $150,000 in early 1998, up from $135,000 three years earlier. The median price for a two-family house was about $195,000, or $15,000 more than in 1994. Median taxes were $900.

Once in, many stay put. Bozena Pietrucha, the owner of the Bo Realty Company on Nassau Avenue, said stability was a sign of Greenpoint's appeal. "Nobody wants to leave Greenpoint," she said, and only a slim inventory of houses had been on the market in recent years.

Realtors say rents that had been about $500 for one-bedroom and $600 for two-bedroom apartments in 1995 were each up by at least $100 by early 1998. Rents are $900 or higher on more desirable streets like those off busy Manhattan Avenue, the main shopping thoroughfare, where the spire of the St. Anthony and St. Alphonsus Roman Catholic Church rises high over stores with apartments above.

It is a wonder of Greenpoint that a prime block like Kent Street between Manhattan and Franklin Avenues, ensconced in a historic district where three- and four-story brownstones are tastefully decorated with flowers and immaculately kept, is not far from a dreary industrial area too desolate at night even for prostitutes. And while birdsongs fill the air on quiet, tree-lined and sun-dappled interior streets, turgid Newtown Creek flows by on Greenpoint's northern and eastern border like a dead river. Its jet-black waters, the color of overused motor oil, are brightened only by the rainbow sheen of gasoline floating on the surface.

Greenpoint, part of an area of Brooklyn purchased by the Dutch West India Company in 1638, was named by sailors for its verdant look as viewed from the deck of passing vessels. Dirck Volckertsen, a ship's-carpenter-turned-farmer who was known as "Dirck the Norman" despite being Scandinavian, built the first house in 1645 near Calyer Street. But it is Norman Street that bears witness to him. Following a long idyll as farmland in a remote corner of the old Town of Bushwick, Greenpoint exploded as a major shipbuilding center in the 1840s. The Union ironclad *Monitor* was built here during the Civil War.

James A. Kenny, a former Greenpoint realtor who recently retired to Florida, said his great-grandfather Daniel Kenny helped build the vessel, the most famous ever to emerge from Greenpoint's docks. Mr. Kenny used to offer a box of cigars to anyone who could name Greenpoint's most famous son or daughter. (His answer is Charles Evans Hughes, chief justice of the United States Supreme Court from 1930 to 1941. Others say Mae West.)

By the 1870s, shipbuilding had nearly vanished, but by then printing, porcelain making, glassworking, iron casting, and petroleum refining had taken root and Greenpoint was alive with factories, foundries, and refineries. In 1867, Charles Pratt, founder of Pratt Institute, began refining Astral Oil, a brand name for "the safest and best" of kerosene for the home market. The Pratt refinery became a part of Standard Oil. In 1911, when the Standard Oil trust was broken, it reemerged as part of Standard Oil of New York, later to become Mobil Oil. Petroleum storage tanks along Kingsland Avenue are all that remain of the former refineries.

The imposing, arch-entranced Astral Apartments, erected by Pratt in 1886 on Franklin Street for his employees and their families, is now a rental residence. "Waste neither time nor money," advises an inscription over a fireplace in the boiler room, what once was the building's reading room.

The fossil fuel tradition is carried on by the Brooklyn Union Gas Company, whose twin tanks—with capacities of 17 million and 15 million cubic feet, respectively—add a note of giantism to a company softball diamond they loom above. Warehouses, importers, recycling companies, and small manufacturers inhabit the industrial area, which still bustles. A mammoth city sewage plant is situated at the foot of Humboldt Street on Greenpoint Avenue.

In the Northside area of Greenpoint, McCarren Park offers soccer and baseball fields and a track. Msgr. McGolrick Park, also in Northside, is loaded with swings, slides, and young mothers wheeling baby carriages.

The St. Stanislaus Kostka Church on Driggs Avenue is the spiritual heart of Greenpoint's Polish community and draws parishioners from surrounding areas. A plaque commemorates a 1969 visit by Pope John Paul II, then the Cardinal Archbishop of Kraków.

Greenpoint is in School District 14, where scores in math and English tests rank below the 50th percentile for city schools. Many Greenpoint students attend the 3,000-student Grover Cleveland High School in neighboring Ridgewood, Queens, where instruction in Polish, Spanish, Italian, Chinese, and French is offered. More than 80 percent of graduates go on to two- or four-year colleges. Eastern District High School in Greenpoint, which had one of the city's lowest rankings in math and English tests, closed at the end of the 1998 school year, replaced by four new high schools offering specialization in such areas as business, technology, and the law in the same buildings. Harry Van Ardsdale High School, also in Greenpoint, specializes in building trades and business education and draws students from throughout the city.

Albert Juszczak, the former executive director of the Polish and Slavic Center at 177 Kent Street, said a credit union the center established in 1977 helped Greenpoint through a delicate moment by making mortgage loans to borrowers with little or no credit history. "The banks were not giving mortgages in Greenpoint," Mr. Juszczak said. "A Polish person who wanted a mortgage to buy a home virtually couldn't get it." The center's faith was rewarded. "It's rare that there's a bank foreclosure in Greenpoint," said Bill Kirrane of Bill Kirrane Real Estate on Nassau Avenue. "I don't even have handyman's specials anymore. These buildings are going to be here for at least another 100 years."

PARK SLOPE

Where the past is an abiding presence

BY JOHN RATHER

For children raised in Park Slope, a premier Brooklyn neighborhood richly laden with advantages, impoverished beginnings can never be an excuse for later failures. There is wealth here—visible in blocks of polished brownstones and attested to by recent sales prices. But it is the breadth of its cultural offerings in a 19th-century architectural setting that frames the life of the community. With its exquisite churches, its stellar brownstone row houses, its thriving Seventh Avenue shops and restaurants, and the eclectic spirit of both its people and its neo-Renaissance and neo-Classical architectural styles, Park Slope has succeeded as much as any community in New York City in drawing in newcomers as renters and home buyers.

Its proximity to Prospect Park, the Brooklyn Public Library, the Brooklyn Museum, and the Brooklyn Botanic Garden adds to its desirability; subway links to Manhattan are numerous, and Seventh Avenue, the neighborhood's commercial hub, reflects its variety with cafes, coffee houses, and restaurants of many nationalities—Italian, Vietnamese, Chinese, Thai, and Japanese.

Residents invariably speak of the small-town feeling and social cohesion of Park Slope, a tree-lined, nearly all-residential area especially attractive to families. It is a place, they say, where activities for children are unending, shopkeepers know their customers, and people stop in the street to chat. "It takes me from 20 minutes to an hour to walk to work, depending on how many people I meet," said Lyn Hill, a vice president at New York Methodist Hospital, a 600-bed hospital with 2,700 employees.

The population mix is all-encompassing—whites, blacks, Hispanics, and Asians, and a sizable lesbian and gay community as well. At St. Augustine Roman Catholic Church, one of several architecturally soaring

POPULATION: 58,500.

AREA: 0.9 square miles.

MEDIAN HOUSEHOLD INCOME: $54,300.

MEDIAN PRICE OF A BROWNSTONE: $615,000.

MEDIAN PRICE OF A TWO-BEDROOM CO-OP: $225,000.

DISTANCE FROM MIDTOWN MANHATTAN: 6 miles.

RUSH-HOUR TRAVEL TO MIDTOWN: 30 minutes on the 2, 3, D, F, N, Q, or R subway line.

CODES: Area, 718; ZIP, 11215 and 11217.

Catholic and Protestant churches in Park Slope, Masses are said in English, Spanish, and Haitian Creole. Temple Beth Elohim, a monumental neo-Classic temple completed in 1909–10 with a Reform congregation, attests to the long and continuing Jewish presence here in the neighborhood.

In few other parts of Brooklyn does the past so enrich the present. The 526-acre Prospect Park, on the neighborhood's eastern edge, is thronged on weekends by parents and children.

The 19th-century dwellings of the rich and near-rich, ranging from grand to substantial, make for prime housing stock. Apartment houses are also plentiful, as are co-ops, many of them in brownstones. The grandeur of Park Slope is along Prospect Park West, built a century ago to rival Fifth Avenue. On St. Johns Place between Sixth and Seventh Avenues, uninterrupted rows of three-story brownstones look out from both sides of the street through large bay windows.

Brownstones bought in the early '60s for less than $25,000 by brownstone pioneers, many of them teachers lured from Manhattan's Upper West Side or Greenwich Village, now cost from $500,000 to more than $1 million. "We used to call it the schoolteacher's coup," said Everett Ortner, a retired editor of *Popular Science* magazine. "They were living in millionaires' houses on a schoolteacher's salary." Mr. Ortner and his wife, Evelyn, bought their brownstone in 1963 and were early leaders of the brownstone revival movement.

John Ottavino, an actor, and his wife, Eve, an elementary school teacher, recently paid $500,000 for a three-story brownstone on 11th Street. They rent out the ground floor. "Everyone asks, 'Did you get a good price?' and I don't think there is such a thing as that anymore," said Mr. Ottavino, a former renter. "I paid what I had to pay."

Rentals in Park Slope don't stay on the market long, and prices are going up. "You have to be prepared to act fast," said William B. Rue, a sales agent at Marilyn A. Donahue Real Estate. "Bring your checkbook. Be ready to pull the trigger."

Co-ops also move briskly. Joan B. Martin, a private school administrator, and her husband, David Oppenheim, a public high school teacher, bought a two-bedroom co-op on Eighth Street off Seventh Avenue for

$169,000 in 1997 after renting in Park Slope for 15 years. The co-op had been on the market 10 days. Less than a year later, a similar co-op in the same building sold in a day.

There are a few condominiums. A recent upper-floor renovation at the palatial Montauk Club near Grand Army Plaza created four units. Matthew Miller, the owner-broker of Heights Berkeley Realty, said he recently sold one of them, a three-bedroom unit, for $467,000. The club, whose exterior blends Venetian Gothic style and American Indian motifs, is in the Historic District, which runs along the west side of Prospect Park and is generally the most expensive area of Park Slope.

Lower housing prices are farther from the park and to the south, in South Slope, where Patricia A. Neinast, the manager of Brooklyn Landmark's Park Slope office, said houses in the $200,000's can still be found.

Park Slope, part of District 15, has six elementary schools. One that is highly regarded locally, Public School 321, with about 1,300 pupils in prekindergarten through grade 5, tallies scores well above city averages in math and reading standardized tests. The school has one computer lab and 20 classrooms with computers. It offers inclusion classes for general and special education students.

P.S. 39, with about 475 students in kindergarten through grade 6, also scores above average on citywide tests. The school also has one computer lab, and computers in 18 classrooms.

The 900-student Middle School 88, where the percentage of students at or above grade level in reading and math tests was below the city average, has a gifted and talented program, two computer labs, and 16 classrooms with computers. M.S. 51, which is generally at or above the city average in the citywide tests, has gifted and talented programs.

The 3,500-student John Jay High School has been striving in recent years to improve academically but still has far to go. SAT scores in 1996, the most recent year for which figures were available, averaged 391 in verbal and 388 in mathematics, compared with the citywide average of 448 and 465, respectively. About two-thirds of graduates go on to higher education. The school has research and honors programs and a broad range of extracurricular activities, from sports to music.

Park Slope accounts for about two-thirds of the 750 students at the Berkeley Carroll School, an independent college preparatory day school for nursery through grade 12 and a major attraction for current and new residents. More than 90 percent of students taking advanced placement exams earn college credit. Tuition ranges from $6,450 for preschool to $15,520 for grade 12. Admission is competitive.

The 150-student Poly Prep Lower School for nursery through grade 4 is a small, child-centered private school that sends graduates to 650-student Poly Prep Middle and Upper Schools in Bay Ridge. Tuition at the lower school ranges from $3,000 for two mornings a week in nursery school to $12,500 for fourth grade.

St. Francis Xavier Elementary School has 500 students in kindergarten through grade 8. Tuition is $1,800. There is an after-school program for children of working parents.

At the all-girl St. Saviour High School, with an enrollment of 280 and established in 1917, about 98 percent of graduates go on to college. Tuition is $4,100. St. Saviour Grammar School, for girls and boys, had 445 students in prekindergarten through grade 8 in the spring of 1998. Tuition was $2,075. There is an after-school program from 2:30 to 6 P.M. for $70 weekly.

The Brooklyn Conservatory of Music, in a 117-year-old Victorian Gothic mansion on Seventh Avenue at Lincoln Place, is one of the oldest community music schools in the country. It offers private and group instruction for voice or instruments in styles from classical to jazz.

The farmland and hills that are now part of Prospect Park and Park Slope were scenes of bloody engagements during the Battle of Long Island in August 1776.

In the 1850s, when its 200,000 inhabitants made Brooklyn the third-largest city in the country, sentiment grew for a park to rival Manhattan's Central Park. The state legislature appointed Frederick Law Olmsted, the landscape architect for Central Park, and Calvert Vaux.

By then Edwin Clark Litchfield, who made a fortune in railroads, had purchased land for development in Park Slope. The opening of the park in 1874 and completion of the Brooklyn Bridge in 1883 established Park Slope, a name that describes its parkside location and topography. The pace of housing development quickened during the late 1870s and the 1880s, when mansions rose along the park and sturdy row houses marched down side streets to the west. It crested prior to World War I.

But by the 1920s, mansions were being razed for apartment houses, and brownstones were going out of fashion. By the end of World War II, many had been carved up into rooming houses. Through the '50s, middle-class families moved to the suburbs and urban decay set in. In the early '60s, brownstone pioneers, recognizing bargains, arrived to renovate and restore fading brownstones and eventually reverse the area's precipitous decline. Park Slope has been on the rise ever since.

BROOKLYN

PROSPECT LEFFERTS GARDENS

Rich architecture and racial harmony

BY JOHN RATHER

A story of racial harmony set against some of the finest residential architecture in Brooklyn resounds from the wide, parking-friendly streets of Prospect Lefferts Gardens. Situated near the southeast corner of Prospect Park in the Flatbush section, the racially mixed, predominantly middle-class, richly West Indian neighborhood holds at its core a 600-home historic district, designated by the Landmarks Preservation Commission in 1979 and restricted by deed covenants to use as single-family homes.

People who live there say the Historic District, where longtime residency has been common, promotes a stability welding the district and surrounding streets into a seamless whole that defeats the black-white racial divide common elsewhere. "There isn't that friction here," said Lenore Briggs, the owner and director of the Lefferts Gardens Montessori School on Rogers Avenue, where 50 children aged 2½ to 6 attend classes.

The housing bargains, real estate agents declare, are remarkable. "There is a wonderful relationship between price and value," said Paul John Skrobela, associate broker at the William B. May Company. He said two- or three-story houses in the district generally ranged from $200,000 to $300,000. The median price for a one-family home was $220,000 in 1996, up $10,000 from a year earlier. By early 1998, it had increased by $20,000, according to local realtors. They said the market was active. "People who are looking in Park Slope can get just as nice a house here for a lot less," said Mary Kay Gallagher, an independent broker from Prospect Park South. "And I mean a lot less."

For all that, the area, which draws its name from Prospect Park, the Lefferts family, and the nearby Brooklyn Botanic Garden, is surprisingly unheralded. "It's sort of a little secret," said Harriet A. Robertson, an associate broker at Century 21 Joseph T. King Realty in Park Slope.

POPULATION: 29,621.

AREA: 0.75 square mile.

MEDIAN HOUSEHOLD INCOME: $42,550.

MEDIAN PRICE OF A SINGLE-FAMILY HOUSE: $240,000.

MEDIAN PRICE OF A TWO-FAMILY HOUSE: $190,000.

DISTANCE FROM MIDTOWN MANHATTAN: 7 miles.

RUSH-HOUR TRAVEL TO MIDTOWN: 35 minutes on the 2, 5, D, or Q subway line.

CODES: Area, 718; ZIP, 11225.

In contrast to the mostly Tudor Forest Hills Gardens in Queens, another architecturally notable area, houses in and around the Prospect Lefferts Gardens Historic District range freely, if with restraint, through revival styles popular from the 1890s to the 1920s, when most were built. Most are modest versions of style-setting, opulent homes built for the rich before and during this period on Manhattan's Upper East Side.

Brick, brownstone, and Indiana limestone exteriors in Romanesque Revival, Colonial Revival, neo-Georgian, neo-Tudor, and neo-Federal style share single blocks. Uninterrupted stretches of the district's signature limestone row houses, with their rounded bays, give way on some streets to free-standing homes, some quite large. Everywhere, cartouches, foliate panels, classical moldings, and other detailing enliven the eclectic mood.

Built for the professional middle class in the late 19th and early 20th centuries, when farms in the old town of Flatbush sprouted a final crop of houses, the area now called Prospect Lefferts Gardens grew apace with the coming of new rail links to Brooklyn and Manhattan. The Brooklyn, Flatbush & Coney Island Railroad, originally designed for seasonal excursions, was by the turn of the century an electrified commuter line serving Flatbush. The opening of the Brooklyn Bridge in 1883 and the area's proximity to Prospect Park, built in the 1860s to rival Central Park, had already set the stage for development.

In 1893, James Lefferts, a descendant of the Dutch family that settled here in 1660, when the area was part of the Dutch settlement of Midwout, divided his estate into 600 building lots. To ensure that only high-quality, single-family homes would be built in the area, to be called Lefferts Manor, deeds carried restrictive covenants. The covenants halted the march of two-family houses at the borders and barred commercial development, which explains the absence of stores. Prospect Lefferts Gardens shopping areas are along Nostrand Avenue and Flatbush Avenue. The covenants also withstood legal challenge and resulted, a century later, in a housing stock in generally good repair, and unaltered by interior subdivisions even during the depths of the Great Depression.

Two-family houses are the norm outside the district, where prices are lower. Owners frequently live in one unit and rent the other. Rentals in two-family houses or in the area's liberal sprinkling of five- and six-story apartment houses ranged from $700 to $900 for two bedrooms in early 1998.

Mr. Skrobela, who has lived in the Lefferts Manor section of the Historic District for more than a decade, described the community as economically and ethnically diverse, and—as from its beginnings—mostly middle class. "You may have a Transit Authority worker living on the same block as the head of a college math department," he said.

"It's a very integrated community racially and attracts people for whom that's important," said Barbara L. Solomon, who moved into the Historic District from the Upper West Side in the early 1980s with her husband, Eliot, the former president of the Lefferts Manor Association. "Some people say they don't understand this place where black lawyers, doctors, and real estate agents live next to white ones," she said. "It seems to be terribly unique, and I'm not quite sure why."

Many blacks moved in during the late '50s and '60s, sometimes encountering "hate fences"—high corrugated plastic barriers erected by whites in that era. But the white flight that occurred in other areas did not happen, and eventually the hate fences fell. Today, Asian and Hispanic residents add to the mix.

The neighborhood was once heaven for Brooklyn Dodger fans. When the Dodgers played at home, the din from nearby Ebbets Field filled the air. There was pandemonium in 1955 when the Dodgers won their first World Series at Yankee Stadium. "We all ran out of our houses screaming," said Ms. Gallagher, the realtor, who used to live on Maple Street.

In some ways, life here is no more perfect than in many other inner-city areas. People know distant popping sounds in the night may not be firecrackers. And at the Honey Bee Farm fruit and fish store on Flatbush Avenue, a burly fruit-watcher employed by the Asian owners draws the line at chasing young crackheads. "An orange is not worth a knife in the heart," he said.

But for the untimid, there is much consolation: eye-pleasing architecture, ample curbside parking, proximity to Prospect Park, the Brooklyn Botanic Garden and the Brooklyn Museum, good subway links to Manhattan, and a self-contained neighborhood where people knew each other. "You have friends who are friends with your other friends," said Jennifer Plassman, a volunteer at the Maple Street School preschool for children 2 to 5, a parent cooperative on Nostrand Avenue. Enrollment ranges from 20 to 30 children.

Prospect Lefferts Gardens is in School District 17, an academically challenged district whose schools have generally ranked below average for city schools in reading and math scores. In 1996, according to the most recent figures available, three elementary schools and one middle school in the district were under scrutiny by the New York State Board of Regents because of failure to meet statewide academic performance benchmarks. At P.S. 92 on Parkside Avenue, only about 26 percent of students were at or above grade level in English. The school has also lagged in reading in recent years but does slightly better in math on standardized tests. About 1,250 children attend prekindergarten through eighth grade. Three city high schools—Prospect Heights, Erasmus Hall, and George Wood Wingate—are near Prospect Lefferts Gardens. In recent years, all have been below city averages in mathematics and verbal scores on the SATs.

Some residents send their children to nearby private schools. The Berkeley Carroll School in Park Slope, with 750 students in prekindergarten through grade 12, offers academic rigor and a summer day camp for children aged 3 to 8. In 1996, it was designated a blue-ribbon school by the U.S. Department of Education, the only private or public school in Brooklyn to win the accolade for general excellence. Packer Collegiate Institute in Brooklyn Heights, also from prekindergarten through grade 12, prepares its 800 students for top-rank colleges, as do Berkeley Carroll and another institution, St. Ann's School, both competitive-admission schools for gifted children.

For more than 25 years, house-proud residents of Prospect Lefferts Gardens have thrown open their doors once a year to visitors during annual tours. Tickets cost $15 at curbside or $10 in advance from the Lefferts Manor Association at 135 Midwood Street, Brooklyn, NY 11225. "We want people to know about our neighborhood," said Robert A. Marvin, a tour organizer. "It's still relatively unknown." Mr. Marvin said he and his wife, Elaine, purchased their limestone-and-brick row house with its Renaissance Revival exterior with Romanesque touches after taking the tour in 1974. "I'm sure if we hadn't gone on that tour, we wouldn't be living here now," Mr. Marvin said. He added that they were only the third owners since the house was built in 1899.

WILLIAMSBURG

Trendy ambience and Manhattan views

BY JOYCE COHEN

At certain hours, Bedford Avenue seems calm for a thoroughfare. But at other times, as when it is so crowded that there are lines for Sunday brunch, you could maybe—maybe—mistake it for a Manhattan streetscape.

O.K., maybe not. But it is close. There is that lovely Manhattan skyline, stretching across the East River, just a subway stop away. There is the unmistakably trendy ambience encroaching upon what was long a working-class neighborhood. There are even visitors from Manhattan, well aware of the area's reputation as a new Bohemia. Hipness, though, is no consolation to some residents, who fret about ever-more congestion, rising real estate prices, and irrevocable alterations to the area's cherished sense of community.

It is still possible to find affordable rent and a sense of space in Williamsburg. But change is fast afoot here, especially in the Northside neighborhood that centers around Bedford Avenue near the first stop on the L train. The area, discovered by the city's artistic community in the early 1980s, is now absorbing its second wave of artists. Even the surrounding sections are starting to feel the shift as pioneers venture to the Southside, home to a large Hispanic population as well as a big group of Hasidic Jews, and to East Williamsburg, predominantly Italian.

Williamsburg is a patchwork of a place, with houses and shops jumbled together with factories, warehouses, and weedy lots. Nine public housing projects, with a population of 17,000, dot the Southside. The largest, the 20-building Williamsburg Houses, opened in 1938. The massive loft spaces that drew the original artists are rarely available anymore. Paul Campbell, an artist, recalled that when he moved to Williamsburg in 1981, "it was much quieter at the time artistically, but it was equally vital."

POPULATION: 126,801.

AREA: 3 square miles.

MEDIAN HOUSEHOLD INCOME: $25,196.

MEDIAN PRICE OF A TWO-FAMILY HOUSE: $200,000.

MIDRANGE RENT FOR A ONE-BEDROOM APARTMENT: $1,100.

DISTANCE FROM MIDTOWN MANHATTAN: 5 miles.

RUSH-HOUR TRAVEL TO MIDTOWN: 15 minutes on the L, J, M, or Z train, including switches to uptown trains.

CODES: Area, 718; ZIP, 11211 and 11206.

Mr. Campbell now lives elsewhere but has retained a studio in Williamsburg. "Culturally," he said, "the area is very rich."

It is not only that several unusual galleries have moved in. North Sixth Street Video invites neighborhood filmmakers to contribute their videos, which are lent for free. Max & Roebling, a Bedford Avenue boutique, sells jewelry and accessories from local designers. And the Brooklyn Brewery, where ongoing events include such things as a contest for "Art on a Bar Coaster," has a room that displays the work of local artists.

Physically, though, Williamsburg is dreary. The prevailing style of architecture—rows of attached frame houses, usually four floors or less—is undistinguished. But you never know what is inside. "It could be a dump, or it could be a palace," said Suzy Kline, owner of Kline Realty.

By early 1998, a typical two-bedroom rental was $1,100. Rents were about $100 less as recently as a year earlier, and $200 less two years earlier. Single-family houses are uncommon and rarely come up for sale. A two-family house is likely to cost in the range of $200,000, up about $25,000 in a year.

Most of the lofts available are for commercial use only, said Kenn Firpo of Kenn Firpo Real Estate, and the few that do come on the market need extensive renovations. "When someone has a great loft to live in, they don't move out," he said. Demand for space has been so strong that, in the fall of 1997, Mr. Firpo raised his fee for apartments in the prime Northside area to 12 percent of a year's rent. For apartments in the rest of Williamsburg, he charges 10 percent of a year's rent. One month is the going rate for the area's other brokers, though Kline Realty charges 15 percent for lofts.

In other areas of Williamsburg, there are signs of creeping gentrification. Rents remain lower, but they are rising quickly. In tumbledown Southside, a small basement studio apartment might rent for $625, while a one-bedroom might start at $750. "There's so little available," said Ms. Kline, and real estate brokers expect demand to intensify.

Perhaps the most common type of Williamsburg housing is the railroad flat. Many buildings have not been renovated, and their interiors can be raw, says George Pappas, manager of M.C.R. Realty. Be prepared for ugly linoleum floors, bathrooms without sinks, and fuses that cannot handle a microwave and an iron simultaneously. But the renters, who tend to be single and in their 20s, do not seem to mind. Many are already familiar with Williamsburg through friends.

Gretchen McGowan took over a friend's apartment in 1994. Moving from Manhattan, she felt her four-room apartment was almost too big. "I didn't know what to do with all this space," she said.

The different ethnic groups in her Northside neighborhood, which houses many recent Polish immigrants, coexist comfortably, said Ms. Mc-Gowan, who works in film production. "We may not have much to do with each other, but we're compatible," she said. "Not cohesive, but compatible."

Most new arrivals have no children; people do not move to Williamsburg for the schools. Children in the ethnic enclaves usually attend nearby parochial schools. At the District 14 public elementary schools, standardized reading and math scores fall close to the citywide mean or just below it. In 1995–96, Regents scores at the neighborhood's two high schools, Harry Van Arsdale and Eastern District, were among the lowest in the state. By the start of the 1996 school year, in fact, Eastern District had ceased to exist as a high school; its Grand Street campus was restructured into several smaller high schools centered around the areas of legal studies, progress, and enterprise and technology.

Williamsburg was named for Jonathan Williams, an early surveyor of the area. In 1855, at the suggestion of Williamsburgh's mayor, Abraham J. Berry, the city became part of Brooklyn. (That is when the final "h" was dropped, though the Williamsburgh Savings Bank retains it. Its first headquarters, at 175 Broadway, at Driggs Avenue, is now a Republic National Bank branch.)

In the mid-1800s, Williamsburg was a fashionable resort area, with hotels, clubs, and beer gardens near the Brooklyn ferry attracting wealthy industrialists and professionals. The neighborhood's nature changed with the 1903 opening of the Williamsburg Bridge and the 1905 inauguration of trolley service over the bridge. Working-class Jews and other eastern European immigrants flooded in from the crowded Lower East Side; they were followed by various groups of working-class immigrants, including Puerto Ricans working in the factories. In 1957, the Brooklyn-Queens Expressway opened, slicing through the neighborhood.

Subway transportation to and from Manhattan is convenient. The L train, of course, has its first Brooklyn stop at Bedford Avenue. The J, M, and Z lines, to Lower Manhattan, stop at Marcy Avenue and Broadway. The B39 bus shuttles across the Williamsburg Bridge, terminating at Delancey and Orchard Streets in Manhattan.

As recently as a dozen years ago, it was hard to find even basic services in Williamsburg. There is still a dearth of banks and ATM machines. But the area abounds with coin laundries and convenience stores; Bedford Avenue even features Sarkana Discount Art Supplies (the name means red in Latvian). So far, chain stores are nonexistent. But fresh food and well-regarded restaurants flourish, including the L Cafe, Oznot's Dish, Vera Cruz, Plan Eat Thailand, and the landmark Peter Luger Steak House, in its original 1887 location. A movie theater on Broadway, the Commodore, shows first-run pictures for $6. It is easy to furnish an apartment and a closet on the cheap, what with the Salvation Army, Moon River Chattel, which was once known as the Olde Age Junk Shoppe, and Greenpoint Used Clothing & Furniture, also known as Sidney's. Domsey Warehouse Outlet, in the former Schaefer Brewery, is crammed with used clothing.

The place for outdoor recreation is McCarren Park, near Greenpoint. It has 35 acres of ball fields, tennis courts, and playgrounds.

Williamsburg's other open space, the waterfront, is not quite so refined. A sweet molasses smell sometimes emanates from the Domino sugar plant, but the garbage business, which occupies parts of the waterfront, has been known to generate a stench, depending on wind and weather. The foul smell has diminished in the last several years, but trucks still thunder down the streets at all hours, said a community activist, Inez Pasher, a longtime resident. But concerns about garbage remain; people worry that transfer stations to process residential garbage will move in now that the Fresh Kills Landfill on Staten Island is scheduled to close in 2001. And some people, especially those living near the Brooklyn-Queens Expressway, complain that their homes are perpetually coated with grime.

Plans to develop the waterfront, now zoned for heavy industrial use, have come and gone. Its future is anyone's guess. Currently, community groups are preparing to recommend zoning changes for possible development. They favor a mix of housing and light industrial use, said Ron Webster, a member of Community Board 1 and chairman of the Greenpoint-Williamsburg Waterfront Coalition. The idea is to prevent the waterfront from turning into a city dumping ground. "People don't want any more transfer stations or other uses that will add more pollution," Mr. Webster said.

Though the Hispanic and Hasidic groups that share the Southside are united on many environmental issues, they disagree on housing, with the Hispanic groups seeking affordable housing along the waterfront, and the Hasidim wanting market-rate housing. Everyone, however, wants housing low enough not to block the sweeping waterfront views.

Street crime has dropped in recent years. Only occasionally do drug dealers gather on corners. Racial conflict and gang violence are minimal, according to the police. In the 90th Precinct, which covers the Southside and East Williamsburg, robbery and burglary rates both fell dramatically in the mid-1990s, though burglary rates rose a bit in 1997. The 94th Precinct, which covers the Northside as well as Greenpoint, had fewer crimes overall and saw even more dramatic drops in the mid-1990s. In 1997, however, cases of burglary and auto theft were each up about 15 percent over 1996.

Williamsburg is the site of one of the city's historic indoor pools, the 1922 Metropolitan Pool and Bathhouse, at the corner of Bedford and Metropolitan Avenues. It was reopened in the fall of 1997 after a $4.88 million renovation. The building, which includes a 30- by 75-foot swimming pool, two new locker rooms, a community room, and a fitness area, was originally designed by Henry Bacon, architect of the Lincoln Memorial in Washington.

ASTORIA

Where the piano meets the bouzouki

BY JOHN RATHER

Umbrellas are the only concession to rainy, windy days along Astoria's Steinway Street, where a seemingly unending expanse of small shops and eating places of every description fairly bristles with shoppers undeterred by bad weather. In this throbbing community, no rainstorm is enough to suppress a sunny disposition. With its brightly colored canopies and double-parked cars, Steinway Street is only one of several main thoroughfares in Astoria, a Greek-American stronghold in northwestern Queens known for its shopping, safe streets, more than 200 restaurants, nightlife, affordability, and good subway connections to Manhattan.

The Steinway Piano Company, an economic bulwark since the company moved here from Manhattan in the 1880s, still provides jobs for craftsmen at its factory on 19th Avenue in Astoria's main industrial area. But the humble bouzouki, not the Steinway grand, is the instrument that best sets to music a neighborhood where Greek is heard as often as English along Ditmars Boulevard, another commercial hub. For Greeks, Greek-Americans, and lovers of Greek cuisine and culture from throughout the metropolitan area, Astoria is a siren song and the place to be. "They all come to Astoria for the food and the entertainment," said George Delis, the district manager of Community Board 1.

Among the restaurants are Elias Corner, serving Greek seafood; Minore, a Greek nightclub with live bouzouki music and traditional Greek cuisine; and the Taj Mahal, with Indian cuisine. At the popular Athens Cafe on busy 30th Avenue, patrons at small tables with marble tops drink coffee and munch on Greek and European pastries while gazing through large windows at the passing scene, always a busy one.

In a working-class setting that has been home to many immigrants

POPULATION: 121,531.

AREA: 3 square miles.

MEDIAN HOUSEHOLD INCOME: $40,742.

MEDIAN PRICE OF A TWO-FAMILY HOME: $300,000.

MIDRANGE RENT FOR A TWO-BEDROOM APARTMENT: $900.

DISTANCE FROM MIDTOWN MANHATTAN: 6 miles.

RUSH-HOUR TRAVEL TO MIDTOWN: 25 minutes on the N subway line; 35 minutes on the Queens Surface bus to the Manhattan side of the Queensboro Bridge; 25 minutes on the Triboro Coach, $3 one way.

CODES: Area, 718; ZIP, 11102, 11103. 11105. and 11106.

in its history, new waves of ethnicity are always pouring in. Around Broadway, near Astoria's ever-open-to-interpretation border with Long Island City, recent immigrants from Bangladesh, the Philippines, Ireland, Colombia, India, and China lead the transformation. Americans of Italian, German, Irish, and Polish extraction have been at home in Astoria for decades, and a Hispanic and African-American presence has been growing.

Its convenient subway links to Manhattan have also made Astoria increasingly popular with young people who work or study across the river but want larger, more affordable apartments than they can find there. Above 31st Street, the N line subway lumbers along elevated tracks through the middle of town to the last stop on Ditmars Boulevard. The ride back to midtown Manhattan takes less than half an hour. Rows of two- and three-story, redbrick, attached and semidetached houses stretching off on both sides are typical of the two-family housing that predominates. Another subway connection to midtown, the R line, stops at Steinway Street and 46th Street.

A decade ago, some developers thought that the subways, coupled with Astoria's work-ethic stability and the allure lent by the Greek presence, made this architecturally plain-hewn community ripe for gentrification. Except for the huge Shore Towers condominium, it never happened, and Astoria churned on with a vitality and momentum of its own. "Astoria keeps moving," said Gregory Fiasconaro, a broker at G. M. Dynasty Realty at 35-04 30th Avenue. "It's so close to the city, it's like the step-brother."

Even some who left are coming back. "A few years ago, a lot of Greeks started moving out to Flushing and Bayside," said Angelo Langdakis, a broker at Owners Club Realty at 31st Street and Ditmars Boulevard, recounting an exodus others said reached out to towns like Port Washington and Glen Cove on Long Island. "But they still hung around this area because of all the big stores and restaurants and night life. Driving back and forth was difficult, so many of them moved back."

The median price of a two-family home was $250,000 in early 1996, but had moved rapidly upward by the fourth quarter of 1997, when some realtors said $300,000 was closer to the median.

A shrewd buyer can cover annual taxes, averaging about $2,000, and most of the mortgage by renting the upstairs and basement of a two-family house, according to Mr. Langdakis. "With today's interest rates, someone putting down a 10 percent payment can almost live for free by renting the second floor and the basement," Mr. Langdakis said. Basement rentals are illegal but extremely common, brokers and others said. "Ninety-nine percent of the houses have finished, rentable basements," Mr. Langdakis said. But the upstairs apartments, often rented out by owners living on the ground floor, are at the core of Astoria's active rental market. A midrange price for a two-bedroom apartment was $800 in early 1996. By late 1997, it was up about $100.

Shore Towers, a 23-story, 405-unit condominium on Shore Boulevard overlooking the East River that was built in 1991, advertises "affordable luxury on the Queens coast" with views of Manhattan and East River bridges. A two-bedroom apartment sold for $125,000 at the start of 1996 but was up to $140,000 in the fourth quarter of 1997. The monthly common charge rose from $242 to $278.52 over the same period. One-bedrooms were $99,000 with a monthly common charge of $214.85 in November 1997.

Maria D'Antoni, an associate saleswoman at Crest Haven Realty at 28-17 Astoria Boulevard, said a pent-up demand for houses and apartments in 1996 intensified during 1997. Realtors say the neighborhood's reputation for safety is a draw, and one of the reasons why the housing market is tight.

Astoria Park, near the Triborough Bridge crossing over Hell Gate, has 62 acres of playing fields, tennis courts, and green spaces and the largest outdoor pool in the city.

A major city-owned housing project on First Street near Shore Boulevard, Astoria Houses, has 1,102 apartments and an estimated 3,245 residents, according to city officials. The Ravenswood Houses, another city project with 2,167 apartments and an estimated 4,500 residents, is just beyond Astoria on 35th Avenue near 21st Street.

The American Museum of the Moving Image, which opened at its current location in 1988, celebrates Astoria's long association with films and video. The museum, at 35th Avenue and 36th Street, is next to Kaufman Astoria Studios, a major East Coast film and video production center. The studio is the historic successor to the Famous Players–Lasky Corporation, which opened a studio here in 1920 to produce silent movies for Paramount Pictures. Stars from Rudolph Valentino and Gloria Swanson to Robert De Niro and Meryl Streep have worked there.

The Isamu Noguchi Garden Museum at 32-37 Vernon Boulevard is named for the internationally known sculptor whose studio was at the museum site. Galleries and the outdoor garden display over 250 works by Noguchi, who died in 1988. The museum is open from early April to the end of October.

Athens Square at 30th Street and 30th Avenue, a small city park with an amphitheater that recalls those of ancient Greece, is a unique Astoria feature. Three 23-foot-high white-granite columns, costing $250,000, weighing 14 tons each, and fashioned after the Doric columns of Delphi, arrived in 1996 from Rhode Island, where they were crafted from Georgia stone. They add to an unusual Hellenic park created by a local fund-raising drive that raised $300,000 from the Astoria community. "Athens Square is a beautiful place for the performing arts," said Mr. Delis. He said there was standing-room-only at Greek Night on summer Tuesdays, one of a number of free musical performances.

Germans settled in Astoria during the latter half of the 19th century, followed by the Irish. Italians came after World War I. Greeks followed after World War II. The Greek population surged after a change in immigration laws in 1962 opened the doors to southern Europeans.

Greek Orthodox, Roman Catholic, and Lutheran churches and four synagogues witness the tides of immigration. St. Demetrios, a 69-year-old cathedral on 31st Street and 30th Drive, is the largest Greek Orthodox church in the nation.

There are six elementary schools and three intermediate schools in the area generally considered to be Astoria, which is in School District 30. At I.S. 126, a visual- and performing-arts magnet school at 31-51 21st Street, Spanish and Bengali are the most frequent native tongues of students who speak limited English. The school, built in 1925, has about 1,000 students in grades 6 through 8.

Many Astoria students attend the recently built Long Island City High School, where the principal, William C. Bassell, said an interdisciplinary program in technology, humanities, and the arts began in September 1996. About 80 percent of the school's 3,000 students are from Astoria. The building, which opened in September 1995, is one of the newest public high schools in the city. It has a 1,400-seat theater and a pool. More than 80 percent of students go on to higher education. About 25 percent of students in the class of 1994 took the Scholastic Assessment Test. Average scores of 302 in verbal skills and 389 in mathematics were below the city-wide average. By 1996, the percentage taking the test was higher and SAT averages had risen to 397 in verbal and 438 in math, closer to city averages.

The William Cullen Bryant High School, the other zoned high school for Astoria, has an enrollment of 3,500. In a recent survey, about 78 percent of graduates went on to higher education.

There is one parochial high school in Astoria, the Roman Catholic St. John's Preparatory School, and one Lutheran and five Catholic elementary schools. There is also a prekindergarten-to-grade 12 St. Demetrios school.

Astoria bore the Indian name Sintsinck, meaning "a stony place," when the first settler, William Hallett, arrived in the 1650s. Halletts Cove on Hell Gate is named after the family. During the Revolutionary War, British artillery batteries set up where the Astoria Houses now stand, aimed over Hell Gate at Colonials holding Manhattan. The area owes it current name, but little else, to the fur merchant John Jacob Astor. Despite protests, village leaders adopted the name when the village was incorporated in 1839 to attract investment from Astor in what was then a well-to-do retreat for New York merchants. But flattery, in this case, got Astoria nowhere.

QUEENS

BAYSIDE

A high quality of life within the city

BY JOHN RATHER

In any quality-of-life rating of Queens neighborhoods, long-prosperous Bayside ranks comfortably near the top. But housing prices are also high in this sought-after semisuburban area flanking Little Neck Bay.

A first-rate rail connection to Manhattan, esteemed public schools, a relatively low crime rate, ample public parks, and a generally healthy, if parking-shy, downtown shopping area on Bell Boulevard make for the good life in Bayside, where traffic noise is muted on shady residential streets on which neighbors know one another. "It's a stable environment, great for family living," said William H. Seto, a broker at Goldmark Realty. "You've got good schools, good transportation, good shopping, and low taxes."

One-family detached houses predominate, but condominiums, co-ops, and two-family houses are plentiful in Bayside's varied residential mix.

At newer condominiums like the Bay Club and Baybridge, both in the Bay Terrace section on the north side of Bayside, two-bedroom units begin in the low $200,000's. At the Bay Terrace co-op, a 10-section, 1,326-unit complex, a well-maintained, two-bedroom, 1½-bath duplex sold for $124,000 in summer 1996. Prices were about the same in the fourth quarter of 1997.

Prices for detached single-family houses in upscale, larger-lot areas like Bayside Gables, also on Bayside's north side, range above $500,000. Prices are somewhat lower in nearby Weeks Woodlands.

But a more typical Bayside dwelling is a smallish, two-story, single-family detached house, often with exterior brick and Tudor touches, sometimes with a slate roof, and with a driveway leading to a detached, one-car garage in back. A house nearly matching this description sold in 1996 for $249,000 in Bayside Hills, a 60-year-old neighborhood on Bayside's south side. Built in 1940, it featured oak floors, two bedrooms and one bath downstairs, one large bedroom and an attic upstairs, an

GAZETTEER

POPULATION: 89,418.

AREA: 9.3 square miles.

MEDIAN HOUSEHOLD INCOME: $60,357.

MEDIAN PRICE OF A SINGLE-FAMILY HOUSE: $245,000.

TAXES ON A MEDIAN-PRICED HOUSE: $1,900.

DISTANCE FROM MIDTOWN MANHATTAN: 13 miles.

RUSH-HOUR TRAVEL TO MIDTOWN: 27 minutes on the Long Island Rail Road, $6 one way, $117 monthly.

CODES: Area, 718; ZIP, 11361, 11360, 11364, and 11357.

unfinished basement, and a cathedral ceiling in the living room. Taxes were $1,958.

Peter Pappas, an associate broker at SPEC International Realty, said such houses sold within two months in Bayside's brisk market. "We don't have enough houses," said Barbara Alexander, a broker and owner of Century 21 B & J Alexander Realty. "It's unbelievable, phenomenal, what's going on here." Ms. Alexander said that in late 1997, the scarcity of listings was growing even more acute. "There are hundreds of buyers lined up," she said. She said the median price for single-family homes of $235,000 in mid-1996 was up $5,000 to $10,000 by the fourth quarter of 1997, still slightly below peak prices of the late 1980s.

Average two-bedroom rentals in co-ops, condominiums, and two-family homes ranged from $900 to $1,100 in mid-1996. The range remained the same in late 1997.

Realtors said uttering the words "District 26" was all it took to convince many families that buying in Bayside was worth the strain on their pocketbooks. The district, regularly first in citywide results on standard tests for English and math, is widely known for academic excellence.

The Matinecocks, whose tribal name means "land of the hilly ground," lived in Bayside undisturbed until 1637, when the West India Trading Company began encouraging Dutch farmers to settle on land grants in then-pristine reaches of Queens. An Englishman, William Lawrence, built the first permanent dwelling, a stone farmhouse, upon settling in Bayside in 1644, 20 years before the English wrested control of New Amsterdam from the Dutch. Bayside became part of the Town of Flushing and was occupied by British troops during the Revolutionary War. The hamlet's name first appeared in a deed dated 1798, written as Bay Side.

By the late 1800s, Bayside was firmly established as a rural resort where the well-heeled from Manhattan and other parts of the city flocked for fun. The Bayside House, famous for clambakes, drew crowds and made the area the social capital of Queens during the Gilded Age. It burned in 1906, but the name of its proprietor, Joseph Crocheron, lives on at 45-acre Crocheron Park, where sunbathers bask on sloping greens.

The park, with 10 tennis courts and two baseball diamonds, is one of three major public spaces in and around Bayside. The others are Clearview Park, with its 18-hole public golf course, and the 623.5-acre Alley Pond Park, which has tennis courts, playing fields, running trails, and an environmental center with programs for children.

During the '20s and '30s, when studios in nearby Astoria were churning out motion pictures at a prodigious rate, early stars including Rudolph Valentino, Gloria Swanson, Norma Talmadge, W. C. Fields, and Charlie Chaplin lived in Bayside. Some built lavish homes. James J. (Gentleman Jim) Corbett, the heavyweight boxing champion from 1892 to 1897, lived from 1902 to 1933 in a large three-story home on a street that bears his name. Invariably polite and sharply dressed, the cane-carrying ex-champion gave nickels to ogling kids.

In the post–World War II era, Bayside emerged as a commuter haven on the eastern edge of Queens with a coveted stop on the Long Island Rail Road's premier Port Washington line, where no change at Jamaica was necessary. Getting to the station can be a challenge, since no major parking facilities are in the immediate vicinity. Once there, the rest is easy. The trip from the Bayside Long Island Rail Road station to Penn Station takes less than 30 minutes.

Unmetered side streets are clogged with commuters' cars, not all from Bayside. "Parking is our big problem," said Ben Fried, at 81 years old the chairman of the Bell Boulevard Merchants Association and proprietor of Ben's Hardware since it opened in 1935. "We would triple our business if people were able to park here." Mr. Fried said that by late 1997, new, large retail stores with ample parking in Flushing and other areas near Bayside were sapping some small businesses on Bell Boulevard. "There is not a place to buy a piece of lumber in Bayside anymore," he said.

Long a meeting place for the city's young, Bell Boulevard, Bayside's spinal column, is filled with bars, bar-restaurants, pizzerias, bakeries, bagel shops, and stores. Bell Boulevard leads north from Northern Boulevard, Bayside's other main thoroughfare, to the recently upgraded Bay Terrace Shopping Center, where stores from Barnes & Noble to Victoria's Secret surround a large parking field.

Bayside has a large number of civic groups and some 40 churches and synagogues. In recent times, the area has attracted Korean, Taiwanese, and other Asian-American residents.

Bayside's location within District 26 is a strong unifier and the district's top reputation is a point of pride. In the 1996–97 school year, 78.4 percent of elementary and middle school students read at or above grade level, the highest for any city district.

Many Bayside students attend Benjamin Cardozo High School, which had an enrollment of about 3,600 students in the fall of 1997. The school routinely scores far above other high schools in the city in the number of students meeting state requirements in all subjects tested—96.9 percent versus 76.6 percent in math and 93.3 percent versus 67.5 percent in reading, for example, in one recent year. Thirty percent of its students graduating in June 1995 received Regents Honors Diplomas, as opposed to 4.7 percent citywide. June figures for 1996 and 1997 were comparable. The school also has special course offerings in science, math, and law for top students.

Bayside High School, which has about 2,450 students, has magnet programs in art, and instrumental and vocal music—"One of the largest, most widely recognized music programs in the city," said its principal, Harris B. Sarney. There is also a science art, science, math, and research program and honors and advanced placement courses in many subjects. An honors minischool for academically gifted students is modeled after the Boston Latin School.

Middle School 74, for grades 6 through 8, is a magnet school for global communications and information systems. M.S. 158, for grades 6 through 9, is a magnet school for science, mathematics, and technology and, with P.S. 31, also a magnet school for academically gifted children.

Bayside has 11 public elementary schools, covering kindergarten through grade 5. Private elementary schools include Holy Martyrs, an Armenian school; St. Robert Bellarmine Roman Catholic School; and the Lutheran School of Flushing and Bayside.

Queensborough Community College, which is in Bayside, stages an annual Performing Arts Series. The musical *Mame* and a performance of *Swan Lake* by the St. Petersburg State Ice Ballet were presented in one recent season.

In recent years, Bayside has been living down the raucous reputation of late-night Bell Boulevard. The bad old days peaked in July 1992, when one person was killed and three others wounded in an early morning shootout on the boulevard. The shootings are remembered now as a watershed event that marked the start of heightened efforts to rein in the excesses of a club and street scene that had attracted young adults from across the metropolitan area for more than a generation.

A crackdown by the 111th Precinct on underage drinking, the closing of some of the more rowdy bars, and a gradual evolution of bars into bar-restaurants that catered to an older, more local clientele helped quiet the thoroughfare.

Bayside's appeal as a neighborhood so suburban that it is easy to forget that it is part of New York City was neatly summed up by Howard Rudolph, an insurance claims adjuster in Manhattan encountered while looking for an apartment. He called Bayside a place of character and convenience. "It's also the first grass-and-trees neighborhood outside of the city," he said.

BRIARWOOD

Where cultural diversity is an old habit

BY JOHN RATHER

Friends used to ask Seymour Schwartz why he stayed in Briarwood, Queens, when he could be living in the suburbs of southern Connecticut. "I could have lived anywhere—economically it was no problem," said Mr. Schwartz, 71, a retired pharmaceutical industry executive and president of the Briarwood Civic Association. "But I never felt the need. Here everyone who passes my door greets me. You can't get that in a purely suburban environment." Mr. Schwartz is not alone in placing community togetherness high on the list of Briarwood's virtues. Others remark on convenient subway and bus connections to Manhattan, arrays of stores and shops on Queens Boulevard and bordering roadways, and a relaxed and accepting attitude about cultural diversity, an old habit here.

Bordered by four major roadways, the rectangular Briarwood neighborhood is a predominantly middle-income, multiethnic community of one- and two-family houses interspersed with five-, six-, and seven-story apartment buildings, nearly all now co-ops. The population was 31,587 according to the 1990 census. Rush-hour commutation to midtown Manhattan takes about 25 minutes on the E or F subway train, or 30 minutes on Jamaica Buses QM21.

Realtors say the market for one- and two-family detached and attached houses is strong. "Briarwood is very desirable; people want it, so there's an excellent market," said Jennifer Dupree, the office manager at Century 21 Big M Realty on Hillside Avenue. Bill Blumenthal, a sales agent at Mattone Real Estate in Bayside, Queens, said the upper end of the Briarwood market was in Briarwood Estates in the northwest corner of the neighborhood, an enclave where stand-alone, redbrick one-family houses, some with Tudor touches, mix with large wood-frame dwellings. The median price of a one-family home, $200,000 at the end of 1997, has been

POPULATION: 25,391.

AREA: 1 square mile.

MEDIAN HOUSEHOLD INCOME: $51,678.

MEDIAN PRICE OF SINGLE-FAMILY HOUSE: $200,000.

TAXES ON A MEDIAN-PRICED HOME: $1,100.

DISTANCE FROM MIDTOWN MANHATTAN: 9 miles.

RUSH-HOUR TRAVEL TO MIDTOWN: 23 minutes on the F train, 25 minutes on the E train.

CODES: Area, 718; ZIP, 11435.

unchanged more than two years; the taxes on such a house would be about $1,100 a year. The median price for a two-bedroom co-op was $65,000 in late 1997, up about $5,000 in a year.

Briarwood was long a part of Jamaica, where English settlers arrived in 1656. In 1905, Herbert A. O'Brien launched a development in the area now known as Briarwood Estates. His wife, Adeline, coined the name because of the briars stuck to her husband's clothing when he returned from forays to the wooded site. Briarwood Estates was well established in 1936, when contemporary classified ads showed houses ranging in price from $3,000 to $9,500.

Many homes on the market today were built during the '30s and '40s. A few were moved from the right-of-way for the Van Wyck Expressway in 1949.

Apartment buildings began rising in the early '50s, followed by an influx of new residents from the Bronx and Brooklyn. The number of apartments increased markedly over the next decade, raising Briarwood's skyline but not, residents insist, obliterating its neighborhood feeling. Diane Cohen, district manager of Community Board 8, said recent rezoning protected areas of one- and two-family homes against apartment-house intrusion.

At the Arlington at 139-15 83d Avenue, a 281-unit, seven-story apartment that became a co-op in the early '80s, two-bedroom units range from $50,000 to $60,000. Monthly maintenance is $500 to $600. Two-bedroom rentals start at about $900. The building has 24-hour-a-day doormen and an underground parking garage.

Parkway Village, with 675 apartments in 109 one- and two-story buildings on a 35-acre campus with two private roads, was started in 1946 for employees of the United Nations, which then was briefly based at Flushing Meadows and in nearby Lake Success, Long Island. The complex, completed in 1948, is bounded by Main Street, Union Turnpike, Parsons Boulevard, and the Grand Central Parkway service road. Many of the original tenants remained after the U.N. moved to Manhattan, setting the tone for the ethnic diversity that has been a hallmark of Briarwood.

To the south, near Parsons Boulevard and on hilly streets leading down to Hillside Avenue, Archie Bunkeresque wood-frame houses bunch together, impressive in size if cramped by their neighbors. Otherwise, appearances are deceiving. This is not now and never was Archie Bunker's sort of place.

"You always had dozens of languages in the elementary school," said Ellen Hofstetter, who raised four children in Briarwood. "Here, kids from everywhere play together, and go to each other's houses." Ms. Hofstetter said the local Little League exemplified what was good about the community. "It's a kind Little League," she said. "The parents don't yell at the kids and they have a rule that every kid plays."

The 1990 census listed 41.4 percent of Briarwood's residents as white and non-Hispanic and 14.7 percent as black and non-Hispanic. More than 26 percent were of Hispanic origin, including 5.8 percent who were of Puerto Rican origin. Asians and Pacific Islanders accounted for 15.7 percent, including 4.6 percent of Chinese origin. Briarwood's substantial Jewish population declined in recent years as older Jews retired to Florida, but has recently been revived by Russian immigrants.

At the Briarwood Jewish Center, an Orthodox and Conservative synagogue on 86th Avenue, a Russian congregation now meets in an upstairs sanctuary. "It's always filled to capacity," said Rachel Matalon, a center volunteer. The center offers Hebrew study for children and English classes for Russian immigrants. There are also programs for the elderly.

A Greek community is served by the St. Demetrios Greek Orthodox Church, where 175 pupils from prekindergarten to grade 8 are enrolled at the Jamaica Day School. Courses in religion, the Greek language, and computer literacy are offered. A parochial high school in the church, Archbishop Iakovos, has about 35 students. The school offers Regents test preparation, Greek studies, and Spanish as a second language.

At the Victoria Congregational Church on 87th Avenue, services are offered in Hindi and Urdu as well as English, a reflection of a growing Indian population in recent years. On Queens Boulevard, the recently opened Patel's Food Mart bills itself as "Your One-Stop Indo-Pak-American Grocery Store." It rents videos and stocks Indian spices and sweets. Samosas, deep-fried vegetable patties, are 65 cents each.

The Annam Brahma, a nearby vegetarian restaurant at 84-43 164th Street, offers a vegetable curry luncheon special with basmati rice and dal for $2.95. An eggplant Parmesan dinner with salad and garlic bread is $6.95 on Italian night each Thursday. Soy turkey is a Thanksgiving feature. Traditional American fare is served at the Flagship, a popular family restaurant at 138-30 Queens Boulevard.

Briarwood is in School District 28, where most schools are above city and national averages in math and English. P.S. 117 at 143d Street and 85th Drive prides itself on cultural diversity among its approximately 1,300 students in kindergarten through the sixth grade. The school has a computer lab and recently was one of a handful of city schools to win an Annenberg Foundation grant of $75,000 annually for five years for Arts in Education programs. The school stresses cooperation between parents, teachers, and administrators.

About 1,300 students attend Intermediate School 217 at 85-05 144th Street. The school has programs for gifted and talented, peer tutoring, and peer conflict resolution. Students typically attain scores near the national average on standardized math and English tests.

Hillcrest High School at 160-05 Highland Avenue, the nearest public high school, has about 4,000 students. In a 1994 survey, 56.4 percent of graduates went on to four-year colleges, slightly above the city average. Advanced placement courses are offered in several subjects; scores on the SAT have been near the average for city schools in recent years.

The 550-pupil Roman Catholic St. Nicholas of Tolentine School, covering prekindergarten through grade 8, offers a computer program and intramural sports. There is an advanced math program and an after-school program until 6 P.M. Monday through Friday. Tuition is $3,330.

Nearly all of the 1,550 students at Archbishop Molloy, an all-male Roman Catholic high school at 83-53 Manton Street, go on to four-year colleges, according to Brother Richard Van Houten, the principal. He said SAT scores were typically 150 points above the city average. The school also offers advanced placement courses and has won city championships in many sports. Admission is competitive. Tuition was $4,400 a year in 1997.

In a measure of civic character, Briarwood has remained supportive of a shelter for the homeless that opened in the early '90s at Union Turnpike and 134th Street, even though the community had fought vigorously to keep it out. The shelter, which is run by the Salvation Army, has room for 90 families. Some of the local volunteers had opposed the project when it was first proposed. "From its opening day, it has never been a problem," said Mr. Schwartz of the Briarwood Civic Association, which had sued to keep the shelter out of this middle-class area. Members had feared drug users, unruly people, and a loss in property values. But after losing its case on appeal, "We turned about," said Mr. Schwartz. "We decided to try to make it into a model shelter, and we believe we have accomplished that." Members of the association sit on a shelter advisory board.

"After the shovel hit the ground, people said as long as it's going in, let's make it the best it can be," said Ms. Cohen, the district manager of Community Board 8. "Instead of fighting it, we made it part of the community." Real estate brokers said the shelter has had no impact on property values in Briarwood.

DOUGLASTON

Small-town charms on a city waterfront

BY DIANA SHAMAN

At night, they fall silent to respect sleeping neighbors, but otherwise the bells of the white clapboard Community Church of Douglaston in Douglas Manor ring on the hour and half hour. And in his 25 years, no one has ever complained, said the pastor, Rev. John H. Meyer.

Church bells add yet another touch of small-town charm to this large, yet closely knit, northeast Queens community where many sections resemble New England more than New York City.

"We are basically a one-family area, we are very concerned with the environment, and we are very community-oriented," said Nancy Sakas, the president of the 87-year-old Douglaston Civic Association. "Anyone who comes in here and tries to change our small-town atmosphere has a fight on their hands," Mrs. Sakas added. "We don't give in easily."

Residents say few neighborhoods can match Douglaston's attractions.

Its schools are rated among the city's finest and its housing choices range from $35,000 one-bedroom co-op garden apartments to $1 million-and-up waterfront mansions. It borders on three city parks—one with an 18-hole golf course—and its stores are varied enough to keep even the dedicated shopper happy. Yet midtown Manhattan is only a 30-minute Long Island Rail Road ride away and major highways are right on the doorstep.

Moreover, thanks to thoughtful planning, the community includes an unspoiled waterfront that stretches for over a mile along Little Neck Bay, and it borders hundreds of acres of wildlife and bird sanctuaries in the 635-acre Alley Pond Park to the west and the 90-acre Udalls Cove Park to the east.

For boaters, there is even a sheltered harbor with mooring for 100 boats, which is owned and operated by the Douglas Manor Association,

POPULATION: 15,340.

AREA: 1.9 square miles.

MEDIAN HOUSEHOLD INCOME: $68,200.

MEDIAN PRICE OF SINGLE-FAMILY HOUSE: $350,000.

TAXES ON A MEDIAN-PRICED HOUSE: $2,500.

MIDRANGE RENT FOR A ONE-BEDROOM APARTMENT: $700.

DISTANCE FROM MIDTOWN MANHATTAN: 9.5 miles.

RUSH-HOUR TRAVEL TO MIDTOWN: 30 minutes on the Long Island Rail Road, $6 one way, $117 monthly; 45 minutes on the Queens Surface express bus, $3 one way.

CODES: Area, 718; ZIP, 11362 and 11363.

but that is also open to nonmembers depending on space availability.

The association is made up of Douglas Manor homeowners. It owns and maintains a private waterfront greenbelt including a park, as well as the marina.

Douglaston is a true neighborhood, said Bernard Haber, the chairman of Community Board 11. "You feel you are part of a community, much more so than any other place I've ever lived in," he said.

The 85-year-old Community Church of Douglaston is the unofficial neighborhood town hall, offering meeting space and a variety of cultural and social programs.

The Zion Episcopal Church, rebuilt in 1925 after a fire destroyed the original 1830 structure, also provides space for activities.

Another neighborhood house of worship is the Roman Catholic St. Anastasia Church, built in 1928. Tuition for children in its prekindergarten-through-eighth-grade school is $215 a month.

Douglaston's public elementary schools are P.S. 98, which has 297 pupils, and P.S. 221, which has 796 children in attendance. Louis Pasteur Junior High School, covering grades 6 through 9, has an enrollment of 1,200. From there, students may go on to Benjamin N. Cardozo High School in neighboring Bayside, which has 4,000 students.

"All our schools are in the top 10 in the city, and Cardozo, into which we feed, has an outstanding reputation," said Stanley Weber, deputy superintendent of District 26.

At P.S. 98, 89 percent of the pupils score at or above grade level in reading, and 97 percent score at or above grade level in math. Scores at P.S. 221 are 90 percent and 98 percent, respectively, and at Louis Pasteur Junior High, 84 percent and 89 percent, respectively. Typically, 98 percent of Cardozo graduates go on to higher education.

There are programs for the gifted and talented along with art, music, and dance programs at all grade levels and special law and science courses in the junior and senior high schools. Advanced placement courses are taken by about a third of the juniors and seniors at Cardozo.

Douglaston's different sections are as varied as its housing prices. Douglas Manor, founded in 1906, is the community's oldest, and most expensive, neighborhood. It and neighboring Douglaston Hills lie north of Northern Boulevard, on a peninsula jutting into Little Neck Bay.

Along streets shaded by stately elm and oak—among them a white oak at 233 Arleigh Road that is over 600 years old—stand an eclectic mix of about 800 turn-of-the-century houses. Of these, 615 now form the Douglaston Historic District, recently designated by the city's Landmarks Preservation Commission.

Prices in Douglas Manor start at about $425,000 for a two- to three-bedroom dwelling "with lots of charm," and rise to $1 million for mansions, said Nina Kowalsky, a broker with Bryce Rea Associates in Little Neck.

In Douglaston Park south of Northern Boulevard, detached houses built about 60 years ago sell for $320,000 to $450,000, she said. South of the Long Island Expressway, there are about 400 condominiums in town house–style buildings. Older one- to three-bedroom units sell for $100,000 to $185,000, said Carolyn Meenan, Mrs. Kowalsky's colleague. New two- to three-bedroom units under construction in a 213-unit development called Oak Park are priced from $215,000 to $415,000.

There are about 1,000 co-op units in Douglaston, said Ms. Meenan, most of them ranging from $35,000 for a one-bedroom unit to $85,000 for three bedrooms. But co-ops in high-rise buildings like Wellesly Gardens on Douglaston Parkway north of Northern Boulevard typically start at $125,000 for a one-bedroom and move up to $230,000 for three bedrooms. Typical rents are $750 for one-bedroom apartments in the 300 rental units.

Early Dutch settlers, like the Matinecock Indians before them, were drawn to the area by the rich land and abundant fishing. Farms gave way to estates in the 19th century. In 1835, George Douglas purchased the 1819 Van Zandt manor and 120 acres on the peninsula. When his son, William, donated an outbuilding in 1866 to what was then the North Shore Railroad for use as a train station, the line called its new stop Douglaston and the name stuck.

The former Douglas manor on West Drive and Manor Road, now much enlarged, has become the Douglaston Club, a private club with tennis and a pool.

Beginning in 1906, Douglas Manor was developed as a suburban community for the well-to-do with prominent architects of the day designing many of the houses.

Its designation on June 24, 1997, as a historic district was the culmination of an eight-year effort by residents concerned over the demolition or modernizing of distinguished houses by developers and individuals.

"This is such a special place because the planning that happened here 90 years ago truly shaped the community that followed in a very positive way," said Kevin F. Wolfe, president of the Douglaston–Little Neck Historical Society, which was founded in 1989 to advocate landmarking.

Mr. Wolfe, who is both an architect and a landscape architect, with offices in Manhattan, spearheaded efforts to win the Historic District designation for what he described as an important example of an early-20th-century planned suburb.

"The most extraordinary thing that happened here from a planning standpoint was to make the mile-long waterfront something the home-owners own in common," he said. That foresight has provided spectacular views of the Throgs Neck Bridge and the Bronx from Shore Road.

Mr. Wolfe said his favorite houses in the Manor include an Arts and Crafts–style dwelling at 1114 Shore Road designed by J. Sarsfield Kennedy, built in 1907, and 1102 Shore Road, designed by Lionel Moses and built in 1916. A McKim, Mead & White house at 4 Ardsley Road—recently for sale for $795,000—was built in 1919.

Douglaston has mall shopping at the 344,300-square-foot Douglaston Plaza on the Long Island Expressway and the Cross Island Parkway with a Stern's department store and a Waldbaum's supermarket. A shopping enclave on a strip on Douglaston Parkway north of Northern Boulevard includes a wine store, flower shop, hardware store, deli, and an art gallery.

Neighborhood restaurants include Il Toscano, featuring northern Italian food. Next door is F. Scott's, which has American cuisine and provides entertainment, including jazz, on Friday nights and weekends.

The Douglaston Manor restaurant, at 63-20 Commonwealth Boulevard, is part of the city-owned Douglaston Golf Course. The dining room overlooks the 104-acre golf course with the Manhattan skyline as a backdrop.

Douglaston residents say they must be ever vigilant to preserve their special community. Recently, they were fighting a plan to expand the Long Island Expressway, and a proposal by a developer to build an eight-story apartment building at 43-10 Douglaston Parkway on land zoned for single-family houses.

Past victories included saving privately owned wetlands rimming the Douglas Manor peninsula from development by getting the city to condemn them and create Udalls Cove Park. "This community is one of the most ardent ecological supporters that we have," said Marc A. Matsil, chief of the Natural Resources Group at the city's Department of Parks.

These causes are part of living in Douglaston, said Julia Schoeck, a resident for 36 years and a community activist.

"People who move here grow to love it," she said. "They appreciate what is here and the effort of the people who came before them to make it nice."

FOREST HILLS GARDENS

An "English village" where Tudors reign

BY JOHN RATHER

With its air of medieval mystery, Station Square in Forest Hills Gardens seems more like something out of a dream than the gateway to the most exclusive neighborhood in Queens. The startling Bavarian tower, steeply pitched red-tile roofs, sweeping arcade, and brick-paved plaza create a public space that has drawn visitors since the early 1900s, when the square, designed with Tudor touches by the architect Grosvenor Atterbury and Frederick Law Olmsted, Jr., the landscape architect, was commissioned by the Russell Sage Foundation as the centerpiece of a model suburb.

Forest Hills Gardens has been inhabited from the beginning by discerning buyers of moderate to ample means. It is one of the country's oldest planned communities and the leading American contribution to the Garden Cities movement. The turn-of-the-century movement, inspired by the English visionary Ebenezer Howard, was a humanist reaction to the Industrial Revolution that recoiled from the spread of grid-block tenements in an era when New York City was emerging as a global center. Adherents sought to bring country living to the city while open land still remained. People living in the 175 acres of Forest Hills Gardens are still the beneficiaries.

From Station Square, where the Long Island Rail Road's architecturally compatible Forest Hills station forms one side, curving streets lined by towering trees sweep past parkside row houses and on to elegant, substantial Tudor and Georgian homes painstakingly sited on small lots. Streetlights resembling old English ornamental lanterns add to the English village atmosphere the founders intended. The Village Green and two small parks, Hawthorne and Olivia, offer open space and relaxation to residents.

A motif of towers, Tudor half-timbers, extensive brickwork, red-tile roofs, prominent chimneys, and off-white stucco walls is maintained throughout. Indeed, exterior changes must be approved by the Forest

POPULATION: 3,588.

AREA: 175 acres.

MEDIAN HOUSEHOLD INCOME: $79,551.

MEDIAN PRICE OF A ONE-FAMILY HOUSE: $600,000.

TAXES ON A MEDIAN-PRICED HOUSE: $4,000.

MEDIAN PRICE OF A TWO-BEDROOM CO-OP: $150,000.

DISTANCE FROM MIDTOWN MANHATTAN: 9 miles.

RUSH-HOUR TRAVEL TO MIDTOWN: 14 minutes on the Long Island Rail Road, $4.75 one way, $103 monthly; 26 minutes on the E, F, R, or G subway trains; 45 minutes on the QM12 express bus, $4 one way.

CODES: Area, 718; ZIP, 11375.

Hills Gardens Corporation, a property owners' association formed in 1923 to uphold standards set by Atterbury, who designed many of the early homes in the eclectic Arts and Crafts style popular in the early 20th century, and Olmsted, the son of the landscape architect who designed Central Park.

Neill E. Parker, the former chairman of the corporation's architecture committee, said the high quality of the original design and the corporation's vigilance in preserving it was at the heart of the Gardens' enduring appeal. Robert M. Hof, a partner with his wife, Susanna, in Terrace Realty on Station Square, said the rules boosted values. "People understand that their property value has remained strong because of the iron-clad covenants and restrictions," Mr. Hof said.

Property owners pay annual fees to the corporation to cover such things as maintenance of local streets, which are private. Nonresidents who park in the Gardens may have their cars immobilized by a wheel-locking clamp applied by crews on patrol 24 hours a day. The practice, called booting, was upheld by the courts several years ago. It costs $125 to have the boot removed.

Susanna Hof said most houses ranged in price from $400,000 to $900,000, and sometimes higher. Mrs. Hof said prices were rising in a very strong market at the end of 1997. She estimated the median price was about $600,000. In addition to median city taxes of about $4,000—but ranging from $2,000 to over $5,000—owners pay from $200 to over $2,000 annually to the corporation, depending on property size.

Realtors said the Gardens had long held a reputation as a highly prestigious area. They said it has become more ethnically diverse in recent years. "It's the most affluent area in all of Queens," said Sarah C. Jones of Sarah Jones Realty, also located at Station Square. Mrs. Jones said lower-priced houses were selling within one to two days.

Vacancies are rare at the Leslie, the Gardens' only rent-stabilized apartment building. "You need to know the pope or the rabbi to get in," said Mrs. Jones. The 96-unit apartment house, built in the '40s, is owned by the Helmsley management interests.

Apartment houses on Station Square and along Burns Avenue were converted to co-ops some years ago. A two-bedroom, two-bath apartment with terraces and working fireplaces at the Inn Apartments will sell for $250,000 to $290,000.

Forest Hills Gardens is in a part of Queens once called Whitepot, a name wedded to a yarn about 17th-century English settlers buying the land from Indians for three white clay pots. Some historians say the name is a corruption of Whiteput, with "put" meaning a pit or a hollow in Dutch.

In 1906, the Cord Meyer Development Company bought six farms covering 600 acres in what was called the Hopedale area. Mr. Meyer coined the name Forest Hills in deference to adjacent Forest Park and because the land was higher than surrounding areas. In the same year, the financier and industrialist Russell Sage, a legendary penny-pincher in private life, died at the age of 89, leaving $90 million to his wife, Margaret Olivia Slocum Sage. Mrs. Sage founded the Russell Sage Foundation, which in 1909 bought land from Cord Meyer where Forest Hills Gardens was to be built on a profit-making basis for people of moderate wealth and according to Garden Cities principles.

The early rural atmosphere changed in the '20s, when the Gardens' popularity brought a rush of new houses. Despite the pace, they were clearly regulated by the community corporation. In 1913, the West Side Tennis Club arrived from Manhattan. The club and its 43 courts remain, but the last of the major tennis tournaments departed in 1977, when crowds and traffic outgrew the club's historic stadium and the U.S. Open moved to Flushing.

The gym and pool at the Gardens Community House, which has a day-care center, is open to all neighborhood residents.

The Church in the Gardens, a nondenominational Christian church designed by Atterbury, was a gift from Mrs. Sage, whose given and maiden names were adopted as street names. St. Luke's Episcopal Church and the First Church of Christ, Scientist are also in the Gardens. Synagogues and Catholic and Protestant churches are nearby in Forest Hills and Kew Gardens.

P.S. 101, also known as the School in the Gardens, has 600 students in grades K–6. Many walk to classes, an advantage of a place designed for pedestrians. Built in 1927, the school adheres to architectural standards set by the Sage Foundation, which constructed it for the city. A four-story brick tower with a clay tile roof, copper leaders and gutters, and a spiral staircase rises above the three-story brick building. Antique, 1920s-style bronze chandeliers with Tiffany glass illuminate the auditorium. Light streams through windows on all four sides of the oversize gymnasium. "It is an unbelievable building," said the principal, Kenneth G. Joseph, who said the school was regularly in the top 10 for city schools in test results on standardized tests. "It sets a tone and gives a sense of history and stability."

Russell Sage Junior High School in Forest Hills, where 1,400 students are enrolled in grades 7 through 9, is regularly among the top 10 city schools for scores on standardized tests. It offers accelerated programs in science and math. The 4,200-student Hillcrest High School in Jamaica, the zoned school for Forest Hills Gardens, has an honors premedical science program. About 94 percent of the school's graduates have gone on to higher education in recent years, said the principal, Stephen M. Duch. Mr. Duch said that Hillcrest's school-within-a-school programs included the School of Entrepreneurship, the School of Law and Community Action, and the Math-Science Research Institute.

At Forest Hills High School, a law and humanities program emphasizes social studies, English, and law. Judges and lawyers address classes. The school, designed for 2,100 students but now enrolling 3,500, operates on an 11-period day because of overcrowding. More than 90 percent of its graduates go on to higher education.

A commercial area on Austin Street, just beyond the Continental Avenue railroad overpass, brings shopping near but keeps it out of sight. The area is filled with specialty shops, restaurants, movie theaters, and a small supermarket. If for the view alone, the best coffee in the Gardens is found at Lucien's, a gourmet restaurant with two small outside tables set out on Station Square during warmer months. With its sweeping view of Station Square's cobbled commons and surrounding fairy-tale English village buildings, there cannot be another view like the one from these tables in all New York.

Village residents strive to maintain the square. Driven to action by what they called "the obvious and severe signs of deterioration around the station," a band of Gardens residents formed a group called Friends of Station Square a few years ago to polish this architectural gem. With volunteers and financial support from other residents and businesses, the group planted shrubs and flowers around the square, among other projects. The group's graffiti busters pounce on graffiti almost before it dries. Members also kept up the pressure for a long-planned Long Island Rail Road project to repair sections of the station wall that began to collapse in 1990, forcing the closing of one stairway. Repair work was finally begun in 1997. The 83-year-old, Tudor-style station, designed as an integral part of Station Square, was paid for in part by the Russell Sage Foundation.

Another project restored the clock in the Forest Hills Inn tower. The clock's feathery chimes add a poignant feeling to the square.

JAMAICA ESTATES

An enclave that treasures its trees

BY DIANA SHAMAN

The first thing that strikes a visitor to the enclave in eastern Queens that is Jamaica Estates is its hilly streets lined by huge oak, maple, elm, and chestnut trees. The Jamaica Estates Company, which developed the community's 503 acres at the turn of the century, laid out lots to preserve existing trees. Some are now more than 200 years old.

The neighborhood's eclectic housing offers something to suit almost every taste, if the buyer can afford it. Next to a slate-roofed 90-year-old Tudor there may be a modern ranch or split-level built in the 1960s, and clapboard Colonials rub shoulders with brick Georgian-style mansions.

But fine schools, convenient transportation, reasonable taxes, and a strong sense of community cemented by an active homeowners association have created a strong demand and a shortage of houses on the market.

"Our homes are beautifully kept, our lawns are manicured, and we have lots of flowers," said Leslie Weinberg, whose husband, Barry, is chairman of the board of the Jamaica Estates Association, the homeowners group.

The predominant housing stock is detached one-family dwellings, though some rental and co-op apartment houses can be found along the southern edge of the community on Wexford Terrace and Highland Avenue. A one-bedroom apartment typically rents for a $750 a month, and one-bedroom co-ops starting at $21,000 are available.

House prices start at around $275,000 for a three-bedroom Colonial or Tudor on a 40- by 100-foot lot, and can exceed $1 million for an unusual property on a large lot. The median price for homes sold in 1997 and early 1998 was $290,000, according to figures supplied by Comps Inc. of Bay Shore, with median property taxes about $2,400.

POPULATION: 12,782.

AREA: 1 square mile.

MEDIAN HOUSEHOLD INCOME: $59,904.

MEDIAN PRICE OF SINGLE-FAMILY HOUSE: $290,000.

TAXES ON A MEDIAN-PRICED HOUSE: $2,400.

MIDRANGE RENT FOR A ONE-BEDROOM APARTMENT: $750.

DISTANCE FROM MIDTOWN MANHATTAN: 12 miles.

RUSH-HOUR TRAVEL TO MIDTOWN: 35 minutes on the F Train; 60 minutes on the express bus, $3 one way.

CODES: Area, 718; ZIP, 11432.

"Property is very important," said Ellen Katz, a broker with ERA United Realty in Bayside. "The more property, the higher the price." One of her listings in late 1997 was a six-bedroom, 60-year-old brick Colonial on a 50- by 218-foot lot with an asking price of $599,000. But another, a four-bedroom center-hall brick Colonial with a very small backyard, was priced at only $399,000. "The house is worth it, but because of the property, people don't want it," Ms. Katz said.

One of the neighborhood's oldest and most unusual houses—built in 1902 and known as Hilltop—was sold in the third quarter of 1997 for $675,000 through Miriam Sand, an associate broker with First Choice Real Estate in Fresh Meadows. The eight-bedroom residence in many ways exemplifies the quirky nature of the community's homes. The property, which borders the Grand Central Parkway service road, is a full acre. The house can be entered on Aberdeen Road, but a second entrance on the service road requires a 40-step climb up a stone staircase. The original owners were French and English, so the front part of the house was built in a Tudor style, and the rear is French Provincial, said Gerald A. Heard, the recent seller, who with his wife, Simone, had lived in the house for 30 years.

Some of the finest examples of larger houses can be found along Midland Parkway, where Donald J. Trump and his four siblings were raised. Mr. Trump's father, Fred, a developer whose activities in Queens included several apartment houses in Jamaica Estates, and his wife, Mary, still live in the large Colonial that has been the family home for over 50 years.

The Jamaica Estates Association keeps a vigilant eye on maintaining the neighborhood ambience. It is, for example, constantly on the lookout for attempts by some homeowners to create illegal apartments in their single-family houses or to otherwise violate building and zoning codes. "We have a very active zoning committee that watches out for this," said Mark J. Lefkof, area chairman for Community Board 8, and the immediate past president of the Jamaica Estates Association, which was established in 1929. "We are very, very adamant that the building codes here be maintained in order to preserve the unique characteristics of this community."

The association subscribes to an armed security service that answers emergency calls from those members who pay dues to support it. Subscribing to the patrol is voluntary, but about half the association's 1,800 members pay the $175 a year fee in addition to the $25 annual dues. Mr. Lefkof said the patrol had been started a decade ago in response to the rash of burglaries. Now, he added, there is "less crime in Jamaica Estates than in many other neighborhoods of the city."

In a 1910 brochure, now at the Queens Historical Society in Flushing, the original developer, the Jamaica Estates Company of Manhattan, noted that "Jamaica Estates is the same distance from Herald Square that Columbia University is from City Hall," and that it could be reached in "an average of 30 minutes." Lot prices started at $2,050 with a liberal discount for cash. A gatehouse built by the developers on Midland Parkway at Hillside Avenue still exists. Inside it is a World War II memorial to local servicemen.

Several of the development company's officers built their own houses in the new community. They included Michael J. Degnon, an engineer who helped design the first New York City subway system, which began operations in 1903. His 12-acre property, which covered a full block between Edgerton Boulevard and Midland Parkway, was purchased in 1925 by the Roman Catholic Passionist monks and became the site of the Passionist Monastery, the Bishop Molloy Retreat House, and the Immaculate Conception Church and School. The monastery was completed in 1927 and the church in 1962.

Prominent among the community's other houses of worship is the Hillcrest Jewish Center on Union Turnpike between Kent Street and Chevy Chase. Its Conservative temple has a 500-seat sanctuary. The center, which has a pool and a gym, offers programs for the young and old, and runs a children's day care center, a Hebrew school, and a summer camp.

One of the two public elementary schools serving the neighborhood, the 440-pupil P.S. 178 on Radnor Road in Hollis, has consistently ranked among the top 10 of the city's elementary schools, with over 95 percent of the children scoring at or above grade level in math and reading. "Our children spend most of their time on very challenging academic material," said Joan Weingarten, the principal. A program for learning-disabled children is also offered.

The other elementary school is P.S. 131 on 172d Street at 84th Avenue in Jamaica Hills, where 64.7 percent of children read at or above grade level, and 80 percent were at or above grade level in math scores.

Children attend seventh through ninth grade at Junior High School 216 in Flushing, which has been designated a magnet school for environmental sciences.

Many of its graduates go to the city's elite high schools, where entrance is by highly competitive examination, said the principal, Frank Schimmel. Others attend Jamaica High School, where special programs include courses in law and finance. In June 1996, 81 percent of Jamaica High's graduates went on to higher education.

The community's private schools include the suburban campus of the United Nations International School in Manhattan. Situated since 1982 at 173-53 Croydon Road, the school has 230 pupils in kindergarten through grade 8. Tuition ranges from $10,500 to $11,000 a year. The Immaculate Conception School at 179-14 Dalny Road—a Roman Catholic school but open to all—has 420 pupils in prekindergarten through grade 8. Tuition ranges from $2,350 for parishioners to $3,125 for nonparishioners. The Mary Louis Academy at 176-21 Wexford Terrace, a college preparatory school for girls that is run by the Roman Catholic Sisters of St. Joseph in Brentwood, has 950 students in grades 9 through 12; tuition is $4,600 a year.

Stores and restaurants along Union Turnpike, the neighborhood shopping avenue, include Vogue & Vintage at Grandma's Attic, which sells antique and contemporary jewelry as well as gifts; shoe stores; boutiques; a baby shop; and various service establishments. A Rite Aid pharmacy recently replaced the Utopia movie theater. For snacks or complete meals, there is the Surrey Kosher Delicatessen & Restaurant, which first opened in 1948, and Rogers Luncheonette, which specializes in salt-free and health-food dishes.

Six blocks east of the neighborhood is the 325-acre Cunningham Park. Along with many nature trails, it has 20 tennis courts, two soccer fields, 27 ball fields, and two boccie courts. Free summer concerts by the New York Philharmonic and the Metropolitan Opera are held on the main lawn bordering 193d Street and Union Turnpike.

"Jamaica Estates was a terrific place to grow up in," said Donald Trump, reminiscing about his old neighborhood. "It was very serene and very beautiful and it had a great feeling of safety and security. And yet it was close to the hub, giving me a good perspective of New York and what New York is all about."

RICHMOND HILL

Working-class, with a touch of nostalgia

BY JOYCE COHEN

In one little pocket of Richmond Hill lie some of the largest, loveliest houses in all of Queens. It is no surprise, then, that the Queens Historical Society chose Richmond Hill to inaugurate its Queensmark program, which recognizes buildings of architectural merit. Most of the dozen designated buildings are homes in the Victorian style. With so many storybook details—balconies, columns, stained glass, even turrets—"this looks more like a neighborhood from the past than most of the other communities in Queens," said Stanley Cogan, president of the Queens Historical Society, which started Queensmark in the fall of 1996. "It has managed to retain a very special nostalgic flavor that to me must be preserved," he added.

The Queensmark buildings are scattered throughout Richmond Hill North, the wedge south of Forest Park and north of Jamaica Avenue. Jahn's Old-Fashioned Ice Cream Parlour, established a century ago, remains near the triangle where Jamaica, Myrtle, and Hillside Avenues meet. Its next-door neighbor, the former RKO Keith movie house, is now a bingo hall. Across the intersection lies another area landmark, the Triangle Hofbrau, which at various times since its 1870 opening has been a hotel and a restaurant but is currently closed. Even the Long Island Rail Road trestle that slices through the neighborhood (it is for a little-used spur line) is a graceful relic, with its long row of slender arches.

Not all of Richmond Hill is so elaborate. The streets are a hodgepodge of houses, with wood-frame homes adjacent to boxy brick apartment buildings, and rows of attached dwellings facing freestanding houses with big yards. Every now and again, a school or church appears. The houses in Richmond Hill South—a much larger area that stretches all the way south to Rockaway Boulevard and east to the Van Wyck

POPULATION: 105,578.

AREA: 3.6 square miles.

MEDIAN HOUSEHOLD INCOME: $49,232.

MEDIAN PRICE OF A SINGLE-FAMILY HOUSE: $160,000.

TAXES ON A MEDIAN-PRICED HOUSE: $1,000.

MIDRANGE RENT FOR A TWO-BEDROOM APARTMENT: $850.

DISTANCE FROM MIDTOWN MANHATTAN: 10 miles.

RUSH-HOUR TRAVEL TO MIDTOWN: 40 minutes on the J or Z train, 31 minutes on the E train, 47 minutes on the A train; 17 to 24 minutes on the Long Island Rail Road from Jamaica, $5.50 one way, $117 monthly.

CODES: Area, 718; ZIP, 11415, 11416, 11417, 11418, 11419, and 11420.

Expressway—tend to be much more modest than those north of Jamaica Avenue.

A two-family Victorian with a private driveway and garage might sell for $220,000 to $250,000, said Tony Novellino, a salesman at George A. Clark Realty on Jamaica Avenue in Richmond Hill North. A two-family Colonial with no driveway or garage could cost $170,000 to $180,000, he said. A private driveway is a major selling point. It could add about $20,000 to the cost of a home, said Alex Karan, of Alex Karan Real Estate on Liberty Avenue in Richmond Hill South. Otherwise, buyers must tolerate the inconvenience of a "party drive" shared with the neighbors.

"It's a big area for first-time home buyers because you can get a very good price and the turnover is very quick," said Mr. Karan. "People buy a home, save up a little bit, and move to a bigger home."

Richmond Hill is a solidly working-class area, with a long history as a haven for immigrants. One famous resident was Jacob Riis, the social reformer and author. In the early part of the century, residents were primarily of German, Irish, or Italian descent. Over the last two decades, Indian, Guyanese, and Indo-Caribbean immigrants have predominated. The neighborhood includes several Hindu and Sikh temples. Each March, the Indo-Caribbean community hosts a parade for Phagwah, a Hindu celebration of spring; in the fall is a smaller celebration known as Dipavali or Diwali, a festival of lights.

Richmond Hill is "rich in tradition, it's well integrated, it's intergenerational, and it's multicultural," said Mary Ann Carey, district manager of Community Board 9. "I think it's a wonderful place to live." The neighborhood, which has a population of around 105,000, has about 1,500 legal apartments, mostly in low- to midrise buildings. But its biggest ongoing problem is the illegal conversion of homes into multiple dwellings. People rent out finished basements, or divide houses into smaller apartments or rooms. And Richmond Hill's houses are so large that "in some of them, you can fit five families," said Ms. Carey.

The conversions, besides violating safety codes, strain the area's resources. For example, the 35,000-student Community School District 27, which includes most of Richmond Hill, has recently been growing by 500 or more students a year. In 1996–97, the district opened two new schools—P.S. 51 for prekindergarten through grade 1, and P.S. 65 for kindergarten through grade 6. The district hopes to have two additional elementary schools within the next five years, said Deputy Superintendent Kenneth Grover. There are gifted and talented programs at P.S. 51, P.S. 56, P.S. 62, and P.S. 100. There is an advanced computer program at P.S. 66. All are within Richmond Hill, which is also home to about a dozen parochial schools and yeshivas.

The 3,000-student Richmond Hill High School celebrated its 100th anniversary in the 1997–98 school year. The school, which specializes in business, is attacking its crowding problem with "end-to-end sessions." Juniors and seniors attend class in the morning, freshmen and sophomores in the afternoon. In 1997, 58 percent of the graduating class went on to four-year colleges, while 28 percent continued on to two-year colleges.

For recreation, there is thickly wooded, 538-acre Forest Park, one of the city's largest. An old clubhouse building, renovated in 1993 and christened Oak Ridge, includes park offices and exhibition space, and is home to the Queens Council on the Arts. The park's 1903 carousel, on the Woodhaven side of the park, was built by the master carver Daniel C. Muller and bought from a Lowell, Massachusetts, amusement park in 1972. It replaced the park's original carousel, which was destroyed by fire in 1966.

Richmond Hill has no movie houses. The closest are in Forest Hills and Ozone Park. There are several large supermarkets and the commercial strips, Jamaica Avenue and Liberty Avenue, are lined with mom-and-pop establishments that sell things more odd than essential; it's easier to find a police uniform or a Halloween costume than regular work clothes. Atlantic Avenue has pockets of strip malls, with just a few national retail stores. There is also the well-known Dallis Bros. Coffee & Teas at 102d Street, with its storefront renovated to look as it did in 1920, when Morris Dallis located his coffee-roasting business there.

Atlantic Avenue has prompted a considerable number of traffic complaints for several years, ever since it was reduced from six lanes to four, with left-turn lanes and a paved median. The median was so shallow that it tempted impatient motorists to drive there, and delivery people to park, maneuvers that will be countered by plans to raise the median by seven inches.

Neighborhood noise is another complaint. "People have celebrations in their homes, with double-parking and drinking in the street," said Margaret Finnerty, president of the Richmond Hill South Civic Association. "It causes a chain reaction of quality-of-life infractions. But the word is getting out that it won't be tolerated, so it is much calmer. We are making headway."

To promote local shopping, Ms. Finnerty's group is erecting signs along Liberty Avenue that say, "Liberty Avenue: The Ideal Shopping Experience." And a merchants' group, the Liberty Avenue Partnership, recently started an "Adopt-a-Basket" program to clean up the avenue. "We didn't have enough garbage pickup," said Ms. Finnerty. "A lot of people put their home garbage there. Garbage cans were overflowing so much that Liberty Avenue was a disgrace." Now, merchants maintain the garbage cans on their corners, emptying the cans and replacing the liners.

"This is a working community where people all care about each other," Ms. Finnerty said. "Everybody wants to make this a better place to live. It has really become the melting pot, this area. All the communities overlap together and the causes are all the same: If you don't have services, your neighbors don't have services. It's a close-knit neighborhood in terms of your community working together."

Community safety is promoted by a nighttime patrol of civilian volunteers organized by the Richmond Hill Block Association. The police warn people about car break-ins and thefts, noting that the area has a lot of thoroughfares, which offer thieves a quick escape.

Getting to Manhattan on public transportation can be time-consuming. The J and M trains run to the Wall Street area, with skip-stop service speeding the rush-hour trip. Still, it's a 40-minute ride. The A train, a local, runs along Liberty Avenue. To catch the E express or the Long Island Rail Road (up to a 24-minute ride), people must backtrack and head east to the Sutphin Boulevard station.

Richmond Hill was farmland until 1867, when it was bought by Albon P. Man, a lawyer, and Edward Richmond, a landscape architect. (It is unclear whether the area was named after Mr. Richmond or after the Richmond Hill area of London.) The neighborhood attracted wealthy businessmen from Manhattan, who built Victorian houses for $2,500 to $5,000.

Today, it's these homes that give Richmond Hill much of its character. "I was looking for a house that was old and historical," said Nancy Cataldi, who several years ago bought a three-story Victorian home that has since received a Queensmark plaque. "We hope more young people will come in to renovate and restore them. It's like an old-fashioned neighborhood. Neighbors look out for one another. People have nice attitudes here."

SUNNYSIDE

Suburbia and an architectural legacy, by subway from Manhattan

BY MAGGIE GARB

Valerie Moylan's 3-year-old daughter and a friend play in the greenery on the patio behind the two-story brick house, snapping the waxy leaves of an overgrown rose bush. When they tire of the patio, the girls march through the Moylan house and out the front door, which faces a lush, sun-dappled courtyard. "I grew up in an apartment on the Upper West Side and we never had all this," said Ms. Moylan, an artist who, with her husband, Christopher, recently bought a two-story brick house on 48th Street in the Sunnyside Gardens section of Queens. "It's wonderful for kids. There are roses growing on the patio, trees and grass just out the front door."

The planned community, which is designated a special preservation district by the Department of City Planning, was designed in the 1920s by a group of urban planners who sought to blend lush park space with urban living. Its 600 two-story row houses are clustered around landscaped courtyards.

The "Gardens," as it is often called, is a 77-acre enclave in the northern corner of Sunnyside, a community of one- and two-family homes and low-rise apartment buildings three miles east of the Queensboro Bridge. Rush-hour commute to midtown runs about 10 minutes on the No. 7 subway and about 25 minutes on the Q32 bus.

Developed largely during the '30s and '40s after the Gardens was built to house working-class families, Sunnyside has in recent years attracted a host of young professional families who wanted to remain near Manhattan but raise their children in a suburban setting. Over the last 15 years, as many of the older, longtime residents died or moved to warmer climates, the population has increased and its average age has dropped substantially.

POPULATION: 25,211.

AREA: 0.54 square mile.

MEDIAN HOUSEHOLD INCOME: $37,951.

MEDIAN PRICE OF A SINGLE-FAMILY HOUSE: $210,000.

TAXES ON A MEDIAN-PRICED HOUSE: $1,400.

MEDIAN PRICE OF A TWO-BEDROOM CO-OP: $65,000.

MIDRANGE RENT FOR A TWO-BEDROOM APARTMENT: $1,000.

DISTANCE FROM MIDTOWN MANHATTAN: 3 miles.

RUSH-HOUR TRAVEL TO MIDTOWN: 10 minutes on the No. 7 subway line; 25 minutes on the M32 bus.

CODES: Area, 718; ZIP, 11104.

In 1997, prices for one-family houses in Sunnyside Gardens, which are 17.5 feet wide and 28 feet deep, ranged from about $185,000 to $280,000, depending on how much previous owners had renovated, said Dorothy Morehead, of Dorothy Raymond Morehead Real Estate. Since rooms are small, many recent buyers have chosen to remove some interior walls, creating open living and dining areas on the first floor. Prices for fully renovated houses increased by about 5 percent in the mid-nineties.

Unrenovated two- and three-family houses run about $200,000 to $275,000, with fully renovated three-family houses going for as much as $400,000. In the late '80s, several three-family homes were converted to one-family, but conversions have slowed substantially in recent years.

Outside the Gardens, the row houses are slightly larger and often have attached garages. In 1997, a one-family house with a one-car garage sold for about $165,000 to $190,000, said Judy O'Rourke Gilpin, a broker for Welcome Home Real Estate. Prices for a two-family house with a two-car garage run from $220,000 to $245,000. Prices for homes outside Sunnyside Gardens increased only slightly in the mid-nineties.

Rents for a one-bedroom apartment in the Gardens run from $750 to $875. Rents increased substantially in the last few years as young couples found themselves priced out of Manhattan's rental market. Outside the Gardens, one-bedroom apartments can be found for as low as $400. Two- and three-bedroom apartments range from $850 to $1,200, but they are hard to find.

Sunnyside is a community of gardeners. The narrow one- and two-family homes have front gardens and rear yards. On almost any block in the neighborhood, a handful of front gardens are ablaze with color from early spring through August.

"We often talk about people who go to the Hamptons or the country every weekend," said Jonas Javna, a retired cantor who, with his wife, Ruth, a retired music teacher, has lived in Sunnyside Gardens for more than 30 years. "All we have to do is step out on our porch here. You can't imagine anything more quiet or beautiful than having a cup of coffee on the porch on a Sunday morning."

The neighborhood's suburban-style environment combined with proximity to Manhattan has made Sunnyside one of the fastest-growing communities in Queens. Parking is almost always available on side streets and, depending on traffic, the drive to midtown can be as short as 15 minutes. But in recent years, growing traffic problems, particularly on congested side streets, have become residents' most common complaint. "Traffic is the hottest issue here right now," said Ms. Morehead. "Nobody wants to move out, but with more and more businesses on the main streets, traffic on side streets has become a problem."

Sunnyside's population hit nearly 30,000 in 1990 and has been growing steadily since. Once largely Irish and Italian, the population has expanded into a rich blend that includes recent immigrants from Latin America, eastern Europe, Southeast Asia, Turkey, and the Middle East.

Along the community's commercial streets, Queens Boulevard and Greenpoint and Skillman Avenues, shops and restaurants reflect the ethnic mix. There is the Pyramid Bakery at the corner of 43d Street and 43d Avenue, which sells Turkish and Middle Eastern foods, including homemade baklava, sugary fig cookies, and frozen falafel. On Skillman Avenue is La Marjolaine, where those who are not worried about calories can find luscious French pastries. The Bliss Street Tavern has Irish folk music on weekend evenings, and the European soccer matches—even when it's not World Cup time—can always be found on the bar television. The neighborhood's first art gallery in at least 20 years, the International Art Gallery and Frames, opened on Skillman Avenue in 1997. In recent years, Indian, Korean, and Mexican restaurants have opened along Queens Boulevard.

Sunnyside children attend elementary school at either P.S. 150 at 40-01 43d Avenue or P.S. 199 at 39-20 48th Avenue. They generally continue at J.H.S. 125 at 46-02 47th Avenue, and then Long Island City High School at 28-01 41st Avenue. The schools are overcrowded, and recent standardized tests found relatively low reading scores, a reflection of the many pupils for whom English is a second language, said Gloria Guzman, the principal at P.S. 150, where the student population jumped from 760 in 1992 to nearly 1,000 in 1997. The school was recently expanded and now includes a computer and science lab. The school encourages parent involvement, sponsoring an English-as-a-second-language program for parents.

Children may also attend two K–8 Roman Catholic Schools, Queen of Angels in Sunnyside and St. Teresa's in neighboring Woodside.

Churches and community groups sponsor an array of programs for children and adults. St. Sebastian's Parish runs a community center that has an indoor pool, workout rooms, and after-school programs.

Sunnyside's crime rate is relatively low, but car thefts have been on the rise in recent years. The neighborhood lacks a first-run movie theater and most restaurants close relatively early. But residents say they feel comfortable taking the subway and walking home through the neighborhood after an evening out in Manhattan.

Originally settled by the Dutch, Sunnyside was a quiet farming community until the turn of the century, when the Pennsylvania Railroad Company began buying land for rail yards. When the IRT completed construction of a subway line through Sunnyside in 1918, working-class families seeking refuge from Manhattan's tenements flocked there.

The architects Clarence Stein and Henry Wright and the landscape architect Marjarie Cautley designed Sunnyside Gardens in the late '20s, seeking to provide low-cost and low-density housing for urban workers. The Gardens houses, which lie north of Queens Boulevard, are jointly owned and maintained by the homeowners. The community is considered one of the most successful planned communities in the United States. Its cohesive design was extolled by Lewis Mumford, the architecture critic and urban historian, who once lived in Sunnyside Gardens. When the Depression struck and homeowners were threatened with foreclosure, Sunnyside Gardens residents organized rent and mortgage strikes. With the prosperity of the 1940s, young couples arrived from Manhattan to raise their families, making the Gardens known, in the words of a newspaper article of the time, as "the maternity ward of Greenwich Village."

When Sunnyside and nearby Woodside were threatened by urban blight during the late '60s and by white flight as crime increased, neighborhood organizations such as Gateway Community Services were formed to combat crime and improve schools. In 1974, Sunnyside was designated a special planned community preservation district by the Department of City Planning.

The original corporation that built Sunnyside Gardens imposed 40-year easements over common areas, including regulations prohibiting most exterior alterations. The community's architectural unity was threatened when the easements expired in 1966: Some residents fenced in their yards; others built driveways or plastered over brick facades. Although a few homeowners continue to balk at the restrictions, the city planning designation effectively halted further changes to the community's original design.

Despite its changes, Sunnyside continues to house two and three generations of its original home buyers. Doris Gilbert moved from Manhattan to an apartment in the Gardens when the community was new. When she had twin sons, she and her husband, Isaac, bought a house facing a courtyard on 48th Street. Both her sons moved away for several years but returned to the Gardens to bring up their families. "I've been in this house close to 50 years," Ms. Gilbert said. "Once you live in Sunnyside, you might move out, but if you have a family, you'll probably move back again."

LIGHTHOUSE HILL

Ocean views and a taste of Tibet

BY JANICE FIORAVANTE

The beacon that gives Lighthouse Hill its name stands on an octagonal tower with a rusticated limestone base and has been guiding ships into New York Harber since 1912. At first, it was not powered by electricity, and horses climbed the hill to bring needed oil to light the beam. Lighthouse keepers had to work pumps to force the fuel up to keep the light burning, said Richard Dyrack, a member of Community Board 2 and a three-decade resident of Lighthouse Hill.

"The light has worked 24 hours a day every day since it opened," said Joseph Esposito, the current lighthouse keeper. "It's a major lighthouse for the Ambrose Channel in lower New York Bay."

The landmarked lighthouse once included a house for its keepers. "They lived in a two-family house next to the lighthouse," said Mr. Dyrack. His wife, Beverly, a broker for Neuhaus Realty of Egbertville, said the house, at 401 Lighthouse Avenue, has been renovated into a three-bedroom, one-family home. It is now occupied by Dr. Neil Nepola, his wife, Rose, and their two sons, Nico, 6, and Adam, 4. "It was institutional-looking with cement floors and walls," said Dr. Nepola, a family physician who moved in with his family in fall 1993 after renovating it into Georgian Colonial style.

Most of the houses in Lighthouse Hill are on one half-mile street, Lighthouse Avenue, at the summit of a hill that runs north-south. Others are on smaller streets nearby. "The neighborhood is removed from highways and surrounded by such special features as Historic Richmondtown at the bottom of the hill," added Dr. Nepola.

Renovating houses could be said to be one of the most popular pastimes on Lighthouse Hill. Mrs. Dyrack described almost every house as having once been renovated into an entirely different style. "In the last five

G A Z E T T E E R

POPULATION: 1,200.

AREA: 0.40 square mile.

MEDIAN HOUSEHOLD INCOME: $69,475.

MEDIAN PRICE OF A SINGLE-FAMILY HOUSE: $395,000.

TAXES ON A MEDIAN-PRICED HOUSE: $3,000.

DISTANCE FROM MIDTOWN MANHATTAN: 17 miles.

RUSH-HOUR TRAVEL TO MIDTOWN: Express bus to downtown, $4 one way, with free transfer to midtown, 1 hour 20 minutes; bus to ferry to N, R, 1, 9, 4, or 5 subway train, 1 hour 30 minutes.

CODES: Area, 718; ZIP, 10306.

years, there's been a tremendous amount of doubling or tripling in the size of homes," said Carl Neuhaus, a broker at Neuhaus Realty. Most of the renovations are of smaller ranches or Cape Cods on lots large enough to permit expansion into larger homes, sometimes after taking the house down to its foundation.

"Houses here are fairly expensive but 30 percent cheaper than those on Todt Hill, which has been considered prestigious for a longer time," Mr. Neuhaus said. Because the houses on Lighthouse Hill originally were more modest, prices were lower. "But lately, as people are adding onto them, property values are increasing," he added. The only multiunit dwelling is a three-family house at 41 Manor Court with two one-bedroom apartments and one studio. There are no co-ops or condominiums.

Among the unusual structures speckling Lighthouse Hill in the center of Staten Island is the only residence in New York City designed by Frank Lloyd Wright. Its hillside site offers spectacular views of the ocean and Sandy Hook, New Jersey. Catherine Cass and her late husband, William, co-president of a personnel agency, called the long, low, prefabricated building they moved into 38 years ago Crimson Beech for a copper beech tree on the property. The home was on the market in early 1998 for $849,000.

Brokers say prices of single-family, detached homes can be as low as $280,000 and range up to $1.2 million. There are a few existing ranches and Cape Cods for sale. But most residences are large customized homes, some on 100- by 100-foot sites. The median sale price in 1996 was $375,000; in the third quarter of 1997, it was $395,000. Price increases averaged 3.5 percent in the mid-nineties. "There's not a lot of turnover on the hill, although currently there's a generational shift that is putting some houses on the market," said Mrs. Dyrack, the broker, who added that annual taxes on a typical house valued at $350,000 would be just under $3,000.

The shift is bringing families with young children, but the community's population remains steady at about 1,200. Vinnie and Ellyn Amessé bought a two-bedroom ranch at 20 Manor Court for $250,000 in 1993 and

154 *If You're Thinking of Living In...*

converted it to a four-bedroom Colonial. The Amessés, who have two young daughters and own a commercial photography studio on Victory Boulevard, are native Staten Islanders who found a sense of community here. "A neighbor will come over and say, 'I've just made this, have some,' or, 'I've just come back from Jersey; here's some corn and berries for you,' " Mrs. Amessé said. "It's wonderful."

The excellent reputation of P.S. 23 was a factor in their decision to choose Lighthouse Hill. Christy Cugini, the District 31 schools superintendent, said pupils in the K–5, 600-pupil Public School 23 were in the upper 5 percent in reading and math scores in New York City. One of its teachers, Barbara Pistor, was among 15 nationwide winners of the Time Warner Cable Crystal Apple Teacher Awards for her use of CNN and C-Span in the classroom. "The school has computers in every classroom, as well as the library, which are networked to each other and to the Internet from two computer labs," said Anthony Polomene, District 31 deputy superintendent. He called the grades 6–8, 1,125-student I.S. 24 in Great Kills "a fine second step for students, as academically elite as P.S. 23," adding that it emphasized language skills and communications arts.

Lighthouse Hill is zoned for the 2,400-student Susan Wagner High School, where reading scores typically show about 70 percent of students reading at or above grade level and 85 percent of its graduates usually go on to higher education.

There are two religious schools in Richmondtown, at the bottom of the hill. St. Patrick's School has 600 students in kindergarten to eighth grade, with tuition of $1,300 for one child, $2,100 for two, and $2,550 for three or more. Rabbi Jacob Joseph School has 150 K–8 students, with tuition at about $4,500.

Among the landmarks on Lighthouse Hill is one of the few 19th-century Greek Revival masonry mansions to survive in New York. The David Latourette House, built in 1836, now serves as a clubhouse for the city's Latourette Park Golf Course. The park is part of the Greenbelt, abutting Lighthouse Hill to its north and west. The Greenbelt is 2,500 acres of forest, streams, and wetlands, of which Latourette Park is 511 acres, including the 125-acre golf course. The Greenbelt master plan calls for the Latourette House to become a restaurant and for a new clubhouse to be constructed. "We hope to evolve the Greenbelt into Staten Island's Central Park," said Thomas A. Paulo, Staten Island parks commissioner.

The Latourette estate is not alone in taking on a new role on the hill. The lighthouse sits on part of what was the Meissner estate. Among the earlier names for the hill were Meissner Hill and Richmond Hill. From the mid-1850s, the Meissner estate, a large Victorian house on 12 acres, graced the hill. Two brothers, Charles and Fred Meissner, were merchants on Beaver Street in lower Manhattan. Part of their property was sold to the government for the lighthouse in the early 1900s. The rest of the Meissner estate, as well as other acreage, was purchased by William Platt, a real estate developer, in the early 1900s. Today Meisner Avenue—minus an *s*—is the principal street leading up the hill from the north.

In the mid-1800s, the site of the Eger Health Care Center, a 378-bed nursing home on the hill, was a private girls' school. In the early 1900s, Chester H. Aldrich purchased the property and converted it to a convalescent home for boys between the ages of 12 and 20 that he operated from 1908 to 1924. The property was sold to the Eger Lutheran Home, an institution founded in Brooklyn by Carl Michael Eger to house Norwegian-American men and women 65 and older. The first residents moved in in 1926. Today, the Eger Home sits on 22 acres and serves people of all backgrounds.

Another landmark on the hillside is the Jacques Marchais Museum of Tibetan Art at 338 Lighthouse Avenue, the only museum dedicated to Tibetan art in the Western Hemisphere. It consists of two small stone buildings constructed in Himalayan architectural style to resemble a mountain monastery, as well as a garden.

The Pathmark Shopping Center in Richmondtown offers everyday items. For serious shopping, the Staten Island Mall is a five-minute drive away.

Lighthouse Hill is a designated natural district, so that any significant changes to the contours of the topography, including the downing of trees, requires approval by the Department of City Planning. Its rural character is attested to by the fact that a "three-foot-high" turkey was signed a couple of falls ago, according to Mr. Dyrack. "The neighborhood adopted her, feeding her until the woods got green enough for her to feed herself," he said. Raccoons, possum, and rabbits are seen regularly and at night the hooting of owls can be heard.

PORT RICHMOND

Eclectic housing, traditional diversity

BY JANICE FIORAVANTE

> Port Richmond is but a country village now.... A trolley runs
> along the shore and one runs up [Port] Richmond Ave.... Stand-
> ing in front of this building there are 18 houses in sight.

This excerpt from a note written by 19-year-old Edmund Joseph Nolan in
1904 was found in a citrate of magnesia bottle when the back wall of the
Port Richmond Library was torn down to expand the structure in 1938 as
a W.P.A. project. The letter was exhibited to commemorate the library's
90th year.

The description remains accurate regarding Port Richmond's location
on Staten Island, abutting the Kill van Kull on the island's north shore. But
today a visitor sees many more houses, several churches, a park, a school,
and a senior-housing center surrounding the library, and the Martin Luther
King Expressway off the Bayonne Bridge defining its western border.
Buses have replaced trolleys, but the village-square design is preserved.

And so is much of the housing stock. "More than 50 percent were built
prior to 1938," said Kathleen Bielsa, housing development coordinator of
the Northfield Community Local Development Corporation. Among the architectural styles represented are Italianate, Colonial, Victorian, Second
Empire, Gothic Revival, and urban row house. The corporation is helping
residents take their first steps toward defining some of the area as a historic district, meeting with the borough's Preservation League. The corporation's first forays into historic preservation were quite successful;
the senior residence is housed in a former public school building. The
reclamation of this 1891 building, which the board of education had abandoned and the city had condemned, began with its becoming a city landmark. The name of the 43-unit Parkside Senior Apartments refers to its

POPULATION: 11,775.

AREA: 0.66 square mile.

MEDIAN HOUSEHOLD INCOME: $50,610.

MEDIAN PRICE OF A SINGLE-FAMILY HOUSE: $159,000.

TAXES ON A MEDIAN-PRICED HOUSE: $1,000.

DISTANCE FROM MIDTOWN MANHATTAN: 18 miles.

RUSH-HOUR TRAVEL TO MIDTOWN: 40 minutes on the city express bus, $4 one way; 20 minutes on the Staten Island Rapid Transit to the ferry; ferry, 50 cents round-trip, 20 minutes, and the 1, 9, N, R, 4, or 5 subway line, 20 minutes.

CODES: Area, 718; ZIP, 10302.

proximity to the village square's Veterans Memorial Park. "I took a tour in the area [with officials from the New York City Department of Housing Preservation and Development], and they were amazed that every block has housing representing different eras from historical to recently built," Mrs. Bielsa said.

The community's commercial strip, Port Richmond Avenue, specializes in home improvement, with such stores as Antique Brass Works and Enjo Architectural Mill, as well as cabinetmakers and furniture, lumber, and home-decorating establishments. "These stores cater to personalized needs with customized products," said Michael Accornero, vice president of the Port Richmond Board of Trade and owner of Community Hardware.

This focus on serving merchandising niches is hard won for merchants here; before the Verrazano-Narrows Bridge or the Staten Island Mall were built, Port Richmond Avenue was considered the Fifth Avenue of Staten Island. The Staten Island Mall's location at the gateway of the island's South Shore signaled a shift in population. With housing developments rising in the middle and south end of Staten Island and the declining interest in downtown shopping avenues, Port Richmond saw stores move away or close. But the area came back with large strip centers, anchored by Pathmark and Waldbaum's supermarkets.

Residents refer to the stores along the southern boundary of Port Richmond as Port Richmond Center and Forest Avenue Shoppers' Town. Both centers are in the process of being refurbished with new signage, shrubs, lighting, and stores. There are many fast-food outlets to satisfy the busy shoppers in the strip centers. But for leisurely dining, perhaps the best-known restaurant is Denino's, serving Italian cusine. And in the summertime, Ralph's Famous Ices at Port Richmond Avenue and Catherine Street is a mecca for those wanting to beat the heat.

Convenient stores and lower house prices—about 20 percent less than the South Shore's mostly newer stock—have attracted younger families to the neighborhood. Rachel Gannon, who owns Rachel Gannon Realty, said young families from the South Shore were leaving town houses with no storage space and looking for detached houses with yards. In Port Richmond, "single-family detached homes predominate, with two-families and a few semidetached newer homes in spots," she added.

Single-family houses can cost from as low as $79,000 for a "fixer-upper," according to Mrs. Gannon, to as high as $225,000 for "a big Tudor." And new semidetached homes and town houses are being built within the community, she added.

Single-family houses recently listed or sold, said Patricia Turvey Dellomo, owner of Turvey Dellomo Associates, range from $130,000 to $185,000, with two-family houses at $150,000 to $190,000. Prices have increased by 5 percent in the mid-nineties. The median sale price in 1996 was $149,000; in the third quarter of 1997, it was $159,000.

These prices are attracting city employees like firefighters and sanitation workers. "They're in their price range," said Mr. Accornero, noting that a fireman and two sanitation workers and their families had recently moved to his block.

This is reversing the declines of the '60s, '70s, and '80s, which hit their nadir five to 10 years ago, when schools were shutting down because of a lack of students. Public School 20 abandoned its building for a new one. St. Mary's of the Assumption Roman Catholic School saw its population plummet from 268 in 1973 to 78 in 1988, and in 1989 the building was converted to an early childhood center for 3- and 4-year-olds. But St. Roch's Catholic School held on and still serves students from kindergarten to fifth grade.

Now grade schools have to cope with crowding. Cheryl Accornero, Michael's wife, is former president of the parents association for P.S. 21, which Justin, 9, attends. "When our daughter Amanda, who is now 12 and attending the Morris Magnet School for the Arts, I.S. 61, for journalism, was in kindergarten, P.S. 21's population was 250 and now it's 450," she said. The school added prefabricated buildings and made do with busing its second and third graders to the Michael Petrides School in Sunnyside, about 20 minutes from Port Richmond. "Justin was among the children who went—he loved it and we worried," she said with a laugh.

"But under normal circumstances all the children at our school walk to school—there's no busing—we want to keep kids close," Mrs. Accornero added.

Intermediate School 51, with 1,350 students, has two computer labs with 66 computers and two computers in the library for research. "We've put four computers in each of 10 classrooms and intend to do the same for every classroom as soon as the resources become available," said the principal, Arnold Raffone.

Port Richmond High School recently added a wing and renovated the rest of the school, said Robert Mathews, president of the school's alumni association and a former teacher who taught there for 30 years. The school opened in 1928. As part of the renovations, the school added a television production studio, robotics lab, and universal weight room. Typically, 90 percent of Port Richmond High's graduates go on to college.

"I'm a great believer in public education and I'm delighted that my children are growing up with Mexicans, Albanians, African-Americans, Asians, and Indians," Mrs. Accornero said. The ethnic diversity of the schools reflects that of the neighborhood. Newer immigrants have been attracted to the area by rentals in its older four- and five-story walk-ups as well as by cottage-style one-family homes.

The newcomers follow an earlier influx of Scandinavians who were drawn to the community as shipbuilders during World War I. By the early '30s, many shipyards were forced to close and some Scandinavians returned home. In the '30s, the neighborhood library, referred to locally as the Port Richmond League of Nations, added collections in Norwegian, German, Spanish, Polish, and Italian. In 1937, the *Directory of New York State Manufacturers* listed 34 medium and large concerns in the Port Richmond area. And by 1942, the shipyards were back, working 24-hour shifts, before their demise in the '50s.

The Scandinavian Lutheran Zion Church, which was built in 1921, was sold in 1966 to become the St. Phillip's Baptist Church, with a predominantly black congregation. The area's other houses of worship include Temple Emanu-el, built in 1907, and the Reformed Church, built by the Dutch in 1715, destroyed by fire during the Revolutionary War, and rebuilt in 1787. The current structure is its third, built in 1844. Its burial ground dates to 1704.

"This is an area that doesn't give up," said Joan Catalano, executive director of the development corporation. "There's lots of community spirit—it's a community working together."

Long Island

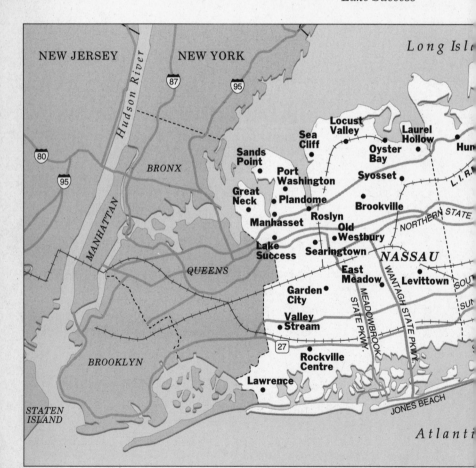

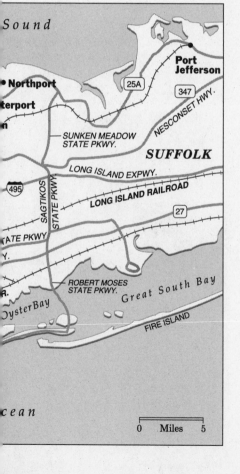

BROOKVILLE

Country tranquillity convenient to the city

BY VIVIEN KELLERMAN

In 1923, there were 22 estates in what is now the Village of Brookville. Many of them were broken up after World War II, but the area has retained its quiet elegance with zoning that bans commercial development and requires at least two acres for residential property.

Residents say that along with its tranquillity, Brookville also offers convenience, with abundant shopping nearby and access to all the major roads and to the Long Island Rail Road a few minutes away in Hicksville.

Prices for homes, from ranches to huge Georgian Colonials, range from $500,000 to several million dollars, said Faith Kanen, owner of Old Oak Realty in nearby East Norwich. Housing prices have climbed steadily throughout the 1990s, with a whopping 27 percent increase between 1996 and 1997, when the median price for a single-family house was $822,000, and median taxes were $14,091.

The 100-acre Uris estate near Route 107 is the only large parcel being developed in the village. In the late 1980s, Ms. Kanen said, the property was bought for $11 million by a developer who lost it to foreclosure. The property was auctioned off and some two-acre lots that went for $400,000 at the time fetched $600,000 only a few years later, she added. Many of the lots are now being built upon.

Stewart Senter, a developer who has built in Brookville for the last 18 years, said that the Uris property, now Broadhollow Estates, had been subdivided to accommodate 40 houses. His houses range in price from $1.5 million to $3 million and in size from 5,000 to 20,000 square feet, he said.

In addition to building new homes, his company has been renovating older homes in Brookville. People buy in Brookville because of its schools and because property is so valuable, he said.

Susan and Todd Katz chose Brookville after living in Rockville Centre

POPULATION: 3,779.

AREA: 4 square miles.

MEDIAN HOUSEHOLD INCOME: $145,755.

MEDIAN PRICE OF A SINGLE-FAMILY HOUSE: $822,000.

TAXES ON A MEDIAN-PRICED HOUSE: $14,091.

PUBLIC SCHOOL SPENDING PER PUPIL: Jericho, $16,506; Locust Valley, $14,385.

DISTANCE FROM MIDTOWN MANHATTAN: 25 miles.

RUSH-HOUR TRAVEL TO MIDTOWN: Seven minutes to Hicksville, then 40 minutes on the Long Island Rail Road, $7 one way, $154 monthly.

CODES: Area, 516; ZIP, 11545.

for 23 years. The couple, who have two grown sons, said they wanted a larger piece of property. In 1992, they found an 1,800-square-foot ranch on 2.6 rolling wooded acres. The house was in such bad condition, Mrs. Katz said, that they essentially paid for the land and tore the structure down. Three years of work with architects, builders, and decorators resulted in a 7,500-square-foot home that Mrs. Katz said had no defined rooms and a lot of open space.

Mr. Katz, a lawyer, works 10 minutes from the house. Mrs. Katz said her job had been building the house. "We just happened on Brookville," Mrs. Katz said. "But I'm glad we did. We have a wonderful house that sits on a hill, and when I drive down this road, I think I'm in the country."

Brookville residents are served by two school districts. The Jericho School District has three kindergarten-through-fifth-grade schools, one middle school, and one high school. With an enrollment of 2,295, it accounts for about 75 percent of Brookville's students and serves other small communities. The Locust Valley School District serves the rest of Brookville, along with residents of five other communities.

Henry Grishman, Jericho's superintendent of schools, said that because enrollment rose in the last several years and was expected to grow 5 percent annually until the turn of the century, the district reopened one of its buildings that had been leased for the last decade. This building, the Seaman Elementary School, serves Brookville students.

Mr. Grishman said that typically 97 percent of the district's high school graduates go to college. Moreover, at least one student a year during the 1990s has been a Westinghouse Science Competition semifinalist.

The district offers close to two dozen advanced placement courses, with about 87 percent of the high school population typically completing at least one such course each year during the mid-1990s.

Computer instruction begins in kindergarten, and every elementary school classroom has three computers. Once a week after school, hundreds of students participate in a cultural arts program taught by teachers and run by parent volunteers, Mr. Grishman said. The program provides a wide array of subjects, including art, dance, and cooking.

"We are a small school district and we spend a great deal of attention treating students individually, whether they're 4 or 18 years old," he said.

The Locust Valley School District, with a 1997 enrollment of 2,132, serves about a quarter of the students who live in the northeast area of the village. It has two schools for kindergarten through second grade, two schools for third through sixth grade, a middle school, and a high school.

Tom Mohen, who served as president of the district's board of education during the 1996–97 school year, said the district had a program for elementary students that brought local professionals into the classroom to introduce students to careers. Examples might be lawyers taking children to spend a day in court, a filmmaker helping a class to produce a film, or a travel agent helping youngsters plan a trip. In another program, students set up fund-raising projects or visit nursing homes.

In 1996, he said, the district developed a five-year plan to upgrade the computer system. The plan includes developing a districtwide web page and setting up e-mail for teachers and parents.

Mr. Mohen said that 90 percent of graduating classes typically go on to higher education and that during the mid-1990s, an average of 20 percent of the high school students took advanced placement courses.

The Long Island Lutheran Middle and High School, with an average enrollment of 500 students in grades 6 to 12 during the mid-1990s, is also in Brookville. The school is affiliated with 22 supporting congregations that underwrite some of the tuition costs. In 1997, tuition for students from those congregations ranged from $3,720 to $4,920. Tuition for others ranges from $4,820 to $6,070.

The 305-acre C. W. Post campus of Long Island University in the village has 46 buildings, among them five mansions on estates that once belonged to Marjorie Merriweather Post, heiress to the cereal company; J. N. Hill, a director of the Northern Pacific Rail Road; William Hutton, brother of E. F. Hutton; and Charles V. Hickox, a philanthropist. The campus, which was founded in 1954, enrolled some 4,572 undergraduates and 3,886 graduate students during the 1997–98 school year.

The Tilles Center for the Performing Arts, a 2,200-seat concert theater on the campus, offers jazz, rock, folk, orchestral, and chamber music, dance, and lectures by prominent figures. Recent performers at the Tilles Center have included Michael Feinstein, Carol Burnett, Marvin Hamlisch, and the stars of the Kirov Ballet.

Brookville has a four-acre bird sanctuary and a 16-acre nature park with horse trails, walking paths, and benches. Outdoor education programs for public school students are provided at a 20-acre property operated by the Nassau County Board of Cooperative Education adjacent to the nature park. The private 107-acre Tam O'Shanter Club, with an 18-hole golf course, is also within the community.

The village is patrolled by a 41-member police force shared by five other villages, each with its own police commissioner and deputy commissioner.

For shopping, the Broadway Mall in Hicksville is about seven minutes away, while the Miracle Mile in Manhasset is 12 minutes away. Residents also shop along Route 107 in adjoining Jericho.

The area was settled in the 17th and 18th centuries by English and Dutch farmers. In 1732, the Dutch built a church at what is now the intersection of Wheatley and Brookville Roads. There were many springs and a brook on the property and it is said that wolves gathered there to drink. Thus, the Dutch called it Wolver Hollow. Four different structures have been built at the site over the years. At present, the Brookville Reformed Church, dedicated in 1924, stands there.

By the early 1900s, the beauty of the area as well as the accessibility to New York City attracted wealthy city residents who bought farmland from the descendants of the Dutch and English farmers. Lavish mansions sprang up and the North Shore of Nassau County soon became known as the Gold Coast. Estates were owned by several Vanderbilts and Deering Howe, first mayor of the village. Some of the original mansions are still occupied.

In the 1930s, many of the estate owners joined to incorporate into villages to protect the two-acre zoning. Brookville was incorporated in 1931. Only 25 miles from Manhattan, the sparsely populated village has a population of only 4,000.

Lawrence Cohen, a former chief executive of a maker of health aids and now semiretired, said that the ambience of the wooded rural area had attracted him and his wife, Ilene, to Brookville 12 years ago. "A quiet residential environment of two-acres-plus and no congestion, it's a place where people have a great attachment to their community," he said.

CENTERPORT

By the sea, from cottages to estates

BY VIVIEN KELLERMAN

Beach lovers and boaters who want rural living with an easy commute to the city, a small and acclaimed school district, and an eclectic choice of neighborhoods that range from cottages on winding roads to magnificent waterfront estates and everything in between can find it in Centerport, a hamlet of 5,100 residents in the Town of Huntington.

Although real estate prices have not fully rebounded from the end of the 1980s, when a single-family house sold for a median price of $309,000, during the mid-1990s prices began to rise again. The median price for a single-family house increased from $240,000 in 1995 to $277,990, with median taxes of about $6,800, in 1997.

Andrea Brovetto, a broker with Coach Realty in Huntington, said prices had soared so high in the 1980s, it took some time for prices to level out. Between 1996 and 1997, however, the market became so hot that some houses received multiple offers, sometimes selling for more than the listing price.

Single-family houses in Centerport range from about $139,000 for two-bedroom cottages to millions of dollars for sprawling waterfront homes on several acres. Most homes, however, are in the mid to high $200,000's and are on parcels that range from fractions of an acre to an acre. Some have private neighborhood associations with beaches, while others have access to two town beaches, both in Centerport.

There are about 750 homes in the hilly Huntington Beach community. These are mostly small updated summer cottages on tiny lots. Many of these are on the water or have commanding views of the harbor. The Prospect area offers older, more traditional homes on larger property, some with water views. The hundred or so homes in the Sea Spray section are wide-line brick style and split-levels on well-kept lawns. The Little

POPULATION: 5,100.

AREA: 2.1 square miles.

MEDIAN HOUSEHOLD INCOME: $77,155.

MEDIAN PRICE OF A SINGLE-FAMILY HOUSE: $277,990.

TAXES ON A MEDIAN-PRICED HOUSE: $6,800.

PUBLIC SCHOOL SPENDING PER PUPIL: $11,302.

DISTANCE FROM MIDTOWN MANHATTAN: 37 miles.

RUSH-HOUR TRAVEL TO MIDTOWN: Five minutes to Greenlawn, then one hour five minutes on the Long Island Rail Road, $8.50 one way, $181 monthly.

CODES: Area, 516; ZIP, 11721.

Neck area near the Vanderbilt Museum is fancier, with plush lawns and bigger homes. South of Route 25A, property sizes increase and the area is more wooded, with homes set off the road.

Bull Calf Landing, built in the late 1980s, is a 12-unit condominium. The contemporary-style complex, with some units on the water, has a tennis court. Prices for two-bedroom units increased from $230,000 to $240,000 during the mid-1990s, while three-bedroom units with two baths and two half baths also rose about $10,000 to $299,000. Another 15-apartment condominium with prices starting at $300,000 on Route 25A was completed in the mid-1990s.

Huntington Town homeowners who obtain an annual permit can turn part of the main living area of their home into an apartment. Ms. Brovetto said that most of these were one-bedroom apartments renting for about $800 a month.

Vanderbilt Estates is a subdivision of 17 single-family homes of post-modern, brick Colonial, and Victorian styles on 26 acres directly across the road from the Vanderbilt Museum. Prices in 1997 ranged from $550,000 to more than $1 million.

In 1996, John and Gay Ioria bought a home in Vanderbilt Estates. The couple built their first home in Centerport when they were married in 1985, in part because it was near the Plainview school where Mr. Ioria teaches. Needing more room as their family expanded, the couple moved to nearby Huntington. As their children prepared to enter school, the couple decided to move back to Centerport. Mrs. Ioria, a stay-at-home mother, said the four-bedroom, 2½-bath farm Colonial on one acre cost about $500,000, and they were able to afford it, she added, because they made money each time they sold a house. "I think you get a lot for your money in Centerport," she said. "We looked around quite a bit before deciding to come back. Centerport had it all. But the number one reason is that we wanted the school district."

In the Harborfields Central School District, there is one kindergarten-through–grade 1 elementary school, one of grades 2 through 4, one 5-through-8 middle school, and a high school. In 1997, the district had an enrollment of 2,847 students from Centerport and nearby Greenlawn. Superintendent of Schools Cramer Harrington said that overall enrollment had increased about 15 percent in the last few years, with a whopping 40 percent increase in grades K–2 children. In 1997, to make more room, the district added grade 1 students to the kindergarten center, housed in a separate wing of the high school. Mr. Harrington said the district was doing a feasibility study to determine how it will accommodate the increases as the children move through the ranks.

The per-pupil expenditure of $11,302 in 1997 reflected small increases in the budget during the mid-1990s. But with state aid stagnant over the last several years, and the student population increasing dramatically, Mr. Harrington said increased costs will eventually fall to the taxpayer.

Unlike many other districts, Mr. Harrington said, Harborfields has a system that brings all kindergartners together, with elementary, middle, and high school students centralized in separate schools. "This is probably a more efficient use of buildings than in many school districts on Long Island," said Mr. Harrington, who has been a superintendent of several other Long Island districts. The centralized system, he said, allows easier regulation of class sizes. Teachers can plan their curriculums together and children stay together throughout their school years. The system, he added, saves the district hundreds of thousands of dollars each year.

Mr. Harrington said approximately 300 parent volunteers were involved in the elementary school. "Our parents really are partners in terms of the education of our students," he said. "And I think this is reflected in the graduates we produce," adding that 94 percent of the June graduating class typically go on to higher education.

Much of recreation in Centerport centers around the water. The town has two beaches open from Memorial Day weekend to Labor Day. Centerport Beach has an outdoor shower and picnic tables. Residents pay $15 a season. Senior Citizens Beach nearby and its beach house are reserved for residents over 60 at no cost.

Residents of the Huntington Beach community have the use of a private five-acre beach, boat ramp, and dock. Residents of this community belong to the Huntington Beach Association, which began in 1928 and provides recreational programs for youngsters and holds social events throughout the year. Annual dues range from $65 for a sustaining membership to $325 to moor a commercial boat. There are several other neighborhood associations, some with beaches. Private beaches allow for boat mooring, and Centerport residents can moor their boats in Northport Harbor. There are also two private marinas.

Centerport is the site of William K. Vanderbilt 2d's 43-acre Eagle's Nest estate, which opened to the public as a museum in 1950. The museum has nine historic structures, a collection of decorative and fine arts, a planetarium, and acres of landscaped grounds. The museum and planetarium are open all year. Fees are $8 for adults, $6 for students and seniors, and $4 for children under 12.

The Barn Museum on Fort Salonga Road is run by the Greenlawn-Centerport Historical Association. The museum, open Sundays from May to October from 1 to 4 P.M., contains a farm workshop, farm wagon, and tool exhibit. There is no entry fee. Also on the site and run by the the Historical Association is the Suydam Home, parts of which date to 1767. In the fall of 1997, the house was opened to the public on Sunday afternoons between 1 and 4 P.M. There is no fee, but donations are requested. The outside of the building and one wing have been fully restored. The association hopes to raise another $100,000 to complete restoration.

Except for two small strip centers, at each end of the community, there is little shopping in Centerport. Residents travel to Northport and Huntington, both less than 10 minutes away, for most major shopping.

In 1660, a Quaker, Thomas Fleet, came from England with his family and settled the west shore of Centerport Harbor. The east shore of the harbor was acquired and settled in the latter part of the 1700s by Phineas Sills, a Revolutionary War veteran who served in the first regiment of Minutemen of Suffolk County. In the 1700s and for most of the 1800s, Centerport was an important harbor where schooners carried grain to the mill and took away flour. Timber was also an important export from Centerport.

With the extension of the Long Island Rail Road into Greenlawn in 1868, Centerport changed from a working harbor to a vacation and recreational area. William Vanderbilt acquired the first 24 acres of his estate in 1910. The film star Mary Pickford lived in a house on Route 25A and Sergei Rachmaninoff, the Russian-born composer, began summering in Centerport in 1940, when he was 67.

The first major development was in 1928 when the Fleets, descendants of the original settler, and others sold land that was to become the Huntington Beach community. The first homes were mostly summer residences, but soon the Centerport area was developed for year-round living.

EAST MEADOW

An emphasis on community

BY VIVIEN KELLERMAN

Residents of East Meadow work hard for their community. Among their accomplishments have been the forming of a volunteer civilian patrol to keep crime at bay and the turning of an ordinary sump into a bird sanctuary. Some years ago, when it became apparent that there was not enough housing for elderly people with limited incomes, local groups helped create almost 1,000 units. "We never say, 'Not in our backyard,'" said Norma Gonsalves, president of the Council of East Meadow Community Organizations, a coalition of 34 local groups.

Indeed, with a Nassau County park, jail, medical facility, and children's shelter, plus federal military housing, all on East Meadow soil and all draining much-needed tax money from the local school district, residents could throw up their hands and say, "No more." Instead, Ms. Gonsalves said, East Meadow residents take pride in their community's low crime rate, abundant shopping as well as accessibility to major parkways, and a school district that keeps its tax rate down while providing excellent education. "We don't look at what we don't have," Ms. Gonsalves said. "We focus instead on what we do have. And what we have is a community that cares."

Raymond McCloat, superintendent of the East Meadow School District, said it had controlled spending, which worked out to $10,755 per pupil in 1996–97, by keeping administrative costs to a minimum. "We have to keep the per-pupil expenditure down in order to allow us to continue our programs," he said. Among those programs are courses in advanced science research, preengineering, advanced computer language, and law, the latter beginning in grade 9 and ending with an internship in a legal office or government-related community service in the high school. A program for the gifted and talented begins in grade 3 and continues with

POPULATION: 38,689.

AREA: 6.3 square miles.

MEDIAN HOUSEHOLD INCOME: $72,009.

MEDIAN PRICE OF A SINGLE-FAMILY HOUSE: $170,000.

TAXES ON A MEDIAN-PRICED HOUSE: $5,300.

PUBLIC SCHOOL SPENDING PER PUPIL: $10,755.

DISTANCE FROM MIDTOWN MANHATTAN: 25 miles.

RUSH-HOUR TRAVEL TO MIDTOWN: 10 minutes to Westbury or Merrick, then 43 minutes on the Long Island Rail Road, $7 one way, $154 monthly.

CODES: Area, 516: ZIP, 11554.

honors programs in middle and high school.

With an enrollment of 7,800, East Meadow is the largest public school district in Nassau County. It serves all of East Meadow and small parts of both Westbury and Levittown. It has five elementary schools for kindergarten through fifth grade, two middle schools, and one high school, which typically sends 87 percent of its graduates on to higher education.

At its peak in 1968, the district had 18,000 students. In the next two decades, enrollment declined, but it is rising once again. Since 1992, 500 students have been added to the district, with 700 more anticipated in the next five years.

Although over the years the district has closed three of its buildings and now leases one to the Board of Cooperative Educational Services, Dr. McCloat said he did not anticipate a problem. "There'll be a few bumps along the way," he said. "But we won't need to do major work."

A wide variety of housing is available in East Meadow. Richard Krug, manager of the community's Coldwell Banker Sammis Realty office, said that prices for single-family homes ranged from $130,000 to more than $300,000 for newer custom homes or those extensively renovated.

Rental apartments in East Meadow are scarce, with only 90 units in two buildings. Two-bedroom apartments rent for $750 a month, and three-bedroom units rent for $1,200.

In Meadowlanes Estates, an 87-unit, two- and three-bedroom town house co-op, prices for a two-bedroom are about $140,000, while three-bedroom units sell in the range of $180,000. There are also two condominiums with a total of 93 units. Prices range from $70,000 for a studio to $160,000 for a three-bedroom duplex with a basement and a garage.

Most of the rental and co-op apartments, nearly 1,000 units, have been reserved for those at least 62 years old. There are two co-op complexes for this age group, with a total of 678 units, with 102 more to be added at the Knolls on Salisbury Drive in 1998.

Maximum income guidelines for these units are $40,000 for a couple and $25,000 for a single. There are also 100 rental units subsidized by the Town of Hempstead. Maximum income levels for these apartments are $26,600 for a couple and $23,300 for a single.

After deciding to move out of their Queens Village home, Dr. Harold Claude and his wife, Rose, spent nine months looking for a house on Long Island. A friend recommended East Meadow, and the couple, with their three children—Harold Jr., 10, Larissa, 5, and Caroline, 3—searched the area. In late 1996, the family moved into a three-bedroom modified ranch across the street from a park. Dr. Claude, a pulmonary specialist, works in Manhattan, about a one-hour drive away. Mrs. Claude, 42, is a student in respiratory therapy at Malloy College in Rockville Centre, about a 15-minute drive away. In addition to good schools, Mrs. Claude said, the family liked East Meadow because it offered good shopping and neighborhoods safe for children.

For recreation for both children and adults, the community offers Senator Speno Memorial Park and Veterans Memorial Park, with ball fields, playgrounds, and a giant pool, available to families for $140 a season. The village is also the site of Nassau County's 930-acre Eisenhower Park, which is open year-round. Among that park's offerings are three 18-hole golf courses and several athletic fields for team sports like baseball, softball, football, soccer, rugby, lacrosse, field hockey, and cricket. There are also 16 tennis courts, three playgrounds, a lake, and a special activities center for the elderly. A 50-meter pool was scheduled to be opened in 1998, and the Harry Chapin Lakeside Theater offers free outdoor summer entertainment.

Shopping in East Meadow is spread out essentially along a seven-mile stretch of Hempstead Turnpike and along one mile of East Meadow Avenue. There are at least a dozen restaurants, several supermarkets, and the larger chain stores.

In 1655, Thomas Langdon reported to the Hempstead Town meeting that he had surveyed the East Meadow and found it suitable for grazing and watering cattle. He advised that efforts be made to exterminate the wild beasts that preyed on domestic animals and that cowherds be hired to care for the cattle. This was accomplished by 1658, and for the next 200 years, East Meadow, part of the Hempstead Plains, was essentially used as grazing land for cattle and sheep. Around 1850, a number of large estates and farms began to spring up in East Meadow, continuing until about 1915. The largest of these was the 2,500-acre farm of Sarah Ann and Peter Crosby Barnum.

The early 1920s saw the first real building boom in East Meadow, with real estate organizations bringing in busloads of city dwellers for all-day picnics to promote their properties. Once development began, there was no holding it back. On April 18, 1955, a record was set when three new 20-room elementary schools were opened simultaneously to 1,450 children—while painters and electricians continued to work around them.

The Hempstead town supervisor, Gregory Peterson, moved into East Meadow in 1950, when he was 5. He remembers new developments springing up among forests and farms. "We used to ride our bikes to the woods," he said. Except for a one-month stint in an apartment in Hempstead Village, Mr. Peterson has never left East Meadow. In 1971, after marrying Linda Karanfilian, a schoolteacher, the 31-year-old assistant district attorney decided to try his hand at politics, and after taking "every nickel we had from the wedding and all our savings," they bought a house "in the same neighborhood where I used to deliver newspapers when I was a kid," Mr. Peterson said.

The couple have lived there ever since, raising three daughters, who all went through the same school system as their father. Mr. Peterson's parents live a block away, while his brother and sister-in-law also live nearby. "I have really grown to appreciate East Meadow in my adult years," Mr. Peterson said. "It's like a fine wine. It gets a little better all the time."

GARDEN CITY

From "Stewart's Folly" to thriving suburb

BY VIVIEN KELLERMAN

In 1869, when Alexander Turney Stewart bought 9,000 acres of treeless land in what was then known as the Hempstead Plains, the acquisition was called Stewart's Folly. Undaunted, he brought in and planted trees, laid out wide streets, built a railroad to Bethpage—it later became part of the Long Island Rail Road—and began putting up hundreds of homes and a first-class hotel. He called his dream Garden City but did not live long enough to see it come to fruition.

Today, in the community he started, all the public schools have been declared excellent by the federal Department of Education, the residents have a choice of five L.I.R.R. stations from which to make a 40-minute commute to New York City, and the 21,515 residents have a shopping district known as the Fifth Avenue of Long Island.

"So many of the people I know graduated from my high school, went off to college, and then if possible, mortgaged themselves to the hilt to get back here," said Janet Downey, who returned to Garden City with her husband, Edward, a stock trader, and their children, William and Kevin, in 1993.

Mrs. Downey said she liked the variety of recreational programs the village offered for her children and the diversity of municipal services.

"There are always trucks going up and down the street, cleaning the road, trimming the trees, repaving—you name it," she said. "They even pick up my garbage in the back of the house."

The couple moved from nearby West Hempstead into a 60-year-old four-bedroom, three-bath Tudor on a 90- by 110-foot lot, for which they paid $575,000.

If there is a downside to living in Garden City, Mrs. Downey said, it would be that no matter where you live it can be noisy. "There's always a

POPULATION: 21,515.

AREA: 5.3 square miles.

MEDIAN HOUSEHOLD INCOME: $99,461.

MEDIAN PRICE OF A SINGLE-FAMILY HOUSE: $400,000.

TAXES ON A MEDIAN-PRICE HOUSE: $9,500.

PUBLIC SCHOOL SPENDING PER PUPIL: $13,150.

DISTANCE FROM MIDTOWN MANAHATTAN: 22 miles.

RUSH-HOUR TRAVEL TO MIDTOWN: 40 minutes on the Long Island Rail Road, $6.25 one way, $135 monthly.

CODES: Area, 516; ZIP, 11530.

train station or school nearby," she said. "But those are also the things that make living here so desirable."

And, yes, there are a lot of schools. In addition to the public school system, there are two Roman Catholic schools, a private preparatory school, a community college, and a university.

The Garden City School District has two primary schools (kindergarten and first grade), two elementary schools (grades 1–5), one middle school (6–8), and a high school. Enrollment has been increasing since 1989, from 2,870 then to 3,441 in 1997, said the superintendent, Lee Wilson, but class size has been maintained at an average of 22. Per-pupil spending in 1997 was $13,150, increasing about 2 percent a year during the mid-1990s.

Dr. Wilson said that each of the five schools had been recognized as a National School of Excellence by the Department of Education. During the mid-1990s, the average SAT score of high school seniors was 1045, compared to 993 statewide, and 98 percent of the high school graduates went on to higher education. During this same period, the district also had two National Merit Scholarship finalists and two Westinghouse Science Talent Search semifinalists.

Dr. Wilson said that during the mid-1990s, more than 3,000 people a year participated in over 200 adult-education classes. "In light of the many other opportunities in this area and for the size of the community, that so many people chose to take classes here must mean we're doing something special," he said.

Other educational choices include St. Joseph's Roman Catholic School, with an enrollment of 438, which serves pupils from preschool to grade 8. Tuition starts at $850. St. Anne's Roman Catholic School, with an enrollment of 482, also serves prekindergarten to grade 8. Tuition starts at $814.

The Waldorf School is a college preparatory coeducational day school that serves preschool to grade 12. In 1997, it had an enrollment of 270, with tuition that ranged from $3,000 to $10,500.

Nassau County Community College offers more than 50 programs leading to a two-year associate's degree or a one-year certificate. In 1997, it had an enrollment of 21,000 full- and part-time students. Tuition was $84 a credit or $1,110 full-time.

Adelphi University has been in Garden City since 1929 and is the oldest private institution of higher learning on Long Island. It has an enrollment of 5,500 full- and part-time students. Undergraduate tuition is $7,000 a semester full-time.

About two-fifths of the taxes in Garden City are borne by commercial property owners and their tenants, said Bertram Donley, executive vice president of the chamber of commerce. There are about 50 office buildings in Garden City, most occupied by brokerage houses, law firms, banks, insurance agencies, or corporations.

Most shopping is on Franklin Avenue, which has over the years attracted branches of such stores as Saks Fifth Avenue and Sears. Seventh Street, the "Main Street," offers myriad food and services. Some of the more popular restaurants in town are Newport Grill, Seventh Street Cafe, B. K. Sweeney's Steak House, and Orchid, a Chinese restaurant.

Mr. Donley said there was very little industry, except for some warehouses. "Garden City always stands out because it manages to retain its residential character with low-key commercial businesses," he said.

The Garden City Hotel has been part of the community for as long as there has been a community. The first building burned down in 1899 and was rebuilt in 1901. In its heyday, it played host to presidents, royalty, explorers, and other celebrities. It was torn down in 1973, and in 1983 the new Garden City Hotel opened.

The real estate market in Garden City has rebounded. In the late 1980s, the median price of a one-family house was $242,500. After the recession, it dropped to $210,000. But over the past several years, prices have increased about 5 percent a year, with the median price of a house in 1997 at $400,000, and median taxes at $9,500.

Bob Krener of Taylor-Warner Real Estate said that in 1997, one-family homes could go as high as $1.97 million, which might buy a 5,000-square-foot house on one acre. The low end might be a 1,400-square-foot Cape Cod for $240,000.

There are seven co-op apartment buildings, most of them about four stories high. They have a total of 768 units. The largest is Cherry Valley, a 1970 apartment conversion on 15th Street, with 192 units. A one-bedroom unit in Cherry Valley sells for about $70,000. A two-bedroom goes for about $100,000. Prices in co-ops can go up to $250,000 for a two-bedroom unit in the Carlyle House on Stewart Avenue—named, of course, for Alexander Turney Stewart. Prices during the mid-1990s have remained stable, with the median price of a two-bedroom unit at about $150,000.

The condominium market is quite strong, Mr. Krener said, increasing about 4 percent a year during the mid-1990s, with the median price of a two-bedroom unit at about $350,000 compared to $300,000 in 1993. Prices ranged from $150,000 for a one-bedroom unit at Tudor Gardens, one of three condominium buildings in the village, to $300,000 for a one-bedroom at the Wyndham, the newest and most luxurious of the buildings.

There are three rental apartment houses with a total of 239 units in Garden City. Rental prices have increased at a rate of about 2 percent a year during the mid-1990s, with one-bedroom apartments in 1997 ranging from $1,150 to $1,500 and two-bedroom apartments ranging from $1,800 to $2,200.

Lenita Manthey and Arthur Flynn looked at homes in Garden City for only three weeks before buying a three-story English-style town house on Franklin Court for $330,000.

Franklin Court was built in 1912 to house employees of a newly completed Doubleday publishing plant. Ms. Manthey, who comes from Minnesota, likes it for its privacy.

"My background is a small community," she said. "I'm used to a country environment."

The couple run a telemarketing company from their home and came to Garden City because Mr. Flynn had previously lived there. "But even he didn't know about this area," Ms. Manthey said.

As an incorporated village, Garden City is governed by a mayor and seven trustees. Village residents receive services that include police, a paid and volunteer fire department, public works, sewer district, garbage removal, and recreation.

In addition to operating five neighborhood parks that are each supervised by a recreation attendant, the city offers the Garden City Community Park, with four lighted tennis courts, miniature golf, outdoor swimming pools, a clubhouse, a sauna, and lockers. Family membership for the pools in 1997 was $330 a season.

Although Mr. Stewart did not live to see his dream completed, dying seven years after he began the project, his widow and their extended family of nieces and nephews carried it on through the Garden City Company, which they formed in 1893 (and which still exists today, as a real estate company). In 1919, Garden City was incorporated and has been a thriving community since.

GREAT NECK

*Stately homes and country living,
28 minutes from Manhattan*

BY VIVIEN KELLERMAN

Country living just 20 miles and only 28 minutes on the Long Island Rail Road from Manhattan seems like an impossibility. But in the Village of Great Neck, where stately trees and neatly landscaped lawns flank neighborhoods of stone-and-brick homes, residents enjoy spacious, relaxed living.

Add to this an acclaimed school district, convenient shopping, and abundant parks, and Great Neck, known to the locals as the "old village," continues its long history as a desirable place to live.

The village, in the Town of North Hempstead, is part of the Great Neck Peninsula, a collection of villages and unincorporated hamlets surrounded on three sides by water. Although the community, which is south of Kings Point, has its own municipal services, it shares a school and parks district with the rest of the peninsula.

Jeroen and Robin Bours, who have two school-age sons, Benjamin and Aaron, spent 18 months looking for a home in Great Neck. Although prices in the village were higher than the couple planned to spend, they said, they were so impressed with the area, they refused to look anywhere else. What made their task difficult, Mr. Bours said, is that homes were snatched up almost as quickly as they came on the market, putting increased pressure on them to make a quick decision.

"When we saw our house the second time, there was a line of real estate people with customers, waiting to get in," Mr. Bours said. He and his wife wound up spending in the mid-$300,000's for a 1951, four-bedroom, two-bath expanded ranch.

Mr. Bours said two important factors in their decision to move to Great Neck were the school district's reputation and the proximity to

POPULATION: 9,331.

AREA: 1.3 square miles.

MEDIAN HOUSEHOLD INCOME: $79,015.

MEDIAN PRICE OF SINGLE-FAMILY HOUSE: $360,000.

TAXES ON MEDIAN-PRICED HOUSE: $4,800.

PUBLIC SCHOOL SPENDING PER PUPIL: $17,806.

DISTANCE FROM MIDTOWN MANHATTAN: 20 miles.

RUSH-HOUR TRAVEL TO MIDTOWN: 28 minutes on the Long Island Rail Road, $6.75 one way, $135 monthly.

CODES: Area, 516; ZIP, 11023.

Manhattan, where he is an art director and his wife is an administrator at Mount Sinai Hospital.

Stan and Marylou Jorgensen moved to Great Neck from Manhattan in 1968 after visiting friends who lived in the village. "I remember being impressed with the beauty of the village and thinking that it would be a good place to raise children," Mrs. Jorgensen said. It was also a good commute, she said; her husband, a commercial artist, worked in Rye, New York, about 40 minutes away.

In 1992, after raising two children in Great Neck, the couple sold their home and moved to a village apartment. Two years later, they bought another Great Neck home, smaller than their first; the three-bedroom, two-bath, completely rebuilt 1950 ranch cost $303,000 in February 1994.

Mrs. Jorgensen, a fund-raiser for the United States Merchant Marine Academy in Kings Point, said that Great Neck offered her everything she wanted in a community. "We live within walking distance of the post office, shops, parks, the community pool," she said. "It's all here."

Great Neck's single-family homes come in a wide range of styles. Prices begin at about $225,000 and go up to about $600,000. Post–World War II ranches and Cape Cods with basements and garages go for about $350,000.

David Lurie, owner of Lurie Realty, said that many homes had been updated or even gutted and rebuilt, and that many tract homes no longer looked anything like they did when they were first built.

Great Neck has no condominiums, but the village has several two- and three-story co-op and rental apartment buildings. Apartments in the 10 co-op apartment buildings, which have a total of more than 500 units, sell for about $60,000 for one-bedroom units and $110,000 for two-bedroom units. There are three rental apartment buildings with a total of 181 units. One-bedroom rentals are about $900 a month; two-bedrooms are about $1,500. Mr. Lurie said that co-op and rental apartment prices have increased about 1 percent a year during the 1990s. A two-bedroom co-op in 1997 sold for about $112,000, while a two-bedroom apartment rented for about $2,000. Apartment availability, however, was scarce.

Mr. Lurie said that most buyers coming into Great Neck were moving up, and that many had children. He said that although prices for single-family homes dropped about 30 percent during the recession, they had firmed up, and demand for homes has been strong. During the 1990s, he said, median prices for single-family houses increased about 1 percent a year, reaching $360,000 in 1997. Taxes on a median-priced home are about $4,800 a year.

Like most Long Island school districts, enrollment in the Great Neck Union Free School District has been increasing during the 1990s, reaching an enrollment of 5,700 in 1997. Superintendent of Schools William Shine said that the district will probably have to ask the residents to approve a bond issue in order to reconfigure the elementary school buildings to accommodate the increase in enrollment.

From 1990 to 1997, typically 95 percent of the district's high school graduates went on to higher education. The district also has an alternative high school and a prekindergarten-kindergarten school, housed in separate buildings.

The district's kindergarten program consists of classes with 20 students attending four half days and one full day a week. One day a week, groups of five students continue on with the teacher until 3:30 P.M. Dr. Shine said this aspect of the program gave youngsters a chance to bond with the teacher and get special attention.

Students in Great Neck come from more than 40 countries, Dr. Shine said, adding that during the mid-1990s, an average 23 percent of the high school's graduating class were born outside this country, many of them in Russia, Israel, or Iran.

Dr. Shine, who has been superintendent since 1983, said that the district has had only three superintendents since 1940. "I think that says something about the stability of the community," he said.

There are several houses of worship, some of which have long been fixtures of the community. All Saints' Episcopal Church was erected in 1889; St. Aloysius Roman Catholic Church is more than a century old. Temple Beth-El, Great Neck Synagogue, St. Paul's A.M.E. Zion Church, and Bethel Baptist Church are all within village borders. The village also has three Iranian synagogues, with two more to be added on the peninsula.

Among the most popular features of living in the village are the 21 parks in the Great Neck Park District, which covers the Great Neck Peninsula. Residents within the park district have access to all the parks.

The Parkwood Sports Complex on Arrandale Avenue has three outdoor swimming pools, four indoor and five outdoor tennis courts, and an indoor ice-skating rink. The pools are open from Memorial Day until the weekend after Labor Day, with district residents in 1997 paying from $175 to $185 for a season family pass.

Great Neck House, a cultural center, also on Arrandale Avenue, offers free movies, live performances, museum and art exhibits, classes, lectures, and card and game tables. The 8.5-acre Memorial Field, on Fairview Avenue, has 16 tennis courts, six basketball courts, paddle tennis, and several ball fields.

The superintendent of parks and recreation, Richard Aranello, estimates that taxes to pay for the park district in 1997 averaged $296 a year for a family. The facilities in the park district are open only to residents of the peninsula, who are issued free photo ID's.

The village also offers plenty of shopping; there are about 250 stores of all kinds, most of them on Middle Neck Road.

Records show that in 1644, a small group of colonists from Connecticut negotiated a deed with the Matinecock Indians for lands extending from Little Neck Bay to Hempstead Harbor. By the late 1600s, the Dutch had completely settled most of Great Neck, where pastureland was used for cattle ranching.

With its proximity to Manhattan, the community thrived. In 1862, the Long Island Rail Road began service in Great Neck, cutting the traveling time to the city by hoof or sloop from seven hours to a little more than an hour. Until 1899, when Nassau County was created, Great Neck was part of Queens. In 1922, Great Neck was incorporated as a village. After World War II, many large farms were sold, and the population increased from 4,010 in 1930 to 7,759 by 1950.

The population of Iranian immigrants in Great Neck has been growing since the 1979 Iranian revolution and the overthrow of the Shah. The 1980 census listed 872 people of Iranian descent in the Town of North Hempstead; by 1990, the number had grown to 4,474, most of them in the Village of Great Neck or on the Great Neck Peninsula. The peninsula now has the largest Iranian population in the metropolitan area.

For all its growth, a country feeling still remains in Great Neck. "When you walk down Main Street to the post office, everyone knows you," said Richard Stancati, chairman of the Great Neck Business Association. "It has a nice hometown kind of feeling to it."

HUNTINGTON VILLAGE

Vibrant downtown with an artistic flair

BY JOHN RATHER

There are places on Long Island where traditional downtown shopping districts have faded and decayed, their vitality siphoned off by malls and strip shopping centers. With its solid lineup of shops, restaurants, and local businesses, Main Street in what is universally called Huntington Village, a thriving hub on the north shore of western Suffolk County, has avoided this fate despite competition from nearby shopping monoliths like the Walt Whitman Mall on Route 110.

Instead, busy Main Street remains the backbone of what is technically not a village but the hamlet of Huntington. It is also the main thoroughfare through the history-laden center of a lively community of almost 18,000 people that is more cheerfully comfortable than posh. Detached older homes on half- and quarter-acre lots are tucked onto properties that are well tended without being highly manicured.

The venerable old downtown, where young Walt Whitman once trod, supports a bona fide nightlife and accoutrements like a chocolatier, a tobacconist with a wooden Indian by the doorway, and the Book Revue, a bookstore that stays open until midnight on Friday and Saturday. These and other touches—oddities like Condom Sense, a shop for contraceptives and erotically shaped pasta, among other things—would be enough to give the hamlet a distinct identity. But this is only half the story.

Foot for foot, Huntington has the greatest concentration of arts groups for miles around. Fliers for concerts, plays, dances, movies at the Cinema Arts Centre, meet-the-author or -artist receptions, and gallery exhibits festoon shop windows around Main Street. "I really do think that we are the cultural capital of Long Island," said Cynthia B. Clair, the executive director of the Huntington Arts Council, which serves 85 groups in the Town of Huntington, the larger area that sprang from the original

POPULATION: 17,885.

AREA: 8.4 square miles.

MEDIAN HOUSEHOLD INCOME: $80,084.

MEDIAN PRICE OF A SINGLE-FAMILY HOUSE: $250,000.

TAXES ON A MEDIAN-PRICED HOUSE: $5,000.

PUBLIC SCHOOL SPENDING PER PUPIL: $13,286.

DISTANCE FROM MIDTOWN MANHATTAN: 40 miles .

RUSH-HOUR TRAVEL TO MIDTOWN: 58 minutes on the Long Island Rail Road, $8.50 one way, $181 monthly.

CODES: Area, 516; ZIP, 11560 and 11765.

village. "We have quite an active cultural scene within the village, and the village serves the whole town."

One pillar of culture, the Heckscher Museum of Art, is in a Beaux Arts building in 18.5-acre Heckscher Park. The town park has a small lake, playgrounds, playing fields, and an outdoor amphitheater built in 1979 where free concerts and plays are staged from June through August.

A location about 40 miles from midtown Manhattan makes the commuting trip for the city-bound on the Long Island Rail Road from Huntington almost an hour.

Detached houses dominating residential areas are often more than 50 years old. "We call them oldies but goodies," said Janet D. Smiley, branch manager at Coldwell Banker Sammis in Huntington. Mrs. Smiley said features like front porches and dentil moldings have made older homes the most sought-after properties in a seller's market. Newer homes are scattered throughout the residential areas. Many were built on land subdivided from the plots surrounding larger Victorian dwellings, some erected before the turn of the century.

"This part of the town is pretty much the way it was back before World War II," said Huntington Town Historian Stanley B. Klein. His office is in the Soldiers and Sailors Memorial Building, built in 1892, on the east end of Main Street. Mr. Klein said the hamlet was remarkable, among other reasons, for preservation of its Colonial-era Village Green, a four-acre expanse farther to the east that is now owned by the town. The Arts League of Long Island, founded by local artists in 1955, hosts its annual arts festival at the green during the third week in June.

Prices for detached homes ranged from the mid-$100,000's to more than $2 million during the mid-1990s, and were trending modestly upward by late 1997. The median price for a one-family detached house was about $250,000 through that year, up about $20,000 from five years earlier. Median taxes for one-family homes are about $5,000.

A large co-op complex, the Huntington Village Cooperative, has 244 units in 15 two-story brick buildings erected in 1950 around a grassy commons. In 1997, one-bedroom units were selling for about $85,000 to $90,000, two-bedroom units for $120,000 to $130,000. Ann Lewis, an associate broker at ReMax North Shore Real Estate, said the apartments, for which there is a waiting list, attracted older couples and single people of all ages.

Average prices at the eight condominium complexes, with a total of about 180 units, range from $200,000 to $350,000 for two-bedroom apartments.

A key attraction of the community is the 4,000-student Huntington School District, which encompasses the Huntington hamlet and surrounding areas. It includes a kindergarten center opened in 1996 offering a full-day program.

In an unusual arrangement, the district has three schools for pupils in grades 1 through 3. An assistant superintendent, Steven Tribus, said the approach reduced class sizes and allowed the teachers to better target the educational needs of the children in these grades. There are two intermediate schools for grades 4 to 6 and a junior high school for grades 7 and 8. The junior high recently started a program under which groups of students are matched with a group, or team, of the same teachers in both years. "Parents can meet with the team," Mr. Tribus said. The program was recently introduced in grade 6, he said.

Huntington High School offers programs in music and art and advanced placement courses in English, physics, biology, social studies, math, and several other subjects. The high school has four computer labs, including one for music. There are two computer labs in the junior high and computers are widely available in the lower grades.

More than half the graduates earned Regents diplomas during the 1990s. In recent years, about 85 percent have gone on to college. SAT averages for the 1995–96 school year were 530 in verbal and 517 in math, both above state and national averages. Scores were similar for other recent years.

A Science Research Program begun at the high school in 1996 yielded a Westinghouse Science Talent Search semifinalist in 1997. District spending per pupil was $13,286, according to 1997 state figures.

A Roman Catholic school, St. Patrick's, has from 600 to 650 students in prekindergarten through grade 8. Among its offerings are opportunities to play in its band, sing in its chorus, and help produce the school newspaper. In the 1997–98 school year, annual tuition was $1,785 for parishioner students in grades 1 through 8, $2,300 for nonparishioners. Kindergarten tuition is $1,740 for morning sessions, $1,385 for afternoon sessions. Prekindergarten tuition is $670 for one day a week up to $2,020 for four days. Parishioners have priority.

The community traces its history to 1653, when three Englishmen, Richard Holdbrook, Robert Williams, and Daniel Whitehead, bought six square miles of land in the Huntington area from the Matinecocks. Many early settlers came from the New Haven colony. The purchase price, according to the historian Richard M. Bayles, was six bottles, six coats, six hatches, 30 eel spears, 30 needles, six shovels, 10 knives, and a clutch of wampum.

The name Huntington recalls the wealth of game and good hunting in the area's wooded, rolling terrain. From the beginning, the hamlet was the residential and commercial center of what became the Town of Huntington, which was briefly joined with Connecticut during the early 1660s.

It was also where important chapters of local history were written. In late July 1776, at the first public reading of the Declaration of Independence in the village, local patriots showed their enthusiasm by hanging an effigy of King George III from a gallows and exploding it with gunpowder.

In 1782, possibly in an act of late revenge, British troops under the command of Col. Benjamin Thompson, an American Loyalist, knocked down more than 100 tombstones on Burying Hill to make way for a fort they grimly named Fort Golgotha. The troops tore apart the old Presbyterian church, stripped a barn, and felled orchard trees for wood for the fort. They used the tombstones for tables and ovens. Loaves of bread baked in these macabre ovens, the story goes, bore mirror-image inscriptions from the stones. At war's end, the offending fort was dismantled and the cemetery was returned to its former use. It is now in the National Register of Historic Places.

The town's borders originally stretched from Long Island Sound 20 miles south to the Atlantic Ocean. But in 1872, with the approval of the town's residents, the southern portion became the Town of Babylon.

In 1838, young Walt Whitman, born in outlying West Hills, founded *The Long Islander*, a weekly town newspaper published continuously ever since under subsequent owners.

Early-20th-century photos of a firemen's parade on Main Street show two-story commercial buildings that are still standing and in use today. But the passing parade has changed a bit. The Long Island Pride Parade, a gay, lesbian, bisexual, and transgender parade, has held annual marches down Main Street since 1990.

Main Street, which is also Route 25A, has had to grapple with heavy traffic barreling down its four lanes. Visitors relying on a pedestrian crossing by the library may have to quick-step to reach the far curb safely. Some drivers stop; some don't.

The hamlet's U-shaped borders touch upon the shores of Huntington Harbor. The slot of the U, now the neighboring hamlet of Halesite, is where the British arrested Nathan Hale as a spy shortly after he came ashore from Connecticut in September 1776.

LAKE SUCCESS

Family-centered first home of the U.N.

BY JOHN RATHER

There could be few more suitable places to study the evolution of the Long Island ranch house than Lake Success, an expensive, family-centered village in western Nassau County where the expanded ranch is something of an art form. Older Colonials, Tudors, contemporary designs, and eclectic styles are also found among the more than 800 houses in the 1.8-square-mile village, the most southerly of nine villages that make up the Great Neck area. But the many variations of enlarged and upgraded ranches and split-levels stand out on winding streets, harking back to the 1950s, when development in the more-than-70-year-old village surged.

In addition to its well-kept residential areas, which are patrolled by its own small police force, attractions that make Lake Success a sought-after community include the village-owned 18-hole golf course, stable housing values, and buffered proximity to major roadways.

"The village is always a strong market," said Florence Bromley of Florence Bromley Inc., the only real estate company within the village boundaries.

"With the golf and the easy commute, it's probably the best area we have right now in Great Neck," said Hildy Sanders, a broker and owner of Trylon Realty of Great Neck. "You get a lot of doctors because it's so near the hospitals," she said, referring to Long Island Jewish Medical Center in Hillside, Queens, and North Shore Hospital in Manhasset.

Membership in the golf club, automatically extended to residents, costs $1,500 annually. Nonresidents may join the club, but there has been a waiting list more than a decade long in recent years. The village also has an outdoor pool and 11 tennis courts.

Housing prices range from the high $300,000's to over $1 million but are typically between $500,000 and $700,000. The median price of a

POPULATION: 2,569.

AREA: 1.8 square miles.

MEDIAN HOUSEHOLD INCOME: $124, 292.

MEDIAN PRICE OF A SINGLE-FAMILY HOUSE: $550,000.

TAXES ON A MEDIAN-PRICED HOUSE: $7,000.

PUBLIC SCHOOL SPENDING PER PUPIL: $17,806.

DISTANCE FROM MIDTOWN MANHATTAN: 16 miles.

RUSH-HOUR TRAVEL TO MIDTOWN: 27 minutes from Great Neck on the Long Island Rail Road, $6.75 one way, $135 monthly.

CODES: Area, 516; ZIP, 11020 and 11042.

one-family home of $550,000 in 1996 was up marginally by the last quarter of 1997 in a seller's market, but inventory was slim. Zoning restricts housing to single-family dwellings. There are no condominiums, co-ops, or apartment houses, and house rentals are rare.

The ingrained habit of home improvement shows in prices. Two houses of similar age and style, originally bought for a similar price and located on the same street, may now vary in price by $75,000 because one has been more extensively upgraded.

A commercial and industrial area along Marcus Avenue, away from residential neighborhoods, provides revenues that keep village taxes relatively low. Total property taxes on a $550,000 house, realtors said, were around $7,000.

The lowest housing prices are in areas near the Long Island Expressway and the Northern State Parkway, where traffic noise is constant. Both roads cut through the village. North Hempstead Turnpike, more frequently called Northern Boulevard, is on the village's north side. More expensive homes are found in the Windsor Gate neighborhood and along the southern shore of Lake Success, the body of water that gives the village its name.

Some village residents were upset when the 33-story North Shore Towers (34 stories tall when penthouses on each of the three towers are included) was built in the mid-seventies. For newcomers to parts of Lake Success where they dominate the horizon, its three towers looming imposingly in the not-too-distant background across the Queens border take some getting used to.

"The shadow comes right across the synagogue," said Rabbi Scott Hoffman of the Lake Success Jewish Center, exaggerating slightly. In fact, he said, many members of the Conservative synagogue live in the towers. The center has a preschool program for children aged 2 to 4, a kindergarten-through-seventh-grade Hebrew school, youth programs, and adult-education courses.

Mayor Roberta Chavis said that her village, just 16 miles from midtown Manhattan, was one of several in Nassau County that had gained an agreement from New York State transportation officials to ameliorate residential impacts when the expressway is expanded to add high-occupancy-vehicle lanes. The agreement gave residents living near the road a voice in where sound barriers are situated, among other things. Widening was expected by 1999.

It takes about an hour to drive the roughly 16 miles from the village to Manhattan during the morning rush hour, and half that time when the traffic is light. Many commuters drive instead to the Long Island Rail Road station in Great Neck for a half-hour trip to Penn Station.

With virtually no retail outlets of its own, Lake Success is served by what Madeleine Bodner, president of the Century 21 Madeleine Bodner Real Estate Agency in Great Neck, called "incredible Great Neck shopping" in boutiques, gourmet food stores, and specialty shops near the railroad station. Miracle Mile in Manhasset, where Lord & Taylor and other larger stores are situated, is also close.

The 45,000-square-foot main branch of Great Neck Public Library seats 380 people and offers a silent study room, computers, electric typewriters, meeting rooms, and a children's media center. The main branch and three smaller branches house 350,000 volumes, more than 12,000 recordings, and more than 9,000 videos. The library subscribes to more than 1,200 periodicals and more than 50 newspapers.

Lake Success is in the academically solid Great Neck School District. Its youngsters attend the nearby 1,000-student, 110-acre Great Neck South High School, one of three high schools in the 5,700-student Great Neck School District. From 1990 to 1997, an average of 95 percent of graduates went on to college. Spending per pupil was $17,806 in 1997 state figures. The amount is high even for Long Island's North Shore.

Advanced placement courses, independent-study programs, and honors, Regents, and accelerated classes are offered in many subjects. The school also offers its students a computerized online database retrieval system with Internet access in its newly renovated library media center. During the 1997–98 school year, it had four computer labs, each with 15 or more computers, and six computer clusters, each with three or four computers. Average SAT scores are typically in the high 500s, exceeding state averages by 70 points in verbal and 80 points in math.

A middle school for grades 6 to 8 is located in the village. The district also has four elementary schools. An early childhood center has kindergarten classes and prekindergarten programs for 3- and 4-year-olds. The grade schools offer small classes, enriched courses in art, computers, industrial arts, music, reading, and science, and a program for the gifted. Each elementary school has a computer lab and at least one computer terminal in every classroom. The district's Cumberland Adult Center in Lake Success offers many courses, trips, and special events.

The government's construction of a vast plant in Lake Success for Sperry Gyroscope on Marcus Avenue in 1941 troubled the then-rural community. The plant, straddling the village border with New Hyde Park, marked the beginning of a corporate and industrial presence in the area. In 1946, part of the plant in Lake Success became temporary headquarters for the United Nations, giving the village name international recognition. Nevertheless, as late as 1948, when the village population was 936, Lake Success remained little removed from its past as farmland and estates of the Phipps and Vanderbilt families.

In the '50s, housing development arrived in earnest. "When I moved here in 1953, it was getting built up very quickly," said Sylvia Bareish, the village historian. "My street had been owned by a farmer."

A key moment came in 1956, when village voters approved buying 113 acres of the Deepdale Golf Club for $1 million. The club's course, created in 1926 by William K. Vanderbilt, was a casualty of the newly constructed Long Island Expressway. The purchase saved the land from housing and gave the village its own course. (The Deepdale Club reemerged in North Hills.)

The once heavily forested Lake Success area was within the realm of the Matinecocks, who named the lake "Sacut" in honor of a chief. Dutch and, beginning in 1644, English settlers followed during the Colonial period. In 1732, a Dutch Reformed Church became the first building erected in what later became Lake Success. After the Revolution, the area around what was then called Success Pond became known as Lakeville, and the lake became popular for swimming and fishing.

Its popularity as a summer resort continued into the early 20th century, when the Vanderbilt and Phipps families purchased about half the area that now makes up the village. The area, which incorporated as Lake Success in 1926, was the western terminus of the original Vanderbilt Raceway, later the Motor Parkway toll road. The old clubhouse Vanderbilt built on the shores of the lake is now the village hall.

The lake, actually a kettle pond formed by a retreating Ice Age glacier, is a surface expression of the groundwater that lies in aquifers beneath all of Long Island. In the mid–19th century, Brooklyn briefly contemplated importing water from the lake. But when a test trench was installed, the lake level dropped sharply and the plan was quickly abandoned. The lake gradually filled again.

LAUREL HOLLOW

Affluent privacy on the sound

BY JOHN RATHER

Weatherworn bungalows with leaky plumbing, sagging roofs, and tiny yards would probably sell briskly, and at a price, in Laurel Hollow, a village of 2,000 people on the North Shore of Long Island's Nassau County. The grateful buyers would include young families willing to put up with deprivation for the right to send their children to the Cold Spring Harbor Central School District, a system with a reputation for strong academics. Others would leap at the chance to live in a premier setting where the school district's reputation is only one factor that keeps land values high. But there are no humble dwellings in the nearly all-residential, 2.9-square-mile village, where the zoning law calls for two acres of land for each new house. Instead, newcomers must ante up mightily for far finer homes scattered about the hills and vales of this very private and expensive North Shore Long Island coastal community perched on the west side of Cold Spring Harbor.

Selling prices, though sometimes tens of thousands of dollars below asking prices, are daunting, rarely falling below $450,000 for ample starter houses, Laurel Hollow style. Prices top $2 million for small estates with panoramic water views. The median home price of $750,000 in 1996 and 1997, up by $200,000 from earlier in the decade, was inching upward again by the last quarter of 1997. In a strong market with limited listings, young families were bidding up prices. The falloff between asking prices and sale prices had also lessened, realtors said. Taxes on a $750,000 home were about $15,000, though, as in most Nassau communities, they vary widely from house to house, depending on age, improvements, and other factors.

Scarsella's Florist on North Hempstead Turnpike is the village's only retail business. For shopping, residents go to Syosset, Huntington, Oyster Bay, or Cold Spring Harbor. There are no co-ops or condominiums, and

POPULATION: 1,998.

AREA: 2.9 square miles.

MEDIAN HOUSEHOLD INCOME: $207,407.

MEDIAN PRICE OF A SINGLE-FAMILY HOUSE: $750,000.

TAXES ON MEDIAN-PRICED HOUSE: $15,000.

PUBLIC SCHOOL SPENDING PER PUPIL: $13,639.

DISTANCE FROM MIDTOWN MANHATTAN: 30 miles.

RUSH-HOUR TRAVEL TO MIDTOWN: 50 minutes on the Long Island Rail Road from Syosset, $7 one way, $154 monthly; 52 minutes on the Long Island Rail Road from Cold Spring Harbor, $8.50 one way, $181 monthly.

CODES: Area, 516: ZIP, 11791 and 11771.

rentals are rare. Rail commuters to Manhattan, 30 miles distant, ride 50 minutes on the Long Island Rail Road from Syosset or 52 minutes from Cold Spring Harbor.

Carol L. Tintle, the manager and vice president of the Daniel Gale Real Estate Agency office in Cold Spring Harbor, said that fine schools and appreciating property values have made the village extremely attractive to families of means with school-age children. "There are few places you can live that are so lovely, and where you also have private beaches, moorings, your own police force, and small public schools," she said.

The village hall faces the village beach on Cold Spring Harbor. Boat moorings are free for residents. A 12-member police department patrols village roads. "We certainly don't have an extremely high crime rate, but most certainly over the years the village has seen every crime imaginable," said Police Chief Chester J. Smith, a 30-year veteran.

The exception to the village's halcyon existence, Chief Smith and others in the village said, is the chronic mayhem on Route 25A, the North Hempstead Turnpike, where traffic accidents are frequent on a sloping, curving section of road spiraling down toward the harbor. The New York State Department of Transportation recently resurfaced the road, a job last done more than 20 years ago, to improve traction in wet weather. Plans for other changes are still being debated. "They assure us they are going ahead with lights and traffic controls, and that's all we really want," Mayor E. Richard Droesch said. The road, harrowing to enter or exit even in dry weather, divides the village roughly in half.

On the north side, the wooded, older section where baronial homes are set back in rolling nooks and longtime residency is common, many homes vanish behind a veil of leaves and other greenery each spring. The terrain is not typical of Long Island. "It's like a Vermont kind of feeling," said Arlene Canestro, a salesperson at Coach Realty in Commack.

Visitors may experience déjà vu driving on undulating, uncharted, mazelike, one-lane privately maintained roads, where what looks familiar may have been passed minutes earlier. "If you don't know where you're going, you may have a problem," said Alyssa M. Nightingale, a broker at the Buyer's Agent: Nightingale & Partners, in Cold Spring Harbor, a buyers' agency.

The newer south side, annexed to the village in the 1950s, is easier to navigate and slightly more affordable. Large ranches and other residences, many of them built within the last 40 years, give the impression of being blown up to twice the normal size to fill their large lots.

Some purchasers raze existing houses and build new ones. Frank S. Urso, the owner and broker of Long Island Village Realty in Syosset, referred to a house on the market for $625,000 as "something that allows people to come in, buy the land, and get into the school district."

"Come back in a year or two and you'll probably see a new Colonial here," Mr. Urso said.

A feeling of calm and space pervades the village. "It's a beautiful place to raise children," said Eleanor A. Foxen, who raised seven children as a resident. "But if you want a next-door neighbor to talk to, it isn't an over-the-back-fence kind of community. Remember, you are on two acres."

The village incorporated in 1926 to gain control of beaches that drew crowds of outsiders, some of whom offended residents by changing clothes in their parked flivvers. The founders discarded the original name, Laurelton, because the post office confused it with the Laurelton section of Queens. The second choice, Laurel Hollow, appears on land deeds dating to the early 18th century and fits the village's rolling terrain and still ubiquitous mountain laurels.

Inhabited first by the Matinecock Indians, settled by the Dutch in the early 17th century, and later controlled by the English, the Laurel Hollow area is linked in history to the nearby hamlet of Cold Spring Harbor, the nation's 27th-largest whaling port from the 1830s to the 1860s, when kerosene ended the market for whale oil. The Cold Spring Harbor hamlet, on the eastern, Suffolk County side of the harbor, is a lovely place of Colonial architecture, antiques stores, boutiques, and quirky one-of-a-kind shops.

According to the Cold Spring Harbor School District, which serves Laurel Hollow, George Washington stopped in Laurel Hollow during his Long Island tour of 1790 to observe construction of the Bungtown School. Its descendant, the West Side School, is an elementary school attended today by village children. The school, for grades 2 through 6, strives for a relaxed and homey atmosphere for its 259 students.

The district emphasizes innovative teaching methods for reading and writing and programs that allow students in different grades to mix. Special programs at the DNA Learning Center in Cold Spring Harbor are offered in collaboration with Cold Spring Harbor Laboratory.

In response to rising enrollment, the district, which also includes the Village of Lloyd Harbor and northerly areas of the Towns of Huntington and Oyster Bay, opened the Goosehill Primary School in Cold Spring Harbor in 1993. About 260 students are enrolled in kindergarten and first grade. The district, with about 1,600 students in early 1997 and nearly 100 more by the year's fourth quarter, has a combined junior and senior high school for grades 7 through 12.

The high school, a five-building, 75-acre harborside campus with about 700 students, offers 25 honors courses as well as many advanced placement courses, including art and music. Tutorials and independent-study programs are available to selected students. Among the high school's special programs is a three-year sequence in architectural and engineering drawing.

Students consistently score far above national and state averages on standardized tests, the district said. About 95 percent go on to higher education. In recent years, median SAT scores were about 580 in verbal and 600 in math. Both scores are about 90 to 100 points higher than median scores for New York State.

All but a handful of the village's nearly 600 homes are in the district, whose lines cross the Nassau-Suffolk county line. The few exceptions are in the Oyster Bay School District.

Like a giant within the village gates, the Cold Spring Harbor Laboratory is a commanding presence in Laurel Hollow. An internationally known center for cancer, neurobiology, and genetic research, the private, not-for-profit lab employs 577 people, including more than 200 scientists, and occupies a 100-acre waterfront campus that has been a biological research lab since 1890. The current lab president, James D. Watson, co-winner of the Nobel Prize in 1962 for discovery of the DNA structure, is one of many Nobel Laureates and eminent scientists who have studied and lectured at the facility.

LAWRENCE

Civic awareness, public pleasures

BY VIVIEN KELLERMAN

In the early '50s, when it became apparent that developers were eyeing the thousand-acre marshland that borders the southeastern portion of the Village of Lawrence, residents banded together to raise enough money to buy the land and give it to the community for preservation. A more recent example of civic involvement was the response to the influx of young families who had been renovating and expanding older homes, sometimes to twice their original size. Concerned about the integrity of their neighborhoods, the village trustees, with assistance from the Lawrence Association, took measures to limit the size of houses.

Bordering Queens and just across the Reynolds Channel from Atlantic Beach and the City of Long Beach, Lawrence is just minutes away from their beaches and is within easy reach of both Manhattan—55 minutes by Long Island Rail Road—and Kennedy International Airport. Its amenities include a village golf and tennis club as well as a marina, two private golf and tennis clubs, a museum, and a nature preserve.

Such factors, as well as its highly rated schools, have resulted in a thriving housing market. Early in 1997, two families got into a bidding war over a 50-year-old center-hall brick Colonial that went on the market for $830,000. The house, set on a hill, ultimately sold for $880,000. Morton Haves, of Morton Haves Real Estate in nearby Hewlett, recalled that in 1995, someone driving through the village stopped at a Tudor mansion that was not even for sale, knocked on the door, and offered to buy the house for $2.1 million. Mr. Haves said the shocked owner sold it.

While detached houses near the train tracks may sell for as little as $380,000, prices in 1997 were generally up near $800,000 and often topped out at over $2 million, Mr. Haves said. One 5,000-square-foot house being built on speculation will go on the market for $1.7 million. The median

POPULATION: 6,961.

AREA: 3.8 square miles.

MEDIAN HOUSEHOLD INCOME: $106,157.

MEDIAN PRICE OF A SINGLE-FAMILY HOUSE: $577,800.

TAXES ON A MEDIAN-PRICED HOUSE: $15,000.

PUBLIC SCHOOL SPENDING PER PUPIL: $17,250.

DISTANCE FROM MIDTOWN MANHATTAN: 20 miles.

RUSH-HOUR TRAVEL TO MIDTOWN: 55 minutes on the Long Island Rail Road, $6.25 one way, $135 monthly.

CODES: Area, 516: ZIP, 11559.

price for a one-family house in 1997 was $577,800. Taxes were correspondingly high, averaging about $15,000.

The neighborhood called Back Lawrence, an area of minimum one-acre zoning with many estates that date to the early part of the century, takes up about a quarter of the land in the village. Lawrence Bay Park, about 120 homes built in the late '50s, is a mix of split-levels, high ranches, and Colonials.

There are 10 co-op buildings along Central Avenue with about 500 units in all. At the 130-unit Plaza, which has a pool and an exercise room, units ranged in price in 1997 from $125,000 for a one-bedroom to $195,000 for a three-bedroom. The other buildings, which have smaller apartments, have units priced from $30,000 for a one-bedroom to $70,000 for some two-bedroom units. There are also two condominium buildings with a total of 81 units. These range in price from about $135,000 for one-bedroom units to $205,000 for two-bedrooms. Rental apartments are scarce. When available, one-bedroom units run about $950 a month and two-bedroom apartments go for about $1,200.

Despite a rise in the number of young families moving into the community, Schools Superintendent Stewart Weinberg said that public school enrollment increases had been small because 2,400 youngsters within the district attend private Orthodox Jewish schools. "If they were here, we would need extra space," said Dr. Weinberg. Partly because calculations of spending include transportation and books for the private school students as well as operating costs of an outstanding public school system, 1997 per-pupil expenditures in Lawrence were high, at $17,250 a year.

The 3,850-student Lawrence Public School district has one early-childhood center, four elementary schools serving grades 1 to 5, one middle school covering grades 5 through 8, and one high school. In addition to Lawrence, the district serves Cedarhurst, Inwood, Atlantic Beach, and portions of North Woodmere and Woodsburgh. Typically 90 percent of the Lawrence High School graduating class goes on to college. In 1996, the high school produced six Westinghouse Science Competition semifinalists. Two became finalists and one ultimately became a winner.

The Lawrence district, which has a gifted and talented program for pupils in grades 3 to 5, offers middle and high school courses in Hebrew, French, Spanish, and Italian, as well as one year each of Japanese and Russian.

Lawrence also has one of the most extensive adult-education programs on Long Island, its more than 225 courses including subjects such as "New Age Theories and Practice," golf, karate, and "Passover Treats." Diane Beller-Harris, who runs the program, said that in a typical semester, 1,200 district residents and 700 others were taking classes.

Within the village, there are three Jewish private schools. Rambam Mesivta is a boys' high school with 160 students and a tuition of $9,500 a year. The pre-K–grade 8 Brandeis School serves a Conservative population and has about 450 students. Tuition ranges from $4,000 to $8,000 a year. The Hebrew Academy of the Five Towns and Rockaway has its kindergarten-to-grade 8 campus in Lawrence; its high school is in neighboring Cedarhurst. Total 1997 enrollment for both buildings was about 1,850; tuition ranges from $6,000 to $11,000 a year.

Lawrence has long had a large and active Jewish community, and in recent years has seen a significant growth in numbers of Orthodox families. The need for convenient houses of worship has led to the entire Five Towns area of Lawrence, Cedarhurst, Hewlett, Woodmere, and Inwood becoming a center for synagogues and Jewish schools.

Daniel and Elise Vitow and their children, Joshua and Jennifer, moved to Lawrence from Staten Island in 1989. Dr. Vitow, principal of the Hebrew Academy's high school, said he had chosen Lawrence because it is a good environment to raise children, "especially modern Orthodox children." The religious school is clearly central to the Vitows' family life. Joshua graduated from his father's school; in 1997, Jennifer moved from the elementary school into the high school. Mrs. Vitow teaches science in the high school.

Dr. Vitow praises the village government for being responsive to the needs of its residents and for providing efficient and well-managed services. "It's a wonderful place to live," he said. "It's close to the city, close to everything, yet we feel very safe here."

For recreation, the village has its own 18-hole Lawrence Golf Club, with nine tennis courts, a restaurant and catering hall, and a 134-slip marina, where in 1997, fees started at $1,100 a year for a 20-foot boat; boats up to 80 feet can be accommodated. In 1997, membership in the golf club ranged from $1,750 to $2,450 a person for residents; for nonresidents, the range is $3,175 to $4,875.

There are also two private clubs: the Woodmere Country Club, with nine tennis courts and an 18-hole golf course, and the Rockaway Hunting Club, with an 18-hole golf course, 25 tennis courts, and a squash court. The

Cedarhurst Yacht Club and the 40-acre Lawrence Beach Club in Atlantic Beach are available to Hunting Club members.

Beaches in Atlantic Beach and Long Beach are accessible by the Atlantic Beach Bridge, which carries a $1.25 one-way toll; a 40-trip book costs $15.

In addition to Hicks Beach, the preserved marshland purchased by the residents four decades ago, the village owns an additional 69-acre nature preserve. This adjoins the Lawrence Golf Club and the man-made four-acre Dixon Pond at the south end of the causeway.

Rock Hall, built in 1767, is a two-story museum decorated with 18th- and 19th-century furnishings. It sits on three acres of formal gardens.

The 70-year-old, 1,100-member Lawrence Association monitors both school district and local and town government board meetings. A monthly newsletter covering these meetings is sent to residents of the community. The president of the civic group, Michael Kimmel, said that one of its current goals was to spruce up the two-block-long commercial district. The village has applied to Nassau County for funds for planting and benches, among other improvements. Another function of the group is to work with the Port Authority of New York and New Jersey in limiting hours of use for certain runways at nearby Kennedy Airport.

Until 1870, Lawrence was known as Rockaway Neck. The area was named Lawrence when three brothers, Alfred, George, and Newbold Lawrence, purchased large tracts of land that they donated to the South Side Rail Road Company. From its inception, the village was a planned community, geared to the fashionable and wealthy. It has been the home of industrial magnates like E. H. Harriman, owner of the New York Central Railroad; Russell Sage, the banker; George Wickersham, President William Howard Taft's attorney general; and Henry L. Stimson, Franklin D. Roosevelt's secretary of war. By 1886, there were more than 100 mansions in the village. An 1890 census indicates that the population was 697. A century later, population was nearly 10 times that figure.

In 1887, the village was incorporated. At about that time, members of the Hunting Club, founded a decade earlier, began riding to hounds. The last fox was killed in 1898, and in 1900 the club built a golf course, but retained its name to this day.

LEVITTOWN

An enduring symbol of suburban promise

BY VIVIEN KELLERMAN

At the start of the 1950s, Jim and Flora Mullens would drive from their home in New Jersey to Jones Beach on Long Island, often taking friends and relatives. One day, while driving along Wantagh Parkway, a guest looked at a sprawling new development called Levittown and said, "I've read that someday this will be the slums of Long Island."

In 1953, when Mr. Mullens, a draftsman, got a job at Republic Aviation in Farmingdale, he and his wife moved to Levittown, buying a basic two-bedroom Cape Cod on a 60- by 100-foot lot for $8,600. Forty years later, having reared their daughter, Katherine, they are still there and, to the surprise of many, Levittown has become anything but a slum.

Recalling her move, Mrs. Mullens said: "It was a kind of a miracle. We came from the city and all of a sudden we had a house with grounds and plants and young friendly families all around us."

The couple praise the developer, William Levitt, for having planned a community that included donated land for nine "village greens," which started out as combination shopping centers, swimming pools, and playgrounds. Only three still have shopping. The scattering of the greens around the community, Mrs. Mullens said, meant she did not have to learn how to drive because "everything was in walking distance."

Then, too, Mr. Mullens said, the community is only 10 minutes from the Hicksville Long Island Rail Road station, from which a trip into the city is only 40 minutes, and from Jones Beach or Bethpage State Park and only 5 to 10 minutes from the Southern State, Wantagh, or Bethpage Parkways.

"Of course, it's changed a lot," said Mrs. Mullens, "but I think it still tries to be the same kind of community today."

Some of the changes are that by 1997, nearly 11 percent of the residents were over age 65, Asians had increased from 0.17 percent of the

POPULATION: 54,000.

AREA: 6.9 square miles.

MEDIAN HOUSEHOLD INCOME: $71,078.

MEDIAN PRICE OF SINGLE-FAMILY HOUSE: $150,000.

TAXES ON A MEDIAN-PRICED HOUSE: $4,350.

PUBLIC SCHOOL SPENDING PER PUPIL: $11,212.

DISTANCE FROM MIDTOWN MANHATTAN: 30 miles.

RUSH-HOUR TRAVEL TO MIDTOWN: 10 minutes to the Long Island Rail Road Hicksville or Wantagh station, then 40 to 50 minutes; $7 one way, $154 monthly.

CODES: Area, 516; ZIP, 11756.

population in 1980 to 2.6 percent, and the Hispanic population had increased from 1.5 percent to 4.9 percent.

Perhaps no Long Island community is as well known around the world as Levittown. A few years ago, said Lynn Materrese, president of the Levittown Historical Society, a reporter from Tass, the official news service of the then-still-intact Soviet Union, came to Levittown. "They wanted to know what William Levitt did so they could duplicate something like it in Russia," said Mrs. Materrese.

What Levitt did was develop a community of affordable homes designed to serve returning servicemen and their families at the end of World War II. He had to persuade the Town of Hempstead to change an ordinance requiring basements in houses. He also built homes on lots of 60 by 100 feet, 10 feet wider than the minimum lot size.

The first 2,000 homes were built in 1947. By the time Levittown was completed five years later, 17,447 one-family houses had been put up. These included a two-bedroom, one-bath Cape Cod or ranch with room for expansion. Each house came with a washing machine, and the ranch had a fireplace that opened to the kitchen and the living room. The houses began as rentals for $60 a month and soon were selling for $6,500 and up. Fifty years later, the population had grown to 54,000 and the median price for the same house was $150,000, with taxes of about $4,350.

Despite changes, Levittown today is much as it was nearly half a century ago, though few houses are unchanged from the basic design; most have been expanded more than once.

Lisa and Sean King moved into a Levitt Cape Cod after their marriage in early 1997. Mrs. King, a substitute teacher in the Lawrence School District, about 45 minutes away, grew up in Levittown and said there was little question about where she would settle down. Mr. King is a ground-crew worker for American Airlines at La Guardia Airport, an hour's commute.

For $115,000, they bought a three-bedroom, one-bath handyman special Cape Cod that Mrs. King said had to be gutted. "My folks are here and so are a lot of my friends," Mrs. King said. "I've been through the school system and I know what it's like, and it's the kind of place where I'd like to raise a family."

The Levittown School District has six elementary schools, two middle schools, and two high schools, a 1997 total of 6,995 students and a per-pupil expenditure of $11,212. Alan Groveman, assistant superintendent of business, said that although enrollment has been increasing at about 100 students a year during the mid-1990s, space is not yet a problem. He said the district had a gifted and talented program for grades 4 to 6 and offered several advanced placement courses for high school students. During the 1990s, an average 87 percent of high school graduates went on to higher education.

The district also has a vocational high school. It is housed in the Levittown Memorial Educational Center, which also has special education programs and the district's administrative offices. The vocational high school offers more than a dozen programs, including auto mechanics, culinary arts, printing, and drafting. Half of its 500 students are Levittown residents; the rest are from other districts, which pay Levittown tuition for the service.

Of the 17,000-plus homes, about 3,300 are in the Island Trees School District, which in 1997 had 2,400 students in two elementary schools, a middle school, and a high school. It, too, has a gifted and talented program for grades 4 to 6, and Dr. Peter Egan, assistant superintendent of schools, said that since the mid-1980s, the percentage of students going on to higher education has increased from 68 percent to 91 percent.

Paul Schmidt, an agent with Century 21 Dallow Realty, said Levittown was still a community for first-time buyers, with houses ranging from around $120,000 to $190,000. Houses that are priced well sell in about two months. The biggest drawback, said Mr. Schmidt, are the high taxes. "We have no industry here, and school taxes are very high," he said. Median taxes for a one-family house in 1997 were $4,350. There are five garden apartment complexes with a total of 278 units. The largest are Cambridge Village, with 78 units, and Kensington Lane, with 80. Prices for both remained stable during the mid-1990s, with one-bedroom units selling for about $99,500 and two-bedrooms for about $103,000.

In 1992, the Town of Hempstead approved an ordinance that lets people over 60 convert part of their home into an accessory apartment. By 1997, 58 people had received permits for these apartments.

The 250-unit Levittown Senior Center is a subsidized Hempstead Town housing project for those over 60. To be eligible for these apartments, the 1997 income level was no more than $29,100 for singles and $33,300 for couples.

At the center is a town-operated activity center open five days a week for anyone in Hempstead Town over 60; free bus transportation to the center is available. The center offers free arts and crafts and classes in language and creative writing.

In addition to shops in three village greens, there are about 200 stores along Hempstead Turnpike and the major north-south roadways, said Edward Szala, who served as president of the Levittown Chamber of Commerce between 1993 and 1994. Most are neighborhood stores, but there is also a Caldor, a Kmart, and a Lord & Taylor outlet. Mr. Szala said that there had been a constant turnover but that few stores were empty.

Restaurants often mentioned are Domenico's and Portofino, both Italian; Old Country Buffet, which, as its name suggests, serves country-style food such as fried chicken and mashed potatoes; and Landmark Grill, a popular steak house.

The area's settlement history dates to 1635, when Capt. John Seaman and Robert Jackson together bought 1,500 acres from the Matinecock Indians and settled on the land with their families.

One part of Levittown was originally named Jerusalem. Another, smaller, section was called Island Trees. The thickest settlement came in the early 19th century, and most residents then were farmers.

By the time William Levitt came around, potato farming was a primary source of income, but the crops eventually fell victim to disease and many farmers sold their land and moved away.

LOCUST VALLEY

A golden reminder of a genteel past

BY JOHN RATHER

Locust Valley and the surrounding villages are in the heartland of Long Island's famous Gold Coast, a North Shore expanse where the fabulously wealthy and socially prominent built magnificent estates in woods and on rolling terrain beginning in the late 19th century. Life was never so grand again after the stock market crash of 1929, and by the end of World War II, when servants had grown scarce, many of the old estates had been subdivided or turned into clubs or parks. The carriage trade that once supported the area is gone. But regal manor houses still rise from the woodlands and fields along many twisting, two-lane roads.

The area remains one of the wealthiest in the country, a vestige from another age that largely escaped Long Island's post–World War II suburbanization because of strict curbs on development set in place by village founders.

A bias against development or unwanted change, backed by tough village zoning laws, still runs deep. "You can't cut a tree down here without having quite a bit of controversy," said Edith Hay Wyckoff of Matinecock, the founder, editor, and publisher of *The Locust Valley Leader*, a weekly newspaper that celebrated its 50th anniversary in 1997.

In the strictest sense, Locust Valley refers only to an unincorporated hamlet where the post office, 65,000-volume library, Long Island Rail Road station, firehouse, shops, boutiques, and a Gristede's food market are located. Small-lot capes, ranches, and Colonials in the surrounding unincorporated area sell in the $200,000 to $400,000 range, as affordable as it gets in the area. But it is generally agreed that the villages of Lattingtown, Matinecock, and Mill Neck, where homes are much more expensive, are also a part of what is called Locust Valley. With few exceptions, zoning in these villages is two-acre and five-acre.

POPULATION: 7,909 (Locust Valley, 4,081; Lattingtown, 1,966; Matinecock, 875; Mill Neck; 987).

AREA: 10 square miles.

MEDIAN HOUSEHOLD INCOME: Unincorporated Locust Valley, $71,006; Lattingtown, $126,786; Matinecock, $109,211; Mill Neck, $118,000.

MEDIAN PRICE OF A SINGLE-FAMILY HOUSE: $650,000.

TAXES ON A MEDIAN-PRICED HOUSE: $10,000.

PUBLIC SCHOOL SPENDING PER PUPIL: $15,125.

DISTANCE FROM MIDTOWN MANHATTAN: 33 miles.

RUSH-HOUR TRAVEL TO MIDTOWN: 70 minutes on the Long Island Rail Road from the Locust Valley station, $7 one way, $154 monthly.

CODES: Area, 516; ZIP, 11560 and 11765.

There are 7,900 residents in the 10-mile-square area encompassing the three villages and the Locust Valley hamlet that lends its name to the sum of these parts. "People who live there will say they live in Locust Valley," said Bonnie Devendorf, an associate broker, manager, and vice president of Daniel Gale Associates in Locust Valley, a Sotheby's International Realty affiliate. Home prices in these villages range from well above $500,000 to several million dollars.

Mrs. Wyckoff, whose newspaper serves, along with the Locust Valley School District, as a unifier of the wider area, said that a still broader definition included Upper Brookville, Old Brookville, and even Brookville. The exact borders will be left for others to ponder, with a caution from Mrs. Wyckoff about calling the area the Gold Coast. "No one who knows anything calls it that," she said.

Real estate values are clearly gold-plated. The median house price was $650,000 early in 1997, up about $15,000 from five years earlier. By the last quarter of 1997, prices were holding, and the market was brisk. Taxes on a typical $650,000 house were about $10,000 in the fourth quarter of 1997, though tax figures vary greatly from house to house.

There are no condominiums or co-ops. Rentals for single-family homes or for estate cottages in the villages range from $3,000 to $4,000 monthly, when they can be found. A large apartment in a house in the unincorporated area of Locust Valley was on the market in early 1997 for $1,200 a month.

Locust Valley's old link to the fate of the stock market remains. "Our market is somewhat driven by Wall Street, and, of course, Wall Street has been doing very well lately," said Mrs. Devendorf, who said upper-end sales had been strong in 1996 and 1997. Patrick H. Mackay, the president of Piping Rock Associates, another real estate company serving Locust Valley, said a plunge on Wall Street could chill the area's currently hot housing market in a New York minute. "We were so stagnant here after the market crashed in October 1987," he said, recalling that sales declined by 35 percent to 40 percent from 1988 to the end of 1991.

Locust Valley is tucked away from major highways. Signposts are scarce on undulating roads that seem designed for sport utility vehicles. There are few directional signs, and traffic is light. Commuting time to Manhattan, 33 miles away, is 70 minutes on the Long Island Rail Road from the Locust Valley station.

The first European settlers arrived in Locust Valley in the 1660s and settled permanently after the Matinecock Indians made land deals with Capt. John Underhill, who named the area Buckram, and others. The origin of the name Buckram is obscure, but it may refer to a coarse cloth used in clothing, book binding, and wrappers, which may have been produced in the area.

In 1725, Quakers built a meeting house near the intersection of Piping Rock Road and Duck Pond Road near the Matinecock and Glen Cove border. It was destroyed by fire in 1985. A new meeting house on the site replicates the original. The name Buckram endured until 1856, when, according to Mrs. Wyckoff, the president of the Long Island Rail Road, Oliver Charlick, forced a change. "He said he would not have the railroad stop at a place called Buckram," Mrs. Wyckoff said. "People decided they would rather have the train than the name." The name Locust Valley was chosen, she said, "because we have locust trees all over the place."

Trees of many varieties, exotic shrubs, and flower beds are plentiful at the Bailey Arboretum in Lattingtown, a 42-acre Nassau County Park on a former estate with a mid-19th-century Gold Coast mansion. The arboretum is open from April to November.

Two exclusive private clubs, the Creek and the Piping Rock Club, are also located in the area. The Creek, in Lattingtown, a preserve for the wealthy from its beginnings in the 1920s, has an 18-hole golf course, tennis, swimming, croquet, paddle tennis, and a health spa. There are about 500 members. Piping Rock, an elite club begun by wealthy sportsmen some years earlier, also has an 18-hole course and other amenities, and was famous for its horse shows until they ended in the 1960s.

The Locust Valley School District serves Locust Valley, Lattingtown, Matinecock, Bayville, and parts of Mill Neck, Muttontown, Old Brookville, and Upper Brookville. Part of Mill Neck is in the Oyster Bay School District. "We have a small district which can provide students and parents with a more personal touch to education," said Anthony L. Singe, the Locust Valley district superintendent. About 2,100 students were enrolled in kindergarten through 12th grade in the 1997–98 school year. Spending per pupil was $15,125.

The district offers a full complement of advanced placement courses. About 60 percent of students receive Regents diplomas. About 90 percent go on to higher education. Average scores on the SAT in recent years were 540 in verbal and 570 in math, according to the district. Both scores are significantly above state and national averages.

The middle school, for grades 6 through 8, emphasizes an interdisciplinary curriculum. Two elementary schools, for students in kindergarten through grade 5, have computers in every classroom and special programs for academically gifted children beginning in fourth grade.

Locust Valley also has two private day schools with strong reputations. Friends Academy, situated on 65 acres across from the Quaker meeting house, has 700 students in nursery and prekindergarten through 12th grade, most drawn from a radius of 15 miles. Though few students are Quakers, instruction in Quaker beliefs and philosophy is part of the curriculum. Friends is the only independent school in Nassau County that competes with public schools in sports. Tuition ranges from $7,000 to $14,000, depending on grade and not including books and meals. A new theater-and-arts center and commons is to be joined by a new library, and projects to enlarge and renovate the middle and upper schools are in the works.

The Portledge School, situated on 62 enclosed acres on the former Coffin family estate in Locust Valley, has 350 students in prekindergarten through grade 12, with most also drawn from about a 15-mile radius. Admission is competitive at both schools, and virtually all graduates go on to college. Tuition ranges from $3,350 for prekindergarten to $14,950 in upper grades.

A visit to Locust Valley begins best in the commercial area along Forest Avenue and Birch Hill Road, where shops are decorated with live greenery for Christmas and all the wreaths are real. The area's old original name and equestrian past survive at the Buckram Stables Cafe, one of several taverns and restaurants in the downtown area. Reservations are recommended at Barney's, one of several standout restaurants. The name recalls the hulking fire chief who lived in the house long before it became a sophisticated yet rustic restaurant.

Locust Valley and surrounding villages, with their fields, woods, and sparse residential development, are part of an environmentally important 45-square-mile groundwater recharge area. The Long Island Regional Planning Board designated the area as one of nine special groundwater protection zones in a 1992 report. Tap water in the zone is as pure and sweet as the costliest bottled waters, some people say. "It's fantastic, the best water ever," said Joan Bruce, an administrative assistant at the Locust Valley Water District. The district serves about 2,400 households in Locust Valley, Lattingtown, Matinecock, and part of Mill Neck. "We don't chlorinate. Nothing is added," said Ms. Bruce. "The quality is way above anything required by Nassau County or the state, and the taste is very good."

MANHASSET

A prosperous enclave of gracious living

BY JOHN RATHER

From the crest of Manhasset Avenue, it is possible to view two features that help make well-to-do Manhasset a blue-chip area. On one side, beneath an overpass, Long Island Rail Road tracks lead to Manhattan, a brisk 28-minute commute on spiffy express trains that run, after one stop in Great Neck, uninterrupted to Penn Station. Nonexpress trains make the trip in about 40 minutes. Down a sweeping entrance road on the other side, the clock tower of Manhasset High School, one of Long Island's most highly regarded public schools, rises from a handsome campus. Ninety-five percent of the graduating seniors routinely go on to higher education, many to colleges and universities rated highly competitive.

"There is no doubt our schools and our commute to the city are two of our best points," said Diane Harragan, the president of Blaich House and Home Realty. But in Manhasset, she and others said, there is much more.

An air of unquenchable prosperity, subdued but unmistakable, pervades distinct neighborhoods where roomy, sturdily constructed, single-family houses, many built during the 1930s or earlier, have been upgraded, expanded, and improved.

By tradition, Manhasset is defined as an 8.5-square-mile area roughly within the Manhasset School District. Home to 18,000 residents, it includes an unincorporated area and all or most of five villages: Plandome, Plandome Heights, Plandome Manor, Munsey Park, and Flower Hill. A sixth village, North Hills, is partially within the Manhasset School District.

At the end of 1997, median taxes were in the $6,000 range for a median-priced $550,000 house. But, in a pattern typical of Nassau County, taxes varied considerably for houses in the same price range. In late 1997, taxes on houses in Strathmore Vanderbilt valued at $659,000, $710,000, and $719,000 were $7,000, $7,700, and $8,160, respectively. In Munsey Park,

POPULATION: 18,010.

AREA: 8.5 square miles.

MEDIAN HOUSEHOLD INCOME: Unincorporated area, $89,838; Munsey Park, $145,838; Plandome, $153,070; Plandome Heights, $98,485; Plandome Manor, $183,478; Flower Hill, $141,107.

MEDIAN PRICE OF A SINGLE-FAMILY HOUSE: $550,000.

TAXES ON A MEDIAN-PRICED HOUSE: $6,000.

DISTANCE FROM MIDTOWN MANHATTAN: 17 miles.

PUBLIC SCHOOL SPENDING PER PUPIL: $16,783.

RUSH-TRAVEL TO MIDTOWN: 28 minutes on the Long Island Rail Road express trains, $6.75 one way, $135 monthly.

CODES: Area, 516; ZIP, 11030.

taxes on houses valued at $589,000 and $559,000 were $8,100 and $9,000.

Realtors said they had no doubt what was driving the vigorous market in which median house prices gained about 5 percent between the summer of 1996 and fall of 1997, with increases even greater in villages such as Plandome—record gains on Wall Street, a leading economic indicator for Manhasset-area real estate.

Villages and unincorporated areas are pleasing to the eye and triumphantly intact. Homes built by William Levitt before World War II give a strong unifying element to the Strathmore and Strathmore Vanderbilt unincorporated areas, where "every house is magnificent and very different," said Carole Belley of Lovejoy Real Estate. The homes are notably grander than those that Levitt went on to build in Levittown. Scrupulously maintained early-19th-century homes rise from landscaped splendor in older villages, where Colonials, Dutch Colonials, and Tudors shine.

Then there is Manhasset Bay, where sailing is a passion. Private clubs include the Manhasset Bay Yacht Club and the Port Washington Yacht Club for sailing, boating, tennis, and dining. For golfers, the Plandome Country Club has an 18-hole course. One village, Plandome, has its own dock and a village green with tennis courts.

The 36-acre Long Island Science Museum on the Leeds Pond Preserve offers educational programs emphasizing field and lab studies on its wooded grounds.

And the Miracle Mile, a regional shopping hub on Northern Boulevard, features the tony 193,000-square-foot, 50-store Americana at Manhasset shopping plaza, including Giorgio Armani and Barneys on one end and stores like Lord & Taylor and Barnes & Noble on the other.

But on nearby Plandome Road, where a new clock tower on a commercial building is a recent adornment, Manhasset's traditional downtown shopping area and its enduring hometown feeling have not been eclipsed.

Some longtime Plandome Road staples have been lost. Wright Hardware, a mainstay since 1921, left a gap and a vacant storefront when it closed. But the old downtown is generally thriving and other familiar haunts remain. The Manhasset Theater triplex movie house, which, with its Art Deco design, opened in 1935, is still a focal point.

Annie V. Holdreith, a sales agent at O'Connell Real Estate, said Manhasset reminded her of a New England village. But the economy, she and others said, is tied to that other island. "Other towns can be affected by the Long Island economy," Ms. Holdreith said. "Here, we are driven by the Manhattan economy because of all the people who work in the city."

While Manhasset is overwhelmingly white, a black community has deep roots in an area once known as the Valley. The A.M.E. Zion Church on Community Drive, built in 1833 and now a Town of North Hempstead designated historic landmark, served free blacks and Matinecock Indians before the Civil War and still holds services.

North Shore University Hospital is also on Community Drive, as are a number of commercial buildings.

Manhasset has a full array of civic organizations, Protestant and Catholic churches, and Jewish synagogues. The Friends Meeting House on Northern Boulevard, an old Indian trail, marks a Quaker presence that dates to the 17th century.

The nearby Onderdonk House, built in 1836, is a town landmark and a leading example of Greek Revival architecture. It was the home of Judge Horatio Gates Onderdonk, grandson of Adrian Onderdonk, the town's first supervisor.

Home prices tend to be lower in unincorporated areas of Manhasset, though the Whitney estate and other grand properties are in these areas south of Northern Boulevard. But in general, prices tend to be higher in the villages of Plandome Heights, Munsey Park, and Flower Hill, and highest in the villages of Plandome and Plandome Manor.

House rentals, when they can be found, range from $2,000 to more than $3,000 a month for a three-bedroom house. They are far higher for larger homes. The 200 or so condominiums on Shelter Rock and Searingtown Roads sell from about $400,000 to $800,000.

Stone Hill, a housing development under construction on the former William S. Paley estate on Shelter Rock Road, will offer custom homes for around $1 million. Nearby, homes at the Grace Wood development on the former W. R. Grace estate start at $750,000.

Many Manhasset children attend private schools, but the general feeling here is that Manhasset public schools, with about 2,300 students, are equal or superior to them. Spending per pupil was $16,783, according to 1997 state figures. In 1996, voters approved a $21.5 million proposal to reconstruct, enlarge, and improve public school buildings.

Nearly three-quarters of Manhasset High School graduates have earned Regents diplomas in recent years. Graduating classes typically number less than 200. Advanced placement courses, honors classes, and advanced research programs are offered. More than 80 percent of students participate in extracurricular programs. And there are more than 60 athletic teams.

The middle school, for seventh and eighth grades, is in the high school complex. There are two elementary schools for kindergarten through sixth grade, the Munsey Park School and the Shelter Rock School.

St. Mary's Roman Catholic School on Northern Boulevard teaches kindergarten through 12th grade and also has prekindergarten programs. About 95 percent of graduates go on to college. Eight hundred and fifty students attend the high school. Tuition was $4,450 for the 1997–98 school year. The ice hockey team won state championships in 1996 and 1997.

Sister Mariette, the assistant principal at St. Mary's, said the school attracted students from diverse economic and cultural backgrounds. About 450 pupils attend elementary classes. Extended-day programs through the eighth grade run to 6:30 P.M. Tuition ranges up to $2,700.

The name Manhasset, first applied between 1835 and 1845 to an area previously known as Little Cow Bay, was derived from the Indian word *Manhansett*, meaning "island neighborhood." The Matinecocks called the Manhasset area Sink Sink, meaning "place of many stones." By the 17th century, the British and Dutch were disputing ownership. In 1640, English settlers from Lynn, Massachusetts, sailed into Cow Bay, now Manhasset Bay, but were chased off by the Dutch. They sailed on to Southampton.

Shelter Rock, a large glacial boulder with a ledge that once sheltered Matinecock Indians from wind and rain, is still visible along Shelter Rock Road.

On the eve of the Revolutionary War, residents of the north shore of Hempstead split with their Loyalist neighbors to the south. Many joined the Continental Army or local militias. In 1784, in a reflection of the split, the state legislature formed the northern area into the Town of North Hempstead. The town hall, not built until 1907, is on Plandome Road in Manhasset, opposite a park where the old Plandome Road School once stood.

A trestle crossing the valley brought the Long Island Rail Road to Manhasset in 1897. But not until 1924, when a new station was dedicated at its current site, did downtown Manhasset begin to grow. By the 1930s, Manhasset was already established as a prosperous commuter town. Another station is in Plandome.

Manhasset housing prices soared in the mid-seventies and have been climbing, with few pauses, ever since. "In the early 1970s, you could get together $25,000 and move here," said Charles M. Studness, a Manhasset resident. "Now entry people need a lot more resources."

NORTHPORT

Charm snuggled along a North Shore harbor

BY VIVIEN KELLERMAN

Nestled on a harbor that shares its name, the Village of Northport, with its eclectic Main Street shopping, its dock and gazebo, and its tree-lined hilly streets that rise 175 feet above sea level, is a popular summer tourist destination. But despite the summer hordes, Northport manages to remain very much a community. Residents take pride in the village's charming blend of homes, local shops, school district, village hall, private police department, and location away from the highways, on the North Shore of Long Island.

Frequently, even those who move away often manage to return to this village, which is part of Huntington Township in western Suffolk County. George and Vaughan Costsonas were both born in Northport and lived there until 1974, when they were married. In 1994, they bought a house in the village that they planned to rent out. But their teenage children, Keri and Christopher, liked the village so much that the family decided to move into the house, and rent out the one they occupied in bordering Eaton's Neck. The family moved into a 35-year-old three-bedroom, three-bath ranch that has a finished basement, sits on one-half acre, and cost $240,000. "It's a quaint, different world here," said Mr. Costsonas, who has a computer business 25 minutes away in Melville. "It has a nice mix of old shops and new. It's just a great place to live."

In 1997, single-family houses in Northport ranged in price from $200,000 for a small 1950s Cape on a 50- by 100-foot lot to more than $1 million for a 6,000-square-foot waterfront home on one acre, said Billy Byer, the owner of Adelaide Byer Realtors. Prices rose about 5 percent a year between 1993 and 1997, when the median price was $225,000 and median taxes were $4,800. Mr. Byer said that, reflecting an active real estate market, houses that were not overpriced sold quickly, and few houses

POPULATION: 7,571.

AREA: 2.3 square miles.

MEDIAN HOUSEHOLD INCOME: $76,256.

MEDIAN PRICE OF A SINGLE-FAMILY HOUSE: $225,000.

TAXES ON A MEDIAN-PRICED HOUSE: $4,800.

PUBLIC SCHOOL SPENDING PER PUPIL: $12,386.

DISTANCE FROM MIDTOWN MANHATTAN: 40 miles.

RUSH-HOUR TRAVEL TO MIDTOWN: 75 minutes on the Long Island Rail Road, $8.50 one way, $181 monthly.

CODES: Area, 516; ZIP, 11768.

were for sale. New residents, he said, were mostly young professionals with children.

In 1994, the village celebrated its centennial; when it was incorporated in 1894, the population, now about 7,500, was about 1,000.

Village homes reflect the changes the years have wrought. "Northport is unusual in that you could have a big house next to a small one, an old one next to a newer one," said Mr. Byer.

Although most of the homes in the village are custom built, Northport Bay Estates, which was built on an old sandpit in the '60s, has about 150 ranches, Colonials, and farm ranches on one-acre lots. Some have waterfront locations. Prices range from $275,000 to $450,000.

The village has three condominium complexes. At the 66-unit waterfront Harbor Point, prices in 1997 ranged from $450,000 for a two-bedroom unit to $800,000 for a five-bedroom unit. The complex has man-made ponds and its own marina. Greentree Estates has 46 town house units priced from $225,000 to $275,000. At Fairwind, the third condominium in the village, 20 units of waterfront and water-view town house apartments were selling in 1997 for $325,000 to $550,000.

There are four rental apartment complexes with a total of 90 units in the village, as well as apartments in private homes. Bayview, a four-story building on the harbor, was built in the early 1900s. The apartments, all two-bedrooms, rent for about $1,000, plus the cost of heating. Prices for other village apartments range from about $650 to $975 for a one-bedroom and $800 to $1,000 for a two-bedroom.

A recent returnee to Northport is Edward Yule, who grew up in the village. At one point, he and his wife, Victoria, lived about five miles away, in South Huntington, but dreamed of moving to Northport. For a while, they weren't sure they would make it. "We had a budget of the low $200's, but there was nothing around," said Mrs. Yule, a ticket agent who works at the Sea Cliff Long Island Rail Road station, about a half hour away. Mr. Yule, a lawyer, works about 30 minutes away in Islip. In 1994, they found a 100-year-old three-bedroom, 1½-bath Colonial that sits at the top of a steep hill, for which they paid $209,000. "It's very pretty here," Mrs. Yule said.

"But with two young children, one reason we wanted to come to Northport was because the school district is so excellent."

There are nine schools, six K–5 elementary, two 6–8 middle, and one high school with a 1997 enrollment of 5,438 in the Northport/East Northport School District. The district serves Northport, the unincorporated hamlet of East Northport, Asharoken, and Eaton's Neck, and had a 1997 per-pupil expenditure of $12,386.

Superintendent of Schools William Brosnan said that enrollment has been growing for the last several years, and to accommodate the increase, in 1995 the district reopened a building it had closed years earlier, moving the existing middle school students into it. The district then closed the smaller building. Dr. Brosnan said that if current projections of 400 additional students in the next ten years are accurate, the district will have enough space without having to make any additional changes.

Most Northport students attend the Ocean Avenue Elementary School, while all attend Northport Middle School. A few younger students go to the Norwood Elementary School.

The district has a comprehensive computer program that begins in elementary school. A program for gifted and talented students is housed at three district schools, including Ocean Avenue Elementary. Students from other district schools are bused to these three.

Dr. Brosnan said the Northport Middle School emphasizes writing and has a computer lab and an arts and literary magazine, *Imagine*, that has won several awards, including first place in the 1994 Columbia Scholastic Press Association competition.

Dr. Brosnan said that an average of 89 percent of the district's graduates go on to higher education. Since 1995, high school students have been engaged in a statewide pilot program that allows students to receive, via satellite, live television programs from around the world. Dr. Brosnan said students studying foreign languages can tune into news programs in that language.

Although the village does not have a historic district or any structures in the National Register of Historic Places, it does have an active historical society, formed in the '70s. The group runs lectures, an annual holiday party, and spring and summer walking tours of Main Street. The society holds its meetings in the village museum, a 1914 building financed by Andrew Carnegie that once served as the village's library. In addition to rotating exhibits, the museum, which opened in 1974, has a permanent exhibition celebrating the area's history.

For recreation, Northport's park at the dock offers a turn-of-the-century atmosphere featuring a playground, a gazebo, and free concerts every Thursday evening in summer. Scudder Park, on Beach Avenue, has a beach and picnic area, and Steer's Park and Beach, off Eaton's Neck Road, has four baseball fields and two soccer fields. The Town of Huntington operates Asharoken Beach, which adjoins Steer's Beach. To use village beaches, residents must obtain a parking sticker; the cost is $5 a season.

One of the most popular annual village events is Cow Harbor Day, which gets its name from Northport's original name. Sponsored by the chamber of commerce, it is held the last Sunday in September, attracts about 15,000 people, and includes parades, games, and boat races in the harbor.

There are about 75 shops in Northport, the majority of them on Main Street or Fort Salonga Road. The eclectic mix includes antiques, arts and crafts and gift shops, art galleries, beauty salons, clothing stores, delicatessens, and health-food stores. The million-square-foot Walt Whitman Mall in Huntington is about 10 minutes away.

There are more than a dozen restaurants within the village confines. A popular destination is the Sweet Shop, an old-fashioned luncheonette opened in 1929 by George Panarites. His daughter Georgia Pappias and son Peter G. Panarites run the store, which features homemade ice cream, malteds, and egg creams.

For all its charm, one of Northport's perceived advantages can also be a drawback. It is relatively isolated, situated about 15 minutes from the nearest parkway, the Northern State. The nearest railroad station is in nearby East Northport, where a ride into Manhattan is 75 minutes.

Northport traces its modern history to 1650, when travelers from New Amsterdam reported their discovery to the Dutch government. Six years later, the area was purchased from Chief Asharoken of the Matinecock Indians by three Englishmen, and soon after, a small colony flourished with farming and shellfishing. By the 1830s, the name Northport was beginning to replace Cow Harbor, and shipbuilding had became a major industry. The Village of Northport was incorporated in 1894, the same year the Northport Electric Light Company was founded. Northport was the first village in Huntington Township to convert to electricity. In 1911, the company merged with others nearby to form the Long Island Lightning Company.

In 1902, the Northport Trolley line began operating. The trolleys ran until 1924, when buses were introduced. The tracks have been preserved as a reminder of the village's past.

OLD WESTBURY

The way things were is how they are

BY VIVIEN KELLERMAN

In 1929, owners of estates in Old Westbury offered to contribute $175,000 toward development of the Northern State Parkway to make it "worthy of the best traditions and standards of the region." In return, the state agreed to create a five-mile bulge in the road, avoiding Old Westbury.

In the world of high society on Long Island's Gold Coast, the Graces, Whitneys, Guests, Phippses, and other families would gladly pay to protect their community. And the desire to maintain the privacy and prestige of this North Shore village is still strong today.

With no commercial development, four-acre minimum zoning, miles of horse trails, palatial estates, rolling hills, an active polo club, and a 30-member police force to protect it all, Old Westbury, just 45 minutes from Manhattan on the Long Island Rail Road, is as desirable as it was when the rich and famous discovered it at the end of the last century.

The Village of Old Westbury was first settled in 1658 and called Wood-edge. Several years later, Quaker settlers renamed it Westbury after their town in England. The area remained virtually isolated until the end of the 19th century, when prominent New York families began buying the land. Many of the old estates have been broken up and sold, but half a dozen still remain and their occupants live much the way they did in the village's heyday.

Although it takes up 17 percent of Nassau County's land, Old Westbury has only 4,300 residents, less than 1 percent of Nassau County's population. More than half of the village's 5,440 acres belong to a private school, several public schools and colleges, houses of worship, and country clubs.

The manor house and 190 acres of the 530-acre estate established by William C. Whitney is now the Old Westbury Golf and Country Club. (The

POPULATION: 4,345.

AREA: 8.4 square miles.

MEDIAN HOUSEHOLD INCOME: $198,611.

MEDIAN PRICE OF A SINGLE-FAMILY HOUSE: $1.1 million.

TAXES ON A MEDIAN-PRICED HOUSE: $20,000.

PUBLIC SCHOOL SPENDING PER PUPIL: East Williston, $15,483; Jericho, $16,506; Westbury, $13,118.

DISTANCE FROM MIDTOWN MANHATTAN: 20 miles.

RUSH-HOUR TRAVEL TO MIDTOWN: 45 minutes on the Long Island Rail Road, $7 one way, $154 monthly.

CODES: Area, 516; ZIP, 11568.

Glen Oaks Club is the only other golf club in the community.) The remaining acreage of the estate houses the New York Institute of Technology.

The State University of New York bought the 650-acre estate once owned by a millionaire sportsman, F. M. Ambrose Clark, and turned the property into the SUNY Old Westbury campus.

But not all the property can be absorbed in this manner, and so as the land is subdivided for homes, the village has adopted restrictions to preserve open space. One rule requires developers to provide a 10-foot-wide easement for horse trails on their property.

"Old Westbury has a long history with horses, going back to polo matches on the estates," said John Shalam, president of the Old Westbury Horsemen's Association. Mr. Shalam said there were about 25 miles of horse trails in the village and that about 25 percent of the 175 members of the association used them. "A lot of people become members in order to support the concept of the trails," he said.

A polo field on Whitney Lane is the site of summer matches run by the Meadowbrook Polo Club. The field is also used for an annual association fund-raiser. Riding exhibits, jumping, and a polo match are open to all village residents.

Eleanor Simpson, who served intermittently as mayor since 1976, with her last term ending in 1996, said that to prevent overdevelopment, minimum zoning was changed in 1987 from two acres to four in most cases. Moreover, any development is scrupulously controlled. The effect has been to create a community where the median price of a house is more than $1 million, and the annual median property tax by 1997 was $20,000.

Home prices did drop about 20 percent during the recession, but they are back up now, said Sandy Binder, owner of Daniel Gale Associates, Inc./Sandy Binder Division, in nearby East Hills. While some of the estates could take years to sell, she said, the general market for houses in the village has been strong, with only 8 percent of the village's 900 homes on the market in 1997. During the mid-1990s, a building boom began as several large estates were sold and subdivided. Three- and four-acre lots sold for prices that ranged from $650,000 to $975,000.

Single-family homes in the Old Westbury Pines area off Glen Cove Road start at about $600,000. Built about 40 years ago, these are 3,000-square-foot ranches with three bedrooms and 2½ baths on one acre. An 18-year-old ranch of 6,000 square feet with three bedrooms, 3½ baths, and an indoor pool recently sold for $1.1 million.

At the high end is a former Whitney estate, a brick manor home on 19 acres with a pool, indoor and outdoor tennis courts, two caretakers' cottages, and a four-bedroom guest cottage. In the mid-1990s, the property was sold for $6.525 million.

When Dr. Richard Taubman and his wife, Laurie, were looking for a house five years ago, they wanted wide-open space and serenity. An obstetrician with two offices, each about 10 minutes from home, and an affiliation with Long Island Jewish Hospital, 15 minutes away, he found that Old Westbury offered him all he and his wife wanted. Mrs. Taubman, who works in her husband's offices, said the house they bought has a deck outside the master bedroom that overlooks woods in the back. "You stand outside and hear all the beautiful sounds," she said.

The Taubmans' two children, Carley and Eric, attend the East Williston Union Free School District, one of three school districts serving Old Westbury. The district has one K–4 elementary school, one 5–7 middle school, and one high school, with a total enrollment of 1,500.

The superintendent of schools, David Helme, said that approximately 600 children from Old Westbury generally attend schools in the district. About 95 percent of the district's graduates go on to higher education, nearly all to four-year schools.

An arrangement with the Cold Spring Harbor Laboratory and the Winthrop University Hospital nearby allows students from the middle and high schools interested in science to work with mentors on specialized projects. In 1994, the high school had one semifinalist in the Westinghouse Science Competition. Computers are in elementary-grade classrooms as well as in the library.

Other Old Westbury students attend the Jericho Union Free School District, which has four schools, two K–5 elementary schools, one 6–8 middle school, and one high school, with an enrollment in 1997 of 2,573, said Henry Grishman, superintendent of schools. Computer instruction begins in kindergarten and every elementary classroom has three computers. Once a week after school, pupils may participate in a cultural arts program. Taught by teachers and run by parent volunteers, it provides a wide array of subjects, including art, dance, and cooking. Mr. Grishman said that during the 1990s, an average of 46 percent of each year's high school graduates have been recognized by the College Board for their exceptional achievement on the college-level Advanced Placement Examinations. Mr. Grishman said that generally about 175 Old Westbury students attend Jericho schools.

Another choice is the Westbury Public Schools, but less than half a dozen Old Westbury students generally enroll there. Two-thirds of the 534 Old Westbury students attend private schools, according to the 1990 census. Old Westbury is the site of the School of the Holy Child, a private, independent Roman Catholic day school with an enrollment of 170 students, and tuition ranging from $3,300 to $11,000 a year, depending on grade. It offers a nursery and classes through eighth grade.

There is no commercial development within the village except for one diner–gas station built at the time that the Northern State Parkway was being completed. Shopping is within easy reach either in Garden City to the south or Manhasset and Great Neck to the west.

The 100-acre Old Westbury Gardens, with a mansion that was once the home of the financier John S. Phipps and his wife, Margarita Grace, is now owned by the J. S. Phipps Foundation. It has a large expanse of formal gardens, and concerts, lectures, and other special events are offered from April through December with admission $6 for adults and $3 for children 6 to 12. The estate is open Wednesday to Monday from 10 A.M. to 5 P.M.

A good deal of energy in Old Westbury is spent on keeping development appropriate. This energy included taking on the state when it wanted to widen the Long Island Expressway. Village trustees were successful in getting the state to agree to leave the natural vegetation in place and not build walls. Moreover, the width of the road is 30 feet narrower than the state had projected. "It takes constant vigilance that is carried over into all our boards—planning, architectural review, and zoning—to maintain the village's integrity," Mayor Simpson said. "We have legislation to protect what we have now and into the future."

OYSTER BAY

A waterfront hamlet awash in history

BY VIVIEN KELLERMAN

Nestled along Oyster Bay Harbor on Long Island's Gold Coast is Oyster Bay, population 7,000, a hamlet of tree-lined streets, a downtown shopping district, a Long Island Rail Road station from which a trip to Manhattan is 90 minutes, and so many historic structures and landmarks in and around it that it is a wonder it has remained essentially a small town.

Around it are the exclusive villages of Cove Neck, Oyster Bay Cove, Centre Island, Mill Neck, Locust Valley, and East Norwich—all but Mill Neck and Locust Valley sharing a school district with Oyster Bay. But Oyster Bay itself is an eclectic mix of working-class and professional people whose homes range from subsidized low-income and rental housing for the elderly to huge one-family houses on two acres. Except for occasional handyman specials, homes rarely sell for less than $250,000, said Barbara Lippman, owner of Cove Realty in Oyster Bay. The median price for a one-family house in the last quarter of 1997 was $300,000 and typical property taxes for such homes were $5,000.

"Houses priced between $250,000 and $500,000 sell almost immediately, especially if they are in good shape," said Ms. Lippman. "Higher-priced homes are not selling that quickly," she said, "but overall, not many houses are coming on the market anyway."

Most of Oyster Bay was developed as subdivisions in the '50s and '60s. Forest Estates, a community of about 50 split-levels, ranches, and Colonials on quarter-acre lots, and a swimming pool, is typical. House prices there range from $325,000 to $425,000. Houses in Sherwood Gate—about 40 custom homes on two-acre lots built in the mid-1980s—were selling in 1997 for about $825,000.

There are two rental complexes in Oyster Bay with a total of 366 units. The larger, Norwich Gates Townhouses, has 348 units. One-bedrooms rent

POPULATION: 7,050.

AREA: 1.2 square miles.

MEDIAN HOUSEHOLD INCOME: $66,590.

MEDIAN PRICE OF A SINGLE-FAMILY HOUSE: $300,000.

TAXES ON A MEDIAN-PRICED HOUSE: $5,000.

PUBLIC SCHOOL SPENDING PER PUPIL: $15,867.

DISTANCE FROM MIDTOWN MANHATTAN: 28 miles.

RUSH-HOUR TRAVEL TO MIDTOWN: 90 minutes on the Long Island Rail Road from Oyster Bay, or 10 minutes to Syosset, then 60 minutes on the Long Island Rail Road, $7 one way, $154 monthly, for both stations.

CODES: Area, 516; ZIP, 11771.

for about $1,100 and two-bedrooms for about $1,300. The other, Frederick Apartments, has 18 units in one building; one-bedrooms are $850 and two-bedrooms $1,000. Rents during the mid-1990s remained stable.

Condominium prices were also relatively flat during the mid-1990s. The 34-unit Landmark Colony, within walking distance of the beach, is a Victorian-style condominium complex in five attached town houses built in the late 1970s. Two-bedroom, two-bath units there started, in 1997, at about $250,000.

The market is slow for the two co-op complexes, and prices in the mid-1990s actually decreased. One-bedroom units at the 156-unit Top of the Harbor that sold for about $80,000 in 1994 were going for about $60,000 three years later. Two-bedrooms that had been $100,000 went for about $80,000. Rental prices of $1,000 to $1,200 for the units remained unchanged. At the 80-unit Lexington Estates, units sell for about the same price but cannot be rented out.

Dr. Francis Banta, superintendent of the Oyster Bay–East Norwich School District, which had a 1997 enrollment of 1,480, said that studies project that an additional 200 students are expected by the year 2005. The district, which had a 1997 per-pupil expenditure of $15,867, has one K–3 elementary school, one 4–8 middle school, and one high school. It serves the bordering villages of Cove Neck, Oyster Bay Cove, and Centre Island. To deal with increased enrollment, in 1992 the fourth grade was moved to the middle school. Also, to maintain small class sizes, the number of grade sections was increased. In 1997, voters approved a $9.760 million 20-year bond issue that will go toward adding space and other structural improvements.

Typically, 90 percent of the high school's graduates go on to higher education. And of a graduating class that is generally less than 100, one or two students become National Merit Scholarship finalists a year.

Computers are an integral part of the district's educational system, and instruction in computer use begins in kindergarten. "The educational program is very rich for such small enrollment," said Dr. Banta. "And youngsters are not anonymous in such a small setting."

Jan Milhauser, who lived in Manhattan for 10 years, did not want to leave the city. But after three incidents, including one in which she was attacked while pregnant, she decided it was time to move. She and her husband, David, were careful about where they would move with their two school-age daughters. They headed toward Oyster Bay because Mr. Milhauser, the part-owner of a metal-stamping business in Richmond Hill, Queens, often bicycled there. Before buying, however, Mrs. Milhauser visited the schools and was impressed with what she saw. In August 1991, the family moved into a 30-year-old four-bedroom, five-bath, two-story house on two wooded acres in Oyster Bay Cove for which they paid about $800,000. Mrs. Milhauser said it was the best thing she had ever done. "This is the most phenomenal community," she said. "It has everything I could want."

Shopping and restaurants are a big part of life in Oyster Bay. Although somewhat run-down, with vacant stores and some buildings in need of repair, the shopping district, comprising about 100 storefronts—most of them retail, but also including several offices like insurance brokerages—is undergoing a seven-to-10-year revitalization program, said Gregory Koke, president of the chamber of commerce. This is to include moving a Long Island Rail Road maintenance building from its current site to make it easier to get from the downtown to the waterfront.

Oyster Bay has several fine restaurants. Among them are Mill River Inn, rated by Zagat in 1996 as one of the best on Long Island; Bookmark Cafe, which is located in the restored Theodore Roosevelt summer White House (so called because it was used for offices when the resident was vacationing at Sagamore Hill); and Canterbury Ales, which serves light meals.

The weekend after Columbus Day, the chamber of commerce sponsors its Oyster Festival. More than 130 arts and crafts exhibitors display their wares. Oyster-shucking and oyster-eating competitions are part of the activities. Free shuttle buses from the Syosset Long Island Rail Road station to downtown and the waterfront are available.

Oyster Bay has two museums. Raynham Hall, circa 1738, a Colonial saltbox with Colonial and Victorian period rooms, is open 12–5 P.M. seven days a week between May and August. The rest of the year, it is open Tuesday through Sunday from 1 to 5 P.M. Admission is $3 for adults and free for children 6 and under. The Earle-Wightman House, circa 1720, has a hands-on room for children with changing exhibits. The museum is open Wednesdays and Saturdays from 9 A.M. to 1 P.M. and on Sundays from 1 to 4 P.M. Admission is $1.50 for adults and free for children under 12.

The Earle-Wightman House is also the home of the Oyster Bay Historical Society. Ten houses in Oyster Bay have been given landmark status by the town. Three—Raynham Hall, the Oyster Bay Post Office, and the First Presbyterian Church—are also in the National Register of Historic Places. Nearby in Cove Neck is the 90-acre national historic site of Sagamore Hill, estate of President Theodore Roosevelt, with its 23-room Victorian mansion. There is also the small Old Orchard Museum, housed in a building built by T.R.'s son, Theodore Jr. The grounds of Sagamore Hill are open daily, with hours varying with the seasons. Tours of the house are conducted Wednesday through Sunday, 10 A.M. to 4 P.M. Admission is $5 for adults, with no charge for children under 17.

The 400-acre Planting Fields Arboretum and William R. Coe Hall, a 65-room English medieval- and Elizabethan-style estate—technically in Upper Brookville but carrying an Oyster Bay address—also are open year-round. Hours and admission vary depending on event.

The 45-acre Roosevelt Memorial Park and Beach has a beach, pavilion; picnic areas; tennis, handball, and basketball courts; a children's play area; and boat launching ramps. Two residents in 1997 paid $25 for a season sticker. The town has 97 boat slips that are rented from April to November and for which there is an eight- to 10-year wait. Town residents can also pay $20 a season for a mooring in the harbor, for which there is no waiting list.

In 1653, three Englishmen bought the tract of land that now includes Oyster Bay from the Matinecock Indians. In addition to acquiring title from the Indians, a patent was issued in September 1677 creating the Town of Oyster Bay. The Colonial hamlet thrived from the start and became a busy seaport.

Fifty years after the original land grant, ships were sailing to such distant ports as the West Indies. The Oyster Bay line of the Long Island Rail Road began with a station in Glen Cove in 1868 and about that time Oyster Bay was discovered by the Roosevelts, the Beekmans, the Fosters, and others. The end of the line was the Oyster Bay station, which was built in 1888 and is still in use.

PLANDOME

An affluent yet homey community

BY JOHN RATHER

In the small, highly prized North Shore village of Plandome, a bargain is a house on the market for under $600,000. Prices two and three times higher are not uncommon. But for those who can afford the price of admission—and some local realtors say would-be buyers are lined up for certain houses that are not now and may never be for sale—ownership in Plandome means a stake in an affluent yet homey community where mooring rights, membership in the village field and marine club, and a place to park at the village's own Long Island Rail Road station make life all the sweeter.

"You are not just buying a house, you are buying a unique community," said Carole Belley of Lovejoy Real Estate in Manhasset. "And the community comes with all these advantages."

Quiet, family-centered, orderly without being stuffy, well kept without being compulsively manicured, safe and self-contained, Plandome exudes a sense of place distinctly its own. "Plandome just is," said Vera Pulese, an associate broker at Accents on Real Estate, Better Homes & Gardens in Manhasset. "It's one of those places that has whatever it is that makes a place perfect."

The Village Green, a sward of open space lined by pines, is at the heart of life in Plandome. It has been a playing field for generations of young children and teenagers. Several hundred villagers gather here for a picnic, games, and prizes on the Fourth of July, the most festive occasion on the village calendar. Winners of events like the slow bicycle race and the 100-yard dash earn ribbons and cheers.

The green, an early example of Long Island land preservation, was purchased by the village in 1930 for $46,000. It stretches down from the Village Hall, a municipal mansion and one-time elementary school with chocolate-brown trim and a porch overlooking two carefully tended

POPULATION: 1,063.

AREA: 0.5 square mile.

MEDIAN HOUSEHOLD INCOME: $153,070.

MEDIAN PRICE OF A SINGLE-FAMILY HOUSE: $800,000.

TAXES ON A MEDIAN-PRICED HOUSE: $10,000.

PUBLIC SCHOOL SPENDING PER PUPIL: $16,783.

DISTANCE FROM MIDTOWN MANHATTAN: 21 miles.

RUSH-HOUR TRAVEL TO MIDTOWN: 35 minutes on the Long Island Rail Road Port Washington line to Penn Station, $6.75 one way, $135 monthly.

CODES: Area, 516: ZIP, 11030.

tennis courts reserved for village residents.

Village offices and the two-truck Plandome Fire Department, an all-volunteer force established in 1913, share space inside. An iron hoop that once served as a fire alarm still hangs from its wooden frame by the firemen's garage. A towering pine is decorated with lights for the Christmas season.

Zoning excludes commercial development. There are no apartments, no co-ops or condominiums. House rentals, when they can be found, are usually for limited periods. A three-bedroom, 2½-bath house will fetch $3,000 a month. Larger homes go up from there. Rentals often involve owners who were transferred but plan to return.

People who live too long in Plandome may acquire an aesthetic sense that is offended by less ideal settings. This may be a reaction to residing among the 431 Colonial, Dutch Colonial, English Tudor, and large ranches and split-levels that line Plandome's lightly traveled, leafy streets, where there are no sidewalks.

Henry W. Cavaliere of Cavaliere Real Estate in Manhasset, a licensed property appraiser familiar with the village, said a typical Plandome dwelling was a large Colonial built in the 1920s or '30s with a center hall, a large formal dining room, a living room, four or five bedrooms, two or more baths, full attic and basement, a detached two-car garage, and taxes of $8,000. He said it would sell for more than $800,000, up $200,000 from little more than two years ago.

Mrs. Belley said a three-bedroom, 2-bath Colonial with an attic room, a family room, a living room, an eat-in kitchen, a screened porch, a two-car garage, and taxes of about $7,000 recently entered contract for $700,000.

"There's been a surge in the values in Plandome," said Mr. Cavaliere. "it's difficult now to find a house in the old section of the village for less than $750,000."

Indeed, by the last quarter of 1997, the median price for homes in the half-mile-square village had risen to $800,000, an all-time high, with taxes on a median house averaging about $10,000. Brokers attributed the rise in house prices to gains in the stock market. Even at these record prices, they said, listings often touched off bidding wars that ended in sales higher than original asking prices.

Most houses don't remain on the market long, several realtors said. "Of course, there is always that white elephant, but most times houses there go quickly," said Lee G. Jehle, an associate broker at Blaitch House and Home Real Estate in Manhasset.

"*Quickly* is not the word," said Connie Liappas, a sales associate at Blaitch. "It's *magical*."

The Plandome railroad station, a short walk from home for many commuters, is the second westbound stop on the Port Washington line. There is almost always a seat, and rarely a need to double-fold newspapers, until Great Neck or beyond. Electrified coaches rustle by with cozy efficiency. The station road has its overpass, so there are no train whistles. The morning commute to Manhattan takes about 35 minutes.

Resident commuters pay only $5 a year to park in the village's station lots. Cars of nonvillagers are ruthlessly ticketed and towed away. "I park in the same spot every day," said Joseph N. Rizzo, the former president of the Plandome Field and Marine Club. Membership is open to residents.

Residents pay small annual fees for use of the tennis courts and to maintain a mooring at the village beach on Manhasset Bay. The southern tip of the Plandome Country Club, a private club with an 18-hole golf course, is in the village. The Reconstructionist Synagogue of the North Shore is also within Plandome borders. All other development is residential.

Nearby houses of worship include the Manhasset Congregational Church, St. Mary's Roman Catholic Church, the Manhasset Baptist Church, Christ Church (Episcopalian), Church of Our Saviour (Lutheran), the Manhasset Friends Meeting House (Quaker), the Community Reformed Church (Reformed Church in America), the North Shore Unitarian Universalist Society, and Temple Judea of Manhasset.

There is little in Plandome to disturb the peace. "It's got to be one of the safest places in the world to live," said Police Officer Thomas B. Sikes, a crime analyst for the Sixth Precinct of the Nassau County Police Department. "There just don't seem to be any problems at all." The village, which was incorporated in 1911, abolished its own police department in 1976 and is now patrolled by the county force.

Shops, delis, gas stations, restaurants, dry cleaners, the Manhasset movie theater, and longtime establishments like Maclennan Pharmacy and Manhasset Sport Shop are a short ride away on Plandome Road in Manhasset. Lord & Taylor is one of several department stores on nearby Northern Boulevard, which is also Route 25A.

Plandome is in the Manhasset School District, in an area of North

Shore public schools where high academic standards and placement of graduates in competitive colleges is a tradition, according to Alice Willett, the executive director of the Nassau and Suffolk School Boards Association. State figures in 1997 showed spending per pupil was $16,783.

With 2,300 students in grades K–12—there are fewer than 200 students in graduating classes at Manhasset High School—Manhasset is one of Long Island's smallest districts. It maintains a full schedule of sports, music, and extracurricular and academic programs. There are more than 60 interscholastic teams.

About 95 percent of graduates go on to higher education. About 90 percent of the approximately 100 teachers in grades 7 through 12 hold advanced degrees. The district has 210 faculty members, including teachers, guidance counselors, and specialists in subjects like music and art.

The district and its school and community association award scholarships to high school juniors to pursue summer programs of their choice ranging from Outward Bound to university study in the United States and abroad. Eight to 10 students are selected each year.

Most Plandome children attend the 780-student Shelter Rock Elementary School. Children in Upper Plandome, an area up the hill from the railroad station, attend the 500-student Munsey Park school. A middle school for grades 7 and 8 is next to the high school.

The Dutch West India Company purchased lands including what is now the Village of Plandome from the Rockaway Indians in 1639. Would-be English settlers from Lynn in Massachusetts were chased off by Dutch troopers shortly after they arrived by water in 1640. Later, under English rule, Plandome was part of the Cow Neck pasture shared by Colonial farmers. A troop of Hessian soldiers encamped in Plandome during the Revolutionary War.

An early English landowner, Matthias Nicoll, devised the name Plandome. In Latin, it means plain home. Grace Jayne, Plandome's village historian, said the true meaning might be "estate on the plain," a reference to the Nicoll homestead.

Four New York City neighbors, a lawyer, a stockbroker, an architect, and a teacher, formed the Plandome Land Company in 1905 on 90 acres they purchased from a local landowner. Teachers were targeted in early real estate promotions. Today, stockbrokers, lawyers, and architects, together with doctors, other professionals, and business entrepreneurs, inhabit Plandome.

Mr. Rizzo said the Latin translation of the village name didn't fit modern Plandome. "These homes are very far from simple," he said. "People here work very hard to maintain the integrity of the community."

PORT JEFFERSON

A historic village with a seagoing past

BY VIVIEN KELLERMAN

It used to be that only during the summer would the Village of Port Jefferson be clogged with visitors, who came by ferry across Long Island Sound, or by car or train, to spend a day or a weekend. But the village, with its cluster of restored Victorian and Cape Cod houses perched on the hilly winding tree-lined streets that overlook the harbor, is now a tourist destination for all seasons.

Despite its tourist-filled downtown streets, the community of 8,000, which has its own beaches, a country club, a small but progressive school district, a Long Island Rail Road station from which a trip to Manhattan is one hour and 55 minutes, and even two hospitals, has been and remains a popular place to live.

"The market here is extremely strong," said Pat Nicklaus, a sales agent with Cornell/Petsco Real Estate in the village. Prices in 1997 ranged from about $160,000 for a three-bedroom 1960s development house to close to $1 million for some waterfront residences. Newer custom-built ranches and Colonials ranged from $225,000 to $275,000. Ms. Nicklaus said that with a shortage of houses for sale, the median price for a single-family home in the village by the third quarter of 1997 was inching up from $220,000, with taxes on such a house of about $5,150, and that she expected it to continue to climb for the foreseeable future.

The market for 19th-century homes that hug downtown is strong, giving them a higher median price range of about $250,000. Taxes for these homes, however, were lower, around $3,000 to $4,000. Demand for these houses is high, she said. "There are always a few of these on the market, but never an abundance," she added.

While most open space in the village is gone, there is still some new construction. Jefferson Landing, built in 1996, with 30 houses ranging from

POPULATION: 7,952.

AREA: 2.6 square miles.

MEDIAN HOUSEHOLD INCOME: $77,159.

MEDIAN PRICE OF A SINGLE-FAMILY HOUSE: $220,000.

TAXES ON A MEDIAN-PRICED HOUSE: $5,150.

PUBLIC SCHOOL SPENDING PER PUPIL: $20,009.

DISTANCE FROM MIDTOWN MANHATTAN: 65 miles.

RUSH-HOUR TRAVEL TO MIDTOWN: One hour and 55 minutes on the Long Island Rail Road, $10.75 one way, $214 monthly.

CODES: Area, 516; ZIP, 11777.

$300,000 to $440,000, sold out quickly, Ms. Nicklaus said.

The village has several condominium complexes with a total of more than 450 units and a price range of $125,000 to $400,000. At the largest, the 264-unit Highlands, a two-bedroom, 2½-bath town house recently sold for $125,000. At the Riviera, where some of the 95 units have water views, prices range from $200,000 to $400,000. Both complexes have swimming pools. There are also five rental apartment complexes with 322 units; one-bedrooms in 1997 averaged $800, two-bedrooms about $1,100.

Laurie and Thomas Crawford have lived in Port Jefferson since 1983, moving there shortly after they were married. In 1995, when the family, which included their two school-age children, Stephen and Emma, had outgrown their house, they traded up to a 61-year-old three-bedroom, 1½-bath Cape Cod on a .75-acre lot, for which they paid $152,000; taxes are $2,200. "The taxes are affordable, and the village has a wonderful sports program that our kids take advantage of," said Ms. Crawford, a veterinarian's receptionist in Port Jefferson whose husband is a Nassau County road construction crew member. Ms. Crawford also praised her children's school, which she called "small and personalized."

In 1997, there were 1,123 students enrolled in the Port Jefferson School District, which has one kindergarten-to-grade 5 elementary school and one middle-senior high school. A few years ago, the district closed a building that had been used as a middle school. That building has been rented out to the Board of Cooperative Education Services, which is using it as an alternative middle school for at-risk students from Suffolk districts, said Albert Noonen, the district's business administrator.

Despite its size, said Mr. Noonen, the district offers 12 advanced placement courses and four computer labs in its middle-senior high school, swimming instruction for all elementary school pupils, and at least one computer in each grade-school classroom. In addition to French and Spanish, the district offers five years of Latin. Typically, said Mr. Noonen,

92 percent of the district's high school graduates go on to higher education. The per-pupil expenditure in 1997 was $20,009.

Our Lady of Wisdom, a kindergarten-to-grade 8 Roman Catholic day school, is also in the village. Tuition for students who live in its parish or one of three nearby parishes is $2,400. Prekindergarten and nursery school programs are also available. Also in the village is the private, non-profit Maryhaven Center of Hope, a residential school for the developmentally disabled, aged 5 to 21.

A sports program for children includes soccer, softball, baseball, and basketball. A sports program for adults includes a softball team for players over 40. Community members can swim in the elementary school pool, or at one of two beaches.

The village also offers a program for residents 60 or over that provides free door-to-door transportation and activities such as crafts, exercises, parties, and day and overnight trips.

The village also hosts numerous annual events. These include summer concerts on the dock, where such performers as the Peter Duchin and Count Basie Orchestras have appeared. A Charles Dickens Festival in December celebrates the season with house tours, and culminates with fireworks on New York's Eve. The Harborside Arts and Crafts Festival draws as many as 20,000 people to its annual one-day event in late May.

In 1980, Theater Three, a repertory company, moved into the village and later bought an old vaudeville theater on Main Street. The company presents eight shows a year. The Greater Port Jefferson Arts Council uses the Theater Three building for annual film festivals. The group, which was formed in 1987, also sponsors programs that include music, dance, art, cinema, writing, and poetry. Annual membership is $10 for an individual and $15 for a family.

While most residents do the bulk of their major shopping in surrounding communities, they have a wide selection of stores in the village. There are about a dozen restaurants, two specialty-food stores, and several clothing stores.

A few years ago, in an attempt to keep the village from taking on a honky-tonk look, the trustees voted to limit fast-food restaurants to at least 200 feet from one another. Pat Doohan, the office manager for the Port Jefferson Chamber of Commerce said that this seems to have worked, with merchants offering a wide array of goods and services.

The Bridgeport & Port Jefferson Steam Boat Company has two ferries that annually transport 750,000 people across the sound. Service is available all year long, and prices depend on the number of passengers in a vehicle. The company also offers moonlight sails and charters.

In 1655, English settlers bought the land that is now the village from the Setauket Indians, who called it Suwasett or Land of the Small Pines. Because much of it was marsh, the settlers called it Drowned Meadow. John Willse, a Setauket shipbuilder, started a trend by opening a shipyard at Drowned Meadow in 1797. By 1840, Beaver Creek had been diverted and a long wharf was built out several hundred feet into the salt meadow. Land alongside the wharf was filled in and stores were built.

In 1832, the name of the village was changed to Port Jefferson when it was a thriving port and shipbuilding center. The decline of the whaling industry, along with the invention of the steamboat, brought an end to the days of wooden shipbuilding in Port Jefferson. By the turn of the century, the area had become a playground, with beaches, anchorages, and marinas. A group of businessmen, including P. T. Barnum, founded the steamboat line. Nevertheless, for the first half of the century, growth stagnated, and Port Jefferson took on a seedy look.

In 1963, village residents decided to take matters into their own hands by incorporating, and revival began. Stores got a face-lift, new construction sprang up, and historic structures were restored. Improvements continue to this day.

Tourists may pick up a map showing historic houses, now privately owned, that were the homes of shipbuilders or ship captains. The John R. Mather House Museum, circa 1840, is the former home of the Mather shipbuilding family and now houses the Port Jefferson Historical Society. The parklike grounds contain original outbuildings such as a tool shed and marine barn.

Mayor Robert T. Strong said the village had recently bid on five acres of prime waterfront land owned by Mobil, which in the past had been used to store oil. If the bid is successful, he said, it would be converted to some as yet undetermined public use. While such development would encourage even more activity, he said it would only benefit the community. "I think we are keeping the line between tourism and residential living," said Mayor Strong. "Everyone works together—chamber, government, churches, and school district—to keep a level pace between commercial and residential development. For all its activity, Port Jefferson is still predominantly a residential village."

PORT WASHINGTON

Solid comfort, in distinct enclaves

BY JOHN RATHER

Two contrasting aspects of Port Washington strike a visitor to this North Shore area notable for its extensive waterfront, top schools, easy commute to the city, and strong sense of place.

As it traces a sweeping turn below the highly regarded Port Washington Public Library and on toward the softball diamond and band shell in Sunset Park, lower Main Street exudes a long-settled hometown charm. Shops invite lingerers, and Manhasset Bay, with its boating pleasures, shimmers just beyond. It is a place to slow down and watch a sunset from the town dock.

But the pace quickens on Port Washington Boulevard, a raceway for impatient suburban drivers in late-model cars who give no quarter in their cutthroat quest to arrive first at the next traffic light. The boulevard is a link to regional shopping on Northern Boulevard and to the Long Island Expressway, but no place for sightseeing.

But the essence of Port, as people here affectionately call it, is tree-lined interior residential streets of single-family homes, where a substantial, well-tended but unpretentious look prevails. Even modest Cape Cods, when they may be found, seem a bit more grand in this setting.

Occupying the old Cow Neck Peninsula with neighboring Manhasset, Port Washington—a hybrid without its own governing body—is composed of an unincorporated area and four villages: Baxter Estates, Manorhaven, Port Washington North, and Sands Point. It also includes part of a fifth village, Flower Hill. The population, when all these areas are combined, is about 15,500.

Unincorporated enclaves have names, like New Salem, Salem, Monfort Hills, Beacon Hill, and the Park section, as well as distinct identities.

POPULATION: 15,506.

AREA: 4.2 square miles.

MEDIAN HOUSEHOLD INCOME: $85,057.

MEDIAN PRICE OF A SINGLE-FAMILY HOUSE: $446,250.

TAXES ON A MEDIAN-PRICED HOUSE: $7,000.

PUBLIC SCHOOL SPENDING PER PUPIL: $15,236.

DISTANCE FROM MIDTOWN MANHATTAN: 19 miles.

RUSH-HOUR TRAVEL TO MIDTOWN: 38 minutes on the Long Island Rail Road, $6.75 one way, $135 monthly.

CODES: Area, 516: ZIP, 11050.

All areas are within North Hempstead, one of Nassau County's three towns.

Housing prices soared in Port Washington during the real estate boom of the mid-eighties, slumped by 1990, and have now resumed their steady upward climb. "We are probably back up to where we were in 1989," said Robert L. Harding, Jr., the co-president of the Manhasset and Port Washington Real Estate Board.

Mr. Harding, whose agency bears his name, and other brokers said home prices varied widely. "The range is from anywhere slightly under $200,000 to $700,000, not counting Sands Point, where prices go up to several million dollars," said Mary Ann Jacobi, a sales associate at Douglas Elliman/Town & Country Realty. Mrs. Jacobi said prices were rising in the last quarter of 1997. "We are getting prices sellers never expected to get," she said.

Ruth Leonard of the Ruth Leonard Agency said there were limits to how low the market went. "For $200,000, you would find a piece of junk," she said. But the splendor of Sands Point homes and mansions, she said, was beyond compare. She has lived there since 1956.

An associate broker at Charles E. Hyde Realty, Diane E. Andersen, said sales formed a bell curve in Port Washington, with most in the $300,000's and $400,000's. She said some who sold remained, reflecting deep attachment that is a common thread in the community. "People don't move out, they move around," she said. "I've had people move across the street." Sales were especially strong during 1997, she said.

The median price of a one-family house, including Sands Point, was $425,000 at the end of 1996. By the end of 1997, after a brisk year for sales, prices were up about 5 percent. Average taxes on median-priced home are in the $7,000 range.

The housing mix includes two-family homes in Manorhaven and several condominiums, co-ops, and rental apartment buildings. Condominium prices for two-bedroom units range from $185,000 to $250,000 at the four-building, 58-unit Carleton Bay condominium. At Capri Cove, a luxury condominium on the waterfront, two-bedroom units sell from $300,000 to $375,000.

Two-bedroom units at the Port Harbor condominium, where at least one resident per unit must be 55 or older, were selling for about $370,000 at the end of 1997.

At the Tom's Point co-op, one-bedroom units sell in the range of $110,000. At Madison Park Gardens, a garden-apartment rental complex converted to a co-op, prices range from $100,000 to $200,000. Two-bedroom apartments rent from $1,300 to $1,475 a month at the 60-unit Soundview Gardens and the 250-unit Wildwood Gardens, adjoining complexes near the Soundview Marketplace Complex.

Port Washington sends forth weekday legions to climb aboard Manhattan-bound trains for a sleek, no-change-at-Jamaica trip west to the city. It bears repeating that for the Port commuter, there is no standing in the morning, and no worry in the evening about sleeping past home. The station is the branch line's eastern terminus. The morning commute to the city takes 38 minutes.

Port is no mere bedroom community, its denizens insist. The town, they say, hums with civic activism and celebrates itself with a cascade of events, some drawing North Shore neighbors.

The float-filled "Pride in Port" parade is an annual event. The five-mile Thanksgiving Day Turkey Trot draws hundreds of runners. There is an annual harborfest. In warm weather, outdoor concerts are held at the Sunset Park band shell.

The band shell is a local institution with an interesting history. The way Grace Pearsall used to tell it, John Philip Sousa, who lived in Sands Point, inspired her in a dream to go forth and build a band shell.

Mrs. Pearsall, a community-spirited leader and something of a town crier, awoke to begin a fund-raising effort that resulted, in 1967, in the opening of the band shell in the small park overlooking Manhasset Bay adjacent to the North Hempstead town dock.

Donors included local civic groups, but the inspired Mrs. Pearsall also attracted support from a disparate group of patrons, including Richard M. Nixon, Gene Krupa, and Princess Grace of Monaco. "She sent handwritten letters to everybody," recalled Floyd D. Mackey, whose wife, June Rivers Mackey, is Mrs. Pearsall's daughter. The Mackeys now head an all-volunteer group that presents a popular concert series at the band shell during spring and summer.

Among the performers in recent years have been the high school band; the elaborately costumed Long Island Mummers, a band dominated by banjos but including drums and glockenspiel; the Long Island Banjos; the American Concert Band; and Rhythm, Reeds and Brass, a 1940s-style big band.

"We want children to remember that at one time there was something like this in the town where they grew up," said Mr. Mackey.

The 150,000-volume Port Washington Library, which has 25 computers available to its patrons, presents educational and cultural programs year-round.

"This is a place you can live your whole life," said Christina Cronin Southard, the former editor of *The Port Washington News*, who grew up here. "That's why people are so passionate about this town. They see it as their lifelong home, even after the kids are finished school."

But schools are a magnet for young families. Dr. Albert F. Inserra, the superintendent of the Port Washington School District, said that in a typical year, about 70 percent of the graduates from the 4,100-student system are accepted at colleges rated very competitive to most competitive.

"It is quite a remarkable school system," he said. "What is taken for granted here is exceptional elsewhere." An array of academic and advanced placement programs is offered. Spending per pupil is approximately $15,200.

Entering students come from more than 30 ethnic backgrounds, reflecting growth of the Asian and Hispanic populations. Recent state figures showed that 70.5 percent of students were white, 2.4 percent black, 14.8 percent Hispanic, and 9.8 percent "other."

The district has four elementary schools, a middle school, and the Paul D. Schreiber High School. A Roman Catholic school, St. Peter of Alcantra, enrolls students in prekindergarten through grade 8. Tuition ranges from $1,300 to $2,000 yearly.

There are two Catholic churches, nine churches of other denominations, and five synagogues.

The Port Washington police district, created by the state legislature in 1921, covers unincorporated areas and the villages of Baxter Estates and Port Washington North.

"We don't have many serious crimes here," said Police Chief William J. Kilfoil, commander of the force. "A homicide is a rare event." A 1995 annual report listed 14 arrests for selling drugs.

Other areas are patrolled by Nassau County police, except for Sands Point, which has a village force.

The all-residential Sands Point, population 2,500, with its mansions and shoreline expanses, is one of the wealthiest communities in the country. Mayor Leonard Wurzel said about 45 of the village's 850 homes changed hands over three recent years.

In 1994, the village, the East Egg of F. Scott Fitzgerald's *The Great Gatsby*, purchased for $12.7 million the 210-acre former Guggenheim estate from I.B.M., which had used it as a country club and conference center. It is now a club for village residents, offering golf, swimming, tennis, and dining.

The first English settlers arrived in the Port Washington area from

Connecticut in 1643. Early farmers used the peninsula for pasture, building a fence in 1658 that stretched from Manhasset Bay, then called Cow Bay, to Hempstead Harbor. Dairy and oyster farming were mid-19th-century livelihoods.

In the 1850s, residents changed the area's name from Cow Bay to Port Washington to commemorate George Washington's visit in 1790 to nearby Roslyn. Beginning in the 1860s, sand mined from the shores of Hempstead Harbor was used in New York City, first for sidewalks, then for skyscrapers and subway tunnels.

When the railroad arrived in 1898, "Port Washington developed into a suburb rather quickly," said Joan G. Kent, the president of the Cow Neck Peninsula Historical Society. She said Victorian homes built near the station, now part of a Town of North Hempstead Historic District, marked an early stage of the transformation. Today, the railroad is near the center of the busy downtown area.

Port Washington has a wide array of ethnic restaurants. But a favorite of both residents and visitors is Louie's Shore Restaurant.

Four yacht clubs and a string of marinas line the Long Island Sound shoreline. The Town of North Hempstead rents out 160 moorings to owners of boats up to 25 feet long for $100 each per year, but there is a waiting list. A town beach on Hempstead Harbor, Bar Beach Park, has a playground, basketball courts, a boat ramp, and a picnic area. Manorhaven Beach, a town park, has swimming, softball, basketball, boccie, and a boat ramp.

The water is always near. "We are off the beaten track on the end of a peninsula here, and the water plays a big part," said Mr. Harding.

LONG ISLAND (NASSAU)

ROCKVILLE CENTRE

People power

BY VIVIEN KELLERMAN

Since 1898, the Village of Rockville Centre has had a municipal power plant that residents say bills them at half the cost they would have to pay if a private company lit up their homes.

The power plant (run by the village's Electric Department), a respected school system, a commute of only 30 minutes to Manhattan on the Long Island Rail Road, easy access to Long Island beaches, a bustling shopping district, several community parks, and a variety of well-established residential neighborhoods have made Rockville Centre, with its 24,000 population, a most sought-after community.

Joanne Harms, owner of the local Harms Real Estate Agency, said there had been an excess of homes for sale during the recession at the early part of the decade. But since 1993, she said, the market has turned around. Many buyers are returning to the area where they grew up. "I'm selling to my childhood friends," she said.

Most of the village was developed between 1920 and 1950. Home prices range from about $225,000 to $1 million, generally lowest at the southern end of the village and higher at the northern end. The median price of $298,000 for a single-family house in 1997 reflected an increase of about $50,000 since 1990. Taxes on such a house are about $6,200.

One of the oldest neighborhoods is Canterbury, in the northern section of the village, a 60-year-old area of large brick center-hall Colonials and Tudors on a quarter to a third of an acre. Prices range from $350,000 to $1 million. A newer section of Canterbury, built about 40 years ago, has smaller Colonials, ranches, and split-levels priced from the low $300,000's to high $500,000's.

In 1929, the first large multifamily complex, the 78-unit Tudor Apartments, was built in Rockville Centre. Since then, five subsidized housing

POPULATION: 24,064.

AREA: 3.3 square miles.

MEDIAN HOUSEHOLD INCOME: $75,781.

MEDIAN PRICE OF A SINGLE-FAMILY HOUSE: $298,000.

TAXES ON A MEDIAN-PRICED HOUSE: $6,200.

PUBLIC SCHOOL SPENDING PER PUPIL: $11,264.

DISTANCE FROM MIDTOWN MANHATTAN: 25 miles.

RUSH-HOUR TRAVEL TO MIDTOWN: 30 minutes on the Long Island Rail Road, $7 one way, $154 monthly.

CODES: Area, 516; ZIP, 11570.

projects and 48 other multifamily complexes have been erected, ranging from garden apartments to high-rises. More than 2,700 apartments were constructed, about half of them eventually converting to co-ops. In 1997, rentals for one-bedroom apartments averaged $900 a month, with two-bedrooms renting for about $1,100.

During the mid-1990s, one-bedroom co-ops ranged from $60,000 to $80,000 and two-bedrooms from $80,000 to $120,000. Three-bedroom town house co-op units sold for about $150,000.

The 84-unit Park Lane, a garden apartment that is the only condominium project in the village, was constructed in the '80s. Units range from about $200,000 for a one-bedroom unit to the high $200,000's for two-bedrooms.

Charles and Colleen Leone lived in nearby Oceanside when they were first married. Mr. Leone, chief financial officer for a money management firm in Manhattan, said that when they were looking for their first home, Rockville Centre's proximity to the city and to both the Southern State Parkway and Sunrise Highway was important. When friends told him how much money he would save on electricity, he was sold. In July 1994, the couple and their daughter, Natalie, moved into a remodeled three-bedroom, 2½-bath 1920's center-hall Colonial for which they paid $290,000.

"The neighborhood has a lot of kids and my wife and daughter are very happy," said Mr. Leone. His favorite part, he added, is not paying bills from a private power company.

As a new pupil in the Wilson Elementary School, Natalie Leone becomes part of the 2 percent to 3 percent rise in enrollment each year that has been straining the district's elementary schools for the last few years.

To keep up with the increase, voters approved a $14 million bond issue in 1996, of which $9.5 million is to be used to add space to existing buildings. Superintendent of Schools William Johnson said that the spending would have little impact on taxes, since the district recently paid off other debts.

Dr. Johnson said there were five K–5 elementary schools, one 6–8 middle school, and one high school, with a total district enrollment of 3,200. The district has a gifted and talented program for grades 3 to 6. As part of an emphasis on writing, elementary students write and publish books that become part of the school's library.

Dr. Johnson said that the district also put a strong emphasis on science, noting that the middle school has a reptile zoo. It includes two caimans (close cousins of the alligator), two Burmese pythons and a boa constrictor, and is overseen by the school's 80-member science club. "The kids are standing in line to join," said Dr. Johnson.

He also noted that the high school has a television studio run by a teacher and about 100 students that provides two to four hours of programming nightly on a dedicated cable television station serving the village. The high school also participates in a program of shared televised courses: Rockville Centre provides Latin, Russian, and TV journalism to other districts, while the school receives a statistics course.

Typically about 95 percent of the the district's graduates go on to higher education, said Dr. Johnson. Per-pupil spending in the 1996–97 school year averaged $11,264.

The Roman Catholic St. Agnes Cathedral School has also seen an enrollment increase, with 905 students in grades K–8 in 1997, up from 854 two years earlier.

Rockville Centre, the seat of the Diocese of Rockville Centre with its imposing 1935 modified Gothic cathedral, is also the site of the four-year coed Roman Catholic Molloy College, founded in 1955 by the Sisters of St. Dominic of Amityville.

In 1891, the first commercial bank operated on the South Shore of Long Island was started in the village, which now is a financial and business center with more than 10 banking institutions and more than 400 retail and service shops.

Steve Ruchman, president of the chamber of commerce between 1994 and 1996, said that except for Woolworth's, Play World, and Rainbow Shops, all large stores that closed in 1997, Rockville Centre has kept its vacancy rate down to less than 1 percent. He gave much of the credit for the business district's viability to the addition of a five-screen cinema (the village already had a two-screen movie house) about six years ago, noting that there are now more than 50 food establishments in the village.

Rockville Centre also has a thriving Guild for the Arts, which began about 15 years ago and today has about 600 members. Frank Meyer, president of the guild, said it sponsors 13 different events, including four symphony performances and three plays, all held at the district's schools. The guild also sponsors an arts and crafts fair at the Village Green the first week in June.

In 1976, the Phillip House, the Victorian home built in 1882 for a retired sea captain, became a museum. The rooms of the house have been restored, with two rooms used for exhibits.

The village has eight parks, the largest of which is the 100-acre Centennial Park at Mill River, which has five baseball diamonds, two soccer fields, basketball courts, a children's playground, and paths along the Mill River. There is outdoor ice-skating at the Donald F. Browne Park, which also offers nature trails and picnic areas. A lighted roller rink, playground, and ball fields are available at the William B. Hinkley American Legion Memorial Field.

A village-operated recreation building has a full-size gym, auditorium, game rooms, and classrooms. To use the parks or the recreation building, residents must obtain an annual pass for $5.

Jim Heaney, a spokesman for the village, said that with the growth of the village, the existing electrical generating plant cannot meet the demands of the community, so the village now purchases part of its power from the New York State Power Authority at what he calls competitive prices.

While unwilling to say how much village users pay for electricity, he said that it was far less than what they would pay to a private company.

Reckouackie Indians were early inhabitants of what is now Rockville Centre, long before the arrival of Dutch and English settlers in the late 17th century. The territory, which included East Rockaway, Oceanside, and Lynbrook, was called New Rockaway.

Population increased slowly until the establishment of a grist mill, when it became a busy commercial center. By the beginning of the 19th century, there were six mills serving the needs of the region's farmers and salt miners. In 1849, a post office was established, and New Rockaway became Rockville Centre.

The arrival of the Long Island Rail Road in 1867 heralded the entry of Rockville Centre into the modern era. In 1893, residents voted to incorporate the village. Major development followed the creation of the power plant in 1898 and flourished until shortly after World War II, when most of the available land was gone.

ROSLYN

A *wide price range in historic neighborhoods*

BY JOHN RATHER

"**C**arpe Diem," advises the sundial inscription on the wall of Bryant Library in the Village of Roslyn, one of four villages in the comfortably affluent and richly historic North Shore area known as Greater Roslyn. The message seems fitting for a community that has seized not just the day, but its own past, bringing 18th- and 19th-century homes into the present in excellent condition.

About a third of the Village of Roslyn is a historic district clustered around and near Silver Lake, a duck pond reflecting surrounding hills that once prompted Long Island Rail Road publicists, with some exaggeration, to dub the area America's Switzerland.

The century-old Roslyn clock tower, a 50-foot-high, Egyptian-style red granite edifice rising in the village center above antiques stores, homey restaurants, and fancy shops on Old Northern Boulevard, ranks for some with the Montauk Point lighthouse, the Big Duck in Flanders, and the water tower at Jones Beach State Park as among the most recognized of Long Island landmarks.

The country atmosphere in the harborside village is disturbed only by busy traffic on narrow roads that seem designed for horse-drawn carriages. "It's just a very rustic place," said Ida Farriella, a sales associate at E. F. Realty. "You wouldn't realize you were so close to Manhattan."

In addition to Roslyn Village, Greater Roslyn is generally described as including the surrounding villages of Roslyn Harbor, Roslyn Estates, and East Hills, as well as unincorporated Roslyn Heights and a portion of the Village of Flower Hill within the Roslyn School District. "It's a loosely held term," said Florence Wohl, co-president of the Greater Roslyn United Civic Associations. "The major thing we all have in common in this area is that we love it."

POPULATION: 22,830.

AREA: 6.5 square miles.

MEDIAN HOUSEHOLD INCOME: $119,941.

MEDIAN PRICE OF A SINGLE-FAMILY HOUSE: $380,000.

TAXES ON A MEDIAN-PRICED HOUSE: $7,000.

PUBLIC SCHOOL SPENDING PER PUPIL: $15,498.

DISTANCE FROM MIDTOWN MANHATTAN: 24 miles.

RUSH-HOUR TRAVEL TO MIDTOWN: 55 minutes on the Long Island Rail Road from Roslyn, $7 one way, $154 monthly; 28 minutes on the Long Island Rail Road from Manhasset, $6.75 one way, $135 monthly.

CODES: Area, 516; ZIP, 11548, 11576, 11577, and 11579.

Nearly 23,000 people live in Greater Roslyn. Values for single-family homes vary greatly. In some neighborhoods, houses under $500,000 are hard to find. But there is diversity in the market and bargains may be found. The median price of about $380,000 in 1996 was up $15,000 from five years earlier. By the fourth quarter of 1997, prices were holding steady but demand was brisk, local realtors said. Average taxes on a median-priced house were $7,000.

Roslyn as it is today began evolving in the 1930s, when bedroom communities sprang up as the old estates, woods, and farmlands around present-day Roslyn Village were sold off. The pace of development accelerated after World War II. East Hills, the largest village in Greater Roslyn, was once the site of Harbor Hill, the 480-acre estate of Clarence H. Mackey, the philanthropist and inheritor of a fortune made in silver mining. In a gargantuan Gold Coast chateau now razed, the Mackeys hosted the Duke of Windsor in 1924 and Charles A. Lindbergh in 1927 on his return from his solo flight from Long Island to Paris.

Greater Roslyn housing styles range from historic Federal homes on Main Street and East Broadway in Roslyn, to half-century-old, slate-roof Colonials in the Norgate section of East Hills, to king-size ranch houses in the northern section of Roslyn Harbor, and to more than 600 Levitt-built slab homes in the Country Club neighborhood of Roslyn Heights. "You can go from the mid-$200,000's in parts of Roslyn Heights to over a million in parts of Roslyn Estates, East Hills, and Roslyn Harbor," said Linda Wohl, a broker and partner at Sterling Properties who is not related to Florence Wohl. "But all of the incorporated villages have high-end and low-end houses."

While detached housing predominates, co-ops, rentals, and condominiums are also available. At Roslyn Gardens, a 379-unit co-op in Roslyn Village, a two-bedroom unit sold in 1996 for $72,000, according to James J. Miller, a sales agent for Insignia Management Services, which manages the co-op. Prices were about the same at the end of 1997. At the Chalet, a nearby rental building with a doorman, a commanding view of the harbor from balconies, and about 60 one-, two-, and three-bedroom units, one-bedrooms start at $1,500. At the 150-unit Summit at High Point Condominium in Roslyn Heights, three-bedroom apartments range from the mid-$400,000's to the mid-$500,000's.

Prospective buyers might be well advised to listen at roadside before committing. While lawn mowers and leaf blowers are the loudest sounds on some streets, traffic noise is never-ceasing in areas close to the Long Island Expressway, Northern State Parkway, Northern Boulevard, and Searington Road.

Train service doesn't rate high on the list of local amenities. The Long Island Rail Road's Oyster Bay line, which serves Roslyn, is a diesel line that requires a bothersome change at Jamaica, Queens. "It's not one of the reasons people come to Roslyn," said Mrs. Wohl of Sterling Properties. "They come in spite of it." Many commuters contrive to board in Manhasset for direct service to Penn Station on the Port Washington line, renting car space in private garages near the Manhasset station. Others go to the Mineola station or carpool to Shea Stadium, then ride the subway to Manhattan. Still others battle the Long Island Expressway all the way to the Queens Midtown Tunnel. The rail commute takes 55 minutes from Roslyn and about 30 minutes from Manhasset.

The Roslyn School district, one of several top-notch North Shore districts, is a strong unifier of the area's far-flung villages. It also has strong local support. Spending per pupil in the district was $15,498, according to 1997 state figures. Roslyn High School offers 12 advanced placement courses. In recent years, about 85 percent of students have scored high enough on their course exams to win college credits. About 95 percent of all graduates go on to college.

During recent years, SAT scores have ranged about 70 points higher in verbal and 100 points higher in math than national averages. Students are required to perform 40 hours of community service to graduate. Many far exceed the minimum, school officials said.

A bowl in the nurse's office is filled with free condoms as part of the district's AIDS education program. Barry Edelson, a school spokesman, said Roslyn was the only district in New York outside New York City to make condoms available to students.

The 2,800-student Roslyn district, currently completing a $10.9 million building-improvement project, has a preschool and kindergarten center, two elementary schools for grades 1 to 5, and one middle school for grades 6 to 8. Enrollment in lower grades has been increasing as more young families move to the area.

Roslyn began as a port for Hempstead, settled by English colonists from Stamford, Connecticut, beginning in 1643. By 1701 or thereabouts,

Hempstead farmers were bringing their grain to a grist mill in what was then and still remains the center of Roslyn Village for shipment to New York and New England. The old grist mill, a popular tea room earlier in this century, still stands on Old Northern Boulevard. It is now owned by Nassau County.

On April 24, 1790, President George Washington stopped for breakfast at the home of Hendrick Onderdonck, a grist-mill and paper-mill owner, as he returned to Manhattan after a brief Long Island tour. The old Onderdonck House is now the George Washington Manor, where patrons dine in the room where Washington breakfasted.

In 1844, residents petitioned to change the village name from Hempstead Harbor to Roslyn after William Cairns noted a resemblance to Roslin to his native Scotland. By the 1850s, steamboats linked Roslyn to Peck's Slip in Manhattan, a three-hour trip for early commuters, including William Cullen Bryant, the poet, essayist, and for 50 years the editor of *The New York Evening Post*.

The Bryant Library, a Greater Roslyn linchpin and repository of Bryant's writings, offers an avalanche of lectures, films, performances, and exhibits. The library maintains a satellite gallery for the Heckscher Museum of Art, which is located in Huntington. The gallery exhibits recent works by Long Island artists.

Shopping is limited within Greater Roslyn but abounds on its borders. Roslyn Estates, for example, is very near the upscale Americana at Manhasset shopping center. For others, Wheatley Plaza in Greenvale is nearer. Roslyn Village has waged a long battle against a developer with plans to build a supermarket in vacant land near the harbor.

Preserving Roslyn Village's historic atmosphere and the houses that create it has been a cause with heroes of its own. It never took long for new homeowners in Roslyn Village's historic district to meet Roger Gerry, a retired Navy captain and oral surgeon who made a crusade out of protecting homes from owners' decorating whims. "Dr. Gerry would be knocking on the door at six in the morning, wanting to know what you were doing," said Millard B. Prisant, a former president of the Roslyn Landmark Society. The society, founded by the late Dr. Gerry, is dedicated to maintaining the village's spectacular stock of historic homes, and to finding owners who will share in the commitment. "A house to us is not just a commodity," said Mr. Prisant.

Another group, the Roslyn Preservation Corporation, buys homes in the district, restores them immaculately, and offers them for sale with protective covenants. The Landmark Society hosts a house tour each year on the first Saturday in June. Many of the homes are decorated and furnished in period fashion.

SANDS POINT

Lush, convenient, and on the waterfront

BY VIVIEN KELLERMAN

In 1953, Leonard Wurzel, then the executive vice president of Loft Candies, took a ride out to Long Island with his wife, Elaine, and their two sons, Mark, now 46, and Lawrence, now 44, on what they thought would just be a day in the country. A friend suggested a trip through Sands Point, and while there, they stopped to look at some model homes that had caught their eye. Mr. Wurzel said he did not think he could afford to live in such a beautiful community. But to his surprize, the house, at $42,000 with extras, cost less than he expected, and by the end of the day, the Wurzels had purchased a four-bedroom ranch on one acre. Forty-four years later, the retired candy executive, now mayor of the village, is still delighted by his community. "Sands Point was then and still is Long Island's best-kept secret," Mr. Wurzel said.

With only 850 homes on 4.2 square miles, the lush, hilly waterfront community at the tip of what is known as the Cow Neck Peninsula is both private and close enough to the city to make it a commuter's dream.

Residents say they chose Sands Point over other exclusive villages because, for all its isolation, it shares an acclaimed school district and is close to shopping and restaurants in Port Washington next door, giving residents a sense of community. A 21-member private police force, backyard trash pickup, village parks, recreation, and boating are also important drawing cards.

Diane Andersen, a real estate agent at Chuck Hyde Real Estate in Port Washington, said that prices for detached homes start at $600,000 and can soar into the millions. Homes are on a minimum of an acre, with two the average. Recently, a ranch house that Ms. Andersen said needed a lot of work sold for $900,000, primarily because of its water view. "People will

POPULATION: 2,459.

AREA: 4.2 square miles.

MEDIAN HOUSEHOLD INCOME: $193,089.

MEDIAN PRICE OF A SINGLE-FAMILY HOUSE: $811,000.

TAXES ON A MEDIAN-PRICED HOUSE: $18,000.

PUBLIC SCHOOL SPENDING PER PUPIL: $15,236.

DISTANCE FROM MIDTOWN MANHATTAN: 18 miles.

RUSH-HOUR TRAVEL TO MIDTOWN: Five minutes to Port Washington, then 44 minutes on the Long Island Rail Road, $6.75 one way, $135 monthly.

CODES: Area, 516: ZIP, 11050.

pay almost anything for water view," she said. "They come in and literally rebuild the entire house."

While the community is a mix of older homes, those built in the early part of the century and after the war, development continues as estates are sold and broken up. Six new houses are being built on Backus Farm, a 17-acre site at the end of Middle Neck Road, with prices starting at $1.3 million. Kean Development, a Cold Spring Harbor developer, is building 16 homes on 50 acres of former governor W. Averell Harriman's estate. Houses, on two acres, start at $1.5 million.

The median price of a one-family house in 1997 was $811,000, up from $734,000 in the previous year; in 1992, the median price was $802,000. Taxes on a median house in 1997 were $18,000 a year.

Ms. Andersen said there had been an influx of young families into Sands Point. This increase is reflected in the schools, where the superintendent of the Port Washington School District, Dr. Albert F. Inserra, said enrollment was outstripping earlier predictions. In 1993, it was thought that enrollment would increase by 400 pupils by the turn of the century. It has since risen more than 500, to 4,100. "We have added space to our elementary buildings, and now we are at the point of considering reopening a building we closed several years ago," Dr. Inserra said.

The district, in which per-pupil spending in 1997–98 was $15,236, has four elementary schools, one middle school, and one high school. One elementary school is in Sands Point; all other schools are in Port Washington. Each elementary school has a full-time teacher to work with children in a gifted and talented program. The high school offers a science research program that in one recent year produced eight semifinalists and two finalists in the Westinghouse Science Competition.

Over 90 percent of a typical graduating class goes on to higher education. In 1996, the district embarked on a $1 million-per-year computer upgrade program that will continue into the beginning of the next century.

Some Sands Point children attend the Roman Catholic St. Peter of

Alcantra school in Port Washington, covering prekindergarten-through-eighth-grade students. Tuition ranges from $1,300 to $2,000.

Marc Silbert moved from Manhattan to the village with his wife, Peggy, and their two sons, Ryan, now 17, and Adam, now 10, 12 years ago. Mr. Silbert, a public relations executive in Port Washington, said that when the children reached school age, the couple decided it was time to move to the suburbs. For the price of an acceptable co-op in Manhattan, he said, "I could get a couple of acres." Although both Mr. and Mrs. Silbert had grown up in Great Neck, they said they decided on Sands Point because they liked, among other things, its diversity. Indeed, students entering the school district come from more than 30 ethnic backgrounds. "The schools are great, and even though Sands Point is private in its own way, it's still convenient to everything," Mr. Silbert said.

Mr. Silbert is president of the Sands Point Civic Association, to which 75 percent of the village residents pay $20 in annual dues, and many members make additional donations. The dues and donations are used for beautification projects such as the planting of 6,000 daffodils and 19 trees in one recent year. "I suppose you could say the village is beautiful enough and does not need all this extra attention, but there is nothing wrong with gilding the lily," he said.

In 1691, three Sands brothers, John, Samuel and James, arrived in what was then known as Cow Neck, the area that encompasses the peninsula. John and Samuel had adjacent farms at the foot of Cow Neck, now Sands Point. Not much is known about Samuel, but John, a sea captain, owned 500 acres of Cow Neck and built his house on the south side of what is now Sands Point Road. The house, with an additional three-story wing, is still privately owned. Across the road, to the north, there is a half-acre family burial ground containing the remains of Captain Sands and his descendants.

During the Revolution, Cow Neck settlers waged guerrilla warfare while acting as spies for George Washington. After the war, the population of Cow Neck grew. As traffic on Long Island Sound increased, many ships and lives were lost, and so in 1809, one of the first Long Island lighthouses was built in what is now Sands Point. The lighthouse has been preserved and the house adjacent to it is being expanded. Both are under the same private ownership.

The modern community of Sands Point began with the arrival of the railroad in Port Washington, in 1898. Soon after, newcomers began arriving to build elaborate homes. By the second decade of the 20th century, Sands Point competed with Newport, Rhode Island, as America's summer social capital. In addition to the Guggenheims and the Goulds, Sands Point, said to be the East Egg of F. Scott Fitzgerald's *The Great Gatsby*, also boasted among its residents the composer John Philip Sousa, the publishers Condé Nast and William Randolph Hearst, and the journalist, editor, and speechwriter Herbert Bayard Swope.

On July 23, 1917, Sands Point became the first Cow Neck village to be incorporated. On May 23, 1932, Harbor Acres, a 300-acre tract of land that had been one of the largest estates in the area, was annexed to Sands Point.

In 1971, Nassau County acquired two estates—127 of the 162 acres that included Castlegould and Hempstead House, and Falaise, the 90-acre estate of Harry Guggenheim, a philanthropist and heir to a mining fortune whose uncle Solomon built Manhattan's Guggenheim Museum. The county turned the estates into the 217-acre Sands Point Preserve, which includes the original restored mansions and several outbuildings and features exhibits and special events. Nature trails take advantage of the unusual setting, and outdoor programs run between May and October.

The Isaac Guggenheim estate, built in 1916, now belongs to the village, which runs it as the Village Club of Sands Point. The mansion houses a restaurant, a conference center, and meeting rooms. The 210-acre property includes a nine-hole golf course, 12 tennis courts, and a swimming pool. Membership is open primarily to village residents, and opens to others only if no residents are waiting to join. A family golf membership is $4,200, tennis $750, swimming $500.

Originally owned by Isaac Guggenheim, the estate stayed in the family when Isaac's brother Solomon purchased it at auction in 1924 two years after Isaac's death. After Solomon's death in 1948, a group of private builders purchased the property, but they were unsuccessful in their plan to build homes on one-acre parcels. In 1953, I.B.M. bought the estate as a country club for employees and their families. Corporate cutbacks forced the company to sell, and in 1995, the village acquired it for $12.7 million. "Sands Point is the kind of place where you don't necessarily bump into each other on the street," said Mr. Silbert, the civic association president. "But the village club has become a magnet where you may introduce yourself to someone, only to find out they live next door."

SEA CLIFF

Arts, crafts, a harbor, and history

BY VIVIEN KELLERMAN

If you make a wrong turn, you can easily miss Sea Cliff, a crowded village—population 5,000 on only 1.1 square miles—of Victorian, Queen Anne, and Carpenter Gothic homes overlooking Hempstead Harbor. But despite its small size, Sea Cliff has become a cultural center with a growing reputation. In addition to being the home of many artisans and arts and crafts shops, the village is the site of an annual arts and crafts tour and a huge arts and crafts festival.

It is this atmosphere that appeals to residents. But there are other things they like: their much-praised school system, the one-hour commute to Manhattan by Long Island Rail Road, and the relatively low school taxes, made possible by a Keyspan Energy power plant in nearby Glenwood Landing, which is in the same school district.

A typical two-bedroom, one-bath cottage on a 40- by 60-foot lot sold for about $165,000 in 1997, according to Wayne McCann, owner of Harmonious Homes, a real estate brokerage, with annual taxes of $1,200. Larger homes on larger parcels, or with a water view, can sell for as much as $1 million.

Although a quarter of Sea Cliff's 2,000 dwellings are multifamily—some of them old hotels that have been converted to residential units—even here the market is tight, Mr. McCann said. One-bedroom units rent for about $800 a month, two-bedrooms for about $1,000, and three-bedrooms for about $1,400. Three-bedroom, 1½-bath one-family homes rent for about $1,600 to $2,000 a month.

Schools and architecture are among the strongest attractions for home buyers. In the mid-1990s, empty-nesters seeking smaller homes created a strong buying market for the village's quaint Victorians. Among the

POPULATION: 5,048.

AREA: 1.1 square miles.

MEDIAN HOUSEHOLD INCOME: $66,321.

MEDIAN PRICE OF A SINGLE-FAMILY HOUSE: $342,000.

TAXES ON A MEDIAN-PRICED HOUSE: $3,833.

PUBLIC SCHOOL SPENDING PER PUPIL: $15,967.

DISTANCE FROM MIDTOWN MANHATTAN: 23 miles.

RUSH-HOUR TRAVEL TO MIDTOWN: One hour on the Long Island Rail Road, $7 one way, $154 monthly.

CODES: Area, 516; ZIP, 11579.

first-time buyers, Mr. McCann said, at least half, couples in their late 20s and early 30s, had children and were drawn to the village by its schools. "We're getting a lot of first-time home buyers coming from Brooklyn, Queens, and Manhattan," he said.

Richard and Beth Carraro moved to Sea Cliff in November 1992 with their daughter, Tamantha. Although the couple grew up in Roslyn, they moved to Manhattan in 1979 and left only when it came time to rear a family. Mr. Carraro, an advertising copywriter in Manhattan, said they had looked in many areas, including Westchester County and Connecticut. But every time they visited their parents in Roslyn, about three miles away, they would stop in Sea Cliff to check out the market. On one visit, they found an almost completely updated four-bedroom, two-bath, 100-year-old Victorian on a 40- by 60-foot lot, and they bought it for $235,000. "We always liked Sea Cliff," Mr. Carraro said. "It's a great place to raise kids."

Michael McGill, superintendent of the North Shore School District, which serves Sea Cliff, Glen Head, Glenwood Landing, Old Brookville and parts of Greenvale and Roslyn Harbor, oversees five schools—three K–5 elementary schools, one 6–8 middle school, and one high school, with a 1997 total enrollment of 2,400 and a per-pupil expenditure of $15,967. Although enrollment has grown by 600 since 1989, Dr. McGill said, the average elementary class size, 18, remains the lowest in Nassau County. To meet its growing needs, the district has added classrooms in recent years, paying for the expansion with a $7.6 million bond approved by voters in 1993.

Typically, 97 percent of North Shore High School graduates go on to higher education, and Dr. McGill said about a third of them are accepted by the most competitive schools in the country, such as Yale, Georgetown, and Princeton. More than 90 percent of all students are involved in arts, athletics, or community service. "Each school is a small community of learning in which adults know students very well and give them a tremendous amount of personal support," Dr. McGill said.

The small-community feeling is evident in the shops along Sea Cliff Avenue downtown, where galleries and crafts stores complement one another. Along Glen Cove Avenue, stores offer a wide range of goods, including sporting goods, clothing, boating supplies, and hardware. John Alcina, a board member of the Sea Cliff Business Association, said there were about 200 stores and businesses in the village. Since an economic downturn in the late '80s and early '90s, when rents become too high and empty stores all too familiar, Mr. Alcina said, the business community has rebounded. In 1997, the village qualified for a Nassau County Main Street Revitalization grant to install new sidewalks, lighting, benches, and paving.

Adding to the village economy are two well-known annual events. Since 1970, an annual street fair of arts and crafts has been held on the first Sunday in October. Sponsored by the North Shore Kiwanis Club since 1980, the one-day event has 260 exhibitors and hosts 30,000 visitors.

The second event is the arts and crafts tour. Ward Bell, 84, a wood carver and lifelong Sea Cliff resident, got the idea for it from his daughter, Barbara, an artist. She decided one year to display her work at home and invite friends to a Christmas party. The next year, another artist followed suit. Others heard about the idea and then, coordinated by Mr. Bell and four other artists, the annual tours began. They operate during the first two weekends of December from 11 A.M. to 5 P.M., with maps showing artists' studios and galleries provided by local merchants.

The village's cultural identity is also enhanced by three musical groups. The Sea Cliff Chamber Players was founded in 1970 by two residents, Herbert Sucoff and Barbara Speer, and now plays more than 30 concerts a year, not only in Sea Cliff, but throughout Long Island and in Manhattan. Well-known guest artists often participate. The North Shore Community Orchestra, made up mainly of village residents, plays three concerts a year at North Shore High, some in conjunction with the North Shore Community Chorus. Both the orchestra and the chorus are financed by the school district and private donations.

Despite its small size, Sea Cliff has 16 neighborhood parks. Most are greens, but some have ball fields and playgrounds. Memorial Park, at Prospect and Sea Cliff Avenues, commands an unobstructed view of Hempstead Harbor, Long Island Sound, and the New York and Connecticut shorelines. There is ice-skating at Scudder's Pond on Shore Road, which has lights for night skating. Sea Cliff has its own municipal beach, and residents can obtain a family membership for a seasonal parking sticker good from Memorial Day to Labor Day.

Harry Tappen Beach on Prospect Avenue is operated by the Town of Oyster Bay. In addition to 500 feet of beach, there is an outdoor swimming pool and boat launch. In 1997, a pool membership for a family was $130.

Beach parking stickers were $25 a season. Varying rates were available for nonresidents for both the pool and the beach. The town also rents out 272 boat slips. In 1997, rents ranged from $60 to $65 a foot for residents, and $70 to $75 for nonresidents. There is a short waiting list for boats longer than 34 feet. The village does not provide boat slips but offers boat-rack rentals.

Because of the concentration of old homes, residents work to preserve landmark buildings. Close to three dozen buildings have been designated local landmarks, said Jerry Izzo, vice president of the Sea Cliff Landmarks Association. Almost all those buildings have also been declared national landmarks. At the end of May each year, the association sponsors a house tour, for which it charges $12. Proceeds are used for grants to homeowners who want to do restoration work on their houses.

Village Hall on Sea Cliff Avenue is part of a complex that includes a museum and library. Built in the 1920s in the Gothic style, the complex was originally the Sea Cliff Methodist Church, its parsonage, and other buildings. The village bought the buildings in the '70s.

In 1668, Joseph Carpenter, who was probably from Connecticut, bought most of what is now Sea Cliff from the Indians. The land was farmed and over the years more settlers came. Little is known of life in Sea Cliff from the end of the Revolutionary War until after the Civil War. Although rail service began in 1867, trains did not stop in the Village during the winter for some time. Sea Cliff began to take its present shape in 1871, when the Grand Metropolitan Camp Ground Association bought 240 acres from James Carpenter, a descendant of Joseph Carpenter, as a summer meeting place for Methodists. The association's tent sites, mostly at the north end of the village, faced narrow streets in a gridiron pattern. The sites eventually were sold and became homesteads.

At the turn of the century, Sea Cliff was a popular resort area. By the 1920s, many of the summer residents had bought houses and settled in the village. Indeed, two-thirds of Sea Cliff's houses were built before 1940, more than in any other community in Nassau County. Throughout the '40s and '50s, the population growth slowed, stabilizing at about 5,000 people.

SEARINGTOWN

Classic suburb keeps its appeal in the '90s

BY JOHN RATHER

"Nassau County, the Fastest-Growing County in the U.S.," proclaimed the once-ubiquitous signs the county's Department of Public Works posted at its myriad projects during the 1950s and into the early 1960s. Searingtown, an unincorporated area in the county's Town of North Hempstead that extends downward like a clenched fist from the Northern State Parkway, sprang into existence during this explosive era. There is no aggression in the fist. It is only grasping the good life that three suburban generations have lived in Searingtown, drawn by proximity to the city, tidy neighborhoods of one-family homes, and a strong public school system.

Good location, residency within the highly regarded Herricks Union Free School District, and a North Shore address make for relatively high prices today in an active real estate market where young families, including a growing number of Asian-Americans, are the most frequent buyers. Aging suburban pioneers, not infrequently Italian-Americans and Jews, long the dominant ethnic groups, have been retiring to Florida or to condominiums outside hamlet borders. But a large Jewish community remains and appears to be growing. The turnover adds pace to a real estate market in a landlocked hamlet where population has remained steady at around 5,000, with some fluctuations, for three decades.

Prices of houses range from the low $300,000's to $600,000 and above, but most go for around $400,000. Taxes are typically around $7,000, but can vary significantly for homes of similar value. Most lots are a quarter of an acre.

A 1942 map shows Searingtown all but taken up by Bloodgood Nurseries, the Shelter Rock Country Club, a handful of estates, and a large parcel owned by the Nassau County Boy Scouts. Traces of the now-vanished Vanderbilt Motor Parkway—the private, banked-curve racetrack, toll

POPULATION: 5,319.

AREA: 0.9 square mile.

MEDIAN HOUSEHOLD INCOME: $104,320.

MEDIAN PRICE OF A SINGLE-FAMILY HOUSE: $400,000.

TAXES ON A MEDIAN-PRICED HOUSE: $7,000.

PUBLIC SCHOOL SPENDING PER PUPIL: $12,072.

DISTANCE FROM MIDTOWN MANHATTAN: 17 miles.

RUSH-HOUR TRAVEL TO MIDTOWN: 50 minutes on the Long Island Rail Road from Albertson, $7 one way, $154 monthly; 30 minutes on the Long Island Rail Road from Manhasset, $6.75 one way, $135 monthly.

CODES: Area, 516: ZIP, 11507, 11576, and 11030.

road, and prototypal high-speed, limited-access roadway built by William K. Vanderbilt early in the century—still showed on the map, looping through the soon-to-be transformed hamlet.

Then came the ranches, high ranches, split-levels, Colonials, and, more recently, contemporaries as Searingtown quickly grew to become a stable, upward-trending, all-residential new suburb, near major highway links to the city and regional shopping centers, including the upscale Americana at Manhasset, not much more than a mile north of the hamlet on Searingtown Road.

The hamlet is near the Long Island Expressway and other major links to Manhattan, other parts of the city, and Kennedy and La Guardia Airports. The commute to Manhattan on the Long Island Rail Road from Albertson takes about 50 minutes.

Searingtown's original housing stock endures today, but it is improved, expanded, upgraded, and greatly appreciated in value. "When I started 18 years ago, homes were in the 150's," said Lenora Weiss, an associate broker at East Brook Realty. "Now those same homes are in the 400's and I think we're beginning to get even higher prices." Median house prices rose steadily during the 1990s to reach $400,000 by the fall of 1997, up about $40,000 from five years earlier. But inventory was low, according to Ms. Weiss. "We just don't have enough listings," she said.

There is also some new construction. At Homestead Estates, a 29-unit development on the southern edge of the hamlet, new houses in Victorian, Colonial, traditional, and contemporary designs are priced from $600,000 to $700,000 and above, with taxes from about $11,000 to $12,000. Larry Magid of his family's Magid Realty, who built the project with his brother, Marc, and his father, Abraham, said low mortgage interest rates and the surging stock market were spurring sales. The Homestead Estates property includes the Sackler House, a Town of Hempstead historic landmark built in the 1920s using timbers, doors, and other parts from an 18th-century Dutch farmhouse in Flushing, Queens, that was damaged by fire.

The dwelling has been preserved and is now occupied by Abraham and Sally Magid.

Larry Magid, who grew up in Searingtown, said the hamlet was entering a time of rapid change. "It's the beginning of a big turnover now," he said. "That's why we are trying to establish ourselves here."

Orthodox Jews are part of the change. Searingtown is one of a handful of Long Island communities with an *eruv*, an enclosed area in which Orthodox Jews are permitted to carry objects and do other tasks that are normally prohibited outside the home from sundown Friday to sundown Saturday and on certain religious holidays. The fence along Northern State Parkway is part of the border of the *eruv*, which was established in 1995.

"We have had a number of families move in since the *eruv* was erected," said Rabbi Tzvi Kramer of Congregation Zichron Eliezer on Shelter Rock Road. "It's one of the first things they ask about before they move." Searingtown also has a Conservative synagogue, the Shelter Rock Jewish Center.

The hamlet has no commercial district. There are no apartment houses, condominiums, co-ops, or attached housing. Searingtown Pond Park, off Searingtown Road with a small duck pond, is the only park.

But South Shore ocean beaches are not far and Nassau County's Christopher Morley Park is a short distance north on Searingtown Road. The park has a swimming pool that becomes an ice rink in winter, a nine-hole golf course, jogging trails, and playing fields. Golf fees are $8, or $4 for the elderly.

While all of the hamlet is within the Herricks district, which sends more than 95 percent of its graduates on to higher education, there are three ZIP codes and impressionistic borders that become especially cloudy on the east, where the cape-filled, somewhat less expensive hamlet of Albertson is situated.

Sudha Bhalla, a sales agent at Century 21 Laffey Associates in Roslyn Heights, said the schools were a siren song for buyers. "They all have it in mind that Searingtown is in the Herricks district," she said. "They all know that in advance."

The 3,600-student district is not modest about its central role. "Our standardized test results are always among the best in Nassau County," said Superintendent Sidney A. Freund. He could have added that Nassau results were always among the best in the country.

The district has three kindergarten–grade 5 elementary schools, a middle school that was recently awarded a blue ribbon for excellence by the Education Department, and a high school on a 35-acre campus in Searingtown at which a number of advanced placement courses are offered. Spending per pupil was $12,072, according to 1997 state figures.

In addition to academics and a full sports program, the district emphasizes musical education and has a music honor society. About 80 percent of students in grades 3 through 12 are involved in musical performances, the school said.

The elementary and middle schools offer an enrichment program for academically superior students. Students chosen for the program are taken out of regular classrooms and enrolled in accelerated classes in all disciplines.

Students in Herricks schools also come from Albertson, North New Hyde Park, Williston Park, Manhasset Hills, Roslyn, and Roslyn Heights. Most of the more than 300 teachers have one or more advanced degrees.

The hamlet derives its name from the Searing family, once numerous in the area and among the first parishioners at the Methodist church that was erected in 1788. "It was a hotbed of Methodism and the Searings were the moving force," said Roger Wunderlich, a professor of Long Island history at the State University of New York at Stony Brook and editor of the *Long Island Historical Journal.*

The historic Searing-Roslyn Methodist Church on I. U. Willets Road, although altered and expanded, still stands and includes parts of the original structure. But the area is now considered part of Albertson. The congregation shares church space with the Holy Light Korean United Methodist Church.

More recently, Searingtown reinforced ties with Japan. When Emperor Akihito and Empress Michiko of Japan made a 16-day, 10-city tour of the United States in 1994, they made just one official visit on Long Island—to the National Center for Disability Services, an internationally recognized nonprofit facility with educational, rehabilitation, training, and job-counseling programs for people with disabilities. It has had links to Japan since the 1950s, when it became a model for Japanese disability centers. The center operates the tuition-free Henry Viscardi School for prekindergarten through grade 12. About 220 students with disabilities attend. There are also continuing-education programs serving more than 2,000 adults.

SYOSSET

*A range of housing and a
plus for hockey fans*

BY VIVIEN KELLERMAN

This well-established hamlet in the township of Oyster Bay placed three high school students as semifinalists in the 1994 Westinghouse Science Competition, a better showing than some entire states make. Syosset has an acclaimed school district, and also boasts a convenient 50-minute commute to New York City on the Long Island Rail Road, downtown shopping, accessibility to highways, and tightly knit residential neighborhoods.

The hamlet is so desirable, said Andrew Mensch, an owner of Century 21 Birch Tree Realty in Syosset, that during the 1990s, demand for houses by first-time buyers and those moving up to more expensive homes has exceeded the supply on the market. While the price spread for single-family homes has ranged during the mid-1990s from $180,000 for a three-bedroom, one-bath ranch to almost $1 million for luxurious homes on an acre or more, the median price for a single-family home has increased about 1 percent a year, reaching $261,500 in 1997. Taxes on a median-priced home are about $5,300.

Syosset is essentially made up of two sections, one north and one south of the Jericho Turnpike. The northern area is more wooded and hilly with a mix of homes and lot sizes. Homes here range from $500,000 to $600,000, with some smaller ones that start in the low $200,000's.

South of the Jericho Turnpike, where there are several large developments, the area has more of a planned-community feel. A typical three-bedroom, 2½-bath split-level house in this area ranges from $180,000 to the low $300,000's.

Hidden Ridge is a 15-year-old, 215-unit town house condominium complex. In 1997, two-bedroom units ranged from $230,000 to $250,000, while three-bedroom units sold from the high $200,000's to the low $300,000's. Most of the units have formal dining rooms, two-car garages,

POPULATION: 19,240.

AREA: 5 square miles.

MEDIAN HOUSEHOLD INCOME: $88,312.

MEDIAN PRICE OF A SINGLE-FAMILY HOUSE: $261,500.

TAXES ON A MEDIAN-PRICED HOUSE: $5,300.

PUBLIC SCHOOL SPENDING PER PUPIL: $10,234.

DISTANCE FROM MIDTOWN MANHATTAN: 28 miles.

RUSH-HOUR TRAVEL TO MIDTOWN: 50 minutes on the Long Island Rail Road, $7 one way, $154 monthly.

CODES: Area, 516; ZIP, 11791.

and basements. The gated community has a clubhouse, swimming pool, and tennis courts.

There are no co-ops or rental complexes in Syosset, although occasionally condominium units come on the rental market. Rents were increasing during the mid-1990s from about $1,800 a month for a two-bedroom unit in 1995 to $2,000 two years later. Three-bedroom units increased about $100, to $2,300.

In 1994, 29 new contemporary and Colonial houses were built on property next to Hidden Ridge. These four-bedroom homes with 2½ baths and 3,000 to 3,500 square feet of space on a quarter acre were priced from $350,000 to $500,000 and were sold out in nine months. Three years later, the prices for the same houses had increased about $100,000.

"There is a broad range of houses in Syosset, which gives people the ability to move up in house and keep the kids in the same school district," Mr. Mensch said.

It was the desire to stay in the school district that motivated Anne and Mitchell Margolis to buy a single-family home in Syosset after living in a condominium in Hidden Ridge for five years.

Mr. Margolis, a real estate developer in Manhattan, and his wife moved to Syosset from Great Neck in 1987 to be near their parents. He said Syosset was a convenient commute for Mrs. Margolis, who works as a product manager in Melville, only five minutes away.

But with a growing family, which now includes sons Adam and Lawrence, Mr. Margolis said the school district was the most important reason for staying in Syosset.

When the family learned that a new subdivision would be developed near the condominium complex, they decided to buy. In August 1993, the Margolises moved into a four-bedroom contemporary Colonial on a quarter acre.

"We bought this house as much for the neighborhood as anything else," Mr. Margolis said. "The average ages are 30 to 40 years old with lots of small kids. It's a perfect place to raise a family."

In 1996 and 1997, the Syosset Central School District was named number one among 600 suburban school districts in the country by *Expansion Management* magazine, a publication for companies planning to relocate.

Dr. Carole Hankin, superintendent of schools, said the district did not apply to the magazine for placement in the listing, but she said the rating was deserved. "The success of our school district is the strong input of our parents," she said. "Everyone works together for the education of our children."

In 1997, the district had 5,300 students in seven K–5 elementary schools, two middle schools, and a high school. Per-pupil spending in 1997 was $10,234.

The district has a K–7 gifted and talented program and child-care programs before and after school, which in 1997 had 311 students enrolled. Although the program has grown during the mid-1990s at an average of 8 percent a year, the cost of $3.25 to $5.25 an hour, depending on program usage, has remained stable during the mid-1990s.

Dr. Hankin said that the district's emphasis on science has grown from a strictly voluntary program to one that also includes an enriched four-year program for all high school students. She said typically, the district sends 99 percent of its graduates on to higher education.

The downtown shopping area of Syosset, with 56 stores plus three banks and eight restaurants, runs along Jackson Avenue from the Jericho Turnpike to the Long Island Rail Road station. A popular spot is Cardinale's bakery, which has an attractive dessert parlor; late Saturday evenings, there is a wait for a table. An additional 60 or so stores are in strip shopping centers nearby. The Syosset Triplex, which once was Long Island's Cinerama theater, is the local place for films.

A proposal to turn 39 acres of land near the Long Island Expressway into an upscale shopping center has been bandied around for the past several years. Some local civic groups have opposed the development, saying it would bring increased traffic into the area. Among the stores that have expressed an interest in the idea are Lord & Taylor, Nordstrom, Neiman-Marcus, and Bloomingdale's.

Andrew Adias, a pediatric dentist who opened his practice in 1987, said he chose Syosset because the community was growing, with young families moving in. In 1997, Dr. Adias, his wife, Andrea, and their son, Matthew Salimbene, moved into a 45-year-old three-bedroom, two-bath expanded Cape on a quarter acre in a country setting. They paid $275,000.

"We love it," Dr. Adias said. "We're here to stay. It's a great neighborhood, quiet, peaceful, pretty, and near to just about everything. I'm very happy with the school district. Matthew is doing real well."

Another attraction is the 46-acre Syosset-Woodbury Community Park on the Jericho Turnpike in Woodbury, which is shared by residents of

Syosset and Woodbury. It has two swimming pools, two playgrounds, lighted ball fields, miniature golf, a roller-skating rink and picnic areas. In 1997, residents could buy a family pool pass for $140 a season. Other residents of the Town of Oyster Bay paid $170.

The park is also the site of the Syosset-Woodbury Community Center, where there are programs for the elderly and for preschoolers. Programs are open to Syosset and Woodbury residents, and workshops include bridge, dance, and crafts. Fees are $20 to $30.

A free entertainment is watching the New York Islanders hockey team practice at its training center, Ice Works, on Underhill Boulevard.

In 1648, a man named Robert Williams bought land known as East Woods from the Matinecock Indians. Not much is known about Mr. Williams, except that he also established Hempstead eight years earlier. The first people to settle in the area were primarily Quakers seeking religious freedom.

By the Civil War, the area was divided among 13 prominent families, among them the Schencks, Borums, Van Sises, and Sanfords, who farmed the land.

By 1847, mail leaving the village was postmarked Syosset, although there is no record of how or why the East Woods name was discontinued or why this name was selected.

The name, however, caused a furor among the town's fathers, who were split in their feelings about it. Some thought it was a crude Indian name and tried to get it changed. After some debate, the Syosset name was officially adopted in 1855.

In 1854, the Long Island Rail Road was extended from Hicksville to Syosset. Once the railroad came to town, Syosset became a major stop on the North Shore. Wealthy landowners built estates in the area. Most of the estates are gone, having been sold off and subdivided before World War II. Population exploded to 16,000 in 1956 from 4,000 in 1950, with the hamlet's population now at 19,000.

Henry Marzolo has seen Syosset grow since he moved there in 1919, when he was 3 years old. He remembers when farmland dominated the area and the Van Sise general store and an ice-cream parlor were the only two stores in town.

Mr. Marzolo, a retired plumber who joined the Syosset volunteer fire department in 1938 and has been fire commissioner since the 1960s, said that the first house built by his father in 1928 carried a mortgage of $2,200. The first home he bought in 1947 cost $6,500. He bought his current home in 1968 for $32,500. He laughs when told how high the median-priced house is today.

"It's changed so much," he said. "But it's still a great place to live."

VALLEY STREAM

Family-centered and hugging Queens

BY JOHN RATHER

With nearly 35,000 residents living along its tightly packed streets of one-family houses on small lots, Valley Stream is the third most populous village in New York State. It is also among the more affordable communities in Nassau County, one of the most expensive housing markets in the country.

For considerably under $200,000, a compact, detached, well-maintained Cape Cod, Colonial, or ranch-style house, typically built in the '50s or '60s, may be purchased in this middle-income, low-to-the-horizon area where public schools send about 90 percent of graduates on to higher education.

Local real estate brokers say good schools—there are three high schools to choose from—and a short commute to the city from the village's two Long Island Rail Road stations are key attractions. Young families, often from Queens and Brooklyn, are frequent buyers. "The key selling point is proximity to Manhattan while still being on Long Island," said Robert R. Miller, broker-owner of Century 21 Miller & Miller in Valley Stream.

Villagers speak of amiable, family-centered neighborhoods where children are once more much in evidence, as they were during the village's suburban boom time 40 years ago. But residents pay a price for living east of Queens, which abuts the village. Property taxes are more than twice those west of the border. "They feel suburban living is better for their families, so they are willing to pay higher taxes," said Dorothy L. Potter, broker-owner of Valley Stream Realty and a village resident for 33 years.

In early 1998, the median price for a one-family house was $170,000; taxes on a median-priced house were about $4,800. Prices ranged from $150,000 to $300,000.

POPULATION: 34,957.

AREA: 3.4 square miles.

MEDIAN HOUSEHOLD INCOME: $65,390.

MEDIAN PRICE OF A SINGLE-FAMILY HOUSE: $170,000.

TAXES ON A MEDIAN-PRICED HOUSE: $4,800.

PUBLIC SCHOOL SPENDING PER PUPIL: $12,185.

DISTANCE FROM MIDTOWN MANHATTAN: 15 miles.

RUSH-HOUR TRAVEL TO MANHATTAN: 32 minutes from the Long Island Rail Road Valley Stream station, 40 minutes from the Gibson station, $6.25 one way, $135 monthly.

CODES: Area, 516; ZIP, 11580, 11581, and 11582.

Mayor Jim Darcy, a villager since the age of 2, said higher taxes must be weighed against the benefits of living in an intact hometown with a vivid history, where people care enough to contribute, as they did recently, toward medical expenses for a native son with leukemia.

A large number of civic and service groups, village sports programs, including midget football, two local papers—*The Valley Stream MAILeader* and *The Valley Stream Herald*—and a local chamber of commerce intent on revitalizing downtown areas add energy and texture to village life.

While single-family detached homes predominate, there are some other housing choices. At the 89-unit Gibson Gardens Cooperative, a brick complex near the Valley Stream railroad station, the asking price for a two-bedroom co-op is $65,000, with monthly maintenance of $900. One-bedroom units are $50,000, with maintenance of $780. Some sponsor-owned units rent for $1,200 and $1,000, respectively.

The average cost of a three-bedroom unit in the smattering of condominium units in the village is about $155,000.

The main village-owned recreation area, the 36-acre Hendrickson Park, has three outdoor swimming pools, a fitness trail, tennis and handball courts, and lakeside promenades. Seasonal pool passes are $125 for a family and $55 for single adults. The nine-acre Barrett Park is in the 1920s vintage Gibson neighborhood south of Sunrise Highway. (East of it is the North Woodmere section, which juts out into Woodmere in the shape of a musical note.) The park has two baseball fields, a playground, a roller hockey rink, and handball and basketball courts. The 13-acre Fireman's Memorial Park has baseball and football fields and is a center for local sports teams. These parks are free for village residents.

The 97-acre Valley Stream State Park, which is partially in the village, has basketball courts, softball fields, picnic tables, bike paths, and walking trails. Admission is $4 a car or $39 for an annual pass.

The predominantly Republican village is in the Town of Hempstead, the home base of the powerful Nassau Republican Party. It has its own justice court but relies on the county's Fifth Precinct for police services. The police say it is a low-crime area.

In May and June, street fairs are held downtown on the last Thursday of the month. A summer concert series that has featured the West Point band one week and the Great South Dixieland Jazz Band the next, is offered at the Village Green by Central Avenue and Sunrise Highway, where the Valley Stream Fire Department Carnival and Casino is also held.

Small businesses and franchise outlets crowd Merrick Road, Central Avenue, and Sunrise Highway. But for serious shopping, there is the 200-store Green Acres Shopping Center at the village's southern boundary. Anchor stores include Macy's, Sears, Caldor, and JCPenney.

Valley Stream's beginnings date to 1640, when the Dutch West India Company bought land the village now occupies from the Rockaway Indians. In the 1840s, Robert Pagan, a local shopkeeper, led a successful effort to gain a local post office to spare residents the trip to Hempstead. Inspired by the village's valleys and streams, he coined the name Valley Stream, which was quickly adopted. Carol C. McKenna, the president of the Valley Stream Historical Society, said the name was unique in the United States. "We are very proud of that fact," she said.

In the early 20th century, the village gained renown as a place for fast living. People called the downtown area Rum Junction. There was also Cookie Hill, a coy reference to another area's saucy reputation. And Merrick Road, which runs through the heart of the village, was dubbed the Great White Way of Nassau County. The legendary nightclub entertainer Texas Guinan greeted customers at one of two well-known roadhouses with her trademark "Hello, sucker." Rudy Vallee and Guy Lombardo performed at the other.

The village incorporated in 1925, midway through a decade of early growth. By then, William R. Gibson, a builder of houses and apartments in the Ridgewood, Richmond Hill, and Elmhurst sections of Queens, was already erecting homes for white-collar workers from the city in the neighborhood that still bears his name. An architecturally matching Long Island Rail Road station, paid for by Mr. Gibson in exchange for a guarantee of rail service, opened in 1929. It is also named for him.

By the mid-fifties, village population was 36,000 and space was at a premium. Mayor Arthur J. Hendrickson, a titan in village history, negotiated purchase of 36 acres next to Valley Stream State Park for creation of the village park named in his honor.

Schools have always been a top priority for the village. But the organization of local public schools is a bit confusing. The Valley Stream Central High School District, one of only three high school districts on Long

Island, is comprised of three high schools. There are also three separate elementary school districts, Districts 13, 24, and 30, with a total of 10 schools.

Most students in the village attend Valley Stream Central High School, not to be confused with the central high school district. But students may now attend either of the other two high schools—Valley Stream North and Valley Stream South—with the permission of the district superintendent. Nearly 70 percent of the high schools' Class of 1997 graduates earned Regents diplomas.

Combined enrollment for the elementary and secondary schools is about 8,400. The schools also serve North Valley Stream and parts of Elmont, Franklin Square, Malverne, and Lynbrook.

A district program encourages students to take the most rigorous academic program appropriate for their abilities. School officials say this accounts for the high percentage of Regents diplomas. The high schools offer advanced placement programs in 16 subjects.

Valley Stream Central High School teaches grades 10–12. A separate junior high school, Valley Stream Memorial, teaches grades 7–9. Valley Stream North and Valley Stream South are combined junior-senior high schools for grades 7 through 12. The district has no middle schools. Average annual spending per pupil was $12,185 in 1998.

The central high school district and the three elementary school districts are currently studying consolidation into a single school district or two districts for grades K–12. "We are trying to decide the best path to take," said Martin G. Brooks, the interim superintendent of the central high school district. He said tricky school tax questions were involved. Overcrowding has become a problem in some elementary schools in the past four years, he said.

There are two Roman Catholic schools in the village. About 300 students attend Holy Name of Mary School. Tuition ranges from $830 to $1,870 for nursery through prekindergarten, $1,870 to $3,720 for the higher grades, depending on grade and the number of students from one family attending. Nonparishioners in kindergarten through grade 8 pay $2,800 to $4,300.

Blessed Sacrament School has about 425 students in nursery classes through grade 8. The school has a new computer laboratory, and an extended-day program for students of working parents is planned. Tuition for grades 1 through 8 is $2,190. Varied fees apply for nursery through kindergarten. Nonparishioners are charged $2,580 in kindergarten through grade 8.

Villagers always know which way the wind is blowing. When it is from the east, flight paths for John F. Kennedy International Airport shift, bringing jet noise. But east, some point out, is not the prevailing wind direction.

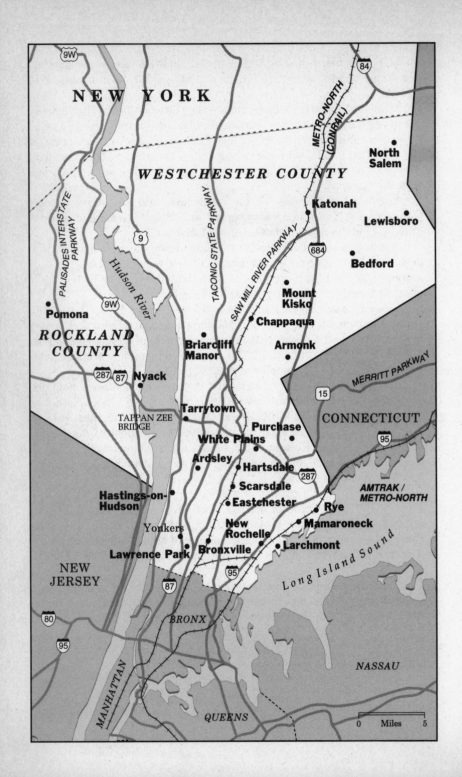

Westchester and Rockland Counties

Ardsley

Armonk

Bedford

Briarcliff Manor

Bronxville

Chappaqua

Eastchester

Hartsdale

Hastings-on-Hudson

Katonah

Larchmont

Lawrence Park West

Lewisboro

Mamaroneck

Mount Kisco

New Rochelle

North Salem

Purchase

Rye

Scarsdale

Tarrytown

White Plains

The Nyacks

Pomona

ARDSLEY

A small-town feel, ringed by highways

BY MARY McALEER VIZARD

With a downtown isolated by highways, the one-square-mile Village of Ardsley in Westchester County is surrounded by higher-profile neighbors. But what the small community offers is cherished by its residents, especially its natives.

Kathleen Canfield and her husband, Philip, who both grew up in Ardsley, lived briefly in Tarrytown, but decided they wanted to raise their family in Ardsley. About the time of the birth of their first child, a daughter, in the summer of 1997, the couple closed on a four-bedroom Cape Cod/Colonial a few blocks from the house where Ms. Canfield grew up. "I can see my old bedroom window from the house," Ms. Canfield said.

The small-town feeling of Ardsley—the population is estimated at 4,400—combined with what she called "phenomenal" schools, is the main draw for the Canfields. "I had such a great childhood here, I wanted that for my child," Ms. Canfield said.

Fred N. Arone, the unofficial historian for the village, remembers a time when it seemed that everyone who lived in Ardsley was also born there. "Now most of the middle-aged people I overhear in the coffee shop reminisce about childhoods in the Bronx or in Queens," he said. "It's changed. They come here for the schools, are willing to pay the high taxes, then once the children are out of school, they move on to greener pastures."

One such newcomer, Peter Rosenberg, moved to the village in 1995 from the Riverdale section of the Bronx. "My children were just starting school, and we thought it was time to get into a really good school system," Mr. Rosenberg said. He said he and his wife, Abbe, had looked all over Westchester before they found "a community of concerned and involved parents" in Ardsley. "We weren't looking for schools with the

POPULATION: 4,434.

AREA: 1 square mile.

MEDIAN HOUSEHOLD INCOME: $93,830.

MEDIAN PRICE OF A SINGLE-FAMILY HOUSE: $301,583.

TAXES ON A MEDIAN-PRICED HOUSE: $7,100.

PUBLIC SCHOOL SPENDING PER PUPIL: $12,158.

DISTANCE FROM MIDTOWN MANHATTAN: 22 miles.

RUSH-HOUR TRAVEL TO MIDTOWN: 36 minutes on Metro-North's Hudson line, $6.50 one way, $141 monthly.

CODES: Area, 914; ZIP, 10502.

highest scores," Mr. Rosenberg said, "We also didn't want a competitive and stressful atmosphere for the kids."

The Ardsley School District, which encompasses parts of Hartsdale, Scarsdale, and the unincorporated section of the Town of Greenburgh, has three schools: the kindergarten-through-grade 5 Concord Road Elementary, the Ardsley Middle School, and the Ardsley High School. Average per-pupil spending in 1997 was $12,158.

Of the 109 students in the Class of 1998, 80 percent went on to four-year colleges and 18 percent went to two-year schools.

Each school has its own library and in 1997 a new 6,000-square-foot library opened at the high school. "It's a double-tiered structure with a skylight," Ms. Callahan said. "We're also in the process of renovating the middle school library."

When considering school districts, Mr. Rosenberg remembers being particularly impressed by Ardsley's facilities. "When I saw the elementary school library," he said, "it seemed like a temple of learning."

The village's housing is eclectic. Since much of it was developed after World War II, there are a large number of ranches and split-levels tucked into discrete neighborhoods beside older sections of Colonials and Victorians.

Prices generally range from just under $200,000 for a "cottage," said Cheryl Mathew, a sales associate at Hudson Affiliates, to the "high $600,000's." The median price of a house in the first quarter of 1998 was $301,583; taxes on a median house were $7,100. Most houses are on small 100- by 100-foot lots, Ms. Mathew said. In some sections, the houses have substantially more property. On Winding Road Farm, where houses are set far back and sit on two acres, prices range from $500,000 to more than $1 million.

At Ardsley Estates, a 34-unit development just outside the village boundaries but within the school district, four-bedroom Colonials were sold for $700,000 to $900,000, according to Christine Sciarrotta, a marketing director with Toll Brothers, the project's builder.

There are also two condominium developments. Stonegate, a 27-unit complex, has three- and four-bedroom brick Georgian-style town houses priced from $325,000 to $355,000. Ardsley Court, a 39-unit condominium converted from a 1912 schoolhouse, has one- and two-bedroom apartments priced from $120,000 to $180,000. Some are multilevel.

The Canfields were pleased that they were able to buy their home for $230,000. "It needs a lot of work, but it was a better deal than we expected to find," Ms. Canfield said.

Lucy Grinson, 91, came to live in Ardsley with her husband, Eugene, in 1954. "It was a tiny town in those days," Ms. Grinson said. "You could let your dog loose to run through the open meadows." In some sections of Ardsley today, the vegetation is still so lush and dense that it is more like the country than a bustling suburban community.

One such area is referred to as the "original 21 acres," a hilly swath of land developed by a group of architects and other professionals in 1946. "We were looking for interesting terrain in a wooded area with natural boundaries and no through traffic," said Stanley Torkelsen, who is still a working architect and living in the house he and the group helped design. "We came up with a module house, with a plank roof and exposed beams," Mr. Torkelsen said. They built 13 of the same houses, each on 1.33 acres.

The result is one of the most unusual developments in Westchester. For the most part, low-slung wooden houses sit unobtrusively on heavily landscaped property. The houses practically disappear in the foliage. "They were all the same style originally," Mr. Torkelsen said, "but over the years, people made changes. Some still have the original character." While they rarely sell, Ms. Mathew said prices would range from $600,000 to $700,000.

Ardsley has several public green spaces, including the 12-acre Ashford Park, which is a focal point for the community. It has four tennis courts, a soccer field, a softball field, and a basketball court. The 12-acre McDowell Park, with an ice-skating rink, has a picnic pavilion and a playground. And the county operates the 172-acre V. Everit Macy Park, which has a picnic pavilion, two ball fields, and a basketball court.

Despite such attractions, Ardsley is in many ways a forgotten village. Sandwiched in between Dobbs Ferry and Hartsdale, it's a place people drive through to get somewhere else. Once a true village center, the crescent-shaped downtown is now bordered by the Saw Mill River Parkway and New York State Thruway on one side and Route 9A on the other.

The village was profoundly affected by the building of both the Saw Mill River Parkway, which opened in 1930, and the New York State Thruway in 1955. To make way for the highways, whole sections of the village were obliterated, according to Mr. Arone, the village historian. The construction of the Thruway and the Ashford Avenue Bridge, which connects the village to the highways, resulted in the virtual destruction of the old Ardsley, according to Mr. Arone. "Approximately 40 buildings and structures were demolished or were moved to new locations," Mr. Arone said.

Of course, the highways also make Ardsley more accessible for commuters, which is a major advantage to some. "The location is so convenient, you can get anywhere so easily," said Mr. Rosenberg, who commutes to Manhattan daily to his job as a television executive.

An earlier construction project that passed directly through the area also had a lasting impact on what was to become Ardsley. The New Croton Aqueduct, bringing water to New York City from reservoirs in the country, was built between 1854 and 1893. After the aqueduct was completed, many of the Irish and Italian workers settled in the area. And discussions began on incorporating the village, which was officially approved in 1896.

Certainly not pedestrian-friendly, Ardsley's downtown consists of several restaurants, a deli, a pizza parlor, and a few real estate offices. One recent addition is Starbucks, which moved into a vacant storefront on Route 9A. "That really enlivened that section of town," said Mayor Samuel J. Abate, Jr. "It's great to drive by at night and see people sitting outside enjoying themselves."

"One of our biggest problems is traffic," the mayor said. "It's an unfortunate reality that Route 9A is our downtown, but we have to find ways to alleviate the bottleneck there." He said he would also like to upgrade the downtown with a program of facade improvements and establish laws limiting the size and design of signs.

"There's been a renewed interest in the downtown with the opening of Starbucks," the mayor said. "We need to have a plan in place to make sure any future development turns out the way we want."

ARMONK

Rugged beauty, healthy tax base

BY TESSA MELVIN

Tucked away in the up-country region north of White Plains, Armonk is separated from that city by seven miles of watershed wilderness. The hamlet of Armonk makes up more than two-thirds of North Castle, a sprawling 26-square-mile town that encompasses two other hamlets, Banksville and North White Plains.

Visitors are often surprised by the unusual array of restaurants, gourmet food stores, and take-out establishments filling storefronts along Main Street. The eating places rely on the sizable office neighborhood hidden in the surrounding hills, including I.B.M.'s corporate headquarters, which has overlooked Armonk for 33 years.

The business sector, including tenants at the Westchester Business Park adjacent to I.B.M., and the town's largest taxpayer, New York City, supply a quarter of the tax base in the Town of North Castle. Corporate tax support will increase in 1999, when the Swiss Re Corporation moves into its new $100 million United States headquarters, now under construction. That tax support has spurred the development of numerous small residential subdivisions folded into the rugged terrain.

Settled in the early 17th century by Quakers fleeing religious persecution, Armonk, a derivation of a Siwanoy Indian name, remained a farming community for much of the next 200 years. The railroad passed it by, and so did the Industrial Revolution. It was the perfect location for the estates of wealthy New Yorkers. And New York City officials bought vast acreage for their developing water system, building the Kensico Reservoir in North White Plains in 1915. Today, Armonk remains an area of rugged beauty, with large stretches of protected open space. It is bordered by Interstate 684 and Route 22 and is surrounded by seven communities, including Greenwich, Connecticut.

POPULATION: 2,867.

AREA: 16.3 square miles.

MEDIAN HOUSEHOLD INCOME: $94,343.

MEDIAN PRICE OF A SINGLE-FAMILY HOUSE: $570,000.

TAXES ON A MEDIAN-PRICED HOUSE: $8,970.

PUBLIC SCHOOL SPENDING PER PUPIL: $11,625.

DISTANCE FROM MIDTOWN MANHATTAN: 35 miles.

RUSH-HOUR TRAVEL TO MIDTOWN: 40 minutes from North White Plains on Metro-North's Harlem line, $6.50 one way, $141 monthly.

CODES: Area, 914; ZIP, 10504.

The development of transportation has made Armonk a magnet for corporate and residential development, although its growth has not always been smooth. In 1946, residents defeated efforts to build the United Nations headquarters there. But as White Plains attracted big companies, Armonk was tempted as well, eventually welcoming the International Business Machines Corporation. The company's arrival raised real estate values and enriched the local culture, providing funds for various community projects, including the acquisition and preservation of the 300-year-old Smith Tavern, headquarters for the North Castle Historical Society.

Residents breathed a loud sigh of relief in 1995, when I.B.M., the town's second-largest taxpayer, quashed rumors about its possible departure and announced instead it would build a new 300,000-square-foot headquarters on part of its existing property. Big Blue, whose 400-acre headquarters property lies mostly in Armonk, supplied 8 percent of the town's $12,543,000 budget in 1997.

With its proximity to transportation, the White Plains commercial hub, and surrounding corporate parks, Armonk's residential real estate market has thrived. Down at Armonk Hardware Store, business is brisk as contractors line up to buy materials they need to complete the various subdivisions under construction. Among them: Sands Mill, a 42-unit project that will sell its five- and six-bedroom units for an estimated $975,000 to $2 million, and the Thomas Wright development, 28 units of luxury five- to nine-bedroom homes on 100 acres a mile north of town. Ten of the homes are completed and have been offered for sale at prices ranging from $1.5 million to $3 million.

Presiding over three decades of development, and then some, is the town supervisor, John A. Lombardi, whose 36 years in office is a Westchester County record. He oversees a town he calls "properly zoned and framed for the way it is growing," adding that his job has been to monitor the unfolding of his predecessors' plans. The 73-year-old supervisor said he wanted to ensure "enough growth to maintain the tax base." In this decade, town taxes have increased only three times, each increase less than 3 percent. But Mr. Lombardi said that maintaining the residential-office mix was getting more difficult.

Mr. Lombardi and the Conservation Board have doubled the amount of public parkland in North Castle, with Armonk's total now at 292 acres. The town's newest park was donated by I.B.M. in 1996. The 23 acres include four ball fields and tennis, paddle tennis, and basketball courts. In downtown Armonk, a 20-acre park is named for Mr. Lombardi; other parks include Wampus Brook Park, with a gazebo and stocked pond for children's fishing, Whippoorwill Ridge, Cats Rock Park, and Clark Field. The hamlet also has two private country clubs, Whippoorwill and Canyon.

Not all has gone according to plan. In 1988, under pressure from Westchester County, town officials proposed Armonk's first multifamily zone in an area they said could accommodate 409 units of housing. Outraged residents forced the plan to be scaled back almost by half. The new zoning paved the way for Wampus Close, Armonk's first homeowners association, with 18 units built in 1993 and sold in less than a year. It was followed by Whippoorwill Ridge, a homeowners association with 55 two- and three-bedroom units, including 28 attached town houses and 27 detached single-family homes on old Route 22 a half mile from town. The two-, three-, and four-bedroom units border a 70-acre nature preserve and include a recreation center with two pools, a tennis court, and a clubhouse. The Armonk Planning Board recently approved Whippoorwill Hills, a 76-unit multifamily development being built near the business district.

Large, single-family homes, many from 4,000 to 6,000 square feet and clustered in small subdivisions, are increasingly common in Armonk and sell for $800,000 to $1.5 million. The market is brisk, said Barbara Greer, an associate broker at the Armonk office of Houlihan/Lawrence. The median price for a single-family home for the year ending in August of 1997 was $570,000. Single-family homes sold in the previous 12 months for a median price of $500,500. Taxes on homes around this median price vary. On one single-family Colonial with five bedrooms on a quarter of an acre that was built in 1993 and that sold in May of 1997 for $649,000, taxes were $9,267. On a three-bedroom town house built in 1994 in Wampus Close and sold two years later for $510,000, taxes were $7,444.

One of Armonk's most desirable neighborhoods, said Ms. Greer, is Windmill Farm, site of a 1,000-acre farm 43 years ago. The land was developed in stages, resulting in 350 homes ranging from small Colonials and ranches to larger homes of varying styles, many of them on the farm's five lakes. Home prices range from $400,000 to $839,500 and include access to the Windmill Club, with its water sports, tennis courts, childrens' programs, and clubhouse.

Lisa and Larry Salko bought their four-bedroom Colonial on Long Pond Road in 1993, returning to the Windmill Farm neighborhood where

Mr. Salko grew up and from which he commutes to Manhattan to the family-owned textile business, the Salko Corporation. Their home is a quarter of a mile from Long Pond, where their children, Jake, 7, and Jennifer, 5, have learned to fish and to skate. Although the Salkos were attracted to Armonk because of its schools, "a community with all these amenities and a real neighborhood feeling is hard to find these days," Mrs. Salko said.

Although water is one of Armonk's attractions, protecting its purity is one of the hamlet's biggest problems. About 90 percent of Armonk residents rely on wells for their drinking water, and groundwater contamination is a constant worry. The Conservation Board has proposed groundwater protection areas and regulations that could limit development in some places. Public water now supplies downtown Armonk after dry-cleaning solvent contaminated 24 wells seven years ago, prompting a $2 million federal superfund cleanup. The state's Department of Environmental Conservation has delayed the building of Heritage Square, a retail center approved by the town five years ago, pending final cleanup.

Armonk residents are proud of the Byram Hills school system, which regularly produces National Merit Scholars and has an academic program that stresses science, technology, and the environment. Students at the H. C. Crittenden Middle School regularly qualify for state science competitions, while selected high school students participate in research projects. In this decade, the high school has produced three Westinghouse Science Talent Search finalists and 11 semifinalists. Typically, 98 percent of the graduating class goes on for more education and 10 percent to 15 percent receive some level of National Merit recognition.

A number of special traditions contribute to Armonk's character, including the June Fol de Rol, sponsored by the Lions Club. The event attracts 30,000 people for two days of jazz, a flea market, and rides. The annual October Art Show, sponsored by the Armonk branch of the North Castle Library, draws nearly 200 artists each fall. Funds from the show helped build the library's Whippoorwill Room, a 185-seat theater in which the library offers a popular Tuesday-night movie series.

BEDFORD

New England, 44 miles from Broadway

BY TESSA MELVIN

Dirt roads may cost three times as much as paved lanes to maintain, but most Bedford residents gladly pay the price to protect their horses' hooves and the ambience of this area of gracious estates and rustic farms 44 miles from Manhattan. Thirty-two miles of dirt roads, popular with wild turkeys and foxes as well as horses, lace the countryside and wind past the stone walls that define the town's character. Many are in Bedford Village, the 317-year-old historic center of the Town of Bedford, which also includes Bedford Hills and Ketonah.

Living in any of these hamlets is a state of mind more than an address. Indeed, local officials say no one really knows the size of Bedford Village, though the assessor said that a third of the parcels in the 39.3-square-mile town were in the hamlet.

Separate school, park, tax, and fire districts overlap, though there are three libraries, three "village" parks, and three post offices (and ZIP codes). Some residents of Bedford Village have Mount Kisco mailing addresses, although they recently won the right to use "Bedford Corners" as their new address. They still share a ZIP code with Mount Kisco.

Residents in each hamlet share a police department and town government. They also share four-acre zoning, which covers 78 percent of the town; increasingly stringent watershed regulations, which limit development; and an appreciation for town history, which is symbolized by the Bedford Oak. The large tree at Hook and Cantitoe Roads is depicted on the Bedford town seal and predates the town's founding in 1680.

The town's major cultural institutions, the Katonah Museum of Art, the John Jay Homestead, and Caramoor, are in Katonah. Bedford Hills is the town's business hub, a big estate area and the seat of town government. Bedford Village is its historic center.

POPULATION: 4,842.

AREA: 39.3 square miles.

MEDIAN HOUSEHOLD INCOME: $145,511.

MEDIAN PRICE OF A SINGLE-FAMILY HOUSE: $525,000.

TAXES ON A MEDIAN-PRICED HOUSE: $9,300.

PUBLIC SCHOOL SPENDING PER PUPIL: $15,900.

DISTANCE FROM MIDTOWN MANHATTAN: 44 miles.

RUSH-HOUR TRAVEL TO MIDTOWN: One hour on Metro-North's Harlem line from Bedford Hills or Katonah, $8.75 one way, $193 monthly.

CODES: Area, 914; ZIP, 10506, 10507, and 10536.

"There aren't any borders," said Jeffrey Osterman, Bedford's director of planning, building, and related services. "The only way to define them is tongue in cheek."

The town has 17 separate zoning districts, but Bedford Village places the most restrictions on its retail area, where lots are kept small and new shopping centers and even restaurants are all but impossible to build. There are, however, three restaurants: Bistro 22, with contemporary French cuisine; the Butcher & the Baker, a seafood-and-pasta family restaurant; and the Village Inn.

Twenty years ago, a square mile in the center of the village, with a triangular green surrounded by 18th- and 19th-century buildings, was listed in the National Register of Historic Places. The designation followed more than a half century of work by the Bedford Historical Society to preserve the architectural and political history of a New England–style town that the railroad and industrial progress had spared.

The Bedford Village Historic District includes all the buildings on the green, now the center of the retail area, many built when Bedford was one of two county seats and the political hub of northern Westchester. Among the historic buildings is the courthouse, built in 1787. Once used by Aaron Burr and John Jay, it is the oldest county government building in Westchester.

The heart of the district was established by 22 Puritan farmers who arrived from Stamford, Connecticut, in 1680, chipped in £2 each to buy a three-acre tract from Chief Katonah, and laid out Bedford Village around the green as part of the colony of Connecticut. In 1700, King William gave Bedford to New York.

"Bedford Village is really defined by the green," said William Carlebach, who for many years headed the town committee that oversees all changes in the character of the district. "The majority of people here look on this village as a New England hamlet, no longer in New England, with a charm and beauty everyone recognizes."

The Bedford Historical Society owns and maintains most of the historic buildings around the green, conducts tours, and finds retail tenants whose businesses are in keeping with the character of Bedford Village. Rental income provides 75 percent of the society's budget, said Lloyd Bedford Cox, Jr., former president of the society and the third generation of his family to live in the village.

There is an old-style double-screen movie theater in the center of Bedford Village that shows first-run films, including those starring village residents like Glenn Close and Richard Gere. Above it are 25 studio and one-bedroom apartments, the only legal apartments in the village.

Finding a home in the village can be difficult. Right behind the Historic District, houses sell for $400,000 to $1 million, said Kathy Needell, a broker with Ginnel Realty, adding that homes in some parts of the hamlet can cost $10 million. The median price of a single-family home was $525,000 in 1997, up from $522,500 a year earlier. Houses around that median include a four-bedroom historic house built in 1790 on 2.27 acres that was on the market in late 1997 for $525,000, with taxes of $9,300. A second four-bedroom colonial, built in 1997 on three acres, was on the market for $440,000, with taxes of $9,000.

Realtors agree there are not many moderately priced homes in Bedford Village and no lower-income housing. "There's a demand for housing we don't have," said Muriel Ten Dyke, a broker with Renwick & Winterling.

Illegal apartments abound, many in converted barns or on estates. "There are so many, we can't even count them," Mr. Osterman said, despite a four-year-old ordinance permitting accessory apartments. One-bedroom apartments can rent for $1,800.

Some unusual estate properties become available on occasion, Mrs. Needell said, including an eight-bedroom Victorian house built by R. H. Macy, founder of the department store, for his daughter and her husband, James F. Sutton, in the late 1880s. The house, with its four acres landscaped by Frederick Law Olmsted, sold in 1994 for $1.3 million along with its guest cottage, carriage house and playhouse, a pool, and a two-stall stable.

More modest homes are available in the Farms, a 38-year-old development off Route 22 south of the Historic District. Many of the 69 homes, mostly on one- and two-acre lots, sell for $325,000 and up. The property is next to the 26-acre Bedford Village Park, which has four tennis courts, two paddle courts, a pool, two ball fields, and a small creek that is damned for boating and fishing. Homeowners can walk to the Mianus River Gorge, a 555-acre nature preserve owned by the Nature Conservancy.

When the weekend ends, commuters pay $193 per month to board trains from either the Katonah or Bedford Hills stations for the hour commute to Manhattan.

Village residents are delighted to have a neighborhood elementary school, the Bedford Village Elementary School, which reopened in 1991 after being closed for a decade. The reopening of the school, on the edge of the Historic District, has given the village renewed life, said Bruce L. Dennis, superintendent of the Bedford Central School District. "People talk to each other more now," he said.

Early in 1997, voters approved a $17.8 million bond issue to expand and update the district's schools and make space for a growing school population. A new library media center and cafeteria complex will be added to the Fox Lane Middle School and six rooms added to the Bedford Village Elementary School.

Dr. Dennis oversees a 60-square-mile school district with 3,093 students from Bedford Hills, Mount Kisco, and Pound Ridge, in addition to Bedford Village. With an enrollment that is 20 percent members of minorities, the school district "offers an environment for people who want their children educated in the real world," Dr. Dennis said. The district spends $15,900 per pupil.

Students attend one of five elementary schools before coming together in the sixth grade in Mount Kisco at the Fox Lane Middle School and High School. About 90 percent of the district's high school graduates go on to college. The district supplies free transportation to 661 students enrolled in private schools in the area. The schools include the pre-K–9 Rippowam Cisqua School, which is considering adding a high school, the 6–12 Harvey School, and the K–5 St. Patrick's Roman Catholic School.

The Bedford Riding Lanes Association, with more than 300 members, maintains a 325-mile network of contiguous trails throughout the town and in neighboring Pound Ridge. The system is one of the largest in the country.

Historic preservation can be controversial. Village residents took to the ramparts a few years ago to prevent the state from installing a traffic light at one point of the green's triangle, where several accidents—one of them fatal—had occurred. They lost, but the state agreed not to redesign the green.

A lack of off-street parking has left the retail area in the Historic District without a pharmacy or hardware store, said former town supervisor Joseph M. Del Sindaco, a resident of the hamlet. "Bedford Village should consist of more than real estate offices and antiques shops," he said.

But Mr. Del Sindaco said he respected his neighbors for being purists. "They don't like quaintness, but authenticity is very important," he said.

BRIARCLIFF MANOR

Sweeping vistas and subdivided estates

BY TESSA MELVIN

From the top of Scarborough Ridge, sweeping views of the Hudson River take in the broad expanse of Haverstraw Bay to the north and the skyscrapers of Manhattan 23 miles to the south. That vista—without the skyscrapers—attracted Sint Sinck Indians, Dutch and English farmers, and 19th-century estate owners with names like Vanderbilt and Webb.

Today, most of Briarcliff Manor's large properties have been converted into smaller lots in a village that won a county planning award in 1985 for its adaptive reuse of estates. Beechwood, the former riverfront estate of Frank A. Vanderlip, a banking executive, is now a homeowners association whose members read in the mansion's library, swim in its pool, and stroll beneath its copper beech trees.

Up on the ridge, the Renaissance Revival mansion designed by Stanford White for Commodore Cornelius Vanderbilt's granddaughter Margaret and her husband, Elliott Shepard, is now the clubhouse for the Sleepy Hollow Country Club. The Ridgecrest section, bordering the club, is one of the most sought-after sections of the village.

"The view of the Hudson is drop-dead," said Elizabeth M. Biggar, manager of the Prudential–Carolyn A. Dwyer Agency in Briarcliff Manor. Ridge lots are half an acre to an acre, but homes with good views sell for around $1 million, she said.

The ridge divides Briarcliff Manor from Scarborough, a hamlet with its own post office, railroad station, and identity. East of the ridge, Briarcliff Manor owes its special identity to its founder, Walter Law, a carpet manufacturer whose influence over the village proved so great that in an article in 1902, *The New York Times* called him "one of the few American millionaires to own villages of their own." Arriving in 1890, Law bought up most of the small farms dotting the area. By 1900, his Briarcliff

POPULATION: 7, 271.

AREA: 5.75 square miles.

MEDIAN HOUSEHOLD INCOME: $126,488.

MEDIAN PRICE OF A SINGLE-FAMILY HOUSE: $450,000.

TAXES ON A MEDIAN-PRICED HOUSE: $9,700.

PUBLIC SCHOOL SPENDING PER PUPIL: Briarcliff Manor Union Free School District, $13,596; Ossining Union Free School District, $12,000.

DISTANCE FROM MIDTOWN MANHATTAN: 23 miles.

RUSH-HOUR TRAVEL TO MIDTOWN: 45 minutes to an hour on Metro-North's Harlem line from Pleasantville or Hudson line from Scarborough, $7.50 one way, $163 monthly.

CODES: Area, 914; ZIP, 10510.

Farms employed virtually everyone in the area and supplied much of the metropolitan area with high-quality milk, American Beauty roses, and bottled water. His employee population made the area eligible to become a village and in 1902 Law applied to the state and got a village charter for Briarcliff Manor. He became one of the new village's first trustees; his son, Henry, was mayor from 1918 to 1936.

One business venture made Briarcliff Manor internationally famous. Through the first third of the century, the Briarcliff Lodge, Law's resort hotel, which had 150 rooms when it opened in 1902, played host to a glittering clientele and served as a country getaway for such prominent New Yorkers as J. Pierpont Morgan, F. W. Woolworth, and Jimmy Walker, as well as the actresses Mary Pickford and Tallulah Bankhead. When it closed in 1936, it had about 200 rooms. Guests took golf lessons from Gene Sarazen and tennis lessons from Bill Tilden and swam in a pool that Johnny Weismuller and Gertrude Ederle used for their Olympic trials in 1924. Two years later, the Winter Olympic trials were held at the lodge using snow brought in by train from Canada.

Today, the future of the lodge, which became the main administrative building of King's College, and its surrounding 52 acres in the center of the village is uncertain. Financial problems forced the college to close in 1994. Current zoning restrictions will limit future development to 30 luxury homes or an elder-care site, according to Lynn M. McCrum, the village manager.

In the village as a whole, plans for several subdivisions, which had been gathering dust during the formerly sluggish economy, have been approved and are now being built. Twenty-five of the planned 136 two- and three-bedroom town houses at Scarborough Glen had been completed by the fall of 1997. Ranging in price from $155,000 to $275,000, the homes have a village post office address, but most are located in the Ossining School District.

New developments wholly within the Briarcliff School District include the 82-unit Wyncrest town house development, which includes 14 moderately priced units for village employees, and a proposed 87-unit project on the former Briarhall Country Club property. Donald Trump, the developer, hopes to build 87 large semidetached three- and four-bedroom luxury homes on the site he owns surrounding the golf course, although new approvals will be required.

Residents worry about a sudden development boom, but Mr. McCrum, village manager for 25 years, said the village had established careful land-use policies. "Briarcliff has changed very little since I arrived," Mr. McCrum said. "I take that as a compliment."

While the total of town, village, county, and school taxes is relatively high, Mr. McCrum said, so is home-buyer interest in Briarcliff Manor. "We are just in such a good location," he said. Briarcliff Manor is 15 minutes northeast of White Plains, served by two railroad stations, and intersected by the Taconic Parkway and Routes 9 and 9A. It lies in two towns, Ossining and Mount Pleasant. The monthly commutation ticket cost of $163 is the same from both the Scarborough and Pleasantville Metro-North railroad stations.

Because land is expensive, with lots ranging from $250,000 to $350,000 an acre, there is little moderately priced housing, Mr. McCrum said. Voters approved a bond issue to pay for a $2.67 million water filtration system in 1993 but turned down plans for a new library, believing the nearby Pleasantville Library is sufficient.

Among the recently completed luxury developments is Briar Vista, with 14 custom-built one-family homes on one-acre sites, and the nearby Unicorn at Sleepy Hollow, with 30 homes. All sell for $600,000 to $1 million.

These homes adjoin the Estates at Rosecliff, a 12-year-old planned community where 116 three- and four-bedroom one-family homes have been built on a 152-acre wooded estate once owned by Edward Walker Harden, who went from financial editor of *The Chicago Tribune* to a millionaire investment banker. With homeownership—prices range from $525,000 for a three-bedroom house to $600,000 for a four-bedroom—comes the use of Harden's Italianate mansion, pool, and gardens.

Most homes in Briarcliff Manor are one-family, although three mostly two-bedroom condominium complexes have been built in the last decade. There is one three-story rental apartment complex, Briar House, with 66 two- and three-bedroom units, including some duplexes.

Agents say finding a home in Briarcliff Manor is extremely difficult. "We need listings!" Mrs. Biggar said, adding inventories are extremely low. Single-family homes sold for a median price of $450,000 in the first quarter of 1998, Mrs. Biggar said, up from $320,000 in the first quarter of 1997.

Two- and three-bedroom starter homes in the Old Village and Crossroads area near the elementary school sell for $300,000 to $400,000 but are rarely available, Mrs. Biggar said.

More expensive homes are found on Linden Circle overlooking the Hudson River in Scarborough, on plots laid out by the firm of Frederick Law Olmsted. At Chilmark, the 250-acre former estate of V. Everit Macy, a Standard Oil heir, the Macy family planned the estate's transition to one-family homes whose owners, as an association, jointly own a swimming pool and tennis courts.

About a third of the village's children, including most Scarborough residents and all those in Chilmark, attend Ossining public schools. Real estate agents say the two systems are equal, but buyer preferences for the Briarcliff Manor schools have inflated prices for homes in the district, they say.

The Ossining School District is comparatively large, with 3,718 students in its three elementary schools and its middle and high school. Ossining High School, selected as one of the state's 10 best in 1985, sends 81 percent of its graduates to college. The high school has a fully licensed cable television studio and offers college-level courses sponsored by Syracuse University in addition to an extensive advanced placement program. The school district spent $12,000 on each student in 1997.

The Ann M. Dorner Middle School, named a federal Blue Ribbon School of Excellence in 1989, has special honors programs in mathematics and science starting in grade 6 and foreign language study in grade 7.

An unusual feature of Ossining's educational program is the Ossining Plan, which lets students progress through the grades as a cohesive group. Developed in response to the district's large multicultural population and with the community's endorsement, the plan keeps all students in a particular grade at the same school, encouraging a wide ethnic and racial mix.

The Briarcliff School District has 1,300 students in the K–5 Todd Elementary School, the new middle school school, and the high school. The district spent $13,596 per pupil in the 1997–98 academic year.

Briarcliff High School sends about 93 percent of its seniors on for more education and often produces National Merit Scholars, including three in the Class of 1997. Briarcliff High School was the first in Westchester County to require seniors to contribute 120 hours of community service before graduation.

Briarcliff Manor residents have a wealth of recreational opportunities in the village, including 167 acres of parkland, plus biking and hiking on Old Croton Aqueduct Trail and the County Bike Trail. Two stables provide horses to ride on the grounds of the nearby 801-acre Rockefeller State Preserve.

The village's five parks have 10 tennis courts and three paddleball courts. The village pool at Law Memorial Park is open to all residents.

Three smaller retail areas provide a typical assortment of laundries, grocery, hardware, and liquor stores, and pharmacies. On North State Road, Amalfi's Restaurant offers Italian specialities and fresh fish dishes.

BRONXVILLE

*A craggy square mile intent
on retaining its village identity*

BY TESSA MELVIN

Just 2.5 miles north of the New York City line lies a village with distinctive turn-of-the-century homes and an excellent school system within a single craggy and wooded square mile.

Established almost a century ago in the path of a crowded city spilling northward, Bronxville, part of the Town of Eastchester, has fought hard and successfully to preserve the integrity of its village life against urban encroachments. The 6,000 residents in this village of one square mile began a year-long centennial celebration in April of 1998.

Almost fully developed by 1940, Bronxville now looks much the way it did then. The average house is over 50 years old and there are only two or three vacant building lots. The first major new building project since then, 100 town house and duplex rental units, is being constructed on Parkway Road across from the railroad station. The one- to three-bedroom Tudor-style apartments are expected to rent for $1,500 to $3,000 a month.

The village's success as one of the nation's first planned communities and one that has been able to protect and enhance its quality of life has given it its reputation as "a suburb endlessly copied and never matched," as Victor Mays called it in his *Pathway to a Village: A History of Bronxville*.

Although the minority population is increasing, the village is still 92 percent white and predominantly Republican. Democrats have won village positions but have never captured the mayor's post.

Bronxville's children often return as adults to rear their own families. Among them are Michele and Douglas Bond, who returned with their two young children in 1992 to renovate a five-bedroom Colonial home near Pondfield Road. "We had a good experience, and we wanted to give that same experience to our children," Mrs. Bond said, adding that the village is little changed since she was a child. While taxes are high, the Bonds,

POPULATION: 6,010.

AREA: 1 square mile.

MEDIAN HOUSEHOLD INCOME: $113,834.

MEDIAN PRICE OF A SINGLE-FAMILY HOUSE: $783,000.

TAXES ON A MEDIAN-PRICED HOUSE: $17,000.

PUBLIC SCHOOL SPENDING PER PUPIL: $14,167.

DISTANCE FROM MIDTOWN MANHATTAN: 15 miles.

RUSH-HOUR TRAVEL TO MIDTOWN: 28 minutes on Metro-North, $5.75 one way, $126 monthly.

CODES: Area, 914; ZIP, 10708.

both products of Bronxville schools, say the cost is reasonable, given the quality of the system. "It's worth it, because we know what's coming for our children," she said.

If the Bonds look forward to what is coming, they also appreciate what is past. And that past, a colorful village history, is reflected in the residential architecture—an impressive array of Tudor, Italianate, and shingle-style homes, including some carefully restored 19th-century estate homes. One notable example is a Greek Revival house on White Plains Road built by Alexander Masterton, an early resident and prominent businessman who quarried marble in nearby Tuckahoe for use in New York City buildings.

Other homes were designed by leading early-20th-century architects, including Lewis Bowman, whose well-proportioned houses, many with low-hanging rooflines, can be found nestled into the landscape throughout the village.

Lawrence Park, a historic district on the hill above the business district, was listed in the National Register of Historic Places in 1980. The district and much of the rest of the village, including Lawrence Hospital, part of the downtown, and Sarah Lawrence College, just outside municipal borders, owe their existence to William Van Duser Lawrence, a 19th-century developer.

In 1890, Lawrence set about creating an exclusive colony for established artists. With the help of the architect William A. Bates, he divided a hilly 86-acre estate into irregular plots, turning its cow paths into curving yellow-brick streets while retaining its rocky slabs, giant elm trees, and wildflowers. The two men produced gabled Victorians and shingled eight-bedroom "cottages" with verandas, screened porches, and balconies overhanging the winding streets. Fences were forbidden and friendly neighborhood relations were encouraged.

Getting into Lawrence Park was not easy. "You cannot come to our Park anyway unless some of us know and like you," Alice Wellington Rollins, a noted author of the period, observed. "You must be either a Genius or a Delightful Person to be eligible at all for such privileges as we extend."

Many wanted the privileges, and between 1890 and 1920 two dozen prominent painters, writers, and architects did come, including the muralist Will H. Low, the society portraitist William T. Smedley, and the "poet of Wall Street," Edmund Clarence Stedman.

The colony is gone now, but the homes remain; they are houses that a former Lawrence Park resident, the late *New Yorker* critic Brendan Gill, called "joyous." Such homes, he wrote, "make one feel good simply to look at them."

Owning one is now open to anyone who can afford it. There were nine sales in Lawrence Park in 1997, ranging from a small ranch that sold for $665,000 to a Lewis Bowman Tudor that sold for $2.9 million.

Concerned about the ability of young families to afford Bronxville, Lawrence built several multifamily houses, setting a pattern evident today in which newcomers often buy relatively modestly priced starter homes.

The 2,385 housing units in the village are almost equally divided between one-family and multifamily dwellings, the latter mostly clustered around the railroad station.

Co-ops can be an especially good buy. Among those recently listed for sale: a one-bedroom on Parkway Road for $48,000 and a three-bedroom duplex for $475,000.

One-family homes, usually on small plots, are often quite large, with four or more bedrooms. In 1996, said Laura Stichter, an agent with Houlihan/Lawrence, such homes sold for an average of $830,202.

The median price of all homes sold in Bronxville in 1997 was $783,000, up from $742,500 for the previous 12 months. A four-bedroom, three-bath Colonial built in 1935 on a third of an acre and needing work was on the market at the end of 1997 with an asking price of $699,000 and taxes of $14,515. A second four-bedroom, 3½-bath Colonial built in 1967 on a third of an acre was on the market for $795,000, with taxes of $19,205.

The single "big magnet" that draws residents willing to pay such high prices, Ms. Stichter said, are the schools. The Bronxville system has its grade school, middle school, and high school all under one roof in a U-shaped building. The 1,300-student system is consistently ranked among the top five school districts in Westchester County.

The high school graduated 82 seniors in June of 1997, all headed for higher education, including four who were named National Merit Scholars. Verbal college board scores averaged 520 and math averaged 607.

Class sizes are among the lowest in the county, said Superintendent John A. Chambers, averaging 20 students. Kindergarten enrollment in the fall of 1997, 113, was the largest in 30 years, as Bronxville experiences the "baby boomlet" surging across the county.

Bronxville's education system is based on a philosophy of integrated learning, or "having to show what you know," Mr. Chambers said, a philosophy that found full expression in 1993, when Patrick English, an 18-year-old Bronxville senior, ran for mayor, capturing 42 percent of the vote.

The community "prizes education," Mr. Chambers said, adding that the Bronxville Community Foundation, established in the early '90s to counter declining state aid, has raised more than $1 million, with most donations averaging $1,000.

Concordia College, a Lutheran-sponsored four-year college with 500 students, offers adult education and has a program for the community's gifted children.

Planning for the future is a "delicate balance," said Bronxville's mayor, Nancy Hand, "because we live in such a densely populated community." With little room to increase the tax base, the village must continue to depend on its residents for its revenues, the mayor said.

Residents agree they get a lot for their money, including a Georgian-style library complete with wing chairs, fireplaces, and antiques. Adding to the array of recreation services supplied by the town of Eastchester, Bronxville offers its own summer day camp and an extensive tennis and paddle tennis program that annually draws more than 1,000 participants.

Almost everybody in Bronxville walks into the commercial district on Pondfield Road, drawn by its old-fashioned-looking triplex movie theater and its gourmet food shops and restaurants, including Marichu, which features Basque cuisine, Pane e Vino, and the Scarborough Fair Cafe.

Zoning ordinances are strictly enforced. Despite grumbling by merchants, signs in store windows are strictly regulated, and garage-sale and tradesmen signs in residential neighborhoods are prohibited.

In an effort to limit parking, a continuing problem throughout this small municipality, local ordinances require members of the health professions to use existing office space or go elsewhere.

Among the more noted village events are November's villagewide Paddle Tennis Superscrambles Tournament and the dinner-dance and community Christmas pageant on the lawn of the Dutch Reformed Church. And many youngsters are signed up for Miss Covington's dance classes in the grand ballroom of the Women's Club.

From her vantage point in the Abijah Morgan house on White Plains Road, the oldest house in the village, Frieda Riggs, 90, recently surveyed her 59 years in the village, where three generations of her family live and where she continues to volunteer. "Communities cannot make up for their own lack of background," Ms. Riggs said, adding that "Bronxville is special."

"The school system, the unusual architecture, and the great artists have all come together in a special way," she said.

CHAPPAQUA

A hamlet that cherishes its schools

BY TESSA MELVIN

Chappaqua is a tiny hamlet, a post office address for 3,500-plus households nine miles north of White Plains in the Town of New Castle. But the "real" Chappaqua meanders into six postal districts and two towns—an educational state of mind for people sharing a common school district with a national reputation.

Residents willingly pay high taxes to send their children to the Chappaqua public schools, consistently ranked among the nation's top systems. Voters regularly support growing school budgets, including a $10.5 million bond issue in 1994 for technology development and capital improvements.

"The Chappaqua school budget hasn't been turned down in memory," said Polly M. Kuhn, former supervisor of the Town of New Castle, which includes Chappaqua. "Sixty percent of our residents have no school kids, but most of them vote for the budget. It's part of the identity of their house and a belief there that public eduction is to be supported."

The popularity of the schools combined with an eight-year-old master plan detailing an ambitious building program has made New Castle the fastest-growing community in Westchester County. Eighty percent of New Castle's residents live within the school district and over half live in the hamlet of Chappaqua.

A few of the town's children attend schools in the Ossining and Pleasantville districts. "If you think you are buying a house in Chappaqua," said Caroline Corwin, the town clerk, "be sure to check with the tax assessor before putting your money down."

The schools' reputation and a "baby boomlet" have caused enrollments to increase 20 percent between 1991 and 1997. Housing developers are eager to keep up. Robert C. Kirkwood, chairman of the town Planning

POPULATION: 17,798.

AREA: 24 square miles.

MEDIAN HOUSEHOLD INCOME: $135,495.

MEDIAN PRICE OF A SINGLE-FAMILY HOUSE: $486,000.

TAXES ON A MEDIAN-PRICED HOUSE: $11,000.

PUBLIC SCHOOL SPENDING PER PUPIL: $13,713.

DISTANCE FROM MIDTOWN MANHATTAN: 38 miles.

RUSH-HOUR TRAVEL TO MIDTOWN: 50 minutes on Metro-North, $7.50 one way, $163 monthly.

CODES: Area, 914; ZIP, 10514 for Chappaqua.

Board, said that most of the planned homes would be "very upscale," ranging in size from 5,000 to 8,000 square feet, many with individual tennis courts and pools. Approvals will not come quickly, Mr. Kirkwood said, since much of the remaining available land in the town is located on steep slopes, including some that drain into wetlands.

The building boom in Chappaqua that began in the early 1990s has unsettled longtime residents, Mr. Kirkwood said. Many, Mr. Kirkwood among them, are concerned that development is putting undue pressure on available roads and recreation facilities. "Traffic downtown after school and on weekends is a nightmare," he said, adding that community pressure is building to "revisit the master plan."

Parking in the hamlet's commercial district is made more difficult, since it is divided into two separate shopping areas by Route 117, which makes a 90-degree turn in the middle of town. Officials are working on a plan to improve the area.

The hamlet's sudden growth has put pressure on Chappaqua's Metro-North Railroad parking lot, where there is a long waiting list for the 75 nonresident slots. New Castle residents pay $180 annually for their 1,125 spaces. Nonresidents pay $450 annually. Commuters pay $163 per month for their rail trip into Manhattan.

Growth has been good for business, which includes several fashionable clothing stores and the Second Story bookstore.

Growing slowly from its beginnings as a Quaker farming community, Chappaqua was protected from development through much of its early-20th-century history as wealthy New York businessmen, bankers, and lawyers looking for country estates bought vast amounts of farmland. Among these early estate owners were Billy Rose, the impresario and theatrical producer, and A. H. Smith, president of the New York Central Railroad.

Much of Chappaqua's rural beauty is still intact, protected by rolling hills combined with strict local laws limiting building bulk, protecting trees, and limiting steep-slope construction. Much of the new housing is tucked into these hills, developments that newcomers find hard to spot.

New residents can choose from an array of detached homes and condominium town houses within reach of one of six private swim clubs scattered throughout the town, most with tennis courts. Annual dues are about $1,000. There are also seven town-owned parks.

At Apple Hill Farm, 56 two- and three-bedroom condominium town houses spread across 32 acres, surrounding three tennis courts and a pool. These units, which sell for $211,000 to $290,000, were the first multifamily housing built in Chappaqua, following a 1977 lawsuit.

Among other condominium developments, Old Farm Lake, an easy walk from the station, offers 175 one- to three-bedroom town house units, most with fireplaces and garages, selling from $219,000 to $335,000.

The 150 New England–style town houses at the Highlands at Riverwoods have won several design awards. Situated on the border of Mount Kisco, the complex still fits within the boundaries of the Chappaqua school system. The two- and three-bedroom units range in price from $450,000 to $550,000.

A bit farther south, Random Farm, Chappaqua's largest development, has 105 detached houses. The four- and five-bedroom residences have 3,200 to 4,000 square feet of space and sell for $600,000 to $900,000.

One of the older and most prestigious sections of Chappaqua is the Lawrence Farms East section east of the north-south Saw Mill River Parkway, which bisects the hamlet. Several homes are within sight of the Reader's Digest corporate headquarters and many border one of two private clubs, Whippoorwill or the Mount Kisco Country Club. Others border Crabtree's Kittle House, a well-regarded area restaurant and inn.

Just opposite the Kittle House is Heathcote Manor, one of the area's newest subdivisions. The 16 homes straddle two school districts with homes in the Chappaqua district starting at $770,000. Houses on the Mount Kisco side start at $599,000.

The median sales price for single-family homes throughout the hamlet in 1997 was $486,000, up $6,000 over the previous year. One 2,500-square-foot, four-bedroom home built in 1962 on one acre sold in 1997 for $485,000, with property taxes of $10,233. A five-bedroom home with 3,000 square feet on half an acre built in 1956 that sold in 1997 for $486,000 had property taxes of $11,879.

Newly constructed homes tend to be larger and have significantly higher taxes. One four-bedroom Colonial with 4,200 square feet built in 1997 on one acre sold a year later for $804,000, with taxes estimated at $18,090.

The schools are the main attraction drawing residents, Bill Holmes, principal broker and founder of Holmes & Kennedy Real Estate, said, adding, "At the same time, they are seeking the quality of life that a relatively rural community like ours has to offer along with its proximity to Manhattan." Marcy Corbett and her husband, Michael Silverstein, were looking for a home outside Manhattan where their three children, Lauren, 17, Kaelyn, 14, and Brett, 12, could enjoy sports. In 1991, the family rented a four-bedroom Colonial with two acres in the Lawrence Farms neighborhood, a home they now own. "These kids needed a life," said Ms. Corbett, vice president of a boy's apparel company in Manhattan, adding she had to convince her husband to give up city living. Today, Mr. Silverstein, vice president of sales for the In-Style clothing concern in Manhattan, also heads the Triple A Division for Little League baseball, and Ms. Corbett has become active in school affairs.

"It's a country atmosphere close to the city," Ms. Corbett said, adding that the school tax bill was a welcome change after paying private school tuitions for their children. The family found the sports they wanted, with full schedules for each of the children, and a good deal of parental involvement. "We run from cross-country to soccer to baseball," Ms. Corbett said with a laugh. "Now, we have no life."

The big drawing card is the school system, which attracts many of its parents as volunteers. "The word has gotten out that we know what we are doing," said Donald C. Parker, superintendent of schools and a parent of two students and one graduate.

The educational program includes Socratic seminars for fourth graders and interdisciplinary courses in the high school combining art, physics, and social studies. Students attend one of three elementary schools, the Robert E. Bell Middle School, and the Horace Greeley High School, named for Chappaqua's most famous resident, founder of *The New York Tribune* and a presidential candidate.

The senior class participates in activities ranging from juggling to advanced Russian, produces substantial numbers of National Merit Scholars, and has sent an average 94 percent of its graduates on to higher education over the last five years. The district spent $13,713 per student in 1997.

Dismissing concerns that the Chappaqua school system generates an excessive amount of academic pressure, Dr. Parker said: "Our program encourages students to become self-motivated. What emerges are students who want to do things, who want to take extra courses. As a parent and as an educator, I think this is an exceptional school system."

EASTCHESTER

Rich housing mix in rustic Westchester

BY MARY MCALEER VIZARD

In "The Lake Isle of Innisfree," the poet William Butler Yeats contemplates a life of solitary reflection on a little wooded island off the coast of Lough Gill in County Sligo, Ireland. A great place to "live alone in the bee-loud glade," he wrote, "where peace comes dropping slow." It might seem odd to connect those sylvan sentiments to the populous Westchester County town of Eastchester. But that's just what a 1930s developer did when he named one of the town's former reservoirs Lake Innisfree. A community of apartments, detached houses, and town houses now known as Lake Isle has since grown up around the lake. "It's one of the most beautiful spots in town," said Jim Cavanaugh, the town supervisor. "It's lushly landscaped. And the residents have beach rights, so it's almost like resort living so close to the city."

Eastchester is rife with such neighborhoods of well-tended lawns and extensive landscaping; most have primarily single-family homes, but some also come with condominiums and co-ops. "We probably have one of the widest selections of housing options in the county," Mr. Cavanaugh said. "Houses in every price category, a few hundred condominiums, and 2,300 co-op units."

Lake Isle, probably the most exclusive neighborhood, is also a micro-cosm of the scope of housing available. Some houses on the lake sell for more than $1 million, said Carol Mele, a sales agent with Prudential Ragette in Eastchester. "But more often they're in the $600,000's and $700,000's." In other unincorporated areas, she said, detached houses range in price from $250,000 to $600,000.

Lake Isle's highest-priced houses are mostly contemporaries and split-level ranches, built in the '50s and '60s, Ms. Mele said, "on a nice piece of property and with a dock." There are also 225 co-op units in

POPULATION: 17,711.

AREA: 3.5 square miles.

MEDIAN HOUSEHOLD INCOME: $77,264.

MEDIAN PRICE OF A SINGLE-FAMILY HOUSE: $275,000.

TAXES ON A MEDIAN-PRICED HOUSE: $7,000.

PUBLIC SCHOOL SPENDING PER PUPIL: $12,925.

DISTANCE FROM MIDTOWN MANHATTAN: 20 miles.

RUSH-HOUR TRAVEL TO MIDTOWN: 34 minutes from Metro-North's Crestwood station, $5.75 one way, $126 monthly.

CODES: Area, 914; ZIP, 10707, 10708, 10709, and 10583.

Interlaken Gardens, priced from the high $60,000's for a one-bedroom to $130,000 for a two-bedroom. At Townhouses at Lake Isle, 85 town homes range from the mid-$200,000's for a two-bedroom with den to the low-$400,000's for a four-bedroom.

All residents of Lake Isle have beach rights. But only owners of detached homes may become members of the Lake Isle Shore Club, which has a pool and lake access. Families pay annual dues of $650.

"There are three homeowner associations representing the houses, co-ops, and town houses and they all work together to protect the water quality and make sure everyone is respecting the environment," Mr. Cavanaugh said.

The Town of Eastchester encompasses the villages of Bronxville and Tuckahoe, each self-governed but sharing some town services. What remains is known as the unincorporated area or the "town outside."

"It's easy to get confused," Mr. Cavanaugh said. "Eastchester suffers from an identity problem." The north end, for instance, has a Scarsdale ZIP code. "It's commonly referred to as Scarsdale," he said. "There are also sections with Bronxville and Tuckahoe ZIP codes."

Mr. Cavanaugh hopes that the 1997 adoption of Eastchester's first comprehensive master plan will help bolster its image. "We were the only municipality in Westchester without a master plan," he said. "Its purpose is to guide growth, although we don't have many vacant parcels. We also want to create transition zones between commercial and residential areas. There is too much mixed use in some of our neighborhoods."

The so-called Scarsdale section is the site of the Vernon Hills Shopping Center, which includes Lord & Taylor, Laura Ashley, Ann Taylor, and a recent addition, Encore Books, which has a cafe offering weekend folk and jazz concerts. Eastchester's only movie theater, the Plaza, on Garth Road, has recently reopened after being shut for years while undergoing an extensive renovation. The single-screen theater had specialized in second-run and art films at reduced prices. In its new incarnation, it will show first-run movies. "It has new seats and a new projector," Mr.

Cavanaugh said. "It's one of the few old theaters left that hasn't been carved up."

Eastchester was a farming community at the outbreak of the Revolutionary War through the mid–19th century, when it started to develop into a suburban enclave. One of the few historic properties remaining is a one-room schoolhouse, built in 1835 of "Tuckahoe marble," an indigenous granite stone. Originally on White Plains Road (Route 22), the building was moved in 1869 to its present location at the intersection of California and New Rochelle Roads. It remained a functioning school until 1884. The modest pitched-roof building has been restored by the Eastchester Historical Society and is now its home, complete with period furnishings. School groups are invited to spend a day at the school to study as children did in the 1800s. And public tours are also available by appointment.

At one time, Eastchester took in the northwestern section of what is now the city of Mount Vernon as well as Bronxville and Tuckahoe. In 1853, a group of New York businessmen incorporated 375 acres as the Village of Mount Vernon. It became a city in 1892. Bronxville was incorporated in 1898 and Tuckahoe in 1903, leaving the unincorporated area to fend for itself. As a result, perhaps, it developed in a haphazard way, never establishing a real town center—although the intersection of Mill Road and Route 22, near the town hall, is generally accepted as the downtown.

Growing up in Eastchester in the '60s and '70s, Laura Slavin remembers a sleepy suburb without a whole lot to do. "As a teenager, I always felt I had to go into Manhattan to socialize and find any excitement," she said. When Ms. Slavin, now a Manhattan resident, returns to Eastchester, she said, "I'm amazed by the traffic and all the activity there is now"—pointing particularly to the Vernon Hills Shopping Center, where the popular Alex & Henry's Restaurant is noted for its political and fund-raising events.

The housing market is active, according to Claire D. Leone, who has a real estate agency bearing her name. "I'd say the hottest price category is $275,000 to $325,000," Ms. Leone said. "If we get a listing in that price, it's gone." The median house price in early 1998 was $275,000; taxes on a median house were about $7,000.

Even with the scarcity of land, there has been a surge in single-family home construction in recent years, according to Joseph Vohnout, the town engineer. "In the last two years, we've had 12 to 18 new homes built on scattered sites," he said. "Normally we have two or three in the same period."

Even co-ops, laggards on the housing market in Westchester in much of the '90s, have benefited by the surge in the housing market, Ms. Leone said, especially those along Garth Road, which is lined with prewar buildings converted from rentals. One building, developed as a co-op in 1929, is doing particularly well, according to Ms. Leone. The 46-unit Kragswold "is very elegant," she said, with doormen and Oriental rugs in the lobby. Its one- to three-bedroom apartments have fireplaces, high ceilings, and formal dining rooms. Prices range from $80,000 for a one-bedroom to $295,000 for three-bedroom apartments. "We've been getting empty-nesters who sell their homes and want to stay in the area," Ms. Leone said. "But we're also getting young people."

One of Eastchester's draws is its school system. Most of the town is in the Eastchester School District, but one section sends its children to the Tuckahoe schools. Dru Galella, and her husband, Daniel, moved from Tarrytown to be settled in the Eastchester School District by the time their 3-year-old daughter, Christiana, was ready to attend. "We zeroed in on Eastchester because the schools are great," Ms. Galella said. "And from where we live, my daughter can walk to school."

Eastchester has five schools, one for preschool and kindergarten only, two elementary (grades 1 to 5), a middle school (6–8), and a high school. Per-pupil expenditure is $12,925, according to Stephen Lieber, deputy superintendent of schools.

The district is one of the few in the county to offer Latin, as well as French, Spanish, and Italian, starting in seventh grade. "We go all the way to Latin 5," Mr. Lieber said. "We also have a thriving foreign exchange program where high school students travel to Massa, in Italy, and Italian students come here." Starting in 1998, students have also been able to travel to Cuenca, in Spain.

One of the town's unusual features is its 116-acre Lake Isle Park, featuring an 18-hole golf course, six tennis courts, and five pools. There are individual fees for tennis, golf, and the pool, but for an annual fee of $1,575 a family gains access to all amenities, including golf. There are also two private country club golf courses—Leewood and Siwanoy—several smaller parks, and green patches throughout the town for passive and active recreation.

At one time, Eastchester was called "the cradle of American golf," since it spawned some early golf champions, such as Will MacFarlane and Johnny Farrell, winners of the U.S. Open in 1925 and 1928, respectively.

HARTSDALE

A suburban mix, with farms

BY MARY McALEER VIZARD

In warmer weather, when Alan Hochberg looks out his window, he can see a tractor tilling the land on a farm across the street from his home in Hartsdale, a hamlet in the Town of Greenburgh. "It's amazing to me that I'm living in southern Westchester and I'm right near a farm," said Mr. Hochberg, administrator of the Scarsdale Synagogue/Tremont Temple. He and his wife, Faye, a lab technician in the Bronx, moved from that borough 13 years ago. "It was always our dream to come up here," he said, "and it's been everything we've dreamed of."

Hartsdale has a 17-acre and a 15-acre working farm, both on Secor Road and both operated by Westchester Greenhouses & Farms, a local company that sells produce and flowers from a roadside stand. "I don't know of any other farms in the area," said Joseph Chiocchi, the company's owner. "There are other nurseries, but no one else who cultivates their own produce and flowers."

The farms are in a section called Poet's Corner, whose 26 streets, all named for poets, are lined with single-family homes. The majority of the houses are Cape Cods, ranches, and some Colonials, built mostly in the '50s and '60s, with a scattering from the '20s.

The presence of farms lends a sense of spaciousness to what would otherwise be a traditional suburban community. Hartsdale has several similar neighborhoods of single-family homes scattered throughout its two-square-mile area. Around its train station are several apartment buildings, most of which have been converted into co-ops. The hamlet also has condominium complexes and a highly diverse population. Mr. Hochberg says much of Hartsdale remains unchanged from when he first arrived. "The essence of Hartsdale is the beautiful mix of people," he said. "And everyone works hard to maintain our quality of life."

POPULATION: 9,332.

AREA: 2 square miles.

MEDIAN HOUSEHOLD INCOME: $81,419.

MEDIAN PRICE OF A SINGLE-FAMILY HOUSE: $267,500.

TAXES ON A MEDIAN-PRICED HOUSE: $7,350.

PUBLIC SCHOOL SPENDING PER PUPIL: $15,569.

DISTANCE FROM MIDTOWN MANHATTAN: 21 miles.

RUSH-HOUR TRAVEL TO MIDTOWN: 45 minutes on Metro-North's Harlem line, $6.50 one way, $141 monthly.

CODES: Area, 914; ZIP, 10530.

Paul J. Feiner, the town supervisor, added: "People don't say, 'I live in Greenburgh.' They always identify with the section, whether it's Hartsdale or Elmsford [another hamlet]. In fact, most people think of Hartsdale as a village."

Its central business district near the train station is a collection of small, mostly local shops. Some have been there for more than 30 years. Hartsdale Liquors, for instance, has been at its present location on West Hartsdale Avenue, the hamlet's main street, since 1933. Richard O'Leary has owned and operated the store since 1959. "Since the apartment buildings went co-op, there's not as much turnover," Mr. O'Leary said. "It's a more stable customer base. And recently, there has been an increase in the number of Asians. They're excellent customers." The hamlet has been a magnet for the Japanese in particular, reflected in the number of Japanese shops and restaurants.

"Just about every ethnic group is here," said Dorothy Jensen, president of Dorothy Jensen Realty. Ms. Jensen opened her real estate office in Hartsdale in 1995, after selling in the hamlet for years at another office. So far, she said, business has been "phenomenal." "Buyers come up primarily from the city to find a single-family home, priced between $225,000 and $250,000," Ms. Jensen said. "Most people who buy here have incomes in the $65,000-to-$85,000 range."

The fact that Hartsdale is a moderately priced community makes it vulnerable to market fluctuations, said Stephanie W. Bellino, president of Blum & Bellino Realtors, in Hartsdale. "Many of our customers are in middle management, which makes them uncertain about their job security," Ms. Bellino said. "When interest rates come down, everybody comes in. But if they blip up, they're all gone again." Ms. Bellino said that in general, prices for single-family homes range from around $179,000 for a two-bedroom, one-bath ranch to $376,000 for a four-bedroom, 3½-bath Colonial on a half acre. "That's about the range," she said. "Most sales fall in the middle." The median price of houses sold in the first quarter of 1998 was $267,500; annual taxes on such a house would be about $7,350. In addition, there is a wide range of co-ops and condominiums. Most co-ops are within walking distance to the train, Ms. Bellino said. Their prices can range from $50,000 for a one-bedroom to $219,000 for a three-bedroom. Condominiums, which usually offer amenities like pools and tennis courts, are priced from $139,000 for a one-bedroom to $329,000 for a three-bedroom, Ms. Bellino said.

Hartsdale was once part of the Manor of Philipsborough, presided over by Frederick Philipse, a Dutch merchant. The Odell House, at 425 Ridge Road, served as Comte de Rochambeau's headquarters during the Revolution, and George Washington is said to have planned strategy there for the Battle of Yorktown with the French general. John Odell, Washington's guide to Westchester, purchased the house in 1765. His descendants deeded it to the town in 1965, and it is now a museum.

After the Revolutionary War, the third and last lord of the manor, also Frederick Philipse, a great-grandson of the first lord of the manor and a Tory, fled to England. The state confiscated all of the family's 90,000 acres stretching from the Bronx to the Croton River and later resold it at auction to tenant farmers and other buyers.

One of the successful bidders was Robert Hart, and what is now the intersection of Central Park Avenue and West Hartsdale Avenue (now known as the Four Corners) was once Hart's Corner. In the 1870s, the surrounding area became known as Hartsdale.

In the 1880s, the hamlet was made up of several large estates owned by prominent New York families. The Woodlands Junior/Senior High School, for grades 7 through 12, is on 190 acres of the former 500-acre estate of Felix Warburg, the financier. In 1956, his widow, Frieda Schiff Warburg, donated the land to the school district.

In addition to the Woodlands school, the Greenburgh Central School District No. 7 also includes three K–8 elementary schools. There are also two Roman Catholic schools, Sacred Heart, for kindergarten through eighth grade, and Maria Regina High School.

The Woodlands Senior High School was designated a New York School of Excellence in 1995 by the state Department of Education, according to Elizabeth Weinberg, district clerk. It offers advanced placement courses in biology, calculus, French, Spanish, English, and American history. It also has a research-projects room, funded by Texaco, for use by science students. Texaco employees serve as student mentors, Ms. Weinberg said.

Parents living in Hartsdale, as well as sections of White Plains and Elmsford, send their children to Woodlands. Eighty-seven percent of students go on to college, Ms. Weinberg said. And average SAT scores are 482 for the verbal portion and 480 in the math. The entire district's per pupil expenditure is $15,569.

Patricia Garner and her husband, Melvin, have been living in the area for 21 years. "When we first came here, we both worked in the city and just came home to eat and sleep," Mrs. Garner said. After they had children, a son, now 19, and a daughter 16, "we got more involved in the community," Ms. Garner said, adding: "The supervisor really gets people involved. If you're upset about something or want something done, he says, 'You're on that committee.' " Ms. Garner is now co-chairwoman of a downtown beautification program. "We want to spruce up the area, get coordinated signage, and make it more inviting for shopping," she explained.

The closing of a Gristede's in 1995 dealt the central shopping district a severe blow, with business shrinking by 40 percent, according to a report prepared by the town Planning Department. After a two-year struggle to find another food operator, a 6,500-square-foot I.G.A. supermarket opened at the same site in late 1997. "I turned away other potential tenants for the space," said Toby Ritter, whose family owns approximately 25,000 square feet of space in downtown Hartsdale. "I wanted to hold out for a supermarket because I felt that was in the best interest of the community."

Between Central Park Avenue and the train station, Hartsdale is comprised mostly of co-ops. "There are 2,500 families along that strip," said Michael Paschkes, who is also on the beautification committee. "Many of these people are senior citizens and they need to be able to walk for their groceries. That's why it is so important to have a food store downtown."

In 1995, the town began operating a farmers' market by the train station, open from 9 A.M. to 1 P.M. on Saturdays, from July through November. And large, full-service supermarkets, as well as every other kind of shopping imaginable, are available within a five-minute drive along Central Park Avenue.

One of Hartsdale's main attractions is its ample recreational opportunities. There are 19 tennis courts and 7 pools at Anthony F. Veteran Park, in nearby Ardsley. Residents can also swim at the Fairview-Greenburgh Community Center, in White Plains. There is also ample open space with the 170-acre Ridge Road Park, owned by the county; the 86-acre East and West Rumbrook Park, half of which is a nature preserve; the 25-acre Secor Woods Park; and the private Scarsdale Golf Club.

Another celebrated feature is the Hartsdale Canine Cemetery, on Central Park Avenue, which was created in 1896 by Samuel Johnson, a New York City veterinarian. More than 40,000 pets are interred there, including those of Al Jolson, George Raft, and Irene Castle. The cemetery has also accommodated birds, mice, and even a pet lion, which was buried there in 1912 by a divorced Russian princess, Vilma Lwoff-Parlaghy.

HASTINGS-ON-HUDSON

Close to the city, but in a world of its own

BY MARY McALEER VIZARD

Every morning when he walks from his home to the train station, Tom Quinn is reminded of why he moved to Hastings-on-Hudson. "First of all, I walk through the heart of the downtown," Mr. Quinn said. "This isn't some nightmare subdivision with no center." Then he stands on the platform and can see the Palisades across the Hudson River and the Manhattan skyline to the south. "It's comforting to me to know that the city is so close."

Many of the people who live in this southernmost river village in Westchester County feel the same way. "I like the fact that it feels like the Upper, Upper West Side," said Kevin Dawkins, a video producer who moved here from a co-op in Central Park West. "Unlike the image of Westchester as an upper-class enclave, this is a nicely mixed environment with a lot of interesting people."

Another West Side transplant, Harry Stein, a writer, said the move to Hastings wasn't that big a leap. "For one thing, one isn't the only writer here," he said. "And, as everybody knows, writers will do anything to avoid writing. And I can find all sorts of people to talk to during the day to help me do that."

Hastings, which was incorporated in 1879, was originally known as an industrial community, the site of cable-and-wire manufacturing, stone quarries, and sugar refineries. In recent years, however, it has become known as a bedroom community of New York City that attracts young families with a proclivity for the arts. "Everyone seems to be from either the West Side of Manhattan or Park Slope [in Brooklyn]," said Mr. Quinn, who is a senior writer with the Ford Foundation, in Manhattan. He and his family moved to Hastings from the Riverdale section of the Bronx in 1994. "My neighbors are from Park Slope," Mr. Quinn said. "When they

POPULATION: 7,799.

AREA: 2 square miles.

MEDIAN HOUSEHOLD INCOME: $78,337.

MEDIAN PRICE OF A SINGLE-FAMILY HOUSE: $375,000.

TAXES ON A MEDIAN-PRICED HOUSE: $9,000.

PUBLIC SCHOOL SPENDING PER PUPIL: $12,384.

DISTANCE FROM MIDTOWN MANHATTAN: 20 miles.

RUSH-HOUR TRAVEL TO MIDTOWN: 35 minutes on Metro-North, $6.50 one way, $141 monthly.

CODES: Area, 914; ZIP, 10706.

heard we were from Riverdale, they asked, 'How did you get here?' I mean, we lived seven miles from here. But it's less about geography than cultural attitudes."

The village has a dance studio and several bookstores, art galleries, and artists' studios. It has been home to such celebrated artists as the painter Jasper F. Cropsey and the sculptor Jacques Lipchitz, whose work *Between Heaven and Earth* adorns the lawn in front of the village library. Cropsey's home, called Ever Rest, is now part of the Newington-Cropsey Foundation Gallery, on Cropsey Lane. It displays the works of Cropsey primarily, but also exhibits the works of other painters of the Hudson River School. It is open to the public by appointment only.

The Creative Arts Council, a volunteer group, plays a prominent role in the community. It gets local musicians to give music lessons at the public schools, conducts artists' studio tours, and runs film programs and once-a-month get-togethers for artists in Hastings and from the surrounding area to "meet with each other, get support and feedback on their work," said Jane Cameron, the council president.

Ms. Cameron and her husband, Jamie, a lawyer, found Hastings almost by accident when they were looking for a house over a decade ago. They were living on the Upper West Side of Manhattan with their young son. "We found this great stone coach house," Ms. Cameron said. "We didn't know anything about the village, except we'd heard it was low-key with intelligent people, not a country club atmosphere." The couple, who now have three children, are firmly entrenched in village life. "Raising children in a village like this is a wonderful political and social education for them that they couldn't get in a large city or many other settings," Ms. Cameron said.

Mary Allison, who is the village historian and has lived in Hastings since the mid-seventies, said one change she had noticed lately was more young children on the streets. "I see a lot of baby carriages," she said. These young families are snatching up the village's Tudors and Colonials as fast as they can come on the market, according to Robin Friedman, manager of the Irvington office of the Houlihan/Lawrence brokerage concern.

The majority of homes were built in the '20s and '30s and fit into the "charming older home with character" category, said Arthur G. Riolo, a broker with Peter J. Riolo, in Hastings. Prices can range from $209,000 for a two-bedroom Colonial to $1.75 million for homes on two to four acres along Broadway, he said. "I wish I had more houses priced in the $400,000's," Ms. Friedman said. "That seems to be the category everyone wants." The median price for a single-family house is $375,000, for which property taxes would be about $9,000, Ms. Friedman said.

There are also town house condominiums at Hastings Landing, where three- to four-bedroom units run from the high $300,000's to the low $400,000's. Co-ops at River Glen are also town houses, with fireplaces. One-bedrooms are priced at $125,000, Mr. Riolo said, and two-bedrooms at $200,000. There are also less expensive co-ops available in converted buildings, with one-bedroom units at $60,000 and two-bedrooms at $85,000.

The Hastings public schools are the K–4 Hillside Elementary School, the 5–8 Farragut Middle School, and the Hastings High School. The district has experienced dramatically rising enrollment in recent years, especially in the lower grades, says Schools Superintendent John J. Russell. As a result, the fifth grade moved to the middle school in 1996 to ease crowding.

"We've renovated the entire school building to take advantage of the additional space," said Hillside Principal Marilyn Wishnie. "We didn't get too much additional classroom space, but opened up common areas that we use for a multitude of purposes." The district draws heavily on the diversity of the community to benefit even the elementary students, Ms. Wishnie said. "We have a mentoring program where residents teach extra-curricular courses on architecture, writing, science, even bird-watching."

The district places a heavy emphasis on music and the arts, Ms. Wishnie said. "Every year, the fourth grade puts on an original musical, and the performances are fantastic," she said. Per-pupil expenditure for the Hastings schools is $12,384.

In addition to the public schools, there's the K–8 Roman Catholic St. Matthew's School and the Greenburgh-Graham School for troubled children.

Hastings is believed to have been named by William Saunders, a prominent resident who is said to have been born in the English town made famous in the 1066 Battle of Hastings. In the 1830s, Saunders operated one of the first factories in town, the Saunders Patent Axle & Brass & Iron Turning Factory.

As the waterfront industries thrived, immigrant laborers poured into Hastings. Germans came to work in the sugar refineries. Poles, Slavs, Hungarians, Czechs, Russians, and others settled in the village working for chemical and manufacturing plants. By 1891, the National Conduit &

Cable Company was on the riverfront making cable for early electrical-utility companies. In 1929, the Anaconda Company took over the business and operated it until 1975, when the plant closed down. The building's hulking shell has been a blight on the Hastings riverfront ever since.

The Atlantic Richfield Oil Company of Los Angeles, which took over Anaconda, has acknowledged responsibility for cleaning up the site, according to Village Manager Neil P. Hess. "There's been a toxic buildup over the years," Mr. Hess said. "The area needs an extensive cleanup. The company is now negotiating with the state Department of Environmental Conservation."

One bright spot on the waterfront in recent years was the establishment of the MacEachron Waterfront Park, a 1.3-acre passive green space on the riverfront. There are also several other parks, including Draper Park, which contains the home of John W. Draper, a scientist credited with taking the first photograph of the moon.

The largest green space is the 49.9-acre Hillside Park, which has a pool, four tennis courts, nature trails, and a pond for fishing and ice skating. The village recently acquired an adjacent 48 acres called Hillside Woods. "That's 100 acres of open space in the center of town," Mr. Hess said.

The old Croton Aqueduct, which runs from the Bronx to Croton, slices through town parallel to the river. It is now used as a hiking trail and by joggers and cyclists.

Village residents take pride in the fact that the village has no fast-food restaurants or major department stores. There is, however, Hastings Prime Meats, on Main Street, which sells imported specialty foods and has been likened to a small-town Zabar's. Across from the train station are two popular restaurants, Buffet de la Gare, for French cuisine, and Maud's Tavern, for pub fare.

The village's only supermarket is a Food Emporium, A&P's upscale subsidiary. Residents must travel a few minutes outside Hastings to Central Park Avenue or White Plains for more extensive shopping. "We call Central Avenue the 'Great White Way,'" said Mr. Riolo. "We're glad it's close, but we're also glad it's not here."

WESTCHESTER

KATONAH

Estates, reservoirs, culture, and comforts

BY TESSA MELVIN

Shortly after Philip Batson and his wife, Deirdre Courtney-Batson, bought
their 1870s Victorian house with its crenellated tower on Bedford Road 14
years ago, they learned where they really lived. "Oh, you just bought
Jimmy Williams's house," neighbors would tell them, referring to the harness maker who lived there 120 years before.

The past has defined the Batson house as it has modern Katonah. The
beige frame house with its pink and purple trim is one of 55 houses moved
between 1895 and 1897 to Bedford Road, an area now in the National Register of Historic Places. The houses were moved from the original village
a half mile away, the foundations of which now rest at the bottom of the
Cross River Reservoir, which supplies water for New York City.

The centennial was vigorously celebrated in 1997 with the help of
New York City, which permitted tours to the above-water portion of the
old village, now part of the city's watershed.

The Inundation, or the Move, as the event is popularly known, and the
presence of the reservoirs have given the new Katonah a particular stamp
shared by no other metropolitan-area suburb. The flooding of old Katonah
gave the hamlet an opportunity to re-create itself and enter the 20th century in an organized and thoughtful way.

That character is much in evidence today, especially in the downtown
business district, with its wood-frame Victorian stores that sell everything
from gourmet foods to Ayurvedic incense. The classic Main Street atmosphere has made Katonah a regional shopping hub for residents seeking
relief from malls.

Katonah is one of three hamlets, along with Bedford Village and Bedford Hills, in the Town of Bedford, a rustic and sprawling area of estates,

POPULATION: 5,260.

AREA: 11.25 square miles.

MEDIAN HOUSEHOLD INCOME: $98,864.

MEDIAN PRICE OF A SINGLE-FAMILY HOUSE: $425,000.

TAXES ON A MEDIAN-PRICED HOUSE: $10,400.

PUBLIC SCHOOL SPENDING PER PUPIL: $11,979.

DISTANCE FROM MIDTOWN MANHATTAN: 44 miles.

RUSH-HOUR TRAVEL TO MIDTOWN: One hour on Metro-North's Harlem line, $8.75 one way, $193 monthly.

CODES: Area, 914; ZIP, 10536.

horse farms, and dirt roads in the northeast section of Westchester County. The town, and Katonah in particular, owes its development—or lack of it—to New York City, which began acquiring land and building dams for an increasingly thirsty city in the mid–19th century.

Today, New York City is the town's largest landowner, with parts of three of the city's reservoirs spread across thousands of acres, providing bucolic vistas and superb fishing. Recently, relations have been strained as the city has enacted new and more restrictive watershed regulations that some fear would restrict development.

But a century ago, Katonah residents generally sympathized with the city's need for water, perhaps especially because that need brought with it the opportunity to sell their land for a hefty sum. One local publication of the time, *The Blue Light*, published in Katonah by the Women's Guild of the Presbyterian Church, editorialized: "New York must have water, and more water, especially if she should follow the example of our town and quit drinking other beverages."

With the help of B. S. and G. S. Olmstead, landscape architects not related to Frederick Law Olmsted, the designer of Manhattan's Central Park, Katonah residents planned two main streets—Katonah Avenue and Bedford Road, a broad tree-lined residential street that paralleled a commercial area on Katonah Avenue. Liquor was banned, as were "vicious dogs" and such "noxious trades" as distilling and tanning.

Today, Katonah Avenue, adjacent to the Metro-North Railroad, includes three blocks of stores, including many of the original two- and three-story Victorians moved from the old village. Some, like the Charles Department Store, are still operated by descendants of the original owners.

Nearly everyone ends up at the Baker's Cafe across from the train station, which features homemade cakes and cookies in a block of similar stores owned and recently renovated by Teddy Wainwright, her sister, Sloan McTavey, and their husbands. Worried about rising rents on nearby blocks, the two sisters charge less than the going rate to keep their neighbors in business. "We did this to support the community we live in," Ms. Wainwright said. "Katonah is kind of the last bastion of a service-oriented small-town place where the kids ride their bikes and where you can buy all you need without going to a mall."

There is still a ban on buying liquor in Katonah—except from Sam Rogers, who owns the former Metro-North station, which is exempt from the ban because it was railroad property. A restaurant in the old station, Peppino's, has a liquor license, as does Mr. Rogers's Katonah Wines & Liquors there.

Despite its careful foundations, the hamlet has not escaped modern perils. Bedford Road is also Route 117, until the early '90s a popular truck shortcut between Harris Road and the busy east-west Route 35. Residents counted as many as 50 trucks an hour, rattling Victorian foundations that had already been lifted once.

After Bedford was added to the National Register of Historic Places in 1984, a move that prevented removal of the grassy center islands or widening the road, the state agreed to spend $8 million for a 1.8-mile bypass, opened in July 1991.

Although town officials have long argued that downtown Katonah needs a $15 million sewage treatment plant, residents, believing they would not directly benefit from it, defeated a bond issue early in this decade. Katonah faces pressure from New York City officials who fear damage to their reservoirs and from local business owners paying the high costs of pumping septic systems.

Real estate values throughout the hamlet have risen steadily in recent years, area real estate agents agree, especially in the Historic District. House prices in the district range from $400,000 to $800,000, depending on the size and condition of the property. The area's charm has attracted such new residents as David Liederman, owner of David's Cookies.

Most of the 5,000 residents of the hamlet live on small lots, some a quarter acre, in or near the village, a relatively dense population mix unusual in a town where four-acre zoning predominates. These houses range in price from about $290,000 to $600,000. The housing market is tight in all parts of Katonah, said Anne Mygatt, an associate broker in the Bedford office of Houlihan/Lawrence. A four-bedroom Colonial on one acre in a subdivision sold for $525,000 in the third quarter of 1997, Ms. Mygatt said, adding that the sale is typical of current residential transactions. The median sales price for a single-family home in the third quarter of 1997 was $425,000, up from $392,500 a year previously. Houses in the village selling for close to the median included a four-bedroom Colonial built in 1964 on 1.1 acres, which was on the market for $439,500, with taxes of $10,393.

Large open-space tracts cover the hills around the hamlet, surrounding the estates owned by such well-known figures as the designer Ralph Lauren, the architect I. M. Pei, and the financier George Soros.

The town has thousands of protected acres, much of them owned by the Nature Conservancy. Just three miles east of Katonah's border is the country-owned Ward Pound Ridge Reservation with its 4,700 acres of hiking trails. Although 85 percent of the dwelling units in Katonah are single-family residences, there is an eight-block area with a number of two-family houses and two condominium complexes. Katonah Hills, a 49-unit complex of three-story Colonials, has a pool and tennis court, while the Wildwood condominiums face the 36-acre Katonah Memorial Park with its pool, ball fields, and tennis courts. There are scattered rental units, many illegal.

Many newcomers are young families attracted by the reputation of the Katonah-Lewisboro School District, with its four elementary schools, middle school, and high school. Spread across a 55-square-mile area, the district serves 3,700 students. District enrollment has grown almost 35 percent in five years in the mid-decade, and voters recently approved a $44 million bond issue to expand and renovate the schools, projects scheduled for completion in 1999. The district spent $11,979 on each student in 1997–98.

Student scores consistently place in the top 10 percent of all school districts in the state, said School Superintendent Karen McCarthy, who cited outstanding art and science programs. Although the 900 students in the high school are required to take only one art course in four years, Ms. McCarthy said, two-thirds enrolled each semester. Writing is emphasized throughout the school system, Ms. McCarthy said, with special workshops for teachers.

Graduations for the senior class have been held in recent years in the Venetian Theater at the Caramoor Center for Music and the Arts, the 100-acre estate of Lucie and Walter Rosen, who established the Caramoor International Music Festival, which has been in existence for more than 50 seasons. The resident St. Luke's Chamber Orchestra has been directed by its musical adviser and neighbor, André Previn.

Caramoor is one of three cultural landmarks on or near Route 22 on the outskirts of the hamlet in a section called the Museum Mile. Abutting Caramoor is the estate of John Jay, the nation's first chief justice. Just up the road is the new, since 1989, home of the Katonah Museum of Art, a well-known regional museum that has received national attention since its founding in 1953. In recent years, exhibitions have featured the works of Milton Avery, John Beerman, Mark Rothko, and local artists.

Louisa Baur is a retired teacher and the widow of one of the founders of the museum, John I. H. Baur, who for several years directed the Whitney Museum of American Art in Manhattan. After living in Katonah for 50 years, Mrs. Baur said, she had reason to stay. "This village has a good feel," Mrs. Baur said. "Katonah has a solid past and we are all still connected to it."

LARCHMONT

Leafy village on the Sound, but close in

BY MARY McALEER VIZARD

Phyllis McGinley, the Pulitzer Prize–winning poet who lived in Larchmont for years, immortalized the village in her poem "I Know a Village":

> I know a village full of bees.
> And gardens lit by canna torches
> Where all the streets are named for trees
> And people visit on their porches.

So enthralled was she that the last line reads:

> And I'd not willingly, I think,
> Exchange it for Arcadia or Camelot.

High praise indeed for the one-square-mile village along the shores of Long Island Sound. Interesting also, considering that Larchmont is often perceived as the quintessential old-world, old-money suburb. And as such, has come in for its share of good-natured ribbing.

Over the years, Joan Rivers has got tremendous mileage doing comedy routines on her supposedly stultifying teenage years in Larchmont. And Jean Kerr wrote that suburban paean, *Please Don't Eat the Daisies*, while living in Larchmont. She and her husband, Walter, the theater critic, moved to Larchmont in the 1940s. Now a widow, Ms. Kerr still resides in the village, in a Gothic-style house a stone's throw from the Sound near the privately owned 12.6-acre Manor Park.

Boston Post Road splits Larchmont into two parts. The oldest section, Larchmont Manor, lies to the south. In 1865, Thomas Flint bought 288

POPULATION: 5,531.

AREA: 1 square mile.

MEDIAN HOUSEHOLD INCOME: $109,480.

MEDIAN PRICE OF A SINGLE-FAMILY HOUSE $460,000.

TAXES ON A MEDIAN-PRICED HOUSE $11,600.

PUBLIC SCHOOL SPENDING PER PUPIL $13,516.

DISTANCE FROM MIDTOWN MANHATTAN 21 miles.

RUSH-HOUR TRAVEL TO MIDTOWN 33 minutes on Metro-North's New Haven line, $6.50 one way, $141 monthly.

CODES Area, 914; ZIP, 10538.

acres between Boston Post Road and the water, turning it into a summer colony for wealthy New Yorkers.

One of the more colorful stories from its heyday as a popular resort involves Douglas Fairbanks, who was supposed to have courted the then-married Mary Pickford on the steps of one of the old resort hotels in the early 1900s. Today, the old hotels are long gone or have been converted into private residences. The streets, named after trees, are lined with stately Victorians, Tudors, Colonials, and even a few Mediterraneans.

"Most of the manor's housing was built between 1880 and 1910," said Judy Spikes, the village historian. Houses in the newer section, north of the Post Road, went up in the 1920s and 1930s.

"The big wave of building after World War II took place just outside the village," Ms. Spikes said. "By that time, the village was already fully developed." The people who live in this area, which is officially part of the Town of Mamaroneck, share a postal zone with the Village of Larchmont and send their children to the same schools. In the village and surrounding area, housing runs the gamut from palatial waterfront mansions selling for up to $4 million to a starter home for less than $350,000, said Marian Misad, a broker with Merritt Associates. The median price for a single-family home in the first quarter of 1998 was $460,000.

"What people sacrifice here is land," Ms. Misad said. "There isn't a whole lot of property, even with the larger homes. On average, houses have less than half an acre."

There are a few condominium complexes, where two- and three-bedroom units range from $325,000 to $450,000, according to Barbara Cleary, Merritt's office manager. Co-ops, most of which are outside the village but within the Larchmont postal district, are priced at from $35,000 for a studio to $249,000 for a two-bedroom unit.

June Allen came to live in Larchmont as a child and has stayed for more than 50 years. Her grandfather bought his house, built in 1872, from Thomas Flint, the 19th-century developer. "At first, we only used it during the summer," Ms. Allen said. "We moved into it full-time in the early 1940s." She and her husband, Bruce, now retired, finally sold the family home in 1996. They have, however, remained in the village, living in a condominium.

Larchmont's earliest history dates from 1661, when John Richbell purchased "three necks of land" from the Mohegan Indians. A hundred years later, Peter Jay Monro acquired the middle neck and built his house on a slight rise or "mont." The village's name came to be because of the Larch trees Monro planted along the western edge of his property to absorb the noises of the passing wagons and stagecoaches along Boston Post Road.

The first train line came down from Boston in 1845, Ms. Spikes said. "It was extended in 1871 or '72 into New York City," she added. "This is what caused Flint to start building." The village was incorporated in 1891.

Proximity to New York City is what attracted Campbell McLaren and his wife, Susan, to Larchmont. They had lived in Greenwich Village for 15 years, and were fearful of "moving to the land of stockbrokers and attorneys and not much else," said Mr. McLaren, a television producer. "We love the city, but it's designed for adults, not children," Mr. McLaren said. "We wanted a place where the kids could be outdoors." The couple and their two school-age children now live in a 1922 "white Colonial with a picket fence," Mr. McLaren said.

Another couple who at one time thought they would live out their days in Manhattan wound up moving to Larchmont for the sake of their 11-year-old daughter. Paul Heacock and his wife, Carol Cassidy, both book editors, had become frustrated with the public schools in their East Village neighborhood. They had taken a temporary work assignment in England, where they admired the schools. "When we returned to Manhattan, things never went smoothly," Mr. Heacock said. "The public schools seemed underfunded on every level, so we started looking for a place to live with better schools." They settled on Larchmont because, in addition to "good schools," Mr. Heacock said, "it's also close enough to the city and we found we could afford it." The couple bought a two-bedroom, two-bath co-op for $90,000 just outside the village but in the same school district.

Larchmont is part of the Mamaroneck Union Free School District, which encompasses the villages of Larchmont and Mamaroneck, as well as the unincorporated area of the town of Mamaroneck. It has four elementary schools, (prekindergarten through grade 5), a middle school (6, 7, and 8), and a high school. Ninety-three percent of high school graduates go on to higher education. Per-pupil expenditure for the district is $13,516.

At the Hommocks Middle School, students can get high school credit for studying French, Spanish, or Chinese. Once in high school, they can add Russian and Italian to the list. "Our Russian Academy makes regular trips to Russia," said Sherry P. King, superintendent of schools, referring to their Russian class. "And the Chinese class and their teacher travel to China every spring."

Mamaroneck High School offers a performing arts program that exposes students to music, choreography, drama, and video, Ms. King said. "As they progress, they start to specialize, but at the same time they continue to work as an ensemble," she added. "They learn that to create a production you need to work together."

There is also the private French-American School of New York, where classes are taught in French. The building housing kindergarten through fifth grade is in the village. The preschool and grades 6 to 10 are in Mamaroneck. Tuition for the 1998–99 school year ranged for $8,400 to $11,050 a year. "A lot of our students are children of United Nations employees, many of whom move to Larchmont specifically because of our school," said Katrine Watkins, one of the school's founders.

Also just outside the village but within the postal zone is St. John and Paul, a Roman Catholic parochial school for grades K to 8. Tuition for the 1998–99 school year was $2,180 for parishioners and $3,050 for nonparishioners.

The Hommocks Middle School has an indoor Olympic-size swimming pool, convertible to outdoor use in the summer and open to residents in off hours. There is also a covered ice-skating rink used both for open skating and hockey. Manor Park, which is owned by the residents of the surrounding community, was developed by Flint in the 1880s. It has a 300-foot sandy beach at Horseshoe Harbor. The village runs tennis clinics and other programs at the 27-acre Flint Park, which has nine tennis courts, several ball fields, and picnicking facilities. There are also several private recreational facilities, including the Larchmont Yacht Club, established in 1880.

Larchmont has two distinct downtowns, one on Boston Post Road and one on Palmer Avenue. Both feature an array of specialty stores and restaurants. On Palmer Avenue is one of the few single-screen movie theaters left in the county. In nearby Mamaroneck, residents can attend concerts and theatrical productions at the Emelin Theater.

Mr. Heacock said he found more cachet in the village than he expected. "There's a French bakery with excellent croissants and pastries," he said. "I think it's here because of the French school. It adds a nice cosmopolitan touch."

Larchmont's mayor, Cheryl W. Lewy, said she had noticed a trend in home design stores opening downtown. "There are several antiques shops, a fabric design center, carpet and flooring places," she said. "They serve our residents, a lot of whom have old Victorians that are in constant need of work. But they also serve as destination stores that attract other customers to the village."

Eileen Dinolfo, owner of Eye of the Needle, a needlepoint craft store, started business 23 years ago. "This is one of the few places I think I could have lasted this long," she said. "It's a very diverse downtown. There's room for many different kinds of stores and we all help each other."

LAWRENCE PARK WEST

A Yonkers locale, a Bronxville pedigree

BY MARY McALEER VIZARD

In the years since Yonkers passed a local landmarks ordinance in 1991, two neighborhoods have been designated historic districts and four structures have received landmark status. Lee Ellman, the city's planning director, says the Lawrence Park West neighborhood could well be next. "It certainly qualifies," Mr. Ellman said, "in terms of its historical significance to the city and the abundance of turn-of-the-century mansions," most of which have been exceptionally well preserved. The nub of the law is that exteriors of structures either individually landmarked or in a historic district can only be changed with the approval of a landmarks preservation board. "Basically we hope to keep them just the way they are," Mr. Ellman said. "Lawrence Park West has been pretty good at maintaining its integrity even without landmark designation."

Barbara Dimpel, a resident for over 30 years, can attest to that. "Nothing's really changed in all that time," Ms. Dimpel said. "The same houses are here. Very few new ones have been added. The only thing that's changed is that we're among the oldest residents now. Not in age, but we've been here the longest."

The neighborhood's history is tied to that of Lawrence Park, about a half mile away in the next-door village of Bronxville. In the late 1800s, William Van Duzer Lawrence, a pharmaceutical magnate, envisioned a community of artists and other creative people who would move from Manhattan and live together in well-designed homes in a countrified setting. Using the Barbizon in the Fountainebleau forest in France as his model, Lawrence bought land and hired architects to help realize his dream of a utopian village. The result was the Lawrence Park neighborhood of Bronxville, which eventually, in 1980, was listed in the National Register of Historic Places.

POPULATION: 4,139.

AREA: 0.5 square miles.

MEDIAN HOUSEHOLD INCOME: $77,654.

MEDIAN PRICE OF A SINGLE-FAMILY HOUSE $429,000.

TAXES ON A MEDIAN-PRICED HOUSE: $8,000.

PUBLIC SCHOOL SPENDING PER PUPIL: $10,856.

DISTANCE TO MIDTOWN MANHATTAN: 16 miles.

RUSH-HOUR TRAVEL TO MIDTOWN: 28 minutes from Metro-North's Bronxville station, $5.75 one way, $126 monthly.

CODES: Area, 914; ZIP, 10708.

By the early 1900s, Lawrence decided to extend that community into 295 other acres he also owned in Yonkers, calling it Lawrence Park West. In 1917, Lawrence built his family home in the Yonkers neighborhood. The redbrick and half-timber mansion called Westlands now serves as the administration building for Sarah Lawrence College, which Lawrence founded in 1926 as a tribute to his wife, Sarah Bates Lawrence, a women's-rights advocate, who died at Westlands that same year.

Because Lawrence Park West shares a post office and ZIP code with its Bronxville counterpart, there are apocryphal stories about residents of Lawrence Park West not knowing they live in Yonkers until they receive a city tax bill. "There's a joke that Sarah Lawrence College has two sets of stationery," Mr. Ellman said. "One identifies it as in Yonkers and is used for dealings with the city. The other says it's in Bronxville and it's used for recruiting and public relations."

But Cliff Theiss, an advertising executive who is president of the Lawrence Park West Neighborhood Association, has no problem with his home's location. "I grew up in Yonkers," Mr. Theiss said. "I've lived in several different sections and worked my way to Lawrence Park West. It just goes to show that you can achieve the American dream without leaving Yonkers." Mr. Theiss said that Lawrence Park West has always been one of the city's showpieces. "It's a beautiful, peaceful, integrated neighborhood," he said. "It's everything you would ever want from a residential community."

Tall mature elm trees form a canopy that shades most streets. Set back from the roads are sprawling Tudors, Victorians, and Colonials with landscaped lawns, often with well-tended flower gardens.

Lawrence Park West residents use a school system supported by the property taxes they pay to Yonkers. For houses that are similar in appearance if not in market value, Lawrence Park West taxes are at about half the level of those in Bronxville, said Joan H. Spencer, a broker with Bronxville/Ley Real Estate. Residents can send their children to

Bronxville's schools if they pay tuition that averages about $11,000 a year. Or they can use a private school or a Yonkers public school.

"We have 60 magnet programs all over the city that parents can choose from," said Elyse David, a spokeswoman for the Yonkers schools. The school closest to Lawrence Park West is the Patricia A. DiChiaro Early Childhood School, a Yonkers public school covering kindergarten through the third grade. It puts a special emphasis on mathematics and science and teaches via an interdisciplinary concept incorporating life sciences in the curriculum.

Many Lawrence Park West residents, though, seem to opt for private schools. Ms. Dimpel's children, now grown, attended St. Joseph's, a Roman Catholic elementary school in Bronxville that charges $2,700 annual tuition. "I know a lot of my neighbors' children went to St. Joseph's," she said. "Or they send their children to other private schools nearby."

For young families, realtors said, the issue of schools does bear heavily on their decision to buy in Lawrence Park West. But not all young families make the school issue their most immediate concern. Thomas Nides and his wife, Virginia Moseley, who moved from Washington, closed on a five-bedroom brick home in 1996 after changing their minds about an apartment they had found in Manhattan. "We were about to sign a lease on an apartment on 61st and Madison," Mr. Nides said, "when we realized we wanted to raise our child in the suburbs and decided to find the closest suburb to Manhattan."

For Mr. Nides, the head of corporate affairs at Morgan Stanley, and his wife, an ABC news producer, proximity to Manhattan was the key factor. "We looked in Larchmont and Scarsdale," Mr. Nides said. "But they're a few minutes farther. And those minutes are precious to us now. We'd rather spend them with our child."

Lawrence Park West has a wide selection of housing price categories, according to Ms. Spencer, even some availability for first-time home buyers. "It has some houses priced in the low $300,000's," she said. "In Bronxville, you can only get a town house for that price."

In general, though, houses tend to run from the mid-$300,000's to the high $900,000's, Ms. Spencer said. Median price for a single-family house is $429,000, with property taxes of around $8,000.

One distinct advantage Lawrence Park West has over Bronxville is the size of most residential lots. "You get more property in Lawrence Park West," said Ms. Spencer. "In general, you get about one-fourth of an acre more."

Near the center of the neighborhood, there's the 8½-acre Sunnybrook Park, a city-owned green space.

The vast majority of Lawrence Park West's houses date from the 1920s and 1930s. Anything newer was built on fill-in lots, Mr. Theiss said.

Examples of homes recently listed for sale included a four-bedroom, 3½-bath Colonial on a half acre for $422,500, with property taxes of $8,448, and a seven-bedroom, 5½-bath Tudor on a half acre for $799,000, with property taxes of $13,234.

While surrounded by commercial development, Lawrence Park West itself is strictly residential. The neighborhood is minutes away from the Cross County Shopping Center and Bronxville's downtown, which has several small shops and a supermarket. And the Vernon Hills Shopping Center in Eastchester is 10 minutes away by car.

Residents were concerned a few years ago when a 14-unit low-income housing project was built on the outskirts of the neighborhood on Midland Avenue. But, Ms. Dimpel said, "that seems to have worked out fine. They're garden apartments and blend right in."

For the most part, there's been peaceful coexistence between residents of Lawrence Park West and Sarah Lawrence, "but we worry about them getting too big," Ms. Dimpel said. In 1987, the city set up a college/university zone, which gave the college permission to develop within their own 40 acres of property, Mr. Ellman said. "But if they want to expand or buy an existing property for university use, it must conform to what is already allowable on that site." In the past, the college has bought homes and converted them to dormitories or classrooms. Ms. Dimpel said she doesn't expect any future problems. "They've been very good neighbors," she said, "with the exception of a few special events where there's been bands and music."

LEWISBORO

Desirable schools amid the horse trails

BY MARY MCALEER VIZARD

In the small hamlet of South Salem, the geographic center of the Town of Lewisboro, there is a tiny commercial center that provides a tableau of small-town Americana, just an hour's drive from Manhattan. It consists of a general store, an antiques shop, and the remnants of a one-pump gas station that no longer operates. Across the street, standing on a slight rise, is the South Salem Presbyterian Church. Founded in 1752, the church, with its Revolutionary-era cemetery, still serves as a focal point for the community of Colonial and Victorian homes that surrounds it.

"From my house I can walk to the general store, the church, the post office, the library, and the town hall," said William Lonergan, a local lawyer who lives in a converted shoe factory built in 1827. "It's definitely a Norman Rockwell kind of thing. I like to think that it's rural, but it's really not. But it's not suburbia either."

The Town of Lewisboro, which is shaped like a boomerang, is spread out across the northeastern quadrant of Westchester County and consists of six hamlets: Lewisboro, Goldens Bridge, South Salem, Waccabuc, Cross River, and Vista. For centuries, the town was involved in border disputes with Connecticut, which helps explain its odd shape. At one time, the territory was referred to as the Oblong. Today, it encompasses a broad swath of territory that includes six lakes and sprawling horse farms, as well as palatial estates, starter homes, and two condominium complexes.

Despite the wide variety of housing, the overwhelming impression while driving around Lewisboro is of being in horse country. Horseback riders can be seen trotting on the town's dirt roads or crossing major roads on their way to a labyrinth of horse trails that snake through town. The Lewisboro Horsemen's Association has successfully cajoled local

GAZETTEER

POPULATION: 13,240.

AREA: 28 square miles.

MEDIAN HOUSEHOLD INCOME: $105,572.

MEDIAN PRICE OF A SINGLE-FAMILY HOUSE $365,000.

TAXES ON A MEDIAN-PRICED HOUSE: $8,500.

PUBLIC SCHOOL SPENDING PER PUPIL : $11,979.

DISTANCE FROM MIDTOWN MANHATTAN: 40 miles.

RUSH-HOUR TRAVEL TO MIDTOWN: One hour and 15 minutes on Metro-North's Harlem line, $8.75 one way, $193 monthly.

CODES: Area, 914; ZIP, 10518, 10526, 10590, and 10597.

residents into allowing horse trails through their property. The trails traverse 1,500 acres of private property.

Riders can also use the extensive trails at the 4,500-acre Ward Pound Ridge Reservation, a county-owned park, a portion of which is in Lewisboro. There are also four town parks, with a total of 179 acres. In addition to hiking and riding trails, the parks have playgrounds, ball fields, and tennis courts.

Recent house sales in Lewisboro range from a low of $80,000 to a high of $2.2 million. In the first quarter of 1998, the median price for a single-family home was $365,000.

"There are little cottages by the lakes that are very inexpensive," said Kenneth Sobel, a broker with Houlihan/Lawrence. "You don't get much house, but they're nice communities and you get the schools." Also on the lower end of prices are condominiums, where one- to three-bedroom units range from $150,000 to $225,000.

More typically, Wall Street couples come up looking for their first single-family homes, and they are prepared to spend money, according to Patrick Browne, a broker with Preferred Realty. "They're two-income couples who were able to sell their co-ops in Manhattan," Mr. Browne said. "They want to be here before their kids start school." For these couples and others, the town's main draw, aside from its bucolic beauty, is its schools. "If not for the reputation of the schools," Mr. Sobel said, "we'd just be a bunch of hicks living 20 minutes farther away than anyone else."

Laurie Wolkin, a psychologist, and her husband, Hal, a vice president with a commodities firm, moved to Lewisboro in 1978. Even though they have moved several times since then, they have always managed to stay in town. "We didn't want to leave the school district," Ms. Wolkin said. The couple recently moved into a new house, which meant that their son, 7, had to change schools within the Katonah-Lewisboro School District. "His teacher called me every week for the first three weeks to discuss how to make his transition easier," Ms. Wolkin said. "It just goes to show the lengths the teachers here go to take care of their students. I was very impressed."

The reason for the Wolkins' latest move was to be in a development where the houses were closer together. "I wanted my son to have other children to play with," Ms. Wolkin said.

That can be a challenge in a town with two- and four-acre zoning. Small sections of town, mostly in the commercial areas and around the lakes, have less restrictive zoning. "You start to feel it when your child is about 5 and says, 'I have no one to play with,' " Ms. Wolkin said. "You go out to the porch and look both ways and he's right. No one's there."

Partly because of a desire to be closer to other houses, many young couples are increasingly opting for new construction, Mr. Sobel said. "People like them because the houses are closer together and the kids can run back and forth," he said.

Lewisboro is adamant about protecting its open space. Half the acreage protected by the Westchester Land Trust is in Lewisboro, a total of 150 acres. "We work with the developers to get them to allocate parts of their property as open space because we're so concerned now about the town losing its rural character," said Susan Henry, whose family, the Meads, were among the town's earliest settlers.

In the late 1990s, "vacant land is being gobbled up left and right," said William Cargain, the town's building inspector. "Building permits are significantly up." One new development in Waccabuc, called Rock Shelter Road, will have 21 homes on approximately four acres each, according to its developer, John Chiardullo. Building lots cost $325,000 to $350,000. "And people can basically build whatever type of house they want," Mr. Chiardullo said.

The town's growth has been reflected in the impact on its schools. "We had to face the fact that we were running out of space," said Schools Superintendent Karen McCarthy. In November 1995, a $44 million bond issue was passed to finance the construction of new classrooms and upgrading of existing facilities at the district's six schools, which include four elementary schools, a middle school, and a high school. The construction, expected to be completed in the spring of 1999, will add 18 new classrooms, as well as new computer and music rooms, libraries, and gymnasiums, Ms. McCarthy said.

When Ms. McCarthy took over as superintendent in 1992, the high school had 746 students. By 1998, there were 948, and by the year 2000, the estimate is for at least 1,200, she said. Average class size in the district is 22, Ms. McCarthy said. And 90 percent to 95 percent of its students go on to college. Per pupil expenditure for the district in 1997–98 was $11,979.

"We have the most exceptional students," the superintendent added. "That's probably due in large part to committed, involved parents who have engendered enthusiasm for learning in their children. The students respect learning and come to school prepared." The district offers a full complement of art classes, including studio courses in ceramics, photography, and video. "I don't quite know why, but our students are very interested in art at all levels," Ms. McCarthy said.

June Cory Patrick, who moved to Lewisboro 50 years ago and now spends her winters in Florida, said she always found the town little changed when she returned. "When I drive back on Route 35, I always notice how everything is the same," she said. "I know there's been construction, but it's back from the roads and you don't see it. The only change is increased traffic."

As the town has grown, one of its main problems is the lack of parking at the Goldens Bridge Metro-North station, the only train station in town. And traffic, according to several residents, can be brutal during the morning and evening commutes. Ms. Wolkin, who commutes to Briarcliff Manor by car, said the trip took about 40 minutes. "The worst times are between 7:50 and 8:15 A.M.," she said. "There's lots of traffic."

Despite its growth, Lewisboro has been able to find new uses for some of its historic properties. The Horse & Hound Restaurant, for example, is housed in a 1749 building on Spring Street in South Salem that was once the home of the town blacksmith, Henry Dauchy Keeler, a descendant of one of Lewisboro's original founding families. During the mid-19th century, Mr. Keeler did a flourishing business in an adjacent shop, shoeing horses and repairing farm implements. After his death, his home was turned into an inn sometime in the early 1900s. In more recent years, the building housed a game restaurant, serving such exotic fare as ostrich, bear, boar, and alligator. "George C. Scott was a regular when he lived around here," said Achilles Alexander, the manager. After closing for five years, the restaurant reopened in May 1996 under the same name but with a new theme. "Game meats went out of favor," Mr. Alexander explained. "Now we're more like an English pub, serving T-bone steaks, fresh fish, and baby-back ribs."

The town has three shopping centers—in Goldens Bridge, Cross River, and South Salem—with supermarkets and convenience stores. Otherwise, people travel 40 minutes to White Plains or 20 minutes to Danbury, Conn., for more extensive shopping. "The closer a house is to 684, the higher its value," Mr. Browne said, referring to the interstate highway. Goldens Bridge, for instance, is highly desirable because of its proximity to the highway, and because it is the only hamlet with a train station.

The exception to that rule may be Waccabuc, Mr. Browne said, which has its own special cachet, with its million-dollar properties and the Waccabuc Country Club. It has been home to Bryant Gumbel, the newsman, and his family, and to Alfred Del Bello, former lieutenant governor of New York. "I'd say it's our highest-end hamlet," Mr. Browne said, "but it's all relative, since we've got million-dollar homes all over Lewisboro."

MAMARONECK

Unusual diversity and the tang of the sea

BY TESSA MELVIN

Nowhere was there greater jubilation when *Stars and Stripes '87* beat the Australians and brought home the America's Cup than in Mamaroneck. The sleek 12-meter craft had been built there at the Derecktor Shipyard by Portuguese, Chinese, and American craftsmen who lived in the village. Boatbuilding and sailing have a long tradition there, and marinas and beach clubs line the shore of the second-largest natural small-boat harbor on the East Coast—sometimes hard to see through the forest of masts from 1,500 boats.

Harbor Island Park, along the water at the foot of Mamaroneck Avenue, is the 45-acre centerpiece and focus of village life. The former island started being changed into a peninsula early in the century with rock removed in building New York City's subway system. Today, there are tennis courts and ball fields, a 700-foot public beach, and several fishing floats. Along a border is the upgraded Westchester County Sewage Treatment Plant, whose Art Deco tower serves as a modern lighthouse. The upgraded plant has helped reduce harbor pollution caused by runoff from the Mamaroneck River.

While pollution is decreasing, village officials took the unusual step in 1993 of installing a floating filter around the public beach, which has kept out flotsam. It was redone in 1997. The village also has a station where heads and bilges can be pumped out free.

Lt. Andrew S. Landau of the village police department's Marine Division, who is in charge of patrolling the village's 9.5-mile coastline, is optimistic. "The Sound has really gotten cleaned up in the last five years," he said. "The lobster population is thriving and even the blue-claw crabs have returned. People are scooping them out in bushels."

Residents are following a tradition started by the Siwanoy Indians,

POPULATION: 17,251.

AREA: 3.24 square miles.

MEDIAN HOUSEHOLD INCOME: $63,729.

MEDIAN PRICE OF A SINGLE-FAMILY HOUSE $306,000.

TAXES ON A MEDIAN-PRICED HOUSE: $7,935.

PUBLIC SCHOOL SPENDING PER PUPIL: Mamaroneck, $13,516; Rye Neck,$12,586.

DISTANCE FROM MIDTOWN MANHATTAN: 23 miles.

RUSH-HOUR TRAVEL TO MIDTOWN: 37 minutes on Metro-North, $6.50 one way, $141 monthly.

CODES: Area, 914; ZIP, 10543.

who named the area where the Mamaroneck and Sheldrake Rivers converge on their way to the sea as "the place where the salt water meets the fresh." Recognizing the value of this snug harbor with its two rivers, John Richbell, a Boston merchant and West Indies trader, bought it from the tribe in 1661 with shirts, wampum, and gunpowder. From the Revolution until the present day, the village has grown because of its harbor, attracting commerce with help from a former Indian trail that is now the busy four-lane Boston Post Road, the New York, New Haven & Hartford Railroad—which arrived in 1848—and the New England Thruway.

Diversity increased as the railroad brought waves of European immigrants from New York City, including Germans, who started a rubber factory, and Italians, many of whom worked in the MacIntosh coat factory creating fashionable coats for New York stores. By 1895, when the village was incorporated as part of two towns, Rye and Mamaroneck, 12 neighborhoods had taken shape; by 1950, most of the land had been developed and most industry had arrived. The village doesn't look much different from the way it did half a century ago—economically and ethnically diverse, with both luxurious estates and overcrowded apartments.

Described as "almost a mini-city" by former village manager Matthew Galligan, Mamaroneck has an unusual diversity for a suburban community. "You can find anything you want in Mamaroneck," said Gloria Poccia Pritts, the village historian, "any kind of house, any kind of people, any kind of food." The nearly 7,000 housing units include a mix of one-family homes, co-ops, condominiums, and rental units, each type constituting about a third of the total. The median price of a single-family home in 1997 was $306,000, up from $292,000 in 1996. A three-bedroom Colonial built in 1924 that sold for $302,000 in late 1997 had taxes of $6,250, while a four-bedroom Colonial built in 1970 sold for $310,000, with taxes of $9,080.

Many houses went up on the former estates of the wealthy Manhattan industrialists who built summer homes along the harbor. Among the most sumptuous is the onetime home of Henry Flagler, who co-founded Standard Oil with John D. Rockefeller. In 1919, Flagler's 32-acre estate on Orienta Point, a peninsula west of the harbor, was acquired by D. W. Griffith, the film director, who ushered in a short but brilliant golden age for the village as a kind of East Coast Hollywood. A silent-screen-era movie studio attracted such early stars as Lillian and Dorothy Gish, who lived in a house that is still on the corner of Bleeker and Walton Avenues.

Today, Flagler Drive leads to a security gate beyond which lies Edgewater Point, with some of the village's most luxurious homes. In the fall of 1997, a baronial six-bedroom home on Long Island Sound with its own dock, beach, and pool was on the market for $3.6 million, said Kathy Spadaro of the Spadaro Real Estate office in the village.

The peninsula is the farthest extension of Orienta Point, the largest neighborhood in the village, with the most one-family homes and town houses and the most beach frontage. Several homes are on the private peninsulas. Fairway Green, a complex of town houses bordering the Hampshire Golf Course, is tucked into the top portion of Orienta Point; two-bedroom units with cathedral ceilings sell for $450,000 to $550,000.

In the fall of 1997, a 114-unit condominium, the Regatta, was being constructed, with two- and three-bedroom units ranging in price from $125,760 to $232,460.

On the eastern side of the harbor, bordering the City of Rye, is Harbor Lawn–Shore Acres, expensive one-family homes on extensive water frontage similar to Orienta Point. Two of the village's 16 beach clubs are there, including the Mamaroneck Beach and Yacht Club, formerly the estate of the New York financier Charles W. Osborn. Some buildings on the estate, designed by Stanford White in 1883, are still intact, including the turreted carriage house.

Rye Neck, the eastern half of the village, encompasses some older homes, including turn-of-the-century houses in the proposed Melbourne Avenue Historic District. Rye Neck is bordered on the north by the 850-acre county-owned Saxon Woods Park.

North of the Metro-North rail line are more one-family homes, many of them historic, and a 52-unit town house complex built in 1992, Top of the Ridge.

Mamaroneck Avenue, which divides the village into nearly two equal parts, is the center of the thriving but somewhat worn business district whose small shops offer a wide variety of goods and services. In the fall of 1997, a downtown face-lift was being planned.

Popular restaurants include Satsumaya, combining Japanese and Western cuisine, Le Provençal, located near the railroad station and featuring French food, and Down by the Bay, an informal seafood restaurant. The Crab Shanty and Chef Antonio's are local favorites. Since 1919, Walter's Hot Dogs on Palmer Avenue has purveyed its offerings from a pagoda complete with copper roof.

Because the village lies in two towns, children attend one of two school systems. In the Town of Mamaroneck, they go to one of two K–6 elementary schools operated by the Mamaroneck Union Free School District, which also enrolls Larchmont children; Rye Neck children have their own K–4 elementary school; and there are separate middle schools through grade 8 and high schools for both systems.

The Mamaroneck system, with 4,297 students, has a high school noted for arts and music programs and a science program that has produced a Westinghouse Scholar. About 90 percent of the seniors go on to higher education.

The Rye Neck district, with 1,150 students, has won state and national recognition for its team approach to school management. Special high school programs include theater arts and such electives as Japanese culture and sports in literature. About 85 percent of the senior class goes on to college.

Students from both systems can use and attend performances at the 282-seat Emelin Theater adjacent to the Mamaroneck Free Library and founded by it. Today, the Emelin operates independently as a performing arts showcase for major actors, musicians, cabaret artists, and other performers.

MOUNT KISCO

A touch of the rural, and an expansive downtown

BY MARY McALEER VIZARD

This northern Westchester village has become something of a movie actor in recent years, capable of playing multiple roles. It stood in for a small town in Indiana during the filming of *In and Out*, starring Kevin Kline, Debbie Reynolds, and Joan Cusack, a contemporary story about a small-town high school teacher on the verge of marriage. Much of the action took place at a downtown bridal shop. Part of *Ragtime*, the film based on E. L. Doctorow's best-selling novel, was filmed in a 14-room Victorian mansion, one of many such distinctive homes that sit high on hills overlooking Main Street.

It is fitting that Mount Kisco should be chosen to represent such disparate stages of Americana, since it's such an amalgam of styles and periods. "Most of the housing was built at the turn of the century," said Susanne Lerch, a broker with the Century 21 Country Living real estate agency. "They're mostly Colonials, Tudors, and Victorians, but we also have 1960s-era split-levels."

Unlike most northern Westchester communities, which tend to be more rural, Mount Kisco has a thriving and expansive downtown center, with mostly local shops mixed in with a few chain stores. On the outskirts of downtown, especially along Route 117, there is a dense commercial concentration, including a cornucopia of car dealerships and the Manufacturer's Outlet Center of Westchester County, a factory-outlet center.

Kem and Lisa Tekinay, who moved from Queens, said they had chosen Mount Kisco because they wanted a community where they could do local shopping and walk to the train station. "We wanted to get out of the city, but we didn't want too rural a place either," Mr. Tekinay said.

When Mount Kisco was incorporated as a village in 1875, it straddled the towns of New Castle and Bedford. It became a coterminous town/

POPULATION: 10,044.

AREA: 3.2 square miles.

MEDIAN HOUSEHOLD INCOME: $60,884.

MEDIAN PRICE OF A SINGLE-FAMILY HOUSE $290,500.

TAXES ON A MEDIAN-PRICED HOUSE: $5,250.

PUBLIC SCHOOL SPENDING PER PUPIL : $15,900.

DISTANCE FROM MIDTOWN MANHATTAN: 38 miles.

RUSH-HOUR TRAVEL TO MIDTOWN: 54 minutes on Metro-North's Harlem line, $8.75 one way, $193 monthly.

CODES: Area, 914; ZIP, 10549.

village in 1978. The municipality, with a population of 10,000, is largely self-contained, offering convenience and major shopping and recreation all within walking distance of most homes. "We're a walking village," said Mayor Mark Farrell. "Our downtown benefits from the diversity of our housing and our population. There's practically any kind of activity imaginable from coffee shops, outdoor cafes, a five-screen movie theater, restaurants, and lots of stores."

Mount Kisco is considered the commercial hub of northern Westchester. People who move here tend to value convenience over style, and want the relative tranquillity of northern Westchester without the isolation.

"I love Mount Kisco," said Susan Smith, a high school guidance counselor at the nearby Croton-Harmon schools, who recently moved with her daughter from the Park Slope section of Brooklyn. "You have a sense of the country while still being in town." Ms. Smith, who bought a town house condominium, said, "I can walk to anything, but just up the hill from my house and I'm on a country lane."

Such sylvan sensibilities can also be satisfied at the 116-acre Leonard Park, a contemplative oasis that features a Japanese teahouse overlooking Wallace Pond. It is equally suitable for quiet meditation or vigorous activity, with four lighted tennis courts, three basketball courts, and numerous playgrounds for toddlers.

Mount Kisco is also home to the Northern Westchester Center of the Arts. Begun as a small, community-focused arts center in Goldens Bridge, the center has grown exponentially. Now occupying a 52,000-square-foot building on Route 117 north of Knowlton Road in Mount Kisco, it offers fine and performing arts classes for children and adults, as well as art exhibitions, concerts, and theatrical performances.

Mount Kisco's earliest history is commemorated by a statue of "Chief Kisco," which stands at the intersection of Main Street and Route 117. He stands on a base that once was a fountain that fed a horse trough. It was presented to the village in 1907 by D. F. Gorham, a strong prohibitionist. The base was inscribed: "God's only beverage for man and beast."

"There really was no Chief Kisco," explained Jane Stewart, the village historian. "He's just a representation and he serves as a great landmark." Actually, little is known about Mount Kisco's Indian past, Ms. Stewart said, or about how the village/town got its name. It became a Quaker settlement in the 1600s, and remained a farming community with a population of less than 200 until the mid–19th century, when the New York & Harlem Railroad opened a station and it began to become a haven for commuting New Yorkers. "It's been changing rapidly ever since," said Ms. Stewart. "A lot of apartment buildings went up in the '50s and '60s. I remember my uncle moved to North Carolina in the '70s because he thought Mount Kisco was becoming a concrete jungle."

What repels some attracts others. Paul McKenzie and Cynthia Mather came to the village specifically because of such development. "I like the large commercial base," said Mr. McKenzie, a consulting architect. "It's a hip little town. If there's a downside, I'd say there's not enough nightlife. It kind of shuts down after 9 P.M." Mr. McKenzie and Ms. Mather bought a remodeled 1917 Cape Cod across from Northern Westchester Hospital Center, where Ms. Mather works as a nurse. "We looked at other places in Westchester, like Croton-on-Hudson, but they lacked a commercial base," he explained. "Mount Kisco offered us everything we wanted within our budget."

Houses tend to range from slightly under $200,000 to the high $600,000's, according to Ms. Lerch. "For anything under $200,000, you'd better be handy," she said. In addition, there are six condominium complexes with about 600 units and seven co-op complexes with about 850 units, Ms. Lerch said. Condominiums range in price from $99,000 for a one-bedroom to $300,000 for a three-bedroom. "You can get a house for the same price," she said, "but not with the amenities like pools and tennis courts."

In the last few years, condominiums sold nearly as well as homes, Ms. Lerch said. "About half of our sales in 1997 were single-family homes, the other half condominiums," Ms. Lerch said. "The people who buy condos tend to be either just starting out or starting over. Sometimes they're downsizing or going through a separation or divorce."

In the same period, co-op sales in her office have increased. "In the last year, we sold 10, which is pretty good considering that in prior years we were lucky if we sold one or two," Ms. Lerch said. "There's also been a slight increase in price."

Despite its northern Westchester location, Mount Kisco also offers an easy commute to midtown Manhattan's Grand Central Station, which is 54 minutes away on Metro-North's Harlem line.

Even with its wide variety of housing options, the village is still growing. There are currently three single-family home developments under construction. The largest is being developed by Toll Brothers, of Huntingdon Valley, Pennsylvania. Called Mount Kisco Chase, it is an 86-home subdivision with four-bedroom homes selling for $535,000 to $600,000. "The price differential has to do with lot size," said Robert Parahus, a vice president with Toll Brothers. "The lots range from one-half acre to two acres. We're targeting the move-up buyer and the empty-nester," he said.

"I think it's a very encouraging sign that a company like Toll Brothers is interested in our community," said Mayor Farrell. "They're creating a whole new neighborhood. And that also helps us attract other kinds of businesses and retailers who might be interested in doing business here."

Mount Kisco's school system reflects the variety in its other offerings. "You have every kind of child, especially in Mount Kisco, where there's a greater ethnic mix," said Bruce Dennis, superintendent of the Bedford Central School District, which also takes in the towns of Bedford and Pound Ridge. "We get the full range of children, from multimillion-dollar homes to children who qualify for the subsidized-lunch program." In the district as a whole, 78 percent of students are white, 11 percent Hispanic, 8 percent black, and 3 percent Asian, Pacific Islander, and other, according to Mr. Dennis. "We consider the diversity of our district to be a real asset," Mr. Dennis said. "It's a very rich contribution to the education offered." Language is strongly emphasized, he said, with Spanish and French starting in the sixth grade and Latin in the ninth. "We also have a very strong English-as-a-second-language program," he added.

Mount Kisco children attend Mount Kisco Elementary or West Patent Elementary and go on to the Fox Lane Middle and High School, in Bedford. "Ninety percent of our children go on to college," said Mr. Dennis. Per-pupil expenditure is $15,900.

The school system is what brought Susan Smith back to Mount Kisco after having lived in Brooklyn for a while. "My older children had gone through the Mount Kisco schools," she explained. "I wanted my daughter to experience the same thing.

"It's just not possible to get this kind of education in other parts of northern Westchester," Ms. Smith said. "My daughter wouldn't be exposed to as many different kinds of people. I think it's invaluable."

NEW ROCHELLE

Lush waterfront, a diverse population, and echoes of Glenn Miller

BY MARY McALEER VIZARD

The picture window of the Rosens' living room commands a sweeping view of Long Island Sound. To one side is open water, to the other, the wooded peninsula of Premium Point in Larchmont and its million-dollar homes. In 1950, Phil Rosen, a builder, and his wife, Rita, bought almost an acre of waterfront property for $7,500. They built a four-bedroom contemporary with open spaces and large windows that make it seem more a beach house than a primary residence. The property is said to be worth about $900,000. "Over the years, we thought about moving someplace else and we looked at different waterfront properties," Mrs. Rosen said, "but we could never find a view this magnificent."

This neighborhood is not usually the first thing to come to mind when people think of New Rochelle, whose reputation as an urban area with all the attendant problems often belies the fact that it is also a shore town with nine miles of waterfront and well-tended neighborhoods of comfortable houses.

The area's original inhabitants were the Siwanoy Indians of the Algonquin tribe. A section of the city is called Wykagyl, a shortening of the name for the Indians who lived just west of the city. In the late 1600s, a group of French Huguenots settled there, naming the town after the French port of La Rochelle. One of the oldest houses in the city once belonged to Thomas Paine, the Revolutionary War pamphleteer. It is now a museum in a two-acre park owned by the Huguenot and Historical Association. In the early 1800s, New Rochelle became a popular resort for people fleeing New York City's sweltering summers. By 1849, when the New York & New Haven Railroad opened a station there, its transformation to suburbia had begun.

POPULATION: 66,498.

AREA: 10.4 square miles.

MEDIAN HOUSEHOLD INCOME: $60,363.

MEDIAN PRICE OF A SINGLE-FAMILY HOUSE $235,000.

TAXES ON A MEDIAN-PRICED HOUSE: $5,800.

PUBLIC SCHOOL SPENDING PER PUPIL : $11,113.

DISTANCE FROM MIDTOWN MANHATTAN: 16 miles.

RUSH-HOUR TRAVEL TO MIDTOWN: 34 minutes on Metro-North's New Haven line, $5.75 one way, $126 monthly.

CODES: Area, 914; ZIP, 10801, 10802, 10804, 10805.

Today, it has many faces, from affluent waterfront enclaves to tree-lined streets of more moderately priced Colonials, Tudors, and ranches to co-op apartment buildings near the downtown. It is still possible to buy a house for under $200,000. Betsy Sutton, an agent with Anthony F. Sutton Realty, recently sold a five-bedroom stucco Colonial with two baths for $175,000. "Houses are very rare in that price range, but they are out there," she said.

More typical, though, is the experience of Kelly and Eugene Young. When they started looking for a house, they didn't think of New Rochelle. "We had looked at 120 houses in places like Chappaqua and Larchmont before we saw an ad for this house," said Mr. Young, a television producer for ABC news. He commutes to his office in midtown Manhattan, which is a 34-minute trip to Grand Central Station, on Metro-North's New Haven line. The Youngs wanted an older home with more than two bathrooms, Mr. Young said, and "the moment my wife saw this house, she said, 'This is it.'"

The house, a 1931 Norman Tudor with a backyard that abuts a nature preserve, was listed at $365,000, but since it needed work, they got it in February of 1992 for $277,000. The neighborhood, Mrs. Young said, has "a real mix of people, which is the kind of environment we want for our child."

Real estate agents say the city is less homogeneous than most Westchester municipalities. According to 1995 estimates, the population broke down to 76 percent white, 18 percent black, and 10 percent Hispanic. There is also a sprinkling of Asians and other nationalities.

"I had one family move from a million-dollar house in Larchmont because they wanted a more diverse population," said Patricia Lampl, a sales associate with Wykagyl/Rittenberg Realty. "So we sold them a million-dollar house here."

Brokers say the best buys in town are co-ops and condominiums. Most co-ops range from $45,000 for a small one-bedroom to $190,000 for a two-bedroom with parking and a pool; condominiums typically cost from $70,000 for a one-bedroom to $250,000 for a two-bedroom.

In recent years, the city's reputation has been tarnished somewhat by its deteriorating downtown. Largely abandoned by shoppers in favor of malls and shopping centers on the city's outskirts, its Main Street has been left with empty storefronts and quiet streets. Mayor Timothy Idoni says this will change now that construction has begun on a 375,000-square-foot shopping and entertainment center to replace the 30-year-old Macy's mall at the intersection of Main Street and Le Count Place in the heart of the downtown. The $106 million project, expected to be completed by spring 1999, will include a 70,000-square-foot supermarket, two ice-skating rinks, a 20-screen movie theater, and Westchester County's first Imax theater.

In the planning stage is a 408-unit luxury rental, to be built in the downtown by Avalon Properties. "We've got to get people living down there," said Development Commissioner Joseph Madonna.

There already are several popular restaurants, such as Del Ponte's for Italian food and Brett's for Continental cuisine.

For years, the city has been hoping to start building an Intermodal Transportation Center in the heart of the city, linking up the various modes of transportation, including Amtrak, Metro-North, and bus service. "We've received $1.6 million from the state and are hoping to get federal financing," said Mr. Madonna, who expects the entire project to cost from $12 million to $14 million.

Shopping was dealt a heavy blow with the closing of Macy's in the New Rochelle Mall in 1992. The nearest department store now is 10 minutes away in the Vernon Hills Shopping Center in Eastchester. There is, however, a Home Depot, Price Club, and many small shops, especially along Main Street and North Avenue.

The city is still trying to recover from several major disappointments over the years. In 1993, it was in the running to be the new world headquarters of UNICEF, the children's relief agency. But the agency chose to stay in Manhattan. Then Donald Trump appeared with a plan to redevelop the 77-acre Davids Island, a former Army base, into a millionaire's retreat, but he withdrew his proposal in March 1996.

New Rochelle has over 40 houses of worship, including the Trinity–St. Paul's Episcopal Church, originally a French Calvinist congregation. The church's history dates to 1710, but its present building was put up in 1862.

The public school district is extensive, with seven elementary schools, two middle schools, and one high school. In addition, there are five Roman Catholic grammar schools and three high schools and three private colleges: Iona College, the College of New Rochelle, and Monroe Business Institute.

The public schools offer a broad-based curriculum, from pre-K to 12th grade, for a total of 9,552 students. Per-pupil expenditure was $11,113 in 1997. And average class size is 24 students. The high school offers advanced placement courses in 14 subjects, including physics, chemistry, and Latin. The high school also has its own television station, planetarium, and Olympic-size swimming pool.

For sports enthusiasts, the city has an abundance of recreational opportunities, including 30 parks with numerous athletic fields and a total of 32 tennis courts. Three of the parks are on the waterfront. The municipal marina has 400 slips and 300 moorings. In the winter, there is ice-skating on Paine Lake, Beechmont Lake, Twin Lakes, and Carpenters Pond. The Five Islands Park, on Echo Bay archipelago, has a 300-seat outdoor amphitheater and park pavilion for outdoor concerts.

There's also the county-owned Glen Island Casino, which in the early 1930s became a Mecca for the Swing Generation. It was during his first engagement there in 1939 that Glenn Miller recorded one of his most memorable sides, "In the Mood." The county-owned casino has been renovated and is now rented out for weddings and banquets. It is also open as a restaurant on Saturday evenings.

NORTH SALEM

Charm, tradition, space, high taxes

BY TESSA MELVIN

Tucked into the northeast corner of Westchester County is a rustic community of graceful horse farms and estates amid thousands of acres of lush woodlands and apple orchards. This is North Salem, 55 miles north of Manhattan, a horseman's paradise of open fields and rugged hills surrounding the New York City–owned Titicus Reservoir. Three-quarters of the land is zoned for four acres or more and there are no sidewalks, sewers, or public water supply. Until a few years ago, there were no numbers on houses.

There is one traffic light and only two gasoline stations, both near Interstate 684. The north-south highway cuts through the town's 22 square miles, dividing the hamlet of Croton Falls on the west from the hamlets of Purdys, North Salem, and Salem Center on the east. There are two railroad stations, at Purdys and Croton Falls, scattered grocery stores, real estate offices, and antiques shops, but no commercial center. Residents shop in Ridgefield, just over the Connecticut line, or at the Danbury Mall, a 15-minute drive east.

"There's a four-acre mentality among many people who move here," said Gail Pantezzi, an agent with Houlihan/Lawrence in Katonah. "It's why they are here. They like the quiet."

But the price of rusticity is on the rise. Although generally acknowledged as one of the most beautiful and undeveloped communities in the metropolitan area, North Salem is also one of its most expensive. There is virtually no commercial tax base and courts have required the town to revise the code to permit more multifamily zones, including some areas designated for affordable housing. After a decade of litigation and mounting court costs, the town acquiesced, and a few years ago, North Salem elected a more flexible town administration, more open to development.

POPULATION: 4,989.

AREA: 22 square miles.

MEDIAN HOUSEHOLD INCOME $86,702.

MEDIAN PRICE OF A SINGLE-FAMILY HOUSE $285,000.

TAXES ON A MEDIAN-PRICED HOUSE: $8,000.

PUBLIC SCHOOL SPENDING PER PUPIL : $12,917.

DISTANCE FROM MIDTOWN MANHATTAN: 55 miles.

RUSH-HOUR TRAVEL TO MIDTOWN: 70 minutes from Croton Falls on Metro-North's Harlem line, 64 minutes from Purdys; $10.25 one way, $211 monthly.

CODES: Area, 914; ZIP, 10560.

At the end of 1997, town officials were completing an amendment to the zoning ordinance to permit greater density on specific parcels and to increase use of the bonus-density option, which gives developers greater density in exchange for adding affordable units.

Very little new housing has been built in North Salem since the court's decision. "There's no guarantee you can build what the zoning allows," said Cynthia Curtis, a member of the town board, who cited the area's steep slopes and other environmental concerns.

The most recent subdivision of any size is Salem Chase, with 53 single-family homes, including five affordable units, which was recently completed off Route 22.

All but 3 percent of North Salem is within the New York City watershed, where new regulations limiting development have been enacted.

Town and school officials are coordinating an effort to improve the tax base and the town hopes to rezone additional land for commercial development. "There is just enough tax money in town to support the school system," said Sy Globerman, the town supervisor. That opinion was shared by Dr. Charles Wilson, former superintendent of schools, and by the current superintendent, Dr. Debra Jackson.

"Our charm is also our Achilles' heel," Dr. Wilson said. "To have this much land this close to New York City is going to cost. This is an absolutely bucolic setting, but the downside is that there are no commercial resources. The homeowner pays the full freight."

Homeowners are willing to pay more than their share to maintain their town's charm, tradition, and open space. For the last two decades, the Open Lands Foundation, an organization of open-space and horse lovers, has been preserving land and has accumulated several hundred acres in North Salem and Lewisboro, just to the south.

Descendants of some of the original settlers still live in North Salem, including the Hawleys, Purdys, Van Scoys, and Keelers, many of them active in the North Salem Historical Society. For more than 70 years, residents have gathered every Christmas Eve for carols around a tree donated by the Keelers.

The biggest business is still related to the land—horses. Unofficial estimates put the town's horse population at around 450, many of them prize jumpers and hunters. The largest commercial operation is at Old Salem Farm, once owned by the actor Paul Newman, where horse shows are regularly held, among them the Pepsi Challenge Grand Prix each May.

The town's most colorful tradition is provided by the Goldens Bridge Hounds, the only remaining hunt club in Westchester County. Throughout the six-month season, and as often as three times each week, the club's 50 members ride to hounds, chasing foxes who appear to know there is refuge in North Salem's three golf courses.

Horse owners worry that development will threaten their sport and traditions. Ron Stewart and his wife, Jayme, recently purchased 43 acres behind their horse farm to prevent it from being developed. "I want farming to be preserved," Ms. Stewart said of her purchase. The Stewarts have lived in North Salem for 18 years, rearing three children on their 118-acre horse farm. Mr. Stewart commutes to New York, where he owns the York Preparatory School and the Learning Annex, the city's largest private adult education program. Mrs. Stewart is author of *How to Get into the College of Your Choice and How to Finance It* (William Morrow).

Mr. Stewart is a member of the Zoning Board of Appeals. Calling the town's earlier efforts to prevent development in North Salem "a period of nimbyism carried to the ultimate," Mr. Stewart said the town was now "eager for controlled development." While the town "is still a little artificial with the hunt, the open fields and all that, housing is getting more diverse," he said, adding, "We are no longer just a rich man's haven."

First-time home buyers can find a wide range of housing options, said Ms. Pantezzi, the real estate agent, including starter homes for less than $200,000. "There's housing here for everybody from $100,000 to $6 million," she said. The median price of a single-family home in North Salem in 1997 was $285,000, up from $260,000 a year earlier. One three-bedroom split-level home near the median was on the market at the end of 1997 for $289,500. With one-half an acre, the home, built in 1956, had taxes of $6,323.

At Sunset Ridge, a 30-year-old development of one-family homes just off Interstate 684, three-bedroom Colonials on one acre sell for $207,000 to $255,500. The homes are built around the only public park, which has baseball and soccer fields, a basketball court, two tennis courts, and a playground. A second town park is planned next to the North Salem Middle-High School on June Road. At the Cotswolds in Purdys, 38 two- and three-bedroom town houses built in the mid-eighties offer large units, ranging from 2,200 to 3,000 square feet. The two- and three-bedroom homes sell for between $235,000 and $285,000.

Many of the town's large estates can be found on Mills and Cat Ridge Roads, prime horse country, where homes sell for $2 million to $3 million.

The rustic privacy of North Salem has attracted some rich and famous people, including Alan Mencken, the Oscar-winning composer. David Letterman, the talk show host, once paid $5 million for a 100-year-old Stanford White Colonial farmhouse on 88 acres.

Several members of the Hearst publishing empire have also owned property in North Salem. All six Hearst properties have recently been sold. One of them, the Snow Hill estate, with a mansion, caretaker's cottage, eight-stall barn, and 117 acres, was purchased by a television producer, Robert Halmi, Jr., for $3.15 million.

The large number of apartments that violate zoning regulations is decreasing since the town began allowing secondary units on private property in 1995. Rents vary, but one two-bedroom unit recently rented for $1,600 a month.

North Salem's elementary school and combined middle and high school enroll 1,300 students, an increasing enrollment that is straining school facilities, now at over 100 percent capacity. The school system offers a wide range of subjects, including an interactive computer project linking high school students to college courses at Mercy College in Yorktown. The school district spent $12,917 per student in 1997. About 80 percent of the senior class go on to higher education.

North Salem offers some unusual culinary and cultural opportunities. The Hammond Museum has exhibitions and concerts, many centered around its four-acre Japanese stroll garden. Two of Westchester County's most noteworthy restaurants are found here—the Box Tree, in a small 18th-century Colonial farmhouse in Purdys, and the elegant French Provincial–style Auberge Maxime in North Salem.

Along Hardscrabble Road is the North Salem Vineyard, where for 32 years Dr. George Naumburg, Jr., a retired Manhattan psychiatrist, has grown grapes. The vineyard annually produces 1,600 cases of wine from French hybrids. Dr. Naumburg welcomes the changes he sees coming to North Salem. "There was a deliberate decision a decade ago to ban all commercial development," he said. "But you can't run a community on single-family homes unless you have very high taxes. Now, it's going to be different."

PURCHASE

Boom times in big-home country

BY MARY McALEER VIZARD

The neighborhood known as Purchase, part of the Westchester town of Harrison, has earned its reputation as an exclusive enclave of baronial houses surrounded by expansive, exquisitely manicured lawns and acres of rolling countryside. A look at the map shows the gridwork of the community with plentiful open space. Yet it is bisected by highways and bordered by more densely populated areas, such as the city of White Plains, the shopping and commercial hub of the county. But time may finally be catching up to Purchase. It is now experiencing an explosion of building, mostly of expensive homes on former estates that are being subdivided at a frantic pace.

"Purchase is the place," said Frank DePalo, building inspector for the Town of Harrison. "That's where all the land is left. People who had five to 10 acres now all seem to be subdividing their property and making lots of money by selling off parcels to developers."

The biggest development is called Park Lane Reserve, a 306-lot subdivision on 400 acres. Begun in 1985, it stalled during the recent downturn in the market and revived in 1993. At the close of 1997, a total of 164 houses had been sold, and 32 were under contract, said Reza Bashirrad, vice president of Park Lane Reserve Development, which is selling lots to individual builders. "Of that, about 150 houses have either already been built or are under construction," said Mr. Bashirrad, who added that all must adhere to strict design guidelines. "No contemporaries," he said. "All must be traditional designs, built with brick or stucco. While there's uniformity, no two houses are exactly the same."

Prices in Park Lane range from $730,000 to $1 million. "This is just what was needed," said Audrey Rapaport, regional manager for the real estate brokerage Houlihan/Lawrence. "There was tremendous pent-up

POPULATION: 4,139.

AREA: 6 square miles.

MEDIAN HOUSEHOLD INCOME: $152,500.

MEDIAN PRICE OF A SINGLE-FAMILY HOUSE $690,000.

TAXES ON A MEDIAN-PRICED HOUSE: $10,000.

PUBLIC SCHOOL SPENDING PER PUPIL : $14,068.

DISTANCE FROM MIDTOWN MANHATTAN: 25 Miles.

RUSH-HOUR TRAVEL TO MIDTOWN: 10-minute drive to Metro-North's Harrison station, then 36 minutes on the New Haven line, $6.50 one way, $141 monthly.

CODES: Area, 914; ZIP, 10577.

demand for houses at this price range."

Another developer, Hickory Pine Associates, is commanding the same prices, but just for land. At Purchase Estates, lots from one to 2.3 acres are priced from $705,000 to $1.5 million. "People can build their own houses," said Billie Prizio, a sales agent with Julia B. Fee, the real estate company that is sales director for the project. The lots are arranged around an 18-hole golf course built by Jack Nicklaus.

In some cases, developers are buying lots and building speculative houses on them. An example of one is a five-bedroom, 5½-bath Victorian selling for $2.9 million. The project is now in its second phase, with 11 houses in each phase. The ultimate size of the development will be 73 houses.

Even more exclusive is Stoneleigh Manor, a subdivision of lavish custom-built homes to be built on lots of 2.5 to 4 acres that are expected to cost from $5 million to $10 million.

"Four projects are now being built, and another three are set to begin in early 1998 if they get all their approvals," said Mr. DePalo. "It's phenomenal. We are booming."

"Resales have also been strong, but only if they're priced competitively," said Ms. Rapaport. "Buyers are very savvy. They know what everything's worth. It's a matter of whether they want to pay more for new construction or buy a resale." One recent example of a resale at a competitive price, Ms. Rapaport said, is a six-bedroom, 3½-bath Colonial priced at $610,000. "There's no new construction available at that price," she added.

In general, resales in Purchase range from a small four-bedroom Cape Cod in the $300,000's to a five-bedroom estate with tennis courts for $1.5 million, Ms. Rapaport said. The median price for a house in Purchase in early 1998 was $690,000, with taxes around $10,000.

The people who buy in Purchase generally fall into one of two categories, Ms. Prizio said. "They either want new construction or something old and charming," she said. "If they want old and charming, they should be prepared to spend another $100,000 to renovate and update, put in central air and the kinds of things most people require today."

One longtime resident, Arthur Shapiro, is worried about the frenetic pace of building. "I think there's a danger Purchase will turn into a heavily populated area and lose a lot of the charm and personality it now has," he said. "Soon when you drive down Purchase Street you'll just see all these big houses. You won't see any green space anymore."

The neighborhood tends to attract chief executives of major corporations and people in the financial and entertainment industries, said Susan Glasgall, a sales agent with Houlihan/Lawrence. Among some prominent residents are the shoe designer Kenneth Cole and his wife, Maria Cuomo, daughter of the former governor, Mario M. Cuomo.

In its humbler days, Purchase was settled by a group of Quakers led by John Harrison, who bought a tract of land from the Siwanoy Indians. These early settlers gravitated to the northern part of the town, which over the years was referred to as "Harrison's Purchase." By the mid-1800s, almost all the original farms had become opulent country estates used as summer retreats by New York City businessmen.

Whitelaw Reid, owner-publisher of *The New York Tribune* and also ambassador to Britain, owned Ophir Farms, which at one time encompassed more than 1,000 acres. Much of it is now occupied by classrooms and dormitories of Manhattanville College and by the Keio High School for Japanese students.

The Purchase campus of the State University of New York was once the estate of John Thomas, the first judge of Westchester County. He is credited with giving the first public reading of the Declaration of Independence in New York on the steps of the White Plains courthouse on July 11, 1776. Soon after that, Judge Thomas was taken from his home by British soldiers and thrown into prison, where he died a month later. His monolith memorial now stands on the grounds of the Purchase campus.

Aside from its role as a four-year college, the state college has a performing arts center, which features theater, dance, and musical performances open to the public, and the Neuberger Museum.

Children can attend the Purchase School, from kindergarten through fifth grade, and then go on to the Louis M. Klein Middle School and Harrison High School. One reason Fran Lerner and her husband, Mark, who moved from Manhattan in 1997, chose Purchase was "because we were thrilled with the elementary school," Ms. Lerner said.

"We emphasize academics at the elementary school but also the arts," said School Superintendent Ronald D. Valenti. "Music classes start in the fourth grade." Per-pupil expenditures in 1997 averaged $14,068. In 1995, the middle school was cited as a National School of Excellence by the Department of Education, Dr. Valenti said. "It's a very prestigious award given only to those schools that have met a high standard of excellence in their programs and in the performance of their students," he said. Ninety-five percent of all students who graduate from Harrison High School go on to college, Dr. Valenti said.

The elementary school, which has 275 pupils, should reach 300 before the year 2000, the superintendent estimated. The district recently added six additional classrooms funded by a $22 million bond referendum, which passed in 1995.

Purchase has no shopping to speak of, and only a few restaurants, including the popular Cobble Stone and George's Hilltop for casual food, and Cobble Creek Cafe for nouvelle cuisine.

Despite the bucolic bent, Purchase is a discreet haven for several large corporate campuses, including those of Pepsico, Texaco, and MasterCard. It also encompasses a portion of the Westchester County Airport. "The tax base is excellent, which is unusual for a community with so little commercial development and so much open space," Ms. Glasgall said.

RYE

Waterfront mansions, New England look

BY MARY McALEER VIZARD

Rye, the smallest city in Westchester County, is renowned for its picturesque neighborhoods of detached homes, its imposing waterfront mansions, and, of course, the Art Deco, county-owned Playland Amusement Park, which is listed in the National Register of Historic Places.

Rye shares with parts of nearby Connecticut a small-town New England ambience and a sense of history. Many people first become acquainted with it through its downtown, which runs along Purchase Street, the city's leafy main road, with a collection of delis, coffee bars, and specialty stores. The city center's low-slung architecture has been preserved through the enforcement of strict city ordinances and architectural guidelines, says Frank J. Culross, the city manager. "We don't forbid chain stores," Mr. Culross explained. "But whatever moves in must fit in with what's already there. Most merchants realize that the existing character works and want to fit in."

When residents wish to do more extensive shopping, they can drive 10 minutes to White Plains or Stamford, Connecticut. There are no movies in town, but local entertainment is provided by the Rye Arts Center, which sponsors community concerts, dance recitals, and amateur and professional theatrical productions.

Representing Rye's commitment to its history is the Square House, built around 1700 and situated at the southern entrance to the downtown. It shares the "Village Green" with the Municipal Building and the Rye Free Reading Library. Once a tavern and inn and a popular stop along the historic Boston Post Road, the building now houses the Rye Historical Society, which sponsors exhibits and special events. Two centuries ago, the Square House was the center of Rye's community life. And, yes, George Washington slept there—twice, in fact, according to diary entries dated

POPULATION: 15,071.

AREA: 5.5 square miles.

MEDIAN HOUSEHOLD INCOME: $92,806.

MEDIAN PRICE OF A SINGLE-FAMILY HOUSE $523,577.

TAXES ON A MEDIAN-PRICED HOUSE: $9,700.

PUBLIC SCHOOL SPENDING PER PUPIL : $13,986.

DISTANCE FROM MIDTOWN MANHATTAN: 25 miles.

RUSH-HOUR TRAVEL TO MIDTOWN: 37 minutes on Metro-North's New Haven line, $6.75 one way, $152 monthly.

CODES: Area, 914; ZIP, 10580.

October and November 1789. He described it as a "very neat and decent inn."

Now listed in the National Register of Historic Places, the building is no longer sufficient to house all of Rye's historical activities, according to David Byrnes, director of the society. In 1992, the society acquired another historic property called the Knapp House, built from 1667 to 1670. It is the oldest existing residential property in Westchester County, according to Mr. Byrnes. "We've been trying to raise $1 million to rehabilitate the house," Mr. Byrnes said. "So far we have $800,000, which we've been using to replace the roof, remove rot, etc." Eventually the society hopes to relocate the city's archives there.

Rye's history began in 1660, when a group of farmers from Greenwich, Connecticut, established a community and named it after their original home in England. By the early 19th century, Rye had become a summer resort, attracting wealthy New Yorkers who built palatial estates along the Long Island Sound. After World War I, Rye began a transformation from summer colony to commuters' community. Summer cottages bordering salt marshes were winterized, and later split-level ranches and more modern styles were mixed in with mansions that at one time sat alone on hills with unobstructed views of the Sound.

"What I love about Rye is its eclecticism," said Audrey Rapaport, manager of Houlihan/Lawrence's Rye office. Its housing runs the gamut from "cottages to castles," she said. There are also 13 condominium complexes with a total of 295 units and eight co-op buildings with 495 units in all.

The largest condominium complex is the 76-unit Water's Edge, where prices for two- and three-bedroom units range for $350,000 to $750,000 for those on the Sound. As for co-ops, the largest is the 162-unit Rye Colony, where the range is from $53,000 for a one-bedroom apartment to $125,000 for a two-bedroom. The most expensive co-op is the 88-unit Milton Harbor House, where one-bedrooms start at $235,000, and $410,000 buys the most costly three-bedroom.

Janice Callahan and her husband, Bob, a radio network executive, lived in Rye for 15 years when they decided to look for a bigger house. "There really wasn't anything available in Rye, so we looked in Connecticut," Ms. Callahan said. But neither she nor her husband wanted to leave, she said, adding that "even our children always tell us how much they love Rye." They wound up buying a house around the corner from where they lived. "It's a lot bigger and older than we had planned on getting," Ms. Callahan said. The 1774 Colonial has nine bathrooms and nine fireplaces with a total of 7,000 square feet, Ms. Callahan said. "It's your quintessential money pit," she said. "But we fell in love with it with its old moldings. And we were able to stay in Rye."

On the other end of the market, Maria Rodrigues, a New Rochelle native, said she always wanted to live in Rye. The trouble was, she and her husband, Brian, were afraid they would find nothing in their $250,000 to $300,000 price range. "People assume you've got to have millions to live in Rye," Ms. Rodrigues said, "but it's not true." In late 1996, the couple and their 4-month-old son moved into a three-bedroom, three-bath, split-level that they purchased for $260,000.

Rye has several extremely exclusive neighborhoods, such as Manursing Island, a gated community of multimillion-dollar mansions, most of which occupy beachfront property. In the warm weather, pleasure boats and yachts bob at docks in front of the homes. But for those Rye residents not blessed with their own water frontage, there is the municipal marina with 398 boat slips.

A fifth of the city is open space, with two miles of coastline, including a city beach, Playland, which has a beach and an outdoor pool, and the 120-acre Marshlands Conservancy. The 47-acre Rye Nature Center offers wooded trails, a bird sanctuary, a nature museum, and a full-time naturalist. In addition, the city maintains three parks with tennis courts, athletic fields, and playgrounds. The municipally owned Rye Golf Club has an 18-hole course, a kiddie pool, and a full-size pool. The family fee is $1,725 for the season; for the pool alone, it is $580.

On one of the few pieces of developable land left in the city, 40 acres off the Boston Post Road, a new project called the Preserve at Rye, is attracting a whole new home buyer to Rye, according to Martha Bentley, manager of the Merritt Associates real estate office in Rye. "It's the only new construction around," she said. "For the people who wanted a new house, even if they wanted to live in Rye, we always had to show them other communities." The Preserve's 38 detached homes, with 3,200 to 5,000 square feet, are selling for $1 million to $1.5 million.

Michael Grasso, a professor of urology at New York University Medical Center in Manhattan, and his wife, Kathyanne, are among the home buyers at the Preserve. The couple had been renting in Manhattan since Dr. Grasso was transferred from Southern California three years earlier.

"One of my sons is starting kindergarten," Dr. Grasso said. "And we thought it was time to find a good school district and a home with some grass for the children to play on."

Many people move to Rye to send their children to its public schools. The 2,202-student district has three kindergarten-through-grade 5 elementary schools, a middle school for grades 6 to 8, and a high school. The high school occupies a 20-acre campus and shares its building with the middle school. Among its courses is one on civilization for ninth- and 10th-grade students. "It tries to weave together literature from Western civilization and history," explained Edward J. Shine, the school superintendent. All of the district's graduates, as a rule, go on to higher education, Dr. Shine said.

Children who live in the Greenhaven section of the city go to the Rye Neck Union Free School District, which also takes in parts of the Village of Mamaroneck.

Rye has two private schools—the prekindergarten-through-grade 12 Rye Country Day School and the Roman Catholic Resurrection Grammar School for prekindergarten to grade 8. Annual tuition at Rye Country Day ranges from $9,500 for prekindergarten to $15,175 for grade 12. Tuition at Resurrection ranges from $2,090 to $3,950 for parishioners (with kindergarteners paying the most) and $2,750 to $4,450 for nonparishioners.

In 1996, voters approved the allocation of $5.4 million for the restoration of the Gothic Revival Whitby Castle, built in 1854 and situated on the grounds of the Rye Golf Club. In recent years, it had fallen into disrepair, and the city plans to use it to house a restaurant and catering business. Another historic property, the Jay Mansion, is now operating as a museum. The 1838 Greek Revival mansion sitting atop a knoll facing the Boston Post Road was once the home of Peter Augustus Jay, son of John Jay, first chief justice of the United States. Now the home and its carriage house are being painstakingly restored by the nonprofit Jay Heritage Center. Both properties are open to the public for tours.

SCARSDALE

Being "comfortable in a lot of ways"

BY TESSA MELVIN

One fine June evening in 1922, a representative of the Suchard chocolate company walked into the Scarsdale Village Board meeting and proposed building a factory on 10.5 acres on Palmer Avenue. His action abruptly ended a debate then going on about the need for a villagewide zoning law, made possible by recent state enabling legislation. "For 20 years, we have been developing a village of homes," said Arthur Boniface, then the board's president. "Nothing in the nature of a factory has come into the village."

And nothing has in the 72 years since Scarsdale became the first suburban community in New York State to adopt a complete zoning law. It has successfully fought off several challenges to its right to be a community of homes alone.

Each spring, ducks swim on ponds and swimming pools behind stately houses. Each fall, residents collect their fallen leaves, from which the village creates 30,000 tons of compost.

Residents enjoy the 500-acre Saxon Woods County Park, with its outdoor pool, hiking trails, and picnic areas; 20 village parks; 25 public tennis courts and six public paddle courts; one public and two private golf courses; four community pools; and more than 300 children's athletic teams, which often play at the 18-acre Crossway Field.

This coterminous town and village 24 miles north of midtown Manhattan was settled in 1702 by Caleb Heathcote, an English merchant. Tudor-style commercial buildings that dominate the small downtown recall the village's heritage.

The Scarsdale Union Free School District is consistently regarded as one of the nation's best, with SAT scores among the highest in Westchester. The high school has been cited by the federal Department of

POPULATION: 16,847.

AREA: 6.4 square miles.

MEDIAN HOUSEHOLD INCOME: $159,642.

MEDIAN PRICE OF A SINGLE-FAMILY HOUSE $580,000.

TAX ON A MEDIAN-PRICED HOUSE: $12,000.

PUBLIC SCHOOL SPENDING PER PUPIL : $14,500.

DISTANCE FROM MIDTOWN MANHATTAN: 24 miles.

RUSH-HOUR TRAVEL TO MIDTOWN: 31 minutes on Metro-North, $6.50 one way, $141 monthly.

CODES: Area, 914; ZIP, 10583.

Education as "one of the 144 exemplary schools to which others may look for patterns of success."

The seven classic school buildings are well kept. School officials completed a $25 million renovation in 1996, redoing all roofs, updating the heating systems, and replacing windows. Scarsdale High School, parts of which were built in 1915, has been substantially renovated.

Reflecting the community's growing international population—Japanese citizens or families of Japanese descent make up 17 percent of the village population—the school has placed substantial emphasis on multicultural understanding. Students participate in a variety of cultural exchange programs and have been treated to performances by such renowned artists as Midori.

Other special programs include the Scarsdale Alternative School, an experimental college-oriented program offering students a smaller setting and a participatory, democratic structure. The district spent $14,500 per student in 1996.

Each year, about 5 percent of the senior class, which numbered 300 in 1997, become National Merit semifinalists or better. The percentage of seniors going on for more education varies between 96 percent and 100 percent. But achievement does have a price. "There is a lot of pressure in this community for kids to succeed," a former school superintendent, Dr. Richard D. Hibschman, once noted. "Sometimes I worry we keep them too busy," he said. "We ought to give our kids more time to play kick-the-can."

Francis M. Murphy has been superintendent of schools in Scarsdale since 1996. Calling Scarsdale students "active" and "engaged intellectually and athletically," Dr. Murphy added, "Generally there is a smile at week's end from a week well spent, but sometimes I worry about the pressure these students apply to themselves in this culture of high achievement."

Schools may be a major—perhaps the major—attraction. But Lowell J. Tooley, village manager for 33 years until his retirement in 1994, once observed, "People move to Scarsdale to be comfortable in a lot of ways.

"They go walking, biking, hiking, and they can shoot baskets and play tennis all over town," he said.

They also participate actively in any of several dozen community organizations. The League of Women Voters, with over 600 members, is the largest suburban chapter in the country. The 900 members of the Town and Village Civic Club, which was founded in 1904, study community issues and help administer the nonpartisan village elections. There are 15 election districts in Scarsdale, and candidates for village posts are chosen by delegates from five groups of three election districts each. Every so often someone tries to buck the system, which has been in place 65 years, and run independently, but none has ever won a village post.

Residents strongly support the Scarsdale Adult School, a 59-year-old evening adult education program with a wide-ranging curriculum. They study music at the 94-year-old Hoff-Barthelson Music School and nature at the 10-acre village-owned Weinberg Nature Center.

They worry about high taxes, problems with downtown parking, and how the downtown development plan proposed by a succession of developers over the last several years, with its mixture of residential and commercial use, would affect the village. A Scarsdale business district committee of landlords, merchants, and village officials is working together to beautify the downtown, improve parking, and make the shopping area more viable.

When a survey done in 1993 showed that residents wanted a local movie theater and more downtown restaurants, they got both. The Scarsdale Plaza Cinema, a traditional-style movie house that had been closed for many years, has reopened, offering first-run films. Two new restaurants in the village include the upscale Scarsdale Avenue Cafe in the heart of downtown, featuring American cuisine, and the Heathcote Tavern at the Five Corners, with a more casual menu. The Parkway Cafe is a popular local hangout that serves unusual omelets, including low-cholesterol varieties. People willing to drive to the edge of town will find Il Cigno, called one of the county's best Italian restaurants by a *New York Times* critic.

Residents pay for their privileges. Without a significant commercial tax base, property taxes are high. Annual taxes on a three-bedroom Colonial listed at $379,500 were $9,700 at the end of 1997, while a six-bedroom Colonial listed at $599,000 had taxes of $11,879.

Nevertheless, the village has had no trouble attracting newcomers. The median price of a single-family house in Scarsdale was $572,500 in 1997, and $580,000 for the first six months of 1998. Seventeen homes sold for less than $325,000 in 1997, said Lynne B. Clark, vice president of Julia B. Fee Real Estate, the largest agency in the village, while 33 homes sold for more than $1 million.

Many of the less expensive homes are in the Edgewood Section, where lots and houses are smaller. The five neighborhoods—Edgewood, Heathcote, Fox Meadow, Greenacres, and Quaker Ridge—share the same eclectic mixture of homes, with some small lots and estates in each one. The estate section is concentrated in the Heathcote area, where homes on three to five acres commonly sell for $1 million and up. Newer homes are mostly located in Quaker Ridge.

There are two co-op complexes. In the 116-unit Chateau, eight four-story buildings put up in the 1920s, two-bedroom units with fireplaces sell for an average of $250,000. The 45 units in the six-story Popham Hall building range from $250,000 to $350,000. The one rental building, at 45 Popham Road, has 64 apartments, with two-bedroom units renting for $2,400 a month.

In 1891, a group of Manhattan investors established the Arthur Suburban Home Company and bought 150 acres in Scarsdale, what its brochure called "New York City's healthiest and prettiest suburb." In addition to "small cottages" for $5,500 or "large cottages" for $8,500, prospects were told a monthly ticket on the Harlem Railroad was only $5.75 or "9 cents a ride." The legacy of this effort to change Scarsdale from a rural town to a residential suburb is Arthur Manor, now a neighborhood within the Edgewood section of the village. Some of the original homes still exist. One of them, a five-bedroom, 1½-bath Colonial built in 1905, sold in the fall of 1997 for $325,000.

TARRYTOWN

Rich history, picturesque river setting

BY TESSA MELVIN

Each year, the cross-country team at Sleepy Hollow High School represents a student body from at least a dozen countries. It trains on the paths of the Rockefeller family estate and it competes under the banner of the headless horseman, the school mascot.

Welcome to Tarrytown, a village with rich and varied historical and cultural roots and a splendid setting overlooking the three-mile width of the Hudson River. The Dutch called this point, the river's widest, the Tappan Zee—Tappan probably for a group of Indians and Zee meaning "sea" in Dutch. Wealthy industrialists built estates on its hills, and its shores drew industries that employed newly arrived immigrants.

The past is present in this eclectic village, home to corporate executives as well as to blue-collar workers. Among the remaining mansions is Lyndhurst, the Gothic Revival jewel of the National Trust for Historic Preservation, designed by Alexander Jackson Davis for William Paulding, a mayor of New York City, and completed in 1838. It was later owned by Jay Gould, the railroad financier.

On the waterfront near the recently restored 107-year-old Victorian railroad station, the county asphalt plant and a recycling plant, among other small industries, still hum. And teenagers knock balls around in the waterfront Losee and Pierson Parks. Nearby are the Washington Irving and Tarrytown Boating Clubs with a total of 320 slips.

"Tarrytown is a wonderful, very mixed community with an even more mixed school system," said Kathleen DeFemia, and administrative assistant at village hall. "My kids have had friends of all different skin colors, and I think it has made them better people—it's what the world is all about."

The world has known about Tarrytown for a century and a half, thanks

GAZETTEER

POPULATION: 11,034.

AREA: 3.08 square miles.

MEDIAN HOUSEHOLD INCOME: $65,750.

MEDIAN PRICE OF A SINGLE-FAMILY HOUSE: $291,000.

TAXES ON A MEDIAN-PRICED HOUSE $7,000.

PUBLIC SCHOOL SPENDING PER PUPIL: $12,651.

DISTANCE FROM MIDTOWN MANHATTAN: 25 miles.

RUSH-HOUR TRAVEL TO MIDTOWN: 38 minutes on Metro-North's Hudson line, $7.50 one way, $163 monthly.

CODES: Area, 914; ZIP, 10591.

to its legendary equestrian ghost. Who does not know of Brom Bones, Ichabod Crane, and the lovely Katrina, made famous by Washington Irving, an area resident. And Tarrytown also has a place in real history: Maj. John André, the British spy, was captured there as he tried to help Benedict Arnold betray West Point.

After a century as an active river port and a regional industrial center, Tarrytown entered its golden age in this century as a mecca for the wealthy. Home to industrial tycoons, including William E. Dodge, a merchant and philanthropist; J. D. Maxwell, an automobile pioneer; and several members of the Lehman banking family; it also attracted Albert Bierstadt, the landscape painter, and Samuel L. Clemens.

With the Rockefellers and other prominent families in North Tarrytown, recently renamed Sleepy Hollow, the area was dubbed "the millionaire's colony." Tarrytown incorporated as a village in 1870, adjacent Sleepy Hollow, then known as North Tarrytown, in 1874.

Modern Tarrytown is a transportation hub connecting Westchester and Rockland Counties with New York City via excellent train connections and the Tappan Zee Bridge, which connects to I-287, Westchester's major east-west highway.

Automobile traffic has also been the village's biggest nightmare. When it was built in 1955, the bridge was considered a boon to development. Office parks sprang up and hotels as well, among them the Tarrytown Hilton and the Westchester Marriott.

But few were prepared for the traffic that threatened to choke off the village as frustrated rush-hour commuters tried to get onto the Tappan Zee by seeking alternative routes through the village. "It used to be a disaster," Ms. DeFemia recalled, "especially on Friday nights. You couldn't even go out for a quart of milk."

Peace returned in 1993, after the state agreed to install a removable barrier on the bridge, freeing an extra lane for Westchester-bound traffic in the morning and an extra lane westbound in the evenings.

A commuter bus service bringing Rockland County residents to the train has also helped, said Eileen Pilla, mayor of Tarrytown for the last 13 years. She presides over a village board that in 1988 approved a revised master plan, in the process rezoning the village near the bridge to reduce density.

"Development was overtaking events," said Mayor Pilla. "We wanted more open space and we wanted to prevent such dense development it would take away from the attractiveness of the community."

Residents hope their historic past and a spruced-up downtown will be keys to their economic future as the region's industrial tax base declines. Taxpayers in the two villages are concerned about the economic impact of the departure of General Motors, which closed its assembly plant in Sleepy Hollow in 1996. Although the plant paid no village taxes in Tarrytown, it has contributed almost 10 percent of the consolidated school budget.

The region has become an increasingly popular tourist destination because of Sunnyside, Washington Irving's home; Kykuit, the Rockefeller family home; and Philipsburg Manor Upper Mills in Sleepy Hollow.

Today, Main Street looks remarkably as it does in photos taken 50 years ago, with three- and four-story Victorian storefronts dominating the street. After the designation of the street as a local historic landmark in 1980, shopkeepers had to get permission to make architectural changes.

Antiques shops abound, mixed with delis, clothing stores, and restaurants featuring Italian, Mexican, and Portuguese specialities.

The most prominent building on Main Street is the Queen Anne–style Music Hall, built in 1885 to bring grand opera and vaudeville to the village and the site of an annual flower show. It is now a thriving performing arts center that has played host to such well-known performers as the singer Arlo Guthrie and the New Orleans Preservation Hall Band.

The clearest sign of diversity is Tarrytown's housing stock, from the tiny row houses in the inner village to the elegant freestanding brownstones on North Washington Street to the rambling Victorians in Wilson Park. About 40 percent of the 4,311 housing units in Tarrytown are one-family, including several Hudson River Victorians with fine river views.

Aside from a scattered lot here and there, little new housing has been built in the village until recently. At the end of 1997, there were 300 rental apartments under construction along Route 119, also known as Tarrytown Road. There is little available land, except for about 220 acres in the south end of the village owned by the Unification Church.

One of the most luxurious condominiums among 12 complexes in the village is Carrollwood, where a total of 208 two- and three-bedroom units surround Axe Castle, once known as Carrollcliffe. The castle was purchased in 1994 by a group of investors headed by Hanspeter Walder, a

Tarrytown resident. Equus, a stylish restaurant featuring regional delicacies, now makes its home in the 100-year-old Norman-style castle and inn, now called the Castle at Tarrytown.

In Tarrycrest, a one-family-home neighborhood, three- and four-bedroom ranches and Colonials sell for $250,000 to $350,000, said Joanne De Cecchis, principal broker at De Cecchis Realty. The median price of a single-family home was $291,000 in 1997, up from $286,000 a year earlier.

Several surround the fields of the Hackley School, a private co-ed day school and five-day boarding school. Others are near the Tarrycrest Swim Club, a private club with tennis courts, and some are near the two Tarrytown Lakes, a backup reservoir where people fish in the summer and skate in the winter.

Beyond the lakes is the Wilson Park neighborhood, which many brokers consider the most prestigious part of town and where some Victorians sell for $600,000 and up. Residents are surrounded by open space, most of it owned by the Rockefeller family, and by the four-year, 700-student Marymount College, a private women's college.

Brian and Carol Kelly bought their rambling white Colonial on a hill in the neighborhood because of its river views and its proximity to both Kykuit, at the end of the street, and the downtown, just a walk away. Mr. Kelly, an advertising executive with Ammirati Puris Lintas, looks forward to weekends when the couple take Sarah, 6, Will, 3, and Quinn, 1, on long rambles at Kykuit, accompanied by Abbie, their golden retriever.

Sarah attends first grade at the John Paulding School in Sleepy Hollow, one of six schools in the consolidated system, each designated for particular grade levels. Sarah and the other first graders will enter the Winfield L. Morse School in Sleepy Hollow for second and third grades.

The Washington Irving Intermediate School in Tarrytown houses grades 4 through 6, and students return to the Sleepy Hollow Middle School in Sleepy Hollow for grades 7 and 8 and spend their last four years in Tarrytown at Sleepy Hollow High School.

Dr. Donald R. Kusel, the district school superintendent, said the system had been building up a surplus to offset the anticipated loss of revenue from General Motors. The district has raised $100,000 from its newly created school foundation for technology improvements and teacher grants.

The 2,131-student district spent $12,651 per pupil in 1997. About 80 percent of the senior class go on to higher education.

It is a system, Dr. Kusel said, that now offers seven languages, including Russian, as well as 17 advanced placement courses, and that has recently instituted new math and language-arts curriculums.

WHITE PLAINS

Balancing tranquillity with tax benefits

BY TESSA MELVIN

Shoppers headed for the Westchester, the luxury mall that opened in White Plains in 1995, use routes planned to bypass most of the city's 13 residential neighborhoods. That pleases the city's more than 50,000 inhabitants, who frequently voice irritation at the traffic jams on the interstate highways that connect White Plains with the metropolitan area. They are as determined to protect the residential tranquillity of their tree-lined streets as they are eager to enjoy the property-tax benefits a varied economic base provides.

The balancing act is difficult, but the city is intent on combining the best aspects of both environments, preserving gracious neighborhoods while serving as the business, retail, and government hub of Westchester County. "White Plains is a place that is carefully trying to straddle polar opposites of city and countrified suburb," said former mayor Sy J. Schulman. "How do we balance our desire to be a dynamic city while preserving the small-town quality of our neighborhoods? We worry all the time."

Preserving continuity, Mr. Schulman said, requires citizens with a "citywide mentality," which the city has in abundance. Many participate extensively in its activities, often through a network of neighborhood associations. Others join civic groups, including the Beautification Foundation, now more than 30 years old, which has raised more than $1 million for gardens, small parks, a carillon, and barrels of flowers donated to participating merchants.

In 1994, the city's call for volunteers to develop a new comprehensive plan attracted 400 residents, and Mayor Schulman observed, "The process was as important as the product. Four hundred people is incredible," he said. "That's 1 percent of the population."

Completed in 1997, the plan described the city as "predominantly

POPULATION: 50,899.

AREA: 10 square miles.

MEDIAN HOUSEHOLD INCOME: $61,318.

MEDIAN PRICE OF A SINGLE-FAMILY HOUSE: $285,000.

TAXES ON A MEDIAN-PRICED HOUSE: $4,750.

PUBLIC SCHOOL SPENDING PER PUPIL: $16,000.

DISTANCE FROM MIDTOWN MANHATTAN: 22 miles.

RUSH-HOUR TRAVEL TO MIDTOWN: 36 minutes on Metro-North, $6.50 one way, $141 monthly; express bus, $4.50 one way.

CODES: Area, 914; ZIP, 10601–10607.

built-up" and outlined a strategy for limited additional commercial development, for more housing opportunities for senior citizens and middle-income families, and for rehabilitating existing house stock.

The Westchester is one of four malls within a few blocks' walk of one another that have helped White Plains recoup some of the sharp losses in property taxes it suffered in the early part of the '90s, when companies including I.B.M., Nynex, and AT&T vacated space or won tax abatements. The million-square-foot mall, anchored by Nordstrom and Neiman Marcus and including Tiffany and F.A.O. Schwarz, has increased the city's retail market to 4 million square feet. The four malls generated $30 million in sales tax revenues for the city in 1996.

Downtown revitalization, which already includes new sidewalks, trees, and lights, has taken on a new urgency with the arrival of the new mall on the edge of the city's business district. Shops and restaurants on Mamaroneck Avenue, the city's main shopping thoroughfare, continue to suffer from mall competition and the loss of area office workers. Macy's department store, which had occupied a prime location on the avenue, has closed and moved to a nearby mall, and at the end of 1997, no new tenant had been found. A movie complex was one of the options being considered for the site. While there are a number of good ethnic restaurants downtown, including the Bengal Tiger, Reka's, España, Fujinoya, and Dawat, the city has no movie theaters. The city council is also considering a multiplex theater by the train station.

If location is everything, White Plains has it all. Halfway between the Tappan Zee Bridge and Long Island Sound, the city is a commuter's dream, with direct access to three major highways. Downtown, a public-transportation hub adjacent to the headquarters of the county's bus system includes express trains to Manhattan, just 36 minutes away by rail. Westchester County Airport is five miles away.

Most of the estimated 200,000 people who commute to White Plains daily are workers headed downtown or to corporate parks ringing the city, students enrolled at Pace University's law school or its Lubin Graduate School of Business, or shoppers.

Originally called Quarropas, or "the White Marshes," by the Siwanoy Indians, White Plains has had a rich past. On July 9, 1776, the Declaration of Independence was adopted by the New York Provincial Congress sitting in the courthouse on Broadway. Three and a half months later, a crucial battle was fought in and around the city.

The most recent notable event occurred a little more than 30 years ago. In 1964, the city launched a massive urban renewal project—now nearly complete—that has rebuilt a third of the central business district. Involving almost $100 million in federal and state grants, the effort has transformed the area, tearing down the library Andrew Carnegie financed, along with blocks of urban blight. New roads have been built and office superblocks created. Residents were moved and 712 units of subsidized housing were built elsewhere. As Renoda Hoffman, the city historian and a lifelong resident, has observed, "There are few small cities in the nation that have changed so quickly and so radically as White Plains."

Today, the central business district includes the 850,000-square-foot Galleria Mall, a modern library and police headquarters, the transportation center (known as TransCenter), an aging county courthouse, a new federal courthouse, and several parking garages. Strict zoning has allowed little more than a corner deli to operate in most residential neighborhoods, and an $11 million neighborhood revitalization program has helped preserve the quality of residential life surrounding the downtown hub.

Kenneth Wyatt grew up on Battle Hill, a fringe neighborhood where his parents still live. Mr. Wyatt, a wine importer with Schieffelin & Somerset in Manhattan, decided to move back to White Plains from Manhattan with his wife, Emmy, a human resources consultant, and their son, James Calvin Wyatt 2d, 4 years old, and their daughter, Caroline, 2, who was born in White Plains. "I feel good about having them grow up where I grew up," Mr. Wyatt said, referring to the city where he was born. "We got a really good residential value." The family now lives in a four-bedroom Colonial in the gracious Soundview neighborhood bordering Scarsdale, where, he said, "our taxes would have been double." A black man whose wife is white, Mr. Wyatt said he chose to return to a city where different races live harmoniously and, he added, "I love my commute. I can leave my house at 6:20 A.M., and I'm at my midtown desk with a bagel at 7:20."

The city needs to pay more attention to its fringe neighborhoods, Mr. Wyatt said. "The value of my real estate is tied directly to the quality of life in other neighborhoods," he said, adding that "my parents are concerned about where they live."

Single-family homes make up about a third of the more than 20,000 housing units in the city, many of them built before 1950. Four- to six-bedroom Tudors, Colonials, and Victorians can be found less than a mile from downtown, some available for under $400,000. Small three-bedroom

Cape Cods can be bought for $250,000, but they are hard to find. The median price of a single-family home in White Plains in 1997 was $285,000, up from $267,000 a year earlier. One four-bedroom home built in 1936 with 2,192 square feet of space and taxes of $5,463 was sold in mid-1997 for $304,000. A newer four-bedroom built in 1992 with 4,000 square feet sold in April of 1997 for $595,000, with taxes of $13,136.

Houses are moving briskly at several developments of recently constructed luxury housing in the south end of the city, led by Toll Brothers of Huntingdon, Pennsylvania, which has revived a number of languishing projects. At the Greens on North Street, four-bedroom Colonials start at $550,000, said Nancy D'Arcy of Houlihan/Lawrence.

Interest in the city's luxury apartment complexes has also revived after several stood partially empty for several years. At the 244-unit Westage Towers, one-bedroom condominiums start at $125,000, two-bedrooms at $235,000, and three-bedrooms at $330,000.

Both the middle school and the high school have been named Schools of Excellence, a federal designation based on the quality of curriculum, students, and teachers. Four years ago, the district was rated among the top 10 in the nation by *Expansion Management Magazine* for families involved in corporate relocation. In the last five years, about 87 percent of the graduating class at White Plains High School has gone on to higher education. Each class usually produces at least one National Merit finalist. The White Plains School District spent an average of $16,000 for each of its 6,100 students in the 1996–97 school year.

The district is participating in two significant national educational reform efforts—calling for higher student performance standards and helping younger students become more responsible. An elementary school program to encourage parent participation in the schools while ensuring racial balance has won national attention. Parents of incoming kindergarten children are invited to select from five elementary schools, each offering a distinct academic emphasis. The Parent Choice program has been so successful, said Dr. Saul Yanovsky, the superintendent, that 90 percent get their first choice, and most others get their second choice. In the 1996–97 school year, in a district that includes a 54 percent minority enrollment, 37 percent of incoming parents chose a school that was not in their neighborhood.

The city provides 200 acres of outdoor recreational space, two outdoor swimming pools, 28 tennis courts, 17 baseball and softball diamonds, and the Ebersole Skating Rink with its attached warming house. County parkland in the area includes the Bronx River Parkway Reservation, with hiking and bicycle trails, Silver Lake Park, and the 18-hole Maplemoor Golf Course.

THE NYACKS

Unusual diversity in a bedroom suburb

BY CHERYL PLATZMAN WEINSTOCK

The Rockland County community known as the Nyacks—the hilly river-front villages of South Nyack, Nyack, and Upper Nyack; the rural hamlet of West Nyack; and an area west of Nyack known as Central Nyack—is not a typical New York bedroom suburb. For tourists, the draw is Nyack itself, with a melange of about 50 antiques and crafts shops, one-of-a-kind clothing and gourmet shops, galleries, and restaurants. For the 16,000 residents, it is an interlocking jigsaw puzzle of cultures, races, religions, socioeconomic groups, and living styles, with 20 houses of worship and 30 different languages or dialects spoken by schoolchildren.

"A lot of people that gravitate to the Nyacks come from Park Slope, Brooklyn Heights, the Upper West Side, and the West Village because it has the diversity they're accustomed to and they like the urban flavor of a place where the schools are complicated," said Jo Baer, broker/owner of Baer & McIntosh Real Estate.

Rev. Richard Gressle of Grace Episcopal Church in Nyack said he had been attracted to the village because its people "think in ways that have been lost in the places I have lived.

"Like it or not, there are enough liberals left out there whose experience from the '60s and '70s is still their road map," he said. "They're out there in the community and they're determined not to fall into that quiescent numbness that seems to have gripped everyone else."

Residents live in housing as diverse as they are. Nyack and South Nyack have a mixture of less expensive, modest homes on quarter-acre lots interspersed with larger, more expensive Tudors and Victorians. Homes in Upper, Central, and West Nyack can be good buys because they are in the Town of Clarkstown, which has lower taxes than the other Nyacks, which are in the Town of Orangetown. Upper Nyack has a larger

POPULATION: Nyack, 7,104; South Nyack, 3,420; West Nyack, 3,409; Upper Nyack, 2,267.

AREA: 6.6 square miles.

MEDIAN HOUSEHOLD INCOME: Nyack, $49,702; South Nyack, $52,520; West Nyack, $94,301; Upper Nyack, $80,417.

MEDIAN PRICE OF A SINGLE-FAMILY HOUSE: Upper Nyack, $300,000; South Nyack, $256,000.

TAXES ON A MEDIAN-PRICED HOUSE: Upper Nyack, $9,464; South Nyack, $9,270.

PUBLIC SCHOOL SPENDING PER PUPIL: Nyack, $13,067; Clarkstown, $11,009.

DISTANCE FROM MIDTOWN MANHATTAN: 25 miles.

RUSH-HOUR TRAVEL TO MANHATTAN: 48 minutes on the Red and Tan bus to the Port Authority George Washington Bridge terminal, $4.35 one way, 20-trip ticket, $77.60; then 20 minutes on the A train.

CODES: Area, 914; ZIP, 10960 and 10994.

selection than elsewhere in the Nyacks of grand homes on lots of one acre or more, Ms. Baer said. The median price of a house in West Nyack, which has many 1950s development homes on one-acre lots, averaged $225,000 through the mid-1990s, mirroring the median price of a home in South Nyack, said Ms. Baer. But in the first quarter of 1998, the median price of a house in West Nyack rose to $230,000, she said, while in South Nyack, the median price rose to $256,000.

In Central Nyack, the median price of a home has remained stable for several years at $128,000, about 30 percent lower than Nyack's. Two-bedroom apartments in the three co-ops in the Nyacks, with a total of 258 units, go for $119,900 to $200,000. Prices of two- and three-bedroom condominiums at the 81-unit Clermont overlooking the river in Nyack range from $205,000 to $790,000 for the triplex penthouse. Two-bedroom prices at three other condominiums, with a total of 85 units, range from $89,000 to $220,000.

"There is a bigger demand for rentals here than the supply," Ms. Baer said. The largest rental building is the 162-unit West Shore Towers on the Nyack riverfront, where one-bedroom apartments average $1,150.

The housing market in the Nyacks was strong during the first two-thirds of the 1990s and, with few exceptions, housing prices appreciated, according to the Rockland County Multiple-Listing Service.

The median price of a home in South Nyack appreciated more than the other villages and hamlets in the Nyacks from 1990 to 1998, going to $256,000 from $154,000, according to the M.L.S. During the same period, the median price of a home in West Nyack rose to $230,000 from $205,000.

In the last part of the decade, demand has been increasing. Throughout 1997 and in early 1998, said Ms. Baer, the realtor, "there has been a dramatic increase in the demand for housing in the Nyacks, especially the high-end houses. This has caused an upsurge in prices of about 15 percent."

Among the appeals of the Nyacks is the easy commute to Manhattan—located only 25 miles away—by car or a one-hour-and-20-minute bus ride to midtown. Another major attraction is the schools.

Sally Witte, a psychologist who lives in South Nyack with her husband, Michael, a cartoonist, and their three children, said the diversity of the school population was one of its advantages. Her experience in a private girls' school in the Midwest never caused her to question her values, she said, "but in this school system, because there are so many kinds of people, you're sort of always having to question what your values are. You're put in a situation where you have to struggle a bit more, but I think you can learn from this heterogeneity." She added: "In many ways, my children's education has been more complete than mine."

Said Roberta Zampolin, superintendent of the 3,100-student Nyack School District, which serves Nyack, Central, South, and Upper Nyack, Upper Grandview, and Valley Cottage: "It's a constant struggle of how to meet all the needs of the different students, but we do a great job if you look at our statistics." The district's Math League ranked number one in the county in 1996. The academic club, Academia Nuts, won the Rockland County championship in 1996 and 1997, said Ms. Zampolin. Typically 95 percent of the high school graduates go on to higher education.

The district has three elementary schools for kindergarten through fifth grade, a middle school for sixth through eighth grade, and Nyack High School. At a time when many schools are cutting back classes in the arts, the high school offers electives in photography and media communications, including television and video production, as well as 10 advanced placement courses. Per-pupil spending in the district averaged $13,067 in the 1997–98 school year.

Students in West Nyack are served by the Clarkstown Central School District, where, said Dr. William Heebink, its superintendent, typically 95 percent of high school graduates of South High School and North High School go on to college. One recent project in the school system was a $13 million program to update its computer capabilities.

The 8,600-student district, which has 10 elementary schools and a middle school, offers an innovative language program that sends sixth graders through 10 weeks each of Japanese, French, Italian, Latin, American Sign Language, and Spanish to help them choose the language they want to specialize in when they reach seventh or eighth grade. The district's public school spending per pupil was $11,009 in 1997–98.

The restaurants that line Broadway and Main Street in Nyack

reflect the overall community's diversity. Among them are pubs, like O'Donoghue's Tavern; Italian restaurants, like Heather's Open Cucina; The King and I for Thai food; Ichi Riki for Japanese food; Southern Comfort for southern home cooking; Three Broadway and the River Club on the Hudson for fine dining; Miriam for vegetarian and light cuisine; and Strawberry Place for breakfasts with the children.

For both the young and their elders, there is the Palisades Interstate Park system just north of the Nyacks, where they can hike on Hook Mountain, bike, picnic, and swim, and the riverside Memorial Park at the end of Burd Street in Nyack, where there are two basketball and two tennis courts, a playground, a boat launch, and a baseball field. And for $5, residents can work a small plot of land in the Nyack Community Garden.

Named by Dutch settlers for the Indians that first settled there, Nyack grew as a river port through the 19th century. The village prospered from a growth in factories, quarries, and shipbuilding. But by the end of the century, prosperity slowed and the village began to decline. With the opening of the Tappan Zee Bridge, in 1955, the Nyacks became more accessible and downtown Nyack showed some signs of revival. But strip malls outside Nyack and, finally, the opening of the 800,000-square-foot Nanuet Mall in 1969 decimated the shopping district. Later, an influx of federal subsidies and innovative business people began to turn the Nyacks around.

Antiques dealers bought up vacant storefronts and Nyack gained a reputation as an antiques mecca, although one afflicted by what merchants call a severe parking shortage.

The Nyacks have been known for their interesting and often famous blend of residents, including actors and actresses, such as Ellen Burstyn and the late Helen Hayes; Jonathan Demme, who directed *Silence of the Lambs*; and Edward Hopper, the artist, who grew up here. In 1996, Rosie O'Donnell, the actress and television personality, bought the Nyack home of Ms. Hayes for $770,500. Ms. Hayes had done extensive renovations, so she called it Pretty Penny.

Another noted Nyack resident is the ghost who is believed to haunt 1 Leveta Place. The ghost was the focus of a state appellate court ruling in Manhattan in 1991 that realtors are required to disclose to prospective buyers accounts of the presence of ghosts in a house.

POMONA

Easy city access in a Ramapo setting

BY CHERYL PLATZMAN WEINSTOCK

From her 10-room Colonial with sweeping decks and a panoramic view of the Ramapo Mountains, Leslie Sanderson enjoys the simple pleasure of greeting the deer that sometimes peer into her window in the morning as the dew sets on her one-acre wooded property. "Compared to Westchester or Connecticut, this style house was a pretty good value at $419,000," said Ms. Sanderson, who with her husband, Nicholas, built their home in the Rockland County village of Pomona in 1990.

Houses in the village's developments are especially appealing because "the homes are not cookie-cutter houses," said Dorothy McNamara, a broker for Century 21 Len Carr Realty in Pomona.

The original old farmhouses, bungalows, and Revolutionary War Colonials on Old Route 202, Route 306, and Camp Hill Road were built on large lots that once drew wealthy people seeking a summer retreat to what was then an unincorporated area, even then known as Pomona. In 1967, part of the community straddling the towns of Haverstraw and Ramapo was incorporated into a village to control zoning.

Many farmers began selling off their land at the end of the '60s and the early '70s, and new subdivisions with one-acre lots for detached houses replaced the orchards that gave the community its name—Pomona was the Roman goddess of fruit. "We did a little pioneering back then," said Sam Schechter, a local developer. "We built and kept most of the trees and foliage when it wasn't fashionable."

Show business is well represented among present and former residents such as Joe Harris, who produced and managed *Sweet Charity*, *Dancing at Lughnasa*, and *Mame*. And Frederick Loewe and Alan Jay Lerner wrote *My Fair Lady* in Mr. Lerner's 1732 home. The house was previously owned by, among others, Charlie Chaplin when he was married

POPULATION: 2,600.

AREA: 2.4 square miles.

MEDIAN HOUSEHOLD INCOME: $117,083.

MEDIAN PRICE OF A SINGLE-FAMILY HOUSE: $279,000.

PUBLIC SCHOOL SPENDING PER PUPIL: $12,700.

DISTANCE FROM MIDTOWN MANHATTAN: 32 miles.

RUSH-HOUR TRAVEL TO MIDTOWN: 80 minutes on the Red and Tan bus to the Port Authority George Washington Bridge terminal, $5.20 one way, 20-trip ticket, $94.40; then 20 minutes on the A train.

CODES: Area, 914; ZIP, 10960.

to Paulette Goddard, and Burgess Meredith when he was married to Ms. Goddard.

Buff Blass, 47, a village trustee and a creative director in advertising, said she was "very, very happy" living in a community with easy access to Newark, La Guardia, and Stewart Airports over the Palisades Interstate Parkway, the Garden State Parkway, and the George Washingon and Tappan Zee Bridges; it's 32 miles from midtown Manhattan. Strip malls along Route 202 just outside the village provide diversified shopping, services, and food outlets, and the huge Nanuet Mall is just a short drive away.

For many of Pomona's 2,611 residents, whose median income is 4 percent higher than the county average, the village, with its 60 acres of parkland, is an amalgam of serenity and challenge. Most people in Pomona get involved, said Deputy Mayor Herbert Marshall, "to produce the best educational product we can in spite of budget and any political infighting that occurs."

"When we built our home we could have gone anywhere," said Ms. Sanderson, who has two children and is co-president of the Grandview Elementary School P.T.A. "I specifically wanted to stay in the East Ramapo Central School District. I know the school district—I went through it. I definitely like it because of its ethnic and cultural diversity. Here my children get a true picture of the real world."

With 9,200 students enrolled in the East Ramapo Central School District, 73 percent of the children represent 50 different nationalities. The district encompasses three towns, including part of the township of Haverstraw, and eight villages, including Spring Valley, which has a concentration of Haitian immigrants. "The only problem that this presents is that there are 500 students enrolled in English-as-a-second-language classes, which are task-intensive and expensive," said Dr. Jack R. Anderson, who retired as the district superintendent in January 1998. "But we try to mainstream students within three years."

Typically, about 88 percent of the district's high school graduates go on to higher education. Seventy percent of all students take the SATs. The average scores have steadily followed the state SAT averages. In 1997, SAT averages were 497 in verbal and 506 in math; the state averages for the same period were 495 in verbal and 502 in math.

"Both of our high schools are in the top 1 percent of all high schools in the United States in regard to the advanced placement courses we offer," Dr. Anderson said, noting that more than 100 college credits were available. But after many years of success, the East Ramapo Central School District, which has 10 elementary schools—five for kindergarten to third grade, five for fourth to sixth grade—three junior high schools, and two senior high schools, has come under fire by some.

"I think the school district does an amazing job in integrating everything," said Scott Shabot, who moved to Pomona in 1983. "But the bottom line is we'd all like it to be better. We serve a wide economic spectrum with all the problems of the urban poor. Sometimes it becomes politics in the school district and educational considerations become secondary."

Harvey Katz, a former school board member and Monsey businessman, disagreed. "We don't have politics in the school system," he said. "I am here to see to it that there is as cost-effective high-quality education in the district as possible."

While East Ramapo is one of five school districts in the state where more students are enrolled in private schools than public schools for religious reasons—9,500 students within the district, from the Orthodox Jewish communities of Kaser, New Square, and Monsey, are enrolled in private schools—the parochial school parents are nevertheless obliged to pay taxes to support public schools. Yet some public school parents see the high proportion of parochial school parents as a threat to the school system, arguing that residents who send their children to private schools are likely to have less of a commitment to public schools.

Not so, said Mr. Katz, who during his term on the school board, which ended in June 1997, was one of four Orthodox Jews who sat on the nine-member board. "Just because my children are not in the public schools doesn't mean I don't care about all the children," he said. "Children are our future, wherever they may be."

The village parks offer quiet, wooded trails, swimming, tennis courts, and fishing. Burgess Meredith Park, dedicated in 1971 and named for the actor who helped incorporate the village, offers residents 21 acres of walking paths, a playground, and a baseball field. The 16-acre Jon Van Den Hende Park has two tennis courts; the 17-acre passive Tamarack Lane Park has trails. The newest addition, the 3.6-acre Secor park, offers a stocked fishing pond. A highlight of the village is the Pomona Cultural Center, a fieldstone building that was a one-room schoolhouse in the early part of the century. Visitors can engage in, among other things, quilting contests and Japanese brush painting workshops.

Not far from the Cultural Center is Camp Hill Road, where George

Washington's soldiers encamped during the Revolution. A short distance to the west of the road is the Ladentown United Methodist Church, built in 1865, one of the oldest still-active churches in Rockland County. The only other house of worship in the village is the Pomona Jewish Center, a Conservative synagogue. A Hindu temple is on the drawing boards.

Carole Novick, proprietor of Carole Novick Realty, said the housing market, with homes in the village starting at $180,000 and going to $1 million and more, was getting stronger. Bruce Sokol, a real estate appraiser, said that home prices had been held down for several years in the '90s in the wake of the bankruptcy of the developer of a 200-lot subdivision, which had allowed construction of homes at lower prices than those paid by many original buyers. A further factor in prices in recent years, he said, has been the multiracial character of the school district, and the conflicts over school policies and spending.

However, Ms. McNamara, the broker, said that for the first quarter of 1998, the median price of a house remained stable at $279,000, the same price it was in the first quarter of 1997, instead of dipping as it traditionally has been doing over the last five years. "There are fewer lots available on the top of the mountain. Those that become available are very desirable and very valuable," she said.

As for prices in different parts of the village, Mr. Sokol said, homes in the Haverstraw section of Pomona are generally less expensive because they are taxed at lower rates. Taxes on a four-bedroom house on the market in the Ramapo section for $268,000 are $8,900. In the Haverstraw tax district, a four-bedroom home for $269,000 is taxed at $6,200.

New Jersey

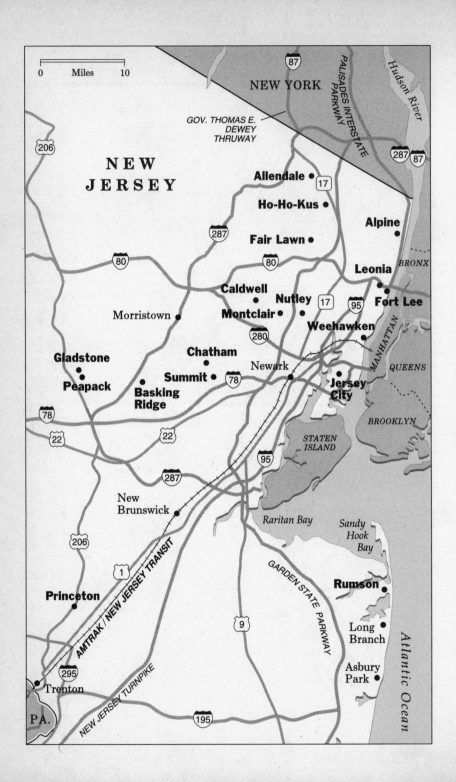

ALLENDALE

A tower symbolizes its aspirations

BY JERRY CHESLOW

A redbrick clock tower presides over an island of flowers at a key inter-section on West Allendale Avenue, the main business street in the 2.9-square-mile Bergen County borough of Allendale. The tower, which matches the new, brick-paved sidewalks of the three-block, 19th-century business district, was the finishing touch of a two-year renovation. It was paid for by private donations in honor of Allendale's former mayor, Clarence L. Shaw, the driving force behind the renovation, which was completed in 1993. "The tower gives the town that traditional feel that I love," said Joan Berndt, who moved to Allendale in 1993 from East Brunswick, New Jersey, with her husband, Bryan, and their two children. Both of the Berndts are certified public accountants.

Allendale is in the heart of heavily populated Bergen County, just 18 miles from midtown Manhattan. It has an estimated population of 6,100 and the feel of a sleepy country hamlet, with tree-lined streets and houses set far back on large, well-kept lots. Most of the houses were built after 1950, as the last but one of the large farms were subdivided into housing sites.

"We chose Allendale because its school system has a very good repu-tation, yet is small enough so that the children don't get lost in it," Mrs. Berndt explained. "We also wanted a town feel. Allendale is small enough for the store owners to get to know you quickly."

Mrs. Berndt said that despite the fact that they had moved into their four-bedroom Colonial on Franklin Turnpike during a blizzard, the neigh-bors had come over to welcome them. She has since joined the Holiday Observers Club, one of three dozen volunteer organizations. The club raises money for holiday celebrations such as an Easter egg hunt and a Fourth of July fireworks display.

POPULATION: 6,160.

AREA: 2.9 square miles.

MEDIAN HOUSEHOLD INCOME: $97,485.

MEDIAN PRICE OF A SINGLE-FAMILY HOUSE: $320,000.

TAXES ON A MEDIAN-PRICED HOUSE: $6,700.

PUBLIC SCHOOL SPENDING PER PUPIL: $8,315.

DISTANCE FROM MIDTOWN MANHATTAN: 18 miles.

RUSH-HOUR TRAVEL TO MIDTOWN: 40 minutes on the Short Line bus, $8.15 one way, $186.20 monthly; 45 minutes on the N.J. Transit train to Hoboken, $5.50 one way, $142 monthly, then 10 minutes on the PATH train, $1 one way.

CODES: Area, 201; ZIP, 07401.

Allendale celebrated its centennial with a parade in September 1994, marking the time in 1894 when it split from the surrounding Orvil Township in a dispute over where a school was to be built. The local history is summed up by a large mural painted on the outside of a building in the shadow of the new clock tower. It shows settlement, the railroad, and strawberries, the mainstay of the farmers until the tourists began arriving in the late 19th century.

The first white settlers were Dutch and English farmers who arrived in the late 1600s. Allendale went through a growth spurt that started in 1848, with the coming of the Paterson & Ramapo Railroad, which allowed farmers to send crops to markets all over New Jersey and to New York City. The station was named Allendale after the railroad's surveyor, Richard Allen. By 1900, much of what is now the downtown had sprung up around the station. And summer visitors had discovered the lakes in the area, leading to the construction of numerous boardinghouses and three hotels on West Allendale Avenue. One of those hotels, the Allendale House, still exists as a rooming house.

"Babe Ruth used to come to vacation at the Allendale Hotel," recalled Stiles Thomas, 71, who has lived his entire life in Allendale. "He was always chasing women in town, including my mother."

Housing is expensive and taxes are a high $2.27 per $100 of assessed valuation. Prices start at about $200,000 for some small three-bedroom Cape Cods and older Colonials on streets such as Mallison Street, Dale Avenue, and Park Avenue near the center of the borough. The median price of a home at the end of 1997 was $320,000, with taxes of $6,700. "It's rare to find anything decent for under $250,000," said Borough Administrator Thomas F. Carroll.

According to Richard Van Houten, a real estate broker who is a descendant of one of the town's early settlers, the typical house in the western section of the borough is a three- to four-bedroom split-level, bi-level, or Colonial on one acre. Such homes go for $325,000 to $375,000. In the San Jacinto neighborhood in the southwestern area, 30-year-old four-bedroom Colonials go for $400,000 to $450,000. A handful of large, five- or six-bedroom contemporaries on one-acre lots on Carteret Road in the southern section are valued at more than $1 million.

There are four condominium communities, the largest of which is the 45-unit Rio Vista town house complex off Allendale Avenue. Prices of the three- to four-bedroom units range from $290,000 to $340,000, according to Mr. Van Houten.

Rentals are scarce and command high prices. Two-bedroom apartments in two-family homes or over stores in the downtown rent quickly for $750 and $900. Some three-bedroom town houses rent for up to $2,000 a month.

The largest piece of borough-owned land is the Celery Farm, a 87-acre nature preserve that was once a celery, onion, and lettuce farm. At the turn of the century, it was sending vegetables to Boston, Philadelphia, New York, and the Campbell's Soup factory in Camden, New Jersey. Most of the property was bought in 1981 for $140,000. Today, it is a bird-watcher's paradise, with more than 225 species sighted in recent years, including the rare black rail, king rail, and bald eagle. "It is a rare jewel in the heart of a developed area," said Mr. Thomas, who is also the marsh warden.

The most widely used recreational site in the borough is the 70-acre Crestwood Park. Purchased in 1972 from the Van Houten family, the property includes a nine-acre artificial sand-bottomed lake, two baseball diamonds, and four tennis courts. The lake is open to residents for swimming from Memorial Day to Labor Day. In 1997, memberships cost $90 for the first adult in a family, $25 for each additional adult, and $8 per child per year.

"My father acquired the property in the 1920s to subdivide it into building lots," said Mr. Van Houten. "The Depression hit and he could only sell one lot. So he developed the lake and charged 25 cents a head admission. At one point, 10,000 people were coming to Crestwood on weekends."

The best-known commercial establishment in the borough is the Allendale Bar & Grill, opened on West Allendale Avenue in 1935. Known to locals as the AB&G, it draws a lunch crowd of corporate executives from all over Bergen County. The downtown's 50 stores include several banks, florist shops, a bagel shop, specialty stores, and one supermarket. For major shopping, residents go to malls in Paramus, a five-minute drive away.

The borough's children attend the K–3 Hillside School on Hillside Avenue and the 4–8 Brookside School on Brookside Avenue. Of the 65 K–8 school districts in Bergen County, Allendale's scored highest on the statewide Eighth-Grade Early Warning Test in 1996, with 70.8 percent of the students scoring as "clearly competent," the top rating.

"Our students come from highly motivated, involved families," explained Dr. J. Thomas Morton, the superintendent. "The parents volunteer to work in the library and as volunteer classroom aides." And, he added, "Allendale voters have never defeated a school budget."

According to Dr. Morton, computers are introduced in kindergarten and are available in each classroom and in computer laboratories in each school. By eighth grade, the students can use word processors and spreadsheets and can access information via computer. The per-pupil cost in the K–8 school system is $8,315 per year, which is about $600 more than the state average.

Allendale's students go on to Northern Highlands Regional High School, which the borough shares with neighboring Upper Saddle River and Ho-Ho-Kus. The school, on Hillside Avenue in Allendale, spends $12,127 per pupil. The superintendent, Dr. Edward D. Westervelt, noted that *New Jersey Monthly* magazine rated his school among the most cost-effective high schools in the state. Of the 68 schools noted, Northern Highlands had the seventh-highest combined SAT scores at 1134.

In 1994, the high school was rated fifth in excellence in the state by *New Jersey Monthly* magazine. In 1993, it received national recognition as a Drug-Free School by the federal Department of Education at a White House ceremony. The agency also recognized Northern Highlands in 1987 as a Blue-Ribbon High School, the highest national academic award. Typically, more than 95 percent of its graduating class go on to higher education.

The high school has several unusual features, including a planetarium, a physical fitness center, complete with exercise machines, and a cultural arts center that includes a ballet room and a fully equipped electronic music studio. "At the beginning of the year, each child is examined and given a computer printout on his or her physical condition, including body-fat percentages," said former superintendent Dr. David Garrahan. "Physical fitness goals are set for each student and when report cards are issued, each receives a computer-printed report on progress toward those goals." Dr. Garrahan said that the fitness program was part of the school's overall program to keep students drug- and alcohol-free.

"We survey our students each year to find out the major deterrents from taking drugs," he explained. "An overwhelming number of students say 'health.' So we emphasize healthy bodies, as well as healthy minds."

ALPINE

Lavish homes in a millionaires' borough

BY JERRY CHESLOW

Alpine is one of the few municipalities in New Jersey where residents do not complain about their property taxes. Because of high property values and a small number of school-age children, they pay 94 cents per $100 of assessed valuation, one of the lowest rates in the state. That is one of the reasons the 6.4-square-mile Bergen County borough has become a magnet for millionaires who build sprawling mansions on lots of two acres or more.

Other reasons cited by Mayor Lawrence M. Manus for the borough's popularity among the very rich are its excellent grade school, its location seven miles north of the George Washington Bridge, and its minuscule population density of less than 300 people per square mile, compared with a countywide density for Bergen County of 3,546.

Alpine has no apartment blocks, just one two-family house, and only three commercial establishments—a restaurant, a gas station, and a garden shop. Residents buy their groceries in supermarkets in neighboring Cresskill and Closter. The closest large shopping center is the Riverside Mall in Hackensack, five miles to the south.

Mail must be picked up from the post office, and very few of the houses have numbers, a fact that often frustrates truck drivers who search for their destinations on nearly deserted streets, passing one heavily wooded, gated compound after another.

"We value our privacy here," explained Dr. Hijung Pyun, a retired radiologist who moved to Alpine from neighboring Tenafly with his wife, Obkay. "That's the major reason we moved here, although the low tax rate was also an attraction." Like many other residents of Alpine, the Pyuns are immigrants, having emigrated from Korea. The borough is also home to numerous Iranians, Iraqis, Israelis, Chinese, and Japanese.

GAZETTEER

POPULATION: 1,908.

AREA: 6.4 square miles.

MEDIAN HOUSEHOLD INCOME: $127,727.

MEDIAN PRICE OF A SINGLE-FAMILY HOUSE: $1.2 million.

TAXES ON A MEDIAN-PRICED HOUSE: $12,000.

PUBLIC SCHOOL SPENDING PER PUPIL: $14,000.

DISTANCE FROM MIDTOWN MANHATTAN: 10 miles.

RUSH-HOUR TRAVEL TO MIDTOWN: 30 minutes on the Red and Tan bus to the Port Authority George Washington Bridge terminal, $3.20 one way, 20-trip ticket, $59.20; then 20 minutes on the A train.

CODES: Area, 201; ZIP, 07620.

Dr. Pyun's custom-built, 7,000-square-foot home in the prestigious Rio Vista neighborhood just west of Route 9W is small by the standards of Alpine, where a house of more than 20,000 square feet is currently under construction on eight acres.

Housing prices listed by the multiple-listing service start at $319,000 for a small, newly renovated three-bedroom Colonial on Main Street and climb steeply to $6.9 million for a 23-room mansion with two bowling lanes, an indoor racquetball court, a five-car garage, and an elevator.

Alpine has been ranked by *Worth* magazine as the 17th-wealthiest community in the United States. Based on real estate sales prices during 1995 and 1996, *Worth* said the median single-family home value was $795,000.

But the mayor said that those figures, and even the current M.L.S. statistics, were deceptively low. "Many of our houses are not sold through the M.L.S.," he explained. "And smaller houses on decent-size lots are often bought for a million dollars and then knocked down so that a larger home can be built on the land." A current estimate of the median price of a home in Alpine is $1.2 million; taxes on such a house would be $12,000 a year.

The rising value of properties is a double-edged sword for some long-time residents, such as the 77-year-old president of the Alpine Historical Society, Robert J. Wilson. An eighth-generation Alpine resident who says that one of his ancestors fought under Lafayette in the Revolutionary War, Mr. Wilson grew up as a fisherman in a small house near the Hudson River. He now lives in a modest 40-year-old Cape Cod on Miles Street, but is under pressure to sell. "Every week, I get letters from realtors offering to buy my house," Mr. Wilson said. "On the other hand, the low tax rate allows senior citizens to stay in their homes."

At some points, the borough has a commanding view of the Hudson River from the cliffs of the Palisades, which appear on the first European map to include the New World. That map was drawn by Gerardus Mercator in 1541 on the basis of a detailed description written by Giovanni da Verrazano, a Florentine navigator who explored the river in 1524 on behalf of France. In the early 18th century, the Alpine area was known primarily for a dock built by a Dutch settler named Frederich Kloester in 1685. It enabled local farmers to ship their produce to New York City. The dock vanished long ago, but one of Alpine's main arteries is called Closter Dock Road.

A winding access road from Route 9W and the Palisades Interstate Parkway leads to the Blackledge-Kearney House on the Hudson River, reputed to have been the site of Lord Cornwallis's landing on November 20, 1776, in an unsuccessful attempt to prevent George Washington from fleeing from Fort Lee with his troops to Valley Forge. The house, which is listed in the National Register of Historic Places, is now a museum containing Colonial-era artifacts and showing a film about the construction of the park.

Just after the Civil War, the Erie Railroad arrived in neighboring Closter, making Alpine more accessible to New York City. It was followed by the construction of several large estates atop the Palisades. Among the estate builders was Charles Nordhoff, the *New York Herald* editor who sent Henry M. Stanley to Africa in 1869 to find Dr. David Livingstone. Nordhoff's wife, Lida, is said to have given Alpine its name because the Palisades reminded her of the Swiss Alps.

The improved explosives that resulted from the Civil War, coupled with new rail transportation, made the Palisades attractive for its trap rock, which could now be blasted loose. Among the many projects that used Palisades rock were the cobbling of New York City streets and the building of the New Orleans breakwater.

In 1899, outrage among environmental groups in both New York and New Jersey over the blasting led the legislatures of the two states to pass twin bills to preserve the rock formations. Land was expropriated and the Palisades Interstate Park Commission was formed in 1900. The final traprock blast took place on Christmas Eve that year.

Large grants from philanthropists, including the Rockefeller and Harriman families, allowed the commission to spend $543,000 to purchase its first 13.5-mile-long stretch of the current 55-mile, 81,000-acre park that starts at Bear Mountain in New York and continues southward to Fort Lee in New Jersey. The park includes hiking trails, picnic grounds, fishing sites, and marinas.

The only public school in the borough is the Alpine Elementary School, covering prekindergarten through grade 8. It has 180 pupils, said the principal, Dr. Mathew R. Glowski, who noted that about a fourth of Alpine's children attended private schools. "Our biggest challenge is convincing parents that our public school is every bit as good as a $15,000-a-year private one," explained Dr. Glowski. The school introduces computers in prekindergarten and French and Spanish language classes in kindergarten. The class size is a mere 13, about half the state average, and each classroom is equipped with one to three computers. Yearly per-pupil spending is $14,000.

The students go on to Tenafly High School, in neighboring Tenafly, which typically sends over 90 percent of its graduating classes of about 230 to higher education. The school offers 10 advanced placement courses in English, mathematics, sciences, foreign languages, and history. Its students scored an average 549 in verbal and 605 in math on the SATs in 1996, which was 52 and 97 points higher, respectively, than the state averages.

The only major borough-owned recreational site is the 10-acre Alpine Swim and Tennis Club off Hillside Avenue. Family memberships cost $450 per year. The club offers a pool open from Memorial Day through Labor Day and a pair of tennis courts that are open year-round.

In 1996, a consortium of Alpine, Rockleigh, and Bergen County paid the New York Council of Boy Scouts $7 million for 134 of its 700 acres in the northern section of Alpine. The property is to be left in its natural state except for a few hiking trails that will be added. And it will continue to be used for Boy Scout camping.

One of the largest estates ever amassed in Alpine was the 200-acre Rio Vista, acquired by Manuel Riondo, a Cuban sugar baron, between 1904 and 1920. Among its outstanding features was a 100-foot-tall stone clock tower that still stands in the new Rio Vista neighborhood.

Among the best-known Alpine estates was the 145-acre summer home of John Ringling, one of the owners of the Ringling Bros. Circus. He purchased the property in 1918 for $125,000. Ringling was famous for entertaining on a grand scale, including an annual circus party, for which performers were brought in from all over New York State. The hundreds of invited guests partied long into the night, fell asleep on the extensive lawns, and awoke to party all over again.

BASKING RIDGE

A hamlet that gobbled up a town

BY JERRY CHESLOW

Despite the presence of large office complexes, including the 1.27-million-square-foot world headquarters of AT&T, Basking Ridge retains its small-town character. Nearly all of the 39 stores and offices in the three-block downtown on South Finley Avenue are converted 18th- and 19th-century houses. The redbrick sidewalk pavers skew just enough to make them seem as if they had been laid a hundred years ago. The signs on the businesses are small and understated, as if to say, "Everyone here knows us."

Indeed, many of the businesses have been in the same families for generations. "We know how just about everybody in town takes his coffee," said Barbara Brush, co-owner of Brush's Deli & Catering, which has been in her family since 1940. At breakfast time, the dozen tables are filled with diverse clients, from city maintenance workers in uniform to professionals in business suits. "Here, everyone's equal, if you make $200,000 or $10," Mrs. Brush said. "Some new people in suits have a hard time getting used to this, so we just pick on 'em until they get it. Then they become our best friends."

Present-day maps show Basking Ridge as a tiny business district in the northeast section of Bernards Township. But over two centuries, about 95 percent of the township became known as Basking Ridge and has a Basking Ridge postal address. "I speak to schoolchildren and they are amazed to hear that they live in Bernards Township and that the police who serve them are Bernards police," said June O. Kennedy, the township historian. "That's how deeply ingrained the name Basking Ridge is."

The recorded history of Basking Ridge goes back to 1717, when John Harrison, an agent of King James II, bought most of what is now Bernards Township from Chief Nowenoik of the Leni Lenape Indians for the equivalent of $50. According to Mrs. Kennedy, the first settlers were English and

POPULATION: 4,041.

AREA: 23.7 square miles.

MEDIAN HOUSEHOLD INCOME: $92,411.

MEDIAN PRICE OF A SINGLE-FAMILY HOUSE: $400,000.

TAXES ON A MEDIAN-PRICED HOUSE: $6,000.

PUBLIC SCHOOL SPENDING PER PUPIL: $8,351.

DISTANCE FROM MIDTOWN MANHATTAN: 35 miles.

RUSH-HOUR TRAVEL TO MIDTOWN: One hour on the Lakeland bus to the Port Authority midtown terminal, $6.60 one way, 10-trip ticket, $60, or on the N.J. Transit train to Penn Station, $8.60 one way, $241 monthly.

CODES: Area, 908; ZIP, 07920.

Scottish Presbyterians escaping religious persecution. The name Basking Ridge first appeared in the records of the Presbyterian church in 1732. The writer noted that wild animals from the surrounding lowlands would bask in the sunlight on the ridge. At that time, the church was a log cabin on what is now East Oak Street. The current Presbyterian church, built in 1839, is the third on the site and is listed in the National Register of Historic Places. The name Bernards Township was given to the area in 1760 by King George II to honor Sir Francis Bernard, provincial governor of New Jersey from 1758 to 1760.

The town is known for a giant, 600-year-old white oak that George Washington and the Marquis de Lafayette picnicked under in the yard of the Basking Ridge Presbyterian Church in 1779. That oak has 35 veterans of the Revolutionary War buried under its branches. In 1923, the tree was badly diseased and State Senator John Dryden organized Friends of the Oak Tree. The group raised $2,400 to clean out the disease, leaving a cavity large enough for four men to stand in. That cavity was then filled with three tons of concrete, which has helped keep the tree healthy to now.

The bottom of the residential market is represented by older two-bedroom "needs work" houses in the southern section of town. One was recently listed at $169,000. The most expensive homes go for about $1.25 million on streets such as Butternut Lane in the new Crystal Ridge neighborhood in the northern section of town.

But the majority of resales are of homes that are 25 to 30 years old. Three-bedroom ranches, bi-levels, and splits on one-acre lots near the geographic center of town sell for $275,000 to $350,000, and four- or five-bedroom 30-year-old Colonials on one-acre lots go for $375,000 to $500,000, according to Diana Boquist, mayor of Bernards Township and manager of the Coldwell Banker Schlott Realtors office on North Maple Avenue. The median price for a single-family home was $400,000 at the end of 1997, with taxes of $6,000. This reflected a 1 percent drop from the end of 1995.

"You can't touch any new single-family homes for under half a million," said Mrs. Boquist. Indeed, a number of "to be built" homes are in the multiple-listing service book at more than a million dollars.

There are 10 condominium complexes, most in the southeastern section, off Spring Valley Boulevard. According to Mrs. Boquist, units start at $90,000 for a one-bedroom in the Spring Ridge Complex and go up to about $400,000 for four-bedroom town houses with finished walk-out basements and two-car garages in the Barons, off South Maple Avenue.

Among the newer residents are Gloria and Richard Flaskegaard and their two children, Kirk, 10, and Brittany, 6, who moved into a five-bedroom, 25-year-old Colonial on an acre in 1994. Mrs. Flaskegaard is a hospital nutritionist and her husband is a marketing executive at a nearby candy company. They moved from a small home on a quarter of an acre in Pleasantville, New York. "I was raised in Iowa and found Westchester too crowded," Mrs. Flaskegaard explained. "When we looked for a home, we were concerned about the schools and transportation. We liked the fact that Interstate 287 and 78 run through the town and that there are two train stations and a bus line into New York City."

Mrs. Flaskegaard said she was impressed that 95 percent of the students in Ridge High School take the SATs and that the school average SAT scores are high. She also liked the relatively small size of the schools.

The largest town-owned park is the 111-acre Pleasant Valley Park off Valley Road. It has one baseball and two softball fields, five soccer fields, six tennis courts, four paddle-ball courts, and an amphitheater where plays are performed in the summer. Next to the park is the municipal Pleasant Valley Pool, consisting of a 50-meter Z-shaped Olympic-size pool, a kiddie pool, and play areas. Family memberships cost $285 per season, after a onetime initiation fee of $375.

In addition to the business district, there is the Lyons Mall shopping center in the geographic center of town, which has a supermarket and about a dozen small stores. The closest mall for serious shopping is Bridgewater Commons, seven miles to the south. The best-known restaurant is the Store on South Finley Avenue in a structure built in 1871 as the Washington House hotel.

The Bernards Township School District serves a total of 2,750 pupils in five schools—two covering K–2, one for grades 3–5, a middle school for grades 6–8, and Ridge High School. In 1997, it budgeted $8,351 per pupil, which reflected a savings over the $8,700 spent per pupil in 1995.

Graduating classes number between 160 and 180 per year, with 95 percent traditionally taking the SATs. In 1996, their mean scores were 552 in verbal and 572 in math—each of which is about 70 points above the national average—and reflect a rise of at least 20 points over the scores of the previous class. The high school offers 28 advanced placement courses, which School Superintendent Dalin K. Showalter says is comparable to offerings at schools with twice the student body of about 700. More than 90 percent of the graduates traditionally go on to higher education. In 1986, Ridge High was one of five high schools in New Jersey to receive the federal Department of Education's School Recognition Award for Outstanding Progress Toward Excellence in Education. In 1997, said Mr. Showalter, "we ran a comparison of our current scores on standardized tests with those of 1986–87, and they were comparable to those when we were recognized nationally."

Residents complain mainly about traffic. With Interstate 78 in the southern section and Interstate 287 to the north, the town is noisy during rush hours. When either of those highways is congested, motorists heading for New York City often cut through town to the other one. The traffic is exacerbated by the presence of the town's only major heavy industry, the Millington Quarry on Stonehouse Road. "People complain about the blasting and about the 700 to 800 trucks a day that go in and out of the quarry with bluestone for the production of asphalt," said Township Administrator H. Steven Wood.

Among the measures being taken to reduce congestion are a widening of Interstate 287, scheduled to be completed in 1998, and the installation of speed bumps on some of the through streets in the center of town. Mayor Boquist said that the town is also exploring the idea of making some of the roads leading to and from the quarry one way. Despite those changes, traffic continues to be a problem, especially because several housing developments are being expanded, bringing more cars into the township.

The municipal building on Collyer Lane, a sprawling, brick Tudor mansion, surrounded by a stone wall, reflects an old-world grandeur with French pocket doors, maple and mahogany paneling, and marble fireplaces. Built in 1912, the house, on 28 acres, was sold to the township by John Jacob Astor VII in 1968 for $140,000.

Behind the municipal complex on South Maple Avenue is the 900-acre county-owned Lord Stirling Park, which includes riding stables where lessons are offered, and the Somerset County Environmental Education Center, which runs educational programs for children, adults, and school groups on the flora and fauna of the Great Swamp along the Passaic River. The park makes up the bulk of the estate of William Alexander, one of George Washington's commanders, who was known locally as Lord Stirling, even though he never officially received the title from the Crown.

CALDWELL

*A "real town" works to
keep its downtown viable*

BY JERRY CHESLOW

Mayor Paul G. Jemas of Caldwell is delighted that a new, beautifully land-scaped Dunkin' Donuts franchise has opened on Bloomfield Avenue to re-place a neglected one that closed in 1996 at the same location. To the mayor, the franchise had become the front line in his battle to keep the quarter-mile-long downtown viable. He considered the boarded-up pink building particularly important because it is right across the street from the 1832 house where President Grover Cleveland was born.

"We are trying to demonstrate to businesses that they can grow and prosper in this town," he explained.

Caldwell's Bloomfield Avenue is similar to many other 19th-century business districts that are struggling to survive while regional malls, super-markets, and large hardware chains grab their customers. There are about a dozen vacant stores, the aging sidewalks are cracking, and many of the facades are hidden behind countless coats of paint and patchwork signs.

Yet Bloomfield Avenue still supports a full-service hardware store, a variety store, 13 banks, bagel stores, clothing shops, hair salons, a travel agency, and shoe-repair stores. There are about half a dozen restaurants, including the Rainbow, an inexpensive diner that serves as a hangout for politicians, police officers, and lawyers.

Mayor Jemas said the 1.2-square-mile borough, 25 miles west of Man-hattan, was investing $300,000 to $400,000 in improvements to the down-town in a three-year program that began in 1996. "We are also working with local banks to enable property owners to get low-cost funding for im-proving their facades," he said.

The borough gets its name from Rev. James Caldwell, who was nick-named the "Fighting Parson of the Revolution" during the Battle of Spring-field on June 23, 1780. When Continental soldiers lacked paper wadding to

POPULATION: 7,697.

AREA: 1.2 square miles.

MEDIAN HOUSEHOLD INCOME: $59,451.

MEDIAN PRICE OF A SINGLE-FAMILY HOUSE: $202,648.

TAXES ON A MEDIAN-PRICED HOUSE: $5,050.

PUBLIC SCHOOL SPENDING PER PUPIL: $9,293.

DISTANCE FROM MIDTOWN MANHATTAN: 25 miles.

RUSH-HOUR TRAVEL TO MIDTOWN: 45 minutes on the DeCamp bus to the Port Authority Midtown terminal, $4.75 one way, 30-trip ticket, $133.95.

CODES: Area, 973; ZIP, 07006.

hold the powder in their muskets, he ran up and down the lines, tearing pages out of a book of hymns, shouting, "Give 'em Watts, boys"—a reference to Isaac Watts, the prolific composer of hymns. The Reverend James Caldwell was also instrumental in the establishment of the First Presbyterian Church, built in 1782 on what is now Bloomfield Avenue. The current building was constructed in 1875, following a fire in a previous structure.

The most expensive section of the borough is the Cedars, in the southwestern area, bordering Essex County's Grover Cleveland Park. Most of the lots along the winding streets are tree-lined, nearly all of the houses were custom-built in the '20s and '30s, and there are no sidewalks. Many were built as summer dwellings for New York City businessmen, including George Morgan, brother of the banker J. P. Morgan.

In 1996, a restored 1875 Victorian on an acre on Knollwood Terrace in the Cedars section went for $585,000. According to Thomas J. Gartland, broker-owner of Gartland Realtors, this was one of the highest prices ever paid for a home in the borough. Mr. Gartland said that most houses in the Cedars go for between $215,000 for some small two-bedroom homes on quarter-acre lots and $390,000 for some renovated four- or five-bedroom homes on half-acre lots.

The closer to Bloomfield Avenue, the more tightly packed the houses are and the lower the values. Near the center of the borough, 1920s two-bedroom bungalows can go for as little as $125,000. Three-bedroom Colonials in the same section fetch $145,000 to $180,000, depending on condition.

According to Mr. Gartland, at the end of 1997, the median price of a single-family home in the borough was $202,648. Taxes on such a home were $5,050.

There are about 300 condominium units in seven complexes. The largest is the 108-unit Parkside Gardens, a converted garden-apartment complex on Roseland Avenue. One-bedrooms go for $75,000 to $80,000, two-bedrooms for $105,000 to $110,000. Apartments in the 40-unit Fells

Manor, which straddles the border with Essex Fells, have 2,300 to 2,400 square feet of space, two-gar garages, decks, and fireplaces. The two- and three-bedroom units sell for $285,000 to $310,000.

Nearly all of the rental apartments are in four high-rise buildings and three garden-apartment complexes on or near Bloomfield Avenue. The largest building is 519 Parkside Avenue, which has 156 units renting for $690 for the smallest one-bedroom to $1,350 for the most expensive two-bedroom.

Among the newer residents of Caldwell are Nanci J. Whitman, her husband, Mark O. Whitman, and their two children, Courtney, 8, and Dylan, 5. Mr. Whitman is a freelance television cameraman who works mainly in Manhattan, a 45-minute bus ride away. Mrs. Whitman is a home-maker. Like many other young residents, Mrs. Whitman grew up in Cald-well, moved away, and then returned, buying a 125-year-old Victorian on an acre of land in 1993. "I love this place because it's a real town," said Mrs. Whitman. "You walk down to Bloomfield Avenue and people know you. In the variety store, they say, 'Good morning, Mrs. Whitman. How are you today?' and they mean it."

Mrs. Whitman walks her children to the 237-pupil Lincoln School, the smallest of the four elementary schools in the Caldwell–West Caldwell School District. "It's small enough for all of the teachers to get to know the parents quickly," she said.

Caldwell, which has a population of 7,800, is within 10 miles of three major malls, Willowbrook, Livingston, and Short Hills. John Collins, who sold his downtown drugstore to a chain after 40 years, said that the down-town must become much more service-oriented, rather than trying to com-pete with superstores and malls. "Recently a dry cleaner moved in and is doing extremely well," he said. "You have to fill the niche that saves peo-ple time."

Mayor Jemas said his administration had reduced municipal real es-tate taxes, mainly through staff reductions, a salary freeze, and a restruc-turing of its employee-benefits package. Despite this, the overall local tax rate actually rose in recent years due to increases in county and school taxes.

Rather than cut services, Caldwell has been combining programs with those of neighboring Essex Fells, West Caldwell, North Caldwell, and Roseland. Together, they make up a region known as West Essex. Among the services Caldwell now shares with one or more municipalities are its recreation program, schools, libraries, a senior citizens center, and a po-lice dispatch service.

Caldwell has seven houses of worship. The oldest congregation is the First Presbyterian Church, established in 1779. Grover Cleveland, who served as the 22d and 24th president, was born in the church manse in

1837, when his father, Rev. Richard E. Cleveland, was the pastor. That house, at 207 Bloomfield Avenue, was built in 1832 and is a national historic site and a museum. Among its artifacts are the president's crib, a dried slice of his wedding cake, and furniture from his White House years. The building is generally open Wednesday through Saturday. Visitors should call (973) 226-1810 for hours.

The most widely used recreational facility is the 5.5-acre Kiwanis Oval behind the municipal building on Provost Square. It has a multipurpose lighted field, a basketball court, a playground, and two platform tennis courts. The largest park is the 18-acre Grover Cleveland Park, off Brookside Terrace. It has bicycle and jogging trails, a pond stocked for fishing in the spring and used for ice-skating in winter, a softball diamond, and four tennis courts.

The Caldwell–West Caldwell School District has about 2,200 students, 30 percent of whom live in Caldwell. School expenditure per pupil in 1997 was $9,293, about $450 above the state average. The district has four kindergarten-to-grade 5 elementary schools, the Grover Cleveland Middle School, and the James Caldwell High School. From 1995–97, the high school graduating classes have averaged about 160 students, 90 percent of whom went on to higher education. On the SATs, the high school seniors typically score about 550 in the mathematics section and 527 in the verbal portion, both of which are about 50 points above the state average. On the Eighth-Grade Early Warning Test, about 95 percent of the students at Grover Cleveland Middle School score "competent" in math, reading, and writing, or 15 points above the state average.

According to Superintendent of Schools Daniel A. Gerardi, the school system has built seven new science labs throughout the district. Science courses through grade 6 are taught mainly in the labs, without textbooks, to make science more enjoyable. Laboratory work represents a greater portion of the class time in the higher grades. The schools have 300 computers, including those in kindergarten. More computer systems will be added and they will be networked together and into the libraries at the various schools to make research materials more accessible, Dr. Gerardi said.

Caldwell is also home to the four-year Caldwell College, a 1,700-student co-ed Roman Catholic institution that has an optional external degree program in which students submit much of their work by phone, fax, or e-mail. The college shares a 60-acre campus with the Mount St. Dominic Academy, a high school for girls.

CHATHAM

Rich past, bustling but homey present

BY JERRY CHESLOW

First settled in the 1720s along the Indian Minisink Trail, where the Leni Lenapes forded the Passaic River, the 2.3-square-mile Morris County Borough of Chatham thrives in its rich past. Main Street, which follows that trail, still has black cast-iron fire hydrants with the date 1889 in raised numbers. Businesses—including banks, boutiques, hardware stores, beauty salons, video shops, and one supermarket—are all small enough to blend in with the town's turn-of-the-century look. Many of those establishments are housed in 19th-century structures. Cafe Beethoven, for instance, at the corner of Main Street and Fairmount Avenue, has a sign telling passersby that the building was put up in 1887 and restored in 1982.

"We are still in some ways an old white-picket-fence community," said Mayor Barbara H. Hall. "And we are trying to take that old-fashioned neighborliness into the 21st century."

"It's a place where many people live their entire lives," said the borough historian, Margaret C. Keisler, who was born in Chatham 83 years ago. Mrs. Keisler remembers sledding down the steep streets that wind among the Watchung Hills. In those days, she says, not only did local residents not lock their doors, but many didn't even own keys to their houses.

There was little traffic in Chatham then. Today, Main Street, which is also State Route 24, is jammed at rush hours as commuters from neighboring municipalities head toward their jobs or homes. But each summer, Main Street recaptures its past with an old-fashioned Fourth of July parade, sponsored by the local volunteer fire department.

While the housing stock ranges from pre-Revolutionary farmhouses to 1950s Cape Cods, Chatham is known for its many Victorians on winding roads lined with oaks, maples, and dogwoods. Some of the largest and

POPULATION: 7,986.

AREA: 2.3 square miles.

MEDIAN HOUSEHOLD INCOME: $84,380.

MEDIAN PRICE OF A SINGLE-FAMILY HOUSE: $320,000.

TAXES ON A MEDIAN-PRICED HOUSE: $5,000.

PUBLIC SCHOOL SPENDING PER PUPIL: $10,035.

DISTANCE FROM MIDTOWN MANHATTAN: 31 miles.

RUSH-HOUR TRAVEL TO MIDTOWN: 50 minutes on the N.J. Transit train to Penn Station, $6.10 one way, $171 monthly; one hour on the Lakeland bus to the Port Authority midtown terminal, $5.90 one way, 10-trip ticket, $53.50.

CODES: Area, 973; ZIP, 07928.

most desirable homes are on Fairmount Avenue, where four- and five-bedroom Victorians can sell for $850,000 and a six-bedroom center-hall Colonial with a pool went for $1 million four years ago, according to Rosemary A. Pucci, a broker with Burgdorff Realty on Main Street. At the other end of the price spectrum was a two-bedroom Cape Cod on Ellers Road, which went for $200,000. According to Mrs. Pucci, young professional couples have begun buying run-down Victorians and restoring them. Prices vary with the condition of the houses. Mrs. Pucci said the bulk of the homes in the borough were 50- to 70-year-old Colonials.

Chatham has about 400 rental apartments in a dozen buildings, mostly on Main Street. Rents for two-bedrooms range from $1,000 to $1,200.

There is one condominium conversion—the 49-unit Chatham Court garden-apartment complex on Main Street near the train station. One-bedroom units range from about $95,000 to $120,000, with two-bedroom apartments selling for about $30,000 more.

European settlement in Chatham began in the early 18th century. Among the first settlers was John Day, a farmer who owned the land near the old Indian ford and built a bridge over the river. By 1750, a village known as John Day's Bridge had sprouted, including cottages, a blacksmith's shop, and flour, grist, and lumber mills. Two houses, now privately owned, survive from that time—the Paul Day House, at 24 Kings Road, and the Daniel Bonnel House, at 34 Watchung Avenue. Another early settler was Israel Ward, great-grandfather of Montgomery Ward, the department store founder, who was born in Chatham in 1843. In 1773, the village and its surrounding farmland was renamed Chatham Township to honor William Pitt, the earl of Chatham, an outspoken advocate of the rights of the colonists in America. In the Revolutionary War, Chatham was the site of four skirmishes, as residents and the rebel army held off British advances on Washington's supplies at Morristown.

The coming of the Essex & Morristown Railroad in the late 1830s led to a growth spurt in Chatham's population. By 1843, there were two trains a day from the borough to New York City. The 1860 census showed that Chatham Township had a population of 2,960. In 1892, Chatham Village found itself at odds with the rest of the township. Although village residents paid 40 percent of the township taxes, they got only 7 percent of the receipts in services. The village had to raise its own money to install kerosene street lamps, and its roads were in poor repair. As a result, the village voted on August 9, 1892, to secede from the township. Five years later, it became a borough.

Many residents still complain about their taxes, especially because they do not cover the cost of garbage collection. The borough has a contract with a private hauler, whose fee is the price of his yellow refuse bags sold at the local supermarket.

By the turn of the century, Chatham Borough, with its easy commute to Manhattan and access to the Passaic River, had become a bustling summer resort with hotels and vacation homes. Manhattan families often stayed in rented houses while the man of the house commuted by train to work in the city. Many of the summer people eventually built homes in the borough.

The easy commute to Manhattan remains a key attraction for newcomers to Chatham. Among them are Janice L. Brooks and her husband, Leonard, an investment banker. They moved from Baltimore in 1995 into a 90-year-old four-bedroom Colonial on Red Road, around the corner from the N.J. Transit train station. "I didn't even realize small towns like this existed anymore," said Mrs. Brooks. "We looked in the area and liked Chatham because it was smaller than some of the neighboring towns."

Mrs. Brooks is president of the 165-family Welcome Wagon Club of Chatham Borough, also known as the Newcomers Club. She says that's her way of paying back the kindness of neighbors. "When the truck was moving our furniture in, two neighbors came over with plates of brownies," she said. "Others introduced their children to our two girls." Their daughters are now 5 and 2½ years old.

Among the attractions for the Brooks family was the highly rated school district that Chatham Borough shares with Chatham Township. In 1997, the School District of the Chathams had a total of 2,280 students in three elementary schools, Chatham Middle School, and Chatham High School. It spent $10,035 per pupil annually. According to Dr. Carol R. Conger, the superintendent of schools, the schools are overcrowded and enrollment is growing. In 1997 alone, it was up by 200 students. Although nine new elementary school classrooms were built two years ago, Dr. Conger says more will be needed.

Computers are introduced in the first grade and are available through the eighth grade. According to Dr. Conger, the school system is now upgrading its technology, with emphasis on the computer as a learning tool. As part of its upgrading, it will join the Morris County Community College Interactive Television Network, which links many of the county's school districts. Dr. Conger hopes to use the network to broaden its electives by sharing some courses with other school districts.

The high school, which typically sends between 90 percent and 95 percent of its graduates to higher education, offers advanced placement courses in history, the sciences, computers, English, and foreign languages. On the 1997 SATs, its students had combined mathematics and verbal scores of 1135, which is about 150 points above the state average.

Mrs. Brooks says that she likes to walk on Main Street and to patronize the local merchants to help preserve the downtown, which has a mix of restaurants on Main Street, including the Bean Curd and Chatham Wok (Chinese), Villa Ristorante (Italian), and Town Square (French). For serious shopping, there is the huge, upscale Mall at Short Hills, which abuts the borough's west side.

The largest patch of green in the borough is a conservation area of forests and wetlands in the northerly sector, where development is prohibited. The largest recreation area is the 14-acre Sheppard Kolleck Park at the end of Main Street, near the current bridge over the Passaic River. Named for the publisher of a Revolutionary War Colonial newspaper, the park has two baseball diamonds, an exercise area, climbing equipment for children, a boat launch, and a trail along the river.

The 72,000-volume Library of the Chathams is in the eight-acre Memorial Park, which has a four-foot-deep swimming pool, a kiddie pool, and a baseball diamond, and is off Main Street in the center of the borough. Dedicated to veterans of all United States wars, the park was cleared and planted by local residents in 1924. "All of the men came out with their picks and shovels," Mrs. Keisler related. "And the women made them clam chowder."

FAIR LAWN

A suburb with some surprises

BY JERRY CHESLOW

Wedged between the Passaic and Saddle Rivers, the 5.4-square-mile Borough of Fair Lawn, 16 miles from midtown Manhattan, is a tightly packed bedroom community of small, well-maintained, sturdy houses. Although 80 percent of its population of approximately 31,000 work outside the borough, residents speak of a feeling of community that caters to individual needs.

Fair Lawn is not flashy. Its most expensive houses are the same type of four-bedroom, 2½-bath Colonials that were built all over northern and central New Jersey 20 to 30 years ago. According to Lewis Sprechman, a broker at Nat Sprechman Realty on Fair Lawn Avenue and a former mayor, homes on the east side of the borough sell for $350,000 to $400,000. The most prevalent house is the expanded three- or four-bedroom Cape Cod, built in the early 1950s for returning servicemen. Such homes sell for $200,000 to $275,000, according to Mr. Sprechman. Some smaller, two-bedroom Capes or three-bedroom ranches can still be had for $150,000 to $170,000.

Houses in the Radburn Historic District, a community planned in 1928, sell for $150,000 for some two-bedroom row houses and up to $400,000 for some four-bedroom detached houses. The median price of a single-family home at the end of 1997 was $189,000, with taxes of $4,600.

Most of the 92 apartments in the four-story Eldorado Village Building in Radburn are rented to Russian Jewish immigrants, who have settled in the borough in large numbers over the last decade.

All Radburn property owners pay common charges based on assessed valuation. The money is used for the maintenance of common areas, including lawns, two swimming pools, four tennis courts, a tot lot, and the

POPULATION: 30,986.

AREA: 5.4 square miles.

MEDIAN HOUSEHOLD INCOME: $67,213.

MEDIAN PRICE OF A SINGLE-FAMILY HOUSE: $189,000.

TAXES ON A MEDIAN-PRICED HOUSE: $4,600.

PUBLIC SCHOOL SPENDING PER PUPIL: $8,690.

DISTANCE FROM MIDTOWN MANHATTAN: 16 miles.

RUSH-HOUR TRAVEL TO MIDTOWN: 45 minutes on the N.J. Transit bus to the Port Authority midtown terminal, $3.25 one way, $92 monthly; 40 minutes on the N.J. Transit train to Hoboken, $3.60 one way, $101 monthly, then 10 minutes on the PATH train, $1 one way.

CODES: Area, 201; ZIP, 07410.

Grange Hall, a former meeting hall for the area's farmers that has been converted to a clubhouse.

Mr. Sprechman said one-bedroom apartments in the borough rented for $800 to $875. Two-bedroom units go for $950 to $1,400. In addition to those in Eldorado Village, there are about 1,300 other apartments, 900 of which are in five garden-apartment groupings, with the remainder in two- to four-family dwellings.

The borough has about 500 condominium units in nine buildings and complexes. The largest is Blue Hill Condos, a 158-unit converted garden-apartment development off Route 4. One-bedroom units go for $80,000 to $100,000 and two-bedroom apartments fetch an additional $20,000.

Among the newer residents in Fair Lawn are Daniel B. and Judith A. Flax and their two daughters, Shoshana and Leora. In 1994, the Flaxes bought a 3½-bedroom expanded Cape on Plaza Road North and moved down from Albany, so that Mr. Flax could take a job as executive director of the Jewish Federation of North Jersey, based in Wayne. Mrs. Flax is a medical technologist, who took a job in a bookstore when the family moved to Fair Lawn. "We chose Fair Lawn because it is safe and has a large Jewish population and an Orthodox synagogue within walking distance of our home," Mr. Flax said.

Fair Lawn has been a magnet for Jews from all over the United States as well as Jewish immigrants from Israel and the former Soviet Union. Although no one has counted the number of Jewish residents, municipal officials estimate that they make up 33 percent to 40 percent of the population. Of the 21 houses of worship, eight are synagogues. To cater to the Jewish community, the borough and the synagogues have jointly strung wire between telephone poles to surround nearly all of the borough to create what in Hebrew is known as an *eruv*, an enclosure in which Orthodox Jews are allowed to use baby carriages and carry objects like keys, canes, and eyeglasses on the Sabbath. There are also a number of small kosher eating places and even a kosher Chinese take-out.

The borough has four shopping streets—River Road, Maple Avenue, Fair Lawn Avenue, and Broadway, which is part of Route 4. Each of the four has one shopping center with a supermarket and about two dozen additional stores. Much of the rest of the shopping is in strip malls and rather disjointed areas along the four streets. According to Bertrand N. Kendall, the borough manager, merchants complain of a lack of parking for their customers and, especially on Broadway, heavy through-traffic that obstructs their business. He said the borough was working on plans to alleviate the parking problems.

The heaviest traffic is along Route 208, which bisects the borough diagonally. Although only four lanes wide, it handles heavy traffic to Manhattan from Morris and Bergen Counties. Often when there are traffic snarls, motorists cut through backroads in Fair Lawn, creating traffic problems throughout the borough. The Garden State Parkway, Interstate 80, and Route 17 are all nearby, giving Fair Lawn easy access to New York City and other points in the state. The borough is also bordered by Paramus, which has some of the largest shopping malls in New Jersey.

The restaurant scene is not fancy. There are about two dozen pizzerias, including a kosher establishment, and four diners. Among the more elaborate restaurants are the Golden Tree (Chinese), Rivara's Grill House (American), and Piccola Calabria (Italian), all on Maple Avenue.

The largest taxpayer in the borough is Nabisco Foods, which has a cookie factory off Route 208 on the northeastern side of town. "You can always tell by the smell whether it is an Oreo or a Lorna Doone day," Mr. Kendall said.

There are a total of 16 public parks, the largest of which is the 30-acre Memorial Park off Berdan Avenue and First Street, which has a pool, two baseball diamonds, two tennis courts, two street-hockey courts, and a trailer that is used as a band shell for free concerts on Sunday nights in the summer.

The Fair Lawn Public School District has has about 4,100 students and spent $8,690 per student in 1997. There are six K–5 elementary schools, the largest of which is the 383-student Warren Point School on Broadway. The 609-student Memorial Middle School on Berdan Avenue serves the west side, and the 337-student Thomas Jefferson Middle School on Morlot Avenue serves the east side. The 1,289-student Fair Lawn High School, serving grades 9–12, is a winner of a National School of Excellence Award (1990–91).

According to Dr. Robert J. Byrne, the superintendent of schools, the schools stress technology education, with computers introduced in kindergarten. The district is a member of the Interactive Television Network of Bergen County, through which 20 school districts share some instructional and teacher-training programs. "Among the classes we share with other schools are filmmaking, government, and Russian," Dr. Byrne said.

The Fair Lawn schools also emphasize science instruction and offer a wide range of advanced placement courses, which allow students to earn college credits while in high school. Among those courses are English literature, American history, calculus, computer science, and biology. Of the senior classes, which average about 300 students, a third generally take advanced classes, according to Dr. Byrne.

The students also score well above grade level on national achievement tests. For instance, a recent fifth grade scored on an eighth-grade level on the California Achievement Test of Basic Skills, a test mandated by the New Jersey Department of Education. On the SATs, the 1997 senior class averaged 517 in verbal and 542 in mathematics, both of which are considerably higher than the state average and reflect a trend of rising scores over the previous two years. Fair Lawn High School typically sends about 70 percent of its graduating class to higher education.

The borough also has one Roman Catholic parochial school, the K–8 St. Anne School on Summit Avenue.

The borough's Radburn section, which is in both the National and the New Jersey Register of Historic Places, is recognized as one of the first modern planned communities in the United States. It was planned in 1928 by architects Clarence S. Stein and Harry Wright, who bought two square miles to construct what they called a "Town for the Motor Age." They had hoped to build a ring of attached row houses and apartments for 25,000 people, surrounding 23 acres of common space and parks. Only about 600 redbrick homes, all of which survive, and a Dutch Colonial Revival brownstone train station on Fair Lawn Avenue were built before two-thirds of the original land was sold off to other developers. "The Great Depression forced the project into bankruptcy in 1933," explained Jane Lyle Diepeveen, the borough historian.

FORT LEE

Atop the Palisades, "Manhattan West"

BY JERRY CHESLOW

In the 65 years since the bridge opened for traffic, it has shaped Fort Lee into more of an extension of Manhattan than its suburb. Arguably New Jersey's most strategically situated municipality, the 2.5-square-mile borough sits at the western ramp of the George Washington Bridge where Routes 46, 1, 9, and 9W, Interstates 80 and 95, and the Palisades Interstate Parkway converge to funnel 100 million vehicles into and out of Manhattan each year. It is 20 miles from both Newark International and La Guardia Airports and but a short drive to Yankee Stadium and the Meadowlands Sports Complex. The rush-hour bus ride to the Port Authority Bus Terminal in midtown Manhattan via N.J. Transit takes roughly half an hour.

The bridge has provided fodder for despair over taxes for three generations. "One-quarter of Fort Lee is taken up by the George Washington Bridge and other Port Authority land and they don't pay us a cent, because they are tax exempt," lamented Mayor Jack Alter. "The bridge translates into revenues of $139 million a year for the Port Authority. We have double the police force a town our size should have, just to deal with the bridge traffic. Why should our citizens have to pay for it?" The borough is negotiating with the Port Authority of New York and New Jersey on possible payment of a portion of the expenses associated with the bridge, according to Mayor Alter, who estimates that it costs the borough about $5 million a year.

Of the 15,300 dwelling units in this multiethnic borough, where about 40 percent of the population is Asian, 6,407 are in 18 co-ops, 3,376 are in 75 condominiums, and the rest are in single-family houses, rental apartment buildings, and a sprinkling of two-family houses. "We probably have more co-ops than any other municipality in New Jersey," said Randy L. Ketive, owner/broker and president of Oppler/Ketive Realtors in Fort Lee.

POPULATION: 33,911.

MEDIAN HOUSEHOLD INCOME: $64,563.

AREA: 2.5 square miles.

MEDIAN PRICE OF A SINGLE-FAMILY HOUSE: $240,000.

TAXES ON A MEDIAN-PRICED HOUSE: $5,856.

MEDIAN PRICE OF A TWO-BEDROOM CONDO: $225,000.

PUBLIC SCHOOL SPENDING PER PUPIL: $8,500.

DISTANCE FROM MIDTOWN MANHATTAN: 6 miles.

RUSH-HOUR TRAVEL TO MIDTOWN: 30 minutes on the N.J. Transit bus to the Port Authority midtown terminal, $2.55 one way, $82 monthly, or 7 minutes to the Port Authority George Washington Bridge terminal, $1.90 one way, $59 monthly, then 20 minutes on the A train.

CODES: Area, 201; ZIP, 07024.

Like many of the people moving into Fort Lee, Jay Greenstone, a Hackensack lawyer, and his wife, Myra, are empty-nesters. The Greenstones moved from their single-family house in nearby Teaneck to a two-bedroom co-op in one of the most prestigious buildings in Fort Lee, the Plaza, in 1991, after their four children had grown and left home. "Myra and I were rattling around by ourselves in a big house," said Mr. Greenstone. "We liked the easy access from Fort Lee to New York City and other parts of New Jersey. The theater district is just 20 minutes away by car. The Plaza is like hotel living. It has a doorman, a health club, and a swimming pool."

The largest co-op complex is the 1,266-unit Horizon House on Horizon Road overlooking the Hudson. According to Stanley Feldman, president of Sword Realty, prices at the end of 1997 ranged from $35,000 for the smallest studio apartments to $160,000 for some large two-bedroom units.

At the lower end of the co-op market is the 1,170-unit Linwood Park Co-ops off Edwin Avenue in the northwestern section, where prices ranged from $12,000 for the least-expensive studios to $55,000 for some two-bedroom units. In the 173-unit Plaza, where Mr. and Mrs. Greenstone reside, two-bedroom units start at about $360,000 and three-bedrooms go for up to about $700,000.

Maintenance charges in co-ops vary according to size, view, and floor. In Horizon House, charges range from $550 for the smallest studio to $3,850 for a four-bedroom penthouse. Linwood Park charges range from $208 for a small studio to $800 for some three-bedrooms; at the Plaza, the charges range from $1,080 for the smallest one-bedroom to $6,119 for a five-bedroom penthouse.

Single-family house prices start at about $165,000 for some smaller two-bedroom houses in the older, less fashionable, northern section of town, known as Coytesville, or near the George Washington Bridge. The most expensive section is the eastern Palisades area overlooking the river, where larger custom homes or restored Victorians sometimes sell for several million dollars. The median price of a single-family home in late 1997 was $240,000; property taxes on such a home were $5,856.

Most of the middle-market single-family homes—1950s brick ranches and split-levels in the center of the borough—were selling in late 1997 for $275,000 to $400,000, depending on location, condition, and improvements.

Among the condominium apartment buildings, the most expensive are four buildings along Palisade Avenue, overlooking the river. They are the 193-unit Buckingham Towers, the 183-unit Royal Buckingham, the 239-unit River Ridge, and the 270-unit Atrium Palace. Atrium units ranged from $280,000 for some one-bedrooms to more than $1.15 million for some three-bedroom, three-bath units. In the Buckingham buildings, recent sales ranged from $185,000 for a one-bedroom unit to $830,000 for a three-bedroom.

Also off Palisade Avenue is the gated Kensington Park community of condominium town houses, where prices for three- to four-bedroom units range from $500,000 to $600,000.

"Co-op prices have been rising because building associations have become more flexible on their policy toward allowing owners to rent their apartments out," explained Mr. Feldman. "So they are not forced to sell at low, sacrifice prices if they want to move and can't find a buyer at the right price."

Fort Lee owes its name to a Revolutionary War visitor. The Palisades were used by General Washington in 1776 to harass the British during the blockade of New York. The Continentals sank hulks in a line across the river from Fort Constitution on the Palisades to Fort Washington in what is now Washington Heights in a futile effort to thwart British passage. In October 1776, when Maj. Gen. Charles Lee visited Fort Constitution, its name was changed to Fort Lee. On November 16, 1776, the British captured Fort Washington and crossed the river, forcing Washington to abandon Fort Lee.

Today, the 27-acre Historic Park occupies much of the fort's onetime site. Part of the Palisades Interstate Park system, it includes a visitors' center, a replica of a Continental gun battery, and a museum with Revolutionary War relics and a diorama.

Fort Lee's public school system, which had 3,431 students in 1997, consists of four elementary schools, the Louis F. Cole Middle School, and Fort Lee High School. According to Superintendent of Schools Alan W. Sugarman, its projected size by the year 2000 is 4,000 students. Dr. Sugarman said that the enrollment was less than 10 percent of the overall population of Fort Lee, reflecting the borough's mainly adult population. He attributed the growth in the school system to a turnover of the single-family home stock from empty-nesters to young families.

The fastest-growing segments of Fort Lee's population, according to Mayor Alter, are Koreans, Hispanics, and Russians. For Dr. Sugarman, this means increased demand for English-as-a-second-language instruction at a time when class sizes are growing. State average sizes for elementary, middle, and high school classes are 21 to 22 students. Dr. Sugarman says Fort Lee's average class sizes are 24 in elementary school, 25.9 in middle school, and 28 in high school.

Despite the overcrowding, Gov. Christine Todd Whitman recently cited Fort Lee's school system as an "example of educational excellence and innovation." In her State of the State message in January 1996, she noted that while Fort Lee spends less than the state average per student, its students score 50 points higher than the state average on SAT tests. In 1997, the borough's seniors scored 486 in the verbal section, which was at the state average, and 613 in the mathematics section, the total of which was about 115 points over the state average.

The program of which Dr. Sugarman is most proud is a cooperative effort with Seton Hall University, Fairleigh Dickinson University, Bloomfield College, and St. Peter's College. Students may take 25 different college-level courses for credit while still in high school. "Since 1984, when we started the program," Dr. Sugarman said, "1,262 students got a total of 3,786 semester hours of college credit."

Fort Lee has three supermarkets and a Main Street with an abundance of restaurants, banks, boutiques, video stores, flower shops, and nail salons. Among the best-known restaurants are Memories (Italian), and JD's Steak Pit, both on Main Street, and Archer's Ristorante (Italian) on Palisade Avenue.

The largest borough-owned recreational facility is the 5.5-acre Constitution Park off Fletcher Avenue in the center of town. It has a baseball diamond, a running track, and playground equipment.

In the 19th century, Fort Lee was known for its Belgian paving blocks, quarried from the area north of where the bridge now stands. They were used to pave the streets of New York City.

During the early 20th century, the borough was the motion picture capital of the world. More than 900 movies were shot in the borough from 1903 to 1927. Among the stars who acted in Fort Lee were Charlie Chaplin, Douglas Fairbanks, Sr., and Mary Pickford. Eventually, the movie industry moved to California, where the weather is more dependable.

HO-HO-KUS

A borough that guards its traditions

BY JERRY CHESLOW

Although it is less than 20 miles from Manhattan and two miles from five major shopping malls in neighboring Paramus, the well-maintained 1.8-square-mile borough of Ho-Ho-Kus has changed little in the last 50 years. Most of its housing stock is turn-of-the-century or earlier. Its last major housing development, the Cheelcroft section, dates to the Great Depression, and a score of its houses are in the National or New Jersey Register of Historic Places. "Many people tell me we are right out of a Norman Rockwell painting," said Mayor Rusty Thompson, who also serves as borough historian. "I guess you could say we're frozen in time."

Reflecting an acquiescence to the nearby shopping malls, most of the businesses in Ho-Ho-Kus are either specialty or convenience establishments, including three banks, a video store, a florist, a couple of delis, and five antiques shops. The 19th-century clapboard, Tudor, and brick downtown business district spreads for six blocks around the intersection of Franklin Turnpike and Sheridan Avenue. In addition to stores, it also has half a dozen two-story office buildings used by professionals such as doctors and lawyers.

The borough's housing stock is almost exclusively single-family detached. The only exceptions are 10 small apartments above stores in the business district and the 24-unit Normandy Court condominium complex off West Saddle River Road, where prices range from about $400,000 for some three-bedroom units to $500,000 for some four-bedroom units.

At the end of 1997, 22 houses were registered for sale in the multiple-listing service, with the most expensive ones on the east side of New Jersey Route 17, which bisects the borough from north to south. The listed homes ranged in price from $249,000 for a small three-bedroom home

POPULATION: 3,977.

AREA: 1.8 square miles.

MEDIAN HOUSEHOLD INCOME: $112,997.

MEDIAN PRICE OF A SINGLE-FAMILY HOUSE: $385,000.

TAXES ON A MEDIAN-PRICED HOUSE: $4,500.

PUBLIC SCHOOL SPENDING PER PUPIL: $9,362.

DISTANCE FROM MIDTOWN MANHATTAN: 18 miles.

RUSH-HOUR TRAVEL TO MIDTOWN: 40 minutes on the Short Line bus to the Port Authority midtown terminal, $6.70 one way, $12.75 round-trip, 10-trip ticket, $49; 45 minutes on the N.J. Transit train to Hoboken, $5.50 one way, $142 monthly, then 10 minutes on the PATH train, $1 one way.

CODES: Area, 201; ZIP, 07423.

on a busy street in the western section to $1.995 million for a large six-bedroom house on the eastern side. "Anything priced at under about $400,000 goes very quickly," said Eleanor Portsmore, a sales associate with Abbott & Caserta Realtors on Sycamore Avenue in Ho-Ho-Kus. Among the most sought-after are the Cheelcroft homes, 50 mainly brick or flagstone Tudors and Colonials on such streets as Gilbert Road and Sutton Drive, which sell for $400,000 to $540,000. They were built by Harold W. Cheel during and after the Depression. His widow, Helen S., still lives in one.

Mrs. Portsmore said she could not accurately gauge the rental market because downtown apartments rarely become vacant. However, she said small, two-bedroom houses rent for about $2,000 a month.

Former mayor Richard M. Sayers says he is disturbed that his children and those of other longtime residents cannot afford to move into the borough immediately after they marry. He says that buyers are willing to pay a premium because the borough has a negligible crime rate. "We have a 14-person police force that patrols around the clock, which is quite a lot for a small borough," Mr. Sayers said.

Lori Lamb, a six-year resident of the borough, also cites a low crime rate. She and her husband, John J., own a large home on 3.5 acres. Their home dates back to 1720 and is listed in the National Register of Historic Places. "Although you know that crime is everywhere, I feel safe here," Mrs. Lamb said. Mrs. Lamb, a former airline hostess and model, and her husband, a real estate lawyer, have three children, aged 5, 3, and 3 months. Recalling that her husband had lived in nearby Emerson, New Jersey, she said: "My husband knew the area and wanted a large piece of property. We started negotiating for the house before we got married and got a call from the realtor when we were on our honeymoon in Germany that we had gotten it."

Mrs. Lamb called Ho-Ho-Kus "a friendly place where people reach out to you." She recalled offers of help that the Lambs had received from neighbors and the pastor of the Community Church, a Protestant church and one of three houses of worship in the borough, just after they moved in.

Like most residents of the borough, Mr. Lamb commutes to work. His office is in Montvale, New Jersey, a 20-minute drive. Many other residents are executives who work in New York City and use the borough's two park-and-ride lots near the train station in the commercial center of the borough.

Some historians say the name Ho-Ho-Kus is a Leni Lenape Indian word that means "Red Cedar," for the dominant tree in the area when the first white settlers arrived in the late 17th century. Others interpret it as "Running Water," for the Saddle River and the Ho-Ho-Kus Brook, which pass through the borough. The earliest Ho-Ho-Kus property deed dates from 1698; the year 1998 marks the borough's 300th anniversary.

Residents carefully guard their traditions, starting with the spelling of the borough's name. A book published in 1983, the 75th anniversary of the formal incorporation of the borough, includes a congratulatory note from President Ronald Reagan addressed to the "Citizens of Ho Ho Kus." A note underneath the letter comments, "Look, Ma, no hyphens!!!"

The first white settler to own property in what is now Ho-Ho-Kus was Albert Zaborowsky, who arrived from Poland in 1662. In 1790, one of Albert Zaborowsky's descendants, John Zabriskie, built a private home on the corner of East Franklin Turnpike and Sheridan Avenue. That house later became a stagecoach stop and inn. Today, the brownstone and clapboard structure is Claude's Ho-Ho-Kus Inn, a highly regarded French restaurant, one of the borough's five restaurants.

The arrival of the Ramapo & Paterson Railroad in 1850 started Ho-Ho-Kus's transformation from an agricultural center to a bedroom community of New York City. In 1870, the borough was put on the national map by the construction of what became the world-famous Ho-Ho-Kus Racetrack, a 23-acre track and fairground facility that was just west of what is now Route 17. Horse and auto races took place at the track until 1938, when they were banned after a fatal accident. The area has since been developed for housing. When Route 17 was built in the 1930s, the residential character of Ho-Ho-Kus was preserved by a zoning ordinance that banned strip shopping centers from the highway in the borough.

One of the oldest houses in the borough, the Hermitage, is now a state museum displaying 19th-century furniture and artifacts. The oldest part of the structure was built in 1747 and was visited by George Washington, Alexander Hamilton, and the Marquis de Lafayette during the Revolutionary War. In 1782, Aaron Burr married its owner, the widow Theodosia Prevost.

Unlike many other school districts in Bergen County, which have replaced aging facilities, Ho-Ho-Kus continues to upgrade its 1936 school building to meet local codes, said Dr. Debra Jackson, the superintendent of schools. Many of the floors of the Ho-Ho-Kus school are hardwood, its desks are older wooden ones, and the wires to link up the classroom computer network run outside the building, rather than inside the walls. "The people here appreciate the woodwork and the fireplaces in the kindergartens," Dr. Jackson said. "It gives the school a nurturing, homelike atmosphere."

The district serves about 500 students in kindergarten through eighth grade and spends $9,362 per pupil annually. At the end of 1997, Ho-Ho-Kus was phasing out an arrangement under which it had to send its high school students to Midland Park. The juniors and seniors were attending Midland Park High and the freshmen and sophomores were in Northern Highlands Regional High School in Allendale. When the switch was being negotiated, former mayor Sayers said Midland Park, which has fewer than 400 students in grades 9–12, was too small and offered too few electives.

Beginning in September 1999, all Ho-Ho-Kus secondary students will attend Northern Highlands Regional High School. Northern Highlands Regional High School, which the borough shares with neighboring Upper Saddle River and Allendale, has an enrollment of about 700 students. The school, on Hillside Avenue in Allendale, spends $12,127 per pupil. The superintendent, Dr. Edward D. Westervelt, noted that *New Jersey Monthly* magazine rated his school among the most cost-effective high schools in the state. Of the 68 schools noted, Northern Highlands had the seventh-highest combined SAT scores, at 1134.

Students in the Ho-Ho-Kus elementary schools generally average in the 90th percentile on state-mandated achievement tests. In 1989, the district received the Blue Ribbon for Excellence Award from the federal Department of Education at a White House ceremony.

There is also a private school for severely learning-disabled students ranging in age from 5 to 21. Tuition for the 100 students at Early Childhood Learning Center, on Franklin Turnpike, is paid by the state Department of Education and local school districts.

There are six parks, the largest of which is the 15-acre East Park off East Saddle River Road and Hollywood Avenue. It includes picnic facilities, walking trails, and a section of the Saddle River, which residents use for trout fishing.

JERSEY CITY

Now as then, a place for new beginnings

BY JERRY CHESLOW

For nearly two centuries, Jersey City, a short boat ride from Ellis Island and the Statue of Liberty, has served as a first American home for hundreds of thousands of immigrants. More than a fourth of its residents are foreign-born, with large numbers from the Arab world, the Philippines, South America, and the Dominican Republic. But Thomas Gallagher, director of the city's Department of Housing, Economic Development and Commerce, notes that there has also been an influx of urban professionals. "They take the PATH train from Exchange Place, near the waterfront, and are at the World Trade Center in Manhattan in two minutes," he explained.

Among those new residents are John and Kathleen Robinson and their 14-month-old son, John Jr. In 1995, the couple moved from a three-bedroom, $2,100-a-month rental in Brooklyn Heights to a similar-size apartment here renting for $1,300. "That savings allowed Kathy to stay at home with our son," said Mr. Robinson, a lawyer who works in lower Manhattan. A year later, the Robinsons paid $208,000 for a renovated four-story brownstone in the upscale Hamilton Park area. But the Robinsons plan to leave the city before their son reaches school age, reflecting a concern over the troubled 32,000-student school system.

The system was taken over by the New Jersey Department of Education in 1989 following disclosures of widespread political nepotism in the appointment of teachers and supervisors. At the time, the city's elementary school pupils had placed 29th in the state's Eighth-Grade Early Warning Test for New Jersey's Special Needs Districts, 28 impoverished urban school districts designated by the state Supreme Court as having special needs that must be financed by the state.

"We have made progress, but still have a long way to go," said Dr. Richard A. DiPatri, the state-appointed district superintendent of schools

POPULATION: 232,785.

AREA: 14.9 square miles.

MEDIAN HOUSEHOLD INCOME: $39,679.

MEDIAN PRICE OF A SINGLE-FAMILY HOUSE: $82,000.

TAXES ON A MEDIAN-PRICED HOUSE: $3,000.

PUBLIC SCHOOL SPENDING PER PUPIL: $7,806.

DISTANCE FROM MIDTOWN MANHATTAN: 2 miles.

RUSH-HOUR TRAVEL TO MIDTOWN: 13 minutes on the PATH train, $1 one way; 30 minutes on the N.J. Transit bus to the Port Authority midtown terminal, $2.55 one way, $82 monthly.

CODES: Area, 201; ZIPs, 07302, 07303, 07304, 07305, 07306, 07308, and 07310.

all of Jersey City. "We are now 14th among the Special Needs Districts. Our attendance rate has risen from 87 percent in 1989 to 91.4 percent last year." Mayor Bret Schundler says conditions in other areas have also been improving throughout the city since 1993. The unemployment rate has fallen by 3 percentage points to 11 percent, he said, and the number of jobs has climbed from 50,000 to 63,000, mostly in financial services and retail. And the city has bought a 26-block stretch of Martin Luther King Drive, the main thoroughfare cutting through some of the city's poorest neighborhoods, and leveled more than 100 boarded-up buildings.

In their place, a new business and residential district called the Hub is to be built, including a 50,000-square-foot supermarket and a post office. The cost of the whole project, expected to be completed by 2001, is estimated at $60 million in federal, state, and local funds.

Jersey City is a state-designated Urban Enterprise Zone, which means that shoppers pay half the normal 6 percent state sales tax. The tax revenue is returned to the city for the improvement of its business districts. Last year alone, the city received $18 million in sales-tax revenue.

Jersey City has long been a gateway to Manhattan. In 1804, Robert Fulton built his shipyard at Green and Morgan Streets and later established a 14-minute steamboat ferry service to Manhattan. In 1836, the Morris Canal was extended to Jersey City, bringing coal from Pennsylvania to fuel a growing industrial base. By the turn of the century, Jersey City was a booming industrial city of 206,000, with four railroad terminals—the Erie, the Pennsylvania, the Lehigh Valley, and the Jersey Central—and a fresh crop of immigrants who had fled revolution in Germany and the Irish Potato Famine. In 1927, the Holland Tunnel was opened, giving the city of vehicle link to Manhattan.

Among the modern-day immigrants here is Adnan Kwara, a native of Syria who owns a small Middle Eastern restaurant and pastry shop in a century-old building on Grove Street with an original tin ceiling. "My customers are as diverse as this city," said Mr. Kwara. "There are Arabs, Jews, Indians, Hispanics, and other Americans." His wife, Amal J. Awad, a life-long resident, likens Jersey City to a university. "A walk down the street opens your mind," she explained. "I love it."

Minds are also opened at two public colleges—New Jersey City University (formerly Jersey City State College) and Hudson County Community College—and the coed Jesuit St. Peter's College.

The 1990 census found that Jersey City had 90,723 housing units, most built before 1940 and fewer than a third owner-occupied. The most expensive area is Port Liberté, a 363-unit gated condominium complex on a finger of land that juts into Upper Newark Bay. Laura Skolar, manager/broker at Century 21 Plaza Realty, said a four-bedroom, three-bath luxury town house there with a private boat slip recently sold for $425,000. One-bedroom units can be had for $110,000.

Close to Port Liberté is the 1.8-million-square-foot Harborside Financial Center on the site of a former rail terminal and Newport, a huge mixed-use complex that includes two office towers, a mall, and five residential buildings with a total of 1,500 rental units and 445 condominiums. When completed, the riverfront complex with its views of downtown Manhattan will include 9,000 residential units.

Some of the better residential areas surround Hamilton and Van Vorst Parks and the Paulus Hook Historic District, where the first permanent white settler, Michael Paulusen, a Dutch trader, built his home in 1633 and started trading with the Communipaw Indians. One-family brick or brownstone row houses range in price from $125,000 to $170,000, according to Ms. Skolar.

A couple of blocks from the parks, housing prices decline sharply, with some single-family homes selling for as little as $75,000. For the city as a whole, the median price of a single-family home was $82,000 in 1998, and taxes on such a house were about $3,000.

Ms. Skolar said most of the rentals are in small multifamily dwellings. One-bedroom apartments in prime areas command monthly rents of about $925, with some two-bedrooms going for as much as $1,200. In other parts of the city, rents can be as low as $500 for a two-bedroom apartment.

One- and two-family frame dwellings that practically touch each other in the Jersey City Heights, Journal Square, and West Bergen sections are considered the middle of the market. Single-family dwellings in those areas range from $70,000 to $110,000, with two-families going for about $40,000 more.

In poorer areas, such as the Greenville and Bergen/Lafayette section, abutting the 1,122-acre Liberty State Park, many new immigrant families are buying their first homes for as little as $40,000 for a one-family and $65,000 for a two-family.

Condominium apartments in small, converted rental buildings are bargains, Ms. Skolar said, noting that she had recently sold a two-bedroom, one-bath condominium apartment in Jersey City Heights for $40,000. She said the owner had paid $124,000 in 1987, when housing prices peaked.

Jersey City has a host of diverse restaurants, including Casadante (Italian) on Newark Avenue in Journal Square, Laico's (Italian) on Pavonia Avenue, Komegashi (Japanese) on Montgomery Street, and the Iron Monkey on Green Street, which serves a mixture of Continental and Asian food from a rooftop terrace overlooking Manhattan.

As for the educational system, Superintendent DiPatri said 10 of the 30 elementary schools were outstanding and nine perform dismally, despite the fact that spending per pupil, at $7,806 in 1997, is comparable to that of much wealthier districts.

As an example of an excellent school, Dr. DiPatri cites School 27, in which 100 percent of last year's eighth graders passed the state's Early Warning Test in reading, writing, and math. But School 27 has 28 students per classroom—six above the state average—and more than 70 percent of the students come from low-income households. "I've made the principal of School 27 my executive assistant and started a no-holds-barred campaign to bring all of our schools up to her standards," Dr. DiPatri declared.

The district's five high schools offer 16 advanced placement courses. The highest-rated secondary is the Ronald McNair Academic High School, which accepts the top 100 graduates from the city's elementary schools each year. Its dropout rate is zero and all but two of last year's 98 graduates went on to four-year colleges. On the SATs, McNair's students had combined verbal and math scores of 1,104, which is 100 points above the state average.

A more typical Jersey City high school is the William L. Dickinson High School, which had a 14.3 percent dropout rate and average combined SAT scores of just 791.

The largest county-owned park here is the 273-acre Lincoln Park, with a multitude of playing fields and 21 tennis courts. The most widely used city-owned park is the eight-square-block Pershing Field off Central Avenue. It contains an ice-skating/roller hockey rink, an Olympic-size swimming pool, a jogging trail, four tennis courts, two basketball courts, two baseball fields, and a refurbished playground.

Jersey City is home to the 19,000-acre Liberty State Park, opened in 1976 as a "shrine to freedom" on the site of a former Central Railroad of New Jersey terminal, the first stop on the mainland for about 8 million immigrants who had landed at Ellis Island. About 3.5 million people visit the park annually. The major attraction is the $68 million Liberty Science Center, which has an Imax theater with a 125-foot screen and three floors of exhibits on the environment, health, and inventions.

LEONIA

Well-read, well-shaded, and well-placed

BY JERRY CHESLOW

A seven-foot-high mural in the auditorium of Anna C. Scott School in Leonia depicts George Washington on horseback, leading a ragtag group of bundled-up soldiers through the snow. Painted by Howard McCormick in 1930, it commemorates Washington's retreat through Leonia on November 20, 1776, after Lord Cornwallis humiliated him in three major battles on Long Island, in White Plains, and in Harlem Heights. At the time, General Cornwallis was in hot pursuit but made a wrong turn in Leonia and allowed the remnant of Washington's vastly outnumbered force to escape.

"Like many a New Yorker traveling through northern New Jersey today, Cornwallis got lost in Leonia," said Carol Karels Lutchin, a borough historian. "He knew Washington was fleeing toward Hackensack and had to cross the Overpeck Swamp via Second Bridge in what is now Ridgefield. But Cornwallis's maps showed the bridge to be a couple of miles south of where it really was."

Leonia is at the northernmost exit of the New Jersey Turnpike, just south of the George Washington Bridge. Although occupying just 1.5 square miles, the Bergen County community has 10 churches, two synagogues, seven parks, a large recreation program, and a four-block downtown on Broad Avenue.

The downtown offers a few clothing stores, two delicatessens, two gas stations, two supermarkets, a bagel store, a hardware store, half a dozen hair salons, and three restaurants but no bars or liquor stores. The sale of alcoholic beverages is banned. On Saturday mornings, Your Place Diner is packed with politicians and longtime residents.

A focal point is the 60,000-volume Leonia Public Library on Fort Lee Road, which also serves as a meeting place for local organizations and societies. "Ninety-seven percent of Leonia residents hold library cards,"

POPULATION: 9,000.

AREA: 1.5 square miles.

MEDIAN HOUSEHOLD INCOME: $73,463.

MEDIAN PRICE OF A SINGLE-FAMILY HOUSE: $245,000.

TAXES ON A MEDIAN-PRICED HOUSE: $6,320.

PUBLIC SCHOOL SPENDING PER PUPIL: $8,083.

DISTANCE FROM MIDTOWN MANHATTAN: 7 miles.

RUSH-HOUR TRAVEL TO MIDTOWN: 25 minutes on the Red and Tan bus to the Port Authority midtown terminal, $2.55 one way, 10-trip ticket, $49.75; 30 minutes on the N.J. Transit bus to the Port Authority midtown terminal, $3.25 one way, $92 monthly, or 18 minutes to the Port Authority George Washington Bridge terminal, $1.90 one way, $59 monthly, then 20 minutes on the A train.

CODES: Area, 201; ZIP, 07605.

said Deborah Bigelow, the head librarian of Leonia, which has a population of 9,000. "That's the highest figure in the state. Per-capita borrowing is also the highest in the state at 12 items per year."

Most residential streets are lined with maples and oaks that form canopies over the roads. For the last eight years, owing to its active Shade Tree Commission, which has veto power over the removal of large trees from private property, Leonia has been designated by the National Arbor Day Foundation as a Tree City U.S.A.

Although settled by Dutch farmers in the late 17th century, what is now Leonia had just 10 farms and a few dozen residents during the Revolutionary War. Those residents were about equally divided between Tories and Continentals, which meant that the farms were constantly being plundered by foraging armies of one side or the other.

Leonia remained a sleepy backwater until 1896, when the Leonia Heights Land Company, headed by Artemus Ward, a New York advertising executive, started marketing building lots to professors at Columbia University. The company put up billboards on the campus and at train and subway stations during the decades-long marketing campaign proclaiming Leonia to be a cultural mecca, "Heaven on Earth," and the "Athens of the East."

By 1925, Leonia's population had swelled from a few hundred at the turn of the century to almost 4,000. Today, the population stands at more than twice that. An early borough historian wrote that, at the time, 80 percent of the adult residents had college degrees.

Among those drawn to the tiny borough near the turn of the century were prominent artists like Harvey Dunn and Charles Chapman, who founded the Leonia School of Illustration. Much later, its residents included five Nobel Prize winners, among them Enrico Fermi, one of the developers of the atomic bomb, and Willard Libby, who discovered radio-carbon dating; Sammy Davis, Jr., Pat Boone, and Alan Alda, the entertainers; and Robert Ludlum, the author. Current residents include artists and other professionals, many of whom work at home, making them available for town activities.

"The town runs on volunteers," Mayor Judah Ziegler said. "The mayor and council are unpaid; the fire department and rescue squad are volunteer, as are the 50 coaches in our recreation program." That program has leagues in baseball, soccer, basketball, and T-ball.

Detached-housing prices range from $170,000 for a rare handyman special to $600,000 for some older Victorians and newer four- and five-bedroom Colonials in the 118-home Golf Course section, built in 1980 on the site of the former Englewood Golf Course. According to Jack McAlear, broker/owner of McAlear Cavalier Realtors, the average home sells for $230,000 to $280,000. The median home price is $245,000, with taxes of $6,320.

"We had a robust market in 1997, which has continued into 1998," Mr. McAlear said. "Last year, 66 single-family homes were sold here. Most of the sellers were empty-nesters and the buyers were young, two-income families."

There are two types of condominiums in the borough: two-story luxury town houses and converted garden apartments. The largest town house development is the 68-unit Meadowview off Grand Avenue in the western section.

According to Mr. McAlear, prices start at $220,000 for some two-bedroom town houses and go up to $290,000 for some three-bedroom units. Both have two-car garages. A typical converted garden-apartment condominium complex is the 52-unit Lakeview on Lakeview Avenue, with a price range of $80,000 for one-bedrooms to $120,000 for three-bedrooms.

One of the larger rental complexes is the 52-unit Leonia Manor garden apartment complex off Broad Avenue. One-bedrooms rent for $900, two-bedrooms for $1,100.

In 1992, Nyree and Robert MacArthur, who have two children, Ian, 3, and Tuleen, 6, moved from New York City to a 100-year-old, five-bedroom Colonial, which Dr. Nyree MacArthur, a psychoanalyst in private practice, says needed an updated kitchen. Dr. MacArthur said they chose Leonia because it was an easy commute for her husband to his job as a research pharmacist at Manhattan's Columbia Presbyterian Hospital, because the population is ethnically diverse, and because the school system has a reputation for quality.

"I like the fact that it is compact and you can walk to the parks, the library, and the downtown," she said. "Yet Leonia is not for everyone. If you want land, forget it. The building lots are small. The downtown is tiny and lacks a lot of the commerce you might want. For instance, it has no bakery and no video shop. It's also too small for anyone to remain anonymous. On the other hand, it's just a short jump to the museums of New York City."

For serious shopping, Bergen County has a plethora of malls. The closest large complex is the Riverside Square Mall, 3.5 miles to the west in Hackensack.

Leonia's 1,650-student school system, which spends $8,083 per pupil annually, grew by 40 students in 1997, reflecting the turnover of housing from the elderly to younger families. A typical high school graduating class is 120, with 95 percent going on to higher education.

The students are about equally divided among the kindergarten-to-grade 5 Anna C. Scott School, the Leonia Middle School for grades 5 to 8, and the Leonia High School, which includes 234 students from neighboring Edgewater.

According to the acting high school principal, Christine Cummings, who is also curriculum coordinator for the school system, technology is stressed. Leonia has high-data-volume Internet lines in the high school and middle school. All three schools have computer laboratories and computers in every classroom. This was made possible by a $4.9 million bond issue passed by the residents three years ago. "You can't teach today's children by yesterday's methods because they will have to live in tomorrow's world," Mrs. Cummings said.

She said the district is a participant in the federally funded Goals 2000 program at the Bergen County Technical School in Hackensack, which provides special courses to the county's top math and science students. The high school offers a dozen advanced placement courses in English, the sciences, mathematics, and federal government studies.

The largest of Leonia's seven parks is the seven-acre Sylvan Park on Grand Avenue, which has four baseball diamonds and a basketball court. It is near the Leonia Pool, a borough-owned facility supported by the annual memberships of $325 per family. The most widely used park is the four-acre Wood Park, next to the library on Fort Lee Road. It has three tennis courts, two basketball courts, a softball diamond, a handball court, and playground equipment.

Among the other widely used facilities is the Civil War Drill Hall, a cavernous building constructed by the New Jersey Blues Infantry regiment as a training center in 1859. The hall is now home to the Players Guild of Leonia, established in 1919 and the oldest community theater group in New Jersey. The hall is in the National and the New Jersey Register of Historic Places as the last existing Civil War drill hall in the United States.

MONTCLAIR

*Seeking urban advantages in
a suburban setting*

BY JERRY CHESLOW

Montclair is a magnet for young urban professionals seeking to raise their children in the suburbs but still thirsting for the culture and diversity of city life. Although just 6.2 square miles in area, it has safe streets, abundant parks, 50 houses of worship, a well-respected art museum, and the 13,000-student Montclair State University. It also has some of the oldest local theater groups in the country, vibrant business districts, and 38,000 trees, one for each resident of the township.

Its housing ranges from tiny Colonials in low-income areas to $2.5 million mansions set back far from the road and hidden behind thick foliage. Many of the mansions lie along the eastern slopes of the Watchung Mountains, which form the western boundary of the town.

Perhaps one of the more unusual draws for newcomers is the racial situation. With a population that is roughly two-thirds white and one-third black, Montclair's residents take pride in the way the races get along. The residents often use the term *lighthouse* to describe the school system's policy of allowing liberal school choice as long as each school maintains a racial balance.

"We moved here because we wanted our children to grow up in a diverse, integrated town with a fully integrated school system," said Robin Ross, a lawyer, who with her husband, Dr. David Marks, a neurologist, bought a four-bedroom Colonial on Highland Avenue in 1994, moving from Hoboken. "At the time, we had a 1-year-old daughter and were expecting twins," Ms. Ross said.

But a dispute that the couple is having with the public school system shows that the search for fairness has its price. Historically there have been sharp public disputes in Montclair over school integration, urban renewal, and transportation, which have often divided people along racial

POPULATION: 38,087.

AREA: 6.2 square miles.

MEDIAN HOUSEHOLD INCOME: $67,381.

MEDIAN PRICE OF A SINGLE-FAMILY HOUSE: $280,000.

TAXES ON A MEDIAN-PRICED HOUSE: $9,500.

PUBLIC SCHOOL SPENDING PER PUPIL: $7,830.

DISTANCE FROM MIDTOWN MANHATTAN: 12 miles.

RUSH-HOUR TRAVEL TO MIDTOWN: 45 minutes on the DeCamp bus to the Port Authority midtown terminal, $4.65 one way, 30-trip ticket, $128; 33 minutes on the N.J. Transit train to Hoboken, $3.60 one way, $101 monthly, then 10 minutes on the PATH train, $1 one way.

CODES: Area, 201; ZIP, 07042.

lines. They are generally resolved through compromise, but sometimes they go to court.

Ms. Ross has filed suit against the school system protesting her daughter's exclusion from a prekindergarten program. Although all students were being admitted three years ago when the Rosses moved in, just 172 of 285 applicants were accepted in 1997 because of budget cuts. Of 172 children selected, 52 were picked based on the need to be prepared for kindergarten. The rest were chosen by what the Board of Education described as a racially balanced lottery. But Ms. Ross maintains that the effect of this was to discriminate unfairly against children from higher-income, better-educated families. "We feel cheated," she said.

The school system has a total of 6,722 students in seven elementary schools, two middle schools, and Montclair High School; per-pupil expenditures in 1997 were $7,830. According to statistics posted on the Montclair Chamber of Commerce web page, 10 percent of students from Montclair go to private schools, twice the New Jersey average.

The public school system is based on "magnet" schools, each of which stresses different subjects and learning systems. For example, the kindergarten–grade 5 Bradford Academy is an information-technology magnet that offers a core curriculum enhanced by courses on information gathering. Other schools offer curriculums for the gifted or courses in science, technology, and the environment. Parents may choose the magnet school, based on ability and interest of their child, with the proviso that racial balance is maintained.

Edna Harris, interim superintendent of schools, characterized both middle schools and the high school as excellent. One middle school is a magnet for the arts; the other is oriented toward science and technology. Of the 1997 graduating class of 348 in the 1,417-student Montclair High School, 85 percent went on to higher education. The high school offers advanced placement courses in biology, physics, mathematics, computer science, foreign languages, English, and history.

The system benefits from a $1 million, two-year technology overhaul that has placed computers in every classroom. Eventually, all classrooms are expected to be networked together and have Internet availability. Montclair State University sends student teachers into the classrooms for experience and helps the school develop new teaching strategies.

Another town issue is transportation. In recent years, there have been complaints in the black community over perceived discrimination in transportation planning. Charles L. Smith, town councilman from the mostly minority Fourth Ward, is angry about N.J. Transit's plans to link two lines that are three blocks apart in the Pine Street area. The plan, known as the Montclair Connection, has been under discussion for more than 30 years and still lacks final approval. "The connection would save time for the passengers, but would go through 17 properties in a working-class neighborhood that doesn't use the train to go to work in New York City," Mr. Smith said.

Claims of discrimination are part of the dynamics of an unusually diverse community, in Township Manager Terence Reidy's opinion. "We have 38,000 people, with 38,000 viewpoints, and each feels it is his civic duty to express his viewpoint," he said. One of the best-known figures in the black community, 77-year-old Rose Catchings, a Montclair resident for 44 years, said she had seen the town "open up" to minorities in housing, education, and local government. She noted that her late husband, Rev. Dr. L. Maynard Catchings, was the first minority president of the local school board. But not enough is being done to combat crime and the drug problem in low-income areas, she said.

Disputing this, Police Chief Thomas J. Russo said that crime of all kinds has been reduced by 20 percent over the last five years to a rate of 48 reported incidents per 1,000 residents annually. There are 112 officers on the Montclair force—23 of them black, Chief Russo noted—and a special task force of nine deals with street crime. Seven officers work in the Drug Awareness Resistance Education program in the elementary schools.

Montclair's early history foreshadowed its current diversity. The first European settlers were the Speers, a Dutch family that in the 1660s built their houses on the mountain slopes in what is now Upper Montclair. Thirty years later, two Englishmen, Jasper and Azariah Crane, left the overcrowded settlement of Newark and built their home two miles to the south.

The Dutch Speertown and the English Cranetown both prospered, sprawled, and eventually met at the current Watchung Avenue. Although no Revolutionary War battles were fought in Montclair, General Washington had headquarters in Cranetown and General Lafayette had headquarters on the heights at Speertown.

In 1868, when the combined towns known as Montclair were part of Bloomfield Township, the section seceded and formed the Township of Montclair. Five years later, the Greenwood Lake Railroad, now part of the N.J. Transit line, arrived to link Montclair to Newark and New York, and from 1880 to 1930, the population soared from 5,100 to 42,000. By then, most of the existing housing had been built.

Recent single-family listings have included a tiny, two-bedroom ranch on Pine Street for $78,000, and, at $1.65 million, a five-bedroom Tudor with a Manhattan view on Lloyd Road.

The median price of a one-family house in 1997 was $280,000, and taxes on a median house were about $9,500.

There are 6,410 rental units in 161 apartment buildings, garden-apartment complexes, and private homes. The largest apartment building is the 135-unit Hawthorne Towers, where rents start at $710 for some studios and go up to $1,300 for the largest two-bedrooms, for which the building has a long waiting list.

There are 10 condominium complexes with close to 500 units. Recent sales ranged from $15,600 for a two-bedroom on Pine Street to $156,000 for a two-bedroom unit on the more prestigious Union Street.

Montclair has seven shopping districts, four movie theaters, and five supermarkets. One of the best-known local restaurants is Blue Sky on Bloomfield Avenue, with an eclectic cuisine that employs exotic spices and mushrooms and goat cheese.

The town has 18 public parks and 152 acres of parkland. There are 21 tennis courts, seven playgrounds, three public swimming pools, six baseball diamonds, and four basketball courts.

Among the more unusual public facilities is the Presby Memorial Iris Gardens in Mountainside Park on Upper Mountain Avenue. Dedicated in 1927, it has more than 4,000 varieties of irises and is in the National and the New Jersey Register of Historic Places.

Montclair has two nature reserves—the 20-acre Alonzo F. Bonsal Wildlife Preserve off Alexander Avenue and the 408-acre county-owned Eagle Rock Reservation, off Gates Avenue, known for its extensive network of nature trails.

Montclair has been known as a cultural center since the 1870s, when the landscape artist George Inness began coming out from Manhattan to paint. Today, it is home to hundreds of artists, writers, actors, and dancers. The Montclair Art Museum, a colonnaded Greek Revival structure built in 1914, has a collection of more than 1,100 pieces of American art and relics, with a heavy emphasis on Indian items.

NUTLEY

Annie Oakley's home, rich in history

BY JERRY CHESLOW

With stories of a speakeasy, a slave jail, artists, and the sharpshooter Annie Oakley, the tiny township of Nutley in New Jersey's Essex County is steeped in its colorful past. Although settled by the Dutch and English in the early 1700s, the township's character was shaped by Irish and Italian immigrants who arrived in the mid–19th and early 20th centuries. They worked in three quarries that supplied brownstone to New York City, 11 miles away, as well as in the many mills powered by the Third River, which bisects the township. The mills and quarries have since closed and the flood plain of the river has been converted into a 100-acre stretch of parks running through the township from north to south.

The parks have a total of 15 baseball diamonds, three soccer/football fields, eight tennis courts, hiking and bike trails, and several ponds that are used for ice-skating in winter and are stocked with trout by the township. The Nutley Parks and Recreation Building, off Park Avenue, is now on one of the quarry sites. When the quarry closed in 1927, the site was used as a landfill and then a circular track for bicycle races. Those events stopped abruptly in 1939, when a rider was killed on the wooden track, which had begun to sink and had become uneven and dangerous.

One of the 19th-century brick mill buildings now serves as the town hall. Outside the building, on Franklin Avenue, is the town well, where residents can fill bottles of clear spring water.

Like many other Nutley citizens, Mayor Garry Furnari is a third-generation resident of the 3.4-square-mile township. The mayor, who was also elected as a state senator in November 1997, lives in the house in which he grew up on Franklin Avenue, the main business street. Mr. Furnari's father operated a beauty parlor in the front section of the house that now serves as the mayor's law office.

POPULATION: 26,584.

AREA: 3.4 square miles.

MEDIAN HOUSEHOLD INCOME: $57,728.

MEDIAN PRICE OF A SINGLE-FAMILY HOUSE: $165,000.

TAXES ON A MEDIAN-PRICED HOUSE: $5,320.

PUBLIC SCHOOL SPENDING PER PUPIL: $7,664.

DISTANCE FROM MIDTOWN MANHATTAN: 11 miles.

RUSH-HOUR TRAVEL TO MIDTOWN: 35 minutes on the DeCamp bus to the Port Authority midtown terminal, $3.80 one way, 30-trip ticket, $107; N.J. Transit bus to the Port Authority midtown terminal, $3.25 one way, $92 monthly.

CODES: Area, 973; ZIP, 07110.

Mr. Furnari's grandmother attended the Park Elementary School, which has since been expanded to become Nutley High School. The mayor's four children, aged 6 through 12, all attend the Yantacaw Elementary School, which he also attended as a child. "We're a very stable community," said Mr. Furnari. "People grow up and want to stay and raise their own families here."

Among the newer residents are Elizabeth and William Garofalo and their three children, Gary, 8, Andrew, 6, and Tori, 2. They bought a four-bedroom Colonial on Rutgers Place in 1992 and moved in from nearby Lyndhurst. "My husband got to know Nutley by running through its beautifully maintained parks," said Mrs. Garofalo, a personal-injury lawyer. "We needed a larger house and naturally considered Nutley. We also liked the school system's small size and the fact that it's easy to get to know the teachers." Mr. Garofalo, an Internal Revenue Service lawyer, bicycles to work in nearby Newark. He also serves as president of the township-sponsored Nutley Soccer League.

Nutley's appearance has changed little since the '40s. The most prevalent housing style is the narrow three-bedroom Colonial, built near the center of town between 1900 and 1930. During the first quarter of 1998, the median sale price was $165,000, on which the property taxes were $5,320 per year. In December 1997, the houses on the market ranged from $108,000 for a five-room Cape that was listed as "needs work" to $276,000 for a three-bedroom Dutch Colonial, according to Louis Costantine, broker and owner of Costantine Realty in Nutley. He said that, except for spot lots, the township was nearly fully built out by the late '50s.

Among the more expensive homes are large turn-of-the-century Georgian Colonials, Tudors, and Victorians, which go for up to $375,000. These homes are mainly in the older, northern section on streets such as Rutgers Place, Highfield Lane, and Satterthwaite Avenue. In 1995, one home was offered for $500,000 but did not sell and was taken off the market. "It would be unusual for us to sell more than six houses in the $350,000-plus range in a year," said Mr. Costantine. "The market just will not support those prices here. However, we have many people who have improved their homes beyond their real value, because they have confidence in the community and want to stay."

Besides Colonials, the township has an abundance of Cape Cods and a handful of two-bedroom bungalows on Ideal Court that can sell for as little as $110,000, according to Mr. Costantine.

The township has about 250 condominium housing units, mostly in converted garden-apartment complexes off River Road and Passaic and Franklin Avenues. Mr. Costantine said prices ranged from $45,000 for some one-bedroom units in the 26-unit Hillside Gardens development on Hillside Avenue to about $175,000 for some three-bedroom town houses with garages in the 16-unit Nutley Heights Complex on East Passaic Avenue.

There are 1,700 rental units in the township, ranging in price from about $700 for some one-bedroom apartments to $1,100 for some three-bedrooms. The largest rental complex is the 225-unit Village Manor on Adams Court.

Among the most famous people to live in Nutley were Annie Oakley and her husband, Frank Butler, both sharpshooters in Buffalo Bill's Wild West Show at the turn of the century. A coin shot by Ms. Oakley during a benefit for the Red Cross in 1894 is on display at the Nutley Museum, an 1875 schoolhouse on Church Street. The museum also has Ms. Oakley's derringer, one of Buffalo Bill's pistols, old photos, postcards, artifacts, and a re-creation of a general store. The museum is open from 2 to 4 P.M. on the first and third Sundays of each month and on Tuesday from 7 to 9 P.M.

Among the more unusual charity events staged in the township is the annual Friends of Abused Children Motorcycle Run, a rally organized by Nutley police officers to raise money for children's charities. The event, held on the third Sunday of July, includes music and a barbecue. Typically, it raises about $35,000.

In the center of the township, next to Memorial Park, is the Enclosure, a historic district in the National Register of Historic Places. It includes four artists' studios, including that of Reginald Marsh, and nine homes dating back to 1872, when the area was an artists' colony.

Nutley's main business district, on Franklin Avenue, includes a number of nail and hair salons, banks, video shops, a sporting-goods store, and a shoe-repair shop. The township has three supermarkets. For major shopping, residents go to malls in Wayne and Paramus and outlet stores in Secaucus, all of which are within 10 miles of the township. Among the best-known restaurants are the Franklin Steak House on Franklin Avenue and the Park Diner on Center Street. Also well known for its meats is Roth's Deli on Franklin Avenue, where John Dinger, the owner, keeps weekly tabs for dozens of regulars. "We see them crossing the street and pour their coffee and start making their sandwiches," Mr. Dinger said.

Mr. Dinger coined the term "lawyer's row" for a stretch of Franklin Avenue where a growing number of private houses are being converted into professional offices. This is a trend that he says indicates that the town is becoming more white-collar, a fact that appears to be supported by the 1990 census, which shows that more than 28 percent of Nutley's adults have some university education.

The 3,900 student Nutley Public School District consists of five kindergarten-through-sixth-grade elementary schools, the largest of which is the 520-student Yantacaw School on Yantacaw Place, the Franklin Middle School on Franklin Avenue, and the 250-student Nutley High School. In the 1997–98 school year, the district was spending $7,664 per pupil annually, which is low by New Jersey standards. Nutley High was cited by *New Jersey Monthly* in September 1997 as one of 62 public high schools in the state that "spend a little and get a lot." Among the indicators measured were scores on the SATs. In 1997, Nutley's students had combined verbal and mathematics scores of 1036, which was about 50 points above the state average. Typically, the school sends between 80 percent and 85 percent of its graduates to higher education.

One of the reasons for the school's cost-effectiveness, according to John Sincaglia, business administrator for the Nutley Board of Education, is that no new school buildings are required. Although most of the current schools were built before the Depression, they are maintained and upgraded regularly. For instance, they were recently wired for computer networks. Mr. Sincaglia says that 100 percent of Nutley's middle school students passed the state's Early Warning Test, which are given to identify pupils who need special help.

PEAPACK AND GLADSTONE

Foxhunting and high-priced homes

BY JERRY CHESLOW

Residents of the 2,200-person Borough of Peapack and Gladstone in Somerset County pride themselves on being nonchalant about the many celebrities who live in the borough and surrounding municipalities. Mayor Mary Hamilton said famous people were "not singled out and can remain as public or as private as they like here." She does have a story about Aristotle Onassis, who rented a home in neighboring Bernardsville with his wife, Jacqueline Kennedy Onassis. "He was an insomniac," Mrs. Hamilton said, "and he would go walking in the borough at two in the morning with no identification. To Mr. Onassis's embarrassment and to the embarrassment of the police chief, he was once taken in for questioning before his habits were known."

The 5.9-square-mile Peapack and Gladstone is in a rural New Jersey area of estates and horse farms of the wealthy. The king of Morocco is one of the borough's biggest landowners, and foxes are still hunted here. But most of the residents live less ostentatious, although well-off, lives. Nick Villa, a broker associate with Re/Max Pinnacle Realty in Bedminster, said that the median price of a single-family home in December 1997 was $490,000, with taxes of $7,950. The most expensive house on the market was a six-bedroom, six-bath home on nine acres on Mosle Road, listed for more than $1.975 million. The least expensive was a four-bedroom, two-bath home on a quarter of an acre listed at $198,000.

In general, the less expensive dwellings are in the downtown areas of the villages of Peapack and Gladstone, which make up the borough. Mr. Villa says that less than half a dozen such houses come on the market each year, and are snapped up.

Borough officials have zoned most of the vacant land for five-acre lots to preserve the rural character and abundant wildlife, including deer,

GAZETTEER

POPULATION: 2,215.

AREA: 5.9 square miles.

MEDIAN HOUSEHOLD INCOME: $86,511.

MEDIAN PRICE OF A SINGLE-FAMILY HOUSE: $490,000.

TAXES ON A MEDIAN-PRICED HOUSE: $7,950.

PUBLIC SCHOOL SPENDING PER PUPIL: $10,005.

DISTANCE FROM MIDTOWN MANHATTAN: 35 miles.

RUSH-HOUR TRAVEL TO MIDTOWN: 70 minutes on the N.J. Transit train to Hoboken, $8.90 one way, $249 monthly, then 10 minutes on the PATH train, $1 one way.

CODES: Area, 908; ZIP, 07977 and 07934.

foxes, and pheasants. A proposal before the council seeks to double the size of new building lots to 10 acres. In the process, housing prices have been kept high.

Mr. Villa says the typical buyer in Peapack and Gladstone is a young, well-established family head who commutes to his office in New York City by train. There are New Jersey Transit stations in both villages. The trip takes about 70 minutes. The typical homes they buy are four- or five-bedroom Colonials on two- to five-acre lots. Several such homes are on the market in the Tiger Hill section off Mendham Road and the Sheep Hill section off Mosle Road. Houses on Tiger Hill go for $450,000 to $800,000 and those on Sheep Hill for $800,000 and up.

"There just aren't enough reasonably priced houses in the borough," Mrs. Hamilton said. "So we are losing our young people. That disturbs me."

There are fewer than two dozen rental apartments, mainly in two-family homes. They rarely become available, Mrs. Hamilton said, and rent for $850 to $1,100 a month.

The one condominium building is the 14-unit Gladstone House, at Main Street and Mendham Road in Gladstone, built in 1923 as an auto dealership. Mr. Villa says no units are now on the market. But he estimates that one-bedroom apartments there sell for $110,000 to $120,000, with two-bedrooms going for about $20,000 more.

The cost of housing may be responsible for the small number of school-age children. In 1980, the Peapack-Gladstone Board of Education voted to close the borough elementary school, which has since been converted into municipal offices. The borough, which does not have a high school, sends all of its 280 or so students to schools in neighboring Bernardsville. As a result, the borough has little influence over school budgets and policy. Its per-pupil spending is $10,005.

Typically, Bernards Senior High School sends more than 90 percent of its graduates to higher education each year, according to its principal, Dr. Lynn J. Caravello. The 1997 graduating class achieved combined verbal and mathematics scores of 1097 on the SATs, which is about 100 points above the state average. Dr. Caravello said that the school's technology program was a model for others throughout the state. It has courses not only in computers, but in robotics, video production, and invention, among other facets of technology, as well.

The private Gill St. Bernard's School, with 500 students from prekindergarten through grade 12, has a 70-acre campus in Gladstone. The tuition ranges from $6,600 for pre-K to $14,400 for high school. Practically all graduates go on to higher education.

One local history speculates that the name Peapack came from the Leni Lenape Indian word *peapackton*—"the marriage of the waters." The Raritan River and the Peapack Brook meet at the eastern border of the borough. Gladstone is named for the British prime minister William Gladstone. In 1701, the Peapack Patent was granted to George Willocks and John Johnstone by the 24 English proprietors of East Jersey, who received their authority from Sir George Carteret, who in turn received his rights from the duke of York. The tract encompassed about 3,000 acres and included what is now Bedminster Township, Bernards Township, and Peapack and Gladstone.

By 1912, the villages of Peapack and Gladstone found themselves in conflict with the rest of Bedminster Township. The villages wanted electric lights, telephones, and fire hydrants and resented being forced to pay for rural roads in the township. The villages petitioned the state legislature for the creation of the borough and the legislature voted to do so on April 23, 1912.

The two villages that make up the borough were sleepy backwaters until 1890, when the Delaware & Lackawana Railroad built an extension to Gladstone. Soon afterward, wealthy businesspeople—among them the railroad magnate C. Ledyard Blair; the multimillionaire Walter L. Ladd and his wife, Kate; and James Cox (Diamond Jim) Brady—built country estates.

The Ladd estate, called Natirar (Raritan spelled backward) was bought by King Hassan II of Morocco in 1983. The king owns 383 acres of borough land. The Brady estate, called Hamilton Farms and once totaling about 5,000 acres, has been reduced over the years by property sales. The Beneficial Corporation, a financial services company that combined with Household Finance to become Household International in 1998, owns part of the former estate.

The Essex Hunt Club is a foxhunting club that evolved into two private clubs, Essex Fox Hounds, which still hunts, and the Essex Hunt Club, a winter recreational club on a property of more than 100 acres that uses an ice rink for figure skating and hockey.

The Hamilton Farms estate, now owned by Household International, is home to the United States equestrian team. Besides being the training site for horses and riders that participate in Olympic events, it is also the venue for the annual I.B.M.-U.S. Equestrian Team Festival of Champions, a four-day extravaganza of horsemanship, including driving, show jumping, and dressage, held in the third week of June.

Just after they were married, Steuart Ellsworth and his wife, Pamela, both from nearby towns, bought the oldest house in the borough, a four-bedroom Colonial with four fireplaces, in November 1992. According to a local history, coins found at their house, 109 North Main Street, suggest that the earliest section was built around 1670. The house was occupied in 1720 by the family of a miller named Johannes Lowrance. The Peapack Brook, which powered the Lowrance grist mill, runs in the backyard of the two-acre property. "We looked for over a year," said Mr. Ellsworth, who owns a company that applies antiglare film to windows. "Since this property is zoned for office and residential, it was perfect for both our house and my business."

Mrs. Ellsworth runs a local travel agency in one of the fewer than two dozen stores in the two villages. "Everyone in the stores gets to know you quickly and you get to know them," Mr. Ellsworth said. The Ellsworths buy small food items at the local deli, the Copper Kettle. For their major food shopping, they travel to the supermarket in Chester, five miles to the north. The closest mall is Bridgewater Commons in Bridgewater, 10 miles south of the borough.

Among the best-known restaurants in the borough are Rudolfo's Ristorante (Italian) on Lackawanna Avenue, Toscana Trattoria (Italian) on Main Street, and Chatfield's Grill and Bar (American) on Pottersville Road. On its front porch, Chatfield's has a full-size 19th-century model of a horse that was originally a harness maker's dummy. Inside, the restaurant has a series of photos of the borough dating to the turn of the century.

Despite the abundance of open land, the borough lacks public parks. Its largest recreation area is the grounds of the former elementary school, which includes two baseball diamonds and a practice soccer field. The two-acre Liberty Park, at Main Street and Park Avenue, is the only real park in the borough. It has a picnic area and monuments to the fallen in the two world wars and the Korean and Vietnam Wars. It also has a man-made pond, complete with swans.

Mayor Hamilton says she often receives complaints from residents about the high volume of traffic on Main Street during rush hours, as residents of nearby municipalities travel to the two train stations. The borough posts police officers at strategic intersections to enforce the 25-mile-an-hour speed limit.

PRINCETON

A historic, and prototypical, college town

BY JERRY CHESLOW

Surrounded by Princeton Township, Princeton Borough is the epitome of a college town. Its downtown grew up north of Nassau Hall, a massive structure with 26-inch-thick brown sandstone walls built in 1756 to house the College of New Jersey, later renamed Princeton University. The 6,000-student university still occupies the entire area south of Nassau Street and owns about one-third of the borough, with 160 buildings sprawling over a 600-acre campus that spills into the township. The downtown of the 1.73-square-mile borough is comfortable for walking, with wide, tree-lined sidewalks and glittering upscale shops.

Just west of Nassau Street, Palmer Square, which once was the site of a busy stagecoach stop between New York and Philadelphia, is dominated by the five-story, 216-room Nassau Inn Hotel, which also has 49 stores and 107 condominium and rental apartments. According to Teri McIntire, director of marketing for the hotel, it sells out a year in advance of every home football game, graduation, or reunion weekend.

The university crowd supports a broad array of restaurants, from the upscale Lahiere's on Witherspoon Street to the Annex, a pub on Nassau Street that caters to student tastes and pocketbooks.

Mayor Marvin R. Reed says that a fifth of Princeton's housing is in three historic districts along Nassau Street and nearby Mercer Street, governed by the Historic Preservation Review Committee. The committee's jurisdiction relates not only to exterior construction, but also to paint and shutters.

"Many couples buy houses in Princeton because one spouse works in New York and the other in Philadelphia," explained Mayor Reed. "We call them two-bonus couples, because they are generally high-income couples who invest their annual bonuses in a down payment on a house."

POPULATION: 12,200.

AREA: 1.73 square miles.

MEDIAN HOUSEHOLD INCOME: $45,495.

MEDIAN PRICE OF A SINGLE-FAMILY HOUSE: $374,000.

TAXES ON A MEDIAN-PRICED HOUSE: $7,700.

PUBLIC SCHOOL SPENDING PER PUPIL: $10,487.

DISTANCE FROM MIDTOWN MANHATTAN: 55 miles.

RUSH-HOUR TRAVEL TO MIDTOWN: 5 minutes from the borough to Princeton Junction on a local shuttle called the Dinky train and then 60 minutes to Penn Station on the N.J. Transit train, $9.85 one way, $14 round-trip, $84 weekly.

CODES: Area, 609; ZIPs, 08540 and 08542.

Prices of Princeton homes match their prestigious address. The least-expensive one listed for sale by the multiple-listing service in early 1998 was a small, three-bedroom Colonial on a tiny lot on John Street, offered at $135,000. But the typical starter home in the borough is a three-bedroom unit that is half of a duplex house, priced at $170,000 or more, according to Susan Gordon, a sales representative with Coldwall Banker Residential Real Estate Services on Nassau Street.

The upper-end dwellings are stately stucco and brick mansions with six or more bedrooms on the western end of the borough with prices starting at about $800,000 and rising to over $2 million.

Among the borough's newer residents are Susanna C. Monseau, an international lawyer from London, and her husband, Marc D., a writer. The couple moved to Princeton from London in January 1995. At first, they rented an apartment and then purchased a three-bedroom half-duplex on Harris Road for $150,000. Mr. Monseau now works in public relations for Johnson & Johnson, the pharmaceutical giant, in nearby Somerset and Mrs. Monseau is employed by a local law firm.

"If we had chosen to live 20 minutes to the south, our money would have bought a four-bedroom house with some land," she said. "But we wanted a place with culture, where you could walk around without the battle of public transport of a major city."

Mrs. Monseau said she was a bit intimidated by the wealth of Princeton, where costly boutiques are replacing traditional shops, such as the F. W. Woolworth's store that recently closed and the only local supermarket, which became a health-food store. "You always worry about whether your child will think that everyone is richer than him," she explained.

Many of the borough's condominiums and rental apartments are situated above stores in Palmer Square. According to Ms. Gordon, studio condominiums now start at about $89,000. The highest-priced condominiums are in 150-year-old Guernsey Hall, a converted mansion off Lovers Lane in the western section of the borough, where a huge one-bedroom, two-bath unit with a library and a one-car garage sold for $650,000 in 1996. A smaller two-bedroom unit in the same building sold for $310,000 in 1997. The largest condominium complex is the 100-unit Queenston Common off Harrison Street on the east side of the borough, where three- and four-bedroom units with garages and basements sell for $189,000 to $300,000.

Apartments in Princeton rent for between $1,200 for some one-bedroom units and $2,500 for two-bedrooms.

Princeton Borough derived its name from its site along the Kings Highway, which connected Kingston, now a part of Princeton Township, and Queenston, an earlier name for New Brunswick. Nassau Hall was named for William III, prince of Orange-Nassau and king of England from 1689 to 1702. During the Revolutionary War, the borough changed hands several times. In December 1776, the British forces under Lord Cornwallis seized Nassau Hall for use as a barracks, hospital, and stable. A month later, George Washington's army defeated the British in the Battle of Princeton, turning the tide in the Revolutionary War. Nassau Hall still bears a scar from a cannonball fired by Continental troops during the battle.

Princeton Borough youngsters comprise about one-third of the 3,100 students in the Princeton Regional School District, which it shares with Princeton Township. The district includes four kindergarten-to-grade 5 elementary schools, the grades 6–8 Princeton Middle School, and Princeton High School. There is also the publicly financed 72-student Princeton Charter School for grades 4–6, which stresses traditional education, eliminating many of the electives in other public schools.

The district, which serves as Mercer County's Educational Technology Training Center for teachers, prides itself on technological achievements. Computers are introduced in kindergarten, where some of the more advanced students learn to draw and even to work the word processors.

The 960-student Princeton High School offers 16 advanced placement courses in history, government, foreign languages, mathematics, sciences, music, art, and computers. Nearly 75 percent of its 83 teachers hold advanced degrees.

In 1997, Princeton High School seniors scored 593 and 598, respectively, on the verbal and mathematics sections of the SAT, each of which was about 85 points above the national average. Eighty-eight percent of the 192 graduating seniors went on to higher education.

Acting School Superintendent Daniel M. Swirsky said that roughly 75 percent of parents in Princeton Borough had university degrees, with a third of that number holding advanced degrees. These parents, he said, are heavily involved in the school system and have high expectations of their children and of the teachers. "We try to meet those expectations by being extremely selective in our staffing," said Dr. Swirsky. "We look for applicants with strong educational backgrounds and proven success. Sometimes we will visit the applicant's classroom in his prior job, to view his lessons in progress."

Princeton University is not the only institution of higher learning in the borough. Others include the Princeton Theological Seminary (Presbyterian), the music campus of Rider University, and the Westminster Choir College, a 400-student, four-year college that prepares students for careers as church musicians and choir directors.

The Institute for Advanced Study, where Albert Einstein was a professor of mathematics from 1932 until his death in 1955, is just across the line in Princeton Township. It caters to postdoctoral scholars.

Borough residents have access to a wide array of cultural institutions, the most famous of which is McCarter Theater. They can also visit the university's Art Museum, Museum of Natural History, and Firestone Library, which has more than five million volumes, 50,000 periodicals, many rare books, and a children's library with interactive exhibits.

Another important borough site is Drumthwacket, official residence of the governor of New Jersey.

One of the most visited historic sites is the Princeton Cemetery on Witherspoon Street. Among those interred there are Grover Cleveland, Aaron Burr, and John Witherspoon, who signed the Declaration of Independence.

The borough has one public park, the 17-acre Marquand Park at the intersection of Mercer Street and Lovers Lane. It is an arboretum with rare specimen trees, picnic grounds, and playground equipment.

RUMSON

*Abundant space, and no
cookie-cutter neighborhoods*

BY JERRY CHESLOW

Flanked by the Shrewsbury and Navesink Rivers and just a mile west of the Atlantic and 45 miles from Manhattan, Rumson has been a magnet for wealthy New York financiers for more than a century. In the 1890s, bankers and industrialists like Jacob Schiff built estates of dozens of acres and commuted by boat across New York Bay to lower Manhattan. "At the time, Rumson Street was the showplace of New Jersey," said Mayor Charles Callman. "People would drive here just to get a look at the beautiful estates, with their large houses and spectacular gardens."

Today, the natural beauty of the 5.2-square-mile Borough of Rumson continues to attract Wall Street bankers, many of whom commute to the Monmouth County community on an Express Navigation ferry from the nearby Highlands to Pier 91 just north of the South Street Seaport. Among the more expensive homes are several built by well-known architects, including Stanford White.

Fewer than two dozen houses were under construction in 1997, with all but a handful being marketed for more than $700,000. The largest property in Rumson, a 30-acre estate complete with 32-room mansion, outbuildings, and stables, recently sold to a Wall Street financier for $3.7 million.

"The profile of the couples moving in here is that they are in their 30s and 40s with one or two children," said P. J. Rotchford, manager/broker at Gloria Nilson Realtors in Rumson. "They know that Manhattan is not where they want to raise their children and can afford something special."

Among the newer residents are Christopher J. Evans, his wife, Deborah, and their 4-year-old daughter. They moved to Rumson from Manhattan in December 1992 because, Mr. Evans said, he "has a thing about being on the water." Their home is a renovated Dutch Colonial on three-quarters

POPULATION: 6,171.

AREA: 5.2 square miles.

MEDIAN HOUSEHOLD INCOME: $80,329.

MEDIAN PRICE OF A SINGLE-FAMILY HOUSE: $390,000.

TAXES ON A MEDIAN-PRICED HOUSE: $7,000.

PUBLIC SCHOOL SPENDING PER PUPIL: Elementary, $7,058; high school, $10,012.

DISTANCE FROM MIDTOWN MANHATTAN: 45 miles.

RUSH-HOUR TRAVEL TO MIDTOWN: 70 minutes on the N.J. Transit train from Little Silver or Red Bank to Penn Station, $8.90 one way, $13 round-trip, $249 monthly.

CODES: Area, 732; ZIP, 07760.

of an acre, backing up to the Navesink River. Mr. Evans says he likes the fact that Rumson has large properties, keeping congestion down. "Many people buy a summer home and use it on weekends, or their wives and kids stay in the Hamptons while they spend the week in Manhattan and go home for the weekend," said Mr. Evans, a 37-year-old Wall Street money manager. "My goal was to have just one house, but it had to be in a recreational environment."

Mayor Callman is quick to point out that many houses are available for less than $150,000. Most are tiny, turn-of-the century converted bungalows or Capes on small lots on streets like Meadowbrook Road, Maplewood Road, and Ward Lane in an area known to old-timers as Cartontown, perhaps because of the small size of its bungalows. Some of the original owners of those homes worked on the large estates prior to World War I, according to George Moss, a borough councilman and local historian.

There are no cookie-cutter neighborhoods in Rumson. On many streets throughout the borough, small ranches, Capes, and Colonials that sell for $200,000 to $300,000 are next to larger, custom homes on more than an acre that sell for a million dollars or more. Mr. Moss attributes this to the way in which large, turn-of-the-century estates were broken up. "After World War I, the men came home from overseas, where they learned that there was a future beyond serving the owners of the large estates," Mr. Moss said. "So the large estates lost their source of inexpensive labor and found it impractical to keep so much land. They started dividing the land and selling off parts of it for construction. That process continues to this day. Therefore, you have mansions near small houses."

A median-priced home would sell for $390,000, with taxes of $7,000 a year. On a home selling for $1.8 million, taxes would be $27,000 to $30,000.

There are only 40 condominium town houses in the borough. They are in a complex called Rumson Park, off River Road. The median price of a two-bedroom condominium in the borough is $210,000, Mr. Rotchford said. The only apartments in the borough are over some of the stores in the business districts and are designated as nonconforming. Rents are about $750 a month for two-bedrooms.

There are three small business districts within a quarter of a mile of each other on River Road, a main thoroughfare that links the borough to Red Bank. They contain the usual complement of banks, boutiques, delicatessens, bagel shops, and hairdressing salons. There is also a wide variety of restaurants, including Barnacle Bill's and Hook, Line and Sinker, both of which serve seafood, Fromagerie (Continental), Briody's (American), Val's Tavern (Italian), and What's Your Beef, a steakhouse. The Rumson Market, similar to an old general store, is a gathering place for locals. No neon lights are permitted in the borough, making many of the business establishments barely distinguishable from local houses.

For supermarket shopping, residents go to neighboring Red Bank, Fair Haven, or Little Silver. The closest large mall is the Monmouth Mall in Eatontown, six miles southwest.

No one knows for sure what the name Rumson means. One old story, vehemently denied by Mr. Moss, is that the borough land was bought from the Leni Lenape Indians in the late 17th century for "some rum." The name may be a shortened version of the Indian name for the area, Narrumsum, which appears on a deed of sale of the land by the 11 Indians to a group of Englishmen from Long Island on April 7, 1665, for $359.

Rumson was mostly a farming community with a few large estates until 1870, when a drawbridge was built across the Shrewsbury River, linking Rumson to the Borough of Sea Bright and convenient boat travel to Manhattan. This set off a wave of estate building by New York society.

Among the institutions founded by the residents of the estates was the Sea Bright Lawn Tennis and Cricket Club on Rumson Road in 1877, just four years after tennis was introduced to the United States. The club, which has 15 courts, is listed in the National Register of Historic Places and has been designated by the Department of the Interior as a National Historic Landmark. The club has a two-year waiting list for membership. The initiation fee is $4,500 per family, with an annual fee of $650 per player. Also in the borough is the Rumson Country Club off Ward Avenue, which includes an 18-hole golf course and tennis courts.

Other recreational facilities include the five-acre Victory Park, donated to the borough in 1920 by Bertram H. Borden, an estate owner and former president of the board of education. The park, off River Road, has two tennis courts, a basketball court, and a large gazebo, which is sometimes used for concerts. The largest park is the 23-acre Meadow Ridge Park off Ridge Road. It has two baseball diamonds, two soccer fields, a tot lot, and walking paths.

In addition, according to Mayor Callman, the Navesink and Shrewsbury Rivers offer some of the finest fishing in New Jersey, including striped bass, bluefish, and flounder.

Rumson's children attend the Deane-Porter School from kindergarten through third grade, followed by the Forrestdale School for grades 4 to 8, which share a campus on Forrest Avenue. In 1997, the district spent $7,058, per pupil, compared with a statewide average of $7,794. At the same time, it pays 10 percent more per teacher in salaries. "We are trying to attract the best and the brightest teachers from across the country," said the superintendent of schools, Dr. Jack Woodbury. "We want them to be good examples for our students. That's one of the best ways to build lifelong learners."

Both Forrestdale and Deane-Porter have 25 computer laboratories and at least one computer per classroom, with some classrooms having five. According to Dr. Woodbury, all graduates of Forrestdale are proficient in the use of both I.B.M.-compatible and Macintosh computers.

On the 1995 New Jersey State Early Warning Test, Forrestdale eighth graders scored seventh highest of the 640 schools in the state. The students also take the Educational Records Bureau Test, which is used mainly by wealthier districts and private schools. In almost all subjects, Rumson students from grades 3 to 8 consistently exceed the average scores of other public schools and match those of most independent schools.

From Forrestdale, the students go on to the 650-student Rumson–Fair Haven Regional High School, which typically sends 95 percent of its graduating seniors to higher education.

There is one parochial school, the Roman Catholic Holy Cross School on Rumson Road, for kindergarten through eighth grade. There is also a nonsectarian private school, the Rumson Country Day School on the corner of Ridge Road and Bellevue Avenue, for the same grades.

By far the most famous resident of Rumson is the singer Bruce Springstein, who has a brick and wood mansion with turrets on five acres off Rumson Road. The house is shielded from prying eyes by large artificially created hills of earth.

NEW JERSEY

SUMMIT

A transit hub with a thriving downtown

BY JERRY CHESLOW

In the early 18th century, what is now Summit was called Poverty Hill because the land was suitable only for hardscrabble farming. But poverty is but a dim memory today. Property values are rising sharply in the six-square-mile Union County city, where the average household income was $171,500 for 1997 and the median was $98,500 according to estimates by city officials. Since May 1996, when New Jersey Transit designated it as its hub for the Midtown Direct train line, the average sale price for a house has risen by $81,000, to $518,000, according to Lois Schneider, owner of a local real estate agency that bears her name. The median price of a single-family home is $370,000, with taxes of $6,200.

Two train lines—one from Chatham and Madison and the other from Morristown—now funnel into Summit, then move directly into Penn Station in midtown Manhattan 25 miles away. Midtown Direct shaves approximately 25 minutes off the commute that previously took passengers 70 minutes to Manhattan via Hoboken and the PATH train.

Mayor Walter D. Long said 28 percent of his town's wage earners worked in the financial, real estate, and insurance industries in New York. Many, he added, earn more than $1 million a year.

House prices range from $106,000 for a two-bedroom handyman special to more than $2 million. Many small houses on prime lots go for $500,000 to $1 million, just to be torn down so that a larger home can be built.

Near the low end of the market, 40-year-old, three-bedroom Colonials, ranches, expanded Capes, and split-levels range in price from about $220,000 to $280,000, according to Mrs. Schneider. They are mainly on the northern, western, and eastern ends of town. The most expensive areas of town are in the northeastern section, where grander Colonials with deep

Summit **427**

POPULATION: 19,441.

AREA: 6 square miles.

MEDIAN HOUSEHOLD INCOME: $98,500.

MEDIAN PRICE OF A SINGLE-FAMILY HOUSE: $370,000.

PROPERTY TAXES ON A MEDIAN-PRICED HOUSE: $6,200.

PUBLIC SCHOOL SPENDING PER PUPIL: $9,200.

DISTANCE FROM MIDTOWN MANHATTAN: 22 miles.

RUSH-HOUR TRAVEL TO MIDTOWN: 45 minutes on the N.J. Transit train to Penn Station, $5.85 one way, $164 monthly; 50 minutes on the Lakeland bus to the Port Authority Midtown terminal, $5.60 one way, 10-trip ticket, $49.50.

CODES: Area, 908; ZIP, 07901.

setbacks on lots of an acre or more sell for $1 million to $2 million, and housing within a walk or bike ride of the train station is in great demand.

"We take sealed bids on choice streets such as Linden Place and Oakland Place in the downtown area," said Mrs. Schneider. "Four- or five-bedroom older houses can go for between $500,000 and $675,000."

The largest co-op apartment complex is the 40-unit Parmally Place on Summit Avenue, where prices range from about $75,000 for a one-bedroom to $175,000 for some two-bedroom apartments.

There are 475 condominium units in town, ranging in price from about $105,000 for a one-bedroom apartment in the 25-year-old Morris Glen condominium complex on Morris Avenue to $575,000 for a three-bedroom luxury town house in the Beacon Square complex on Springfield Avenue. The largest number of condominiums are in the $250,000 range, according to Mrs. Schneider.

The largest rental complex is the 132-unit New England Village, where two- and three-bedroom apartments go for $1,150 to $1,400 a month.

The area that is now Summit was part of the Eizabethtown Purchase, a half-million-acre tract that the English bought from the Leni Lenape Indians in 1664. It stands atop the 450-foot-high Second Watchung Mountain, affording excellent views of the New York City skyline. By the time of the Revolutionary War, the community was known as Turkey Hill, rather than Poverty Hill, because of an abundance of wild turkeys in the area.

The name Summit may have been coined by James Kent, retired chancellor of the Court of Chancery, New York State's highest judicial office, who bought a house on the hill in 1837 and named it Summit Lodge. Another version of the way Summit got its name is that, around the same time, a sawmill owner named James Bonnell gave the Morris & Essex Railroad free right-of-way across his property, on condition that its track would pass near his sawmill. The company bought a special locomotive to pull the railroad cars up to what it called "the summit of the Short Hills."

Although it is only two miles from the Mall at Short Hills, Summit's downtown is thriving. Of its 200 stores, only a handful are vacant and most of the apartments over the stores have been converted to office space. On July 4, 1997, a five-screen movie house opened there. "Our business district is service-oriented," said Mayor Long. "There are 20 restaurants. So when people go to the nearby malls, they come to us for dinner. Our stores are mostly owner-operated, so they provide a very high level of customer service, which keeps the local clientele coming back."

Of the 20 restaurants, 13 are Italian, with the longest-standing being Marco Polo, on Morris Avenue. Among the other upscale restaurants is Soufflé, a French establishment on Union Place. The one establishment known to everyone in town is the Summit Diner, a stainless steel and porcelain enamel structure that was opened in 1938.

Downtown parking, a problem for decades, has become even more difficult with the arrival of Midtown Direct, which runs 20 rush-hour trains through Summit daily. "We are short 500 spaces in our downtown," said Reagan Burkholder, the city administrator. "In the near future, we will be making alterations in parking patterns and will build a new parking garage to remedy the problem."

Midtown Direct has spawned a thriving morning coffee business on Broad Street and Union Place, around the train station. The newest arrival on the scene is Starbucks, which siphons business from two other long-standing coffee operations. "We roast all of our beans in town," said Peter Peoria, manager of the Common Ground Cafe at Ahrre's Coffee Roasterie. "People stop here to buy their beans because they love our coffee. But they want that expensive Starbucks coffee cup to show as they wait for the train."

Residents call their downtown and the 2,800-student Summit public school system the city's main attractions. In 1997, Summit High School sent 93 percent of its 145-student graduating class to higher education. On the SATs, seniors had median scores of 554 in verbal and 552 in math, about 50 points above the New Jersey and national averages for each test. The high school offers advanced placement courses in 13 subjects.

The system includes five kindergarten-through-grade 5 elementary schools, a middle school for grades 6 to 8, and Summit High School. Annual per-pupil spending is $9,200. School Superintendent Dr. Michael G. Knowlton said that the system focused on language skills through the use of literature, rather than books created for pedagogic purposes. "We want the children to want to read," he explained. "So we expose them to fine literature at a young age."

Computers are introduced in kindergarten and every classroom has at least one terminal. The computer systems in all schools were recently upgraded through a $3 million technology program that also provided all schools with Internet access. In addition, the school system is a pioneer in providing students with computers for home use through the Mayor's Partnership for Technology, a volunteer group headed by former mayor Janet Whitman.

"We raised $425,000 for a pilot project and for the first year of operation," Mrs. Whitman explained. "We provided teachers with laptops and training and bought 50 laptops that students were allowed to take home. We also conducted a survey of the incoming freshman class to determine who had what type of computer equipment. We will be purchasing equipment to supplement what they have, so that all Summit freshmen will have the technology needed to prepare them for tomorrow's job market." The partnership is seeking to raise $400,000 more, according to Mrs. Whitman, to expand the program.

Summit has two Roman Catholic schools—the Oak Knoll School of the Holy Child, co-ed kindergarten to grade 6, with girls only from grades 7 to 12, and Oratory Catholic Prep School for boys, covering grades 7 through 12.

The town has three major parks, the largest of which is the 20-acre Memorial Field off Ashland Road. It has three baseball diamonds, a running track, a football field, three soccer fields, and six tennis courts. The one-acre Mabie Playground has new playground equipment bought through an $85,000 fund-raising drive.

The 12-acre Reeves-Reed Arboretum, which is listed in both the National and the New Jersey Register of Historic Places, offers a profusion of flower gardens. The estate was purchased in 1974 from Ann Reed by a group of conservationists for $380,500. The nonprofit Reeves-Reed Arboretum organization received a $426,000 grant in 1997 from the New Jersey Trust for Historic Preservation to maintain the property.

Anne and Jim Poyner and their three children moved from Dallas in 1994, when Jim was hired as an analyst by a Wall Street firm. In 1997, Anne directed *The Music Man* in a fund-raiser for the Summit Public Library. "We had 200 volunteers, including myself, and raised $56,000," said Mrs. Poyner, a homemaker. "That says that we are a town that is willing to commit both its money and its time to good causes."

Mrs. Poyner said that she got sticker shock when purchasing her four-bedroom ranch. "We sold a 4,000-square-foot custom-built Colonial in Dallas for $280,000," she said. "We paid half a million dollars for a 2,500-square-foot ranch that needed work in Summit. But it was worth it. We are in a community with a great school system, where everyone is concerned about education and we are a short train ride from Broadway."

WEEHAWKEN

Insular neighborhoods with expansive views

BY BRET SENFT

The thin trees rustle their protection above the neighborhood called the Shades and rise up the cliffs toward the rest of Weehawken: the Heights and the Bluffs, sitting at varied altitudes ascending north along the Palisades.

It is quiet in the Shades, where reeds break through the sidewalks and tidy two-family houses are passed to the next generation of McLaughlins (many of the clan moved here from Manhattan's Hell's Kitchen in the 1950s) and other families on its four short streets in from West 19th Street and the waterfront. Kelly Devaney, whose husband, Christopher, is the eighth child of Rosemarie Devaney, née McLaughlin, of adjacent Chestnut Street, said: "We're all still very close, everybody. It's all very family-oriented—you know you're very secure down here."

While the insular nature of the Shades is extreme, similar feelings are echoed throughout Weehawken, a town with a population of 12,000 where lifelong residents of German, Irish, and Italian heritage have been joined by an increasing Latino population, now at over 40 percent.

The nearby Lincoln Tunnel and the views along the Palisades cliffs—the George Washington and Verrazano-Narrows Bridges and the Manhattan skyline across the Hudson—have a magnetic hold on its residents. Its location—three miles from midtown Manhattan, with a 10-minute, low-cost commute by mini-van, N.J. Transit bus, or river ferry service—means easy access to New York, without having to be there.

It has been prized real estate since the Dutch bought it from the Lenni Lenape Indians in the early 1600s, and it was still pastoral in 1804 when Aaron Burr killed Alexander Hamilton in a duel on a grassy shelf near the shoreline. (A bust of Hamilton, and the boulder on which he fell, is set atop the cliffs just south of Hamilton Park on Boulevard East.) Development

POPULATION: 11,929.

AREA: 0.8 square mile.

MEDIAN HOUSEHOLD INCOME: $46,637.

MEDIAN PRICE OF A TWO-FAMILY HOUSE: $230,000.

TAXES ON A MEDIAN-PRICED HOUSE: $6,100.

PUBLIC SCHOOL SPENDING PER PUPIL: $7,200.

DISTANCE FROM MIDTOWN MANHATTAN: 3 miles.

RUSH-HOUR TRAVEL TO MIDTOWN: 10 minutes on the N.J. Transit bus ($1.90 one way, $50 monthly) or mini-van ($1.75 one way) to the Port Authority midtown terminal; PATH trains ($1 one way) from Hoboken; 5-minute ferry service ($4.50 one way, $150 monthly) from Port Imperial to 38th Street and 12th Avenue (complimentary bus service to midtown locations).

CODES: Area, 201; ZIP, 07087.

took the form of mansions built in the early to mid–19th century along the bluffs. There was a restaurant in a Rhenish castle on the hilltop and, for a brief decade in the 1890s, an ornate amusement resort. Nothing remains from that era except the Italianate brick water tower on Park Avenue. Its accompanying reservoir was replaced in 1981 by a Pathmark supermarket and a Little League baseball field.

From the early 1900s to 1929, housing for working people filled the town. One-family houses were divided into income-producing units in the Depression, and again in the early 1970s, against the increased tax burden, after the collapse of the waterfront's rail yards and shipyards.

In the Heights, two-family row houses line Gregory Avenue (backing onto the cliffs), with two- and three-family houses on the cross streets west to Palisade Avenue. Fred and Marianne Lorenz raised their three children in a two-family house on Oak Street; when their daughter got married in 1995, the newlyweds moved in upstairs. In 1994, the Lorenzes purchased a three-family house for their sons, one a local fireman, the other a computer graphics illustrator in Manhattan, on Palisade Avenue between Dodd and Jane Streets for $223,000: two family units for the sons, a third for income.

"It's about four blocks away," said Mrs. Lorenz, who was born here, as was her father before her. "You can walk back and forth. You know, you really feel your roots here." As for the ethnic mix in the community, she said: "Our family was Irish-Italian and I have neighbors who are Cuban, South American, Italian, German, Puerto Rican—and everyone's interested in having a nice neighborhood. Everyone gets along fine."

Richard Barsa, finance director for the Town of Weehawken, grew up on Gregory Avenue; his mother is still there, the house overlooking the remaining town reservoir. The Barsas moved out of town for a while when things were not going well for Weehawken. In 1981, a waterfront development scandal led to the conviction of the then mayor, and wrangling between the town council and school board led to contested school budgets and loss of state certification in 1984. Municipal services and town government have since been stabilized, and the school district has its certification back.

Mr. Barsa and his wife, Diane (born and raised on Boulevard East), left for Rutherford with their newborn son. "But it was too quiet," Mr. Barsa said. "Too suburban." Returning in 1986, they bought a three-family house uptown on Louisa Place for $290,000, then a three-family on Bonn Avenue in the Bluffs in 1993 at foreclosure for $290,000.

Mrs. Barsa, a real estate broker with Crown Properties, said that homes in the Bluffs usually ranged from $300,000 to $1 million or more—prices that have held steady for the last several years. "But there are very few homes for sale," she said. "And if it's priced fairly, once it goes on the market, it goes immediately.

"Right now, there are five offers on every property at full price," she said, "and now they've been selling for over full price—it's become like a bidding war."

The median price of a two-family house was $203,000 in 1994 and $230,000 at the beginning of 1998—about a 12 percent increase (taxes on that median-priced house are about $6,100). Taxes have increased in the wake of a ruling involving Port Imperial, the developer Arthur E. Imperatore's complex of a 300-slip marina, a waterfront restaurant, and a two-tiered, 90-tee, golf driving range. "But," Mr. Barsa, the city finance director, points out, "we still have the second-lowest tax rate in Hudson County" (behind Secaucus).

Apartment rentals range from $750 for a one-bedroom in the Heights to $2,000-plus for a three-bedroom with fireplace, stained glass, and original woodwork in the Bluffs, a 25 percent increase over the last five years. "The reason is, we have overflow from Hoboken, which has zero vacancies, and from Manhattan," said Mrs. Barsa.

There are perhaps a dozen co-op and condo buildings. However, "the market for them is very slow," Mrs. Barsa said, "and when they sell, people are taking a loss."

On Boulevard East, where condominiums predominate, said Ilena Hernandez of the local Action Agency real estate firm, prices average $85,000 for studios to $119,000 for a two-bedroom condo. Recent listings at Gregory Commons, a 177-unit condominium in a converted factory atop the Heights with Manhattan views, include a two-bedroom penthouse duplex (1,643 square feet, with two large decks and 2½ baths with Jacuzzis) at an asking price of $329,000.

The school system, with 1,275 students systemwide, is 72 percent Latino, with expenditure per pupil at $7,200 per year, according to School

Superintendent Kevin McLellan. There are two elementary schools, Daniel Webster for pre-K to second grade, and Roosevelt for third to sixth grade (a third school, Woodrow Wilson Elementary, is rented to the Union City School District). Grades 7–12 attend Weehawken High School, with junior-high students in their own section of the building, with a different schedule from high schoolers. Gifted children enter an academically talented program in third grade, at the Roosevelt Elementary School.

About 70 percent of graduates go on to higher education, said Patricia Hannan, high school guidance director. The school declined to provide information on SAT scores.

"I found the school system better here," said Evelyn Rodriguez, who has three children in the school system. Her family moved here from the Bay Ridge section of Brooklyn over a decade ago. "Here there are, like, 20 kids per classroom, totally different from where I was raised," she said. "There are no guns and everybody knows everybody. I never had that growing up."

In recent years, the town has completed a $4.7 million restoration of the sidewalks and parks along Boulevard East; likewise, a $1 million program of new sidewalks and vintage street lamps for Park Avenue, the commercial strip of bodegas, stationery stores, and supermarkets along Weehawken's western border. (For most goods and services, including movie theaters, residents go to nearby towns and shopping malls.)

Restoration of the boulevard provides better access to the skyline views, and zoning ordinances restrict the height and size of buildings on or below the cliffs.

Ferry service to midtown (every 15 minutes day and evening) and downtown (during rush hour), and a 250-slip marina are available to residents of Riva Pointe condominiums at Lincoln Harbor, on a 1,000-foot pier. There are currently 145 units, a health club, and a parking garage. "One-bedrooms are selling in the high $180,000's, two-bedrooms in the $280,000's, and three-bedrooms around $320,000," said Linda Krissi of Realty Line in Fort Lee. A third phase of development, scheduled for 1998, will add 90 more units to create Riva Pointe III.

There had been ferry service in some form here since 1700 until the late '50s. In 1986, service was reinstated with Mr. Imperatore's New York Waterway, with continuous five-minute river crossings from Port Imperial to midtown (38th Street and 12th Avenue) seven days a week for $4.50 each way or $150 for a monthly ticket. A rush-hour ferry to and from Whitehall Street costs $5 one way, or $156 monthly. (There is Jersey-side parking for $5 per day.) Construction is to begin in late 1998 for a new, six-slip ferry terminal at Port Imperial with additional service to downtown and midtown Manhattan (where a new terminal is to be built at West 39th Street) planned to be in operation by 2000.

Connecticut

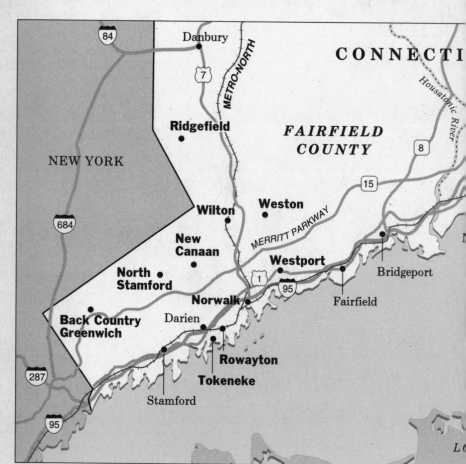

Weston

Westport

Wilton

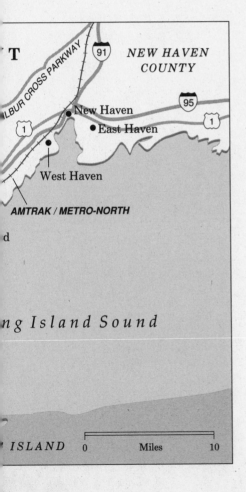

CONNECTICUT

BACK-COUNTRY GREENWICH

Winding roads and deep pockets

BY ELEANOR CHARLES

The farmers and shoemakers who settled the lonely northern reaches of Greenwich in the 18th and early 19th centuries would be astounded to see what has become of their neighborhood.

Renowned as one of America's most prestigious addresses, the back country of Greenwich, the 16.14 square miles bounded generally by the Merritt Parkway to the south (dipping to Clapboard Ridge and Dingletown Roads), Westchester County to the west and north, and Stamford to the east, is not for everyone who is rich. Families of highly placed executives who traditionally shun publicity gravitate to its silent woods and quiet, winding roads, while celebrities tend to prefer the waterfront and a livelier atmosphere.

The legendary great estates are investments that hold their value in recessions and appreciate when times are good. But other back-country homes are equally resilient, whether they are antique farmhouses expanded into handsome residences, large homes on the minimum four-acre lots, or modest houses in the Banksville section on the New York State border.

Among the most famous of the back country's great estates is Dunnellen Hall, until recently owned by Leona Helmsley and her husband, the late Harry Helmsley. Completed in 1918, it was built for Daniel Grey Reid, a New York financier, as a gift for his daughter, Rhea, and her husband, Henry J. Topping, son of the president of Republic Steel. Situated at one time on 208 acres, the 28-room Elizabethan mansion had additional accommodations for 23 servants. The lake was stocked with perch and black bass, and there was an eight-car garage, stables, a pool, a tennis court, a greenhouse, a working farm, and specimen gardens.

It was used to advantage by the Toppings' sons, who entertained

POPULATION: 6,971.

AREA: 16.14 square miles.

MEDIAN HOUSEHOLD INCOME: $188,283.

MEDIAN PRICE OF A SINGLE-FAMILY HOUSE: $1.4 million.

TAXES ON A MEDIAN-PRICED HOUSE: $14,102.

PUBLIC SCHOOL SPENDING PER PUPIL: $9,738.

DISTANCE FROM MIDTOWN MANHATTAN: 33 miles.

RUSH-HOUR TRAVEL TO MIDTOWN: 52 minutes on Metro-North, $9 one way, $196 monthly.

CODES: Area, 203, ZIP, 16830 and 16831.

lavishly and enjoyed the company of movie stars. Don and Henry Jr. each married the actress Arlene Judge, at different times, of course; Don was also married to Sonja Henie, and Henry Jr. was wed to Lana Turner.

It usually takes a year or more for estates to be sold because the market is obviously limited and the owners can afford to wait for the right buyer. A great estate on Crown Lane, on the market for more than four years at $18 million, was reduced to $15.5 million and contracted for sale in 1998. A Georgian Colonial on 14 acres, with taxes of $60,586, it sits on a hill with views of Long Island Sound, has a pool and poolhouse, a lighted tennis court, two guest houses, a greenhouse, and a birch forest.

"It was seldom shown," said Linda Hodge, vice president of Preferred Properties of Greenwich, a company that specializes in marketing high-priced homes. "The price reflects the value of scarce prime land close to New York," she said.

A number of the former great estates have been broken up into smaller parcels, invariably containing large houses with sizable price tags. Together with zoning laws that allow homes to be built on two-acre lots provided that 40 percent of the total property is dedicated to open space, the conversions signal a significant departure from the otherwise rigidly enforced four-acre minimum single-family zoning.

Brad Hvolbeck, owner of Prudential Hvolbeck Real Estate, is the agent for one of the subdivided estates: Conyers Farm, on 1,300 acres along North Street, with about one-third of its acreage in New York State. Two vacant parcels of 10 and 11 acres, both overlooking Converse Lake, were recently for sale at $1.8 million and $3.9 million, respectively. Boating access to the mile-long, 100-acre lake is restricted to properties surrounding it. A 45-acre parcel for $7.8 million has 2,200 feet of lakefront and is subdivided for two homes, and an 11,000-square-foot stone and clapboard Colonial being built on a 15.9-acre lot was priced at $6.25 million.

Conyers Manor—once on the property, but demolished in the mid-eighties—was built in 1904 by Edmund Cogswell Converse. His farm was a highly profitable enterprise employing dozens of local people in its dairy, produce farm, stables, garages, orchards, and stone quarries. The manor was subsequently demolished.

In 1981, the estate of Lewis Rosenstiel, the late chairman of Schenley's, sold the property to Peter Brandt, who redeveloped the property, reviving the name Conyers Farm, into deed-restricted lots of a minimum of 10 acres, some of which have been purchased as horse farms.

Local zoning permits one horse for every half acre. Residents belong to a private association and have sole use of a luxurious clubhouse. In June, July, and September, there are Sunday afternoon polo matches held within the complex on a polo field just off North Street that are open to the public for $20 a car.

Almost half of back-country children attend private schools, two of which are located in the area. The Whitby School American Montessori Center enrolls children from 1 year old through the eighth grade, with annual tuition ranging from $6,840 to $12,900. The Convent of the Sacred Heart, in the main house of what was once Overlook Farm, built in 1916, accepts children of all faiths from age 3 through 12th grade. Tuition is $6,000 to $13,900.

Greenwich has three other private day schools. Two run from pre-K through grade 12, and share co-ed classes in the four years of high school. The Brunswick School has an enrollment of 650 boys, and Greenwich Academy has 720 girls; tuition at both is $10,000 to $16,500. Greenwich Country Day School, with 800 boys and girls in pre-K through ninth grade, charges from $7,500 to $16,300.

The only public school in the back country is Parkway Elementary School, where the curriculum includes art, music, science, physical education, and a computer lab, all in separately equipped rooms. Children maintain their own word-processing files and write stories that are published in the school newspaper or adapted into dance, drama, art, or choral music. Almost 300 pupils in kindergarten through the fifth grade are bused for 15 to 40 minutes each way, depending on where they live. "They are not only from wealthy homes," said Dr. Sandra Mond, the principal, "but from families of stable grooms and housekeepers who live on the estates." In the 1997–98 school year, the town's per-pupil spending was $9,738.

Public school pupils go on to Greenwich High School, where the enrollment, now at 1,950, has been rising in recent years. "We think this was attributable to delayed baby-boomer births," said John Curtin, assistant headmaster at Greenwich High. Another change at the school in recent years has been an increase in advanced placement courses. "A.P. courses have expanded dramatically over the last five or six years, in part because of new subjects like environmental sciences," Mr. Curtin said. "We are now up to 29 courses."

SAT scores in 1997 averaged 532 for verbal and 547 for math, compared with national averages of 505 for verbal and 511 for math.

There are no restaurants or shops in the back country except in Banksville, where a tannery once served a shoemaking cottage industry. The Uptown Luncheonette serves breakfast and lunch to people who work on the estates; Finch's Pharmacy serves coffee; and an I.G.A. market, a dry cleaner, and a hardware store are patronized by area residents.

There is also a general store on Round Hill Road opposite the firehouse, which is home base for about 20 volunteer firefighters. Its equipment is maintained by a $5,000 annual stipend from the town and major contributions from the wealthy residents it serves. An open house fundraiser is held there each October, when children are given rides on the fire engines.

Fairview, Stanwich, and Tamarack, three of Greenwich's seven private country clubs, are in the back country, offering golf, tennis, swimming pools, and dining rooms. Initiation fees range up to $25,000. Bruce Memorial Golf Course is public, operated by the town for seasonal memberships of $40 to $75, and greens fees of $7 to $14, depending on age. Guests accompanied by town residents play for $35 a day.

Anyone who owns or has access to a horse may pay from $25 to $150 a year, depending on age, or $250 a year for a family, to join the Riding and Trails Association, which maintains more than 150 miles of trails and must deal diplomatically with the occasional new resident who does not appreciate the time-honored custom of allowing horses to cross his or her property.

The golf course and the country clubs are part of some 5,453 acres of the back country preserved as open space and owned variously by the town, by land trusts, the Audubon Society, schools, the state, or householders who dedicate land to conservation.

Preservation of open space has been a priority since the 1930s, when the Merritt Parkway, in its design stage, planned to cut a speedway straight across the estate section of Greenwich. When the route was made public, a contingent of influential back-country residents and foxhunting groups persuaded the authorities to change the configuration, creating the loop that peaks at 4.5 miles north of the original course, avoiding damage to many significant properties.

NEW CANAAN

Mecca for architects, and chief executives

BY ELEANOR CHARLES

In much of the 19th century, New Canaan was a community of farmers, blacksmiths, carpenters, weavers, and coopers. One day in 1830, the owner of Hoyt's General Store on Main Street had an attack of temperance and smashed his stock of liquor on the roadway. An astonished citizenry watched as all that good rum, gin, and bourbon sank into the dust. "The general store was where you bought liquor," said Mary Louise King, historian of what is now part of Connecticut's Gold Coast. "The town would vote to be wet or dry, back and forth every few years. We used to have more liquor stores than groceries, and until 1915, we had more Democrats than Republicans."

Some 18th-century houses are still scattered around town, vastly improved as prized antiques. One remaining commercial building, the 200-year-old sawmill by the waterfall on Jelliff Mill Road, continues to crank out fancy wood moldings.

Shoemaking was a principal industry for more than a century, but in the 1870s, the 50,000 handmade pairs produced annually could not compete with new machines in the big cities, and local workers started moving elsewhere to earn a living. By that time, wealthy New Yorkers had begun trickling in to build summer homes. With New Canaan just an hour and 10 minutes from midtown Manhattan, the trickle became a flood of year-round residents during the 1950s exodus from the cities.

In the mid-nineties, *Forbes* magazine ran an article about corporate America's most powerful people "that read like the New Canaan telephone directory," according to the *The New Canaan Advertiser*, a local weekly. Resident chief executives in recent years have included Paul Allaire of Xerox, Robert D. Kennedy of Union Carbide, John W. Johnstone, Jr., of the

POPULATION: 17,675.

AREA: 22 square miles.

MEDIAN FAMILY INCOME: $124,551.

MEDIAN PRICE OF A SINGLE-FAMILY HOUSE: $645,000.

TAXES ON A MEDIAN-PRICED HOUSE: $7,100.

PUBLIC SCHOOL SPENDING PER PUPIL: $9,655.

DISTANCE FROM MIDTOWN MANHATTAN: 41 miles.

RUSH-HOUR TRAVELS TO MIDTOWN: 69 minutes on Metro-North, $10 one way, $218 monthly.

CODES: Area, 203; ZIP, 06840.

Olin Corporation, and David Checketts, president and chief executive officer of Madison Square Garden.

Not surprisingly, the town is a mecca for architects. During the '90s, a house designed by Marcel Breuer sold for around $2 million, and one by Philip Johnson, who still occupies his own famous Glass House, was sold for about $1.25 million. A Frank Lloyd Wright house sold for $3.5 million. "I try to promote the contemporary style," said Barbara Cleary, owner of the Realty Guild, a local agency, "because we have some beauties."

Except for an occasional unwanted visitor breaking into David Letterman's house, life in New Canaan is relatively quiet, and that's how people like it. "Change here is evolutionary, not revolutionary," said Daniel Foley, the town planner. "There is still land to develop, but in small pieces of six to eight acres," he said. Zoning was devised decades ago to confine nonresidential development to the center of town. With land becoming scarce, a phenomenon is taking place throughout the Gold Coast towns, including New Canaan. Existing million-dollar houses on desirable pieces of property are being torn down to make way for the construction of new, larger homes on the same property. "It's the land that is so valuable," said Mr. Foley.

Prices of new homes in recent years have ranged from $500,000 to more than $3 million. In the resale market, "prices are going up at rates approaching 10 percent a year," said Prudence Parris, a broker with Coldwell Banker. "Young couples," she said, "can find resales in the $400,000 to $500,000 range, and larger older mansions on several acres sell for around $4 million." The median sale price increased from $500,000 in 1990 to $645,000 in 1997, with taxes on a median-valued house running about $7,100 a year.

Apartment-building rentals and condominiums (mostly town houses, and comprising 25 percent of the housing) are clustered around the business district of Main, Forest, and Elm Streets. Condominiums can cost as little as $150,000 and as much as $600,000, and some 30 to 40 of them are usually available for rent at $1,200 to $3,000 a month, according to Ms. Parris. Zoning radiates outward, with minimum one-family-home lot sizes ranging from 0.25 to 4 acres.

"Grand and gracious Colonials are going up on speculation and people are buying them before they are halfway complete or at the planning stage," said Ms. Cleary. "Buyers are mostly professional families with young children," she said, adding that alternatives are newer resales, perhaps a raised ranch at $645,000 on one acre, or, along South Avenue, "there are little streets with three-bedroom Cape Cods that come up for sale from $350,000 to $500,000," she noted.

New Canaan's 100 independent downtown shops aim for unusual clothing, silver, sporting goods, art, books, housewares, antiques, and gourmet foods. The *International Herald Tribune* can be found on the newspaper racks of gas stations.

Restaurants have increased at a rate of two or three a year in recent years. Toward the end of the '90s, there were 35 establishments, compared with two luncheonettes in the early 1970s. The Roger Sherman Inn, built in 1740, serves a Continental five-course dinner for $45; L'Abbee, rated as one of the top 10 restaurants in the Zagat suburban survey, charges $80 for a three-course dinner for two without wine. A signature dish is charcoal-grilled sea scallops with confetti linguine, portobello mushrooms, sautéed spinach, and a tomato velouté.

Unlimited play at New Canaan's 13 town tennis courts costs from $10 to $55 a season, depending on age, and a $25 resident's parking sticker admits a carload to Kiwanis Park, where a pond for swimming and ice-skating and a children's playground are available. There are six paddle tennis courts, where season passes cost $10 to $30. The 40-acre Nature Center, six bird sanctuaries, and five parks with baseball diamonds, hiking, and fishing are free for residents. There are also several private country clubs and sports clubs.

Among some 100 civic, cultural, and professional organizations are the Audubon Society, Alliance Française, Gentlemen Songsters, Embroiderer's Guild, Americares (a locally based international relief organization), National Association for the Advancement of Colored People, Business and Professional Women's Club, and New Canaan Bar Association.

The Town Players has its own theater in Waveny Park, a 300-acre public facility where mammoth Fourth of July town picnics are held. The prestigious Silvermine Guild Arts Center, a 75-year-old gallery and art school, presents concerts and lectures as well as exhibitions.

A new auditorium was added to the public library in 1993. According to the library's director, David Bryant, "We have a per capita readership of 17 books a year, about the highest in the state."

The highly rated public school system's 3,200 pupils attend three elementary schools, Saxe Middle School, and New Canaan High School. Annual per pupil expenditure in the late '90s has been around $9,655, and 85.6 percent of high school graduates typically go to college. The latest addition to the high school curriculum is Japanese Language and Culture, a two-year program culminating in a trip to Japan.

Because of an increase in population since 1994 that has added an estimated 600 school-age children, an expansion and upgrading of the elementary schools has been completed at a cost of $27.1 million. Expansion and upgrading of the middle school is in progress at an estimated cost of $26.2 million.

Among independent day schools, St. Luke's, a fifth-through-12th grade college preparatory school, charges $13,160 to $15,200. New Canaan Country School tuition ranges from $5,200 to $14,375 for prekindergarten through ninth grade. St. Aloysius School, a K-8 Roman Catholic school, charges $2,540 for parish children and $3,490 for nonparishioners.

Among six nursery schools and five day-care facilities, the Y.M.C.A. offers programs for children 6 weeks old through 5 years. Maximum hours are 7:30 A.M. to 6 P.M. five days a week, and monthly fees are $750 for children 3 to 5 years old and $1,166 for children 6 weeks to 3 years.

An equestrian school for children and adults is run by the New Canaan Mounted Troop, one of the last junior cavalries in the country. Children may start at age 5 and horse shows are presented periodically in a large indoor ring with a glass-fronted viewing room.

New Canaan's Historical Society, on Oenoke Ridge, is like a Colonial village, with a schoolhouse; the studio of John Rogers, a popular turn-of-the-century sculptor; the first town hall; a tool museum; a library; restored homes; and a printing press.

On Christmas Eve, the town is ablaze with lights and resonant with caroling at God's Acre, the Historic District overlooking Main Street. It was so named because it has three churches, built between 100 and 200 years ago, surrounding a small park that once served as the first settlers' burying ground.

The caroling is traditionally scheduled to start at 6:30, so that it can be joined by late-returning executives, lawyers, and other professionals leaving their commuter trains at the end of the ride from Manhattan.

NORTH STAMFORD

In a bustling city, a rural haven

BY ELEANOR CHARLES

Unlike most rural areas of Fairfield County, North Stamford has the best of two worlds: deep country with a vibrant city just a short drive away. Stamford's urbane downtown, fully emerged from an identity crisis dating back to urban renewal in the '70s, is now established as the business, entertainment, financial, and shopping hub of Fairfield County. Rural North Stamford, which stretches from the Merritt Parkway north, east, and west to Stamford's borders, comprises one-third of its 40 square miles. It was a village until 1949, when it became part of the City of Stamford.

A haven of quiet wooded hills and meadows, punctuated by rock outcroppings, veined with streams and dotted with ponds and lakes, it is entirely residential save for a few grandfathered gas stations, restaurants, and food markets, commercial uses that zoning now forbids.

During the early part of this century, when Stamford was a blue-collar factory town, north end real estate was cheap, bought mostly by working people on modest incomes. Beginning in the '20s, many New Yorkers looking for summer homes turned to back-country Stamford. Among them were Josh Logan, the theatrical producer; Gutzon Borglum, the Mount Rushmore sculptor; Ezio Pinza, Metropolitan Opera star; members of the Sulzberger publishing family; Vivian Vance, the Ethel Mertz of *I Love Lucy;* Alex Raymond, creator of the "Flash Gordon" comic strip; the actor Gene Wilder; the singer Cyndi Lauper; and Jackie Robinson, the baseball star.

Housing now includes subdivisions of raised ranches and Colonials built since the '50s on minimum one- to three-acre parcels, selling for $375,000 to $550,000. Large homes on several acres approach or exceed the $1 million mark. A small district of half-acre lots created before the upzoning in 1951 occasionally has homes that sell for less than $300,000.

POPULATION: 14,622.

AREA: 13 square miles.

MEDIAN HOUSEHOLD INCOME: $133,797.

MEDIAN PRICE OF A SINGLE-FAMILY HOUSE: $420,000.

TAXES ON A MEDIAN-PRICED HOUSE: $7,526.

PUBLIC SCHOOL SPENDING PER PUPIL: $8,900.

DISTANCE FROM MIDTOWN MANHATTAN: 35 miles.

RUSH-HOUR TRAVEL TO MIDTOWN: 45 minutes on Metro-North's New Haven line from downtown Stamford; up to 65 minutes from three outlying stations, $10 one way; $218 monthly.

CODES: Area, 203; ZIP, 06903.

Multifamily housing is prohibited by zoning, and there are about 5,500 single-family homes in the area.

Near the city's northern border a national historic district called Long Ridge Village contains 36 homes and outbuildings dating from 1750 to 1925. Benny Goodman, the clarinetist band leader, lived there for many years.

Incoming downtown businesses continue to bring new residents like Martin Vahsen, an executive with Citibank in Harrison, New York, who will divide his time between Citibank's Stamford office and Harrison. In 1998, he and his family moved into a 10-room Colonial on 1.25 acres next to a bird sanctuary. "It's not cheap, but I got great value and standard of living," said Mr. Vahsen.

Gary Di Silvestri, 30-year-old principal in Di Silvestri Asset Management of Stamford and Geneva, bought a $1.2 million house on 1.5 acres through Juner Properties' Roxbury Road office. It has five bedrooms, five baths, a gym, a three-car garage, two large entertaining rooms, a wine cellar, a music room, a media room, a maid's apartment, and a study. "I looked from Greenwhich to Southport," said Mr. Di Silvestri. "This house was the only one that met European construction standards that matched a custom home I had built in the French Alps."

With existing homes at a premium, new development is accelerating. "Young couples, both working, want new," said Gail Stone of the Long Ridge office of William Pitt Real Estate. "They don't want somebody else's dirt and they don't want major work." North Ridge Associates had that market in mind with custom homes for $900,000 and up on one-acre lots at Heming Way.

Residents of north end subdivisions typify Stamford's traditionally feisty citizenry, organizing over the years into some 20 neighborhood associations involved in lobbying for or against issues that affect them. "The preservation of open space and the proliferation of cell-phone towers are our major concerns," said Kit Martinsen, president of the North Stamford Association. Now that the city recently added 36 acres to an existing 1,646 acres of open space by buying the former Stamford campus of the University of Connecticut, North Stamford residents want the few remaining large tracts preserved. And they are seeking input into the process of approving sites for more than the two existing cellular phone towers in the area. The associations are also fighting the expansion of the private Children's School, citing zoning restrictions on commercial properties.

For north end residents, there is a rich mix of cultural and entertainment activities in downtown Stamford. In their own area, attractions include the Stamford Museum and Nature Center—the former mansion of the late Henri Bendel, the department store owner—with its restored 18th-century barn, animal farm, lake, art and science exhibits, and indoor and outdoor concerts. The Nature Conservancy's trails cover 136 acres of woods and fields, and the Bartlett Arboretum offers 62 acres of specimen trees, plants, flowers, and wetlands, plus lectures and guided nature walks.

On Sunday mornings, the place for gathering and gossiping is Giovanni's sprawling old market, crammed with high-grade meats, vegetables, and groceries. It operates the old-fashioned way, with charge accounts. Giovanni's is also the name of the family's north end steak and seafood house, where Maine lobsters can occasionally run to 18 pounds, serving six people.

An abundance of additional food and household shopping is available south of the Merritt Parkway on High Ridge and Long Ridge Roads, as well as in the 874,000-square-foot Stamford Town Center Mall downtown, which is anchored by Saks Fifth Avenue, Filene's, and Macy's; there is also a freestanding Lord & Taylor between High Ridge and Long Ridge Roads.

Children in North Stamford attend one of three public elementary schools in the north end, each with about 700 pupils from kindergarten through fifth grade; they go on to Turn of River Middle School and either Westhill or Stamford High School. Enrollment citywide increased by 25 percent in the last 10 years, mostly at the elementary level in poor downtown neighborhoods, generating a 20-year integration program in which students are bused to north end schools where Spanish-speaking children learn English and English-speaking children learn Spanish. In 1997, 87 percent of the high school graduates went on to higher education. The school's combined SAT score average of 950 in 1997 was well below the state's 1,116 average and the national average of 1,016.

Among north end day private schools is the Mead School on 13 acres, with 230 children from 6 weeks old through ninth grade. Emotional development is emphasized as well as academics and the arts. The pupil-teacher ratio is 5.3 to 1, and tuition ranges from $3,500 to $15,000 a year.

The Holy Spirit Roman Catholic School has 180 students from prekindergarten through fifth grade, 40 percent of whom are not Catholic.

When appropriate, accelerated or remedial programs are designed for individual pupils. Tuition is $2,540 for Catholics, $3,490 for non-Catholics.

The Bi-Cultural School offers a strong academic curriculum and a parallel curriculum in Judaic studies to 376 children from kindergarten through eighth grade. It ranked first in a NASA math competition, and recently had an advanced math class for one student. Tuition is $6,500 to $7,300.

King & Low–Heywood Thomas, a traditional college-prep school on 40 acres that traces its foundation back to 1865, has 635 students from 18 foreign countries and the United States. Up to 20 percent are in special programs for mild learning difficulties. Tuition from prekindergarten through 12th grade is $8,000 to $15,000.

Children's School, which takes pupils from 3 to 8 years old, is operated in a manner similar to the Montessori philosophy of letting the child select a particular focus. Tuition ranges from $3,900 to $9,900.

Citywide, a full program of children's and adult baseball, softball, and soccer is run by the Recreation Department. Ice-skating at the Terry Conners rink costs $4, children $2: It is free, seasonally, on the north end's frozen ponds. A $10 parking sticker admits residents to three beaches, and a season tennis permit for 45 city courts costs $50. There are also private tennis and swim clubs, and stables that board horses and give riding lessons.

The Sterling Farms and E. Gaynor Brennan municipal courses offer season permits of $20, plus daily play for $10 weekdays and $11 on weekends.

Renee Kahn, a north end resident, said that she and her husband, Samuel, "came up from New York 35 years ago when there were remnants of farms."

"Scenically it's still fabulous," she said, "but the reason we chose to live here was and is the interesting mix of old and new houses, and the mix of people socially, racially, ethnically, religiously, that's been historically constant."

NORWALK

No longer that "hole in the doughnut"

BY ELEANOR CHARLES

In the '70s, the Norwalk Chamber of Commerce tried to attract business to the city by calling it "the hole in the doughnut." "They thought it would appeal to businesses as an undiscovered place on the Gold Coast—a good area on the cheap," said former mayor William A. Collins. But the phrase backfired and just emphasized the economic and social problems that set the struggling city apart from Darien, Westport, Wilton, Weston, and New Canaan—the wealthy residential towns at its borders. Today, benefiting from an influx of corporations moving from or bypassing the expensive Stamford-Greenwich market, Norwalk has drawn corporate employees who found homes in neighborhoods indistinguishable from those in adjacent towns. And over the last decade, Norwalk has established an urban, diversified cachet all its own.

Estates on the wooded, rocky waterfront, handsome back-country Colonials and Tudors, luxury condominium complexes, and a rash of smart, new, clustered single-family houses cost some 20 percent less than their counterparts in neighboring towns. Condominiums and houses needing fix-up or that are situated in marginal neighborhoods can be found at five- and low-six-figure prices.

Alfred Zellerkraut, who is from Marseilles, is typical of the new Norwalk resident. For three years, he worked for a Swiss bank in New York, while living in New Jersey with his family. In late 1997, he was transferred to the bank's new headquarters in Stamford, and after much searching he bought a house from the developer's plans on North Taylor Avenue in Norwalk—2,200 square feet, four bedrooms, on about a fifth of an acre— for $250,000. "I was surprised at prices in Westchester and Fairfield County," he said. "Houses 60 years old in terrible condition cost what I am

POPULATION: 78,225.

AREA: 26.6 miles.

MEDIAN HOUSEHOLD INCOME: $65,796.

MEDIAN PRICE OF A SINGLE-FAMILY HOUSE: $277,200.

TAXES ON A MEDIAN-PRICED HOUSE: $5,000.

PUBLIC SCHOOL SPENDING PER PUPIL: $8,959.

DISTANCE FROM MIDTOWN MANHATTAN: 45 miles.

RUSH-HOUR TRAVEL TO MIDTOWN: 57 minutes on Metro-North's New Haven line, $10.75 one way, $234 monthly.

CODES: Area, 203; ZIP, 06850–06856.

paying. I got a bigger house for less money and I like the location, the coziness of the town."

"We have had lots of buyers from that bank," said Carol Ann Falasca, a Norwalk broker with Coldwell Banker who was not involved in the Zellerkraut sale. "Everybody wants new, and corporate people know that the houses they buy must be resalable—no problems like old lead paint or underground oil tanks." In the fourth quarter of 1997, 532 units of housing in single-family subdivisions, cluster housing developments, and multifamily condominium complexes were being built, proposed, or approved for construction here.

Five homes had been sold and five more were under contract at the 29-lot subdivision at Linden Heights, off the Main Avenue and Merritt Parkway intersection. Priced from $273,000 to $311,000, they offered 42 optional features in addition to three and four bedrooms, full basements, up to 2,260 square feet, and two-car garages. On the upscale waterfront off Canfield Avenue, one- to three-acre building lots with buried utilities, roads, and sewers were available for $965,000 to $1.1 million.

The median price of a one-family house at the end of 1997 was $277,200, up from $249,250 the previous year and $220,980 in 1992. The annual taxes on a house at the median were about $5,000 in 1997.

Silvermine, Wilson Point, and Rowayton are some of the more expensive, established neighborhoods. Heavily wooded and secluded Silvermine has attracted celebrities such as the actress Eileen Heckart, the writers Vance Packard and Evan Hunter, the sculptor Solon Borglum, and Lawrence Eagleburger, a former secretary of state.

Wilson Point contains a private beach club and handsome homes on wooded, hilly roads overlooking Norwalk Harbor. The more densely populated Rowayton, also on the water, has its own shopping district, beach, park, art center, and yacht clubs. "People who can't afford Darien hop over to Rowayton," said Janet Ryducha, a broker with Preferred Properties.

John Delner moved out of Darien after his divorce and into a three-bedroom Colonial at Getner Farms in Norwalk, where homes range in price from $240,000 to $270,000. "It was affordable in my circumstances," he said. "I can stay in the same golf club and see my friends and I have room for my children to visit. The big thing in coming to Norwalk is higher taxes—but properties are priced lower than elsewhere in the area." Taxes vary by about $5 per thousand dollars of assessment in Norwalk's nine taxing districts, and while the mill rate, or amount of tax for each $1,000 of assessed value, is the third highest in the state, there is sufficient compensation in price to satisfy most buyers.

Norwalk's 12 elementary schools, four middle schools, and two high schools, long regarded as inferior by many home buyers, have improved academically. But average SAT scores of 477 in math and 483 for verbal are still below state averages of 507 in math and 509 for verbal. "The top 10 percent of high school graduates score in the high SAT ranges," said Dr. Susan B. Weinberger, spokeswoman for the Norwalk school system. "This year we had a National Merit Scholarship semifinalist and six commendations."

Various steps taken to bring underperforming students up to par include a mentor program in which 800 employees from 44 area corporations invite students, one on one, to spend one day a week at the company. A school-to-work program that creates internships for high school juniors and seniors, college-bound or not, is based on their special interests and coordinated with schoolwork. Both programs have been replicated around the state, even in Gold Coast towns, according to Dr. Weinberger.

Academically and artistically gifted children are placed in special programs from grade 3, and the citywide curriculum contains a comprehensive music and art component through grade 12. Public school spending per pupil was $8,959 in 1998. Brien McMahon High School offers a year of courses in Japanese history, language, and culture, culminating in a two-week trip to Japan. A large number of students from other Fairfield County towns are enrolled in the program.

Norwalk has no private schools, but there are several in adjacent towns.

Inviting to many buyers is Norwalk's emergence as a lively city, with two multiscreen movie theaters, an art movie house, dozens of restaurants catering to a range of pocketbooks and palates, and the boutiques, restaurants, nightclubs, and art galleries of the Historic District on Washington Street. Other draws are the Maritime Aquarium, a symphony orchestra, the Norwalk Museum (a treasury of city history and products, including the original Raggedy Ann and Andy), two large beaches, and 1,200 acres of parklands, ball fields, playgrounds, an 18-hole municipal golf course, and several public marinas.

Norwalk Brewhouse—a microbrewery, restaurant, and brew museum—opened in 1996 near the Historic District for lunch and dinner, serving its own beers. Dinner for two runs around $50. Amberjacks on Washington Street features dry-aged steak and seafood. Dinner for two is about $60. One of several new South Norwalk nightclubs is called the Loft, where cigars, 20 flavors of martinis, and a live band are the principal attractions.

Commuters have a choice of three railroad stations and easy access to the Merritt Parkway, Route 7, and Interstate 95. The South Norwalk station redevelopment was completed in 1996 at a cost of $13 million.

A total of 50,860 people, more than half of Norwalk's population, holds cards at the city's four libraries. Each year thousands of visitors flock to the Scottish Games in July, the SoNo Arts Festival in August, and the Oyster Festival in September. Antique car shows, one of the largest in-water boat shows on the East Coast, hot-air-balloon races and sailboat races, concerts in the parks and on the beaches, are other seasonal events.

Norwalk was founded on land bought from the Indians by Roger Ludlowe in 1640 and declared a town by the General Court of Connecticut in 1651. The city thrived on agriculture for two centuries, until the arrival of the New York & New Haven Railroad in the mid–19th century, stimulating manufacturing and leading to the construction of summer homes for wealthy New Yorkers. "We had a huge hat industry," said Ralph Bloom, the city's historian, "downtown shops, and theaters." But from the late '50s through the '70s, South Norwalk became a haven for drugs and prostitution, damaging the city's reputation. And according to Mr. Bloom, the ubiquitous automobile encouraged people to work, shop, and ultimately live elsewhere.

Beginning in the '80s, however, the redevelopment of South Norwalk turned this around. Residents and shops returned as drug dealers and prostitutes all but vanished. And the neighborhood's prosperity has helped bring about the city's recovery.

An archipelago of 16 islands strung across Long Island Sound off the Norwalk shore range in size from the 1.1-acre Ghost Island that is mostly submerged at high tide, to the 70.2-acre Chimon Island, containing the only heron rookery in New England. Discovered in 1614 by Adrian Block, for whom Block Island was named, several islands are now privately owned as summer or year-round homes. A nonoperating 125-year-old lighthouse in the National Register of Historic Places and the Stewart B. McKinney Wildlife Refuge on 52.8 acres make Sheffield Island a popular spot for summer picnics, boaters, sightseers, and environmental cruise stopovers.

An 1835 house on Tavern Island, still in private hands, was rented in 1938 to Lillian Hellman, who is said to have written *The Little Foxes* there. In 1958, it was purchased by the late impresario Billy Rose, who embellished it with fine art and gave extravagant parties.

RIDGEFIELD

Contemporary Yankee

BY ROSALIE R. RADOMSKY

Ridgefield won't let go of its Yankee roots. "On the surface, it hasn't changed at all," said Sue W. Manning, who has lived here since 1970 and served as first selectman, or mayor, for a decade until 1997. "Houses and shops are pretty much the same. Maybe they're painted a different color, rebricked, or have an added tree." But the 35-square-mile town, which lies in the Housatonic Valley in Fairfield County, also is "a sophisticated, up-to-date place with a small-town atmosphere," Mrs. Manning said.

To Anne Margolis, a sculptor who lived in Ridgefield before moving recently to New York City, "it's like a college town without a campus." Main Street, she said, "is two blocks of enormous houses and genteel, discreet commercial space."

Lining Main Street are huge sugar maples. Set back from the thoroughfare, with its lawns and gray gazebo, is the five-acre Ballard Park. Just down the street, a woman in a Colonial costume gives tours of the Keeler Tavern, built as a home between 1713 and 1723. It became a tavern in 1772, and during the Revolutionary War was a popular meeting place for patriots—and thus a prime target for the British. A British cannonball is embedded in a corner post. In 1907, the architect Cass Gilbert bought the inn and turned it into a summer house. The Keeler Tavern Preservation Society purchased it in 1966.

At times, the charm of the Colonial past clashes with modern traffic. On weekdays, about 18,000 cars traverse Main Street (Route 35), which converges with Route 33 at the Cass Gilbert Fountain, dating from World War I. The fountain has been heavily damaged by collisions and restored twice, most recently in 1989.

A block north of the tavern is the Aldrich Museum of Contemporary Art, every bit as Colonial in style—nicknamed "Old Hundred" for a grocery

POPULATION: 21,311.

AREA: 35 square miles.

MEDIAN HOUSEHOLD INCOME: $102,558.

MEDIAN PRICE OF A SINGLE-FAMILY HOUSE: $450,000.

TAXES ON A MEDIAN-PRICED HOUSE: $5,600.

PUBLIC SCHOOL SPENDING PER PUPIL: $8,712.

DISTANCE FROM MIDTOWN MANHATTAN: 60 miles.

RUSH-HOUR TRAVEL TO MIDTOWN: One hour on Metro-North's Harlem line from the Katonah, N.Y., station, $8.75 one way, $193 monthly.

CODES: Area, 203; Zip, 06877.

and hardware store on the site from 1783–1883, then a bank and a residence—but contemporary in noteworthy exhibitions that include works by emerging artists and movements.

Among the town's residents in recent years have been Maurice Sendak, author and illustrator of children's books, and the actors Robert Vaughn (of *The Man from U.N.C.L.E.* TV series) and David Cassidy (*The Partridge Family* TV series). An earlier resident was Eugene O'Neill, who wrote *Desire Under the Elms* while living in the town.

North of Main Street, at North Salem Road and New Street, is Settlers' Rock, where five scouts from Norwalk and Milford camped in 1708, when they came to survey the land. Later that year, the first settlers bought 20,000 acres from Catoonah, the leader of the Ramapoo Indians. The town was incorporated in 1709. The oldest surviving house, completed in 1714 and now privately owned, belonged to the town's first minister, Rev. Thomas Hawley.

After the Revolution, the town, already known for its inns, built its economy on farming, mills, quarries, and a tannery. Later, hatting shops and shirt factories were established. The town also produced butter, beef, and pork and became a leading carriage maker.

In the years following the Civil War, Ridgefield became a country retreat for wealthy New Yorkers. High Ridge became known as Publishers Row. Among the resident bookmen were E. P. Dutton and Charles Henry Holt. At the end of the 19th century, Italian and Irish immigrants settled in the area to work on public projects and private estates.

The town's greatest growth occurred from 1955 to 1965, when the population expanded nearly fivefold to 23,000. Easy access to Interstates 84 and 684 and to Route 7 drew many newcomers in the '70s, following the shift of corporate headquarters to the suburbs.

"In general, we're slightly less expensive than Wilton, more than Danbury, and comparable to Fairfield," said Chip Neumann of Neumann Real Estate, a family-run firm. "Our major base of buyers for houses are corporate-type executives," he said.

At the high end, a new five-bedroom Georgian mansion with a three-car garage on two acres in the Ward Acres subdivision sold for $1.265 million in early 1998. A four-bedroom Colonial-style 1977 house on 1.6 acres in the Farmingville section was available for $459,000. And a two bedroom 1955 ranch with vinyl siding was offered for $189,000 on 0.29 acre on Great Hill Road.

The sales price of houses increased an average of 9 percent a year in the mid-nineties, according to the town tax assessor's office.

Ridgefield has seven condominiums, the largest with 150 units, and all are within walking distance of Main Street. The units range in price from $100,000 to about $500,000. House rentals start at $1,400 for a three-bedroom split-level, and go to $4,000 for a four-bedroom, 2,500-square-foot neo-Colonial. Apartments, some above storefronts on Main Street, and rarely available, rent from $1,000 a month for a one-bedroom to $1,400 for a two-bedroom.

Among the town's elegant restaurants are the Elms and Stonehenge, both also offering rooms, and the Inn at Ridgefield.

There are 60 civic and cultural organizations in the town, among them the Guild of Artists, the Workshop for Performing Arts, the Ridgefield Symphony Orchestra, and a civic ballet.

Some 50 companies, including service providers and hi-tech computer concerns, operate in Ridgefield. The largest is Boehringer Ingelheim Pharmaceuticals on a 300-acre site in the Ridgebury section in the northern part of town.

There is more than 600,000 square feet of retail space in town, most of it in five shopping areas. One of them, Copps Hill Common, includes the Ridgefield Antiques Center, with 22 dealers. Shoppers also frequent the Ridgefield General Store & Cafe with 15 different sections upstairs and a cozy cafe downstairs serving three-course British teas Wednesdays to Saturdays, 3 to 5 P.M., and Sunday, 10 A.M. to 3 P.M.

Many residents go to the two-screen Bethel Cinema about a half hour away and to the 10-screen Sony Theaters Danbury and three-screen Crown Cine in Danbury about 15 minutes away. There is also the Danbury Fair Mall for serious shopping.

Residents can go for a swim or take aerobics classes by joining the town-run Ridgefield Recreation Center, which took over the former Y.M.C.A. building in 1995. Others drive to the Wilton Family Y around 15 minutes away.

The Wintergarden, an indoor ice-skating rink, which has 20 house ice hockey leagues, eight travel teams, and a figure skating club, completed an $800,000 renovation in 1997. It is open from October to April.

A total of 4,504 students attend seven schools in the Ridgefield system. Sixth graders sample three languages—German, Spanish, and

French—for a year and then select one for the next two years. Eighth graders have consistently scored in the top 1 percent in Connecticut Mastery Tests in reading and math for over a decade.

Ridgefield High School, which offers 14 advanced placement courses for college credit, had 261 seniors in the Class of 1998; of the 1997 seniors, 96 percent went on to higher education, 93 percent to four-year colleges, figures that are typical for recent years. The school has 53 interscholastic teams and 35 extracurricular programs.

The school is one of 24 nationwide public schools participating in the Boston-based "A Better Chance" program, which provides educational opportunities for minority students in the top 10 percent of their hometown class. Seven young women from urban areas around the country participated in the 1997–98 program, living together in a Ridgefield house owned by the program, with a resident director and visiting tutor. The program began in 1987, and 16 of the 17 graduates are attending or have graduated from college.

The Farmingville, Ridgebury, Veterans Park Scotland, and Branchville Elementary Schools cover grades K to 5, the East Ridge Middle School grades 6 to 8. One specialty of the elementary schools is the Art Leap program, which introduces pupils to painting and drawing in the third grade.

The Ridgefield Library, built in 1901, has tripled in size over the last decade. It has 88,000 volumes, attracts some 900 visitors daily, and offers 16 children's programs a week.

The town owns 2,114 acres of open space offering parks, lakes, an 18-hole gold course, Little League fields, and horseback, hiking, and nature trails. The nine-acre Martin Park has a spring-fed pond and beach, and the 30-acre Richardson Park borders Lake Mamanasco, which has a boat launch. In addition, there is Pierrepont State Park with 304 acres.

ROWAYTON

A waterfront neighborhood with a sense of comfortable identity

BY ROSALIE R. RADOMSKY

Rowayton residents liken their neighborhood to a Norman Rockwell painting and to towns along the Maine coast. Everyone in the community, which has 250 boat slips, 120 moorings, and four marinas, seems to know everyone else. "In Rowayton, no one minds if you're fancy or if you're not fancy," said Grace W. Lichtenstein, the former chairman of the three-member elected commission of Norwalk's Sixth Taxing District, which was set up in 1921 by the Connecticut legislature to allow Rowayton residents to tax themselves to supply services not provided by the city of Norfolk, of which the community is a part. Those taxes—the figure is $500,000 for 1998–99—are applied to the parks, beach, and library that help give the community a sense of its own identity, as well as to garbage collection and other services.

"It is a low-key, attractive place to live, and thrives on volunteerism," said Randall Avery, the current chairman of the tax district commission of Norwalk's Sixth Taxing District, who has lived there for two decades.

Wendell Livingston considered it a compromise between Maine and New York when she and her husband, Tom, moved into a 1930s Cape Cod in 1987. When they outgrew it seven years later, they bought a larger 1889 Victorian a half mile away. "We turned a three-family into a one-family house," she said. "Because there are a limited number of houses here that can accommodate a growing family, many of our peers have chosen to enlarge or renovate their current house as opposed to moving to another town. There are small yards, but there's so much going on," said Ms. Livingston, who has a 10-year-old son and daughters 7 and 2. "It's a wonderful place to raise children."

"A typical lot is 0.3 acre and a half acre is considered large," said Gail Van Slyck of Van Slyck Associates, a real estate brokerage.

POPULATION: 3,130.

AREA: 1.5 square miles.

MEDIAN HOUSEHOLD INCOME: $99,698.

MEDIAN PRICE OF A SINGLE-FAMILY HOUSE: $419,000.

TAXES ON A MEDIAN-PRICED HOUSE: $6,650.

PUBLIC SCHOOL SPENDING PER PUPIL: $8,959.

DISTANCE FROM MIDTOWN MANHATTAN: 42 miles.

RUSH-HOUR TRAVEL TO MIDTOWN: One hour on Metro-North's New Haven line, $10 one way, $218 monthly.

CODES Area, 203; ZIP, 06853.

Rowayton's 1,525 houses are a jumble of cottages, Victorians, Colonials, and Capes. Members of its three housing associations—Bell Island, Pine Point, and Rowayton Beach—pay dues for extras such as private beaches and roads. But no house is more than five minutes from Bayley Beach, which all residents can use without charge.

Frank E. Raymond's ancestors moved in 10 generations ago. Mr. Raymond, who remembers skating out of Five Mile River onto Long Island Sound during the freeze of 1934, wrote a history, *Rowayton on the Half Shell*, published in 1990 for the Historical Society of Rowayton.

A variant of its name—Rooaton—appeared in the deed between Chief Runckinheague of the Siwanoy Indians and settlers in 1651, when only a few sustenance farmers and fishermen lived in the area. By the start of the 18th century, blacksmiths, shoemakers, carpenters, and weavers were contributing to its economy. Oystering was dominant by the 1860s, but oysters succumbed early in this century to overharvesting and pollution.

By then, though, Rowayton had become a summer resort. Its drawing card, Roton Point Park, attracted thousands of day trippers from New York. Over the years, they came to hear and see Rudy Vallee, Alice Faye, Glenn Miller, and others, and to ride the airplane swing and Big Dipper roller coaster. The park closed in 1942.

In 1910, James A. Farrell, who became president of United States Steel Corporation, built an Elizabethan-style mansion, which burned down three years later and was rebuilt in granite. The building now houses Hewitt Associates, actuaries. Since 1966, the Farrell family farm buildings have been the community center and the library, which has 33,000 books, including 550 on boating.

Though waterfront houses go for over a million dollars and flood insurance is expensive, the waterfront is coveted. "You can sell land along the water by the square inch," said Douglas A. Bora, Sr., a retired local realtor, whose backyard is the river facing Darien.

Only 27 properties, with a median price of $519,000, were on the market in early 1998. Normally 48 to 52 properties are available, according to Ms. Van Slyck. In 1997, 75 homes sold, with a median sales price of $419,000. There was a jump in prices of 9 percent from 1996 to 1997, but a decline of 17 percent from 1995 to 1996. Property tax on a median-priced house was $6,650. Median prices are somewhat distorted by the presence of one recent luxury development, Thomas Place, whose homes sell for over a million dollars.

Among the houses on the market early in 1998 was a three-bedroom Colonial built in 1920 on 0.14 acre on Dibble Street, selling for $359,000. A three-bedroom ranch listed at $425,000 on three-quarters of an acre along Indian Spring Road, a street known for having larger lots, sold for $398,250 in February. New construction, rare in the neighborhood, included a four-bedroom Colonial selling for $645,000 on a 0.18-acre corner parcel on Witch Lane.

Rowayton's only condominium is a four-unit converted schoolhouse on Thomas Place, a development that also has detached Colonial one-family homes. One of those four-bedroom houses along Wilson Cove was offered at $1.395 million early in 1998. Except for Hilltop Homes, which has 24 one- and two-bedroom units for the elderly and disabled, there are few rentals. About 8 to 10 rentals come up during a year, going for $1,800 to $3,800 a month.

"Rowayton has the best of both worlds," said Ralph Sloan, superintendent of Norwalk public schools. "It's a charming village and has the diversity of the Norwalk school system with 45 percent minority enrollment." Public school expenditure per pupil was $8,959 for the 1997–98 school year.

Brien McMahon High School, with an enrollment of 1,202, attracts students from 10 other towns to its Center for Japanese Study Abroad, which typically sends 50 students to Tokyo each spring, following a year's study. The school also offers nine advanced placement classes for college credit, and usually at least 80 percent of its graduates go on to higher education. In 1997, 50 percent went on to four-year colleges and 33 percent went on to two-year colleges.

Roton Middle School, with 425 students, focuses on team teaching, and offers Japanese to all grades. The K–5 Rowayton Elementary School teaches Japanese to all students and has ties to the Greenwich Japanese School. It also has a renovated wing for grades 3–5 as a result of a $3 million renovation completed in 1995. "It's a caring, extended family," said Leslie Pattengill, its principal, alluding to parent participation. The school has a fine arts and performing arts emphasis for its 381 pupils, and about 200 to 300 parents come in regularly to help out. They also run the annual Rowayton School Carnival to raise funds.

Children also go to private schools in nearby towns. Preschoolers can take advantage of the local Community Cooperative, Five Mile River, and United Church Nursery School. There is also youth soccer and Little League, with all-star teams that play other towns.

Along with having story hours for children 3 and up, a pre-3 program, lectures for adults, and a website (www.rowayton.org), the library doubles as a mini–town hall. Residents pick up applications for the local tennis and paddle tennis associations, apply for Bayley Beach stickers, and line up yearly to buy commuter parking lot permits on a first-come, first-served basis one day in June.

During the annual one-day Trash Bash, a rigorous rite of spring, residents clean up the village. The Memorial Day parade winds down each year with a short speech, followed by hot dogs and soda given away behind the fire station, which houses the 50-member volunteer Rowayton Hose Company No. 1. Homemade strawberry shortcake is also usually sold that afternoon in Pinkney Park, with 2.3 acres along the river, where the annual art show is held.

The River Ramble in mid-July features canoe races, auctions, and the raffling of about 25 pairs of lobsters. Laid-back summer evenings can also be spent on the lawn, where 10 Sunday concerts are held during the Summer Arts Festival through Labor Day weekend.

The block-long commercial strip along Rowayton Avenue has such conveniences as a barber shop, a hardware store, a grocery, and the post office. A block away is Bobs 101, an ice cream store and deli that offers such ice cream flavors as Rowayton rainbow sherbert, Pond Street peach, and East Beach Heath. Bistro du Soleil offers take-out food, catering, and an art gallery.

Although there are no local movie theaters, residents can choose from many within a five-minute drive to Darien, a 10-minute drive in Norwalk, or a 15-minute drive to Westport. Major shopping is done at a Grand Union in Darien and supermarkets along the Post Road in Norwalk.

Fresh fish is available at Rowayton Seafood, which has four tanks holding up to 5,000 pounds of lobster. Its owners run the 60-seat restaurant at Rowayton Seafood in an adjacent building offering views of sunsets over Five Mile River.

Goings-on, from the annual River Ramble to Lobster Bake, as well as other events by civic groups, along with personal greetings, are usually posted on the chain-link fence around the old schoolyard on Rowayton Avenue at Witch Lane. In the fall of 1997, a sheet tied to the fence by an unnamed suitor asked, "Susan, will you marry me? Meet me at Pinkney Park at 2 o'clock." A couple of days later a note read: "She's accepted!"

TOKENEKE

Gold Coast seclusion on the Darien shoreline

BY ELEANOR CHARLES

For more than half a century, Tokeneke (pronounced TOW-keh-neek) has been a secluded residential neighborhood of 1.12 square miles on the Darien shore, where some of the most beautiful real estate on Fairfield County's Gold Coast can be found. Fingering its way around coves, lagoons, and inlets to Long Island Sound, much of its heavily wooded land rises steeply from the water's edge in rugged shapes formed by huge boulders cast up during the Ice Age.

Some 1,000 people live in its Tudor and Norman mansions, Spanish villas, capacious seaside "cottages," and whimsical hideaways, designed by leading architects to nestle into rock or step down a hill, almost always with views of the water, if not directly on it. Currently, 265 homes make up Tokeneke, along with the Tokeneke Beach club—private, but not restricted to Tokeneke residents—and St. Birgitta's Convent, run by an unusual Swedish Roman Catholic order dedicated to hospitality that accommodates guests in rooms overlooking Long Island Sound for a fee of $60 to $140 a day, including all meals.

Commercial establishments are prohibited in Tokeneke, and it is unlikely that more homes will be built unless someone demolishes an existing one to put up another. There is no land for sale nor any that is buildable within the prevailing one-acre, single-family zone. Moreover, restrictive covenants on some properties require approval of architectural plans by the Tokeneke Association. "Living in Tokeneke is like being on a permanent vacation," said Betsy Goss, a broker at the Darien office of Preferred Properties.

Her listings indicate that it is almost impossible to find anything under $700,000 and commonplace to spend up to $4 million. The median price in 1997 was $1.75 million. Darien's property tax rate is among the lowest in

POPULATION: 1,000.

AREA: 1.12 square miles.

MEDIAN HOUSEHOLD INCOME: $180,000.

MEDIAN PRICE OF A SINGLE-FAMILY HOUSE: $1.75 million.

TAXES ON A MEDIAN-PRICED HOUSE: $19,759.

PUBLIC SCHOOL SPENDING PER PUPIL: $9,720.

DISTANCE FROM MIDTOWN MANHATTEN: 37 miles.

RUSH-HOUR TRAVEL TO MIDTOWN: 55 minutes on Metro-North's New Haven line from the Darien station, $10 one way, $218 monthly.

CODES: Area, 203 ZIP, 06820.

the state, at $16.13 per thousand dollars of assessment, making taxes on a $1.75 million house $19,759 a year.

Amity and Michael Wallace and their 2-year-old daughter moved from Princeton, New Jersey, in 1995 into a Tokeneke house that was once the guest cottage of a Mediterranean-style estate where Theodore Dreiser is said to have written *An American Tragedy*. "The school system appealed to us," said Mrs. Wallace. "There's no need for private schools, and the people here are really neighborly." In 1997, the Wallaces sold their house to one of five bidders for more than $30,000 over the asking price of $650,000, and bought a larger, more expensive house in Tokeneke. Mr. Wallace, a Manhattan stockbroker, likes being able to run Max, the family's Labrador retriever, on the community field. And, he said, "we can run and bike on the roads without worrying about traffic."

Robin and Alan Sokolow had lived in Tokeneke for six years. "But when we couldn't expand our house or find another one after our fourth child was born, we moved to north Darien, but kept our membership in the beach club," said Mrs. Sokolow. After two and a half years, they moved back to Tokeneke.

Beginning in the 1860s, when the New York & New Haven Railroad opened up the Connecticut shore to vacationers, and through the 1950s, well-to-do New Yorkers and a coterie of artists and writers gravitated to Tokeneke, building summer homes that were subsequently expanded and embellished into year-round residences. A substantial number of them were built before 1946, when the Tokeneke Association was formed. Membership is not mandatory, but for $35 a year most homeowners join. "They get a directory of the residents," said the current president, William M. Winship, "and they have a number of social events," including a June lobster bake at the beach club, a Christmas carol sing at St. Birgitta's Convent, a winter dinner-dance at the Wee Burn Golf Club in northern Darien, and an Easter egg hunt on the community field.

Named for an Indian chief whose peaceful tribe enjoyed plentiful fishing, hunting, fowling, and gathering, Tokeneke got its first white settlers in the 1640s. They built houses, bred cattle, and farmed the land, and for some 200 years, Tokeneke remained a quiet backwater, except for a brief scuffle toward the end of the Revolutionary War. In 1781, Tories from Long Island landed at Scott's Cove, tramped through Tokeneke woods, and captured about 50 men at church. They were transported back to a Long Island jail, where some captives died. The rest, weakened by disease, were returned six months later in a prisoner exchange.

The enclave's only other unfortunate incident of record occurred in November of 1872. Frederick Kensett, a noted painter of the late Hudson River School, died of pneumonia after rescuing the wife of a friend whose horse-drawn buggy overturned while fording a strip of water separating mainland Tokeneke from Contentment Island. A causeway now joins the island to the mainland.

Nothing else of consequence has happened to disturb the tranquillity of Tokeneke. According to Mr. Winship, "After living here for 30 years, the only changes I've seen here have been substantial capital improvements on some of the houses, and a couple of new ones."

But a few changes are taking place in town. The Darien school system, where the per-pupil expenditure is $9,720, has completed much of a $24 million expansion and renovation program. Holmes Elementary School, warehoused for 10 years, reopened in the fall of 1996, and four additional elementary schools, including Tokeneke School, were reconfigured from separate kindergarten–grade 2 and grade 3–5 schools to all kindergarten-to-grade 5 schools, with an overall capacity of 2,400 pupils instead of the former 1,765.

Middlesex Middle School is to be enlarged to accommodate 1,200 students. Darien High School, already able to handle 1,500 students, will not be expanded. Both schools have had enrollments in the mid- to upper-700s through the late '90s.

"The birthrate has climbed considerably," said Eileen Gress, superintendent of schools, "and more families are moving in with young children."

Combined SAT scores traditionally exceed state and national levels by more than 100 points, and 90 percent of high school graduates typically go on to four-year colleges. "Our emphasis is on fostering basic skills within the context of inquiry and critical thinking," said Ms. Gress, noting that the state and national education departments had cited Darien for excellence in writing, journalism, and drama.

Darien's only private school recently changed both its name and its management, from Plumfield School to Pear Tree Point School, and nearly doubled its student body from 80 to 150 boys and girls from preschool through fifth grade. The day school's tuition ranges from $7,000 to $13,000.

Change has also taken place along Darien's commercial strip on the Post Road from Day Street to Brookside Road. New sidewalks, lighting, benches, spruced-up storefronts, and landscaped parking lots have improved access to the many antiques shops and clothing boutiques, specialty-food and culinary shops, art galleries, coffee shops, and restaurants. The Darien movie theater, closed for five years in a zoning dispute over a multiscreen renovation, reopened with two screens instead of one, and a Dunkin' Donuts and a Starbucks coffee bar are doing brisk business where two service stations had been. "We are seeing planning and zoning approvals for new businesses flow without a lot of obstruction," said Warren Tuttle, owner of the Good Food Store.

Diversions of every kind are available in town. The Darien Arts Council has had regularly scheduled art exhibitions for 38 years, and the Ox Ridge Hunt Club's annual horse show, oldest and grandest in the state, runs for a week in early June. Darien's library contains more than 100,000 books, films, videos, and periodicals, and the Darien Players theater group, a historical society, and a Y.M.C.A. with an indoor swimming pool are popular amenities.

Cherry Lawn Park contains the Darien Nature Center, community garden plots, a softball field, trails, and a wildflower meadow, and at Tilley Park Pond there is ice-skating in winter. Darien also has a commercial indoor ice rink. Three nature preserves with more than 100 acres of greenery to wander through, and seven ball fields, are also available to the public. A $20-per-car annual resident's pass is required at Weed Beach and Pear Tree Point Beach, where a town boat launch costs an additional annual $20 fee. It costs $4 an hour, or $5 on weekends, to play at any of 11 municipal tennis courts, and $12 an hour at five paddle tennis courts that are heated and lit all winter.

There is a waiting list of up to three years for slips at the Darien Boat Club, depending on the size of the boat, but moorings are sometimes available through the harbor master.

In 1952, the state's general assembly established a Tokeneke Taxing District after being petitioned to do so by the association. It requires Tokeneke residents to pay a separate district tax (in addition to the Darien property tax), currently levied at $1.32 for every $1,000 of assessment. The money, managed by a board of directors, pays for private police protection and the maintenance of the enclave's private roads, extending from Tokeneke Road south to include Contentment and Butler's Islands, and from Arrowhead Way east to Indian Trail Road.

"Tokeneke is sought after by people in town," said Betsy Norman, a broker with the Coldwell Banker office in Darien, "and a lot of out-of-staters seem to know about it. It's the first thing they ask for—but they have to get used to the sticker price."

WESTON

Open spaces and a feeling of home

BY ROSALIE R. RADOMSKY

"**W**eston is the ultimate hometown," said Patricia Heifetz, who moved to this Fairfield County town in 1965 and founded a weekly newspaper, *The Weston Forum*, five years later. "I can look out my window and see wild turkeys in my backyard," said Ms. Heifetz, who sold the weekly newspaper in 1992. "One day we counted 60."

Nestled in the hills of Connecticut's Fairfield County, just north of Westport, the town has two-acre zoning, four historic districts, three steepled churches, and 3,500 acres of open space, 25 percent of the entire town.

"It hasn't changed all that much since the '20s and '30s, except it's much wealthier," said George C. Guidera, who has lived there all his 55 years and is the third in his family to serve as first selectman, or mayor.

More than anything, Susan Feliciano enjoys its "sense of history." She and her husband, Jose, the singer-guitarist, and their three children live in an historic 1730 house, formerly Banks Tavern, on four acres along the Saugatuck River. The house relived its tavern role in 1987 for the *The Outlivers*, a 37-minute film made for the town's bicentennial by local volunteers, including Christopher Plummer, as narrator, and the actors James Naughton and Frank Converse.

Outlivers were Weston's first settlers—most of them the younger sons of Fairfield freeholders who left their crowded community, a day's journey away, in the early 1700s. In 1787, the Town of Weston was formed with the North Fairfield parish; the current boundaries were set when the eastern part split off as Easton in 1845. Despite rocky soil, apples, onions, and potatoes were grown and many settles ran grist, cider, lumber, and fulling mills. By 1850, there were nine manufacturers, but 20 years later, only the

POPULATION: 8,813.

AREA: 20.8 square miles.

MEDIAN HOUSEHOLD INCOME: $143,683.

MEDIAN PRICE OF A SINGLE-FAMILY HOUSE: $560,000.

TAXES ON A MEDIAN-PRICED HOUSE: $7,141.

PUBLIC SCHOOL SPENDING PER PUPIL: $10,671.

DISTANCE FROM MIDTOWN MANHATTAN: 45 miles.

RUSH-HOUR TRAVEL TO MIDTOWN: One hour on Metro-North's New Haven line from Westport, $11.75 one way, $254 monthly.

CODES: Area, 203, ZIP, 06883 and 06829.

Bradley Edge Tool Company was still thriving. Like the rest, it faded, and in 1911, it burned down.

Too far from railroads, Weston was no match for industrial hubs like Bridgeport, and its population, which had remained at around 1,000 until the Civil War, dropped, hitting a low of 670 by 1930. It inched up as modern outlivers—artists, writers, and actors from New York—began moving in. The Merritt Parkway reached Weston in 1938 and the population climbed.

Its well-known residents have included the actresses Eva Le Gallienne and Bette Davis, the writer James Thurber, and the choreographer George Balanchine. Today, the writer Erica Jong, Keith Richards of the Rolling Stones, and the actor Robert Redford have homes in town.

In early 1998, the median price of a house sold in Weston was $560,000, according to Sheila Shupack, a broker with William Raveis in neighboring Westport, who has lived in Weston for 26 years, and raised three children there with her husband, Hal, a selectman. Out of 146 listings in early 1998, she said, 47 had a price tag of $1 million or more. The property tax on a median-priced house is $7,141.

Although there are no condominiums or co-ops, a smattering of rentals are available. In early 1998, they ranged from $1,000 for a one-bedroom cottage attached to a larger house on Ladder Hill Road to $5,000 for a 13-room gray wood 1983 contemporary month-to-month rental (also on the market for $999,000) with an indoor pool situated on over two acres on Winslow Road.

Also early in 1998, at the low end a 1780s farmhouse needing work was listed at $329,900 on two acres along Old Western Road. A 1974 10-room contemporary on two acres along Aspetuck Hill Lane overlooking the Aspetuck Valley Country Club sold for $540,000. Available for $2.25 million was a 13-room shingle-style home under construction on 2.43 acres along a cul-de-sac in the new Tall Pines subdivision in lower Weston.

A 1970 seven-room riverfront saltbox with a separate guest house on three acres along Goodhill Road was available for $645,000. At the high end of the market was the former Revlon estate, a restored 26-room Georgian mansion built in 1935, and listed at $4.595 million.

Three public schools share a 113-acre wooded campus with eight athletic fields. The public school expenditure per pupil has been set at $10,671 for the 1998–99 school year.

"We have a huge influx of elementary school students in K–3," said Mr. Guidera. "So we put an addition onto the elementary school and added 11 new classrooms in the middle school. We are looking at adding four to five more classrooms to the middle school. The explosion in school population has leveled out and the high school has plenty of room. We constructed a 4,000-square-foot freestanding administration building on School Road."

"We're a small, primarily college preparatory school," said William Coan, the former principal of Weston High School, which expects to have 416 students in the 1998–99 school year. Mr. Coan, who left the school to head Litchfield District 6 in early 1998, said typically 95 percent of the students went on to higher education in the mid-1990s; 89 percent went on to four-year colleges and 5 percent went on to two-year colleges in 1997.

The high school offers 11 advanced placement classes for college credit and six classes in conjunction with the University of Connecticut. Seventy students participate in the WHS Company, which presents three plays a year; a peer program gives students insight into counseling new students one-on-one.

All grades take swimming at Weston Middle School, which has 761 students in grades 4–8. There are two computer labs, one library research lab, one writing lab, and a program for students in the top 15 percent called the Talented and Gifted (TAG) program.

The K–3 Hurlbutt Elementary School, with 838 children, has four connecting buildings and a new 5,000-square-foot resource center and a new computer center with 25 computers. The school, which also has two computers in every class, teaches Spanish to all third graders, and gives those who qualify a chance to participate in the TAG program.

Preschoolers can be enrolled in programs at the Norfield Children's Center, the Emmanuel Nursery School, and the Westport-Weston Cooperative Nursery School, just over the Weston border. The St. Francis of Assisi preschool is planning to open its doors in September 1999. The Weston Library has 48,000 volumes, is open every day, and holds seven weekly story hours for 2- to 5-year-olds. From June to October, its parking lot had been the site of the Saturday farmers' market in past years. In 1998, its 10th-anniversary year, the market, whose 18 stands feature Connecticut-grown, baked, or created goods, changed its location to the bus loop outside the Hurlbutt Elementary School.

Residents use well water and have no sewers. They also pay a price for keeping out development—not only in property taxes, but also in mileage. Weston Town Shopping Center, which includes a luncheonette, a gas station, and a post office, is convenient for a quick errand, but for serious shopping, movies, and restaurants, residents drive about 15 minutes to surrounding towns.

Westport offers Weston residents Compo Beach stickers at $150 a season and parking stickers for its train station lot at $132.50 (there is a three- to five-year wait).

The only restaurant, Cobb's Mill Inn, on Route 57 North, is in a 19th-century grist mill overlooking a stream. The only other conspicuous commercial enterprise is Weston Gardens, known for landscaping.

More discreetly, many residents work from home at such occupations as writing, sales, law, oil importing, and computer consulting. Under town rules, they must live in the house and devote no more than half the space to their work. With a special permit, they may hire up to two employees.

Weston's volunteer fire department sponsors a Memorial Day parade down Route 57 and a children's Halloween party. There are also church fairs, the Norfield Grange agricultural fair, and the Weston Family Fourth on July 4.

In the winter, children can skate free on private ponds. And, once fishing begins the third Saturday in April, Connecticut residents with $20 state fishing licenses vie for spots along the trout-filled Saugatuck and Aspetuck Rivers; for $20 more (free to Westonites), Bridgeport Hydraulic Company offers fishing along a 10-mile stretch of the western shore of Saugatuck Reservoir.

Weston's Parks and Recreation Department oversees activities at the Middle School's 25-yard pool. It also sponsors Weston Youth Basketball and men's and women's softball leagues and offers aerobics and bridge classes.

Among the private member-owned clubs is the 10.8-acre Weston Racquet Club, with 800 members paying $85 a year ($190 for a family). Ivan Lendl, the tennis star, bought the club's building and land in July 1991 and spent $250,000 redoing the clubhouse and adding six courts. Weston Field Club, where 220 families can play tennis, swim, or trapshoot on 24.5 acres, has a private restaurant.

The town's prime piece of open space is the 1,746-acre Devil's Den, or Lucius Pond Ordway Preserve, run by the Nature Conservancy. Scientists use the decidous forest to study worm-eating warblers, and hikers and cross-country skiers use 20 miles of trails. The 62-acre Katherine Ordway Preserve has three miles of hiking trails and a 10-acre arboretum.

A path along the Saugatuck can be found in 6.2-acre Keene Park, but more popular is 52.6-acre Bisceglie-Scribner Park, whose swimming pond opened in 1993. It has a children's playground and a two-mile jogging trail with 27 fitness stations.

CONNECTICUT

WESTPORT

Martha Stewart has her reasons

BY LISA PREVOST

Widely known as a favorite hideaway of the rich and famous, Westport has a celebrity-driven cachet. And young families are attracted by the town's exceptional school system, a wide range of recreational opportunities, and a strong sense of community.

Westport's popularity and its location just an hour from Manhattan combine to keep prices high—it's difficult to find many single-family homes priced below $300,000. And in mid-1998, about 70 houses, or about a quarter of the homes on the market, were priced above $1 million.

But growth pressures threaten to undermine many of the small-town qualities that have made Westport so desirable. Now that the town is more than 90 percent developed, land is scarce: A recent Planning Department survey found just 350 vacant acres, less than 3 percent of the town, left for development.

Lots are so valuable that developers are buying houses in established neighborhoods only to tear them down to make way for much bigger houses. These modern homes, referred to by disapproving locals as "houses on steroids," are beginning to alter the character of older neighborhoods, said Katherine Barnard, Westport's director of planning and zoning.

Applications for Conservation Commission approval of development on environmentally sensitive lots are rising as green space dwindles. And the student population is swelling so quickly that school administrators expect they will have to bus kindergarteners out of one district to a less crowded school for at least two years until more elementary schools are opened.

Nevertheless, First Selectwoman Diane Goss Farrell is optimistic. A committee is forming to identify land parcels worthy of preservation, she

POPULATION: 23,600.

AREA: 22.4 square miles.

MEDIAN HOUSEHOLD INCOME: $116,615.

MEDIAN PRICE OF A SINGLE-FAMILY HOUSE: $525,000.

TAXES ON A MEDIAN-PRICED HOUSE: $4,800.

PUBLIC SCHOOL SPENDING PER PUPIL: $10,648.

DISTANCE FROM MIDTOWN MANHATTAN: 55 miles.

RUSH-HOUR TRAVEL TO MIDTOWN: 64 minutes on Metro-North's New Haven line, $11.75 one way, $254 monthly.

CODES: Area, 203; ZIP, 06880.

said, and the town has signed a contract to buy 22.8 acres near downtown for future municipal needs.

A native Westporter who once tried out California only to return, Mrs. Farrell said the high demand for land "suggests the town enjoys tremendous vitality."

Westport has cultivated an image as a center of creative energy ever since the early 1900s, when artists, actors, musicians, and writers flocked to its shores to work and play. Previously it was the quiet home of farmers and mill owners who shipped their fresh onions and dried corn on the Saugatuck River, which cuts a broad path through town to Long Island Sound. Wealthy businessmen also maintained a grand presence—Richard H. Winslow, the banker and legislator, thrilled residents every Fourth of July with an extravagant fireworks display at his mansion. But the introduction of the railroad made Westport an attractive seaside outpost for artists in search of affordable living within reach of New York City.

Today, the town is known more for its celebrities than its artists—among the more notable are Martha Stewart, Michael Bolton, Paul Newman and Joanne Woodward, and Marlo Thomas and Phil Donahue.

Westporters themselves tend to pay less attention to their famous neighbors than to more substantive community concerns. "Westport has a very charged, proactive population," Mrs. Farrell noted. Indeed, heated debates erupt easily and often. A pavilion offered as a gift by Westport's sister city in China, Yangzhou, provoked an outcry because of the Chinese government's history of human rights abuses. The Westport Sister City Association decided not to accept the gift.

Parents are intimately involved with the school system, serving with teachers, students, and administrators on leadership councils that work to improve the quality of education. Students at the three elementary and two middle schools have scored well above the state averages on the Connecticut Mastery Tests in recent years. SAT scores for Staples High School seniors in 1997 were also above the state averages at 551 for verbal and

575 for math. Westport offers a program for the gifted in the lower grades, as well as an extensive arts and music program. A host of advanced placement courses are available at the high school level.

According to Joyce Losen, assistant to the schools superintendent, Westport's current student population of 4,130 is expected to increase by 25 percent by 2002. As a result, the town plans to reopen and expand the Green's Farms Elementary School, convert the Bedford Middle School into a fifth elementary school, and build a new middle school. The projects will cost taxpayers an estimated $70 million in bonded debt.

Westport also has two private schools. Landmark Academy offers a preschool for ages 3 to 5; tuition for a five-day-a-week program is $5,150. (Landmark offers classes through grade 8 at its campus in Wilton.) Greens Farms Academy, a co-ed day school, offers a complete program for kindergarten through grade 12. Tuition for the 1998–99 school year is $14,700 for K–5, $15,300 for 6–8, and $16,250 for 9–12.

Westport's neighborhoods have lost much of their individuality over the years, but some clear distinctions remain. Green's Farms is still characterized by expansive lawns and broad porches on the eastern side of town. It is named for John Green, one of five farmers, who, in 1648, first settled the fertile land overlooking Long Island Sound in what became Westport. A former Indian path along the shoreline is now Beachside Avenue, where vast waterfront estates sell for as much as $20 million.

"I've had people from New York who would only look in Green's Farms," said Bunny Mostad, president of the Westport-Weston Board of Realtors and a realtor with Re/Max Heritage in Westport. Prices in Green's Farms start as low as $350,000, generally for houses closest to I-95.

Farther west is the beach area, where home prices have risen considerably in recent years, according to Pat Shavell, managing broker at Riverside-Shavell Reality. Three popular town beaches—Compo, South, and Old Mill—are here, as is the 99-acre Longshore Club Park, a prized recreational area bought by the town in 1960. Houses of every style are squeezed onto small lots in the beach neighborhoods; prices range from about $400,000 to just over $2 million, Ms. Shavell said.

The mouth of the river separates this section of town from Saugatuck, which, like Green's Farms, maintains a separate sense of community. Property along Saugatuck Shores, the finger of land that juts into the sound, is extremely pricey; even outdated split-levels can still go for $1 million because of their location, Ms. Shavell said. There are two private yacht clubs in Saugatuck, Saugatuck Harbor and Cedar Point. The town's main train station is here.

Closer to the center of town in the Historic District is Old Hill, a neighborhood of older homes, most on lots of at least an acre. Prices range from about $400,000 to $4 million. Proximity to the Merritt Parkway makes the location attractive to commuters. Old Hill is also convenient to Westport's thriving downtown.

The retail district's local flavor has been homogenized by upscale chain stores like Eddie Bauer, Laura Ashley, and Williams-Sonoma, but the remaining 19th-century wood-frame buildings still give the district a quaint New England air. The Fine Arts Theater, opened in the 1920s as the first theater in Connecticut to show foreign films, still operates as a movie theater. On the riverfront, National Hall, which housed the Westport National Bank in the 1870s, is now an elegant inn and restaurant.

Condominium developments throughout the town comprise 434 units. But availability is limited, particularly in the desirable Lansdowne and Regent's Park developments, where prices range from about $425,000 for a two-bedroom unit to about $600,000 for a three-bedroom. "As soon as one comes on the market, it's gone," said Ruth Williams, sales manager for the Westport office of William Pitt. She added, "They tend to be places where empty-nesters go."

Westport residents have many recreational and cultural resources. A municipal beach emblem is $20 per car. Compo Beach is the most well equipped, with a large playground, showers and restrooms, and an in-line skating park. Longshore, open only to Westport residents and their guests, offers an 18-hole golf course, three swimming pools, tennis courts, and a waterfront restaurant. Annual passes are $30 a person, with nominal greens and court fees. Other parks include Winslow Park, a 19.5-acre site in a natural state; the 274-acre Sherwood Island State Park, with a public beach and picnic areas; and the Westport Nature Center. The town operates two marinas, the Compo Yacht Basin at Compo Beach and E. R. Strait Marina at Longshore, with a total of 610 slips renting for $432 to $896 a season, depending on the size of the craft. The waiting list has 450 names.

The Westport Library—the third-busiest per capita in the state—recently completed a $4 million expansion that added 60 percent more space for its collections.

The outdoor Levitt Pavilion on the banks of the Saugatuck presents free nightly concerts from June through August. Summer stock theater includes the Westport Country Playhouse and the White Barn Theater. Toquet Hall, a former opera house on Post Road East, was recently refurbished as a coffee house and cultural center for teenagers.

WILTON

Raggedy Ann and Andy's leafy home

BY ROSALIE R. RADOMSKY

When Prohibition was repealed in 1933, residents of Wilton voted to remain dry. But because it was basically a statute meant to keep roadhouses out, the dry law didn't stop anyone from bringing liquor in or from brown-bagging it to local restaurants, which sometimes avoided the prohibition against selling liquor by simply giving drinks to their patrons, without charge. In 1992, restaurants got the official go-ahead to serve liquor when Wilton voted, 4,769 to 4,380, in favor of amending the 1933 ordinance.

The policy of being officially dry did not inhibit the transformation of the 26.8-square-mile town, set amid wooded hills and rivers in Fairfield County, from a farming area to a well-to-do suburb in the years after World War II.

Julian A. Gregory, an 85-year-old lawyer and the 10th generation to live in his family's 1740 farmhouse, recalled the days before the housing boom, when dairy farms and apple orchards abounded. "Kids had paper chases on horseback on Saturday afternoons," said Mr. Gregory, whose parents summered in Wilton in the '20s and '30s, moving there year-round in 1935. Mr. Gregory's ancestor Jachin Gregory, who built the homestead, was among the early settlers. He arrived in 1740, 14 years after some 40 families, most of them from Norwalk, got permission from Hartford, then the seat of the Colonial legislature, to set up what they called Wilton Parish. Local lore has it that they called it Wilton because many had roots in that English town. The Congregational Church, built in 1790 on Ridgefield Road, is the oldest surviving house of worship in Fairfield County.

In the 1800s, townspeople were involved mainly in subsistence farming, though there were a few small grist, lumber, cider, and sarsaparilla mills, as well as home-based hat-, shirt-, and shoe-manufacturing operations and shops. The population peaked at 2,200 in 1860, then fell off when

POPULATION: 16,279.

AREA: 26.8 square miles.

MEDIAN HOUSEHOLD INCOME: $116,512.

MEDIAN PRICE OF A SINGLE FAMILY HOUSE: $454,000.

TAXES ON A MEDIAN-PRICED HOUSE: $6,366.

PUBLIC SCHOOL SPENDING PER PUPIL: $8,400.

DISTANCE FROM MIDTOWN MANHATTAN: 55 miles.

RUSH-HOUR TRAVEL TO MIDTOWN: 78 minutes on the Danbury branch of Metro-North's New Haven line, $11 one way, $241 monthly.

CODES: Area. 203, ZIP 06897 and 06829.

residents found it difficult to make a living there. It hit its modern low point, 1,280, in 1920.

Well-known residents have included Johnny Gruelle, creator of the Raggedy Ann and Andy books, and the 19th-century impressionist painter J. Alden Weir, whose 62-acre farm, next to the Weir Preserve, became a national park in 1990—Connecticut's first. Today, Wilton is home to Dave Brubeck, the jazz pianist, Theodore Bikel, the singer-actor, and the actors Jane Powell, Christopher Walken, and Charles Grodin.

"Most lots are two acres and very wooded," said Robert H. Russell, who is the first selectman, or mayor, and has lived in the community since 1969. "Over 100 houses date from the late 1700s," said Mr. Russell, a retired I.B.M. manager, whose wife, Carol, is the town historian. "Even though it's very countrified and most people have a feeling of privacy and depend on wells for water and septic systems rather than sewers," he added, "the town is very accessible to major business centers in lower Fairfield County and New York."

The town's two train stations—Wilton and Cannondale—offer free parking, and commuters have access to the Merritt Parkway and Route 7.

In early 1998, the median sales price of a house was $454,000, with a property tax of $6,366. "A half dozen out of 54 properties closed at over $1 million," said Susan Bowman Moman, a broker with Reality Seven in town. The median price of a single-family house in 1997 was $415,000, and house prices increased an average of 6 percent from the mid-1990s to early 1998. Mrs. Bowman Moman said that new construction accounted for the upswing in median prices, with the most expensive recently built house being a 14-room Colonial with six bedrooms, close to the town center and selling for $1.795 million.

Six condominium complexes, ranging from 49 to 126 units, offer studios for about $100,000, one-bedrooms ranging from $125,000 to $150,000, and two-bedrooms from $160,000 to $250,000. Silvermine Woods is a condominium around a nine-hole golf course with 24 detached houses, most of them with three bedrooms and two-car garages, selling in the high $500,00 to mid-$600,000 range.

While two-acre zoning was adopted in 1960, there are some smaller lots and small homes, including an 871-square-foot cottage amid pine trees and along a brook on just under an acre on New Canaan Road that sold for $189,500 early in 1998. A nine-room Cape situated on three acres along Washington Post Road went for $454,000. At the high end, standing on six acres along scenic Nod Hill Road, and adjoining 14 acres more of open space, the 1765 Olmstead-Betts House with four fireplaces sold for $1.09 million.

House rentals began at $2,000 for a three-bedroom ranch or split-level and went up to $3,500 for a four-bedroom updated Colonial on two acres in early 1998. Some dozen accessory apartments, not exceeding 750 square feet, on the books at town hall went for $800 to $1,100.

Among Wilton's new developments are Gruman Hill Village, which offered 45 detached cluster homes in the mid-$300,000 range early in 1998. In addition, Crowne Pond offered 26 modular houses ranging from the low $400,000's to the high $700,000's. Avalon Apartments, a 102-unit rental complex that opened in 1996, had apartments ranging from $2,000 for a one-bedroom to $3,500 for a three-bedroom.

The public school budget expenditure per pupil was $8,400 for the 1997–98 year. Wilton High School, with 875 students, offers 11 courses for advanced college placement, and has 54 teams covering 24 different sports. Typically, 90 percent of its graduates have gone on to higher education in recent years; and 85 percent went on to four-year colleges and 6 percent went on to two-year colleges in 1997.

The Middlebrook School, for grades 6 through 8, with 746 students, ranks in the upper 1 percent statewide in math, reading, and writing on the Connecticut Mastery Tests. It will have a new wing following the completion of a $14.6 million expansion in September 1998. Qualified third, fourth, and fifth graders at Cider Mill School, with 667 students, are involved in an enrichment program, and all fifth graders participate in Nature's Classroom, an environmental program.

Children are randomly assigned to one of two adjoining K–3 grade schools—Tilford W. Miller School, which has 600 students, and Ina E. Driscoll, with 596. One principal is in charge of both schools, but each has its own assistant principal. By the year 2000, the schools will serve grades pre-K to 2.

There are three private schools in Wilton; the Roman Catholic Our Lady of Fatima Regional School, pre-K to 8; the Montessori School, pre-K to 6; and the Landmark Academy, pre-K to 8.

Wilton Center, the town's commercial hub across the Norwalk River from Route 7, is where many residents count on meeting someone they know in the aisles of the Village Market, a fixture since 1935. The 15,000-square-foot store, known for homemade salads, cookies, and free coffee, also runs Kids Club, in which 2,000 members get birthday cards and qualify for a free daily treat. A 35,000-square-foot Super Stop & Shop is at the southern end of the shopping hub.

The Wilton Library, built in 1975, now offers 123,000 items, including 114,000 books. The library, originally set up in a post office with 150 books in 1895, has seven weekly story hours, monthly art exhibits, lectures, discussions, and a web site that includes community activities and web pages especially geared to providing students with information relating to their latest school projects.

Wilton Center's smorgasbord of restaurants includes Portofino for Italian fare, Wilton Pizza for a quick bite and live jazz outside on summer evenings, and Happy Wok for Szechuan-style dishes. Elsewhere in town, China Pan offers both Chinese and Japanese menus, and Orem's Diner, around since 1921, is a favorite for weekend brunch.

Cannondale Village—it used to be Cannon Crossing, a pre–Civil War farming village in the Cannondale section restored by the actress June Havoc, a former resident—includes Greenwillow Antiques in an old red barn and the Olde Schoolhouse Grill in a former 1879 one-room schoolhouse. Lambert Corners, along Route 7, is a repository of 10 historic structures dating from 1726 to 1870 and now adapted for retail and commercial use.

Seventeen parks, covering 989 acres, provide recreation, including 37-acre Merwin Meadows, which has a playground, a swimming hole, a basketball court, and a picnic area. The state's 34-acre Quarry Head Park, once a granite quarry, offers views of Long Island Sound. Hiking trails go through 192-acre Town Forest, and 146-acre Woodcock Nature Center, with 2.5 miles of hiking trails, also offers programs on local plants and animals and runs a junior naturalist summer camp.

The Wilton Family Y, which doubled its size as a result of a $2.2 million expansion completed in 1993, has 6,000 members, two-thirds of them from out of town. Its popular day-camp program attracts 700 children a week. Its swim team, the Wahoos, has been state champion for the last decade, and its women's swim team won national championships for three consecutive years beginning in 1995.